GOVERNANCE
IN THE
WESTERN HEMISPHERE

GOVERNANCE
IN THE
WESTERN HEMISPHERE

edited by
Viron P. Vaky

Published with
the Aspen Institute
for Humanistic Studies

PRAEGER SPECIAL STUDIES • PRAEGER SCIENTIFIC

New York • Philadelphia • Eastbourne, UK
Toronto • Hong Kong • Tokyo • Sydney

Library of Congress Cataloging in Publication Data

Main entry under title:

Governance in the Western Hemisphere.

1. Pan-Americanism—Addresses, essays, lectures.
2. America—Politics and government—20th century—
Addresses, essays, lectures. 3. America—Foreign
relations—20th century—Addresses, essays, lectures.
I. Vaky, Viron P.
F1410.G79 1983   327.73   83-16146
ISBN 0-03-069537-6 (alk. paper)

Published in 1983 by Praeger Publishers
CBS Educational and Professional Publishing
a Division of CBS Inc.
521 Fifth Avenue, New York, NY 10175 USA

3456789 052 9876545321

Printed in the United States of America
on acid-free paper

CONTENTS

v

II. BACKGROUND PAPERS

FOREWORD

The Aspen Institute has made Governance—the governability of contemporary societies—a central theme of its program activity for the next decade. Within this framework, the Institute has undertaken a multiyear review of the future of International Governance. We have deliberately chosen the term "governance" to make clear that our interest is not confined to intergovernmental organizations and official relationships, but also includes nongovernmental institutions and patterns of association and interchange.

The report that follows, resulting from a two-year study by the Aspen Institute, is one of few comprehensive analyses of the future of the Western Hemisphere to be published in many years. It is even more special, we believe, because it has been undertaken by a private institution. The distinguished steering committee that carried out the examination, chaired by Viron P. Vaky, includes persons from various backgrounds and professions from a number of countries in the hemisphere. All have served as individuals rather than as representatives of organizations or groups. Most are from the private sectors of their countries, although many have had experience in public life.

The committee, quite rightly, has considered the Western Hemisphere not in isolation, but in a world context. And it has examined all the substantive issues and organizational questions against three fundamental requirements: the preservation of peace, the renewal of economic growth, and the development of human potential. The resulting report deals in concrete terms with a central question: Can the countries of the Western Hemisphere govern themselves with equity and efficiency and participate effectively and constructively in the conduct of international affairs? The report illuminates, thoughtfully and practically, the areas in which the nations of South and Central America, the Caribbean, and North America will have to deal with each other—either in cooperation or in conflict—in the coming decades. It also examines the strengths and weaknesses of hemispheric organizations as regards their ability to help Western Hemisphere nations achieve common goals.

The report contains, along with other proposals, recommendations on the resolution of boundary disputes, needed changes in trade patterns and capital flows, cooperation on migration and immigration issues, natural resource development and use, monitoring of arms transfers, and alterations of international institutions. Although many of the specific recommendations have to do with international public organizations, the committee has emphasized repeatedly the enormous contributions that private sector institutions and informal relationships can make toward the enhancement of shared values and the attainment of mutual objectives.

Although the formal study was completed a year ago, a lively dialogue about the specific recommendations and the general findings has continued in a number of settings in the United States and elsewhere in the Hemisphere. What is most striking about the book that has resulted from the study is this: The premises put forward and the trends identified in 1981, and the suggestions for new and corrective actions proposed by the steering committee in 1982, are very relevant to the dramatic and symptomatic events of 1983. The lesson is an important one: Sensible approaches to urgent and immediate problems in the Americas can only come from comprehensive information and integrated understanding.

The Aspen Institute has been pleased to be engaged in this important enterprise. We are grateful for the special support of the public and private entities, including governmental bodies, which have underwritten the financial costs of the effort. They include the Organization of American States and its Secretary General, the Honorable Alejandro Orfila; the Rockefeller Brothers Fund; the BankAmerica Foundation; the Owens Foundation of Dallas, Texas; the Quaker Oats Company; Sears Roebuck; Levi Strauss; and IBM World Trade Americas/Far East Corporation. The Government of Ecuador, through the courtesy of its distinguished Ambassador to the United States, Ricardo Crespo-Zaldumbide, hosted the steering committee in Quito in April 1981, for a meeting that enriched the discussions and gave special clarity to many of the issues. Southern Methodist University hosted another key meeting. In addition to the contributions of these individuals and institutions, a number of individuals, particularly including the special advisors to the committee, have given unstintingly of their time and counsel. For the Aspen Institute and the steering committee, I express keen appreciation to all those stalwart supporters of the effort.

On behalf of the trustees of the Institute, I wish also to express our great gratitude to the committee members for their good and timely work. They have produced a sound and forward-looking report that should serve, in the months and years ahead, as an important platform on which to build further dialogue about the future of the Western Hemisphere and its international institutions.

Joseph E. Slater
President, the Aspen Institute

September 1, 1983

PREFACE

The central hypothesis of the Aspen Institute's work on International Governance is that the international system, and the interests determining relations among nations, are undergoing a fundamental transition; and that, as a consequence, there is a critical need to examine the implications of this transition for existing international institutions and traditional processes of interaction and for the prospects of bringing peace, well-being, and some order to a rapidly changing world.

Within this framework, the Institute initiated an examination of governance in the Western Hemisphere—in Latin America, the Caribbean, and North America. The Western Hemisphere was chosen because of the region's intrinsic importance and its long history of international association and cooperation. A multinational steering committee, whose composition is shown below, directed this endeavor. We focused our inquiry on two questions:

1. Given the international and hemispheric setting for the 1980s, what are the major problems and requirements with which the region's nations will have to grapple?

2. Which forms of "governance"—from formal institutions and arrangements to informal processes and patterns of cooperation—are most relevant and helpful with regard to the identified problems and needs?

To carry out this inquiry, the committee commissioned a series of papers covering the various issue areas that make up political, social, and economic relationships. These papers are included in this volume. Over a two-year period, three special workshops were held to consider them: one on economic issues, one on social and human resource issues, and one on political and security issues. A fourth special meeting was held in late 1981 with officials and representatives of pertinent international and inter-American organizations to discuss the assessments, conclusions, and ideas that emerged from the earlier workshops. In all, the committee met on eight occasions. Individual members undertook special assignments and consultations, and there was frequent communication within the committee. Our work continued through 1982.

This report is the result of the committee's deliberations. It represents the broad consensus of all the members, although different members would undoubtedly emphasize different points in different ways.

In this study we stressed the need for decision makers to be alert to the probability of unexpected events that can profoundly alter international relations. Little did we realize that between the time of our first analysis and of the completion of our report just such an event would occur: the Malvinas/Falkland Islands conflict. That conflict has already had significant impact on perceptions, interpretations, and policy concepts throughout the hemisphere. And in 1983, the Central American "crisis" has reinforced a major effect of the 1982 war in the South Atlantic: it has made explicit and unambiguous international trends and realities that up to now have been implicit and only partially perceived.

In demonstrating starkly the nature of current international realities, in stripping away old illusions and dramatizing the requirement for constructive cooperation if we are to avoid future confrontations in this nuclear age, these recent crises seem to us to provide a new opportunity to reform and restructure hemisphere relationships on a realistic and constructive basis. More than ever, therefore, we are convinced of the urgent need for peoples and governments to think about and discuss the kinds of problems, requirements, and tasks we have tried to outline in this study.

We tried to write this report from a hemisphere perspective, not from that of any one nation. We submit it to the officials of governments and of international organizations, and to the general public of the American nations, with the hope that it will stimulate further thought, ideas, debate, and actions helpful to the hemispheric community.

The committee wishes to express its deep appreciation to those who have served as special advisors to the project, including Joseph Slater, President of the Aspen Institute, and the other advisors and consultants named hereunder. We express our admiration as well as thanks to Ann Owens who typed many of the background papers, all of the drafts of the report, including the final report, and who, as secretary to the steering committee, aided us in our endeavors in many ways. We appreciate Cynthia Pringshaw's capable handling of myriad details in the course of publishing this book. And we are deeply grateful to Daniel Sherman, also of the Aspen Institute staff, for managing logistical arrangements, and for substantive contributions to the effort, all carried out in his role as coordinator of the project. Finally, we join in expressing thanks to those institutions and individuals who have provided the financial and related support that made possible our pursuit of the study's objectives and the publication of this report.

Viron P. Vaky
Editor
Chairman, Steering Committee
Project on the Western Hemisphere

August 1, 1983

WESTERN HEMISPHERE PROJECT STEERING COMMITTEE AND ADVISORS

Viron P. Vaky
Chairman
Former Assistant Secretary of
    State for Inter-American
    Affairs
Research Professor of Diplomacy
Georgetown University

Nicolas Ardito Barletta
Vice President
Latin America and Caribbean
    Region
The World Bank

Rodrigo Botero Montoya
Former Minister of Finance
Republic of Colombia
Economist and Publisher

Antonio Casas
Director
Petroleos de Venezuela

Jorge I. Domínguez
Center for International Affairs
Harvard University

Gonzalo Facio
Former Foreign Minister
Republic of Costa Rica
Attorney and Professor

John Gallagher
Former Vice President
Sears Roebuck and Company
Goodyear Executive Professor
Kent State University

Georgie Anne Geyer
Syndicated Columnist
Universal Press Syndicate

Augustin S. Hart
Vice Chairman Emeritus
Quaker Oats Company

Felipe Herrera
Former President
Inter-American Development
    Bank
Economist and Banker

Peter T. Jones
General Counsel
Levi Strauss and Company

Joseph John Jova
Former U.S. Ambassador to
    Mexico and OAS
President
Meridian House International

Neville Linton
Christian Action for Develop-
    ment in the Caribbean

William Moody
Director
International Programs
Rockefeller Brothers Fund

Gert Rosenthal
Former Minister of Planning
Republic of Guatemala
Head
Mexico Office
United Nations Economic
    Commission for Latin
    America

Richard Rubottom
Former Assistant Secretary of
    State for Inter-American
    Affairs
Professor of Diplomacy
Southern Methodist University

Javier Silva Ruete
Former Finance Minister
Republic of Peru

L. Ronald Scheman
Assistant Secretary for Manage-
    ment
Organization of American States

Stephen P. Strickland
Vice President
The Aspen Institute

Carmen Delgado Votaw
Immediate Past President and
    U.S. Delegate to the Inter-
    American Commission of
    Women
Vice President of the Commission
    Information and Services
    for Latin America

Sidney Weintraub
Former Assistant Administrator
Agency for International
    Development
Dean Rusk Professor
The LBJ School of Public Affairs
The University of Texas

SPECIAL ADVISORS

His Excellency Ricardo Crespo-Zaldumbide, Ambassador of Ecuador
Mario Garnero, Chairman, Brazil Investments
Joseph Grunwald, The Brookings Institution
Judith Himes, Program Officer, Woodrow Wilson National Fellow-
    ship Foundation
Edgard Moncayo, President, Instituto de Comercio Exterior,
    Republic of Colombia
Hans Neumann, President, Neumann Foundation, Caracas, Venezuela
Marco Pollner, Director, Washington Office, United Nations
    Economic Commission for Latin America

STAFF

Stephen P. Strickland, Project Director
Daniel Sherman, Project Coordinator, Assistant to the Vice President,
    Aspen Institute
Ann Owens, Secretary to the Vice President, The Aspen Institute

LIST OF ACRONYMS

Inter-American Indian Institute (III)
Instituto Indigenista Interamericano (III)

Inter-American Institute of Agricultural Sciences (IIAS)
Instituto Interamericano de Ciencias Agrícolas (IICA)

Latin American Free Trade Association (LAFTA)
Asociación Latinoamericana de Libre Comercio (ALALC)

Organization of American States (OAS)
Organización de Estados Americanos (OEA)

Pan American Health Organization (PAHO)
Organización Panamericana de la Salud (OPS)

Pan American Institute of Geography and History (PAIGH)
Instituto Panamericano de Geografía e Historia (IPGH)

Sistema Económico Latinoamericano (SELA)
Latin American Economic System

Agency for the Prohibition of Nuclear Weapons in Latin America
Organismos para la Proscripcion de las Armas Nucleares en la
      América Latina (OPANAL)

Inter-American Defense Board (LADB)
Junta Interamericana de Defensa (JID)

Inter-American Travel Congresses (ITC)
Congresos Interamericanos de Turismo

Centre for Latin American Monetary Studies
Centro de Estudios Monetarios latino-Americanos

Inter-American Nuclear Energy Commission
Organización Interamericana de Energía Nuclear

Postal Union of the Americas and Spain

Pan American Railway Congress Associations

Organización Latinoamericana de Energía (OLADE)
Latin American Energy Organization

I

Report of the Committee

1

The Global
and Hemispheric Setting

It is no longer news that today's world is different in virtually all its basic structures and conditions from that which existed at the end of World War II—or even a decade ago. But the dramatic nature and extent of the changes hovered over the deliberations of our committee from the beginning of our endeavor, for they affect at every turn any effort like ours, which has been to identify the major issues and needs confronting the nations of the Western Hemisphere.

Our objective has been to consider which forms of governance— institutions, processes, patterns of public and private cooperation— might best assist in the management of such problems and needs. So a full and accurate understanding of the international context within which nations function, specifically the nature of current international dynamics and trends, and of the profound changes that have occurred and are now occurring in the international system, must be the point of departure and continuing point of reference.

THE GLOBAL SETTING

The characteristics of the global changes that have occurred and are now in train may be summarized as follows:

● The *entire* planet has become organized into a system of interacting nation-states for the first time in human history. Nearly 160 independent countries comprise that system today, more than half of them having attained their independence since the end of World War II. They differ in social, institutional and cultural characteristics, and in size, resource endowments, populations, and political and economic capabilities.

There has been a significant diffusion of power and decision in the international system to a growing number of "middle powers" who have increasing capability, *and willingness*, to use their power locally in pursuit of their interests, including the use of force; who have moved beyond the traditional framework of super-power control and influence which was the dominant ordering element in international relations over the past generation; and whose definitions and priorities regarding world or regional stability may differ from those of the big powers.

All of these diversities and disparities have resulted in growing differences in the way each state conceives of its interests and of the policies and strategies needed to advance them.

● Modern transportation and communications technology have enabled transnational contacts among subnational sectors, interest groups, and organizations—in business, scientific, labor, educational, religious, cultural, and other fields—to reach a magnitude, intensity, and organizational form not known before.

The growth and development of multinational corporations have made them major international actors, created a new dimension in the world economy, and provided unprecedented capacities for the marshalling of resources and technology for development, investment, and trade.

The modern international system thus embraces a multiplicity of complex institutionalized and informal interrelationships, official and private, carried on for a variety of functional reasons, some of which are consistent with each other but many of which conflict.

● The growth in the number of nation-states has been paralleled by an explosive growth in the planet's population. Already at an unprecedented level of four billion people, the world's population is projected to grow to between 6 and 6.5 billion people by the end of this century.

Most of this population growth has occurred and will occur in the poorer countries—some 5 billion people will live in these countries by 2000. Most of the developing countries' populations, moreover, is young, which means that the momentum for this growth is already built into the social structure.

● The rapid advances of science and technology have intensified the human predicament. Military weaponry can now destroy our civilization in a few hours. We inflict biospheric damage each day. Yet science and technology have also opened vistas for humankind never possible before.

For the first time in history we possess the technical and scientific knowledge to meet humanity's needs and requirements. But while the demand side is global, the supply side— the means to meet the needs—is still a function of national responsibility.

● These phenomena—technological development, the instantaneousness of communications, the diffusion of power, a global economic system, unprecedented population increases—have all multiplied our capacity to affect each other. They have magnified the international impact of national events and trends and compressed the timeframe within which problems and crises unfold and must be dealt with.

The problems of peace, justice, human dignity, hunger and poverty, economic growth, environmental damage, the relative scarcity of resources, and the surplus of human needs are all issues that can no longer be managed solely in national terms or in isolation from the international environment.

Underlying all these trends is a set of dynamic tensions stemming from simultaneous and conflicting pressures for international cooperation, on the one hand, and for greater freedom of national action and autonomy, on the other. Such tensions are likely to intensify during the coming decade. Thus while interdependence is a compelling condition of international life, different national requirements, changing strategic interests, shifting concepts of values and goals, fundamentally different political philosophies, and newly asserted cultural precepts have all contributed to a fragmentation of the global community and strained systems of world order. Cooperation and mutual concession are becoming harder to put into effect when problems arise, and yet they are more crucial than ever.

All the familiar benchmarks of international order are shifting ground, and new ones have yet to be established.

For the foreseeable future, the international system will be characterized by a continuation of present trends toward the diffusion of power, an increase in revolutionary and irredentist causes, societal change and upheaval in the Third World, and the polarization of key global issues along both "North–South" and "East–West" lines. New sources of strain are also likely to be added—the advent of instability within the major industrial democracies of the West and in the Communist countries of the East, the rise of threats from transnational terrorism, nuclear proliferation, adverse developments in key regional food/population balances, population displacement and refugee migration. The world will be particularly vulnerable in the coming years to both natural disaster and human conflict.

We wish particularly to stress a dimension of current reality that is too often left out of analyses: *the unexpected*.* Given the trends and developments we have outlined, a wide range of events could occur that will not have been anticipated. Some events will be unanticipated because of the inherent difficulty of detecting and monitoring key indicators. Others will simply be unpredictable. Many, however, may be unexpected due to the failure of "imagination" and to institutional blinders that cause analysts and policy makers to ignore or misinterpret key signals. The grinding of the perceptual lenses through which policy is conceived and conducted has frequently reflected outdated diagnoses and prescriptions. The mind often simply refuses to think of contingencies because of their believed "improbability." But the improbable is not impossible; that some improbable events will occur is certain.† Indeed, no one who witnessed within one year the attempted assassinations of the Pope and the President of the United States, the assassination of the Egyptian President, and war between Argentina and the United Kingdom can seriously discount the unexpected, or doubt how the unexpected can shake the world or "change the game."

This suggests the need for focusing not just on *probable* sets of predictions but also on how less probable but still conceivable changes and events, were they to occur, might seriously affect international relations. It emphasizes the need for more imaginative and thorough analyses and more comprehensive information exchanges among nations. It dramatizes the still more fundamental

---

*See Allan Goodman, Chapter 6, this volume.
†Allan Goodman, Chapter 6, this volume.

need for extending the rule of law, especially over the environment, national responses to terrorism, and the management of such phenomena as migration. In a world such as we anticipate for the next decade, the capability of governments and societies to promote legitimacy, development, and political participation will be in short and precious supply.

- Latin America constitutes one of the most successful developing areas of the world. Yet it is also uniquely different from other developing regions, with some consequent potential for finding accommodation in North-South relationships, as well as being the leading edge in growing "South to South" horizontal cooperation.

- With all its diversity, the hemisphere has the historic background and habit of association, and sufficient commonalities, to be conceptually a "separable" region for purposes of such an inquiry.

- The chances for effective cooperation among peoples and governments are as great here as anywhere in the world.

Historically, inter-American relations have been shaped by the region's unique characteristic—the asymmetry of power. The nations of the region have had to relate to and interact—for much of their history in relative isolation from the rest of the world—with the most powerful and richest nation on earth. Most of the history of inter-American relations, in fact, can be written in terms of the process by which the United States sought to legitimize its use of power and Latin Americans sought to cope with it.

As in the world at large, however, profound changes have been under way in the region's dynamics over the past three decades. The premises and realities on which inter-American relations were originally based have altered. Structural conditions have changed significantly. New sets of circumstances and relationships are in the process of creation.

The loss of the United States' substantial global margin of strategic superiority, technological leadership, and economic power has meant the decline of its hegemonic influence in the hemisphere, which was the dominant ordering factor in inter-American relations in the post-World War II period. Simultaneously, significant cumulative growth, sustained over thirty years, has strengthened Latin American economies and institutions, transformed their societies, and enabled them to relate economically and politically to larger world contexts as significant entities in their own right. Power asymmetry still exists, of course, but the tendencies toward greater symmetry are so substantial that the nature of the relationships between the United States and other nations of the hemisphere has been fundamentally altered. Neither the scenery nor the actors are quite the same:

• Latin America has more than tripled its real product since 1950; it is now the most industrialized region in the developing world.

• Its population is almost two-thirds urban and three-fourths literate; its urbanization rate is one of the highest in the world.

• Social and economic indicators show major progress: life expectancy at birth has gone up from below 40 years in 1948 to over 60 now; total gross investment in the region rose from 20% of GNP in 1960 to almost 30% by 1979; industry accounts for almost a third of GNP, more than twice the share of agriculture; women have moved in large numbers into the labor force and into the educational system.

• Latin American economies have become integrated into the world political economy through trade patterns and expanded capital flows, creating new and interlocking relationships with the international system.

• Public bureaucracies are gaining in strength, responsibility, and capacity; universities have grown and diversified with significant advances in graduate studies and independent research centers; public administration schools and technical faculties have proliferated; professional associations have grown in diversity and sophistication; the armed forces have been professionalized.

• The emergence since the 1960s in the English- and Dutch-speaking Caribbean of a number of independent states with few cultural or economic ties to their Spanish-speaking neighbors has resulted in a whole new set of actors in inter-American relations, posing both new challenges and new opportunities for inter-American cooperation.

Even more profoundly, economic and social development has been brought to the center of the region's *political* agendas. Modernization is now a paramount national objective in all the countries of

Latin America and the Caribbean. Political debates center on how societies are to organize themselves to deal with such matters as efficiency, productivity, social justice, employment, welfare, conflicts over distribution of national product, inflation—and the power and bargaining elements that enter into these. Painful dilemmas are posed, such as growth vs. equity, state planning vs. market forces, import-substitution vs. export-led growth models, "trickle down" vs. welfare maximization; and debates arise over the relative need for authoritarian, corporatist, or democratic models of national governance, or eclectic versions thereof. Management of modernization is therefore serious, even grim, business for all the region's developing countries, especially those in which political institutions and processes are fragile or political transitions are under way.

Global indicators, of course, conceal marked differences in the rate and structure of development. While all countries have improved in absolute terms, the relative differences between large and small, richer and poorer nations have grown. And this fact has implications of its own. The larger countries have new industrial muscle and institutional capacity. They are more able to adjust to external economic crises, and to sustain their growth. Their perspectives and interests—and hence their policies, goals, and objectives—are increasingly different from the smaller, poorer countries.

The incorporation of Latin American countries into the world political economy has obviously increased their opportunities for development and broadened their access to resources. But it has also made the region more vulnerable to developments elsewhere. Global economic issues are hence being driven to the top of Latin America's agenda. The financing of current imports, foreign debt servicing, and efforts to sustain short-run growth often supersede in urgency longer-run objectives, such as infrastructure development and sustainable economic growth.

Economic development goals have also spurred persistent efforts for subregional cooperation, economic integration, and common markets built around specific "building blocs." The Andean Pact, the Amazon Pact, the Central American Common Market, and the Caribbean Economic Community are principal examples. The "globalization" of economic issues and the reaching out by some of the larger countries to broader economic contexts have tended to weaken many of these efforts, and the more ambitious economic integration schemes have not prospered. The urge toward horizontal cooperation nevertheless remains a significant factor in hemisphere affairs. Even in Central America, where integration schemes have been disrupted by political turmoil, the pull of desires for joint economic efforts remains strong. In the Caribbean, where ambitious integration plans failed, economic cooperation on a less ambitious scale has nonetheless been institutionalized in five different organizations, including a subregional development bank. The Andean Pact has even developed some political dimensions and rationale. Joint needs have also resulted in some very concrete, if limited and localized, cooperation built around river basin development, as in the case of the River Plate basin. The larger policy groupings, such as the Latin American Integration Association (ALADI) and the Latin American Economic System (SELA) have also increasingly been the focus of planning with regard to horizontal cooperation strategies.

Canada's role in the Western Hemisphere poses an anomaly.* Canada is an active and important participant in the hemisphere's affairs, and it has developed a variety of important relationships: priority attention and concern for the Commonwealth Caribbean; an extensive economic assistance program, especially in the English- and French-speaking Caribbean; active promotion of trade and support for Canadian business in the hemisphere; a unique approach to Cuba and Haiti; and the cultivation of close bilateral relations with Mexico and, to a slightly lesser degree, with Venezuela and Brazil. It has become a participant in the World Bank-led consortium for Caribbean economic development, and it has joined the Inter-American Development Bank as well as some of the OAS specialized agencies. But it has not linked these various elements into a coherent policy framework for hemisphere relations as a whole, and it is still weakly related to the formal institutions of governance in the Americas.

In the past, Canada was reluctant to identify publicly with the United States' preoccupation with political and security conditions in Latin America. Nor did it wish its different orientation toward the region to complicate its special relationship to the United States. Its resources were limited, and the countries of special concern to it were still largely colonies. It was not until relatively recently—its independence from Britain in 1931—that Canada was even able to interact diplomatically with countries in the region. Today, however, the hemisphere has become more pluralistic politically, Canada's resources are greater, its economic interests in the area have expanded markedly, and many of the countries of special interest to it in the Caribbean have become independent. The push toward more intimate interaction in the hemisphere has, in short, become more compelling.

---

*See Robert Jackson, Chapter 7, this volume.

Canadian concerns in the hemisphere have been dominated up to now by trade, economic, and humanitarian interests; it has largely avoided political, security, and strategic questions. There has been a growing sense in Canada, however, that economic links will need to be reinforced by greater attention to political relations in general. Canadian policy toward Latin America and the Caribbean is currently under formal review; the results may have a significant impact on Canadian foreign policy in the decades ahead.

The Western Hemisphere, in sum, is a vital, dynamic, and important region. It is undergoing change and strains, reflecting those in the international system as a whole. Long-range trends in population, resource use, trade and finance, and environmental conditions are inextricably linked with perplexing social, political, and economic problems. The 1980s will be a determining period of challenge for the governments and peoples of the area; how effectively—or ineffectively—they handle their affairs will be relevant to peace and progress of the region and, ultimately, to the larger international order.

2

Principles and Premises

THE INDIVIDUAL AND SOCIETY

The trends and dynamics we have described can be embraced conceptually in an ancient but still elusive dilemma: how to reconcile the needs of both the individual and society. Creativity and human potential are enshrined in the individual. Yet the individual's very being is shaped by and depends on a sense of belonging, of community.

We are accustomed to the synthesis of group and individual in local communities and even national ones, to the image of national ties and mutual interest. But there is no worldwide ethical agreement, no full acceptance of the concept of a global community, which today constrains or enlightens national behavior. Transnational relations depend instead on the concerns of reciprocity, on combinations of interests and fear. The governing motif of most of the nations' foreign policies is the distinction between "us" and "them." Without some stronger sense of international ties, of some larger purpose that can integrate personal and social needs, peace, well-being, and social harmony are in danger.

While peoples and governments may acknowledge the reality of general interdependence, they tend to recoil before the enormity of

the task of creating the consistent patterns of international cooperation logically required by that reality. Too frequently, they opt
instead for "second-best" alternatives as the only "realistic" ones.
The temptation is strong to retreat in frustration into what one
thinks one *can* control; for the powerful to take advantage of their
power in an "everyone for himself" mode, or worse, to assume that
benefits to themselves justify costs to others. But neither a bunker
mentality, nor an effort to enforce one's own interest over conflicting ones, will ensure peace, enduring national well-being, or the
realization of human potential.

With the twentieth century coming to an end in a time of
enormous change and stress, the key to peace and social survival will
clearly have to be found in the capacity to cooperate and so exist for
mutual benefit with those around us. This principle has been the
touch-stone for our inquiry. It has provided the cardinal question, in
a single formulation: What are the specific objectives for which
shared decisions and cooperation are better than unilateral behavior,
and how can that be encouraged?

In examining this question, the Steering Committee posited a
fundamental premise, namely, that the ultimate objectives of
development and modernization, of political and economic policies,
of government and governance must be human ones: to enrich the
lives of human beings; to widen their range of opportunities and
choice; to enable them to realize their potential and to find their
own place; to make them secure in person and property; to give them
participation in making the decisions that affect them; and to impart
a sense of personal dignity and of the value of the culture to which
they belong. We believe that this value orientation is essential to an
improvement of the human situation. And we believe that nothing
less will enable humanity to prosper, and peace to prevail, in the
difficult years ahead.

OTHER PREMISES AND ASSUMPTIONS

Beyond the philosophical view of the centrality of the individual in
any assessment of societal and intersocietal endeavors, the committee has worked from other premises and assumptions. They, as
well as our concrete analyses, have shaped our inquiry and affected
the conclusions and recommendations specified in subsequent pages.

We thus feel the need to set out here a summary of these premises and assumptions:

● *International relations, by their nature, are essentially competitive and often conflictive.* Contradiction, contending interests, competition, self-centered concerns are the realities. *International harmony has to be worked at and painstakingly constructed*; it is not a kind of "natural condition" that will flower if only some "obstacles," such as income disparities or resource deficiencies, are removed from the path.

● *International cooperation, therefore, obviously hinges on nations concluding that it is in their interest, and the achievement of constructive agreements and mutual undertakings depends on the creation of a shared sense that these advance the interests of all.* That sense underpinned the formation of the United Nations and the Bretton Woods institutions, as well as the Organization of American States and the Inter-American Development Bank. *International cooperation can be shown to be a positive sum game*—the premise, for example, that permits progress on trade—*and proposals and recommendations for cooperation must be constructed with that orientation in mind.*

● *The ultimate objective of cooperation—of development, of economic and political policies, indeed of government and governance—must be to enrich the lives of human beings, to provide them with well-being, security, and peace, to permit them widening opportunities to shape their own future.* Individual rights—political, economic, and social—are both the means and ends of governance, of development, of social harmony.

● *The major function that institutional governance can perform is to provide arenas, facilities, services, assistance, information networks, and recommendations (a) to help nations cope with their problems and with each other, and (b) to facilitate and strengthen the intrinsic processes of interdependence— expanded levels of trade, sound financial relations, joint development efforts, cultural and educational exchange, scientific and environmental cooperation.* In political matters, international institutions can provide fora for discussion, consultation, reconciliation, and communication when bilateral channels are broken or impaired—an alternative to conflict. In economic and social issues—including those matters that are predominantly in the realm of domestic policy, such as education and monetary or agricultural policy—international governance processes can provide information, access to the research and experience of others, advice, resources, and opportunities for nations to deepen interaction with others in all these areas. *International governance systems can facilitate the development of norms and rules that will enable nations to deal with problems more constructively through cooperative action than through unilateral behavior.*

● *Nonofficial, nongovernment sectors, institutions, and organizations have an enormous capacity to meet social and economic requirements and needs.* Private entities—foundations, corporations, businesses, private research institutions, educational organizations—are often more flexible, more efficient, and less constrained by political considerations or national jurisdictions than governments. Hence they are able to move more freely and adventurously, react more quickly, and experiment more innovatively. In economic terms, they possess or are able to marshal substantially greater financial and technological resources than official institutions. Many problems, such as specialization of production, tend, in point of fact, to be resolved *de facto* by interacting private groups in a kind of "silent" process of accommodation to mutual interests and circumstance. Substantial progress in meeting the major needs of societies—employment, development, economic growth, scientific/technological progress, food production—will require the energies, creativity, and resources of individuals and private entities. *Private sector participation in international governance is thus vital to effective cooperation and management of problems; and imaginative interaction between private and official sectors is indispensable.*

● *We expect that future kinds and patterns of cooperation and institutional arrangements will have to be varied and diverse, in short, "pluralistic."* The complexities of issues and the congestion of actors and interest groups on the world scene make it unrealistic to expect that with a few great political acts, such as "dialogue" or summit meetings, comprehensive rules and systems can be blueprinted and implemented full-blown. Only rarely, and then usually only after a major crisis, do historical circumstances permit a Bretton Woods. Rather, the process of coping with the world's challenges and problems will be much more likely to resemble a huge "global bazaar,"* in which actors at all levels are continuously engaged in parallel negotiations about strategically related but tactically separable matters. Neat and tidy schemes are intellectually tempting, but they may be unrealistic in the face of the variety and divergencies in the international arena today. Effective cooperation is more likely from all kinds of regional, subregional, multiactor, extranational, and public–private arrangements and networking geared to deal with concrete problems, however confusing the total picture.

● *Experience indicates that international institutions and arrangements work best when they have clearly delineated and specific responsibilities and are essentially "single-purpose."* When the focus of governance is specific and the subject matter disaggregated by problem or issue-field, success is more likely; when it is aimed at many fields simultaneously in comprehensive systems with implicit political obligations and costs, it tends to be resisted.

● *We believe that the regional dimension of international governance is an important linchpin in international cooperation, even with regard to "global" issues.* There is no intrinsic or automatic contradiction between regional and global perspectives. Indeed, regional and subregional activities can be valuable building blocks in reaching and carrying out global programs, because they address the local contexts in which such global issues present themselves. Because global action can frequently be slow and difficult, or become stalemated, regional efforts are often the only alternative if progress on the problems is to be made and frustration avoided. Such efforts can even become "the point of the spear" in getting broader action started again.

● *The realities and impact of history and of power asymmetry place a special obligation and role on the United States.* An appreciation by the United States of the historical/psychological/cultural phenomena involved is essential. The fear of dependency cum vulnerability, and the resentments that accompany a

---

* Aspen Institute, *The Planetary Bargain: Proposals for a New International Economic Order to Meet Human Needs.* Princeton: Aspen Institute Program in International Affairs, 1975.

donor-donee relationship, are deep and real psychological phenomena. *No pattern of cooperation between the United States and the countries of Latin America and the Caribbean is likely to be truly effective unless the United States can fashion a style and substance that effectively conveys to the other American nations a credible relationship of mutual respect and comprehension.* The relative power, capacity, and wealth of the United States, and its position as a crucial supplier of capital, technology, and markets, also give it the ability—and the responsibility—to play a large and, indeed, unsubstitutable role in the inter-American system.

● *Obligations do not, however, all run one way.* If there is asymmetry in power and influence, there is little asymmetry in problems and responsibilities. *Each of the governments of the hemisphere bears an obligation—to its own citizens and to the community of nations—for constructive management of its problems and exploitation of its opportunities, and for responsible and sound internal policies with regard to them. All nations have equal responsibility to contribute—to the extent their capabilities permit—to the resolution of common problems and to constructive cooperation for the benefit of all the citizens of the Americas.*

Our deliberations necessarily and inevitably tended to concentrate on those aspects for which recommendations and suggestions were most feasible, that is, the more formal and institutionalized intergovernmental processes and mechanisms. It was difficult for a group such as ours to move much beyond general exhortation with regard to either domestic measures and policies or the great array of private sector possibilities. But we would not wish that fact to distort perspectives or realities. As a final note to this conceptual framework, therefore, we restate and reemphasize three points already implicit in the foregoing:

First, much of our attention focused on how to facilitate and strengthen the kinds of cooperation that help international activities —trade, investment, development efforts, technological and cultural exchange. It is, of course, these activities themselves that are the major instruments deepening international cooperation. They are thus in a sense both ends and means. Hence, when we stress recommendations for fora, information exchange, and "service" functions, we do not imply that these are the major elements in themselves. We suggest only that they are feasible and practical ways to intensify those very activities—*increased* levels of trade and *greater* joint development efforts, for example—that will in turn be the central instruments strengthening the bonds of interdependence among nations.

Secondly, we repeat our belief that nonofficial, private sectors provide great potential for meeting major needs and requirements. Hence we underline the advisability of governments resorting to, and encouraging, involvement and activity by private sector groups, companies, and institutions in the major issues of the day.

Finally, we note in the following pages that the successful management of many major issues and problems—agricultural production, economic growth, education, public services, employment creation, population planning—depends in a very large degree upon *domestic* policies. We cannot, therefore, escape reemphasizing the responsibility of individual governments in this sense. Societies are, to be sure, responsible for themselves. In this interdependent, nuclear age, however, we affect each other so substantially that responsibility for managing our own affairs constructively becomes an obligation that each of our nations bears for the good of all.

3

The Major Issue Areas: Recommendations

What does the hemisphere face in terms of issues, problems, and requirements? What is the meaning—operationally and conceptually —of current trends? What international cooperative steps and mechanisms might help nations cope with them?

For convenience we have grouped these issues and challenges in three categories: political/security; economic development; and human development. We do not presume to claim a comprehensive survey or treatment. We have focused rather on problem areas that seemed to us to have particular international significance and that could be dealt with under the specific terms of reference of this study. The recitation of even these issues, however, risks appearing to be indiscriminate. We have, therefore, distilled out of subsequent sections, and we restate here very briefly, our conceptual hierarchy of priorities.

There are, in our view, three issue clusters that need to be accorded top priority and attention by the hemisphere community:

● The *preservation of peace* is a fundamental task that it is incumbent upon all nations to pursue. It is a task that can be neither a passing nor a passive pursuit; nor can it be only a reaction to international events. Rather, it is an objective that must be pursued actively and purposefully. Essential in this regard is the need for immediate attention to perfecting procedures for conflict-resolution and peace-keeping, and reversing the drift to international fragmentation and anarchical international behavior, as well as to efforts to resolve existing festering disputes. It will mean, on a broader front, international efforts to deal with nuclear proliferation, terrorism, and arms races, and advancing the conditions of freedom, open political systems, and justice.

● *Renewed economic growth in the world* without which social and political stability and progress in modernization will not be possible. In great part, of course, this depends on sound *domestic* policies and strategies in each nation—and we have already stressed individual responsibility in that connection. Internationally, it requires energetic attention to expanding global trade and capital flows, and to expanded cooperation in food production and in developing and managing natural resources.

● *The development of human potential* is both the end and means of economic development and social peace. Individual governments bear prime responsibility, but cooperation among nations is also urgently required to help countries meet the pressing challenges of providing employment and education/ training to growing populations, as well as to deal with the increasingly complex phenomenon of external migration.

POLITICAL/SECURITY

The institutions, procedures, patterns, and traditions that make up the aggregate "inter-American system" of cooperation and governance developed basically as means for the United States to legitimize and exercise its power and for Latin American countries to contain and cope with that power (see Chapter 1). When the region was relatively isolated from the global dynamics, and the predominance of U.S. power permitted an effective U.S. hegemony, the "system" functioned essentially as an alliance, with implicit bargains and with U.S. power and influence as the overall persuader and arbiter.

Initially, institutions and procedures were fashioned primarily to respond to political and collective security concerns. Subsequently, economic and development concerns were introduced as Latin American countries sought to expand the definition of collective security so as to include them, and as the United States perceived a connection between economic development in the region and the protection of its own security interests in the area.*

In point of fact, cooperation among the nations of the hemisphere, both formal and ad hoc, has had an impressive record of accomplishment. The Organization of American States, a principal linchpin in the inter-American system, has been an invaluable forum for referral of problems, for "cooling off," for maintaining communication among individual members when bilateral channels have been broken. Most importantly, these institutions and processes have by now combined into a deep tradition: They have fostered a habit of cooperation, of acceptance of the rule of law, and of general international order, which has had significant "residual" restraining effects on nations' behavior—even when the tradition is honored in the breach.

As we already have noted, however, changes in the hemisphere and world settings have complicated the conditions under which the system functions:

• The relative decline in the U.S. power position in the world at large has meant a reduced capacity to influence the region.

• Hemisphere politics and economics have been "globalized" as a result of structural changes in the international system to which all nations, including the United States, have responded. The resulting loss of relative isolation has, in turn, linked countries' concerns, alternatives, and opportunities to larger world contexts, thus affecting inter-American priorities.

• Economic development has enabled and induced several of the hemisphere nations, especially the larger ones, to challenge aspects of United States dominance: diversification of political and economic relationships and demonstration of greater independence from U.S. influence represent policy strategies for a large number of these countries.

• Western European countries, Japan, and Canada have all developed significantly increased ties of commerce, investment,

*See Jorge I. Dominguez, Chapter 8, this volume, and Margaret Daly Hayes, Chapter 9, this volume.

finance, and development assistance and have hence become increasingly significant in the calculations and strategies of Latin American and Caribbean countries. European political parties—Christian Democratic and Social Democratic—have intensified links to ideologically similar Latin American political parties, forming a new element in the region's political dynamics.

• With the emergence of several Latin American countries as assertive "middle powers" in their own right, conceptions of national interest have begun to diverge. Consistent with the general global trend of diffusion of power, these emerging powers are increasingly able and prepared to use their growing capacities unilaterally to pursue their interests.

The cumulative effect of all these circumstances on the hemisphere's dynamics has been centrifugal:

• Common definitions, common perceptions of threats and priorities, agreement on the nature of problems have all been rendered more difficult to achieve.

• Common actions are harder to structure. There is a more chaotic note to the system's "tone."

• There are disturbing signs of a growing willingness by American nations to disregard traditional inter-American concepts and principles in pursuit of their own interests, including violations of the nonintervention principle and unilateral use of force.

• Reciprocally, American nations' confidence that the system's mechanisms can effectively meet their needs and interests appears to be weakening. Nation-states, of course, are always reluctant to submit their central political concerns to international organizations or to agree to limitations on their freedom of action. But American states, including the United States, recently have seemed to be more reluctant than in the past to bring major issues to the OAS or to use the organization to advance their principal foreign policy concerns. The trend is to concentrate participation in the system on a "turf protection" basis, that is, to seek to avoid being affected by what might occur in the various fora and to make moderate use of the specialized agencies.

• While U.S. influence has declined, its presence is still sufficiently important to make its "role" in the hemisphere a continuing center of attention and source of controversy. The issue of the U.S. "role," indeed, frequently preoccupies and preempts other matters. The decision by the United States to support the United Kingdom in the Malvinas/Falkland Islands conflict was a significant event in this sense, whose full consequences are yet to be measured. Whatever the merits, necessity, or intent of that decision, it has been duly registered in the memories of present and future Latin American leaders and perceived by them as signaling the primacy to the United States of European over Latin American relations.

But if the hemisphere setting has changed, the nature and seriousness of the political and security problems facing the region's nations have not. If anything, the challenges have intensified:

● Decolonization remains a serious source of potential conflict, as evidenced by the United Kingdom–Argentina conflict. The safety of an independent Belize remains an uncertain question. Decolonization in the Caribbean has also led to independent microstates, whose viability may pose uncertainties among states within the region and beyond.

● Serious unresolved territorial and boundary disputes still exist between American states, and these have at times been at the core of intrahemisphere conflict. Conflicts between Argentina and Chile, Chile and Bolivia, El Salvador and Honduras, and Peru and Ecuador have been the most serious; the first two brought the parties to the verge of war; the third led to war in 1969, and that last resulted in brief fighting in 1981. Potentially serious conflicts also exist between Venezuela and Colombia, Venezuela and Guyana, Chile and Peru, Colombia and Nicaragua. Current tension between Nicaragua and the other Central American governments is a further source of potential conflict. The potential for intrahemisphere conflict in the 1980s, in short, is significant.

● While the level of arms acquisitions has not been large compared to other regions of the world, it does pose potential problems in the context of the disputes and rivalries referred to above. One of the consequences of the war between Argentina and the United Kingdom will undoubtedly be a stimulation of demand by hemisphere military establishments for sophisticated weapons, and a greater willingness of governments to allocate resources for that purpose. The danger of mini-arms races or of arms acquisitions adding to the uncertainties and tensions between nations is palpable.

● Terrorism, and its increasing incidence in Latin America, is a new and exacerbating strain on the system.

● The Malvinas/Falkland Islands conflict demonstrated how deep and persistent in the region are concepts of nationalism, fear of dependency, and feelings of competition between North and South, developed and developing—all of which, in turn, deepens the dilemma between the increasingly pressing need to structure systems of effective international cooperation in this interdependent world, on the one hand, and, on the other, contrary compulsions of autonomy and independence, which render that task difficult to accomplish.

● There has been a resurgence of concern about the East–West struggle's impact on the hemisphere, and in concern about collective security. The United States has specifically raised the question of external intervention in connection with the Cuban/Soviet role in the Central American turmoil. The dilemmas posed are how the East–West question will, in fact, affect the hemisphere: what role global security considerations will impel the United States to play in the hemisphere, what role the United States will seek to get other hemisphere nations to play, and their willingness or unwillingness to accept that role.

The central task confronting the region's nations is clearly to preserve the peace and to foster the political and security conditions that will permit survival, development, and well-being in the region. Operationally, this means improving the mechanisms for resolution of conflict and renewing the commitment to peaceful settlement of disputes, combating terrorism, fostering reasonable arms restraint, halting the illegal flow of arms, precluding the proliferation of nuclear weapons, and advancing the conditions of democracy, freedom, and personal security—that is, human rights.

Conflict Resolution

The hemisphere has a long tradition of dispute settlement, and a strong habit of intermediation as a means of resolving conflict.*

---

*See Mary Reid Martz, Chapter 10, this volume.

Numerous settlement procedures of all kinds have been used in the past, and there is a strong unspoken norm that hemisphere countries do not fight each other, although serious exceptions occurred in earlier years as in the case of the Chaco Wars. Conflict resolution, however, has most frequently been ad hoc and largely informal, even adventitious, and has most often been mounted in response to a dispute reaching crisis proportions rather than as an early preventive measure.

The problem is that reliance on improvised or ad hoc responses to crisis—or allowing disputes to fester—is increasingly unsatisfactory in this modern nuclear age. Indeed, the absence of a clear, effective set of mechanisms and of firm commitment by the region's countries to the principle of peaceful settlement increases the chance of conflict. Given the growth in national capacities, the temptation to gamble by "going to the brink" to press a perceived advantage or interest is heightened, and the invitation to strong parties to take unilateral actions to clear up a problem or advance a "principle," even in the name of collective security, is harder to resist. Yet the weakening of the legal and juridical inhibitions to use of force and intervention can only create more chaotic and anarchical conditions, raising the prospects of conflict. Even if nations believe that sooner or later the traditional impulse to assist in dispute settlements will operate and snatch them back from the brink if conflict is reached, it is not prudent in today's world to let problems go that far. Disputes today can rapidly, easily, and unintentionally get out of hand, and the consequences of being unable to climb down from high horses can be tragic, as the United Kingdom–Argentine conflict in 1982 has demonstrated.

Because the danger of intrahemisphere conflict in the 1980s is substantial, *we recommend*:

● *That in the next General Assembly of the OAS, member governments agree to press for the resolution of all extant border disputes over the next five years and to recommend specific procedures for doing so.* This could include suggestions and procedures for bilateral discussions, arbitration, mediation, good offices, or referral to the International Court of Justice.

● *That the OAS should be prepared to provide technical support for delimitation of land and maritime boundaries as an aid to settlement.*

● *That the OAS General Assembly charge the Permanent Council to monitor all disputes and potential or actual breaches of the peace in the Americas, utilizing the services of its Secretary General. The Secretary General should report on these situations regularly to the Permanent Council. The Secretary General should also be authorized to enlist the assistance of a panel of distinguished statesmen, who can be available to assist him, the Permanent Council, and the parties concerned to assess and try to head off potential conflict.* The Secretary General would be required to report fully on the progress of such activities.

Terrorism

The spread of terrorism and counterterrorism in recent years has added new strains to intra- and interstate relations.* It has also presented individual citizens with serious threats to their personal security and survival. We do not believe that the deliberate creation of terror can be justified. Acts of violence against innocent citizens or efforts to destroy an economy by groups claiming to represent "the people" or "social justice" are not only a self-contradiction, but they are crimes against the human rights provisions of the American Convention on Human Rights and the OAS Charter. Nor do we believe that efforts to combat terrorism by legitimate authorities can in any way countenance the use of counterterrorism. Fighting fire with fire is a pernicious doctrine in these circumstances, and will only sow seeds of deep bitterness and future dissension.

In order to delegitimize terrorism, *we recommend*:

● *That the OAS General Assembly charge the Inter-American Commission on Human Rights with the preparation of an annual report on terrorist activities.*

● *That the OAS condemn terrorist groups as well as all governments that directly or indirectly support them.*

● *That all governments in the hemisphere take all steps, including passing new laws, if necessary, to preclude the use of their territories to train people intent on violent subversion of other governments.*

---

*See Allan Goodman, Chapter 6, this volume.

Arms Transfers*

Latin America is a lightly armed region compared to other world areas, and the level of acquisition of arms is comparatively low. But these facts do not warrant any complacency about the issue. Whatever the level, arms purchases do have negative implications: They divert resources from other uses; they tend to stimulate competitive acquisitions by nations who are parties to territorial or border disputes, and thus risk starting "mini-arms races"; they raise tensions with regard to local disputes; and they may be used to shore up or strengthen dictatorships.

It is unlikely, however, that the demand for arms will decline. The single most important reason for arms acquisition is force modernization and the replacement of aging equipment. This is likely to remain a principal motivation through the 1980s, because the region's military establishments still contain large inventories of aging and obsolescent equipment even after two decades of modernization. Nations, moreover, naturally wish to maintain military establishments commensurate with their perceived politico-economic development. Acquisition of military technology plays a meaningful role in both the internal politics and the diplomacy of each country; considerations of national sovereignty are important factors. The Argentine–United Kingdom conflict will almost surely be seen by governments and military establishments in the hemisphere as legitimating and justifying the national defense argument for increased arms acquisitions. Still another element that feeds the demand side is rising worry about clandestine supply of arms to revolutionary movements, and the consequent resurgence of external security concerns.

Nor is arms restraint likely from the supply side. There is no consensus among major arms suppliers that conventional arms constraints are desirable. Supply and financing are freely available, and the competitors are numerous. Supplies are also easily available in the world arms markets. A new factor, moreover, is that several of the larger Latin American countries are themselves becoming arms producers. As they become producers, they also become weapons exporters, as in the case of Brazil and Argentina.

All the above factors are contributing to a rapid proliferation of arms in the hemisphere that, as a phenomenon in itself, gives cause for concern.

---

*See Caesar Sereseres, Chapter 11, this volume.

It is unrealistic to expect either disarmament or the prevention of arms acquisitions. What *can* realistically be expected is a system for rationalizing arms acquisitions—that is, the establishment of norms to govern arms purchases and a system of consultation to eliminate suspicions and fears. The task of governance, in short, is the *management*—not the prevention—of arms acquisitions.

Accordingly, *we recommend*:

● *That all governments supply the OAS with data every year on military expenditures and weapons systems sales and purchases in the hemisphere. In addition, as is done between NATO and the Warsaw Pact, they should also supply information on the size and location of forces; and they should give advance notice to their neighbors and to the OAS of all major military exercises and maneuvers. The Secretary General would disseminate this information annually in a public document.* The purpose would be to reduce fears and suspicions and shed public light on these matters.

● *That the Andean nations revive the Ayacucho Agreement for conventional arms restraint as a means of establishing norms and standards for future arms purchases, including self-limitations on unnecessarily sophisticated equipment.* Such an agreement could become the nucleus for wider regional agreement.

● *That in order to deal with the problem of illicit arms trafficking from one nation's territory to another's, which is reaching alarming proportions, each member Government be asked to report annually to the OAS the steps it is taking to prevent the use of its territory to transfer weaponry covertly and illegally to others abroad. The OAS should make the same request of Cuba through the UN Secretary General.*

Nuclear Nonproliferation*

Latin American commitment to nuclear power is growing. The question is not whether countries in the region will turn to nuclear energy, but what pattern they will follow when they do. While the drive for nuclear technology has an economic rationale, the issues and ques-

---

*See John Redick, Chapter 12, this volume. This contains an excellent summary of current national programs and hemisphere treaties.

tions it raises are essentially political. The central concern, of course, is that the spread of nuclear technology implies the potential proliferation of nuclear weapons. That is a prospect of such seriousness as to warrant hemisphere-wide concern and attention.

To reduce the risk of weapons proliferation, *we recommend*:

● *That the Treaty of Tlatelolco for the prohibition of nuclear weapons in Latin America be brought into full effect throughout the region.* This will require that the following remaining steps be accomplished: The Government of Cuba should sign and ratify the treaty; the governments of Chile and Argentina should ratify the treaty; the government of Brazil should bring the treaty into full effect as far as it is concerned; and the government of France should ratify Protocol I.

● *That all Latin American and Caribbean governments should adhere unequivocally to full-scope safeguards as administered by the International Atomic Energy Agency (IAEA).*

● *That the three regional agencies having responsibility in this area—the Inter-American Council on Education, Science & Culture (CIECC), the Inter-American Nuclear Energy Commission (IANEC), and the Agency for the Prohibition of Nuclear Weapons in Latin America (OPANAL: the Tlatelolco Treaty executing agency)—coordinate their activities and exchange information fully; they should also determine whether there cannot be a consolidation of functions.*

● *That the governments of the hemisphere consider the multinational cooperative development of a center along the lines of EURATOM under multinational Latin American control, which would seek to develop peaceful uses of atomic energy.*

Human Rights*

Commitment to the central concepts of "human rights" is deep-seated, traditional, and historical in this hemisphere. These principles are included in the OAS Charter and in the UN Charter. The Inter-American Commission on Human Rights was established, by Latin

---

*See Bryce Wood, Chapter 13, this volume.

American initiative, *in 1960,* and the American Convention on Human Rights was signed in 1969 and ratified by the requisite number of states in 1978.

The question, therefore, is not the validity or value of these concepts, but rather how these commitments are to be observed. Experience suggests that this is a question difficult to incorporate into bilateral foreign policies, because inevitably other self-interests intrude. We are agreed, however, that affirmation of support for human rights goals and ideals, and their effective implementation, are essential for the peace, survival, and well-being of the citizens of the Americas. Observance of these traditional commitments will require constant prodding and monitoring, and the marshaling of the "decent opinion of mankind." In this connection, it will be important to remember the distinction between how *people* feel about human rights and how *governments* are likely to react. Because of inherent difficulties in incorporating pressures for human rights into bilateral foreign policies, the question of observance of commitments is a good field for international governance and multilateral management.

In order to continue to advance the rights of humankind in the Americas, therefore, *we recommend:*

● *That governments of the region unequivocally make clear their commitment to the human rights principles incorporated in the OAS Charter, the American Convention of Human Rights, and other juridical instruments, and that they be prepared to express their concern about violations of such rights whether by governments, terrorists, or other groups.*

● *That all nations of the Americas complete the ratification process regarding the 1969 American Convention on Human Rights within the next year* (17 Governments have ratified, and the treaty came into force in 1978). This means that the following governments, which have not yet signed and ratified the Convention, should do so promptly: Argentina, Brazil, Dominica, St. Lucia, Surinam, and Trinidad and Tobago. The following governments, which have signed but not ratified the convention, should do so promptly: Chile, Paraguay, the United States, and Uruguay.

● *That, in the next OAS General Assembly, all OAS member states reaffirm unequivocal support for the Inter-American Commission on Human Rights (IAHRC) and ensure that it continues to have adequate budget and staff resources.* This organization should become the major conscience and instrument of the Americas in monitoring human rights observances.

• *That all governments of the hemisphere affirm their willingness to have the IAHRC visit their country to monitor the state of human rights, and that reports of the Commission be seriously received and acted upon by the General Assembly.*

• *That the countries that have information on the state of human rights in all countries should provide the IAHRC with this to enable the Commission to develop and publish annual information on the status of human rights in all countries of the hemisphere.* Such reports should carry greater weight than national reports. A major purpose of the Commission's work is to ensure that public light is cast in "all dark corners."

• *That nations of the hemisphere support the Inter-American Court on Human Rights.* Only two nations (Jamaica and Costa Rica) thus far have accepted the Court's jurisdiction.

• *That all governments institute systems by which the rights of minorities, especially ethnic minorities, are effectively protected so as to guarantee them equal access to the benefits of democracy.*

• *That the Inter-American Commission on Human Rights, in cooperation with the Inter-American Indian Institute, give special attention to monitoring the human rights of aboriginal people of the hemisphere, and to report regularly to the General Assembly.*

Democracy

Finally, we wish to express our belief that the traditional inter-American ideals of liberty and democracy need firm support and implementation, and that the region's peace and prosperity require it. From the beginning of the institutionalization of the inter-American system during and after World War II, its procedures have sought to enshrine the values of freedom and democracy. These values have been the most uplifting component of official international governance in this region, and formal commitment to them remains a deep-seated ideal throughout the Americas.

This committee frankly admits its bias in this regard. We believe that democracy—that system of government which permits people to participate meaningfully in decision-making structures and to select and change their leaders at regular intervals—is the best and most effective form of government.

The challenge of our times is how to assist nondemocratic governments to make the transition peacefully to more open political systems. No single formula exists, and there are obvious limitations on what an international community can do with regard to essentially domestic questions. Yet the opinion of humankind matters, exhortation matters, and much can be done to assist societies that are themselves prepared and willing to establish democratic governments. As citizens of the Americas, we note, in this spirit, that in the last few years, a number of governments have made important advances in political transition toward democracy, while others have retrogressed. We earnestly hope that all governments in the hemisphere will move rapidly and decisively to establish open political systems, which will permit their people to enjoy meaningfully the basic right of shaping their own destiny through free, fair, and open elections.

ECONOMIC DEVELOPMENT

Development, as we have noted, is the central objective and focus of Latin American and Caribbean nations' economic, political, social, and even security goals. It is not an unrealistic aim. While there were differences among countries, the region as a whole showed substantial economic progress during the past twenty years, both in the growth of productive capacity and in absolute levels of material welfare for the mass of the population. Economic stagnation, relative or absolute, was *not* a characteristic of the region as a whole during this period. The data, in fact, tend to belie some of the conventional myths about the region's development. Social and economic indicators suggest major advances in the material welfare of the majority of the population in most countries, which, although uneven, as between economic groups, have nevertheless reached deep down to the lower-income groups. The stereotype that economic progress has been nullified for the poor majorities by an increasingly uneven income distribution is not borne out by such time series and cross-sectional data as are available.

The countries in the region, in short, have demonstrated real growth capacity and performance, as well as the ability to promote dynamic and large-scale processes of investment and internal economic expansion—indeed, to transform their societies. But development is, of course, an infinitely complex and difficult process, embracing a whole range of fields and even conflicting goals. Most nations, for example, necessarily face an agenda that covers the *simultaneous* need to industrialize, raise productivity, maintain export growth, increase agricultural production, create an internal market infrastructure, expand education and training programs, and face up to vast needs on the health and welfare fronts. Most countries must also deal with great inequalities in their societies between rural and urban areas and between rich and poor.

Development thus generates difficult dilemmas frequently subsumed under the rubric of "growth vs. distribution." We reject the notion that the goals of just distribution and growth are antagonistic; or that absolute trade-offs exist, even though some trade-off decisions may occur at the margin. The empirical data, in fact, suggest that far from curtailing growth to improve income distribution, growth should be speeded up to bring into play the economic and institutional forces that ensure more economically equitable societies—and more equitable at higher absolute standards of living. We believe that equity and growth strategies are interacting poles. Pure growth and free market play will not automatically result in equity; but resolution of social problems, human development, and achievement of structural change are not possible without growth and social sensitivity.

The capacity of states to transform themselves into more equitable modern societies is thus directly related to their ability to stimulate growth. Maintenance of a minimum annual economic growth rate on the order of 5–6%, on the regional average, appears to be needed if major societal and human needs are to be met. That, in turn, will depend on two sets of factors: (a) the state of the world economy, and (b) the effectiveness and consistency of domestic policies and strategies. Major external constraints on growth and development include the impact of energy costs on the balance of payments (for nonoil producers), slowed economic growth in the industrialized countries, consequent declining demand for imports and rising protectionism in developed countries, limits on capital flows, and high external debt and interest rates. Internal constraints turn on the ability to ensure competitive, efficient productive capacity, on sound exchange rate policy, on the capacity to maintain relatively high levels of domestic savings, on avoiding gross distortions of market forces, and on consistency and congruity among various domestic programs and policies.

The complexity of the development process and the nature of the international system of interacting but sovereign nation-states, each anxious to preserve its sovereignty and freedom of action—all make the individual nation's priorities, national context, individual circumstances, and set of value judgments central factors in how well each meets its development objectives. "International" development models or externally devised prescriptions are no longer likely to be acceptable. Syntheses, adaptations, combinations, and eclectic measures on an individual basis will constitute the most likely patterns.

The primacy of national decison-making and national sovereignty in an interdependent world, and the tension built into that circumstance, is a theme that we found to recur over and over with regard to almost every field of international action. With regard to development, it suggests that a basic—and needed—role for governance and international cooperation is providing individual governments with information and services to help check, assess, and evaluate—in short, patterns that will help governments to make wiser policy decisions and enable them to check their ideas against international trends and compare their experience and requirements with those of others. Ways need to be developed to provide governments with more systematic access to data and the experience of others, and with a wider range of services of advice and assistance, to which they may turn if they wish, to help them structure development programs.

Specific observations about particular segments of the economic development issue-cluster are noted below. More detailed discussions of these areas are contained in the papers reproduced in Part II of this volume.

Trade*

The region's economic development goals depend on expanding external trade and financing. Particular importance attaches to the development of active trade with the developed countries, with which the region currently conducts about 70% of its trade. Exports

---

*See Sidney Weintraub, Chapter 14, this volume.

to the industrial countries remain the chief source of foreign exchange receipts for the region, and industrial countries are the chief source of the basic inputs, capital goods, and technology essential to the process of production changes and industrialization. Accordingly, access to the developed countries' markets, which will facilitate the growth of exports of basic commodities, semimanufactures, and manufactures, is an essential requisite for accelerating growth. Intraregional and South–South trade can be a highly valuable supplement, but it will not be a substitute for trade with the developed countries in the foreseeable future.

At the same time, the developing countries now provide the fastest-growing markets for United States exports. Moreover, transforming the industrial base of the United States and other developed countries will have to take into account the developing countries' drive to industrialize. Several of them already compete with industrial countries in a number of industries. If the international trading system remains open, therefore, and the developing countries are able to compete on the world market, they could well become the necessary "engine" of renewed global growth.

From the foregoing, it is clear that promoting freer trade and restraining protectionism are essential for world economic growth, and that they must be the central objectives of international consultation and cooperation. The international body concerned with fostering achievement of these objectives is the General Agreement on Trade and Tariffs (GATT). Trade issues have global, regional, and country contexts, all of which can reinforce each other. In this sense the major attention of the hemisphere should relate to the principles of GATT, which represent the most effective effort made to date to define the rule of law in matters of trade. Those nations that have not done so should adhere to that agreement and play an active role in the implementation of the various "codes of conduct" and, where they fall short, help revise them to meet the needs of the developing countries better. Much can and should be done at the subregional and regional levels to accelerate the reduction of trade barriers and the opening of new markets for lesser-developed nations within the Americas. The extension of nonreciprocal trade benefits to the lesser-developed nations would be of importance in achieving the development goals of the hemisphere.

To strengthen efforts to achieve an open international economy, therefore, *we recommend*:

- *Greater adherence to the articles of GATT by industrialized countries, particularly when trade restrictions are imposed.*

● *Conclusion of a safeguards agreement that will help achieve the foregoing while protecting the trade interests of developing countries.*

● *That hemisphere nations that are not now contracting parties join GATT in order to enhance the region's influence in that body.*

● *That the region's nations sign and play an active role in GATT codes in order to promote freedom of trade as case law evolves under these codes.*

● *That all the more developed countries of the region (as measured by GDP) should grant one-way special tariff and non-tariff preferences to less-developed countries of the region and to those countries whose small internal markets require a large level of exports relative to GDP in order to achieve development goals.* These special preferences should be seen as an interim step to unify preference by all developed countries (including the Lome system of preferences) to the least-advantaged developing nations. *Trade preferences become effective only as preference recipients take the necessary internal measures to improve their productive efficiency.*

● *That the World Bank and the Inter-American Development Bank (IDB) support and cooperate with the Latin American Export Bank (BLADEX) to optimize the financial resources available for nations seeking to develop export capabilities.*

Capital Flows*

The external financing needs of most countries in the region are likely to continue to increase in the years immediately ahead because of (a) the need for large, long-range investments to improve productive capacity, social infrastructure, and human capital; and (b) short-run requirements created by such problems as energy costs, high financing costs, and reduced world demand for exports. External financial gaps are thus likely to grow in the 1980s, and covering them will be essential to sustain needed rates of growth. How to do so in

---

*See Albert Fishlow, Chapter 15, this volume.

the face of uncertain public capital inflows, practical limits on commercial lending in many cases, and differences as to the role of private foreign investment and the conditions needed to attract it will be a central problem. While the massive financial imbalances during the last decade were handled in large part by the rapid growth of private bank credit, the private commercial banking system may not be able to manage all the demands in the future through the same pattern of flows that prevailed in the past. The private sector—and especially private investment—will, of course, remain the largest and most important source of capital, but it is increasingly clear that the multilateral financial institutions will also need to play a crucial supplementary role in helping to channel resources to developing countries.

Yet recent reports from the World Bank Group and the Inter-American Development Bank show a reduced availability of resources, lower than the lending programs envisaged by those institutions and the genuine needs of their borrowing member countries. In these circumstances the multilateral financial institutions operating in the hemisphere will have to give considerable attention to increased forms of cooperation with the capital market financial institutions and the private sector. In the recent past the World Bank Group and the Inter-American Development Bank have widened their cofinancing arrangements with commercial lenders. Although at this stage it would be premature to support any one mechanism to the exclusion of others, we consider that the problem of increasing the lending capacity of those institutions cannot be disassociated from the issue of their capacity to raise funds from the market and to create new methods of financial intermediation.

The role of the Inter-American Development Bank & the World Bank Group in the hemisphere is best understood as cooperative ventures through which industrialized, semiindustrialized and poor countries work together to help both in financing long-term development projects on a cost-sharing basis and in improving the economic environment in the borrowing countries, so that they may be better able to attract and use effectively resources from the international private capital markets. Success in these endeavors will depend to a large extent not only on the role of these institutions as providers of financial resources, but also on their catalytic role in promoting the prudent economic policies that are necessary to facilitate private financial flows of substantial importance. Financial resources and capital by themselves will not, of course, automatically guarantee success. The key will be the efficiency with which those financial resources are utilized. It is in this wider context that the role of the

World Bank Group and the Inter-American Development Bank in the region should be viewed. It is the combination of the roles they play —providing project financing and technical assistance, acting as financial catalysts, promoting institution building, and offering policy advice—that makes their impact in the region unique.

The Latin American and Caribbean countries will, in short, require increasing external resources in order to achieve adequate levels of growth and development. The failure of the multilateral development institutions and of the international financial system to provide the necessary flow of resources will imply very serious consequences for the region. Accordingly *we recommend and urge*:

● *That the nations of the hemisphere, including the United States, maintain their full commitments and obligations to the current replenishment of capital as well as their concessional contributions for the World Bank Group (including the International Development Association) and the Inter-American Development Bank.*

● *That the nations of the hemisphere support the expansion of the lending capacity of the Inter-American Development Bank by increasing the bank resources through a Sixth Capital Replenishment.*

● *That the nations of the hemisphere reaffirm the importance of expanding the World Bank lending program in the hemisphere.*

● *That the OECD countries increase their support of and participation in the Inter-American Development Bank.*

● *That the World Bank and the Inter-American Development Bank explore new mechanisms to increase their lending capacity, including possible prudent changes in their statutory lending authorities, which might facilitate such expansion.*

● *That the Inter-American Development Bank consider establishing a kind of "regional International Finance Corporation" (Multinational Fund for Industrial Development) as a private sector window.*

● *That the Inter-American Bank, the World Bank, and the subregional development banks—the Caribbean Development Bank, the Central American Bank for Economic Integration, and the Andean Development Fund—establish procedures to improve existing cofinancing practices or create new methods of financial intermediation including "financial packages" for joint investment projects in high-priority areas.*

● *That the nations of the hemisphere endorse World Bank efforts to explore all means of mobilizing additional public and private resources to finance expanded energy investments and lending (an energy affiliate)* [see p. 44 below].

Agriculture and Food*

Agricultural development in the region has been uneven and relatively neglected. The result has been some food shortfalls, an increasing need to import basic foodstuffs, both absolute and relative rural poverty, unbalanced economies, and disturbingly wide levels of malnutrition. Food production per capita in the region as a whole is lower currently than it was in the 1961-1965 period. Demand for food, on the other hand, is surging: a 3.7% annual increase in demand is projected over the next ten years.

Reasons for the decline in food production lie mainly in inadequate food pricing policies, limited resource inputs, inadequate technology and training, and inadequate distribution systems. Physical resources—except possibly for energy—are *not* generally a constraint. Indeed, the area's agricultural potential is substantially unrealized. Elements that can raise production levels include increasing irrigation, wider use of fertilizer, use of improved seeds, dissemination of newer agricultural technologies especially in micropackages, adequate credit availability, well-planned land reform, better distribution systems, and better pricing incentive policies. Measures to optimize agricultural development thus lie essentially in the national domestic policy sphere, in policies that will in effect enhance national comparative advantage.

The role international governance can play is essentially a supplementary one, that is, to optimize the availability to national governments of information and services to help them in sectoral planning; availability of financial resources for agricultural investment and nonprotectionist international trade policies would obviously also contribute to national efforts. In this sector, more than in most, information "networking" is an essential element. More systematic

---

*See Montague Yudelman, Chapter 16, this volume.

efforts are required to tap private research centers and to incorporate multinational corporations into constructive government/private sector consultations on technology, production problems, research, and the establishment of data banks. *We therefore recommend*:

● *That the InterAmerican Institute for Cooperation on Agriculture (IICA) develop systematic links, including an information-sharing network, among national agricultural centers and the Consultative Group of International Agriculture Research (CGIAR), which groups the international research centers.*

● *That IICA develop a communications dissemination system—a data bank—to compile information on successful cases of agricultural advances, to which the hemisphere's governments would have access.* Access could be on the basis of a fee to help defray the cost of the service.

● *That multinational corporations and other private sector institutions contribute to agricultural development efforts through consultations with governments and official institutions on technology, production problems, research efforts, and marketing opportunities.* IICA, the international financial institutions, and the subregional development banks should establish the institutional bases for such linkages.

Natural Resource Development*

Collectively, the region probably has as full a complement of natural resources as any other region of the world, and their development is a matter of considerable concern and interest to all the countries in the region. The identification of resources, especially minerals, and the availability of investment capital for their development are perhaps the most urgent needs felt by most countries.

Energy is currently the most obvious and exigent resource issue. The existence in the hemisphere of both oil-producing and oil-importing countries suggests the possibilities of some subregional cooperation to ease the burden on energy-deficit countries. Especially praiseworthy in this regard are three recent steps taken by area oil

---

*See William Glade, Chapter 17, this volume.

producers to assist energy-deficient countries in the region: (a) the Mexican–Venezuelan oil facility to help Central American and Caribbean countries in the importation of needed petroleum; (b) the Trinidad and Tobago facility for Caribbean countries; and (c) the agreement among the state oil companies of Mexico, Venezuela, and Brazil to cooperate through the framework of the Latin American Energy Organization (OLADE) in providing assistance to other Latin American countries for a wide range of petroleum projects, from exploration, development, and production to refining and industrial projects. These are good examples of how cooperation can help nations cope with the serious problems they face.

The potential for renewable energy exploitation in the hemisphere is particularly noteworthy. Vast, untapped amounts of hydro-electric power exist. Wind and solar energy are widely available and could be especially helpful to the smaller, poorer islands and coastal areas of the Caribbean basin. New, more effective ways to harness energy from biomass can be important. Creative—often easy to employ—devices for conserving energy need to be given greater attention in policy formulation. Many creative technologies also exist to reduce resource requirements and economic costs for a range of agricultural, commercial, and home needs, such as new designs for wood-burning stoves that greatly reduce the need for fast-disappearing fuel (wood). Greater communication on the part of innovators of small-scale problem-solving methodologies with intergovernmental agencies, governmental departments, business enterprises, and non-profit institutions could lead to highly beneficial "transfers" and utilization of renewable energy technologies.

Another set of considerations facing nations with regard to natural resources turns on the international impact of some kinds of resource development—for example, water resources, fisheries, and forest resource exploitation. In some instances, such as fisheries, where development involves more than one nation, the matter is international by definition, and the need for agreements or mutually satisfactory cooperative arrangements is obvious. River basin development in the case of international rivers is another good example of this.

Still another set of considerations has to do with the respective role of private and government activities. This is one sector in which government intervention and private sector exclusion are most prevalent. The case of exploitation of subsoil mineral deposits is, of course, one particularly burdened with historical and nationalistic sentiments. However, innovative patterns of public–private sector cooperation are a growing trend; they center usually on the provision of services, technology, and "know-how" by private companies under remunerative arrangements, with retention of ownership and equity by the public corporations.

To help nations develop their natural resources, *we recommend*:

● *That all hemisphere governments support the establishment of a World Bank Energy Affiliate an expansion of lending authority for energy research and exploration and supplement and encourage private investment in high-risk areas.*

● *That all governments establish creative incentives to encourage energy conservation and renewable energy production (e.g., experimentation with indigenous small- and large-scale wind, solar, hydro, and biomass projects), thereby reducing energy imports and increasing energy self-sufficiency.*

● *That intergovernmental agencies, government departments, nonprofit institutions, corporations, and technologists increase communication and joint venturing to widen technology choice (including renewable energy options) in order to solve problems in agriculture, industry, and at home with lower resource inputs, reduced economic costs, and less degradation of the environment.*

● *That the Latin American Energy Organization (OLADE) follow up on the United Nations Conference on Renewable Energy with a series of hemisphere conferences involving participation by state enterprises, governments, and private companies.*

Environment*

There is a growing awareness of the costs of environment abuse. Environmental problems are becoming well documented. Yet mismanagement of critical resources remains a fundamental problem. The main areas of environmental concern are deforestation and land degradation, water resource use, the environmental aspects of tourism

---

*See Kirk Rodgers, Chapter 18, this volume.

and urbanization, such as air, water, and beach pollution, marine resources, and species preservation.

Most environmental problems become international by definition, that is, actions may be national, but consequences are international. In some cases there is a potential for tension between countries and even conflict, as in the case of the excessive use by one party of shared water resources or of acid rain problems. In other cases, environmental problems lead quickly to cooperation because of perceived self-interest, as with boundary water pollution in the Rio Grande or Lake Erie. Instances of joint management and cooperation on environmental matters, such as the U.S.–Mexican Boundary and Water Commission or the River Plate hydroelectric development, can, in fact, provide a wealth of experience, information, and lessons for the international handling of such questions.

A conceptual problem has been the continuing assumption that environment is an "externality" in developing planning. This conception needs to be revised. Environmental factors need to be introduced as an integral part of project planning from the beginning. Both the World Bank and the Inter-American Development Bank have excellent records in forcing environment considerations into development planning, and they should be encouraged to keep doing so. This is an important element, since financial constraints represent an additional problem, that is, environmental measures may be costly at the outset, but corrective measures later are even more so.

Awareness, information, and cooperation are essential to the recognition and prompt management of environmental problems. These are things particularly suited to international governance. Accordingly, *we recommend*:

● *That environmental matters be specifically included in technical conferences and networks recommended above, and that the proposed self-financing "consulting staff" (see Chapter 4, p. 63) specifically cover environment and ecological topics.*

● *That national governments provide the Inter-American Council on Education, Science & Culture (CIECC) with information about successful joint management of environmental matters across national borders for sharing with other governments.*

● *That the OAS legal department should undertake a review of legal problems and applicable principles and law relating to environmental matters*; this information would facilitate future dispute settlement with regard to environmental problems.

HUMAN DEVELOPMENT

Human development—that is, effective programs in the fields of education and training, health and nutrition, and population—has a vital role and *raison d'être* in addition to the direct benefits it confers in these respective areas. Human development is an indispensable *investment* necessary to growth and modernization. The most valuable resource any country has is its people, and, as the World Bank has put it, they constitute "both the means and the end of economic advance."

But human development is a subtle, complex, and interacting process. It is not a matter that can be managed in isolation. It is clear, for example, that the central issue in nutrition lies not just in improving the combination of proteins and calories, but in increasing the amount of staples the poor can afford, which means increasing income and production of these foodstuffs. Human development, in short, is a process inextricably interwoven with a whole range of difficult and sensitive economic, cultural, and political issues and determinants.

The leading edge of human development concerns consists of three mutually reinforcing demographic trends: (a) relatively rapid population growth; (b) urbanization,* and (c) the rapidly increasing size of labor forces.† Each trend is intractable in its present direction for the next decade at least, and each presents unprecedented challenges.

The nature of the problem of overall population growth is altering in the sense that the "problem" is now uniformly recognized and acknowledged and is being dealt with. Population growth rates have begun to drop relatively rapidly, if unevenly, as a result of family planning programs, and especially as the consequences of development—urbanization, better infant mortality rates, and the increase of education for women and the number of women in the working force. The downward trend is likely to continue to the year 2000, when the region's annual population growth rate may be slightly under 2%.

Past population growth, however, has already put in place factors that will result in large future growth in labor forces, heavy urban in-migration, and a built-in momentum for future population

---

*See Alejandro Portes, Chapter 19, this volume.
†See Juan Buttari, Chapter 20, this volume.

growth in those societies where the majority of the people is still under the age of 20. Urbanization and unemployment and poor human resource formation are the most critical manifestations of current demographic problems.

Urbanization rates exceed population growth rates in every country. The trend is probably inexorable to the extent that agglomeration of markets and labor pools is a necessary adjunct to modernization. The problem, therefore, is not how to stop urbanization, but how to promote manageable growth of urban centers and improve conditions of rural life. Sociologists point out that internal migration and urbanization are not intrinsically good or bad; they may be beneficial for migrants, and they may in fact increase the division of labor and thus the fuller integration of the population into the market economy. The rapid rate of urbanization does, of course, have negative aspects, such as peripheral or precarious settlements, housing shortages, problems of providing basic services, deterioration of the environment, and the political dangers—if the agglomeration is in one or two major cities—of making them unmanageable.

The increase in labor forces is so rapid that job creation is a priority concern for almost every country, and unemployment and underemployment constitute a significant political vulnerability. Unemployment and underemployment are becoming largely urban problems, since the major growth in labor forces is concentrated in urban sectors. Almost half of the urban migrants are absorbed into an "informal" system of employment. This informal sector is much more than a survival system and is linked to the formal sector. Many sociologists argue that the informal system has within it some dynamic features relating to accumulation, innovation, productivity, and entrepreneurship. More study of the nature and meaning of the informal economy is obviously needed.

The fundamental issue in all these demographic problems clearly centers on the capacity of the economies to absorb the expanding supply of labor, provide services, and increase real income and opportunity—which can only be sustained through economic growth. These factors, in turn, merge into broad and fundamental questions of domestic policy and culture.

External Migration and Refugees

International migration has surged upward dramatically in the last two decades. It consists of a number of separate flows—refugees, professionals seeking better opportunities, and workers filling labor shortages. A hemisphere map of migration would reveal numerous criss-crossing flows throughout the region—Mexico–United States, Caribbean–United States, Colombia–Venezuela, Colombia–Ecuador, Bolivia–Argentina, Dominican Republic–Haiti. Unfortunately, since much of this migration is illegal, data are hard to come by and are inconsistent.

The pace of external labor migration will probably accelerate in the near-term, with the direction generally toward higher-wage countries. The flow will also get entwined with political refugee flows, such as those from Central America, complicating its management. Such migration flows constitute new strains on the international system and can create serious international complications.

Legal migration has in the past been a source of creativity and needed diversity for the receiving country, although one problem is that such movements have often cost sending countries the loss of persons with relatively scarce skills. The greatest problems, however, stem from illegal migration. These flows cause families to be divided and make the migrants second-class residents in the receiving countries.

Immigration and refugee issues confront virtually every country in the Americas, and their potential seriousness make them issues requiring immediate multinational attention in terms of dealing with problems when they occur as well as of preventing them. Although immigration policy is the sovereign responsibility of each nation, it would be manifestly unwise for any government to make policy without fully understanding its impact on other national interests or its international consequences. Creation of a consultative process and pooling of information among interested governments and international institutions dealing with refugees and migration would appear to be an urgent and prudent step.

Given the foregoing, *we recommend*:

● *That a small, 3- to 5-member, Inter-American Commission on Migration and Refugees, composed of distinguished, prestigious Americans, be established to assist hemisphere governments with regard to migration and refugee problems* (see Chapter 4). There is at present no regional entity functioning in this field; yet the increasing seriousness of the issue does call for special regional efforts to focus on it. We recognize the political sensitivity of migration questions, and we appreciate the fact that management of such matters is a sovereign question. It is not our conception in any way that such a Commission would be a supranational authority, able to prescribe or interpose itself in situations unilaterally. It would be intended rather to *assist* governments—through consultation, suggestions, information exchange, dialogue, study, discussion—in an ombudsman sense. Frequently, an external catalytic agent can prove very useful in matters of such passion and complexity, especially bilateral situations, by clarifying facts, broadening comprehension, suggesting new ideas, devising formula, facilitating bilateral discussions and understandings. The Commission would, in short, be a facilitator and service group available to all governments should they require or request it. The Commission could also link to, work with, and help focus the regional activity of the specialized global agencies, such as the UN High Commission for Refugees. It would promote studies of potential problems to help governments anticipate trends and difficulties.

● *That nations of the region join with ASEAN nations to explore or consider negotiation of an International Convention on Mass Exoduses, which would include condemnation of and sanctions against those nations that show no regard for their own people or for other nations' immigration laws.* Both groups of nations have experienced such phenomena. Consultation between them could suggest ways of preventing a repetition of such massive illegal and dangerous movements of peoples.

● *That the OAS commission a study of the traditional right of asylum, which in many ways has been rendered anachronistic in its present form by the emergence of mass politics and mass exoduses and by the blurring of the lines between political and economic refugees, with appropriate recommendations to member governments.*

Education, Culture, and Science*

1.   The region has seen significant expansion and improvements in the various education systems, which are now reaching most of the population in most places. Problem areas are (a) continuing absorption problems at elementary levels; (b) adult illiteracy; (c) explosive

---

*See Raul Allard, Chapter 22, this volume.

rise in demand for higher education; (d) the need for more vocational and technical training; and (e) the need to accommodate aboriginal populations in a nonalienating process. As in other fields, the response of the challenges of providing adequate education and training to their populations has to come at the national level. International systems, however, can provide support and assistance; there is an elaborate network of international bodies, public and private, global and regional, that deal with educational problems. Systematizing coordination among them and optimizing the flow and exchange of information, research, and experience are needed lines of action.

2. The cultural variety of the inter-American region is great, since there are fundamental differences in inspiration, psychology, style, and ways of acting and of perceiving issues. The peace, growth, stability, and development of the hemisphere depend upon broad mutual understanding of these different cultural values and traditions. It is just as important to the intrinsic strength of the area for Bolivia to know Honduras, for Mexico to know Peru, for Argentina to know Barbados, and for Ecuador to know Jamaica, as it is for any of them to know the United States. The major instruments to achieve this knowledge are the interchange of people and the establishment of networks between institutions in the various countries. Because the smaller nations, particularly, frequently lack the financial or human resources to undertake such efforts, regional institutions are important in terms of assuming much of this role. Cultural questions, however, have not received the institutional attention and development needed from governmental or intergovernmental agencies. Interhemisphere cultural exchanges need to be extended and improved on "North-South" lines as well as in terms of increased horizontal interchanges and the broader exposures that can foster knowledge and understanding.

3. There has been an enormous expansion in the hemisphere of consciousness about the impact and value of science and technology and the necessary role of research and development (R & D). The capacity to absorb and use new technologies is increasing in the larger countries, but the smaller, poorer countries do not have such capacities as a result of weak scientific networks, inadequate skilled personnel to absorb and use information, and limited available resources for investment for these purposes. The requirement—and demand—for human resources and infrastructures to absorb and use new technologies and rapid new advances in science is growing rapidly in all these countries.

Given all the foregoing, *we recommend*:

• *That the Inter-American Council on Education, Science and Culture (CIECC) of the OAS sponsor research on programs focusing on specific needs and emerging problems, such as the needs of women, bilingual education for indigenous peoples, adult education, and so forth.*

• *That CIECC and subregional organizations, such as the Andean Group, jointly establish multinational "centers of excellence" to train specialists of various kinds, pooling resources and using those already in existence,* as Mexican experience and resources in its "green revolution," Brazil on sugar cane derivatives, and Venezuela and Mexico on the petroleum industry. *Similarly, multinational sharing of costly equipment and information systems, such as educational TV or computer centers, should be explored.*

• *That governments make special efforts to encourage private business firms to expand significantly their support of vocational and nonformal "in-the-workplace" education,* and that multinationals, particularly, substantially increase their activities in this regard.

• *That the governments of the hemisphere support international cultural and educational exchanges.* In particular the United States should retain and expand the Fulbright and Humphrey Fellowship programs. Other American nations, such as Argentina, Brazil, Canada, Colombia, Mexico, and Venezuela, should consider establishing comparable programs for the benefit of the less advantaged countries of the hemisphere. *The admission of the group of English-speaking Caribbean states into the inter-American system is a special case, which calls for particular programs to facilitate cultural interchanges between them and the Latin American states.*

• *That CIECC work with the Seminar on the Acquisition of Latin American Library Materials (SALALM), the United States Library of Congress, and similar organizations to promote the effective use of computer-based library technologies, to share language translation facilities and services, to establish networks to facilitate the transfer of these facilities and technologies especially to the poorer countries, and to coordinate the updating of circulation of technical, business, and scholarly journals and books to national and university libraries, that is, "international librarianship"* for information already in the public domain.

● *That CIECC should seek to systematize scientific networking by sponsoring conferences with government, university and professional associations on key issues in the field, and by encouraging subregional cooperation on developing information systems and accessing data banks, including the sharing of costs of equipment and personnel among interested countries.*

● *That CIECC, in cooperation with other UN and subregional organizations, sponsor the task of analyzing the social costs of scientific and technological decisions;* codifying "collective wisdom" on these issues and making it available to national policy planners would be helpful.

4

Intergovernmental Institutions

Institutions are born when there is a felt need for their existence. They flourish if this need persists; when needs change, they perform inadequately or fall into desuetude. Rarely, however, do international institutions die, even when their utility declines. They fade away—not completely—but into a sort of limbo of their own. They survive because there are special groups that favor their continuance, because they have bureaucracies, because of inertia, and because it is often more troublesome to alter treaties that created them than simply to let them exist and just ignore them.

Examples to fit all these descriptions can be found in the Western Hemisphere, where a myriad of official international organizations—world-wide, regional, and subregional; general and specialized—operate in virtually all fields. They constitute perhaps the most elaborate network of public international institutions functioning anywhere in the world.

The period immediately following World War II witnessed a major institutional flowering, with the principal global institutions—the United Nations, the International Monetary Fund, the World Bank, GATT, and other specialized agencies—dating their birth to this period. There is no need to retell here the story of their creation; it is sufficient for our purposes to note that their creation and design grew out of the problems and power relationships of the day. The most important regional institution, the Organization of American States (OAS) was also fashioned at this time. Its original function—and its main present function—was essentially political: peacekeeping, conflict resolution, and, in a more abstract formulation, as an institutional way for the nations of Latin America and the United States to interact with each other, given substantial power asymmetry.

There was a second burst of creation at the end of the 1950s and in the early 1960s, this time focused on the Western Hemisphere and culminating in the Alliance for Progress. The major objective perceived by the countries of the region at the time was to promote economic and social development. The Inter-American Development Bank and the major economic organs of the OAS date their births to this period. Economic and social issues remain at the center of the agenda of the countries of the hemisphere, and the multiplication of institutions in this field is a consequence of this priority. But the pattern of creation, in which there have been mainly births and hardly any deaths, has resulted in a complex structure of overlapping and redundancy.

Institutional overpopulation creates problems, just as biological overpopulation does. It is not only that a plethora of institutions raises questions of duplication, inefficiency, and relevance, but also that each institution represents a demand on limited budgetary and human resources. In a period in which fewer and fewer resources can be expected to be available for international organizations, efficiency and precision in their use are a practical necessity.

We do not intend here to provide a judgment on each international institution in the hemisphere or deliver a verdict on which is needed and which is not. Rather, we have sought to set out some general thoughts as a way of thinking about the complex institutional network and to suggest areas and directions for future actions by governments. We point out also that the comments in the following pages focus on the inter-American system—the OAS and related agencies. This is a choice we made deliberately: The elaborate institutional structure of the inter-American system is a distinct body of institutional governance and therefore conceptually relatively easy to examine; it has a long tradition and history; instrumentalities that can assist the area's nations in coping with problems and the strains of interdependence are already in existence; it is a body of institutions intended to deal with and serve the whole region.

Such a focus does, however, risk distorting the total picture of governance. We do not wish to minimize the contributions and roles of two other dimensions of institutional cooperation—the subregional groupings, such as the Latin American Economic System (SELA) and the economic integration organizations, and the regional activities of global institutions, such as the United Nations Economic Commission for Latin America (ECLA). We recognize the importance of these and, indeed, the pressing need for more systematic coordination and relation of all these dimensions to each other.

Finally, we note that this chapter deals with official institutions. We emphasize again the large number of private sector organizations and entities and private interactions, and the immense resources they command and can bring to bear on regional problems.

For analytical convenience, the discussion of institutional governance that follows is divided into political and economic/social fields.

POLITICAL

This is the relatively clearer, less congested field of activity for institutions. The United Nations and the OAS are the most important international organizations engaged in the field.

The preceding section outlined major considerations in relation to general "political/security" issues. For emphasis we reiterate three broad points here:

- Nation-states are unlikely to submit political concerns to extranational or supernational entities or limit their foreign policy freedom; hence, international institutions are not realistic vehicles for comprehensive political decision making;

- Yet international organizations do have a major value and necessary function in terms of a "service" role, i.e., to provide fora, procedures, and mechanisms for discussion, reconciliation, and venting of pressures, as well as easier and more systematic ways for nations to reach *de facto* cooperative arrangements in face-saving ways than normal bilateral negotiation or intercourse might permit.

- One broad area in which international organizations are especially valuable, even indispensable, is *peace-keeping*, including conflict-resolution and dispute settlement.

As regards peace-keeping, the OAS has a unique purpose, role, and function that is not duplicated by any other institution. Its role is governed by its Charter, by the Inter-American Treaty of Reciprocal Assistance (the Rio Pact), and, within that joint framework, by a number of agreements and treaties relating to mechanisms for dispute settlement. We have already observed that today the mechanism seems to function less effectively than in the past, that American nations' confidence that resort to the system can effectively meet their needs appears to be weakening, and that there is a growing willingness by member states to disregard traditional inter-American precepts and principles (see pp. 24–25). The reasons lie not so much in structure or mechanism as in the political realities of inter-American relations (and of international relations generally), specifically the strong ideological issues coming to the fore in the hemisphere and the fact of power asymmetry.

The answers to this set of problems lie in the political realm, not in the formal, legalistic, and organizational realm. The OAS peace-keeping function will be what the governments want it to be; and governments often find it useful. Governments cannot be compelled to use this, or any, peacekeeping mechanism. But it is essential that the mechanism *be* there. No more urgent requirement exists than having in place the instrumentalities for the hemisphere's nations to consult with each other to secure the peace, especially in the light of expectable new strains in the international system, such as territorial disputes, terrorism, disputes over resources, or refugee migrations. If only one conflict is prevented or curtailed, one source of tension ameliorated, or one dispute resolved, the institution will have more than paid its way.

The flexibility and continuity provided by the mechanisms of the OAS are of particular utility. The annual gathering of the Ministers of Foreign Affairs at the OAS General Assembly provides an unparalleled opportunity, both within and without the official meetings, to discuss the issues of the hemisphere in an informal atmosphere. The principal officials responsible for the conduct of hemispheric relations from all the nations can get to know one another without the requirement of formal state visits. The mechanism whereby the Ministers of Foreign Regulations can be convoked in a Meeting of Consultation by any nation on a moment's notice, with the OAS Permanent Council sitting continuously as back-up, has provided a rapid release valve for tensions on numerous occasions.

The United Nations Charter explicitly concedes the prime peace-keeping, conflict-resolution role to the regional political institutions (Article 52). Consequently, the UN exists in this hemisphere as a residual and heretofore largely unused mechanism. There are pressures to resort to the UN rather than the OAS as ideological issues cause nations to seek support to global fora or as nations perceive the regional mechanisms as unsuited to their interests. A shift of the dispute-settlement, peace-keeping function, *de facto* or formally, to the UN framework would, in our view, be undesirable. It would increase the channeling of world balance-of-power tensions into regional problems. This can only complicate disputes and not facilitate their solution. Regional disputes could easily be transformed in this fashion into larger crises than they intrinsically need to be. For this reason, therefore, *we recommend*:

> ● *that the peacekeeping and conflict resolution machinery of the OAS be maintained and strengthened as the cornerstone of the inter-American system.*

Although we have emphasized the peace-keeping function of the OAS in this section, the OAS clearly provides valuable and needed services and channels with regard to other major issues— defense of human rights, refugees and migration, arms restraint, nuclear questions, terrorism—all of which are crucially relevant to survival and peace. We refer to the various recommendations on these matters in the preceding chapter.

We believe that the system's functioning and efficiency would be improved to the extent that the system's membership could be universal. We believe, for example, that Canada's full participation would be a great asset; we are concerned that some independent countries, such as Guyana and Belize, are excluded because of border disputes with member states; we are disturbed that growing ideological issues with Nicaragua and Grenada present problems as regards their participation. Accordingly, *we recommend*:

> ● *that the inter-American system, and subregional institutions, continue to seek to embrace as many members as is consistent with their continued operation, respecting the varieties of ideologies that are now manifest in the hemisphere.*

> ● *that hemispheric and subregional organizations for economic cooperation and financing continue to provide assistance and to stimulate trade among all present members that meet their obligations to these institutions, notwithstanding the political and ideological differences on other matters that may divide member countries.* We believe that development and economic

activities should be insulated from the winds of other political conflict. Both this and the preceding recommendation are consistent with the OAS principle of ideological pluralism, and the goal of both is conflict containment.

● *that the Government of Canada reexamine its policies toward the hemisphere's formal institutions in order to consider greater participation, and we urge that the OAS, the IDB, and the Caribbean Development Bank give priority to increasing their cooperation with Canadian public and private institutions.*

ECONOMIC–SOCIAL

This field of governance exhibits much greater "congestion" and confusion. In the area of finance, the IDB stands predominant and is effectively coordinating with the subregional banks. But in the area of direct services and policy coordination, questions of duplication, overlap, and inefficiency in cost/benefit terms arise insistently. Our examination of this field leads us to three general conclusions, two of which we pose in the form of general "principles" that could guide institutional creation or continuation in the economic-social area, and the third as a recommendation regarding institutional termination. These are:

1. *International institutions and arrangements work best when they have clearly delineated and specific responsibilities and are essentially "single-purposed."* Cooperation is likely to be more effective if matters are disaggregated by problem or issue field, and the focus of governance is functional and service oriented; to the degree to which an organization aims at encompassing various fields in comprehensive systems with implicit political obligations and costs, it is likely to be less effective and even resisted. This can be stated in reverse. Multifunctional institutions are unlikely to endure in their full vigor unless they resist undertaking subsidiary functions, either formally or in practice, that are not relevant to their principal goals. *We have called this the "functional principle."*

2. *Most functions have a subregional, regional, and global dimension. The institutional framework is strongest when*

each level builds on the others. Global organizations need cooperating regional institutions to build their own strength, while regional and subregional arrangements can facilitate collective responsibility for dealing with problems as they present themselves locally. Frequently regional action may be the only way to make progress on problems when global possibilities are stalemated. Institutional governance can be viewed as ever-widening circles, all touching at one point at their base, but growing ever larger, eccentrically, to the global level. *We have called this the "widening-circle principle."*

The above two concepts are further elaborated in relation to specific institutions, and this will lead us to further recommendations as indicated.

3. *Because it is clearly useful to have a way of terminating as well as inaugurating organizations, we believe governments should institute a "sunset" concept on institutional continuance.* This is a concept that is widely accepted within countries, although it may be harder to practice for institutions that transcend country jurisdictions. It is applicable both to institutions and to individual programs within institutions. Sunset provisions can be effective only if there are periodic, mandated evaluations. These could, for example, take place every ten years or other specified period, at which time governments can make a decision on whether to continue, alter, or discontinue the institution. Since only governments can take action to alter or terminate an organization, the governments, and not the institutions, must carry out the evaluations.

The functional principle can be seen in operation at the *global level*—for example, in the International Monetary Fund, GATT, the World Bank, FAO, ILO, WHO; the *regional level*—for example, the Pan American Health Organization (PAHO), the Inter-American Institute for Agricultural Cooperation (IICA), and the Inter-American Development Bank (IDB); and at the *subregional* level— for example, the Caribbean Development Bank (CDB), the Andean Development Corporation (CAF), the Latin American Export Bank (BLADEX).

There are several reasons why functional organizations have a better chance for success than organizations that have tasks in many fields. A meeting of a functional institution is more likely to attract policy makers from capitals (as the annual IDB, PAHO, and CIECC meetings do), whereas high-level officials are less likely to come to a comparable meeting dealing with a subfunction of a varied institution. [The inability of the Inter-American Economic and Social Council (CIES) to attract senior officials from capitals illustrates this.] Negotiation, when this is the purpose of a meeting, cannot easily be conducted across multifunctional lines. A single purpose also permits more precise delineations of responsibilities, concentration of energy and resources, and clearer definitions of purpose. Relevance, the degree of duplication with other entities, and how valuable governments find the purpose and service offered are all additional factors making for effectiveness.

The stress we have given to functionalism as a main guiding principle of institutional organization in the hemisphere does not mean to underestimate the need for synthesis of different functional issues and the "policy dimension." Interdependence applies to issues as well as nations. Neither economic, nor social, educational, or technological issues can be easily segregated. Effective policies in agriculture, employment generation, industrialization require the coordination of efforts in multiple fields for effective use of scarce resources. No agencies, whether global or regional, economic or social, should be exempt from the disciplines of prioritizing and interrelating their activities. This occurs at present on an *ad hoc* basis within individual countries, but there is clearly a need for transnational coordination, for discussion of policies, and for exchange of experience and views.

Among the Western industrial countries, senior economic policy makers get together periodically, usually annually, in the Organization for Economic Cooperation and Development (OECD). They do not negotiate at these sessions, but they do get to know their counterparts, and, more substantively, each official gets some indication of what the others are contemplating. This permits each to devise his or her own policies with greater knowledge of the outside influence that will act on his or her economy. It may even be possible at times to get another policy maker to revise policies in the light of the impact on others. Somewhat similarly, heads of different economic institutions in the hemisphere meet informally, usually at the time of other meetings, such as the annual IMF and World Bank meetings or the sessions of the IDB.

We note with concern, however, that there is no real truly regional forum for bringing together the most senior economic policy makers of the different countries, even though economic and development issues are of major concern (see Chapter 3), and policy decisions and world trends impact significantly on all. CIES can, in theory, be a forum for bringing together these senior policy officials, but it is not. The plenary sessions of the Economic Commission for Latin America (ECLA) used to serve this function but no longer do this effectively.

We rejected the idea of recommending *formal* coordination among economic policy makers of the hemisphere because we are aware of the full graveyard of past coordination proposals. Yet the desirability of such consultation/coordination is clearly keenly felt. Indeed, the fact that the graveyard *is* full indicates that the need for coordination is still a very alive and recurring issue.

We believe that senior economic policy makers of the hemisphere should meet informally once a year for each to expose his or her policy thinking to the others. It should be a closed meeting, so that statements are made for each other and not for the press. It can work only if it is a professional exercise attracting the most senior officials from capitals. Such a meeting, in short, would be analogous to what now occurs in the OECD and among central bankers, health ministers, agriculture ministers, and even foreign ministers. Such a meeting should include senior U.S. economic policy officials, in the same way these officials now attend ministerial-level meetings at the OECD. Representatives of key international economic institutions— IMF, World Bank, IDB, ECLA—should also attend.

We do not think it of great consequence which international institution sponsors these annual meetings of senior economic officials. The intent is not institutional as much as it is to provide a forum. The forum could be free-standing, for the ministers to organize themselves, but this may be impractical. The institutional locus could rotate each year among the major economic-social institutions of the hemisphere, but this could introduce chaos. In our view, the best way to hold such a meeting to save time and resources may be to have them as an adjunct to the annual IDB meeting, and for the OAS to coordinate them. *We recommend*:

> ● *that the Secretary General of the OAS and the President of the IDB consult on mechanisms to initiate annual, nonnegotiating meetings of economic ministers and to sound out the governments of the hemisphere as to their receptivity to such meetings.*

Mechanisms to provide policy fora in other fields can be operated in a variety of ways, and there are numerous precedents to draw from. The OAS has demonstrated that it can house policy fora for functionally specific activities, provided the principal actors in the respective fields want such a forum. CIECC works because it is the only forum for the education ministers, and they assume responsibility for funding its programs. Similarly, CITEL, the Inter-American Committee on Telecommunications of the OAS, which Canada has recently joined, is working well and coordinating closely with the ITU. This is distinct from CIES, whose economic functions have been largely superseded by the Inter-American Development Bank and which is now redundant with regional and global institutions, thus blurring its purpose. As a result, CIES is a distraction to senior finance and economic officials of the region rather than being seen as a major policy instrument.

The important operational principle that can be extracted from this, therefore, is that a well-designed system of regional governance should provide functionally specific fora for various sectors of interacting national interest. Health ministers, agriculture ministers, labor ministers, education ministers, central bankers, all meet periodically. To the extent that these meetings are not convoked by functionally specific agencies, we believe the OAS should devise the mechanism to do so, as it has done in the case of CIECC, labor ministers, and communications. It would be important, however, for the OAS to define its role clearly in providing the systematic and regular fora for policy making and coordination and not in program execution, as we will discuss further below. *We recommend*:

- *that the OAS give consideration to assuming responsibility to ensure systematic and regular meetings of the Ministers of the principal sectors of the member States for consideration of policy issues.*

Technical assistance is a particularly perplexing segment of institutional governance in this hemisphere. In itself, the management of a flexible, responsive technical assistance operation is a functionally specific capability. For this reason, we have discussed the need for a type of inter-American "consultant firm." At present, technical assistance is offered by scores of organizations—bilateral, subregional, regional, and global. Most of these services are offered with little institutional coordination. What coordination there is must be handled mostly by the country receiving assistance; but by definition, since it needs assistance, the country often lacks the capacity or resources to handle this coordination. Because each entity offering technical assistance—IDB, AID, United Nations Development Program, the specialized OAS agencies—pursues technical and development assistance programs according to its own purposes, programs, recipes and rituals, there is a substantial variation in the kinds and forms of assistance offered, its terms, and the overhead costs. One implication of these circumstances, in our view, is that systematic consultation among these various agencies could lead to a more efficient "sorting out" and coordination and the relative purposes of technical assistance—to backstop loans, the greater need of smaller, less advantaged countries, human needs, and so forth—and more efficient consequent use of resources.

For the OAS, technical assistance activities are governed essentially by the two separate councils, CIES and CIECC, each with its own permanent Executive and Program Committees. There is a relatively cumbersome governmental approval mechanism requiring a large bureaucracy to provide very modest assistance. We have asked ourselves whether the technical assistance function of the OAS is useful to the organization or is best turned over to other existing entities or to an autonomous subbody, such as a Specialized Agency or perhaps a continuing Special General Assembly for Development Cooperation. If organized along the line of a consulting staff or clearing house, it could focus on the needs of the member countries, coordinating the diverse sources of assistance and serving as a resource to the member countries to obtain information on specialized problems and sources of expertise. Accordingly, *we recommend*:

- *that the OAS and the IDB consult with the other major technical assistance agencies of the hemisphere to consider the establishment of a small, joint coordinating staff that could function in the nature of a "clearing house" or as "consultants" for member States*; such a staff could provide and collate information, compile sources, provide data on available technical expertise and professional assistance, offer advice on project formulation and general advisory and evaluative help. The staff could be self-financing by charging a small fee for information provided and services rendered.

The *widening-circle principle* referred to above complements the principle of functionalism and is especially relevant to the ways in which regional institutions relate to global. In this connection, we wish to stress a point that is not self-evident: Subregionalism and regionalism need not conflict with global activities. This is so even in those fields in which much policy must be made globally (such as trade and the workings of the international monetary system), but it is particularly relevant for nonpolitical functional activities such as health, agriculture, energy, education, transportation, telecommunications, and the like. Subregional and regional activities can be valuable building blocks in reaching and carrying out global programs. Where regional agencies may be weak in particular fields, this type of approach can strengthen them and make better use of scarce resources. On the other hand, because global action can be difficult to achieve and can become stalemated relatively easily, given the number of actions, interests, and conflicting objectives involved, regional and subregional actions can become the best way, even the only way, to make any progress on the problems involved.

The *widening-circle principle* is best illustrated by the relationship between the Pan American Health Organization (PAHO) at the regional level and the World Health Organization (WHO) at the global level. PAHO antedates WHO, which gave it bargaining leverage when the latter was created. PAHO and WHO have an agreement under which the programs of WHO in the region are managed by PAHO, and the Ministers of Health of the hemisphere countries meet annually to determine the policies and programs of both PAHO and WHO. This arrangement has worked successfully, and this is what prompted us to suggest generalizing this principle of operation. The PAHO–WHO relationship also conforms to the functional principle.

What other functions might be handled in this manner? One that occurs to us is the Inter-American Institute for Agricultural Cooperation (IICA) and the Food and Agricultural Organization (FAO). Like PAHO–WHO, an IICA–FAO relationship would involve functional and essentially nonpolitical activity, with no necessary conflict between regional and global objectives, but rather a differentiation of regional needs from those of other regions. UNESCO–CIECC and the International Atomic Energy Agency (IAEA) and the Inter-American Nuclear Energy Commission (IANEC) are other possibilities. We also believe that the analogy might be carried downward, that is, OAS activities might be chaneled in subregions through subregional organizations such as the Andean Pact or the Caribbean Common Market (CARICOM).

Because we see merit in these patterns, *we recommend*:

● *that the possibility of extending the PAHO–WHO pattern to other institutions should be explored by member governments and the relevant organizations.*

As we examined the array of regional institutions, it was evident that almost every conceivable function was covered. The one major problem area for which there is no regional institution is that dealing with migration and refugees. This may be unique. We are not aware of any other significant issue or problem area in which there is not a counterpart regional body to the relevant global institution. We are reluctant to suggest the creation of new institutions. However, the immigration/refugee issue promises to reach such serious proportions, impacting on almost all the nations of the hemisphere, that we believe regional processes to facilitate consultation in this area are essential. Accordingly we have recommended above (Chapter 3, pp. 32–33) the formation of an Inter-American Commission on Migration and Refugees for this purpose, and we refer to the discussion and explanations therein.

The institutional structure of the inter-American system and the long history and tradition of regional cooperation in the hemisphere are, in sum, distinct assets for the nations of the region. The framework of the inter-American system, we firmly believe, deserves to be retained and strengthened. It has useful purposes to serve. It is clear, however, that the time has come for a major effort to consolidate and make the regional system more efficient; to eliminate duplication and waste of resources; and to relate the inter-American system more consciously and systematically to both global institutions and subregional arrangements.

The institutions of the system must recapture the allegiance of the nations they serve.

5

Summary and Conclusions

As indicated in the foregoing pages, the range of issues, tasks, problems, and challenges facing the governments and peoples of the hemisphere—indeed, the quality of life itself over the coming years—can be subsumed under three major objectives: the preservation of peace and security; economic growth, development, and modernization; and the realization of human potential.

A central task and major priority facing the peoples and governments of the Americas is the preservation of peace. This is an objective that must be actively and continuously pursued by purposefully seeking the settlement of border and territorial disputes, devising effective procedures for resolving conflicts, engaging governments in rational management of arms acquisitions, stopping the illegal flow of arms in the region, seeking to eliminate terrorism, and preventing the spread of nuclear weapons. A necessary adjunct to the preservation of peace and the containment of conflict is the protection of personal security and human rights and the advancement of the hemisphere's traditional commitment to liberty and participatory government. We have recommended use of the instrumentalities and institutions of the inter-American system in a variety of ways intended to make progress on all these tasks (Chapter 3, pp. 26–33).

Virtually all the nations of Latin America and the Caribbean have made development a national policy goal. It is a realistic aim.

But its attainment, and the ability to handle internal political, economic, and social stress, are all directly related to the ability to stimulate economic growth. In great part this, in turn, depends on sound *domestic* policies and strategies in each nation. Internationally, it is contingent upon expanding external trade and having access to adequate amounts of capital. We have, therefore, recommended that all nations, but especially the more developed, seek to restrain protectionism and promote freer trade; that the institutions and policies intended to promote a liberal world trading system be strengthened and consolidated; that adequate levels of public and private sector aid flows be provided; and that the international financial institutions to be adequately funded (Chapter 3, pp. 38–41). We have also recommended measures designed to increase consultation, share information and experiences, provide technical and resource assistance, and improve the participation of international institutions in the fields of agriculture and food policy, natural resource development, and environmental issues—measures that will enable national governments to make wiser and more effective decisions (Chapter 3, pp. 41–42).

The development of human potential is another major issue cluster. Human development is an indispensable investment necessary to growth and modernization. The most valuable resource any country has is its people, and they constitute "both the means and the ends of economic advance." Individual governments, of course, bear prime responsibility, and most of the areas of human development are essentially matters for domestic policy. Cooperation among nations, however, is also urgently required to help governments in these tasks, especially in their efforts to meet the pressing challenges of providing employment and education and training to growing populations. External migration and refugee flows are also matters of growing international concern, requiring the attention of the region's nations. We have, therefore, recommended measures to be undertaken by international agencies and governments (1) to systematize and expand cooperation, consultation, and information flow with regard to education and training; (2) to expand cooperation in cultural interchanges of people and among institutions; and (3) to improve their capacities to absorb and use new technologies and rapid new advances in science. And we have made recommendations with regard to the migration problems, including the establishment of a new Inter-American Commission on Refugees and Migration (Chapter 3, pp. 48–49).

The long history and elaborate intergovernmental institutional structure of regional governance in the Western Hemisphere constitute distinct assets for the countries of the region. We believe that the framework of the inter-American system deserves to be retained and strengthened. It has useful purposes to fulfill. There is a need, however, for a major effort to evaluate and make the system more efficient; to eliminate waste of relatively scarce resources; and to relate the inter-American system more specifically and in a more coordinated way to global institutions and subregional arrangements. The institutions of the system must reflect the hemisphere's changed realities and demonstrate their relevance to members' needs and aspirations if they are to recapture the allegiances of the nations they serve. We have recommended a "sunset" evaluation procedure to assess the desirability of continuing, discontinuing, or changing the various agencies and organizations; fuller consultation among members' top economic planners and decision makers in a systematic but informal way; the coordination of technical assistance activities in the form of a "consulting firm," which could partially be self-financing; adequate budgetary support by all member states, and systematization of relations with global and subregional institutions (Chapter 4).

Our recommendations necessarily and inevitably tended to concentrate on the more formal and institutionalized intergovernmental processes and mechanisms. But we do not mean thereby to distort perspectives, and we therefore, also emphasize three aspects: (1) While we have concentrated on functional recommendations designed to improve information exchange, consultation, and "service" functions, we recognize that it is the international activities themselves—trade, financing, investment, cultural exchange, development efforts—that are the central instruments that both reflect and constitute the increasing bonds of interdependence among nations. (2) We believe that unofficial, private sectors can provide great potential for meeting nations' needs and requirements; hence, we have urged governments to resort to and encourage the involvement and activity by private sector groups, companies, and institutions in the major issues of the day. (3) In the final analysis, it is the formulation and implementation of wise domestic policies and strategies that will make the major contribution to peace and well-being in our world; hence, in this interdependent world each government's responsibility for managing its country's affairs constructively becomes an obligation that each bears for the good of all.

We fully appreciate the constraints nations and societies feel with regard to such international efforts as we have outlined above. We recognize the problem of limited available resources. We are aware that domestic interests too often seem more compelling than the longer-range, harder-to-prove benefits of international cooperation. But there is an inexorability in the world predicament today. Actions necessary to change adverse trends cannot be postponed without closing important options. Failure to take indicated measures will lead to worsening conditions. We do not have the luxury of "waiting to see" or of settling for "second-best" policies and alternatives. History will not excuse us our failures on the grounds that the required measures were too expensive or too difficult to undertake. And the waste in human potential that our shortcomings can cause will indeed mean lost opportunities to alter the course of history and advance our civilization.

II

Background Papers

6

The Unexpected
and the International System
in the 1980s

Allan Goodman

In the course of the Aspen Institute's review of Governance in the Western Hemisphere, directed by the distinguished steering committee identified elsewhere in this report, twenty papers were commissioned on issue areas on which the committee focused. The papers were especially considered at three workshops on groupings of the issues: economic issues, social and human resources, and political and security issues.

The steering committee has, among its members, knowledgeable individuals in many of the areas assessed; special advisors and consultants joined in the formal and informal deliberations that occurred in the course of the committee's work. But the background papers, compiled in the present volume, helped to ground the discussion in solid information and the seasoned judgment of special experts. They helped to delineate the substantive, procedural, and institutional problems with which the committee grappled in the course of its two-year process, hence they help to underpin the final report itself.

The steering committee, and the Aspen Institute, wish to express again here our gratitude to the authors of the papers for their centrally important contributions to the study and to the report. The papers are presented here in the sequence in which they are referred to in the committee's report.

I

The statesmen of the 1980s will conduct foreign relations against a backdrop of unexpected complexity and uncertainty. Today's fiction is all too likely to become tomorrow's crisis. There are, thus, two papers here. One is written from the perspective of 1981 and discusses the key trends and dynamics that will probably shape foreign policy and crisis management decisions for the rest of the decade. Its focus is on how such phenomena could give rise to the unexpected. Another is written from the perspective of a retired American president, looking back on the 1980s. These reflections are "taken" from draft chapters of his memoirs and focus on what major surprises occurred during the decade and—in retrospect—why.

This chapter was undertaken on the premise that the unexpected event or series of events have frequently and fundamentally changed the range of alternatives and even the framework for considering policy in modern international affairs. As such, this chapter is not designed simply to run out a series of scenarios about the future. Rather it is an inquiry into how the dynamics of projected trends and hypothetically surprising events could create major crises in the international system and change the way in which the nature of power and the requisites of security are likely to be viewed in the 1980s.

My mandate was a liberal one. I was told to "feel free to speculate across the whole gamut of international relations" in order to draw a broad outline of the unexpected and how it could translate into problems and issues that would affect not only the international system but the Western hemisphere in particular. The paper begins with an analysis of those key trends that in my judgment have the potential for confronting the policy maker with unexpected challenges in the foreseeable future (i.e., within the next three to six years). "President Bush" then discusses the major ways in which these trends and dynamics "translated" into surprises for policy makers. Finally, I review briefly the implications such surprises could have for the Western hemisphere and for the ability of existing institutions to cope with the problems with which they could be confronted.

II

I began writing this paper the week that President Ronald Reagan was the subject of a very nearly successful assassination attempt.

It was the third nuclear detonation in as many days over the South Atlantic. But I was no nearer an explanation for the blasts or a strategy to handle the crisis which had emerged than on day one. In these respects, the allies as well as the Soviet Union, faced the same degree of uncertainty.

At least seven groups had claimed responsibility for the blasts, and several had threatened that a fourth blast would occur within a week in a major western city. The PLO (Black September Faction) was the first group to claim credit for the blast, and demanded immediate Israeli military withdrawal from the West Bank and dismantlement of all its settlements. Another PLO splinter group (called Grey Dawn) claimed responsibility for the second blast and demanded that, in addition to Israeli withdrawal, some 321 "political prisoners" detained by Israeli authorities be released. The Basque separatists claimed credit for the second blast, too. In Germany, elements of remnants of the Baader-Meinhof gang claimed responsibility for the first and third blasts, and presented authorities in three European capitals with lists of "freedom fighters" convicted of terrorist attacks and demanded their immediate release. A new group, the "Joint Commando of the Red Brigade and the Japanese Red Army," issued a communique after the third blast, claiming responsibility for the second blast (along with the Puerto Rican "freedom fighters") and presenting authorities in eight countries with yet another list of convicted terrorists that they demanded be released within 72 hours. The Tupamaros claimed responsibility for the second blast threatening others and presented authorities in the Western Hemisphere with a list of some 52 convicted terrorists and other prisoners of conscience and demanded their release within a week.

In addition to these groups and their associated demands, the sovereign governments of Libya, South Africa, Iraq, and the People's Democratic Republics of Brazil and Argentina, were believed by American intelligence to be in some way connected to the blasts.

George H. W. Bush, "August 1985: The Crisis that led to the Collapse of the UN." Excerpt from his draft *Memoirs* (prepared while Mr. Bush was a Distinguished Research Fellow, Center for Strategic and International Studies, and University Professor, Georgetown University).

It was the deepest, most profound tragedy of my life. Throughout the days and weeks of mourning, I grieved for both his family
and the nation. His vision held so much promise for America that
only the cruelest of fates would have snatched it from us so suddenly and so violently. I take some comfort in the fact that he lived
long enough to see a spirit of confidence grow across the land and to
win the re-nomination of our party.

The assassination of the President brought home to all of us
how vulnerable we were to terrorism and how much this evil force
had an impact on world affairs. The radical government of Iran
which trained and armed the terrorists to do this awful act has paid a
grave price. . . .

Bush, "The Death of the President," in *Memoirs.*

A number of other unexpected events occurred in the period immediately prior to that week, which have also shaped my thinking.

When I began "research" on this particular paper I happened to
see that very evening an ABC special called "Soldiers of the Twi-
light," a report on the mercenaries and the growth of mercenary
armies. The report's main message: the modern mercenary had
become a major player in power struggles in the Third World. The
next evening I saw an NBC "news magazine" report on a German
company, "OTRAG," which manufactures rockets and guidance
systems. The focus of the NBC commentary was on the fact that
there is a high degree of suspicion that OTRAG, now under contract
to the government of Libya, is designing rockets and guidance
systems to deliver military payloads for Colonel Qadhafi.

As my "research" continued into the weekend, I ran across an
account of a raid made by a local Florida sheriff on the training
camp of some 24 self-styled commandos who were practicing jungle
warfare on a property adjacent to the Crystal River nuclear plant.
Other news reports of interest included: an account on how the
Techwood Homes Vigilantes, a group set up in Atlanta to police the
black neighborhood where so many children have been murdered,
had been trained by New York City's Guardian Angels (a group of
citizen vigilantes that ride the subway trains in addition to the police
to protect blacks and other minority groups), and that both groups
had been recently visited by a delegation from the Soviet Union,

There was always the possibility that the Soviets would sur-reptitiously try to exceed the limits that we had agreed to at Stockholm on yearly production rates for their *Backfire* intercontinental bomber and on the number of MIRVs in their ICBMs. As the extensive Congressional hearings held in the aftermath of this so-called "intelligence failure" suggested, however, both we and the Congress felt confident that our intelligence could adequately verify the prohibitions of SALT-III at the time we signed this agreement. In the case of both violations, our estimates assumed some lead time before we could be certain that violations had in fact occurred. It is to the credit of our intelligence community that these violations were detected with such rapidity and definitiveness. This is especially impressive given the fact that the factory which produced the excess Backfires was located in Bulgaria, a country which received a relatively low priority in our satellite intelligence collection system.

Bush, "Why Salt-III Failed," in *Memoirs*.

which presented them with small gifts. And finally, about a week into my "research," the State Department acknowledged that Secretary Haig had requested an investigation into the extent to which Americans trained in terrorist techniques are selling their skills and knowledge to Libya and other countries. Moreover, the Associated Press, claiming access to a confidential government report, cited that report as concluding the following: "The United States in effect has become a major supplier of (military) hardware and technology, in support of world-wide terrorism. . . . Former Central Intelligence Agency personnel, military special forces personnel, and U.S. corporations combine to supply products and expertise to whomever can pay the price."

If projected bizzarely enough into the future, these "random happenings could lead to the kind of crisis-driven memoirs a future president might well write. They underscore how present trends in terrorism and nuclear proliferation alone could combine to create serious crises in the international system in the 1980s.

Partly as a result of thinking about this type of crisis as an archetype and partly as a result of examining present and projected trends and strains in the international system, the central theme of this paper is that the unexpected and irrational are going to manifest

---

In a certain sense, no one should have been surprised by the Soviet attack on Japan. The island nation had once before been the landing zone of a defector from the Soviet Air Force who brought in the most advanced aircraft in their inventory. And the extent of Japanese cooperation with allied intelligence agencies (who went over the prize with a fine tooth comb) was a major blow to Soviet security. This time, the prize was the most advanced *experimental* Soviet fighter, apparently proving that they were far ahead of the west (as a result of their long experience with manned missions in outer space) in "stealth" technology.

While a swift, surgical strike force of Soviet Marines stationed aboard the *Kiev* re-captured our prize after only 21 hours in Japan, we got enough of a look at the aircraft to know that the Soviets had made a major breakthrough.

Bush, "Things that go Bump in the Night: Why we built the Phantom II, " in *Memoirs.*

---

themselves in *combinations* of events and problems so bizzare that we will underestimate both their probability and their impact.

It is also essential to say a word about the "methodology" I have used to develop specific examples of events and developments that—if they happened—would have a high probability of being surprises (i.e., unexpected). I have *not* used a "worst case" approach and the events "forecasted" are not meant to be a list of all the adverse things that could happen. Rather, my projections stem from an analysis of the causes of past intelligence failures. The record of intelligence failures is both a measure of our lack of understanding of key dynamics that were shaping the international system and of the inadequacy of many of the concepts and analytical processes that intelligence and policy-making officials alike used to frame their decisions and formulate national security policy.

There are three major sources of surprise associated with past intelligence failures. The first is what I term a failure of imagination. For example, the U.S. government (and many other sources) failed to imagine that the unrest in Teheran and several provincial cities in 1978 could translate into a revolution. The second source of failure stems from institutional blindness. That is to say, the intelligence community was looking at the problem or looking at the indicators but rated the probability of an adverse event occurring as extremely low. This is best illustrated by the judgment reached by the intelligence community in 1962 that the Soviet Union would not put nuclear missiles in Cuba. The third source of failure stems from the difficulty of the target itself. Some things (such as individual psychological motivations or the location and mission of small numbers of troops) are genuinely difficult for even the most sophisticated of intelligence systems to monitor accurately.

By far the largest number of failures occur due to the failures of imagination or institutional blindness rather than the difficulty per se of predicting or anticipating the event. Again this reinforces my suspicion that the conceptual lenses through which we view the international system—especially our openess to thinking about the unexpected and irrational—has a major impact on our ability to anticipate trends correctly.

Throughout this essay, consequently, the term "unexpected" will be used to refer to three major types of unanticipated events. The rarest are those events that occur both without warning and without someone imagining them. The Iranian Revolution, for example, was such a surprise; it was neither anticipated nor forecast by the U.S. government, the international press, or academic specialists. The second type of unexpected events are surprises, but not necessarily unfamiliar ones. That is, a particular event may occur without warning but the type of event was foreseen. Embassy takeovers are a good example. As one analyst of the phenomenon put it, "Seizing embassies became a common form of protest and coercion in the 1970's."* Indeed, some 48 embassies were attacked and taken over by terrorists or militant protestors between 1971 and 1980. So the seizure of the U.S. Embassy in Teheran or the Dominican Republic's embassy in Bogota should not have been surprises in the generic sense. A third type of unexpected event occurs without warning (or warning signs are overlooked) because it is regarded as improbable. The probability of most secessionist struggles succeeding today is officially evaluated as quite low. No one expects, for example, the Kurds (in Iraq and Iran), the Achenese (in Indonesia), the Saharui (in Morocco), the Pathans (in Pakistan), or the Lithuanians (in the U.S.S.R.) to gain territorial and political independence in the foreseeable future. Their success, however, would be a surprise even though their activities and objectives are well known and in some cases well monitored.

---

* Brian M. Jenkins, *Embassies under Siege* (Santa Monica, CA: the Rand Corporation Report R-2651-RC, Jan. 1981), p. v.

The collapse of NATO, precipitated by a withdrawal of the Netherlands and Italy, was in many ways a logical extension of the general concerns that Secretary Haig frequently voiced in Cabinet meetings about the growing lack of cohesion. The Italian exit had been long in coming. It was not surprising, but the timing of it was (following the election of a right wing coalition government). No one expected the new Union Democrats to make an alliance with the communists by pledging Italy's non-alignment. The circumstances of the Dutch withdrawal were equally surprising. The capture of a Pershing II cruise missile by Moluccan "freedom fighters" even for that brief period of crisis until their surrender gave a new and very influential lease on life to the anti-nuclear domestic political forces within the Netherlands and transformed their cause into a general anti-NATO posture.

Bush, "The Collapse of Nato," in *Memoirs*.

III

It is already clear that for the foreseeable future, the international "system" will be characterized by the continuation of present trends toward the diffusion of power (especially within the surviving alliances of World War II and the blocs of the Cold War), the frustration of most revolutionary and irredentist causes, the nihilism of the middle-class young in Europe and Japan, the impact of societal change and upheaval in the Third World on regional security, and the polarization of key global issues along "north–south" lines.

In contrast to their counterparts a generation ago, most texts on international relations today begin by noting that while world politics remain bipolar in a strategic military sense, they have become multipolar in almost every other aspect. The collapse of the international economic system based on the Breton Woods regime, the rise and impact of OPEC and the influence of Arab petrodollars, the growing interdependence between the industrialized countries of the north and the developing countries of the south have not only changed the way all countries look at the requisites of security, but also have complicated—and called into question in some cases—the cohesion of the grand alliances of the post-World War II period. For example, Turkey finds itself in a position today where its identification with the Third World is greater than with the industrialized countries of

Europe or the United States. France, as an extension of its fiercely independent military and economic policies, has developed a link to the Middle East that many members of NATO envy.

By itself, the diffusion of power is neither to be feared nor to be disparaged. It is simply a reflection of the fact that power (i.e., influence) in international affairs is dependent on a complex mix of elements that include military might, economic resources, geostrategic position, internal stability, and the costs and benefits of alliances, and that the weights assigned each will tend to vary from issue to issue. For example, the blurring of the line between domestic and foreign policy contributes an uncertainty about any nation's response in a particular regional crisis.

Internal instability and the rise of challenges to central political authorities is another aspect of the diffusion-of-power phenomenon that calls into question the political will of states to act in predictable ways. In the industrial democracies, challenges to central governments have been manifested for the most part in declining parliamentary majorities, as in Japan, West Germany, Italy, Britain, and France. Other manifestations are persistent labor and student unrest, political violence including terrorism, and what might be called "centrifugal politics" (i.e. , separatism in Britain, France, Canada, Spain, Belgium, and Northern Ireland). Even in the case of the U.S., "opposition to government is the hallmark of American opinion today."*

The importance of this pattern of challenges to central political authorities lies in its implications for the international environment on which national foreign policy initiatives depend. Domestic instability is significant not only because of its immediate effects on ruling elites, bilateral and regional political relations, and East–West competition, but also its significance for addressing such global issues as human rights, responsiveness to LDC economic demands, antiproliferation policies, and arms transfer restraints. The growth of interdependence seems to have coincided with the weakening of central political authorities in many states, making international cooperation on global problems much more difficult to achieve. With little domestic political capital to spare, the compromises so often necessary for longer-term international policies and mutually beneficial adjustments to economic problems may prove too costly in the short term for hard-pressed governments to bear.

---

* Samual P. Huntington, "American Foreign Policy: The Changing Political Universe," *The Washington Quarterly* (Autumn 1979), p. 32.

Power has also been diffused by the rise of a so-called "second-order" powers. Second-order powers include such states as the major members of OPEC and Brazil, Argentina, Korea, India, Egypt, Vietnam, Indonesia, Taiwan, South Africa, who all play an important or pivotal role in a regional or the international economy or occupy a key geostrategic position. Sometimes a state like South Africa does both. The attributes of second-order power status include a clearly defined sense of national and regional purpose, strong political and military institutions (at least as perceived by others in the region), a sizeable enough industrial base to produce some arms and most necessary consumer goods, and to absorb advanced technology, and skilled manpower.*

The significant thing about the rise of second-order powers is the fact that they not only possess the resources that have an impact on the foreign policy and even domestic politics of major industrialized powers, but that they have the will to do so. So the emphasis in the future ought to be on what makes such second-order powers strive for greater regional and international influence, since the possession of any of the attributes listed above is only a necessary rather than sufficient condition for a drive to extend national influence. Consequently, one analyst has suggested that the most important indicators presaging such an effort are:

- An economic development strategy that depends heavily on regional export markets or having assured access to externally located raw materials.

- An ideological mind-set of a dominant elite that their power position depends importantly on spreading their governing values to the leaders of other (often surrounding) countries.

- Perceived danger to the economic or physical security of the potential second-order power if nearby countries are controlled by hostile political forces or subject to chronic political instability.

- The perception that the potential second order power's international bargaining position could be improved by extending its values to other states in its region in order to build a coalition.†

---

* See Saul B. Cohen, "The Emergence of a New Second Order of Powers in the International System," in Schlutz and Marwah, ed., *Nuclear Proliferation and the Nuclear Countries* (Cambridge, MA: Ballinger, 1976).
† L. Keith Gardiner, "The Rise of Second Order Powers: New Focus on Regional Power," Office of Political Research, C.I.A. (August 1976), pp. 1819.

> In retrospect, the world should be grateful that there now exists a Palestinian state (which has so far proved not to be a threat to Israel). And we should take some additional comfort from the fact that the cabal of Arab businessmen who engineered the "oil shock of '86"—and who held out so long—did so without seeking or claiming their government's complicity. This made it possible for us to maintain diplomatic relations in the midst of the crisis, and in effect pitted one group of business interests against another. Finally, we should be grateful to American industry which out of this adversity discovered the process by which today we no longer need rely on imported oil for energy. In retrospect, the Arab move was a cunning one, and reflected their judgement that the life span of the oil weapon was rapidly drawing to an end.
>
> Bush, "The Oil Shock of '86," in *Memoirs*.

As second-order powers push to achieve or extend their influence, in short, they may do so for reasons we fail to anticipate correctly. What threatens a South Africa or a Saudi Arabia, for example, may be quite different from what we think ought to be threatening to them. There is, thus, growing asymmetry in the U.S.–Saudi relationship over the priority that ought to be assigned to the Soviet threat. Americans tend to regard U.S. interest in Saudi Arabia as stemming from oil and as part of the overall rivalry with the Soviet Union in the Middle East. The Saudi perception is quite different and accords a much higher priority to the threats posed by instability in the U.S. (which raises doubts about U.S. willingness to deliver on long-term commitments) and lack of progress on the Palestinian issue.

Another source of strain in international affairs is likely to be the frustration of numerous social, political, religious, and ethnic groups in achieving their objectives (e.g., territorial autonomy, human rights, political power). More than 100 such groups (for whom self-determination is still a major requirement) exist, and they pose varying degrees of threats of dissidence to some 52 sovereign states (see Table 6.1).

A large number of nonstate and transnational groups, in essence, could yet pose significant destabilizing threats both to individual countries and to particular regions. The trend over the past decade, moreover, has been an increase in the degree of assertiveness of these groups as a whole. There are more guerilla wars today fought by these groups than a decade ago. There is more resort to terrorism

TABLE 6.1. Major Peoples with Self-Determination Potential: By Nations

	Population in Millions with (%) of Total	Subnational Consciousness	Assertion or Dissidence[1]	Equality of Treatment[2]
Afghanistan				
Hazara	1 (6)	medium	occasional	fair
Tajik	6 (38)	low	slight	good
Uzbek	1.5 (9)	medium	slight	good
Algeria				
Berbers	4 (21)	medium	cultural	fair
Angola				
Bakongo	1.5 (22)	medium	occasional	fair
Ovimbundu	2.5 (37)	medium	insurgency	fair
Bangladesh				
Hindus[3]	17 (19)	high	slight	fair
Tribal peoples	1 (1)	medium	guerrilla	fair
Bolivia				
Aymara	1 (19)	low	slight	fair
Quechua	2 (38)	low	slight	fair
Brazil				
Indians	.5 (.4)	high (disunited)	guerrilla war	poor
Bulgaria				
Turks[3]	1 (11)	medium	slight	poor-fair
Burma				
Karen	3 (8)	high	insurgency	fair
Shan	2 (6)	high	insurgency	fair
Others (Arakanese, Chin. Kachin, Mon, etc.)	2 (6)	high	insurgency	poor-fair

[1]This is in relation to the dominant national people or ruling clique, not foreign occupiers. Often a subnationality claims to have the whole nation's national interest at heart in its dissidence, and credence may be given to this claim.

[2]Where conditions of violence do not now permit equal treatment, we judge what the situation would be in peacetime.

[3]Nonterritorial. In the case of the Sikhs in India and of South African blacks, only partly nonterritorial.

	Population in Millions with (%) of Total	Subnational Consciousness	Assertion or Dissidence[1]	Equality of Treatment[2]
Burundi				
Hutu[3]	3.5 (85)	high	occasional	poor
Cameroon				
Bamileke	2 (24)	medium	occasional	fair
Western region	1.5 (18)	medium	political	fair
Canada				
French	6 (25)	high	political	good
China (Mainland)				
Chuang	10 (1)	low	slight	good
Hui[3]	5 (.5)	medium	slight	fair
Koreans[3]	1.5 (.15)	medium	slight	good
Miao	3.5 (.36)	medium	slight	fair
Mongols	2 (.20)	high	potential	fair
Tibetans	3.5 (.36)	high	occasional	poor-fair
Uighur	5.5 (.56)	high	occasional	fair
Yi (Lolo)	4.5 (.46)	medium	none	fair
Others	15 (1.5)	?	?	?
China (Taiwan)				
"Taiwanese"[3]	15 (85)	medium	agitation	fair
Ecuador				
Indians (Quechua, etc.)	3 (38)	medium	agitation	fair
Egypt				
Copts[3]	3-4 (7-10)	high	agitation	fair
Ethiopia				
Eritreans	2 (6)	high	insurgency	fair
Oromo (Galla)	2-10 (6-30)	medium	guerrilla war	fair
Sidamo	2 (6)	low	guerrilla war	fair
Somali	2 (6)	high	insurgency	fair (?)
Tigrinya	3.5 (11)	medium-high	insurgency	fair

TABLE 6.1.   (Continued)

	Population in Millions with (%) of Total	Subnational Consciousness	Assertion or Dissidence[1]	Equality of Treatment[2]
France				
Alsatians	1 (2)	high	regional agitation	good
Basque	.2 (.41)	high	agitation & terror	fair
Breton	1 (2)	high	agitation & terror	fair
Corsican	.2 (.37)	high	agitation & terror	fair
Occitanian	2-10 (4-19)	low	none	fair
Ghana				
Ewe	1.5 (13)	medium	potential	good
Guatemala				
Maya	3 (43)	low	guerrilla war	poor-fair
India				
Assamese	11 (1.5)	medium	violent demonstrations	fair-good
Bengalis	53 (8)	medium	potential	good
Christians[3]	15[4] (2.2)	high	none	fair-good
Gujeratis	32 (5)	medium	none	good
Kashmiris	4 (.6)	high	demonstrations (past insurgency)	fair-good

[1]This is in relation to the dominant national people or ruling clique, not foreign occupiers. Often a subnationality claims to have the whole nation's national interest at heart in its dissidence, and credence may be given to this claim.

[2]Where conditions of violence do not now permit equal treatment, we judge what the situation would be in peacetime.

[3]Nonterritorial. In the case of the Sikhs in India and of South African blacks, only partly nonterritorial.

[4]Major overlap with other peoples.

	Population in Millions with (%) of Total	Subnational Consciousness	Assertion or Dissidence[1]	Equality of Treatment[2]
Kannada	28 (4)	medium	none	good
Malayalam	25 (4)	medium	political	good
Marathi	52 (8)	medium	none	good
Muslims	75[4] (11)	high	demonstrations	fair-good
Oriyan	25 (4)	medium	none	good
Punjabis	18 (3)	low	none	good
Scheduled castes[3]	80[4] (12)	medium	demonstrations	fair
Scheduled Tribes (Santal, Naga, Mizo, etc.)	46 (7)	medium-high	passive to insurgency	poor-fair
Sikhs[3]	5[4] (.7)	high	demonstrations	good
Tamil	48 (7)	medium-high	political	good
Telegu	60 (9)	medium	political	good
Indonesia				
Achenese	2.5 (1.5)	high	recent guerrilla war	fair
Batak	3.5 (2)	medium	agitation (?)	fair
Chinese	3.5 (2)	medium	currently passive	fair
Makassarese	2 (1.5)	low	?	fair
Minahassans	1 (.7)	medium	?	good
Minangkabau	6 (4)	medium	?	good
Moluccans (Ambonese)	1 (.7)	medium	terror (overseas)	fair
Papuans	1 (.7)	medium	guerrilla war	poor-fair
Sundanese	21 (15)	medium		fair
Timorese	1.5 (1)	low-high	guerrilla	poor-fair

(Continued)

TABLE 6.1. (Continued)

	Population in Millions with (%) of Total	Subnational Consciousness	Assertion or Dissidence[1]	Equality of Treatment[2]
Iran				
Arabs	.8 (2)	high	guerrilla war	fair
Azerbaijani	7.5 (20)	medium	national partisan	good
Kurds	2 (5)	high	insurgency	fair
Baluch	1 (3)	medium	violent opposition	fair
Turkmen	.6 (1.5)	medium	violent	fair
Iraq				
Kurds	2 (15)	high	insurgency	poor-fair
Shi'ites	7 (53)	medium	agitation	fair
Israel (including occupied territories)				
Palestinians	1.5 (30)	high	agitation & terror	fair
Italy				
Sards	1.5 (3)	low	slight	fair-good
Jordan				
Palestinians[3]	1 (31)	high	potential	fair
Malaysia				
Chinese[3]	5 (36)	high	political & guerrilla war	fair
East Indian	1.5 (11)	medium	slight	fair

[1]This is in relation to the dominant national people or ruling clique, not foreign occupiers. Often a subnationality claims to have the whole nation's national interest at heart in its dissidence, and credence may be given to this claim.

[2]Where conditions of violence do not now permit equal treatment, we judge what the situation would be in peacetime.

[3]Nonterritorial. In the case of the Sikhs in India and of South African blacks, only partly nonterritorial.

[4]Major overlap with other peoples.

	Population in Millions with (%) of Total	Subnational Consciousness	Assertion or Dissidence[1]	Equality of Treatment[2]
Mexico				
Indians (Mayan, Nahuatl, etc.)	5 (7)	low	slight	fair
Morocco				
Berbers	6 (29)	low	slight	fair-good
Saharaui	.1 (.5)	high	insurgency	fair-good
Mozambique				
Shona (lang.)	1 (10)	medium	guerrilla	good
Nigeria (contro-versial census)				
Edo	3 (4)	medium	political	good
Ibibio	3.5 (4)	medium	political	good
Ibo	14 (17)	high	recent insurg-ency	good
Kanuri	4 (5)	medium	political	good
Nupe	1 (1)	medium	political	good
Tiv	7.5 (10)	medium	political	good
Yoruba	17 (20)	high	political	good
Pakistan				
Ahmadi[3/4]	1 (1)	high	agitation	poor-fair
Baluch	2.5 (3)	high	recent insurgency	fair
Christian[3/4]	1 (1)	medium	none	fair
Hindu	1 (1)	high	none	fair
Pathans	7 (8)	high	political (armed partisans)	good
Sindhi	10 (12)	medium	political	good
Peru				
Aymara	1.5 (9)	low	agitation	fair
Quechua	6.5 (37)	low	agitation	fair

(Continued)

TABLE 6.1. (Continued)

	Population in Millions with (%) of Total	Subnational Consciousness	Assertion or Dissidence[1]	Equality of Treatment[2]
Philippines				
Ilocanos	5 (10)	low	slight	good
Muslims	2 (4)	medium-high	insurgency	fair
Pampangans	1.5 (3)	medium	guerrilla war?	fair
Visayans	14 (29)	low	none	good
Rumania				
Magyar	2 (9)	high	cultural	fair
Sierra Leone				
Mende	1 (29)	medium	political	fair
South Africa				
Asians[3]	1 (4)	medium	political	poor-fair
Blacks (Bantu)[3]	20 (70)	medium	political & terror	poor
Coloureds[3]	2.5 (9)	high	political	poor-fair
South West Africa				
Blacks	1 (89)	medium	political & guerrilla war	poor-fair
Spain				
Basque	1 (3)	high	political & terror	good
Catalonians	6 (16)	high	political	good
Galicians	3 (8)	medium	political & cultural	fair-good

[1]This is in relation to the dominant national people or ruling clique, not foreign occupiers. Often a subnationality claims to have the whole nation's national interest at heart in its dissidence, and credence may be given to this claim.

[2]Where conditions of violence do not now permit equal treatment, we judge what the situation would be in peacetime.

[3]Nonterritorial. In the case of the Sikhs in India and of South African blacks, only partly nonterritorial.

[4]Major overlap with other peoples.

	Population in Millions with (%) of Total	Subnational Consciousness	Assertion or Dissidence[1]	Equality of Treatment[2]
Sri Lanka				
Tamil	1.5 (11)	high	political & terror	fair-good
Sudan				
Beja	1.5 (8)	low	mild political	fair-good
Southern Blacks (Nilotic peoples)	5 (27)	medium	political (recent insurgency)	fair-good
Thailand				
Chinese[3]	5 (11)	medium	none	good
Malays	1 (2)	medium	guerrilla war	fair
Turkey				
Kurds	3 (7)	medium	terror	poor-fair
Uganda[5]				
Ganda	2 (15)	high	political & terror	fair
Nkole	1 (7)	low	slight	fair
Soga	1 (7)	low	slight	fair
Teso	1 (7)	low	slight	fair
USSR				
Armenians	3.5 (1)	high	political	good
Azerbaijanis	5.5 (2)	medium	political	fair-good
Bashkir	1.5 (.6)	low	slight	fair
Belorussians	9.5 (4)	low	slight	fair
Estonians	1 (.4)	high	cultural	fair
Georgians	3.5 (1)	high	political	fair-good
Jews[3]	2 (.75)	medium	emigration	poor-fair
Kazakh	6.5 (2)	medium	slight	fair
Kirghiz	2 (.75)	medium	slight	fair
Latvians	1.5 (.6)	medium	cultural	fair
Lithuanians	3 (1)	high	political & cultural	fair

(Continued)

TABLE 6.1. (Continued)

	Population in Millions with (%) of Total	Subnational Consciousness	Assertion or Dissidence[1]	Equality of Treatment[2]
Moldavians	3 (1)	low	slight	fair
Tadzhiks	3 (1)	low	cultural	fair
Tatars (various)	6 (2)	medium	political	poor
Turkmen	2 (.75)	low	slight	fair
Ukrainians	42 (16)	medium	political & cultural	fair
Uzbek	12.5 (5)	high	cultural	fair-good
Polish	1 (.4)	medium	slight	fair
United Kingdom				
Scots	5 (9)	medium	political	good
Ulster Irish	.5 (.9)	high	political & terror	fair
Ulster Scots	1 (2)	high	political & terror	good
Welsh	2.5 (5)	medium	cultural	good
U.S.				
American Indians	1 (.5)	high (diffuse)	political & cultural	fair-good
Blacks[3]	25 (11)	high	political & demonstrations	fair-good
Puerto Ricans (mainland)[3/4]	2 (.9)	medium	political	fair-good
(island)	3 (1.5)	medium	political	good
Spanish-speaking[3/4]	10 (5)	medium	political & cultural	fair-good

[1]This is in relation to the dominant national people or ruling class, not foreign occupiers. Often a subnationality claims to have the whole nation's national interest at heart in its dissidence, and credence may be given to this claim.

[2]Where conditions of violence do not now permit equal treatment, we judge what the situation would be in peacetime.

[3]Nonterritorial. In the case of the Sikhs in india and of South African blacks, only partly nonterritorial.

[4]Major overlap with other peoples.

[5]Presently no dominant people.

	Population in Millions with (%) of Total	Subnational Consciousness	Assertion or Dissidence[1]	Equality of Treatment[2]
Vietnam				
Montagnards	2.5 (5)	medium (diffuse)	guerrilla war	fair
Yugoslavia				
Albanians	1 (5)	medium	political	fair-good
Croats	5 (22)	high	political & terror	good
Macedonians	1 (5)	medium	slight	good
Muslims	2 (9)	medium	slight	good
Slovenes	2 (9)	high	political	good
Zaire[5]				
Bakongo	3.5 (12)	medium	political	fair
Luba-Kasai	3 (10)	low	occasional insurgency	fair
Zimbabwe				
Ndebele	1.5 (20)	high	political (armed partisans)	fair-good

and assassination than a decade ago. Of course, not all of these groups will pose threats at the state level, nor will their actions fore-shadow the kind of long-term internal warfare that exists in Northern Ireland, the Basque region of Spain, and other such trouble spots that are frequently in the news. But even very small and obscure groups and causes can achieve publicity (and some of their objectives) through sensational aircraft hijackings and other hostage incidents. I am thinking here of the South Moluccan "freedom fighters" who hijacked a Dutch train, the Serbo-Croatians who hijacked an aircraft in New York, or the recent incident involving Indonesian separatists in an aircraft hijacking in Thailand. The point to make here is that a bewildering array of causes exists about which very little progress has, is being, and is likely to be made in the 1980s.

The nihilism of the young in Europe and Japan will probably also continue into the 1980s, although its impact on foreign policy is difficult to estimate. Societal dropping-out has led so far not to revolt but to confusion.*

Whatever the magnitude of the problem—and regardless of how it surfaces in the politics of the foreign policy process—European and Japanese leaders acknowledge that they are dealing with a significant unknown with potentially grave consequences for the bases of consensus on which their coalition governments rest.

My own guess is that the internal politics of the counterculture will periodically lead to the kind of outbursts that immobilized France in 1968 (and was partly responsible for dooming the secret negotiations over ending the Vietnam War at the time), and it is in this sense that I think present trends toward nihilism could affect international policies and disrupt international relations in the 1980s.† It is not difficult to imagine widespread disruption (à la 1968) interfering with key bilateral and multilateral negotiations (e.g., European–Middle East initiatives) and diverting the attention of the major participants in these negotiations. What will be difficult is predicting when, where, and why such outbursts occur.

Whatever its current dimensions and dynamics, in sum, the trend toward nihilism by the middle-class young is likely to complicate domestic politics in the industrialized countries and the conduct of foreign policy in quite unpredictable ways. This is especially likely to affect situations requiring governments to mobilize political will for actions abroad or in concert with other countries.‡

Societal change and upheaval is also taking place on a major scale in the Third World. The recent crises in Iran and Central America forcefully brought this fact home to the U.S. government, which had forgotten the insight of then Secretary of Defense McNamara in 1965 that development and security were inseparable. Indeed, it is

---

* See Thomas Forstenzer, "Economic Crisis, Universities and Students in Western Europe," *Prospects* (1978), pp. 283–292.

†There are signs, however, that some elements of the counterculture in Europe have organized into a party and could thereby exert continuing pressure on governments in key regions of particularly sensitive countries. See Elizabeth Pond, "Opposition Party Takes on New Meaning in West German Politics," *Christian Science Monitor* (3 April 1981).

‡ See, for example, the discussion of this in Michael Howard, "Social Change and the Defense of the West," *The Washington Quarterly* (Autumn 1979), pp. 18–31.

The upheavals in Canada, Mexico, and Brazil reminded us that national leadership was perhaps the commodity in scarcest supply during the 1980s. No one would have predicted such fundamental changes in these countries, though with hindsight, the danger signs were there.

In Canada we knew that Mr. Trudeau had underestimated the significance of the Western provinces' demands for higher oil prices. But no one actually expected the provincial parliament to pass the secession motion and then apply for commonwealth status with the US. . . . What surprised me most was Mr. Trudeau's personal reaction to the crisis—to resign and seek deeper knowledge by joining his new wife on a spiritual retreat in India.

Mexico had teetered on the edge of a violent student revolution in 1968. The students were quiescent in the 1970s as they took up jobs in the government and in the business community. But they were sorely disappointed by the 1980s by what the oil bonanza had not brought to Mexican society. Their discontent proved fertile ground for the KGB. And the failure to penetrate the movement that led to the accession to power of the Communist Party of Mexico was among the most serious disappointments I had with our intelligence community. In the wake of this event, I directed a major review and reorganization of our nation's intelligence apparatus. . . .

. . . The return to civilian government in Brazil was short-lived, and in retrospect ushered in the period of instability that led initially to the massive default on foreign loans and later to the rise of a socialist government which paved the way for greater communist influence over the country. . . .

Bush, "The 'Irans' Next Door," in *Memoirs.*

the process by which societies *change* (much more so than what causes some to stagnate) that has proved the most troubling for U.S. interests in recent years and the most destabilizing in key regions of the developing world. And the process of change—its discontinuities, its impact on the nature and scope of expectations, and its impact on the institutions of governance—will continue to complicate and strain the international system of the 1980s.

The dominant "model" today of such potentially troubling societal change is constructed in the image of Iran. That is, modernization, while it improves standards of living, brings unwanted challenges to traditional authorities and institutions with which even the most enlightened ruler will find it difficult to cope. This "inevitably"

China historically has swung between periods of isolationism and periods in which learning from the west and adapting western ways was considered acceptable. My reading of Chinese history is that this is nothing like a cyclical pattern, but rather a reflection of the political complexity and intrigue which goes on away from our view in the largest country on earth.

But when it happened, the second Cultural Revolution was a great personal shock. In part, this was because so many of the officials and other persons I had gotten to know first in Beijing and later in Washington turned out to be in the vanguard of "Double May" movement. It was also a shock because the intelligence community apparently had not a single piece of hard evidence even hinting that such a train of events would be possible. . . .

In retrospect, the seeds of this vast upheaval were sown during the trial of the Gang of Four. The televised accusations were taken personally by the literally millions of Chinese watching the proceedings who had taken action part in the first Cultural Revolution, and still believed in it. . . .

For the foreseeable future, the third of mankind that is China will continue to go through profound political transformations of the sort that we have never been very adept at predicting.

Bush, "Four Horsemen" and "The Disaster in Asia," in *Memoirs.*

stimulates the recrudescence of traditionalism and leads to open conflict between the government and the society. In this vein, Mexico and Saudi Arabia have both been called the next Iran. And several years ago Libya's Colonel Qadhafi predicted that world politics would be increasingly shaped by the struggle on the part of the masses in developing countries for political power and authority. Qadhafi foresaw an "era of the masses" in which the dependence of the industrialized countries on raw materials, coupled to U.S.–USSR competition for influence and strategic footholds in key regions, would give the superpowers a vital stake in the outcome of these struggles. If the period ahead, then, is marked by violent and often unexpected tests of whether governments in key developing countries can manage the process of societal change effectively, all powers will have a stake in the outcome of these struggles.

The state of the so-called north–south dialogue, finally, will continue to complicate international relations in the 1980s.

Ever since the 1973–1974 Arab oil embargo, the developing countries have sought to convert control of raw materials into political influence. While much less successful than many LDCs originally expected, this effort has led to a growing assertiveness on the part of the developing countries over the distribution of both wealth and power in international affairs. OPEC's rise of power and influence, of course, is perhaps the most obvious example of how relations with the LDCs have impacted on the prosperity and the freedom of action of the industrial powers. But comprehensive demands for substantial improvements in LDC terms of trade and in the volume and conditions of aid and investment they receive, and for increases in LDC political authority over international financial institutions, have also contributed to the polarization of important international issues along "North-South" lines. As a result, negotiations between rich and poor nations now affect a wide variety of international economic and political issues.

Galvanized by the example of unilateral OPEC price rises, LDCs have increasingly linked their cooperation in negotiations over law of the seas, the protection of their environment, regulation of the export of nuclear technology, limiting arms transfers, and international measures to combat terrorism to progress on their broader demands. Over the long term, prospects for political stability and economic growth in the developing world will probably remain intertwined in such a way as to make it very difficult for any industrialized country to protect the security of its markets or link certain LDCs into its national security strategy without paying increasing attention to where they stand in and what they want out of North-South dialogue. Finally, the state of North-South relations has been used as one of the yardsticks by which some influential LDCs (e.g., Mexico, Algeria, Nigeria) determine their support of and contribution to efforts to arrive at peaceful settlements of contentious regional issues (e.g., in Central America, the Middle East, Southern Africa) that directly affect the level of tension in international affairs.

Aside from their control of oil, the nonindustrial states probably do not have the leverage—individually or collectively—to extract any of their basic demands against the will of the United States. And they clearly wish to avoid any net loss of the support of the industrial countries for their modernization efforts. But the impact that the growing self-confidence of the LDCs and their occasional resort to pressure tactics have had on the economies and the diplomacy of the major industrial powers—especially on U.S. options to shape changes in the international economic system—suggests that LDC demands for a redistribution of power and wealth from North to South can neither be ignored nor wholly deflected. Hence, the state of North-South relations is likely to be a continuing source of tension in international relations. Policy makers, moreover, should not expect that the debate over "North–South" issues will follow the ground rules set by the industrialized countries. For the emotionalism of today's North–South "dialogue" cannot be separated from its origins as a reaction against colonialism. As Frantz Fannon suggested some time ago, "The natives' challenge to the colonial world is not a rational confrontation of points of view."*

IV

Several new sources of strain are also likely to be added to the international system of the 1980s, including the advent of instability within the major industrial democracies of the West, the rise of direct threats to national security from transnational terrorism, nuclear proliferation, and Third World arms transfers, adverse developments in key regional food/population balances, and the use of population displacement and food allocation policy as siege weapons in major regional struggles.

What follows is speculation on how these sources of strain could play out over the course of the decade. With the exception of the projection of instability within the advanced industrial countries, the phenomena discussed below are familiar in general terms to most writers on international affairs; the surprises (i.e., the unexpected events and developments) that they may presage, however, are less so. Indeed, in the process of "researching" this chapter I was struck by the fact that the present literature on future trends in international affairs generally deals with "straight-line" projections and does not attempt to project discontinuities and abrupt, fundamental changes that could have a major impact on the way most nations perceive threats to their security.

The advent of instability within the industrial democracies of Europe, Japan, and North America, for example, is missing from most contemporary projections of the future and the future sources of conflict.† This is striking given the agenda of socioeconomic prob-

---

* Frantz Fannon, *The Wretched of the Earth* (New York: Grove Press, 1966), p. 33.
† See for example, General Sir Robert Hackett, *The Third World War* (1979); and, Captain John J. McIntyre, Jr., *The Future of Conflict* (Washington: National Defense University Press, 1979).

... The 1980s was also a decade marked by major changes in the relative power of states. No one would have imagined in 1981 that the ability of governments to tackle their domestic problems and restore growth and confidence to their national economies would prove as important as it did. But we were in for a rude awakening.

The fall of the government of Margaret Thatcher in England following the secession of Northern Ireland from the United Kingdom and the collapse of the British social welfare system was deeply rooted in the failure of the English economy. This we had anticipated, and had tried to work with Ms. Thatcher to avert. But the conversion by Ms. Thatcher's successor of the Organization of Commonwealth Countries into a cohesive lobby group for key Third World demands in the so-called North–South dialogue was not foreseen. . . . It was ironic that England's influence over world affairs was never greater in the 1980s than when it joined the Third World.

Bush, from the "Foreword," in *Memoirs.*

lems that must now be tackled. Creating jobs (and with them, a sense among workers in the OECD countries that the quality of life is improving) will present a formidable challenge. Between 1970 and 1980, unemployment in the OECD countries increased from an estimated 9 million to over 21 million. Depending on the rate of growth in real GNP, some analysts believe this figure could increase to over 30 million by 1985, and perhaps double by the end of the decade. Even under quite optimistic assumptions about GNP growth rates, the 1980 figure is not projected to decline until well after 1985.* Whatever the actual figure, three serious problems will result:

• OECD governments paid for offsetting the shock of unemployment by expanding social welfare programs in the 1970s. As a result of the deficits these programs required, the governments of the 1980s probably will not have the funds to continue to expand benefits to the new and chronic unemployed.

• The new unemployed in the 1980s are likely to be older

---

* *OECD Countries: Unemployment in the 1970s and Perspectives for the 1980s.* C.I.A. Research Paper ER 80-10579 (November 1980), p. 10.

Germany had long been considered by Soviet leaders a major security threat. Despite the success of the Soviet campaign to drive a wedge between Germany and the US over the issue of the relevance of linkage to detente, we had clear warning from the intelligence community that the Soviet Union would use all means at its disposal to further weaken the primary relationship on which the military strength of NATO depended. What we did not count on was the unwitting way in which the German leadership played into Soviet hands. The discovery that the *Luftwaffe* had developed a nuclear bomb—leaked to the press by a high Reichchancellor official who turned out to be a "deep cover" Soviet agent—probably fed Soviet paranoia of German re-armament and led to a gross overestimation of the willingness of the US to sanction a European nuclear force available for use outside the NATO context. In any case, in late October of 1983, we received word that members of the German intelligence service had attempted—and very nearly succeeded—in staging a coup against the government of Chancellor Strauss. It was not until several weeks later that we learned that the perpetrators were the elite—and probably the last—of the Soviet deep cover agents, that had done Moscow's bidding since the middle of the second world war.

Bush, "Crisis in Germany," in *Memoirs.*

workers who are quite likely to step up pressure on governments to improve social welfare and unemployment benefits substantially.

● Differing rates of unemployment in Europe may stimulate migration from the southern countries and with it bring widespread ethnic, moral, and diplomatic tensions.

To the potential problem of joblessness must be added the unfinished efforts in most OECD countries to solve the problem of racial and religious discrimination, which in recent days has surfaced in a number of violent outbursts in the United Kingdom, France, and the United States. Assassination of political leaders (of both government and party) is, unfortunately, something that should also be expected to disrupt government, along with revelations of official corruption.

The growth in significance to international affairs of terrorism, nuclear proliferation, and arms transfers to sensitive Third World countries and regional powers are not new phenomena of concern. But neither are they "high-policy" agenda items in most industrialized countries. Rather they are thought of—along with a host of other "key global issues"—as issues over which East–West problems take precedence. Nor are they the ingredients which are usually pumped into a net assessment of U.S.–USSR capabilities or a strategy or options paper for dealing with threats to NATO. Indeed, there exists an almost institutional insensitivity to the very types of trends and problems that could well come to the fore in shaping international relations in unexpected ways. This is the decade, however, in which the key global issues mentioned above are likely to manifest themselves in ways that directly threaten security and the survival of states.

For this to occur, two things need to happen (and are happening). First, terrorism has to become a legitimate instrument of foreign policy. Second, terrorism has to become more lethal.

Terrorism today is *gaining* acceptance as a legitimate weapon in the struggle for political and "social justice" objectives. While I recognize that definitions of justice vary widely from society to society and situation to situation, the point here is that terrorism is no longer as universally or as vigorously condemned as it once was. For example, the Vietnamese, who are in many areas of the world and segments of international society greatly admired for their persistence and ultimate victory over both American and South Vietnamese forces, were practitioners of terrorism par excellence, and to this day they practice a very brutal form of terrorism against the populations of Cambodia and Laos as well as against their own ethnic Chinese minority, which has not been the subject of great censure. Terrorism in the form of assassination, politically motivated kidnappings, and bombings has also achieved such a degree of commonplace that I believe there is growing acceptance of the proposition by many struggling and apparently oppressed forces that the end clearly justifies any means. Perhaps most disturbing of all, I detect growing frustration within the Palestinian Liberation Organization over the lack of progress made since they provisionally abandoned the use of terrorism. This could presage a return by that group to the depredations and violence of the late 1960s and early 1970s. The disturbing thing about that prospect is not the fact that there will be violence and victims, but that world-wide reaction to it will probably be much more subdued, since the Palestinian cause has gained a greater degree of legitimacy than ever before.

Terrorism is also gaining in effectiveness. Especially in those situations involving hostages, one expert has suggested, "there is almost an 80 percent chance that all members of the kidnapping team will escape death or capture. . . . Once they make explicit ransom demands, there is a close to even chance that all or some of those demands will be granted. . . ." His conclusion: "the terrorist tactic of seizing hostages for bargaining or publicity purposes is far from being irrational, mindless, ineffective, or necessarily perilous."* These judgments were reached two years before the seizure of the U.S. Embassy in Teheran. The outcome of that episode, from the terrorists' perspective, could only be a reinforcement of the expectations that the tactic will succeed and that adverse public opinion will not translate into major costs or risks to the operation and the ultimate objectives sought.

There is also some potential that terrorism in the 1980s will cease being only a weapon of the weak or a weapon used by radical, social, and political forces to achieve their objective, and that it will become a weapon used by a growing number of sovereign states. To some extent today terrorism in the form of the application of military and paramilitary violence is used by the governments of El Salvador, Turkey (in the use of its military to combat extremist terrorism), and in Israel (in the use of military and paramilitary forces to intimidate and otherwise repress Arabs living on the West Bank). What I have in mind here could be either a recrudescence of the feeling that was very prevalent in the early 1950s in the United States of "fight fire with fire," or the product of a new strategy for aggressive involvement in internal conflicts in key Third World countries—that is, the use of counterterrorism to "nip them in the bud." The reasoning behind such a development might be that the growth of terrorism from the trends presently projected poses such an enormous threat to security and vital national interests of major countries that it has to be addressed, and that to date experience in addressing it by either defensive measures or by international law and negotiation has proved relatively ineffective. With these arguments "demonstrated," it is not too far a step to advocacy of violent preemptive measures aimed against terrorists.

Another way in which this exceedingly ominous development could take place is in response to a crisis or series of crises in which a state feels that it is literally under assault by terrorism from within and from without and feels that it is left with virtually no alternative other than to fight fire with fire. Italy would certainly be a candidate

---

* Brian Jenkins, et al., *Numbered Lives: Some Statistical Observations From 77 International Hostage Episodes* (Santa Monica, CA: Rand Corporation Papers P-5905, July 1977), p. 1.

country where the day might not be too far off when all those with a stake in law and order would agree to suspend civil liberties and authorize police agencies to counter terrorism by whatever means proved most effective. In such a world, the use of state-sanctioned terrorism as a weapon to preserve law and order could also lead to a reconsideration of the utility and legitimacy of political assassination. Especially in an international system characterized by the kind of nuclear proliferation to be discussed below, the possession of nuclear weapons by a dictator with the proclivities of Idi Amin, for example, would certainly and "reasonably" give rise to arguments within government and intelligence circles that one of the most effective ways of neutralizing the threat that such a psychopathic personality might pose is through his elimination. In sum, I think present trends concerning terrorism already foreshadow an international system in which force plays a much more active role in foreign policy than it does now.

Just as I foresee a potential upswing in both state-sponsored terrorism and the use of terrorism by so-called liberation and progressive forces, I also fear that the international system will be plagued by an upswing in psychopathic terrorism. I have in mind here the terrorism practiced by the Japanese Red Army, the Red Brigades, remnants of the Baader-Meinhoff criminal organization, and other such groups, for whom terrorism becomes a way of life and to whom very few weapons of either individual or mass destruction are denied. Particularly troublesome, it seems to me, is the prospect that it is much more likely, in my judgment, that a psychopathic individual or group will possess the technical skills and "genius" to fabricate a nuclear weapon. This is already foreseen in some of the James Bond literature, where criminal groups succeed not only in stealing nuclear weapons but also sophisticated space-based high-energy particle beam weapons through which they hold the world hostage. Closer to home, and much closer to reality, is the account of the famous Harvard economics student, Dimitri Rotow, who, using publicly available material, drew up a plan for the construction of a fission bomb within a two-month period and then translated these plans into blueprints, which he then had estimated by a local machine shop. The total cost for construction of such a bomb was approximately $1,900. Rotow concluded from this exercise that a reasonably competent man with access to plutonium or uranium could build a fission-type bomb within about a two-month period.*

---

* See Nigel Calder, *Nuclear Nightmares* (New York: Viking Press, 1979).

TABLE 6.2. Future Nuclear Powers

Countries that appear technically capable of detonating a nuclear bomb within the next decade

Who has it	Within 3 Years	4 to 6 Years	7 to 10 Years
United States (1945)	Australia	Argentina	Finland
	Canada	Austria	Iraq
Soviet Union (1949)	West Germany	Belgium	Libya
	Israel	Brazil	Rumania
Britain (1952)	Italy	Czechoslovakia	Yugoslavia
France (1960)	Japan	Denmark	
China (1964)	Pakistan	East Germany	
India (1974)	South Africa	Netherlands	
	Spain	Norway	
	Sweden	Poland	
	Switzerland	South Korea	
	Taiwan		

Sources: U.S. Government Estimates, *The New York Times;* and Joseph R. Egan and Shem Arungu-Olende, "Nuclear Power for the Third World?" *Technology Review* (May 1980).

The terrorism of today—and especially of tomorrow—is considerably more lethal than that of a decade ago. In 1970, the "average" terrorist had access to black market AK-47 and M-16 rifles, mortars, and rather bulky antitank weapons. In 1980, the terrorist's arsenal probably included compact, laser-guided antitank weapons, rocket launchers, a wide variety of antipersonnel weapons, and chemical warfare agents. By 1990, the terrorist no doubt will have access to the full range of precision-guided weapons, some of which could deliver nuclear as well as conventional payloads.* In short, trends in terrorism and nuclear proliferation could be closely related in the 1980s.

---

* James Digby, *Precision-Guided Weapons*, Adelphi Papers, No. 118, London, The International Institute for Strategic Studies, 1975. See also Brian Jenkins, *Terrorism in the 1980s* (Santa Monica, CA: Rand Corporation Papers, P-6564, December 1980), and Barry Smernoff, "The New Faces of Conflict: Some Implications of the Military Innovation Process for 1980–2000," in McIntyre, *The Future of Conflict*, pp. 89–116.

Developing countries technically capable of using nuclear reactors

Reactors in Operation	Reactors under Construction	Reactors on Order	Doing Feasibility Studies Now
Argentina	Argentina	Argentina	Bangladesh
Bulgaria	Brazil	Brazil	Colombia
Czechoslovakia	Bulgaria	Cuba	Greece
Finland	Cuba	Czechoslovakia	Iran
German Dem. Rep.	Czechoslovakia	Egypt	Jamaica
India	Finland	Iraq	Nigeria
Pakistan	German Dem. Rep.	Libya	PRC
South Korea	Hungary	Philippines	Portugal
Spain	India	Poland	Peru
Taiwan	Iran	Romania	
	Mexico	Spain	
	Philippines	Turkey	
	South Korea		
	Spain		
	Taiwan		
	Yugoslavia		

Like terrorism, nuclear weapons and nuclear power will probably achieve a greater degree of legitimacy during this decade. This legitimacy is increasing if measured by the number of states suspected of aspiring to possess their own bomb (see Table 6.2, above) or the number of states intent on building nuclear power plants while taking only minimal security precautions to guard against their seizure.

At the present time there are more than 60 nuclear power plants operating in developing countries and another 60 or so are projected to be on line within the next five years. There are 500 nuclear reactors world-wide; many produce 500 pounds or more of plutonium in a single year. One nuclear bomb requires only about 20 pounds of plutonium.

For my part, I will never forget my visit to a nuclear power installation in a Southeast Asian country. The approach to that installation was made along one of a number of highways fully capable of carrying an armored personnel carrier or a tank. The installation itself was guarded by a single chain-link fence and a

We had been working quietly with the Cubans to clear up the last of the refugee problem and I had personally met with members of the bilateral working group at Camp David to hear them out on a process by which our relations with Havana could be normalized. Most of us believed it would happen this way—through pragmatic dealings with the Cubans on humanitarian and hemispheric issues— and I was myself convinced that Dr. Castro genuinely wanted detente between us. We were also influenced by numerous accounts from the intelligence community to the effect that Cuban leaders wanted to reduce their dependence on the Soviet Union and change their image as a surrogate for Russian adventurism in the Third World. This image had, after all, cost Havana its leadership position in the non-aligned movement. . . .

So it was with considerable shock and surprise that I greeted the news that two Cuban combat brigades led the final wave of the assault which toppled the beseiged government of Morocco's King Hassan.

Bush, "The Gathering Storm in the Middle East," in *Memoirs.*

group of approximately three semiretired guards from the national police. As I observed this level of "security", it occurred to me that any reasonably confident paramilitary organization or opposition group could seize this plant and, provided they had access to or could frighten one of the operators into showing them how to do it, mount a fully credible demand to vent nuclear waste into the atmosphere or in some other way to hold the government of that country hostage to its nuclear power.

Per se, these trends in nuclear proliferation are neither unforeseen nor unanticipated, but what is difficult to anticipate and is most likely to surprise us is the use to which nuclear power could be put for aggressive purposes. Current policy planning and projections fully take into account the fact that if pushed against the wall, Israel, Taiwan, South Africa, or Pakistan may employ a nuclear option. But where I suspect we pay less attention is the prospect that, with considerably less provocation, nuclear power will come into the political calculations of these countries or groups in these countries with particular axes to grind.

So, in essence, there are really two ways nuclear proliferation could threaten national security in the 1980s. One is the threat that other countries or groups will actually produce and use the bomb.

The other, and equally significant to me, is the fact that the nuclear power installations of most countries are relatively vulnerable and probably invite seizure by terrorists or other dissident and opposition forces.

Another key dynamic happening today that will probably be a major contributing factor to unexpected crises in international affairs is that of the massive and unrelenting armament of the Third World. In 1960, approximately six billion dollars' worth of armaments were transferred from the industrialized countries to the developing countries of Asia, Africa, the Middle East, and Latin America. By 1980, this figure had increased to almost $17 billion. And over the period between 1974 and 1978, both U.S. and USSR arms exports to developing countries substantially *exceeded* the total amount of economic aid each gave. In addition, India, South Africa, Taiwan, and South Korea are themselves producers and exporters of arms to developing countries. Indeed, in every region of the developing world (except post-Vietnam Asia), there has been a steady—and sometimes dramatic—increase in arms imports (see Figure 6.1 below).

There are several key dynamics here to watch that have the potential to surprise analysts of international affairs in the future. One is the degree to which the developing countries will not reach their capacity to absorb such arms transfers. It was said by many that by about 1977 the Shah had reached, if not exceeded, the capacity of Iran to absorb the massive amounts of military hardware and new

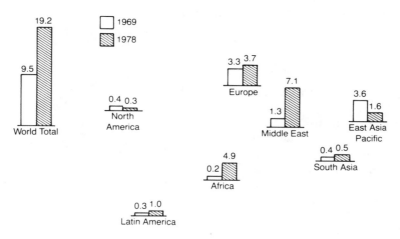

FIG. 6.1:   Regional Arms Imports ($ billions constant '77)
Source: U.S. Arms Control and Disarmament Agency.

weapons systems that he had acquired. Yet, had things gone on, there were serious Iranian plans to continue the purchase of advanced and sophisticated weapons systems. The Shah, his military planners, and most of the U.S. government saw very little that would have prevented Iran from continuing to accept a massive inflow of arms from the West. I think the case of Iran may be somewhat typical of arms sales in most developing countries. That is to say, they will continue at least at present rates, if not substantially expanded ones, especially at a time when many weapons systems are on the verge of becoming obsolete and many others are on the verge of being introduced (such as precision-guided munitions).

Added to this prospect must also be a consideration of the impact that the growth of the world's mercenary forces would have on regional security issues and problems. Today, numerous "Vietnam-" and "Rhodesian-trained" mercenaries are available for hire. The significance of this is not only the large number of people who are available for violence, but the fact that countries are now beginning to have the option of not simply purchasing the services of a white military commander to organize and run native troops, but of buying the services of small armies. Several such "generals" regularly frequent Third World corridors of power, attempting not only to sell their own personal services, but to deliver combat brigades for special missions.

In addition, a well-armed, militarily modernized state becomes a prize for revolutionary forces, worthy of both attack and capture. One has only to think of the vast arsenal that the North Vietnamese inherited in the wake of the collapse of the Saigon government and of the arsenal that a number of regional powers are anticipating acquiring in the wake of the projected internal collapse in Iran to be reminded that relatively small states that are very successful at military modernization and at acquiring weaponry may for this very reason become the subject of subversion or other threats. So it seems to me that arms sales, continuing at the level that they are for the indefinite future, pose major threats not only to systemic stability but also to individual regimes and governments in the Third World.

Finally, I suspect that the general frequency of actual warfare in the Third World in the 1980s will not be anticipated. Western intelligence agencies have been notoriously poor at predicting the willingness and intention of one side in a regional struggle to attack the other.* This has been true many times in the Middle East and in East

---

* See Richard K. Betts, "Surprise Despite Warning: Why Sudden Attacks Succeed," *Political Science Quarterly* (Winter 1980), pp. 551–572.

Asia. Throughout this decade, states who possess the capability to attack their rivals will probably do so. In "predicting" the attack of North Korea by South Korea, Yugoslavia by the Soviet Union, Saudi Arabia by Iran, Taiwan by the People's Republic of China, Jordan by Israel, and Jamaica by Cuba, I have done so to point out that small states rather frequently diverge sharply from the behavior their great power allies wish of them.

New and direct threats to national security are also likely to occur as a result of adverse developments in key regional food and population balances.

Five hundred million persons will be added to the labor force in developing countries between now and the end of this century. Most (70–80%) will not find jobs outside subsistence agriculture, and those in agriculture will probably be underemployed, landless, and very poor. The bulk of these people will live in the low-income countries of Asia and Sub-Saharan Africa. Many will live in cities that tend to be breeding grounds of discontent, disillusionment, and challenges to government authority. By the end of this century, nearly a billion people will be added to the cities of the Third World (see Figure 6.2 below). Some 40 cities in the developing world will be at least 5 million in size; in 1950, only Buenos Aires was that large. Eighteen cities will be larger than 10 million, and Mexico City may well have more than 30 million inhabitants. Such rapid urban growth, coupled to the inevitable dislocations and disappointments that will accompany living in large cities with strained (if not archaic) social services and high rates of un- and underemployment, will place a premium on the ability to control the masses. For some countries, the future therefore is probably a bleak one in terms of political liberties and human rights. But for others, anarchy, such as seen in Iran, may well be the case.

But these problems will just be added to an already "dismal"—to use the World Bank's term—outlook for most people living in the Third World.* The growth of GDP per capita, according to Bank estimates, will exceed the rate of population growth this decade by only one percentage point. In low-income Asia and the middle-income countries of the Middle East, North Africa, and Sub-Saharan Africa, GDP and population growth are either tied, or the former is growing much more slowly than the latter.

In this decade, food shortages should be expected throughout the Third World. Disturbances and challenges to the government will be likely to follow. In the Latin American countries of Argentina,

---

* *World Development Report, 1979* (Washington).

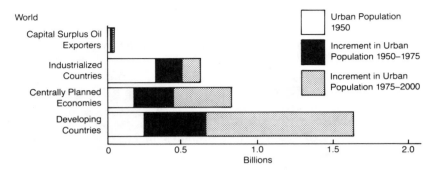

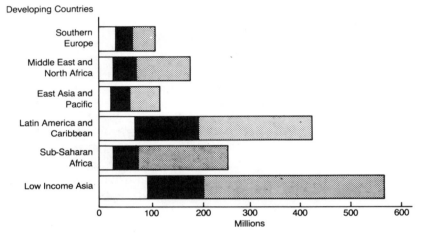

FIG. 6.2: Urban Population Estimates and Projections, 1950–2000

Source: World Bank.

Colombia, El Salvador, Honduras, Mexico, and Guatemala, urban violence and guerilla warfare pose challenges to the government at a time when each of these countries is experiencing a period of urban growth. Other Third World leaders will have to cope with even more violent ethnic and regional dissidence—on the rise in the Middle East, parts of Asia and Africa, as well as in Turkey (a member of NATO)—in which population displacement has been used as a strategic weapons, creating enormous numbers of refugees.*

---

* There are over 17 million refugees today, as compared with 1904, when the estimated world refugee population was less than 8 million.

The famine which gripped the fifth most populous country in the world for nearly three years—and which created the largest refugee population the Asia region had ever known—began imperceptibly. Somewhere in central Java, probably, one farmer too many left his home for the promise of a job in the city, causing a chain reaction that made it impossible for rural Indonesia to produce enough food for its giant cities. Urban slum dwellers who had survived for years on a minimum diet found they could not survive with a hundred calories less. Life expectancy dropped in a matter of two years nearly twenty, as resistance to disease declined.

To this day, I am not sure this terrible disaster could have been avoided. It was not possible for ours or the Indonesian government to know how much food was being produced or when they were on the verge of a crisis. And when the crisis was upon us—and despite the magnificent effort to rush food and medical supplies to Java—the damage was already done. Infant mortality that year was nearly 90%.

Bush, "The Four Horsemen: Harbingers of Disaster in Asia," in *Memoirs.*

In short, as one analyst* has put it, there is

Another vision of potential disaster . . . less dramatically cataclysmic than either nuclear destruction or catastrophic physical breakdown, but not less dangerous for that. It is the prospect of *a slow but probably accelerating slide into chaos* due to social limits on our ability to cope with the complexity inherent in a high technology society. Political, psychological and institutional limitations could condemn the world to a vicious cycle of interlocking crises, *with the institutional structure of society breaking down or becoming paralyzed by the sheer weight and complexity of problems it cannot handle.**

*Maurice Strong, "One Year After Stockholm," *Foreign Affairs* (1973), p. 697 [emphasis added]. See also Council on Environmental Quality and the Department of State; Gerald O. Barney, Study Director, *The Global 2000 Report to the President. Vol. I: Entering the Twenty-First Century. Vol. II: The Technical Report.* Washington: Government Printing Office, 1980.

The coup against Fidel Castro was one event which had few, if any, adverse consequences for the United States and the Western Hemisphere. It illustrates how the unexpected took the heaviest toll against those leaders who when the decade began seemed virtually immune from threats to their power.

The military officers which seized power from Dr. Castro and his associates, of course, did so based on the conviction that he led the Cuban communist revolution astray by too great a reliance on the Soviet Union. And they can be expected to be just as supportive of "revolutionary" and "progressive" guerrilla forces in their hemisphere. But for the immediate future, I would urge my successor to respond positively on a *quid quo* basis to Havana's request for recognition and development assistance while Cuba's new leaders try to rebuild their economy.

Bush, "Giants with Clay Feet," in *Memoirs.*

V

The foregoing trends suggest that the international system of the 1980s will be characterized by the continued diffusion of power, especially within and between present-day alliances. At a minimum, the cohesion of NATO (as well as of the Warsaw Pact), as well as key bilateral relations derived from those alliances, will be severely tested. If the trends noted at the outset shape the international system, we will also witness a number of military conflicts, some of which will have major consequences for security of the United States, the Western hemisphere, and the NATO allies. What constitutes power, and more importantly what brings security, in such an international system will increasingly be a question mark. No leader will be immune from assassination or attempts at it, and for the sake of individual or national survival world leaders can be expected to go through volte face (e.g., the "predicted" denunciation of the Camp David Accords by Anwar Sadat) as frustration with present directions mounts. Since this generalization is meant to apply to leaders in both the communist and noncommunist worlds, some developments in the future need not necessarily be adverse to Western-hemisphere interests. Partly because of the growth in the arms transfers and partly because of nuclear proliferation, the ability of relatively small states to have profound impact on power and security in international affairs will be enhanced, and the problems of other states will become magnified in importance by virtue of the geo-strategic position they

When it happened, few recalled that in 1917 three children in Portugal had predicted it. The catalyst appeared to be less the break-down of the Soviet economy (which we had come to expect in the wake of declining harvests and oil production) than of the social system fashioned by the Communist Party. The Russians had by 1984 become a minority in the army, the cities, and the countryside. The Communist Party couldn't deliver even the most rudimentary relief from the severe food shortages, nor face off dissident, western-looking party leaders in its so-called satellites. The assassination—still never solved—of the Soviet President and the head of the KGB undoubtedly also played a role in shaking faith in the Party. But what surprised us all most was the source of the ultimate breakdown —the underground Christian movement. . . .

Bush, "Forging a New Relationship with the People of Russia," in *Memoirs*.

occupy or the strategic resources they command. Finally, interdependence, in the sense in which this refers to a growing recognition of the need for countries to work together, will probably be a thing of the past. National anxieties and atavisms will come to the fore in such matters as energy policy, trade policy, and military alliance and make definitions of common cause exceedingly difficult.

In reviewing this rather grim series of events, it is essential to point out that they do not necessarily imply an evolution of the international system so adverse to free-world countries that much of what could happen will rebound to Soviet benefit. The events "pre-dicted" do *not* constitute a list of all that might happen of an adverse nature, but rather of the unexpected. Partly because of the immense threat posed to free world institutions, the Soviet Union is the subject of much more intense scrutiny than our own societies. Hence the range of the unexpected is much narrower. The Soviet Union will encounter considerable and anticipated problems in the 1980s— ranging from the decline in its capacity to remain the world's largest oil producer, to its growing inability to feed its population, to the trend toward fragmentation of the Warsaw Pact, to the changing (and unfavorable) demographic balance (of Slavs to other ethnic groups) within the Soviet Army.* So I foresee a decade in which the prob-

* See, for example, Robert Wesson, ed., *The Soviet Union: Looking to the 1980s* (Stanford, CA: Hoover Institution Press, 1980).

lems of the free world—while not unexpected by the Soviet leadership—will not automatically translate into Soviet gains over or confidence about the ability to compete with the United States or other world powers.

VI

There are a number of dimensions along which the implications of this array of unexpected dynamics and events should be drawn. Before discussing these implications, however, it is essential to put this exercise into context. It seems to me that the central question that ought to be asked about such kinds of excursions into the future is not whether the analyst or the particular agency has either a demonstrated track record of being right (say nine times out of ten, or four times out of eight) or even whether the analyst has put together the scenarios in such a way that would make a reasonable leader think that a credible series of events has been constructed. After all, we are talking here about the unexpected, for which present rules of logic and credibility probably will not apply. The critical thing to keep in mind is whether, if any of these projections came true, they would do material harm and significant damage to U.S. and free-world interests. That question more than any other shapes the way in which I have tried to outline the implications of this paper for policy planning and for thinking about foreign policy in both the international and Western hemisphere contexts.

As suggested in commissioning this chapter, my discussion of implications will focus on implications for the Western hemisphere and for existing institutions to cope with the problems ahead.

The unexpected could hit the Western Hemisphere particularly hard. The region is already a major scene of terrorist activity; roughly 25% of all terrorist incidents between 1968 and 1979 occurred in Latin America, including nearly half of the total embassy hostage seizures during the 1970s. The region is also experiencing rapid rates of urbanization; by 1990, it will contain at least three of the world's ten largest cities. Such urbanization will challenge the capacity of existing social welfare institutions and the urban infrastructure itself, which already barely sustains the present population. In its wake could come the collapse of the democratic process in those countries facing both grave challenges from within as well as external efforts to subvert incumbent regimes. Finally, six nuclear reactors are now under construction in Latin American countries (accounting for 25% of the total new reactor construction in LDC's). Three more are on order, and feasibility studies have been completed for reactors in Colombia, Jamaica, and Peru. A combination of geography, tides, and winds could hold countries in both hemispheres hostage to a threat to release nuclear waste material into the atmosphere.

Reaching a net judgment about the ability of existing institutions to cope with the kind of unexpected international crisis that might occur in the period ahead is problematic. Especially if the collapse of NATO occurs, or even if present trends toward dissention within it continue, there may be no collective security focal point for assessing the potential for such crises or managing a response to them. And unless there is a revival of some form of working relationship between the United States and the Soviet Union, the ability of the two superpowers to keep their cool must also be seriously questioned.*

These observations raise even greater questions about the potential for various forms of international governance to provide the network by which such communication and crisis management could be achieved. It is simply hard to imagine, given a world beset by such potential crisis, how we could get from here to there. There is, however, one area that could prove to be the forerunner of greater international cooperation. This is in the area of intelligence cooperation. Even if one considers the scenarios related to terrorism and the potential for terrorism alone, it is clear that only through the exchange of more information about dissident political forces, suspect groups, and psychopathic individuals can such potential crises be prevented. Indeed there is a framework for the sharing of such information that has worked rather well on a limited basis, but needs (if one is fearful of the future) to be substantially expanded. There is a body of international law that makes certain acts uniformly a crime across regions and also provides for the recognition of the legal norms of one country by another. Obviously any such developments as increased international intelligence data sharing or intelligence and police operations ought to be undertaken in the context of wanting to bend over backwards to protect human rights. But I would submit

---

* Indeed, it is my belief that in the 1980s detente will come to play an even more critical role than it has in past history as a means of managing the U.S.-USSR bilateral relationship. Viewed from today's perspective, the argument that the spirit of detente will rise again seems one of the more surprising or irrational events that could happen; in fact, crises and intense competition have been the birth of three out of five previous periods of detente.

that this will be increasingly difficult to do if, as some writers of fiction imagine, computers begin exchanging information on individuals and groups that feel oppressed in one way or another or suppressed by the political systems under which they are governed.

A somewhat more encouraging prospect is held out by William Colby* (a former U.S. Director of Central Intelligence), who has suggested:

> The need today is for a philosophy for the larger discipline of intelligence, private as well as governmental. It must recognize the end of the simple acquisitive stage of intelligence, and of the narrow mercantile insistence on one-sided net benefit in exchanges. It must insist on the recognition of mutual benefit from the free flow and exchange of information, in the fashion that the SALT agreements recognize that both sides can benefit from pledges against concealment and interference with the other's national technical means of verification. It must resist retrograde calls for a "balanced flow of information" as a camouflaged demand to control the information flow and manipulate appearance rather than expand true knowledge and understanding.

I hope Mr. Colby—rather than, for example, the author of *The Forbin Project*—proves prescient.

In any case, improved policy planning and crisis management are essential at both the national and the regional levels. Threat assessment in the 1980s, especially in a region as likely to be as vulnerable to powerful combinations of internal and external pressures as Latin America, can no longer be done effectively without taking into account the way in which problems in one state can easily spill over or be exploited.

We are already in an era in which national power does not equate to military strength nor even to a combination of military prowess coupled to great wealth (either monetarily or in terms of national resources.) But what is even more critically uncertain is the way in which the future and such events and developments as projected here will change basic definitions of security and the measures states will take to achieve it. It seems to me that we are headed for a time in which security has to be defined much the way Robert McNamara did in the early 1960s as a function of social, economic, military, and political developments taken together rather than as separate achievements in each area. It will, moreover, be a time in

---

* "Intelligence in the 1980s," *The Information Society*, I (1981), p. 69.

On the eve of America's civil war, the *Harper's Weekly* of October 1857 editorialized:

> It is a gloomy moment in the history of our country. Not in the lifetime of most men has there been so much grave and deep apprehension, never has the future seemed so incalculable at this time. The domestic economic situation is in chaos. Our dollar is weak throughout the world. Prices are so high as to be utterly impossible. The political cauldron seethes and bubbles with uncertainty. Russia hangs, as usual, like a cloud, dark and silent, upon the horizon. It is a solemn moment of our trouble—no man can see the end.

Much the same could be said about the prospects which we faced in the early 1980s. My successor faces no less complex and uncertain an international system today. But she does so with many resources in international cooperation that we did not have at the outset of this era—and, I personally hope, with far fewer threats and surprises ahead.

Bush, "Concluding Thoughts," in *Memoirs.*

---

which it is very likely that one country's security will be another's threat, and that the responses adopted in one country to enhance security—unless extremely sensitive to the way in which they will be interpreted across boundaries and across cultures—will be as destabilizing as the causes that led that particular country to improve security in the first place.

At best, power will remain elusive. The advantages it confers will be fleeting, its execise will be fraught with complexity and uncertainty, and as Stanley Hoffman has suggested, "calculations of power [will be] . . . even more delicate and deceptive than in previous ages."*

Present, as well as newly emerging, systems of collective security (ranging from NATO to the OAS, ASEAN) will thus be severely tested. The major underwriters of these systems will find themselves asked to defend allies against threats more subtle (e.g., subversion),

---

* "Note on the Elusiveness of Power," *International Journal* (1975), p. 184.

and complex (e.g., nuclear proliferation) than those for which such alliances were originally created. This may require the creation of emergency, "rapid-reaction" forces assigned to organizations rather than states or lead to the breakup of present-day security systems in favor of those created by smaller groups of states who share cultural and political affinities, vulnerabilities, and police forces. With respect to the Western hemisphere per se, the unexpected events of the future may either increase reliance on the United States or be characterized by foreign policies that "see-saw" between nonalignment and close reliance on superpower support (à la Egypt).

At the same time, extending the rule of law, especially over the environment, national responses to terrorism, and the reception to be accorded refugees might also prove a very promising approach to crisis management. Theoretically, international legal systems could operate without regard to grand alliance schemes or even to the relationships between governments per se.* And this may be what Helmut Schmidt had in the back of his mind when he wrote in the most recent issue of *Foreign Affairs*: "stability will only be possible in the unsteady world situation in the 1980s to the extent that governments and politicians, but also businessmen, bankers, and working people can depend on each other's calculability."†

But probably the greatest contribution to coping with the unexpected will be made by the present institutions of governance. In such a world as forecast in this paper, the capability of governments to promote legitimacy, development, and political participation will be in short supply. Whether such events as those listed above occur or not, most states will find the 1980s full of enough surprises to cause rethinking conceptions of national power and the threats to as well as the requisites of security. At the same time, there is at least a better-than-even chance that statesmanship and the capacity of present institutions to cope with this projected environment will prove equal to the task. Viewed from the perspective of today—and scenarios about tomorrow—such a development may prove to be the most unexpected of all.

---

* See, for example, Hedley Bull, *The Anarchical Society* (New York: Columbia University Press, 1977), esp. pp. 250–252 on "Alternatives to the Contemporary States System."
† "A Policy of Reliable Partnership." *Foreign Affairs* (Spring 1981), p. 244.

7

Canadian Foreign Policy and the Western Hemisphere

Robert Jackson

The Canadian government has never directed its foreign policy specifically toward the entire western hemisphere. Instead, at the global levels of political relations, economic development, and defence policy the focus has always been in other directions.

At the global political level, Canada gives priority to developing relations with the United States and the Commonwealth countries, and participating in the United Nations. On economic development issues, Canada's most obvious foreign policy contribution has been a strong and consistent support for the North–South dialogue. At the defence level, because of close ties with Europe, Canada developed a coherent foreign policy with respect to Atlantic and European affairs and participates as one of the original members of the North Atlantic Treaty Alliance. By the same token, Canada joined with the United States to form NORAD for the defence of North America.

The western hemisphere, consequently, has never been foremost in the minds of either Canadian politicians or the public, and as an overall concept hardly exists in the country's foreign policy statements. With the exception of the very close relationship with the United States and a few fragments of regional policies, political relations with the countries with whom Canada shares this area of the globe have generally been bilateral, sparse, and without any coherent policy other than within a broadly defined national economic and humanitarian interest.

At the present time, Canada has no overall hemisphere policy because little effort has been made to link Canadian interests with foreign policy objectives. As this paper demonstrates, Canada does have significant interests in Latin America and the Caribbean, and fragments of a hemisphere policy—priority to the Caribbean Commonwealth, concentrated bilateralism with special attention to Mexico, Brazil, and Venezuela, a unique approach to Cuba and Haiti, an extensive development assistance program, and special close relations with the United States—which could be brought together to form a coherent framework for foreign policy toward the southern part of the hemisphere. As yet, these various fragments of policy have not been linked together to form a coherent whole.

None of this, however, should detract from the fact that, dating back to the nineteenth century, Canada has had extremely close relations with the United States, and also, though to a much lesser degree, with several nations south of the Rio Grande. Today, apart from the dominant relationship with the United States, Canada maintains strong bilateral relations with countries throughout the hemisphere, and on rare occasions has taken foreign policy initiatives in the area ahead of the United States, some of which have been contrary to American policy positions.

Canada has largely avoided the thorny issues of politics and security that plague the southern portion of the hemisphere. As a parliamentary report recently indicated, Canada has a "limited role to play in the resolution of internal struggles in Latin America and the Caribbean".* It is a comfortable position from which the government takes few risks.

To a very large extent, Canada's foreign policy toward Latin America and the Caribbean is dominated by relations with the United States. While the early 1980s witnessed considerable rhetoric from both sides of the border—particularly over fisheries treaties, Canada's National Energy policy, and Federal Investment Review Agency—there is a general recognition that as captive neighbors on this continent, the only reasonable policy is to foster a deep and mutually satisfactory relationship. Canada is a trading nation. The

---

* Minutes of Proceedings of the Standing Committee on External Affairs and National Defence on *Canada's Relations with Latin America and the Caribbean.* Issue no. 48, December 8, 1981, p. 8. Hereafter cited as *Interim Report,* 1981.

domestic market is too small and nearly 31% of the GNP depends on exports. The fact is that 70% of our trade is dominated by markets in the United States.

Although Canada has closer relations with the United States than with all other countries of the hemisphere combined, that is not the subject of this paper. The role of the United States as a superpower and its preoccupation with military security in the hemisphere south of the Rio Grande has never been a role that Canada could—or aspired to—adopt. Canadian–American relations towards the southern part of the hemisphere sometimes coalesce, as with the Caribbean Basin Initiative, and at other times diverge, as they did over continued trade with Cuba after the 1959 Revolution and elections in Salvador in 1982.

The two countries exhibit a general difference in orientation toward the region. The present U.S. administration stresses that instability in the area is externally motivated, whereas Canadians stress economic and social conditions as the root of internal conflict. In other words, the Canadian position is based more on trade, investment, and humanitarian concerns than on security issues. It has also been colored by Canada's different relations with the Soviet Union, an early recognition of Communist China, and the fact that Canada continues to be a member of the Commonwealth.

Canadian policy toward Latin America and the Caribbean is currently under review. Mr. Mark MacGuigan, Secretary of State for External Affairs, outlined the rudiments of Canada's policy in March 1980, in a document that has been irreverently dubbed the Gospel according to Mark. Basing his position on the extreme diversity of the area, Mr. MacGuigan has called for pragmatism and more concentrated bilateralism.

A parliamentary Sub-committee on Latin America and the Caribbean was set up in March 1981, and following extensive hearings published an interim report. In his testimony to the Sub-committee, Mr. MacGuigan called for relations to be less one-dimensional; trade should be supplemented by industrial cooperation and technical exchanges. But in a much overlooked phrase he also called for economic links to be "reinforced by greater attention to political relations on both hemispherical and global questions."* The Sub-committee is expected to produce a more extensive report before

---

* Minutes of Proceedings of the Standing Committee on External Affairs and National Defence on *Canada's Relations with Latin America and the Caribbean*, October 1981.

the end of 1982. In doing so, it has a unique opportunity to structure the future of Canadian foreign policy in the area.*

Since Canadian relations with the hemisphere have never been fully fleshed out and yet are extensive in some areas south of the United States, it seems the best way to proceed is to synthesize Canada's overall relations with the hemisphere by first examining the origins and extent of Canadian hemispheric concerns and then turning to the OAS and security questions. Lastly, the paper discusses bilateral relations on a region-by-region basis.

ORIGINS OF HEMISPHERIC INTERESTS

Contacts between Canada and the countries of Latin America and the Caribbean predate Canadian Confederation in 1867.† Originally, traders from the Maritime provinces exchanged flour and saltfish for sugar and rum. While the private sector set the pace, the government was not far behind. The first official contacts were in 1866, when representatives of the various British colonies in North America visited parts of the Caribbean and South America.

Official commercial agents were sent to Mexico as early as 1887, and although contacts steadily expanded throughout the nineteenth century, in that period the government was not nearly as active as private enterprise in developing relationships. No diplomatic missions, for example, were set up. Before the end of the century, Canadian private enterpreneurs operated throughout much of South America. The Royal Bank opened its first branch in Havana, Cuba, in 1899, at the same time as it opened its first branch in Ontario, and the Bank of Nova Scotia opened a branch in Kingston, Jamaica, in 1889, in Toronto in 1897.

Canadian independence from Britain was won in 1931 with the passage of the Statute of Westminster, and it was only then that Canada could develop diplomatic missions. During World War II, the Canadian government began to take a more direct interest in Latin America and the Caribbean. The first diplomatic missions were set

---

* As well as traveling to the Caribbean and hearing witnesses, the Sub-committee commissioned two academic reports on the area: Edgar Dosman, Liisa North, & Cecilia Rocha, *Canada and Latin America: New Patterns in Development* and Kari Levitt, *Canadian Policy in the Caribbean*, October 1981.

† J. C. M. Ogelsby, *Gringos of the Far North* (Toronto: Macmillan, 1976).

up in Brazil, Argentina, and Chile in 1941. Mexico, Peru, and Cuba followed in 1944 and 1945. In the 1950s and 1960s, the number of diplomatic missions expanded to include most of Latin America and the Caribbean. In 1960, a Latin American division was established in the department of External Affairs.

In 1970 the government published a document called *Foreign Policy for Canadians*, which initiated another increase in activity in Canadian hemispheric relations. By 1977, External Affairs had set up separate bureaus for Latin America and the Caribbean, independent of the one for the United States. While official ministerial visits have taken place since the nineteenth century (generally in the winter months), they were increased in the 1970s. Especially noteworthy were Prime Minister Trudeau's visits to Mexico, Venezuela, and Cuba in 1976, and to Brazil and Mexico in 1981.

In recent years, Canada has maintained continuous diplomatic relations with almost all the countries in the western hemisphere. South of the United States there are 18 missions in 16 countries (three in Brazil), half of which have double or more accreditations; 560 Canadian and foreign personnel are engaged in these operations.*

EXTENT OF CONTEMPORARY
CANADA-HEMISPHERIC RELATIONS

Canadian hemispheric relations continue to be dominated by trade and economic interests. Even the recent foreign policy review mentioned above, which called for closer relations with Latin America, expressed little concern for strategic questions. It identified the mutual advantages for both Latin America and Canada as essentially in trade, investment, and economic affairs, and called for an increase in development assistance.†

While Canada has no coherent foreign policy that embraces the entire hemisphere, the extent of Canada's composite relations with the countries of Latin America and the Caribbean is fairly large. In 1979 (the latest year for reliable statistics on imports and exports to the entire hemisphere), Canada's exports represented

---

* *Minutes.* Issue no. 2, June 9, 1981, p. 8, and appendix 2A:1.
† Secretary of State for External Affairs, *Latin America: Foreign Policy for Canadians* (Ottawa: Information Canada, 1970), p. 6.

about 2.8% of the market share of $87 billion* worth of goods and services. In 1980, this rose by about half a billion dollars to a total of $3.7 billion. Over 33% of these exports were in the form of processed or manufactured goods, many in high-technology fields. In the rest of the world, the ratio of finished products to Canadian exports is only 19%, and this factor partially explains why the Foreign Secretary maintains that economic development and export promotion are the primary objectives of the Liberal government in dealing with the countries of Latin America and the Caribbean.† Mr. Edward Lumley, Minister of State for Trade, has estimated that in 1980 exports to the region kept approximately 150,000 people employed in Canada.‡

Imports to Canada from Latin America and the Caribbean hve increased concomitantly with our exports and amounted to about $4 billion in 1980. Petroleum products accounted for 51% of the imports and much of the remainder was made up of tropical food products. Of Canadian oil imports, 40% come from Venezuela and Mexico. However, the importation of manufactured products is also increasing, particularly from Brazil and Mexico.

Since Canadian banks opened offices in Latin America and the Caribbean in the nineteenth century, investment has been very high. About 75% of Canadian direct investment in developing countries is in this region,§ and Canada provides a strong development aid program here as well. The Canadian global development assistance program, which is now at .43% of the GNP, is projected to rise to .5% by 1985-86. The present government has indicated that this increase will continue to include a priority for the Caribbean. Currently, the total aid disbursement to Latin America and the Caribbean represents about 6% of official development assistance, most of which goes to the Caribbean countries. According to Marcel Massé President of the Canadian International Development Agency, Canada spends about $6 per capita in the Caribbean and 40 cents per head in Latin America. Part of the reason for the differential is the need factor, but other criteria, such as proximity, historic ties, trade relations, and, partly, security have also been considered. Massé calls this distinction a foreign policy decision; "the Caribbean must be an area of concentration because Canadian interests are involved in the area."‖

---

* All figures are in Canadian dollars.
† *Minutes.* Issue no. 1, p. 14.
‡ *Minutes.* Issue no. 2, p. 30.
§ *Interim Report*, p. 6.
‖ *Minutes.* Issue no. 2, p. 87.

The Canadian government also plays a role in supporting private business in Latin America and the Caribbean. It helps to fund the most important organizations—the Canadian Association for Latin America and the Caribbean (CALAC)—in its endeavors. Through the PEMD program, it funds businessmen to make contacts in the area. And, most important, the Export Development Corporation provides considerable sums of money to support business: In 1980, Latin America and the Caribbean consumed 15% of its budget for export insurance, 45% for investment insurance, and 21% of its loan services (exclusive of the United States).

CANADA AND THE ORGANIZATION OF AMERICAN STATES

On several occasions over the years, Canada and the Inter-American System have flirted with each other, but today Canada still remains outside the OAS. In 1910, Eliha Root, the United States Secretary of State, anticipating that Canada would imminently join the Pan-American Union, ordered a chair with "Canada" inscribed on it.* However, the Canadian government turned down the various invitations, until in 1941 the United States actually prevented Canada from joining. This on-again off-again relationship has persisted. Probably the most obvious historic reason that Canada did not join the PAU, however, was that Canada was not totally independent of the United Kingdom until 1931.

When the Organization of American States was formed in 1948, Canada was involved in seeking security through the North Atlantic Treaty Organization and the United Nations. The question of membership in the OAS became significant only in the early 1960s, when Mr. Howard Green was the Canadian Secretary of State. Most of the arguments at that time came down against membership. Proponents maintained that Canada should accept her responsibilities as a member of the hemisphere and in so doing establish prestige in the region and increase trade opportunities. Antagonists argued that Canada should not increase commitments beyond the Commonwealth, NATO, and the United Nations, and warned that if she did

---

* J. C. M. Ogelsby, "Canada and Latin America," in P. V. Lyon and Tareq Y. Ismael (eds.), *Canada and the Third World* (Toronto: Macmillan, 1976), p. 167.

join the OAS, Canada would become embroiled in disputes between the United States and Latin America.

In the early 1960s, President Kennedy invited Canadian MPs to take on their responsibilities toward Latin America. This ended the argument in favor of OAS membership, because the Conservative government in Canada concluded that they would not be pressured by the Americans.* The issue was never seriously raised again as a foreign policy possibility until the 1980s.

While Canada has never been a full member, she has been a "permanent observer" since 1972. Many other countries have a similar status, but only three—Canada, Spain, and Italy—have taken the role seriously enough to set up separate missions in Washington. Observer status has provided a limited but practical forum for communication and cooperation with this body of countries over specific inter-American problems.

Canada does participate actively in six principal agencies of the OAS. These include the Pan-American Health Organization, the Pan-American Institute of Geography and History, the Inter-American Institute for Cooperation in Agriculture, the Pan-American Railway Congress Association, the Inter-American Telecommunications Conference, and the Inter-American Statistical Institute.

Canada is also an active member of other important multilateral organizations. Having joined the Inter-American Development Bank in 1972, Canada has committed over one billion dollars to IDB operations in the first decade of membership. As a member of the Economic and Social Council of the United Nations, Canada has strongly supported the Economic Commission for Latin America.

Thus, Canada has demonstrated considerable interest in parts of the OAS and UN systems but has not chosen to join the main hemispheric organization. Over time, the arguments for joining have become stronger. Much of the stigma of U.S. domination that used to color Canada's view of the organization has abated as countries such as Mexico and Venezuela have become stronger. Parliamentary advocates believe that membership would give a stronger voice in the organization, particularly concerning the overall development strategies for Latin America. Those MPs who tend to be particularly concerned about human rights in Latin America believe that as a member Canada could make a contribution considered to be effective to the Inter-American Commission on Human Rights.†

---

* *Ibid.*, p. 175.
† *Interim Report*, p. 10.

The current arguments against adherence are essentially pragmatic. While bureaucrats may maintain that the six million dollars annually, which would be required to maintain full membership, is not insignificant, the major reason the Canadian government shuns membership in the OAS is the private belief that we could still get caught between the United States and Latin America in disputes, especially in Central America and the Spanish-speaking Caribbean. It is also very doubtful whether Canada would wish to adhere to the Rio Treaty, which binds the members of the OAS in a collective security network. If Canada did join, it would probably attempt to opt out of this treaty. There is also a privately held view among policy makers that the present members of the OAS "do not themselves regard the organization very highly."

At the present time, Canadian diplomats conclude that Canada would not get enough out of the OAS to make joining worth the effort. In order for Canada to seek membership in the OAS, the House of Commons Sub-committee on External Affairs would have to present an extremely cogent argument on the benefits side. While this author believes that benefits for Canada could accrue, especially at the symbolic level, the political thrust to make this foreign policy initiative has not yet developed. This leaves Canada with a philosophy toward the region that can best be called "selective bilateralism," which translates into prudent but rather self-centred policy initiatives. The alternative would be a comprehensive hemispheric policy— one that might mean joining the OAS as a full member. At the present time no such motivation exists. In Mr. MacGuigan's words, there is altogether too much consideration of these more than three dozen independent countries, colonies and territories as a single area: "We must therefore deal with them individually."*

CANADA AND THE CARIBBEAN BASIN

The Caribbean Basin, discussed here as the collection of islands as well as the mainland countries of Central America, has long been an area of particular concern to the Canadian government and occupies an increasingly important place in Canadian foreign, commercial, and aid policy. Whereas the United States has consistently played

---

* *Minutes*, p. 20.

a major role throughout the region, Canada has focused mainly on the English- and French-spreaking areas, where it has developed unique individual relations with the diverse island governments.

Canadian concern in the region is not primarily about security, although, as the United Kingdom withdrew from its traditional role there, the British government has urged both Canada and Venezuela to take more responsibility for security. This applies particularly to the Eastern Caribbean, where oil routes could be vulnerable. The major source of Canada's offshore oil is from Venezuela, and it passes through the Caribbean. The Panama Canal is in the area, and there are also significant Canadian investments throughout Latin America and the Caribbean that must be safeguarded. However, Canada's only contribution to security to date is an extremely modest training program for military, police, coast guard, and emergency planning officials.

Canada, along with Colombia, Venezuela, and Mexico, supports the American proposal of a Caribbean Basin Initiative. The July 11, 1981, joint economic development strategy for the Caribbean Basin is one that Canada had endorsed even before the American initiative. On June 23, 1981, Marcel Massé, President of CIDA, announced that Canada would double aid to the Commonwealth Caribbean over the next five years.* The Canadian government is concerned, however, that the initiative might be misunderstood as a device to mask United States' policy behind the appearance of a multilateral initiative, or that it could become an ideological tool aimed at particular countries. From the Canadian government's perspective, the Initiative is merely a statement of political will to encourage aid to those countries that are suffering from economic difficulties. Canada's total aid contribution to all of the Caribbean Basin is expected to be approximately half a billion dollars between 1981 and 1986.†

CANADA AND THE CARIBBEAN

Canada's major relations in the interrelated basin have been with the Commonwealth Caribbean, Haiti, and Cuba, but even here Canada has taken a low-key back-seat role to the United States and the United

---

* See Massé's statement to Fourth meeting of the Caribbean Group for Co-operation in Economic Development, June 23, 1981.
† See the *Joint Communiqué*, Caribbean Basic Initiative, March 14–15, 1982.

Kingdom. Relations with the Commonwealth states developed from historical links with Britain and today are primarily political and not commercial. In recent decades, Canadian trade and investments have decreased, so that only retail banking and offshore financial activities retain a significant Canadian economic involvement. Fifteen years ago the Commonwealth Caribbean represented over half of all Canadian investment in developing countries; it is now down to 20–25%. Imports are down basically because Canadian markets for bauxite, alumina, and sugar are now being filled outside the Caribbean. Canadian exports to the area in 1980 totaled only $286.4 million.

The aid picture is quite different. Canada and the United Kingdom are the oldest bilateral donors in the Eastern Caribbean and helped to set up the Caribbean Development Bank in 1970. Canada's aid commitments continue to be of paramount importance. In 1981–82, Canada provided $55 million in official development aid to the wider Caribbean, of which $46 million was allocated to the Commonwealth states. In fact, the Commonwealth Caribbean is the highest per capita recipient of Canadian assistance.

In January 1981, Mr. MacGuigan announced that there would be a major increase in aid for the Commonwealth Caribbean and that the agreements between Canada and the CARICOM (Caribbean Common Market) would be strengthened. This policy was elaborated in Marcel Massé's press release of June 23, 1981, which announced that Canada would contribute $350 million in aid between 1981 and 1986; of this sum $270 million is to be in the form of official bilateral aid.

Historically there have been two main types of Canadian aid in the area: balance of payment support, where CIDA extends a line of credit, as in Jamaica, and project aid. Aid in the Eastern Caribbean is almost exclusively in the latter category. Traditionally, Canadian aid has been for infrastructures such as schools, roads, airports. However, since 1977 there has been a shift to projects that will generate employment, food supply, and relief for the poor.

Canada's position is that her interests are best served by treating the Commonwealth Caribbean as an area of special priority among the countries of the Third World. The intention is to work both bilaterally and multilaterally to increase economic assistance and to help to overcome the effects of a declining standard of living. The present policy also stresses the need for regional integration of the English-speaking islands, recognizing that interdependence is necessary, and that all will benefit by sharing services wherever possible.

Canadian relations with Haiti are quite different from those with the Commonwealth islands. As the country with the lowest per capita income in Latin America and the Caribbean and the only other country in the hemisphere with French as an official language, Haiti has received Canadian support for cultural, humanitarian, and political reasons. Canadian missionaries have been active there for about 40 years, and currently there are over 600 of them providing vital social services. There is also a growing Haitian community in Quebec.

An aid program was initiated in 1973 and has allocated $41 million to date. In fact, Haiti has become the largest single recipient of Canadian development assistance in the region. The government is currently reexamining this case because of violations of human rights, refugees, and economic conditions in the country, but it is expected that aid to Haiti and the Dominican Republic will reach about $50 million between 1981 and 1986. Trade relations are not significant.

Canadian relations with Cuba are primarily commercial. Trade that began in the nineteenth century has grown to the point where Cuba is Canada's fourth most important hemispheric market. Despite protestations from the United States, Canada exports far more to this one island than to all the Commonwealth Caribbean states combined. In 1980, exports to Cuba were $475.3 million, with a large favorable balance of trade for Canada.

Canada and Mexico were the only countries in the western hemisphere to maintain relations with Cuba after the 1959 revolution, and Canada has continued to maintain trade relations despite the U.S. embargo. The fact that contact has been maintained could eventually be helpful in any negotiations over the current explosive situation in Central America. Although the Canadian government has made it clear that it disagrees with the ideological commitment and many of the policies and activities of the Cuban government, it does not openly condemn Cuba as the source of conflicts in the Caribbean or Central America. Although Cuban activites may escalate the violence, Canada considers the basic problem as being the backward economic and social conditions that foster the violence and political turmoil in these countries.

Mr. MacGuigan has said that Canada "endeavored to maintain a correct but productive relationship" with Cuba. The countries have had a joint economic committee for many years, and a cooperative agreement for athletic and sports training. Despite these contacts, relations, aside from trade, are not currently as cordial as they were in the mid 1970s. Aid was formally terminated in 1979, ostensibly because the per capita income of Cuba was too high to make them eligible. In 1978, for the first time, Canada imposed visa requirements on Cubans.

CANADA AND MEXICO

As fellow neighbors on the North American continent, Canada and Mexico share many mutual problems and interests. However political relations, though excellent, are relatively recent, having only been built up gradually over the last 15 years. Mexico is viewed as an important stabilizing element in the Caribbean and Central America. In fact, Mr. MacGuigan recently forecast that Canada's relationship with Mexico "will be the mainstay of our relationship with Latin America".*

Oil is an important element in the flourishing trade between the two countries. Canada is currently receiving about 50,000 barrels a day from Mexico and will increase that amount until 1990, by which time Canada aspires to be self-sufficient. Canadian imports from Mexico in 1980 amounted to $344.9 million, an increase of 65.5%. Canadian exports to Mexico in 1980 were $482 million, a 104% increase over the previous year.

Rapport between government leaders of the two countries is excellent. In 1980, an important industrial energy cooperation agreement was signed, which set up mechanisms to discuss and develop cooperation in trade and industry. Cosponsorship of the North-South summit in Cancun, Mexico, in 1981 was another significant milestone for the two countries.

Following President Ronald Reagan's 1980 campaign suggestion that a North American Accord be formed between Canada, the United States, and Mexico, leaders of the three countries did meet to consult about their respective policies. There is an implicit agreement now between the three heads of government and their staffs that regular tripartite meetings should continue. Privately, however, Canadian officials continue to be concerned that President Reagan wishes to expand this accord into a new organizational framework, and there is little disposition in Ottawa to accept any new formalized arrangements for Canadian, U.S., and Mexican policy formulation.

---

* *Minutes.* Issue no. 1, p. 23.

CANADA AND CENTRAL AMERICA

Canada has few historical, commercial, or cultural links with any Central American countries, and there is little significant Canadian investment there. However, in view of the escalation of destabilizing events in the area, Canada has been moving to increase trade and development assistance. On February 12, 1982, the Department of External Affairs forecast that development assistance to the six countries would be increased to approximately $106 million between 1981 and 1986.

The mission in San Jose serves five countries south of Guatemala and was established primarily for trade promotion. Exports to Central America are currently about $100 million a year. There are no significant Canadian investments in the region except through INCO, which has about $250 million invested in Guatemala. Apart from this there is a total of only about $20 to $30 million invested throughout the region.

With the exception of Costa Rica, the area has a history of coups, rigged elections, and human rights violations that have generated considerable humanitarian concern in Canada. The Sub-committee's interim report on Canada's relations with Latin America and the Caribbean called for Canada "immediately to commit itself to a substantial increase in its assistance to Nicaragua beyond current food aid."* Help was also urged for Costa Rica, which has been facing an acute balance of payments problem.

The Canadian government supported the March, 1982, elections in El Salvador but sent no official observers. The Sub-committee, on the other hand, called for preelection negotiations between all parties, an internationally supervised cease-fire, and an internationally supervised electoral process. They considered that the injection of an East–West dimension into the area would foster a dangerous atmosphere of confrontation and polarization and undermine cooperative attempts to solve the problems.† Meanwhile, Canada has been active in the U.N. and other forums, pressing for human rights in the area. The current Canadian quota for refugees from the Latin American region is 1,000 a year, and so far demand has not exceeded that number, but it could well become an issue in the near future.

---

* *Interim Report*, p. 15.
† *Interim Report*, p. 19.

CANADA AND SOUTH AMERICA

Canadian relations in South America are strongest in Brazil and Venezuela. Brazil has become, after a long historic commercial relationship, Canada's largest export market in Latin America. In 1980, Canadian exports reached $893.3 million, of which wheat was the major component. The Canadian government is actively promoting this relationship and developing a range of other contacts in agriculture and industry, as well as developing new cultural affairs programs.

The relationship with Venezuela is based mainly on oil. It supplies the largest amount of Canada's imported petroleum. In 1980, Canadian exports amounted to $652.9 million, mainly in automobiles and parts, and imports amounted to $2.1 billion. After the change in government in Venezuela in 1979, relations between the two countries lapsed somewhat, and Canada is concerned to broaden contacts and develop more active political consultations. Venezuela is increasingly important in the Caribbean basin area, and Canada has encouraged both Venezuela and Mexico in their offer of oil to non-oil-producing countries in the area.

There are relatively few political contacts with Argentina, Chile, Paraguay, or Uruguay, the four military governments in the south of the continent. Most contacts are with Argentina, with whom Canada has a commercial, economic, and industrial cooperation agreement to promote Canadian sales in areas such as communications, construction, agriculture, and mines. The sale of a Canadian-built CANDU nuclear reactor was noteworthy. Canadian companies are currently bidding on a major hydroelectric project in Argentina, but since the 1976 military coup there has been relatively little ministerial contact.

Chile constitutes a small but growing export market for Canada. Exports increased 14.5% to $105 million in 1980. However, there are limited government contacts. There are virtually no contacts with Uruguay, and few with Paraguay, although there has been a recent and first ever visit by a Canadian minister to that country.

Canada has given priority instead to the mainly democratic Andean Pact countries, Venezuela, Colombia, Ecuador, Bolivia, and Peru. Venezuela has already been mentioned. Colombia and Peru are countries of concentrated CIDA activity, and they can anticipate a Canadian development program of several million dollars there over the next few years. Normal relations, which were temporarily suspended, were reestablished in 1980 with Ecuador, and also in Bolivia following the 1980 coup.

CONCLUSION

Because of the dominant East–West ties and a very strong relationship with the United States, Canada has not formulated an overall hemispheric policy. Instead, Canada has developed bilateral relationships to varying degrees, as well as fragments of unrelated policies for particular areas of this part of the globe.

Canadian policy toward Latin America and the Caribbean is currently under review, and the House of Commons Sub-committee report, which is due shortly, has a unique opportunity to make a significant impact on Canadian foreign policy in the decades ahead. There appear to be two possible strategies in restructuring and defining a more comprehensive policy. One entails joining the OAS and accepting the framework established by that organization; the other is to mould together the many fragments of policies that already exist into a tighter, more comprehensive whole. The latter option might or might not include membership in the OAS.

Which choice is made will hinge primarily on two factors, the first of which is domestic. If the Sub-committee presents a cogent argument for joining the OAS, it is not impossible that the government will adopt the recommendation. However, Secretary of State MacGuigan has already called for more "concentrated bilateralism," with special significance for Mexico, Brazil, and Venezuela, and without a strong and convincing case his department's penchant for the "status quo" seems the more likely option.

Canada's future policy will also depend to a large extent on whether the United States becomes further embroiled in El Salvador and elsewhere in Central America. There is a very strong humanitarian element in Canadian domestic politics, which will make it difficult for the federal government to shift toward joining the OAS (or similar policies) if there is any chance that Canada will be drawn into disputes between the United States and other countries in the hemisphere over security questions. Canada's special policies toward Cuba and even El Salvador illustrate the continuing gulf between the U.S. administration and Canada in the western hemisphere.

Over the years, Canada has maintained a reasonably low profile in the Caribbean and Latin America, and, on the whole, relationships are good. Being free of hegemonic power designs in the area, Canada has earned considerable respect and credibility, which could be a significant resource if the Canadian government could develop a coherent and integral foreign policy for the region.

8

Political Relations
in the Western Hemisphere

Jorge I. Dominguez

INTRODUCTION

Political relations in the Western Hemisphere* have come to combine
four clusters of issues. This mixture is unique in the history of the
hemisphere. The first, oldest cluster is the set of political relations
inherent in the geographic location and in the history of international
political relations of the hemisphere since independence. The second
cluster includes the consequences for the western hemisphere of the
Cold War and its evolution in politics and in ideology. The third and
fourth clusters are more recent. The third includes the results of new
problems, opportunities, and issues stemming from the breakdown of
U.S. hegemony. The fourth is the change in the economic development agenda in the hemisphere. Outcomes in all the clusters indicate
changes in the international relations of Caribbean and Central and
South American countries in the 1980s.

I am grateful to the Aspen Institute and to the Center for International Affairs,
Harvard University, for research support, and to my colleagues on this Aspen
Institute project for their excellent comments on an earlier draft.
* For the purpose of this work, purely bilateral U.S.–Canadian relations are
excluded.

The existing international institutions in the western hemisphere respond to some degree to each of these clusters; they are also conditioned in their effectiveness by the outcomes of these political relations. The effectiveness of the hemispheric international institutions, however, is rather more variable. I will argue that the search for greater international institutional effectiveness in the area of western hemisphere political relations may be somewhat illusory. By their very nature, political relations are of central concern to states and thus not likely to be delegated enough to international or supranational organizations. The latter's principal role is to provide arenas and facilities for states to cooperate, or to reconcile differences, in order to minimize violence and advance joint interests. It is in these secondary, albeit still important, areas of politics where institutional effectiveness might be enhanced. Thus I will discuss also some strategies of organizational decentralization, some of which may include countries beyond the Americas.

THE FIRST CLUSTER: GEOGRAPHY AND HISTORY

Political relations in the western hemisphere, as elsewhere in the world, have been shaped in part by territorial and boundary disputes and by the search for political influence over neighbors near and far. The consolidation of a South American "balance of power" system in the mid-nineteenth century responded to the twin concerns of territorial expansion, defense, and consolidation, on the one hand, and the search for influence, resources, and allies, on the other hand. While subregional conflicts emerged from the very moment of independence, the consolidation of a continental South American international subsystem occurred approximately during the 1860s, when concurrent wars were fought by both the Atlantic- and Pacific-coast countries. In addition, Great Britain regulated relations between South America and the outside world during the bulk of the nineteenth century.*

In North America, the United States, Great Britain, Russia, Spain, France, and Mexico had all partaken of a kind of "balance of power" system in the first half of the nineteenth century. Spain's retreat to the Caribbean in the 1820s, the U.S. victory against

---

* See Robert N. Burr, "The Balance of Power in Nineteenth-Century South America," *Hispanic American Historical Review* 35, no. 1 (February 1955): 37–60.

Mexico and the U.S. acquisition of the Oregon territory in the 1840s, France's refocusing on Europe in the late 1860s as Prussia moved to unify Germany, and the U.S. purchase of Alaska, established U.S. predominance in North America.

In a Central America wracked by regional warfare, the British established an early role mediating between Central Americans and the outside world and, at the same time, establishing formal and informal protectorates along Central America's Caribbean coast. As early as 1850, however, Great Britain had to concede an equal share of influence over Central America to the emerging power of the United States in the Clayton-Bulwer Treaty.*

Within the greater and lesser Antilles, the colonial status quo was maintained because it suited the interests of most of the major powers and reflected the weakness of the mainland Spanish-speaking states. Great Britain, France, the Netherlands, Denmark, and Spain remained colonial powers in the western hemisphere's mediterranean.

The hemisphere's international politics changed slowly in the century that followed the consolidation of U.S. predominance in North America, of a balance of power system in South America, of an hegemonial condominium in Central America, and of colonial fragmentation in the Caribbean. The main trends were the expansion of the power of the United States and the decline of continental warfare.

As the twentieth century opened, the United States spread its political and economic power to Central America and to the Spanish- and Danish-speaking Caribbean. The United States purchased the Danish West Indies. U.S. protectorates were established over Cuba, Haiti, and the Dominican Republic; Puerto Rico was annexed to the United States. Panama was helped to become independent from Colombia while remaining a U.S. protectorate as the Canal was built. British territorial control in Central America was eventually limited to its colony of Belize, while the importance of its economic impact on Central America came to trail that of the United States.†

In the last third of the twentieth century, the United Kingdom continued its territorial withdrawal from the Caribbean. In the 1960s, 1970s and 1980s, independence was granted to Jamaica, Trinidad–Tobago, Guyana, Barbados, Bahamas, Grenada, Dominica, St. Lucia, St. Vincent–Grenadines, Antigua–Barbuda, and Belize. Independence is likely for other territories. The Netherlands has also granted inde-

---

* For a critical discussion, see Samuel F. Bemis, *The Latin American Policy of the United States* (New York: Harcourt, Brace and World, 1943), pp. 106–8.
† See Dana G. Munro, *Intervention and Dollar Diplomacy in the Caribbean, 1900–1921* (Princeton: Princeton University Press, 1964).

pendence to Suriname; the rest of the Dutch Antilles may become independent in the 1980s. Only France shows no signs of withdrawal from the Caribbean; its possessions are formal departments of France. But the most dramatic impact of the legacy of colonialism recently has been, of course, the Argentine–British clash in 1982 over the future of the Falkland or Malvinas island archipelago.

As Europe has withdrawn from Central America and the Caribbean, the United States has advanced. U.S. influence, in turn, was transformed in the late 1920s and the 1930s. The earlier spread of U.S. influence had led to territorial annexations, and later to imperialism—the physical military occupation and the indirect governance of formally independent territories that became U.S. protectorates. By the mid-1930s, in contrast, the United States formally adhered to the principle of nonintervention; it terminated its military occupations and abrogated formal protectorate arrangements.* U.S. hegemony took its place. The United States expected international political loyalty and openness to U.S. trade and investment. In return, the United States provided certain special benefits (such as through the sugar quota system and eventually economic assistance, reaching a peak with the Alliance for Progress) and implicit or explicit military defense. U.S. economic and political influence remained considerable in Central America and in the independent countries of the Caribbean. As the English- and Dutch-speaking Caribbean countries gained independence, the United States also assumed responsibilities implicitly for their military defense and for increased economic assistance as well as continuing its markedly important role in trade and investment.†

In South America, the "balance of power" system, the continuing though diminishing British tutelary role, and the focus on national development of the major South American states, contributed to a decline in the practice of international warfare by the late nineteenth century. Unlike in most of Africa and Asia, European efforts to establish new colonies were short-lived, and failed. The wars that broke out in Europe in 1914 and 1939 were fought eventually in all continents except the western hemisphere, most of whose countries allied with the United States and the United Kingdom or remained neutral but experienced no war on their soil.

---

* Bryce Wood, *The Making of the Good Neighbor Policy* (New York: Columbia University Press, 1961).
† Virginia R. Domínguez & Jorge I. Domínguez, *The Caribbean: Its Implications for the United States*, Headline Series no. 253 (New York: Foreign Policy Association, 1981).

Several factors contributed for a long time to the maintenance of South American interstate peace. One was Brazilian foreign policy. Brazil succeeded over time in increasing its territory substantially, but it did so through negotiation and without recourse to war. Because Brazil borders on every South American country except Chile and Ecuador, this outcome had a major impact on keeping the continent war-free. The principal cases of warfare, or close threat of warfare, in the twentieth century have not involved Brazil.*

A second factor was the development of techniques to cool off border disputes. Some disputes were put "on ice" for years, or were submitted to slow negotiation or to arbitration by third parties, or at times governments simply agreed to disagree. An unfortunate consequence of these otherwise valuable conflict-containing procedures has been, however, that many of these issues have lingered until our own time.

A third factor was the fole of intermediaries in South and Central America, especially during economic crises. For example, since the end of the War of the Pacific (involving Chile, Bolivia, and Peru) in 1883 (Treaty of Ancón), the only periods of frequent warfare and severe violent territorial conflicts in South America coincided with the economic crisis from the late 1920s to the early 1940s and again, apparently, in the early 1980s. A prolonged war broke out between Paraguay and Bolivia, and shorter and more limited wars between Peru and Colombia and between Peru and Ecuador. From 1925 to 1942, there were ten instances when 35 countries acted as intermediaries to cool off or resolve border or territorial disputes. The United States did so seven times, European countries five times, South American countries 18 times, and Mexico and Central American and Caribbean countries five times. While European countries served as intermediaries only in South America, intermediaries from South and Central America contributed to settle some disputes not only in their own subregion but also in the other. Therefore, an informal intermediary system had evolved already before the foundation of the Organization of American States.†

From 1942 until 1981, South America was free of war, although countries at times appeared to be on the edge of war (and

---

* For a discussion of contemporary Brazilian foreign policy, see Ronald M. Schneider, *Brazil: Foreign Policy of a Future World Power* (Boulder, Colorado: Westview Press, 1976).

†Jorge I. Domínguez, "Mice that Do Not Roar: Some Aspects of International Politics in the World's Peripheries," *International Organization* 25, no. 2 (1971), pp. 190–94.

there were some isolated border incidents). Both in 1941 and in 1981, war broke out briefly between Peru and Ecuador over the same issue. In 1941, Peru consolidated its hold over the territory that is now its border with Ecuador; Ecuador sought unsuccessfully to regain some of that territory in a one-week war in 1981.* War broke out again in 1982 between Argentina and the United Kingdom over the Falkland (Malvinas) islands. Intermediaries played a role in containing the conflicts in the 1980s, too.

A final factor, especially in Central America, was that the United States became an informal guarantor of interstate peace as it withdrew from its imperial rola. U.S. hegemony included an expectation that the United States would maintain a kind of "international order" to prevent war in the region.

This oldest cluster has implications for the 1980s:

1.   There remain many unresolved territorial and boundary disputes, which have been at times at the core of interstate relations. Conflicts between Argentina and Chile, Chile and Bolivia, El Salvador and Honduras, Guatemala and Belize, and Peru and Ecuador have been the most acute in recent years; the first two have led to troop mobilizations close to war, the third led to war in 1969, and the last to a brief war in 1981. Other serious conflicts exist between Venezuela and Colombia, Chile and Peru, Colombia and Nicaragua, and Venezuela and Guyana.†

2.   The larger states still seek alignments and influence over the smaller states as a heritage of the "balance of power" styles in which South American diplomats are steeped. Argentina and Brazil, in particular, have practiced this kind of diplomacy with regard to Uruguay, Paraguay, and Bolivia, occasionally intervening in their internal affairs.

3.   Decolonization remains a problem of declining but still substantial importance. The safety of an independent Belize without the continued presence of British troops depends in the long run on the willingness and ability of successive Guatemalan governments to accept the way decolonization has occurred, namely, to respect Belize's independence and integrity. Negotiations between Argentina

---

* For historical studies, see Bryce Wood, *Aggression and History: The Case of Ecuador and Peru* (Ann Arbor: University Microfilms International, 1978); and David H. Zook, Jr., *Zaramilla–Marañón: The Ecuador-Peru Dispute* (New York: Bookman Associates, 1964).

† Jorge I. Domínguez, "Ghosts from the Past: Territorial and Boundary Disputes in Mainland Central and South America since 1960," (Cambridge: Center for International Affairs, Harvard University, unpublished).

and the United Kingdom over the Falkland or Malvinas archipelago broke down and led to war in 1982. The continuing fragmentation of federations among Caribbean islands has led to independent microstates that may not be economically or politically viable, thus posing problems for relations among states within and beyond the region.

Decolonization may also alter the character of those hemispheric institutions, such as the Organization of American States (OAS), that operate on the principle of one-state/one-vote. The linguistic, cultural, and political traditions as well as the needs and interests of new Caribbean members differ from those of the older members. Moreover, because the Charter of the OAS operates in part as an alliance against countries that have unresolved territorial disputes with members, the charter institutionalizes the conflict between some recently independent English-speaking countries and their Spanish-speaking neighbors. Guyana and Belize have been excluded from membership because of their disputes with Venezuela and Guatemala, respectively.

4. The infrequency of interstate warfare in the western hemisphere has depended to a considerable degree on the policies of the United States and Brazil. No institutional arrangement suffices that fails to take into account the importance, for different reasons, of these two actors.

5. The overwhelming presence of the United States in the affairs of the hemisphere has also been a major source of political conflict and disruption. The fears and the hopes of many, especially in Central America and the Caribbean, for U.S. intervention remain sources of interstate friction as well as fueling internal disputes within countries. The United States was also viewed by Argentina historically as a rival for influence in southern South America and as the ally of Argentina's main local rival, Brazil. That is one reason why U.S.–Argentine relations, while not always bad, have never been close and sometimes have been exceedingly poor (especially during the Second World War and its immediate aftermath).*

6. The habit of intermediation as a means for conflict resolution has long been accepted in the western hemisphere. Roles of go-between, mediation, arbitration, and judge have been played by different actors in varying ways. To give only recent examples, the Vatican's efforts to fashion a solution to the Beagle Channel disputes between Argentina and Chile, and the role of the guarantors of the

---

* For a discussion of contemporary Argentine foreign policy, see Edward S. Milenky, *Argentina's Foreign Policies* (Boulder, Colorado: Westview Press, 1978).

1942 Rio Protocol in affirming the Peru–Ecuador boundary in 1981, have helped to preserve the peace. The infrequency of interstate warfare had generated norms that states in the western hemisphere do not go to war with each other. One worry about the brief war between Peru–Ecuador in 1981, and about the Argentine–British clash of 1982, beyond their bilateral relationships, is their impact on the weakening of these norms not broken in South America since 1941.

THE SECOND CLUSTER: THE COLD WAR'S EFFECTS

The end of the Second World War (when almost all western hemisphere countries allied with the United States) and the opening of the Cold War provided a context and a partial justification for the formalization of relations among Latin American states with each other and with the United States. The Organization of American States (OAS) and the Inter-American Treaty of Reciprocal Assistance (IATRA) emerged principally in response to the World War that had just ended and to the desire to institutionalize preexisting conflict resolution and collective security procedures in the Americas. Neither the Treaty nor the OAS are exclusively heirs to the Cold War. However, as the actual experiences of the OAS and the Treaty unfolded, they became a part of the formal institutional machinery of the Cold War in the Americas.*

These hemispheric institutions and procedures can be described, as they have actually been applied, as an implicit bargain between the United States and the Latin American States: the Latin Americans were to be loyal to the United States internationally and were to acquiesce (however unhappily) in the "new international economic order" the United States was building in exchange for U.S. nonintervention in the internal affairs of Latin American countries. Moreover, the new institutions and procedures were to assume explicitly the peace-keeping role that the United States had born implicitly among

---

* For a discussion of the first years of the formalized inter-American system and its relations to Cold War issues, see J. Lloyd Mecham, *The United States and Inter-American Security, 1880–1960* (Austin: University of Texas Press, 1961); and John C. Dreier, *The Organization of American States and the Hemisphere Crisis* (New York: Harper & Row, 1962).

Central American and independent Caribbean states. Indeed, between 1945 and 1965, the Caribbean basin (including the islands and the portions of the South and Central American mainland that border on the Caribbean sea) accounted for the overwhelming number of inter-state conflicts subject to inter-American conflict-resolution procedures. Many of these conflicts were directly related to Cold War issues. The most prominent ones were Guatemala in 1954, the Dominican Republic in 1965, and a host of Cuba-related cases.*

The coming to power of the revolution in Cuba, and the consolidation of its revolutionary government, reinforced the latent Cold War features of the inter-American system, to the detriment of its conflict-resolving features. In particular, the brief act of war (a naval blockade) supported by inter-American procedures against Cuba in 1962, and the imposition of collective inter-American sanctions on Cuba between 1964 and 1975, emphasized the alliance features of the inter-American system under U.S. primacy. The U.S. intervention in the Dominican Republic in 1965, later endorsed by the OAS, raised the question whether the original bargain on which the OAS was founded had been broken: Instead of restraining U.S. intervention, the institutionalized inter-American system had become a mechanism to legitimate U.S. intervention and U.S. policies toward Cuba and to enlist Latin American cooperation in the implementation of controversial U.S. policies.

The perception that the OAS, in the words of the Cuban government, was little more than the U.S. Ministry of Colonies, has had severe consequences for the long-term effectiveness of the institution.

1. It has made it less likely that states that prize their foreign policy independence would choose to bring their disputes for settlement before the OAS. Most South American states and Mexico have made little use of the existing inter-American institutional machinery.

2. It has made it much less likely that states that perceive themselves to be in an ideological minority within the Organization will take their issues before it, and it makes it less likely that they would accept OAS judgments that are detrimental to them. Since revolutionary victories in 1979 in Grenada and Nicaragua, conflicts have arisen in the

---

* Joseph S. Nye, Jr., *Peace in Parts: Integration and Conflict in Regional Organization* (Boston: Little, Brown, 1971), pp. 129–54.

eastern Caribbean and especially in Central America, respectively. The OAS will be necessarily ineffective and unhelpful in settling disputes that arise involving Grenada and Nicaragua to the extent these two states do not trust it.

3. The issue of the role of the United States has come to overwhelm the OAS to the detriment, and at times to the exclusion, of other issues. It has made it virtually impossible for the OAS to consider, for example, the possibility of collective peace-keeping interventions similar to those undertaken by the United Nations. As the then Assistant Secretary of State for Inter-American Affairs explained to the U.S. Congress, the refusal of the OAS in June 1979 to consider sending a peace force to Nicaragua to expedite a transition from the Somoza to a post-Somoza regime: "This reflected how deeply the American states were sensitized by the Dominican intervention of 1965, and how deeply they fear physical intervention."* Even if this proposal should have been rejected on its merits, the point is that a discussion on the merits became virtually impossible because the "real issue" became U.S. intervention.

The inter-American system has had also another dimension, however. Its procedures sought to enshrine the values of freedom and democracy on whose behalf the Allied Powers claimed to have fought in the Second World War. While that claim was part illusion and part reality—during and after the war—the values that have come to be described most recently as "human rights" are also the more uplifting component of the immediate postwar legacy. Despite great difficulties, these remain shared values of the Americas—and a source of severe conflict within and between countries.

The Cold War legacy and, in particular, the Cuban revolution's coming to power had other organizational consequences. There was a burst of policy creativity in the late Eisenhower administration that was built on during the Kennedy and Johnson administrations. The Inter-American Development Bank emerged in that context; this older idea could become policy only with a new Cold War shock in the western hemisphere. The Eisenhower administration policies that

* Viron P. Vaky, "Statement before the Subcommittee on Inter-American Affairs, Committee on Foreign Affairs, U.S. House of Representatives," June 26, 1979, p. 11.

eventually led to the bilateral and multilateral features of the Alliance for Progress emerged in a similar setting.* Thus the two most creative periods of institution-building in the western hemisphere—the late 1940s and the late 1950s—can be directly traced to Cold War concerns.

It is too early to assess how effective or long lasting may be the Reagan Administration's Caribbean basin initiative. It already shares with earlier policies several key features: it is clearly innovative in some respects (e.g., regional one-way trade preferences); it builds on on the policies of preceding administrations; it is firmly rooted in Cold War fears; and it enlists the participation of several countries of the hemisphere. It differs notably so far from earlier innovations in that it lacks institutional features.

THE THIRD AND FOURTH CLUSTERS:
THE HEGEMONIAL BREAKDOWN AND THE
"DEVELOPMENT" AGENDA

Political relations within the western hemisphere have also been affected by policies toward development and by the consequences of economic development. The development that has occurred in some of the larger Latin American countries (notwithstanding persisting problems) has enabled and induced several of them to challenge aspects of U.S. hegemony. Many Latin American states have attempted since the 1960s to redraw the terms of the implicit bargain on which the post-World War II inter-American institutions had been founded. They have sought to extend their scope to cover economic issues. The two-fold, and at times contradictory, goals were to restrain economic intervention by the United States and to enlist U.S. assistance in economic development efforts. Changes in the charter of the OAS are examples of the former. Demands for a "new international economic order," either generally or through special concessions from the United States, are examples of the latter. Demands by the larger states to be consulted (over energy, trade, monetary policies, or embargoes) may reflect a lasting change toward foreign policy independence.

---

* For a personal discussion, see Milton S. Eisenhower, *The Wine is Bitter: The United States and Latin America* (Garden City, N.Y.: Doubleday, 1963).

Albeit contradictory in some respects, these initiatives had a common theme that has remained difficult for the United States to address. That theme was the demand for increased statism. On the one hand, the U.S. government has been asked to restrain the free flow of its enterprises as they spread overseas, and the consequences of their actions and their policies. On the other hand, the United States government was to agree to procedures for international economic arrangements that increased the weight of all states over internal and international economic transactions—commodity indexation, special trading and tariff preferences, etc. Thus a new layer of ideological conflicts over a "proper" political economy came to complicate inter-American relations. Although some Latin American states became less statist in the late 1970s and early 1980s (especially Chile and, less so, Argentina), the inter-American politico-economic agenda had remained tilted toward statism.

The international context also changed. Military parity with the Soviet Union, even at the nuclear level, replaced the earlier U.S. superiority. The international economic order built in the late 1940s was shaken. The international monetary system has been altered substantially. The practice of state takeover of foreign-owned enterprises, under certain conditions, has come to be accepted and has become a major source of the spread of state-owned enterprises the world over, including in Latin America. The relative economic power of the United States declined as Europe and Japan recovered from the ravages of war. In addition, high and persistent rates of economic growth in most western hemisphere countries allowed the larger countries to play new roles in world affairs. As their economies became necessarily internationalized beyond the hemisphere, so did their political concerns. Some of the consequences of this economic growth—such as the rise in exports of manufactured products—created new conflicts with a rising protectionism in the industrial countries precisely because many of the newly dynamic Latin American export sectors competed with the declining manufacturing sectors in the United States and Europe.*

The globalization of politics and economics for western hemisphere countries led to a further relative decline in the significance of inter-American institutions. Many of the new targets of opportunity were necessarily beyond the hemisphere. Many of the desirable changes made within the inter-American institutions sought precisely to downplay their specific hemispheric character, such as in the

---

* Jorge I. Domínguez, ed., *Economic Issues and Political Conflict: U.S.–Latin American Relations* (London: Butterworth, 1982). See especially chapters on investment, trade, and technology transfer disputes.

expansion of the membership of the Inter-American Development Bank to non-American countries. This step, taken in response to a U.S. initiative, exemplifies how globalization is a result of a structural change in international relations to which the United States as well as Latin American countries respond. Globalization is a general process, *not* an "anti-yankee" policy. Nevertheless, many of the new conflicts that have emerged with the United States have weakened so much the bases of inter-American solidarity—essential for any such organization—that Latin American governments decided to create the Latin American Economic System (SELA) to exclude the United States from membership. And many of the long list of inter-American institutions, associated formally or informally with the OAS, deal at best with narrow technical issues not at the center of the emerging international concerns.

The search for international influence by the largest South American states also yielded important benefits for the containment of interstate war. In order to improve their prestige in the world community and to avoid costly disputes, several larger South American states made some territorial concessions to their smaller neighbors in exchange for expanded political influence, trade, and investment benefits. This occurred between Brazil and Paraguay, Argentina and Uruguay, and Venezuela and Guyana, among others. This behavior was also evident in U.S. relations with Mexico (return of Chamizal) and Panama (return of the Zone and eventual transfer of the Canal); in a treaty with Colombia, the United States has withdrawn its claims over disputed Caribbean cays. The norms of war avoidance were strengthened by these trends.*

Subregional institutions suffered, however. Regional economic integration for Latin America as a whole, or for smaller regions, such as the Andean countries or Central America, or among the newly independent Caribbean countries, proved to have less promise than had been hoped. Some of the most promising regional economic integration schemes have been disrupted for political reasons. In Central America, war between Honduras and El Salvador, and revolution in Nicaragua and El Salvador, have severely weakened integration efforts. Among the Andean Pact countries, the Chilean defection, military coups in Bolivia, and the brief war between Ecuador and Peru (both under civilian rule) have imperiled the Pact. Among the Caribbean islands, virtually all the more ambitious integration efforts have failed. While there is still an important contribution that some limited integration efforts might make, the future no

---

* Domínguez, "Ghosts from the Past."

longer shines so brightly on them. Their problems illustrate the difficulties of institution building even when the United States is formally absent.

The international agenda was affected as well by changes concerning energy and the law of the seas.* The rise in energy prices led to a heightened search for energy sources. An unexpected consequence was to give a new dimension to the old boundary and territorial disputes in the hemisphere. Because rivers often serve as boundaries as well as sources of hydroelectric power, energy and boundary politics combined to reinvigorate old disputes. The most prominent has been over La Plata river basin development; the 1979 agreement over hydroelectric development between Brazil and Argentina was thus a great breakthrough.

Changes that have been, in effect, taking place in the law of the seas responded in part to the long-standing policy preferences of Pacific coast South American countries for extending maritime jurisdiction to 200 miles. They had sought this goal to protect national fishing zones. With the rise of commercially viable offshore hydrocarbon recovery technologies, the law of the seas became linked to some energy issues, reinvigorating boundary disputes, too, and extending them further. This has become an issue of rising concern in the maritime boundary disputes over the Beagle Channel between Argentina and Chile, in the British–Argentine dispute over the Falklands (Malvinas), and in the maritime boundary problems that Colombia has had with Venezuela and Nicaragua. It matters, too, to the often resource-poor islands of the Caribbean. A maritime economic zone with a radius of 200 miles would multiply by several orders of magnitude the resources possibly available to these islands. At the same time, these small, and often poor, island countries find it difficult to delimit maritime boundaries and then to enforce their rights.

CHOICES AND DILEMMAS IN THE 1980s: IMPLICATIONS FOR INTER-AMERICAN INSTITUTIONS

If present patterns were to continue unaffected, the international organizations of the western hemisphere—with the possible excep-

---

* For a discussion of nuclear energy issues, see John R. Redick, Chapter 11, this volume.

tion of the Inter-American Development Bank—are likely to find themselves in the 1980s in a pronounced decline. Recent trends have reinforced the long-standing tendency that political relations of central concern to states are never likely to be delegated substantially to international organizations. The more politically ambitious regional integration efforts floundered in the late 1970s or early 1980s. There is little prospect that efforts of group countries will succeed if they go much beyond rather technical, economic collaboration.

The larger South American countries and Mexico show little inclination to make use of the Organization of American States, or related fora, to advance their central foreign policy concerns. Their main policies appear to be to prevent being injured by what might occur in these organizations (e.g., human rights condemnation) or to make moderate use of some of the more specialized agencies. The increased ideological polarization in Central America between Nicaragua and its northern neighbors is likely to make it less likely that the OAS could continue to play a conflict-resolution role in the one subregion where its efforts had been more successful. The persistent exclusion of Cuba from the Organization makes it impossible to use it as a forum for discussion among countries that may have severe ideological differences. The persistence of a "Latin" culture within the OAS and associated organizations prevents the incorporation of the non-Latin Caribbean basin countries as truly full members. Already 13 of the 30 active OAS members (Cuba remains suspended) are non-Spanish-speaking countries. The OAS may have a non-Spanish-speaking majority by the mid-1980s.

The emergence of more capable states in most western hemisphere countries has gradually altered the content of their foreign policies. They look now for greater diversification in their international relations, necessarily leading beyond the Americas. They look as well for greater independence from the United States, as many always have; such a policy is all the more feasible now as the relative economic, political, and military power of the United States has declined and more international opportunities have become available. Diversification is not a code word for anti-Yankeeism. With few exceptions, the network of relationships has expanded principally to include Western European countries, Canada, and Japan, rather than the Soviet Union and its close allies. Nevertheless, these trends lead inexorably to a relative decline in the importance of inter-American institutions to member countries. What are some issues, then, that must be considered, not to reverse but to accommodate the future?

1. A central question in the hemisphere's history during the

past quarter-century has been the "fall-out" of the relationship between the United States and Cuba. A rationale for inter-American organizations, on the Latin American side, had been to contain the United States. Originally focused on military and political intervention, this concern spread to economic issues in more recent years. Thus inter-American institutions and procedures have a long history of considering the United States as "a problem." At the same time, they also have a long history of considering the United States as a source of possible political, military, or economic solutions. For example, the U.S. government provides the largest single source of funding for the OAS, the IADB, and other inter-American institutions. The U.S. armed forces continue to provide, implicitly or explicitly, for the military defense of the entire western hemisphere (with the exception of Cuba, Grenada, and Nicaragua), enabling beneficiary countries to forego large military expenditures (and, of course, inducing Cuba, Grenada, and Nicaragua to increase such expenditures!). Inter-American organizations, then, face an inherent contradiction in the roles expected from the United States.* In similar fashion, Cuba has been a persistent problem for inter-American institutions. It was under collective sanctions between 1964 and 1975, and it remains suspended from membership. One operational question is how these institutions might respond to the U.S.-Cuban relationship.

Inter-American institutions can become a tighter alliance in an international climate of renewed Cold War. This will, however, bring renewed strains within the organization, because many Latin American states do not subscribe to the U.S. definition of international problems. From Argentine and Brazilian trade with the Soviet Union despite Soviet political and military actions in Africa and in Asia, to Mexican commitments to foreign policy independence, and to the probable need (under this option only) to suspend another founding member such as Nicaragua, this policy would entail a radical surgery that would alter the nature of the organization without assisting in the resolution of disputes. Indeed, new disputes would be fostered.

Alternatively, the inter-American institutions could abandon explicit ideological commitments linked to a Cold War orientation and may readmit Cuba to the organization. This might lead to a further decline in U.S. interest and to the transformation of the OAS

---

* Jorge I. Domínguez, "The United States and Its Regional Security Interests: The Caribbean, Central and South America," *Daedalus* 109, no. 4 (Fall 1980): 115-33.

into no more than a regional version of the United Nations. Nor is it certain that Cuba would wish to join an organization where it has so few allies. This trend, then, might make the organization more irrelevant.

A third strategy may be to move toward multiple political and military institutional arrangements in the western hemisphere. Under the joint auspices of the United Nations and the Organization of American states, periodic meetings would be held, involving all countries in the western hemisphere; other countries could be invited as observers. Staffed by both Secretariats, this would provide a forum for discussion of issues that cannot be handled within the OAS because of Cuba's absence. Cuba, the United States, and other countries would talk about issues of specific relevance to the western hemisphere that matter greatly to them and that are not addressed now, bilaterally or multilaterally.

It is unclear, however, what might be gained from this approach that is not already available to these countries through the United Nations alone. In addition, not only would this procedure be administratively and politically complex, but the engagement of the UN in the western hemisphere's affairs might make it more difficult to resolve problems that do not now have a high global ideological content and that could be more simply addressed within a regional setting.

Because there are serious difficulties with various alternatives, however, it may be necessary to acknowledge that inter-American institutions cannot be expected to have much impact on the central Cold War questions within the hemisphere: U.S.–Cuban relations.

2. Changes could also occur at the military level. Under a revised Inter-American Treaty of Reciprocal Assistance (IATRA), signatories would commit each other not only to the common defense, but also to provide information to the OAS Secretary-General on weapons systems acquisitions and sales and to demand that extrahemispheric countries that sell weaponry to hemispheric countries provide comparable information to the OAS Secretariat. This mechanism is somewhat akin to that of the Tlatelolco Treaty on nuclear nonproliferation.

Signatories would also provide the OAS Secretariat with information on military expenditures every year. In addition, as is done between NATO and the Warsaw Pact, signatories should also supply information on the size and location of forces, and they should give advance notice to their neighbors and to the OAS Secretariat of all major military exercises and maneuvers. The Secretary-General will make the information public.

The United States would continue, of course, to supply a defense "free ride" to signatory countries. The United States would adhere to the amended Treaty's provisions for information on arms sales; the United States would not object to arms transactions between Treaty signatories and NATO or other countries not allied with the Soviet Union, provided all suppliers comply with the new arms control provisions.

These changes would continue to allow some countries to belong to the OAS, but not to a military alliance. It would allow countries to withdraw from the Treaty but remain in the OAS. It would provide for hemispheric defense. It would remove arms sales as a political irritant in U.S. relations with European or American allies. And it would enhance arms control procedures and reduce the likelihood of accidental warfare.

However, given the past difficulties of arms control agreements among the Latin American countries and separate controversies about the kinds and nature of commitments entailed in the IATRA, it is not clear whether much would be gained by coupling these two. It may be simpler and more propitious, albeit still difficult, to negotiate arms control agreements separate from the Treaty; this strategy might also make it easier to engage Cuba in an arms control agreement. Even separately, however, the difficulties of negotiating such agreements cannot be underestimated, given the historical record.*

3.   Although they have been battered by difficulties and they are limited in scope and efficacy, the conflict resolution functions of the Organization of American States remain invaluable.† This is the single most important *political* reason for the preservation of the OAS. "Mere talk" in itself is valuable as an alternative to warfare. An international organization may dispel fears and track rumors, facilitating communication among states whose bilateral channels are broken or impaired. It may provide information on how others have settled similar disputes. The further development of norms and rules to strengthen the presumption that countries in the western hemisphere do not go to war with each other remains an essential task—to which the United States, not just the other members, must, of course, be subject as well. The provision of resources as go-betweens, mediators, arbitrators, or judges is still a very important contribution

---

* See Caesar D. Sereseres, Chapter 10, this volume.
† See Mary Jeanne Reid Martz, Chapter 9, this volume.

by the OAS. These five tasks—talk as an alternative to warfare, communication, information, norm and rule building, and resource provision—must be enhanced as the core services of the inter-American organizations. The extension of maritime economic jurisdictions to 200 miles gives added importance to this long-standing need.

To cope with conflict resolution, the inter-American system needs to consider whether this function is best served exclusively by western hemisphere countries, or, instead, whether this is a service to be performed *for* such countries. The former is the current norm. The latter alternative might modify OAS procedures. Dispute-specific settings and procedures might be established. The parties to a dispute might agree that only a subset of OAS member countries would discuss their grievance. For example, two disputing Central American countries could choose to limit the council or assembly with jurisdiction, and the set of mediators, to South American countries only. At no moment would all OAS Ambassadors or all Foreign Ministers of the western hemisphere discuss that dispute. When the parties cannot agree, each party will have the right to name at least one-third of the participants in councils, assemblies or mediating teams dealing with a dispute. Henceforth, such participants might be drawn from countries that do not belong to the OAS. A possible illustration would be a dispute involving Nicaragua. It might choose to guarantee that Cuba, Sweden, and Mexico are participants in a dispute-specific council not to exceed nine countries, and that at least one of the three belongs to a three-member mediation team reporting to this small council. Extrahemispheric powers that have been asked to become OAS Observers would also be available for these services. They would be urged to make voluntary financial contributions to a conflict resolution fund, beyond contributions they now make to other funds. At least one nonhemispheric government might participate in all future mediation teams, unless the disputing parties request otherwise.

These procedures could lend much greater flexibility to the OAS. They could incorporate dispute settlement procedures which, often only because of their historical origin, are now outside the OAS (Peru–Ecuador Rio Protocol, Beagle mediation, ect.) in ways satisfactory to the parties. They would enhance the ability of the OAS to deal with its own political minorities without destroying the organization. They would widen the network of mediators. They would improve the record for impartiality. They would make it more likely that mediating countries would be knowledgeable, hard-working, and responsible. They would not duplicate existing U.N.

procedures; on the contrary, they would provide certain procedural guarantees to both parties that are currently absent in U.N. procedures.

A new conflict-resolution fund, financed from voluntary contributions by OAS members and Observers and by fees for services rendered, would finance teams of experts, appropriately equipped, who would render technical services to members that request help in land and maritime boundary delimitation. A sliding scale of fees would be charged, depending on the countries' capacity to pay. These technical services would supplement the political procedures.

This strategy, however, might not add much to what is already available, and it might prove to be too politically or administratively cumbersome. The political minorities within the hemisphere might prefer a pure U.N. setting to anything under the auspices of inter-American institutions. Moreover, it is not evident that much would be gained, and complexity would be added and political risks incurred, by attempting to insert the Ecuador–Peru dispute, or the Beagle channel dispute, within the confines of the OAS. Nor is there any guarantee that extrahemispheric powers would wish to commit themselves to involvement in specifically political disputes far from the areas of close concern to them.

4. The countries of the western hemisphere share many common political values pertaining to democracy or human rights, but they share common practices much less. There are often insoluble contradictions between the goals of promotion of human rights and the resolution of political conflicts among states. To condemn a "gross violator of human rights" at the same time when its acquiescence to international conflict resolution is needed presents, to say the least, difficult diplomatic obstacles.*

The evolving inter-American policies in recent years have emphasized the strengthening of the Inter-American Commission on Human Rights and the strengthening of its reporting to the OAS. The net effect of the latter procedures has been to exacerbate conflicts within the OAS and to dilute the impact of the Commission recommendations. An alternative approach would be to sever altogether the connections between the Commission and the Organization. A separate independent agreement would govern the affairs of the Commission, which would have its own financing from members.

---

* Bryce Wood, "Human Rights Issues in Latin America," in Jorge I. Domínguez, Nigel S. Rodley, Bryce Wood, Richard Falk, *Enhancing Global Human Rights* (New York: McGraw-Hill, 1979).

This would have four advantages. First, the Commission would be authorized to receive funds from all governments, members or not, and from foundations, religious organizations, and ordinary citizens. Second, it would issue its own reports according to its own judgments. It would not be forced to set aside or to dilute its findings to preserve unity within the OAS (which, in turn, is necessary to perform the OAS conflict resolution functions). It would remain free to investigate human rights violations occurring in any country in the hemisphere, whether a signatory to the treaty establishing the commission or not. Third, a stricter separation between the OAS and the Commission would also allow the former to perform its conflict-resolution work more effectively. The OAS would be less likely to be faced simultaneously with motions condemning Argentina and Chile for human rights violations at the same time that their cooperation to dispute settlement procedures is sought. Finally, separation would make it less likely that the Commission's powers be gutted in the years ahead. Because only countries that believed in the Commission's work would be expected to be active in its internal affairs, the Commission's enemies would not be within its midst, as they necessarily are in the OAS.

There are, however, serious costs that would be incurred if this strategy were adopted. The Commission's newly-found influence has stemmed precisely from forcing governments to consider its judgments and to vote on them. Separation from the OAS would risk making the Commission marginal or irrelevant to the affairs of the hemisphere; at best, it would not differ from existing private international human rights organizations. Moreover, the Commission is now well funded within the OAS system. The withdrawal of "southern cone" countries might bankrupt the Commission. It would have to compete for money with other human rights nongovernmental organizations, and the consequence of such competition might be to impoverish them all. Finally, it is important to attempt to preserve the hemispheric norm that all countries must be formally committed and accountable to human rights values; that is best accomplished within the existing framework.

5. Although economic and social issues are beyond the scope of this work, one strategy to cope with the complexities of the OAS could be to transfer many of the OAS' economic tasks to the Inter-American Development Bank. Other tasks should come under the authority of new, independent councils, organizations, or foundations that welcome the participation and financial contributions of extrahemispheric governments and of the private sector. This

approach, it has been suggested elsewhere,* can apply to such diverse topics as banking, energy, state enterprise services, migration and academic and cultural exchanges.

There is, however, a serious danger with attempting to overload the work of the Inter-American Development Bank. The Bank's basic mission is development financing. That basic mission work might be seriously compromised if the Bank were asked to address explicitly political issues that deal with all economic relations in the hemisphere. It is also unlikely that many Latin American countries would agree to remove all economic responsibilities from the OAS, precisely because they believe that economic security themes are at the heart of OAS politics. It might also not be cost-effective for the Bank to handle the small sums now often disbursed under OAS auspices, and it might be counterproductive to deprive the OAS of the opportunity to use economic incentives as a means of facilitating political agreement, especially among small countries.

6. There are also internal organizational matters. The Organization of American States must determine to what extent it is an alliance against states that have unresolved territorial disputes with member countries (Guyana and Belize). I personally believe these clauses should be dropped from the Charter. But if this change is made, some countries may wonder about the Organization's value to them if the OAS does not assist them in their territorial politics. Some may argue: What else could be more important to a state than its territorial domain?

There is also an organizational trade-off between relying upon permanent ambassadors who may have limited influence within their own governments, or on procedures to call meetings (in the absence of permanent ambassadors) of high-ranking government representatives who can commit their governments to a course of action. The value of permanent ambassadors is two-fold: speed of initial response in a crisis and continuing attention to detail. The cost of permanent ambassadors is that they constrain the Organization's Secretariat in the performance of tasks so much that paralysis and patronage overwhelm efficiency. Instead, a strong and flexible secretariat with a cosmopolitan outlook may be needed. The secretary-general, as a chief executive, could be given the authority to initiate conflict resolution procedures and to commit resources subject to a later

* See my earlier memorandum prepared for this Aspen Institute project, "The United States and Latin America: Issues and Organizations," pp. 6–11.

approval by a meeting of consultation to be called as soon as possible. Similar meetings could oversee the OAS' general affairs. Permanent ambassadors would thus not be required. Member countries, however, have been reluctant to delegate such authority in the past to the secretariat; nor is it guaranteed that relying instead on ambassadors accredited to the U.S. Government would solve the problem of ambassadorial involvement in too much detail.

CONCLUSIONS

The issues before inter-American institutions are complex enough that easy formulas are not available. It is important, however, to affirm again the essential political contributions of the inter-American system in at least three areas: to help preserve peace among states and provide for collective security thereby, to advance the common heritage of human rights, and to preserve an internationally moderate military regime that is neither expensive nor war-prone nor interventionist. These are the values that have been best served by the hemisphere's international political institutions and procedures. They can still perform important, though admittedly subsidiary, services. They are the fundamental reasons why states in the Americas are better off cooperating, at least for these purposes.

The inter-American institutions, however, must also recapture the allegiances of the governments that they serve. My own view is that the preferred strategy would favor decentralization and globalization of some of the political aspects of the inter-American system of organizations. More flexible ad hoc arrangements, conscious of the increasingly global context within which the international relations of the countries of the Americas now exist, are needed. The goal should be to create a more flexible system at whose hub the OAS would remain, but that might entail an array of independent but associated organizations concerned with the western hemisphere but with stronger global links. While some changes in formal arrangements might be in order, the promotion of decentralization and globalization can occur within existing organizations and procedures in order better to reflect the reality of inter-state relations in the 1980s.

The time may be especially ripe for new initiatives. The two periods of greatest international organizational creativity in the hemisphere had coincided with the origins of the Cold War (late 1940s) and its implantation in the hemisphere (late 1950s). No two historical periods are identical, and the Cuban government's international role is certainly one major difference between the early 1980s and earlier times. But the Cold War has always led governments in the hemisphere, and especially the U.S. government, to focus attention and resources on matters of collective concern. It has generated the need and facilitated the political mobilization to bring about useful changes. As the Cold War has reappeared generally and in the western hemisphere in the early 1980s, the political incentives to induce organizational innovation may again be at hand. These are the tasks for the decade ahead.

9

Collective Security and the Global Balance

Margaret Daly Hayes

"The logic of collective security is flawless, provided it can be made to work..."

Hans J. Morgenthau

One of the most persistent and perplexing dilemmas in the United States' relations with its Latin American neighbors has been the definition of mutual interests that would bind the group of nations into an alliance, or some less formal systemic relationship, to meet world problems with a unified posture. The existence of shared interests and perspectives vis-à-vis extrahemispheric and even intra-hemispheric events was, for a long time, a basic assumption of U.S. relations in the hemisphere. In the mid-1970s the concept of a special relationship among the Western Hemisphere nations was challenged. "Globalists" argued that no special relationship existed, or had ever existed, or should exist. Now, as the decade of the 1980s

The ideas expressed in the paper are the author's and are not necessarily representative of the opinions or positions of the Committee on Foreign Relations, United States Senate.

takes form, political leaders in all the major countries are looking for ways to build upon perceived common interests while permitting a political plurality to coexist simultaneously.

Especially since World War II, collective security has been an element, although not always the dominant element, of U.S. politico-military relations with the countries of Latin America. In this period there has developed a considerable mythology about the nature of the inter-American System, the commitment of individual members of the System to it, and the role the System can or should play on the world scene.

In reviewing earlier patterns and assessing the directions security relations might take in the future, this paper argues that:

1. the concept of collective security as generally understood in the classic literature is not commensurate with the reality of U.S.–Latin American relations and is inappropriate as a means for guaranteeing U.S. security interests in the region;

2. the United States has real security interests in the hemisphere, but these are defined in political and economic terms rather than military terms, except in crises; and that

3. new ways for guaranteeing U.S. security interests must be sought, and these may lie in promoting greater Latin American independence of the United States rather than closer security relations.

COLLECTIVE SECURITY IN THE HEMISPHERIC CONTEXT

The concept of collective security was codified, in the aftermath of World War I, in the Covenant of the League of Nations. It represented an effort to dissuade all nations from ever again engaging in the type of aggressive behavior that led to the Great War. Hans Morgenthau notes that

> the organizing principle of collective security is the respect for the moral and legal obligation to consider an attack by any nation upon any member of the alliance as an attack upon all members of the alliance. . . . Aggression calls the counteralliance into operation at

once, and, therefore, protects peace and security with the greatest possible efficiency.*

But the principle of collective security as applied in the Western Hemisphere responded to different purposes than did collective security in the League (or later in the United Nations or even the NATO context). The idea belonged almost exclusively to the United States, and when it was initially broached as a principle for hemispheric cooperation, it was in the context of U.S. efforts to ensure for itself access to resources and bases in the hemisphere in the event of war.

The collective security idea emerged in the hemisphere in response to the rearmament of Europe in the 1930s. Jack Child notes that prior to the late 1930s, the United States practiced an exclusively unilateral approach to hemispheric defense. "Color" and "Rainbow" plans were drawn up, largely as staff exercises, for the unilateral U.S. intervention in several Caribbean and Central American countries, as well as Mexico, in the event that U.S. interests in the Caribbean Basin were threatened.†

Beginning about mid-1930, the State Department began to make efforts to persuade the U.S. military departments to consider broadening relations with the Latin American militaries, in part to counter the obvious impact that European military missions had traditionally had in the region. By 1938, with war imminent, the hemispheric defense concept was stimulated by and became entangled with U.S. preparation for continental defense and participation in the war. Child observes that at the time the discussion of collective security in the hemispheric context represented an "adroit manipulation" of what was then fiercely isolationist U.S. public opinion.

Under-Secretary of State Sumner Welles used the opportunity to promote his own vision of multilateral hemispheric security institutions. Child notes that Welles was increasingly successful in persuading his State-War-Navy Standing Liaison Committee military colleagues that some sort of inter-American military cooperation had to be established if there were to be a full measure of political, diplomatic, and economic cooperation in the hemisphere. In particular, it was argued that access to the bases so vital to the Rainbow

---

* Hans J. Morgenthau, *Politics Among Nations*: 5th edition (New York: Albert A. Knopf, 1973), p. 193.
† John Child, "From 'Color' to 'Rainbow'": U.S. Strategic Planning in Latin America, 1919–1945." *Journal of Interamerican Studies and World Affairs* 21:2 (May 1979).

plans could only be guaranteed through cooperation with the Latin nations and their military establishments.

Although the United States pressed determinedly for a mutual security defense pact in the hemisphere it was not immediately successful. In 1936, in Buenos Aires, the 1904 Roosevelt Corollary of the Monroe Doctrine, which defended unilateral U.S. intervention in states in the hemisphere, had been abandoned. Moreover, the principle that "in the event that the peace of the American Republics is menaced" members of the inter-American System should "consult together for the purpose of finding and adopting methods of peaceful cooperation" was adopted.* In 1938, ministers attending the Lima Conference adopted a statement of hemispheric solidarity stating the intention of the American Republics to help one another in case of foreign attack, direct or indirect, on any one of them. In 1940, in Havana, ministers stated clearly that an attack by a non-American state on any American state would be considered an attack on all and that the states would consult on appropriate defense measures. In January 1942, after Pearl Harbor, ministers met at the third Meeting of Consultation and created the Inter-American Defense Board, the organ to be charged with studying and making recommendations for hemispheric defense. The board represented, in part, a victory for Sumner Welles' concept of a multilateral institution responsible for coordinating hemispheric defense programs.†

Thus, with the threat of the war, the Latin American states were more willing to commit themselves to a doctrine of collective, mutual security. All but Argentina and Chile broke relations with and/or declared war on the Axis by 1942, and while few of the nations had resources to commit to the war effort, most cooperated in intelligence efforts and in granting requests to the United States for base rights. Brazil sent units to Italy and cooperated in antisubmarine warfare off its critical northeastern coastline. A Mexican air squadron served in the Philippines.

---

* Interestingly, the U.S. Secretaries of War and Navy were opposed to the creation of the multilateral institution for defense cooperation on the premise that coordination would be difficult and the Latins might use it to pressure the United States for weapons it could not spare. The military departments favored continuation of a unilateral approach to hemispheric defense. Their intransigence resulted in the creation of a board with only advisory capacities. Its principal function proved to be symbolic of political-military unity in the hemisphere. See Child, *op. cit.*, p. 37.
† C. Pope Atkins, *Latin America in the International Political System* (New York: The Free Press, 1977), p. 327.

In the aftermath of World War II, U.S. and Latin American interpretations of collective security began to diverge. In 1945, in Mexico, the Act of Chapultepec broadened the definition of aggression against members of the collective security alliance to include attacks by any state, meaning, most pointedly, intervention by the United States. The war over, U.S. attention turned from the hemisphere, where there was no threat, to the balance of power in Europe, where, in the early days of Cold War, the United States would be the principal guarantor of the balance. This strategic balance of power has been the primary focus of U.S. security emphasis ever since.

In the context of U.S. global security concepts, the hemispheric community has served principally as a pawn in the global balance. The Inter-American Treaty of Reciprocal Assistance, signed in Rio de Janeiro in 1947, embodied the concepts of collective security that had been defined in the war effort and that would be included in Chapter VII of the United Nations' charter. But where the authors of the United Nations' charter attempted to overcome the impotence of the collective security clauses of the League Covenant by giving the Security Council the authority to convene a military force, the Rio Treaty, like the League document, contained no provision for a combined command authority to enforce the collective security.

Thus, like the Inter-American Defense Board before it, the Rio Treaty was primarily symbolic. U.S. security interests in the region remained unilateral. Child cites documents from the joint chiefs of staff* indicating as early as 1945 that U.S. post-war strategic objectives in Latin America would be:

cooperation with the Latin American military to enhance the defense of the Panama Canal and Western Hemisphere;

preservation of peace in the Hemisphere;

continued flow to the U.S. of Latin American strategic materials;

access for the U.S. to key air and naval bases in Latin America;

U.S. military mission in every country;

standardization of Latin American military equipment along U.S. lines;

training of Latin Military in U.S. military schools;

avoiding the unnecessary diversion of U.S. military resources to the Western Hemisphere.

---

* Op. cit., p. 73.

For the United States, the Rio Treaty served the purpose of uniting Latin American nations behind it in the increasingly bitter Cold War, of guaranteeing the United States access to bases in the event the Cold War should heat up, and permitting the United States to focus attention away from the immediate neighborhood of the hemisphere and toward the reconstruction of Europe. Latin American priorities were different and were stated both in Rio and subsequently, more vehemently, in Bogota. There the Latin American countries defended a definition of collective security that included a U.S. commitment to economic assistance in the hemisphere. The collective defense pact, to which they could contribute very little, would serve as a *quid pro quo* for contribution to their economic development. To the United States, the collective security commitment meant an alliance against aggression from outside the hemisphere. The Latins were less concerned about the Cold War threat and more concerned about aggression from within the hemisphere, principally from the United States.

The United States tended to use the apparatus of the inter-American system to legitimize its own preferences for collaboration, which would be based on bilateral mutual assistance agreements as called for in plans developed by the multilateral Inter-American Defense Board. In the 1950s, mutual Defense Assistance Agreements were signed with most Latin American nations. In exchange for training and equipment, the Latin Americans agreed to use the material exclusively for hemispheric defense and to facilitate the supply of strategic resources to the United States and to limit their trade with the Soviet Bloc.

With its attention focused on Europe and Japan, U.S. economic assistance to Latin America remained comparatively low in the 1950s. At the same time, the United States became the dominant economic partner for nearly all the nations of the hemisphere. On all dimensions, the hemispheric relationship became lopsidedly favorable to the United States, a process that nearly guaranteed Latin American resentment.

By the 1960s, elements of the Cold War, in the form of leftist insurgencies, were translated to the hemispheric context, and the quality of U.S. attention changed. Communism in the hemisphere was perceived to represent a direct challenge to U.S. interests. An elaborate apparatus of economic and security assistance was developed in short order to deal with the challenge to U.S. exclusivity. Economic assistance responded not so much to concern for the economic development of the region, but rather to the belief that economic development could contribute to the security of friendly, democratic institutions in the region.

Meanwhile, as if to confirm Latin America's own perceptions and concerns about its security, in the 30 years from the end of World War II to 1975, the United States used military force for political purposes on 217 separate occasions. More than one fourth of these interventions occurred in Latin America and virtually all of them in the Caribbean Basin, for the most part to impede the coming to power of leftist governments thought to be hostile to the United States. From 1965 (the Dominican Republic Intervention) to 1981 (U.S. trainers sent to El Salvador) the United States relaxed its security focussed interest in the region and adopted a more distant relationship, one focussed principally on economic growth. By the end of the 1970s, however, regional tensions, especially in the Caribbean Basin, were once again high as revolution and violence took hold of several Caribbean islands and Central America. In 1979 the United States sought to involve collective security doctrine to stave off the revolutionary military victory in Nicaragua. The Organization of American States rejected the initiative, however. By March 1981, the United States once again sent U.S. military personnel—trainers—to Central America to aid resistance against a leftist insurgency.

This long history of the origins and basis of the collective security concept in the hemisphere is reviewed in order to argue that collective security as practiced by the United States in the hemisphere context (1) was not collective, (2) was fundamentally self-serving, and (3) was contrary to the expressed preferred definition of the Latin Americans, who emphasized economic and social security over military and political security.

Given these problems and differences, collective security as we Americans have understood the concept—a security concept based on a common contribution to defense efforts and a mutually satisfying definition of security interests—has been untenable in the hemisphere from the beginning. In the early days of the alliance-making effort, the imbalance in power was so great that the region represented not an alliance of peers but rather a covey of nations under the U.S. umbrella. Since the early days of the arrangement, the Latin American states have attempted to broaden the definition of security to include economic security concerns as a *quid pro quo* for acquiescing to the U.S. definition of political and military security. In the 1950s and to the mid-1960s, the Latin American states were willing to go along with U.S. mutual security goals defined primarily in terms of anti-Communism in the global Cold War context. But from mid-1960 and through the 1970s, the circumstances of Latin American relations with the United States had changed enough that the Latin Americans could begin to assert more strongly their own perceptions of security.

Amendments to the Organization of American States' (OAS) charter submitted in 1967 specifically downgraded security considerations by lessening the relative position of the security-related agencies and upgrading the importance of economic and social agencies in the organization. A 1973 OAS General Assembly resolution referred to the inter-American system as outmoded and unrealistic and sought proposals for its restructuring. In 1975, the Protocol of San Jose reiterated the concept of ideological pluralism within the hemisphere, stating as one of the purposes, "to reaffirm and strengthen the principle of non-intervention as well as the right of all states to choose freely their political, economic and social organization."* At the same time, the Latin Americans succeeded, over U.S. opposition, in including amendments to the Charter and to the Rio Treaty, establishing the concept of collective economic security for development with Peru, noting that "security is founded in development and without development there is no security."† Subsequently, the Latin Americans have reversed their positions on the imposition of sanctions against Cuba, a cornerstone of U.S. security policy in the hemisphere. They resoundingly defeated a U.S. invitation to send an OAS peacekeeping force to Nicaragua and in other ways have generally failed to support U.S. efforts to define hemispheric collective security in U.S. terms.

CONTEMPORARY U.S. SECURITY PRIORITIES IN LATIN AMERICA

The concept of collective security clearly has become inadequate for defining the nature of or rationale for U.S.–Latin American relations. The previous pages have suggested that this is in part

---

* Atkins, op. cit.
† Atkins, op. cit.

because the United States and Latin American countries perceive *threat* differently, in part because they perceive *security* differently. Latin America does not perceive itself to be a target of Russian strategic weapons; the United States does. The United States is not threatened by shifts in the world economy in the ways that Latin Americans are. To state that past definitions of security are presently inadequate is not to say that the United States does not have security interests in the region. On the contrary, as in other parts of the world, U.S. security interests in Latin America, narrowly defined, are conditioned by political and economic relations as well as purely military considerations. Some areas of the world have a security importance almost exclusively because of their economic importance—the Persian Gulf or southern Africa, for example. Others—Japan, Poland, Yugoslavia—are also important because of their geographic locations. An invasion of Poland or Yugoslavia would exacerbate perceptions of threats to Western Europe and the NATO alliance, whether or not the invaders intended to cross the border into NATO territory. A threat against Japan would invite the isolation of the United States and its allies from Asia.

Although Latin America has played only a minor role in postwar U.S. strategic planning, the United States does have clear interests within the hemisphere that are often overlooked in assessing its importance. First and foremost, the United States has a major interest in the friendliness and tranquility of the region. It has only a mild interest in the economic and political development of the region. It has a major, crucial interest in avoiding instability and hostility in the region. In short, when things go wrong, U.S. security interests are threatened. When they go right, U.S. security interests are not much affected. Rather than being constant, U.S. security interests are largely contingent and residual, and, moreover, they have been preserved with a low level of attention, because there has traditionally been only a low level of threat in the region. Although they are secondary, the United States also has economic and political interests in Latin America. It is today the most developed of developing world regions. By 1985, the regional economy will be the size of Europe's in 1970. The United States is still the single largest trading partner for the region, while Latin America provides approximately 14% of both U.S. imports and exports. It also provides a number of important raw materials to the United States and receives over 18% of all U.S. private investment abroad, far more than any other developing region. U.S. banks are committed to billions of dollars of loans in the region.

The United States has compelling political interests in maintaining good relations with the nations of Latin America. As part of the Western Hemisphere, and in the immediate U.S. geographic sphere of influence, Latin America has long been perceived as a key element in the U.S. political following in the world. While the inter-American system is not as closely knit today as it once was, and Latin American states are on record as seeking to diminish their dependence on the United States, the hemispheric community still figures importantly in our own and others' perceptions of the East-West balance. The Soviet Union has always recognized the importance of western hemispheric solidarity and has taken advantage of every opportunity to embarrass the United States when cracks appear. The United States has demonstrated a less clear understanding of the importance of the hemispheric community in measuring its own relative weight on a world scale. In the last decade it engaged in a number of actions, including arms control, trade, nuclear energy, and human rights policies, the perhaps unintended consequences of which were to undermine hemispheric cooperation and lessen Latin American commitment to the inter-American system. Nevertheless, although the Latin Americans at times resist the conclusion, and at other times use it as leverage against the United States, they continue to figure importantly in the global assessment of U.S. political weight in the world. Failure to achieve their support and collaboration represents a net loss in U.S. weight in the international balance of power. This applies whether one speaks of Southern Cone countries such as Chile or Argentina, or of Mexico or Panama, which are nearer to home.

On closer examination, at least three separate areas of U.S. security interest in Latin America can be identified—the Caribbean Basin and Gulf of Mexico, East Coast South America, and, finally, West Coast South America.* The intensity of U.S. interest in each region is determined in large part by proximity to the continental United States; proximity to other areas of security concern; and the political, military, and economic capabilities of the member states.

The focus of security interest in each area is quite different, reflecting the different objective political and economic conditions in the regions. In the Caribbean islands and in Central America, the United States is intensely concerned that political instability will result in the emergence of hostile, possibly Communist, states that

---

*See Margaret Daly Hayes, "Security to the South: U.S. Interests in Latin America," *International Security*, Vol. 5, No. 1 (Summer 1980).

could provide shelter to a more adventurous Soviet fleet, harbor offensive weapons aimed at the United States, or serve as listening posts to monitor our military movements in the area. A repetition of the Cuban revolution of 1959, of the Cuban missile crisis of 1962, or of the Cienfuegos submarine base incident of 1969 is clearly in the minds of defense planners and policy makers when they observe present instability in Nicaragua, El Salvador, and elsewhere in the Caribbean Basin.

In the South Atlantic, policy makers are also concerned with defense of U.S. interests from Soviet offensive actions. In this arena, the potential targets of Soviet action are important sea lines of communication around the horn of Africa. Because of the importance of such supply lines to the industrial economies of Europe, the South Atlantic plays an important role in scenarios for the defense of Europe in prolonged conventional war. U.S. defense planners are concerned that the greatly expanded size of the Soviet blue-water fleet challenges Western ability to defend these important supply lines.

Finally, domestic instability and border conflicts are the factors that attract attention to the West Coast South American countries. While their role in global security strategy is less salient, they again could play an important role in logistic support to the U.S. fleet in time of war.

PROGNOSIS

While U.S. definitions of its security interests in the hemisphere have remained fairly constant over time, Latin American perceptins of their security needs have changed dramatically in recent years. As the countries have developed politically and economically and as their international roles have become more complex, U.S. and Latin American national interests have begun to diverge. U.S. options for implementing a narrowly defined, U.S.-oriented interpretation of collective hemispheric security are increasingly limited. The major factors influencing present changes in Latin American security perspectives include the following points:

● The Latin American nations' emergence as economic and political entities in their own right, with extensive international contacts, makes the traditional U.S. claim to exclusive rights within the hemisphere both incongruent with current reality and intolerable to Latin American nationalists.

- Because the United States has been the historically dominant power in the region, and because the Latin American nations were demonstrably dependent upon the United States, perceiving themselves subject to U.S. political will, their leaders are often motivated to place as great a distance between themselves and the United States as possible in order to demonstrate their new national political independence. Diversification of political and economic relations is now a major goal of all countries in the region.

- U.S. pursuit of *detente* with the Soviet Union has made the traditional Cold War rationale for collective security less meaningful. At the same time, increasing trade opportunities in the Eastern bloc and China have made ideological hostilities economically costly and inconvenient. The Latin Americans now see economic *opportunities*, rather than threats in the Communist-bloc countries.

- The emergence of the Third World nonaligned movement has made North-South issues more important than East-West issues, and close political alignment with a superpower is less desirable.

- The major Latin American, particularly South American, countries successfully weathered political instability in the 1960s. This has made them more confident in dealing with domestic political problems, reduced their fear of insurgency, and freed them to pursue other security interests.

- Differences over specific U.S. policies—including arms transfers policies, trade questions, human rights observances, recognition of Cuba, and other issues--have suggested to the Latin Americans that U.S. policy is not responsive to their needs and that their interests and those of the United States are not necessarily congruent.

- The perception that the United States lacks a coherent vision of Latin America's role in the hemispheric or global security balance has led to an increasing emphasis on individual national security questions, including defense against traditional regional rivals as well as consideration of projection of national influence beyond the region.

- Many Latin American nations, particularly those in South

America, are economically and politically stronger than ever before and wish to exercise their own control over their international and security affairs. This has been demonstrated by their active roles in pressing positions on the recognition of Cuba, the Panama Canal, or in the recent crisis in Nicaragua, and by their pursuit of independent military capabilities that reduce their dependence on foreign suppliers.

• At the same time, the political and economic problems of the poorer, less economically viable states is causing them to become increasingly unstable and to attract most of U.S. attention in the hemisphere. The narrow U.S. security focus on Central America—and East-West interpretation—concerns many Latin American states and drives a further wedge between them and the United States.

In this context, Latin America's new capabilities represent both a challenge and an opportunity for the United States. The challenge lies in achieving a definition of international security by the major Latin American actors that is in concert with and complementary to that of the United States. Given present Latin American determination to establish political, military, and economic independence and identity from the United States, this is not an easy, but also not an impossible task. The opportunity lies in the advantages the United States can accrue by having firm political relations and sharing responsibilities with the nations of the hemisphere. While the inter-American System was never envisioned as an alliance system such as NATO, certain aspects of that more mutually responsible relationship have become both more realistic and more desirable with the growth of Latin American capabilities and changes in the international system.

Politico-military alignment with the United States is far from the top of the Latin American agenda at the present time. The Latin Americans will be likely to avoid such entanglements until the direction of U.S. policy in the region is more apparent. They seek a strong commitment of equality in any newly intensified relationship and will strike a hard bargain for their cooperation. It is in their national interest to do so. If the United States is to take advantage of this opportunity to bolster its own security interests, it will have to undertake a substantial shift in its policy toward the region. The level and quality of military relations will have to improve, changes in arms transfer policy will be necessary, as will, very likely, aspects of U.S. nuclear policy. Explicitly security-related policies will need to be backed by much more generous economic arrangements. Policies for South America will have to be very different from policies for the Caribbean Basin. Latin American economic and political initiatives will have to be encouraged and supported.

A security relationship that is appropriate will have to be based on a clear understanding of the Latin American countries' political and economic aspirations as well as their individual capabilities. Economic development is the prime motivating national goal in the region today. This will bring continuing change to the system, increasingly separating the more advanced countries (Brazil, Mexico, Argentina, and Venezuela) from their less endowed neighbors. Security considerations, particularly concern over external threats, will be minimized at the same time as economic development permits the countries to acquire new military capabilities, making possible more broadly conceived defense purposes. These changes offer an opportunity to the United States to share responsibilities for regional security with the Latin Americans on a more mature and equal basis. While the Latin Americans are likely to insist on greater autonomy of decision making within the system, their collaboration can be encouraged and their capabilities enhanced in areas where they interface with U.S. global security and contingency requirements.

A reevaluation of the foundations and purposes of inter-American collective security arrangements requires a thoughtful and unemotional examination of what U.S. real, current, and future political, economic, and military interests in relation with the nationals of the hemisphere are.

A restructured inter-American system will have to address the issue of Latin American interests in hemispheric relations directly. The strengths of the alliance lie in the projected economic powers and capabilities of its members. Latin American interests are best served by remaining outside the arena of East–West conflict, and relatively independent of North–South issues as well. They occupy a critical position in which they can maximize benefits from both relationships. U.S. interests may be best served by remaining as much as possible outside Latin American internal and intraregional conflicts. Given traditional U.S. dominance of the hemisphere, the Latin Americans are eager to diversify their political and economic relations to regions outside the hemisphere. Economically powerful Europe and Japan have been the principal substitutes for the United States. Thus the new Latin American relations remain within arenas of U.S. interest. The Third World and the hemisphere itself is becoming increasingly important in Latin American economic relationships, too. At the same time, the United States remains a critical link in the relations between the countries in the region and their extra-hemispheric partners. Continued mutually beneficial economic relations provide the principal rationale for future political and military cooperation. As Cordell Hull noted in comments on the structuring of military alliance with Latin America in World War II, "The political line-up followed the economic line-up."*

FUTURE HEMISPHERIC SECURITY RELATIONS

Continued economic development will bring changes to the inter-American system that will affect both United States and Latin American security interests in a number of ways.

- As economic development is achieved, hemispheric contacts with other developed and developing world countries will increase, and U.S. influence will be diminished in the region. Nevertheless, the United States will continue to be the dominant single economic partner.

- Latin American countries will seek to acquire military capabilities commensurate with their perceived politicoeconomic development status. They will increasingly have the industrial and financial wherewithal to acquire military hardware and technology on the world market. Arms control policies selectively targeted, either intentionally or unintentionally, at the region will be unsuccessful and have a negative impact on U.S. influence in the region.

- The major powers within the hemisphere can be expected to develop independent military capabilities over the next two decades. They will build these capabilities slowly, without assuming substantially greater defense burdens than in the past. While their capabilities will be primarily intended to provide for domestic defense, they will also be available for greater participation within a broader defense role in the region.

- As their industrial capabilities advance, the Latin Americans

---

* Stanley E. Hilton, *Brazil and the Great Powers, 1930–1939* (Austin: University of Texas Press, 1975).

will increasingly pursue acquisition of state-of-the-art technologies in their dealings with weapons-producing nations. Brazil and Argentina are already doing so. Ultimately, acquisition of nuclear capabilities is likely, either through purchase or development of indigenous models.

• Insofar as they become weapons producers, the Latin American nations will also become exporters, as Brazil and Argentina have become already. The economics of production will dictate this development, and it will enhance their position both within the region and with other world regions.

• The Latin American countries are unlikely to become overtly hostile or unfriendly to the United States. Relations may be characterized from time to time by coolness and indifference, however.

• In the event of a clear external aggression, members of the hemispheric community will probably draw together, as they did during the world wars or during the period of Cuban revolutionary activism in the region. In other circumstances, they will prefer only loose political and security relationships.

• The gap between the dominant powers in the region—Mexico and Brazil—the secondary powers—Venezuela and Argentina—and other countries will widen, and no single hemispheric policy will be appropriate for dealing with the differences. Rather, unique policies will be required for each group and its members. At the same time, the Latin American countries will be likely to be supportive of each other for a long time to come.

In view of the continuing development of Latin American economic, political, and military capabilities, the United States has clear interests in maintaining and promoting harmonious and cooperative relations with the members of the region. Latin America figures as an important element in the United States' overall network of allies, despite periodic differences. As the regional economies develop, the hemisphere will become one of the economically most powerful components of the international system. The continued importance of Latin American raw materials to the U.S. economy, the United States' strong economic interests in the region, Latin America's growing importance to the European and Japanese economies, and its leadership role in the Third World all emphasize the region's importance to the United States.

10

Conflict Resolution and Peaceful Settlement of Disputes

Mary Jeanne Reid Martz

> ... for Latin America, nonintervention is a positive concept if for no other reason than it has been Latin America's juridical shield against aggression for the last 150 years. It is not abstention versus use of force; rather, it means political imagination, diplomatic negotiation and technical cooperation as alternatives to the extremes of do nothing or blast everything.
>
> Carlos Fuentes, *New York Times* Op-Ed Article, "Dominoes Again?," 9/19/80

INTRODUCTION

Given disparities of size, population, and sheer power existing among the Western Hemisphere nations, there has long been an inclination, both outside as well as within the region, to view its conflicts undimensionally. Presumably, controversy has been associated with the divergent interests and the unique mixture of affection and animosity between Latin America and the United States which has been a reality for over a century. Alternatively, but scarcely less simplistic,

---

The views expressed in this paper are those of the author and do not necessarily reflect the views of the U.S. Department of State.

has been the assumption outside the hemisphere that inter-Latin American disputes could be controlled, if not indeed resolved, by the United States, should it feel inclined to do so. Yet the reality has never been thus.

In this century there has been only one protracted war—that in the Chaco, 1932–1935. Regional mechanisms to cope with disputes and contentiousness have been developed with greater flexibility, creativity and success than in any other Third World area. Granted the occasional assertion of United States power and diplomacy, there has nonetheless evolved within the Organization of American States (OAS) a rich heritage of both institutions, customs and precedents for the avoidance of minimization of conflict. Yet today pacific settlement of disputes and conflict resolution[1] have never been more demanding in both importance and complexity. Contemporary science and technology have transformed many aspects of hemispheric life; political relationships and linkages are complicated by swirling pressures of ideological and politico-military international rivalry; previously unimaginable problems stemming from energy sources (or lack thereof), nuclear power, social upheaval, and revolutionary fervor have dramatically deepened the crisis of hemispheric and sub-regional conflict.

In assessing contemporary circumstances and elaborating upon alternative courses of action, brief introductory comments are in order as a means of placing the present situation in historical context. Thus, we will first give a summary review of the evolution of hemispheric disputes and conflict resolution procedures. This will pave the way for an illustrative itemization of today's multi-variegated problems and sources of conflict. We will then reassess existing mechanisms and organs. Alternative suggestions for a re-orienting of approaches to the pacific settlement of disputes in the Western Hemisphere within the context of the realistic needs and demands of the 1980s will be discussed.

POSTWAR CONTROVERSIES AND SETTLEMENT MECHANISMS

Between 1948 and 1959, controversies brought before the OAS for resolution to a considerable extent reflected historic rivalries and border disputes antedating World War II. Added to this milieu was the political polarization resulting from opposing democratic and dictatorial ideologies in the postwar period. These controversies usually involved the smaller states of the Central American/Caribbean area.

In 1959 the arena for potential conflict widened, with the coming to power of Fidel Castro. Old conflictual issues remained on the scene, but newer ones infused with the ideological dimension of communism surfaced. Over the next decade, these issues ranged from allegations of Cuban conspiratorial activities against neighboring countries to proven indirect but substantial involvement by Cuba. On several occasions these controversies were viewed by the United States as hemispheric security questions increasing the difficulties of crisis management and encapsulation.[2]

Increasingly over this twenty-year period, events were interfaced with a widening of perspectives and a more self-conscious nationalism on the part of the Latin countries, produced at least in part by rapid advances in transportation and communications. This situation altered the context of even historic disputes, so that in 1969 the war between El Salvador and Honduras became what can be considered a watershed in the evolution of postwar hemispheric disputes. While the boundary dispute itself dates from independence days, armed conflict developed as a more direct result of modern demographic pressures, illegal migrations, and real or imagined inequities in the regional economic scheme, the Central American Common Market (CACM). Thus, the basic issues were economic and social rather than political, ideological, or personal in nature. Nurtured and exacerbated by developed mass media, these underlying problem areas coalesced to bring about what is relatively uncommon in this hemisphere—interstate war. It was more than ten years before a Peace Treaty was arranged, and even now over one third of the border remains undefined.

During the decade of the 1970s, the role of the OAS within the area of pacific settlement of disputes or conflict management has been deemed by many—scholars and diplomats, North Americans and Latin Americans—as irrelevant. Nevertheless, at least during the 1950s and 1960s, that organization functioned in a fairly visible and effective fashion, defusing many potentially volatile situations. Today there are some claims that that is the only defensible role for the OAS.

The old Inter-American Peace Committee (IAPC) and the ad hoc committees of the Provisional Organ of Consultation and the Meetings of Consultation were mandated varying degrees of authority throughout the 1950s and 1960s, operating with a flexibility, informality, and privacy that led to a relatively successful record in the management of conflict. They aided in investigations (Haiti-Dominican Republic, 1950), extended mediation and conciliation services (Dominican Republic–Haiti, 1963–1966), led peace observation missions (Costa Rica–Nicaragua, 1955), threatened sanctions (El Salvador–Honduras, 1969), actually imposed sanctions (Venezuela-Dominican Republic, 1960), arranged ceasefires (Costa Rica-Nicaragua, 1948–1949 and 1955–1956, El Salvador–Honduras, 1969), helped reestablish peace and order (Panama, 1964), and formulated terms of settlement (Costa Rica–Nicaragua, 1948–1949, and Honduras–Nicaragua, 1955).

These ad hoc committees focused a certain amount of limited public attention and pressure on the participants and, even though they did not generally produce a final resolution of the underlying causes of the disputes, provided an invaluable "cooling-off" period during which the supposed healer of all wounds—time—could effect its ministrations. Only in those cases involving collective security issues—that is, those in which real or perceived conflicts of interests existed between the United States and the Soviet Union, such as in Guatemala in 1954—did the mechanisms prove inadequate to the challenge of conflict management.

The volatility of the Caribbean during the course of the 1950s and 1960s would doubtless have led to greater violence and more serious confrontation, had it not been for the crisis management skills of OAS diplomats. While OAS mechanisms functioned less visibly during the 1970s and early 1980s than in prior decades, they extended precedents already set, functioning relatively well on an even more ad hoc basis, founded much of the time on the long-established friendships fostered by the OAS as an institution and on "corridor work" performed as a result of those friendships.

It is, in fact, crisis management—whether formal or informal—resulting in semiisolation or encapsulation of a conflict that has been the primary focus of OAS conflict resolution procedures. Generally, in the past, following the termination of a "crisis" situation, pacific settlement efforts lost their efficacy with resolution of problem areas left to the exigencies of bilateral negotiation. In fact, while the range of tactics and techniques employed by OAS agencies to manage crises has expanded, that organization has increasingly acted in a cautious manner in the area of conflict resolution. This attitude has largely been the result of three factors. First, there is a growing independence and nationalism on the part of individual members, resulting in a greater resort to the traditional "American" doctrine of nonintervention.[3] Related is a fear that formal OAS institutions will broach issues—such as border disputes—that concerned Latin American nations do not want opened to debate. Second, whereas the most successful efforts in the past were directed toward disputes among the smaller countries, today even those types of disputes tend to engage the interest of larger powers. At the same time that non-intervention is stressed in the OAS, both intra- and extracontinental states are taking more of an interest in regional interstate disputes and in situations of internal strife. Thirdly, there are now large and internationally mature states in the hemisphere that are for the most part immune to the type of U.S. pressure that years ago might have persuaded them to accept OAS settlement procedures.

CONTEMPORARY PROBLEMS AND THE POTENTIAL FOR CONFLICT

A perspective on the decade of the 1980s swiftly leads to identification of a multitude of problems ripe in potential for dispute and contention. For the sake of clarity, problems may be subsumed under three broad rubrics: (1) attitudes and approaches to hemispheric affairs on the part of relevant actors; (2) substantive policy issues; and (3) global phenomena. The specific character of the latter two classifications cannot be properly assessed without recognition of the attitudinal context in which they are found.

Attitudes and Approaches toward Problems

A central quality to the thinking of many hemispheric states is a growing sense of self-assertiveness in foreign policy, coupled with declining dependence on the United States. This is buttressed by a tendency in a number of countries to devote greater attention and higher priority to foreign affairs than has been the custom in the past. Among the more striking examples are Mexico, Venezuela, and Brazil.

With the first, a heightened sense of nationalistic independence and foreign policy activism emerged during the administration of Luís Echeverría (1970–76), grew apace under José Lopez Portillo (1976–82) with the added economic muscle acquired through petroleum riches, and can be expected to continue with his successor. Venezuela has demonstrated a rising concern with foreign affairs, first notable under the presidency of Rafael Caldera (1969–74), extended through Carlos Andrés Pérez' expression of petro-*bolívar* diplomacy (1974–79), and, since 1979, continued with the Christian Democratic government of Luís Herrera Campins. Brazilian energies and initiatives have been manifested for the better part of a decade, whether receiving preferential treatment by the Nixon and Ford administrations or responding cooly to the human rights emphases of Carter. Without detailing these cases or extending the number of illustrations, the basic point centers on the indisputable sense of national sovereignty and self-assurance with which specific foreign policy problems and issues are viewed.

At the same time that the dependence of some Latin American nations on the United States is weakening, Latin American perceptions of a primacy of U.S. interest in the collective security aspects of the OAS have been intensifying in the last two decades. To the contrary, in the late 1960s and throughout the 1970s, Latin member states have pursued the goal of an OAS as a forum for the promotion of their economic development. As real or imagined conflict of interest on economic issues continues and grows, the potential for an underutilized OAS in noneconomic areas and a fragmented pacific settlement system could increase. Conversely, however, members could come to view peaceful settlement as the only rationale for the OAS and emphasize that function.

The influence of international movements and ideologies constitutes another element that has increased dramatically and can be expected to mark the years ahead. The Christian Democratic impulse has been a major factor in Venezuelan foreign policy under Herrera, and has helped to shape policies in El Salvador, Nicaragua, and throughout the Caribbean. Former president Caldera, recently named the head of the regional movement, symbolizes the doctrinal interests of the movement. There are sympathetic chords struck by the Carazo government in Costa Rica and, to a degree, by the Ecuadorean administration, in which the Christian Democrat Osvaldo Hurtado as vice-president played an important role. Venezuelan initiatives within the Andean Pact have been shaped by such interests, although with declining effect at this writing.

Social Democratic parties, as well as Christian Democratic ones, increasingly view themselves as part of an international movement. Venezuela's major opposition party, Acción Democrática, has hosted a conference of the Socialist International in Caracas, and stands as a leading outpost in Latin America. Former president Pérez, during his term a staunch supporter of the *sandinistas*, was a prominent guest at the first anniversary celebration of the ouster of Somoza in July 1980 at Managua, and has maintained ties and contacts with leaders of the Revolutionary Democratic Front (FDR) in embattled El Salvador. The attitudes and statements of eminent European Socialist leaders concerning the turmoil in the latter country resound in several Latin American countries.

The Latin American Catholic Church has seen the rise of what might be termed a liberation theology, which has also played a strong role in war-torn El Salvador. The ambiguity of the position of the Church has resulted in a situation in which many see Salvadoran civil strife as based less on Marxism and more on the teachings of Popes Paul VI and John Paul II, who have both spoken forcefully on the right to justice of Latin America's poor.

A less doctrinally-oriented influence is presented by informal hemispheric groupings of both democratic and authoritarian regimes. Venezuela, Colombia, and Ecuador under Jaime Roldós have sought to project the concerns of individual freedoms, human rights, electoral competition, and constitutionalism. While the effort to develop the Andean Pact as a champion of such interests has been eroded by the reluctance of the Peruvian government and diminished by the antagonism toward Bolivian military rule, it will remain a consideration in the years ahead. In a more unsystematic fashion, something of the same may be said of a certain commonality of interests and attitudes emanating from Argentina, Brazil, Uruguay, and Chile. Without overstressing the point, there is a clear competition of regime orientations between the southern cone countries and those in northern South America.

In the light of such inclinations—both pragmatic and doctrinal —an accompanying deterioration in reliance upon formal hemispheric procedures has emerged. There is a preference to subregional and even bilateral efforts, rather than the over-arching context of the OAS. With the former, we have noted the prodemocratic activism of the Andean Pact. A less clearly-defined context is nonetheless present in Central America, further complicated by the presently conflicting preferences of Mexico and Venezuela.

Authoritarian regimes have made common cause on specific issues, including dealings with the present government in La Paz and in the trilateral economic and infrastructural projects of Argentina, Paraguay, and Brazil.[4] Moving to the Caribbean, the Caribbean Common Market (CARICOM) and a host of other subregional agencies have attempted a variety of collaborative approaches to substantive problems. If the purportedly leftist surge appears to be receding in the wake of the Seaga victory in Jamaica, the importance of subregional attitudes are no less significant than they were in the recent past.

There is concomitantly a willingness to deal with issues either on a purely bilateral basis, or, at the least, with the involvement of a reduced number of states. Argentina and Chile have sought the assistance of the Vatican in arbitrating the Beagle territorial issue; a renewal of Venezuelan–Guayanese negotiations following the 1982 expiration of the existing agreement may well seek the aid of a third party. In contrast, the border dispute between Colombia and Venezuela at the moment sees the former suggesting outside arbitration, to which Caracas responds by insisting on bilateral negotiations.

More complex is the situation between Ecuador and Peru. While the former did succeed in bringing the matter to the OAS, in actual practice it has fallen to the four guarantors of the 1942 Protocol of Rio, as Peru preferred. But the major point, whatever the specifics of such issues, is the tendency to deal with problems at a narrower and less generalized level than was once customary.

At the same time, however, there remains an inclination to *deal* with disputes rather than to fight. Many OAS officials argue that this is due to the presence of that organization as a backup mechanism—that is, it represents a "court of last resort" or "supreme court" within the system. It is suggested that in the 1981 conflict between Ecuador and Peru the parties were willing to fight initially because they felt that the very existence of the OAS would keep the hostilities from becoming too bellicose. Moreover, papal mediation in the Beagle dispute resulted largely from informal OAS efforts.

All of the preceding underlines the relative decline of United States power and influence, a diminution of interest in the direct participation of formal hemispheric-wide agencies, and a growing assertion of national diplomacy. This relates to a fragmentation of the system of conflict resolution, which is central to questions of governance in the years ahead. It also must help to inform consideration and assessment of contemporary disputes, the substance of which could also call further into question the entire fabric of institutionalized conflict resolution as it has existed in the post-World War II years.

Substantive Disputes

These in turn can be broken down into subcategories for the sake of convenience. First, consider longstanding disputes, often reflecting historical differences that resist resolution. Several have already been cited: the border dispute between Ecuador and Peru; the Beagle controversy of Argentina and Chile; and the Gulf of Venezuela controversy between Colombia and Venezuela, which is exacerbated by such related problems as Colombian *indocumentados* living in Venezuela and the continuation of cattle-smuggling. The recently negotiated accord on the status of Belize—with Guatemala centrally concerned and Mexico more than a disinterested bystander—may have been placed in jeopardy by internal disorder.

The host of differences between Honduras and El Salvador, bluntly restated by the 1969 soccer war and its aftermath, may have only been shelved temporarily as a result of the internal upheaval in El Salvador leading to a Peace Treaty in 1980. The border dispute is not completely resolved, and the treaty places a five-year time limit on negotiations. Meanwhile, the conflict in El Salvador has sent a sudden influx of thousands of Salvadoran refugees from the war zones into Honduras, possibly shaking the foundations of the peace accord. In late 1979, Nicaragua's decision to revive long-standing claims to the Caribbean islands of San Andrés and Providencia and the cays of Roncador, Quitasueño, and Serrana touched off a strong protest in Colombia.

Latent historical rivalries based on long tradition and nationalistic sentiment must be considered. Among these may be numbered those involving Argentina and Brazil, Costa Rica and Nicaragua, Chile and Peru—further complicated by Bolivian calls for an outlet to the Pacific. Chile refuses even to recognize OAS competence to discuss Bolivian claims. With rising assertiveness in individual foreign policies and greater independence from Washington, existing power rivalries become more vocal, while new configurations have also crossed the horizon. The accord between Mexico and Venezuela over the supplying of petroleum does not veil the competition and rivalry between the two nations as they vie for influence in the Caribbean and Central America. Guatemala, its government dismayed by events in El Salvador and Nicaragua, will not only attempt to defend its own viability but can be expected to increase its influence as it nears the status of an oil-exporting country. Moving to an even broader level, there is the sometimes veiled but insistent jealousy and apprehension on the part of Spanish-speaking South American nations toward the burgeoning Brazilian giant and its heightened role in continental affairs.

Adding to the panoply of historically based issues confronting the inter-American system are potential problems relating to economic and social development (sometimes subsumed under the rubric of collective economic security), and the flow and control of public and private investment and technology transfer—the problems surrounding which have thus far eluded settlement procedures. With both legal and illegal migrations expanding in the last quarter of this century, demographic issues will offer a fertile field for conflict. Should the Law of the Sea Conferences fail to produce a global accord on a sea regime, old bilateral fishing disputes are likely to take on new meaning, while sea bed development can provoke even greater controversy.

The proliferation of small and perhaps in many cases politically and economically nonviable states in the Caribbean has also enlarged the arena for possible conflict. Conditions of internal disorder and strife such as in Central America have much broader repercussions.

Recent developments all bespeak an expanded definition of the national interest in a number of countries, often manifested in greater concern over—and a declining reluctance to become involved in—the affairs of neighboring states. Three examples are offered: multilateral influences on U.S.-Panamanian negotiation of the Canal treaties, external involvement in Nicaragua's civil war, and involvement in the labyrinthine eddies of Bolivian politics. In the first, the three democratically elected presidents of Venezuela, Colombia, and Costa Rica provided frequent advice and diplomatic assistance to the Panamanians. Venezuela's Pérez—his role enhanced by Jimmy Carter's public recognition as "my number one adviser on Latin America"—was especially active. In addition to publicly reported meetings with Omar Torrijos, he also hosted the Panamanian privately on several occasions during the course of negotiations.

During the *sandinista* confrontation with Somoza, regional pressures were multiple. Venezuela under Pérez again provided both public support and quiet material assistance, with the latter channeled through Panama and Costa Rica. Costa Rica, while placed in an awkward and ambiguous position, could not avoid at least implicit involvement, owing to geographic contiguity and the ease with which its northern border could be crossed and recrossed. There was also the less well-documented but presumed encouragement of both the Cuban government in favor of the *sandinistas* and that of Guatemala, Honduras, and El Salvador on behalf of the Somoza regime. Thirdly, Bolivian politics has historically drawn attention from Brazil and Argentina. Since the advent of the Banzer government in 1971, both rival giants have periodically exerted pressure in a variety of ways, perhaps most recently with the Argentine enthusiasm for the annullment of electoral results through approval of the military *golpe de estado* in July 1980.

Global Phenomena

In a final category we can briefly mention factors—some of which have already been alluded to—that bear an extrahemispheric or universalistic quality and relate to the globalization of regional politics. In political terms, the most obvious relates to the Soviet Union and to international Marxism. Without dwelling on the Soviet–Cuban relationship or the implications in Nicaragua and El Salvador, suffice it to note the importance of Marxist objectives and strategies as they impinge upon the Western Hemisphere. While constituting in many ways a collective security issue, the impact of the role played by the Soviet Union and its surrogates within Latin America can scarcely be ignored.

Other influences from outside the region include the economic interests and activities of Japan and of Western Europe. Here, too, we confront factors that in a sense lie beyond our principal focus but are nonetheless germane to questions of potential conflict and intentions for the resolution thereof. Traditionally, Western European states have maintained an economic interest in the hemisphere; political interests are now increasingly engaged. The willingness of European manufacturers to enter into licensing agreements that allow Latin American countries to build up their own armaments industries adds a new dimension to possibilities for violent confrontations. Moreover, when Japan seeks to expand investment in Mexico while increasing its purchase of oil in the country, it is not without ramifications for other issues. In similar fashion, the mutuality of interests between West Germany and Brazil as expressed from 1977 on with regard to nuclear power proved both controversial and a source of acrimony between Washington and Brasilia.

This particular difference, of course, leads to recognition of more generalized issues over nuclear proliferation. The rivalry of Brazil and Argentina has incorporated the component of nuclear power, an arena into which Venezuela and possibly others will later be drawn. Recognition of the nuclear issue also leads naturally to consideration of energy problems that are of global derivation. With the vast majority of Latin American countries increasingly burdened by the financial problems ensuing from their status as oil importers, internal pressures and domestic problems become ever more unsettling. Thus, Trinidad–Tobago could charge Venezuela with mounting a new wave of imperialism in the Caribbean; Mexico might be taxed by other Caribbean ministates with attaching too many strings to its providing of oil; Ecuador and Peru could speculate hopefully about the presence of untapped reserves in territory that both claim for their own. Colombia and Venezuela are even now unsuccessfully negotiating over their disputed border, under the waters of which substantial holdings of petroleum are believed to lie.

Summary

In this section, we have attempted to identify problems and issues according to three separate but interrelated dimensions. Examples have been cited on a nonexhaustive basis for illustrative purposes. While the potential sources of disharmony may not be more intense than in the past, the weight of the evidence, it would seem, points to a proliferation of existing and potential conflict in the near future. Under these circumstances, it now becomes our task to consider and assess the strengths and weaknesses of existing instrumentalities for the reconciliation of competing interests.

AVAILABLE INSTITUTIONS

Regional Mechanisms

The OAS

Interest in procedures for inter-American pacific settlement date back at least to 1889, although present mechanisms find their inception in the Inter-American Treaty of Reciprocal Assistance (Rio Treaty) and the OAS Charter of 1947 and 1948, respectively. The inter-American peace system has never functioned as its founders intended, however, because the Inter-American Treaty for Pacific Settlement (Bogota Pact), which was to have been the cornerstone for peaceful settlement, has been hamstrung by its administrative complexity and rigid procedures, by reservations, and by a lack of will for its utilization on the part of those states who have ratified it. More recently, the majority of American republics have been unwilling to attempt revision of the pact on the ostensible grounds of the complexity of the task.

The response of the peace system to the failure of member states to employ the procedures of the Pact of Bogota was the utilization of the collective security instrument, the Rio Treaty, as the primary agent for conflict resolution *inter se*. In their capacity as organs under the Rio Treaty, the Meetings of Consultation of Ministers of Foreign Affairs, and especially the Permanent Council of the OAS Acting as Provisional Organ of Consultation, played significant roles in the past.

Meetings of Consultation have never been held under Article 7 of the Rio Treaty, which provides that inter-American conflicts be dealt with by peaceful means. Rather, they have been held in cases of "an aggression which is not an armed attack . . . or any other fact or situation that might endanger the peace of America" (Article 6).[5] Thus, the meetings actually held have been more attuned to the problems of probing the sources of aggression and applying, or threatening to apply, sanctions than to traditional approaches to pacific settlement. This has resulted in producing a grey area between collective security, on the one hand, and pacific settlement, on the other. Article 39 of the 1948 Charter and Article 59 of the Amended Charter provide that the Meeting of Consultation is "to consider problems of an urgent nature and of common interest to the American states" as well as serve as Organ of Consultation under the Rio Treaty.

As far into the past as 1902, hemispheric states, fearing U.S. domination of the Washington-based organization, declined to encumber the new Governing Board of the Bureau of American Republics with political functions, preferring to have disputes dealt with on an ad hoc basis. This attitude continued until the 1945 Chapultepec Conference, when the Governing Board was given wide powers to take action on every matter affecting the effective functioning of the inter-American Republics. On the eve of the Ninth International Conference in 1948, a reaction had set in. Specific competence for dispute settlement was again denied the OAS Council. The effect of the U.S. role in the Dominican Crisis of 1965 was further instrumental in stymieing a proposal by Committee III of the Second Special Inter-American Conference for increased Council authority.

Nevertheless, under Article 12 of the Rio Treaty, the Council in its role as Provisional Organ of Consultation for the Meeting of Consultation of Foreign Ministers has played a vital role. It was envisioned, and indeed it has occurred, that certain cases might, by their urgency, not allow the convocation of a foreign ministers' meeting. While the role of the Council in the area of pacific settlement has been of considerable controversy, its function in that field was nevertheless expanded over the years as it acted as provisional organ.

In the majority of cases the Council has acted as provisional organ without convening the consultative meeting. Past experience suggested that in functional terms the provisional organ proved its adequacy essentially in cases where settlement was unlikely to prove inordinately difficult. Today the Permanent Council, under the Amended Charter, functions even more through ad hoc arrangements than in the past in the realm of pacific settlement.

While under the Amended Charter the General Assembly can undertake to deal with disputes among members, the necessity for urgency militates against the calling of a special meeting of the General Assembly, thus leaving the way open for Council action. The 1970 Charter in theory further expanded the role of the Permanent Council by delegating to it specific functions in the field of pacific settlement, authorizing it to consider matters or implement decisions delegated to it by the General Assembly or the Meeting of Consultation. Nevertheless, in the 1970s its role has been limited in scope. The Permanent Council can offer good offices but cannot conciliate disputes. Only with the consent of the concerned parties can the Council investigate the facts and recommend settlement procedures, while authority to function at the request of a third party is lacking.

In the early 1950s, when the self-approved statutes of an independent Inter-American Peace Committee (IAPC) allowed any American state to bring a dispute to its attention if circumstances made negotiation impracticable or if no other pacific settlement procedure was in progress, the IAPC was a relatively effective organ in the area of pacific settlement. Changes in its statutes in 1956 allowing it to act only at the request of a party to a controversy and only with the consent of all the parties to the conflict diluted its authority and effectiveness. Enlarged investigative functions granted to the IAPC by the Fifth Meeting of Consultation in 1959 were terminated in 1965 largely as a result of its vital role in the exclusion of Cuba at the Eighth Meeting of Consultation in 1962. The 1970 Amended Charter replaced it with a new Inter-American Committee on Peaceful Settlement subsidiary to the Permanent Council, which it is intended to assist. In fact, the reconstituted committee has not considered substantive disputes; in 1971, at the height of the fishing dispute between Ecuador and the United States, the only attempt ever to use its offices failed.

For the most part during the first two decades after the creation of the OAS, open hostilities were averted in an atmosphere in which contending parties were keenly aware of the availability of qualified, experienced, and often informal agencies. On many occasions it was remarked at the OAS that the sheer existence of settlement machinery deterred open warfare. Excluding conflicts relating to the Cold War, which generally fall under the rubric of collective security, or those otherwise directly involving what the United States considered its security interests during the two postwar decades, the OAS did deal with the most violent of hemispheric conflicts in an effective manner. It was, of course, hardly a picture of unrelieved success. Antagonisms based on commitments to different ideologies or personal antagonisms and on historical boundary disputes did not readily lend themselves to immediate resolution. Nevertheless, conflict was managed in the sense of easing tensions for a substantial period of time, and controversies were contained by hemispheric mechanisms.

By the beginning of the 1970s, much of the formal authority of OAS settlement organs had been diluted. As member nations—many of whom had never been comfortable with a grant of political functions to a Permanent Council or with broad powers to an IAPC—saw increasing danger of intervention in domestic affairs brought on by regional interdependence, they adopted a more cautious attitude toward pacific settlement procedures. In terms of governance, this attitude evolving over the past more than three decades has resulted in an inter-American peace system increasingly reliant on informal methods of conflict resolution.

Thus, in the early 1970s war may have been only narrowly averted when the OAS sent a small, unpublicized, and informal group to British Honduras to verify the size of the British garrison and alleviate tension. Despite the fact that Chile refuses to recognize OAS competence in the controversy over Bolivia's access to the sea, the overwhelming majority of members felt no reluctance to keep the matter on the agenda and urge a resolution. That regional organization's rich tradition and experience in peaceful settlement techniques is still credited by most hemispheric diplomats today with discouraging the use of violence between member states. As the penultimate decade of the twentieth century opens, however, the possible sources of conflict have multiplied and new complexities have been added, which will test the suasive character of the existence of the OAS.

The Andean Pact

From the avowedly political standpoint, the Andean Pact toward the close of the 1970s attempted to play a role in alleviating hemispheric conflict. Strongly propelled by Ecuador's Jaime Roldós Aguilera following his August 1978 inauguration as elected president, the Pact voiced strong antipathy toward the Somoza regime and proffered moral support to the *sandinistas.* Joining with the democracies of

Colombia and Venezuela and, from August 1979, Peru as well, the Roldós administration also sought to exercise influence on behalf of the insurgents in Salvador. This was accompanied by the outspoken advocacy of democracy and human rights in the hemisphere, and since the July 1980 military *golpe* in Bolivia, several Pact members have attempted to pressure that government to convene democratic elections. In the process, Bolivia has effectively withdrawn from participation in the Pact. President Fernando Belaúnde Terry has taken a dim view of such a political role for the Andean Pact and, disenchanted with many of the economic provisions, has turned diplomatically toward Chile. The renewal of hostilities between Ecuador and Peru in the disputed Cordillera del Cóndor region in early 1981 has further weakened and effectively fragmented the Pact. Whether or not it survives as an economic entity, its political role as an instrumentality for pacific resolution of conflict appears virtually nil for the foreseeable future.

The Central American Common Market (CACM)

Initially successful as an integration scheme on a modest scale but never intended as a pacific settlement agency, the purported unity of the CACM was shattered by the eruption of war in 1969 between El Salvador and Honduras. Efforts by the group to mediate the dispute were unavailing, and even before the overthrow of President Somoza and the advent of civil strife in El Salvador, the CACM had been relegated to a secondary economic role while proving unable to handle political disputes.

States as Mediators

A striking development in recent years has been the return to the pre-OAS practice of reliance on individual states as mediators of disputes. In several instances, and through a variety of mechanisms, such nations as Venezuela, Mexico, and Argentina have attempted to moderate conflict. Ranging from the encouragement of negotiations in El Salvador to the rejection of an offer by Venezuela's Herrera to mediate the Ecuador–Peru dispute in January 1981, this proclivity has assumed far larger proportions than was customary. It not only offers another outlet for conflict management, but suggests a move away from OAS mechanisms and generalized pessimism over the effectiveness of formal institutionalized diplomacy.

The United Nations

Under the U.N. Charter (Articles 33 and 103), while all U.N. members have the right to resort to that organization to resolve their disputes, there is also a recognition that regional possibilities for settlement should be explored before action is to be taken by the Security Council. Although Article 20 of the original OAS Charter and Article 23 of the Amended Charter commit the American states to submit controversies to peaceful settlement procedures set forth in the Charter before referral to the U.N. Security Council, there is no question of the right of the United Nations, under the terms of its Charter, to initiate an investigation at any stage of an inter-American controversy. Nevertheless, claims (primarily by the United States) to a type of primary jurisdiction within the OAS have prevailed, with the United Nations relegated a residual authority to be exercised only if the regional organization has clearly failed to keep the peace. Thus, to date the United Nations has not played a real role in hemispheric conflict resolution. Increasingly, however, since the institutionalization of Marxism in Cuba in the early 1960s, minority leftist forces involved in regional controversies and/or conflict have pressed for a hearing in the U.N. Security Council.

ALTERNATIVE APPROACHES

In the light of an increasing diversity of hemispheric nations in terms of political outlook, economic interest, and independence, combined with a sharpening of a series of bilateral disputes, the already existing tendency for extracontinental influences to impinge on regional issues is likely to increase. If at the same time the inter-American peace system becomes fragmented through lack of interest or reluctance to utilize its mechanisms in the face of such complex problems, the historic peace of the Americas can be shattered. How can the inter-American peace system be strengthened in order to avoid armed conflict in the region?

1. *More extensive reliance on the United Nations*

Frequently in the past the Soviet veto in the Security Council and the impotence of the General Assembly have been cited as reasons for keeping inter-American disputes out of the United Nations. In a work published in 1979, Tom Farer urged a gradual restoration of Western hemisphere peacekeeping (and by implication crisis management) responsibilities to the U.N.[6] Arguing that the region would then cease to appear as the special province of the United States, he contended that endowing the Security Council with responsibility would actually reduce Soviet freedom of action by compelling the Soviet Union to take public positions and by exposing it to international criticism. Nonetheless, while it is true that in the event of armed conflict collective self-defense under Article 51 of the U.N. Charter is not subject to veto, the possibilities for settling a dangerous conflict not yet involving armed conflict are. Moreover, as indicated by Ernest Haas,[7] subjecting strictly hemispheric disputes to the scrutiny of a U.N. General Assembly or Security Council would tend to reduce the ability to encapsulate and isolate the controversy from world pressures, thereby complicating rather than ameliorating the dispute.

2. The strengthening of other non-OAS regional institutions

The failure of the Andean Pact and the CACM to become effective instruments for peaceful settlement has been elaborated. Similarly, it is unlikely that the Latin American Economic System (SELA) could be used for settlement purposes. These organs, all designed for economic uses, may well not be suitable for a conflict resolution role in a region where economic diversity sets the stage for even broader conflict. Nevertheless, it is possible that these institutions, and others as they are created, could establish networks for dealing with some controversies on a subregional level with the OAS acting as a "court of last resort."

Efforts to expand the powers of the Inter-American Defense Board or the Central American Defense Council (CONDECA) seem doomed to failure. CONDECA has never contributed to the easing of regional tensions, and attempts on the part of various military regimes to expand the power and significance of the former, or even institutionalize it by incorporating it into the OAS Charter, have been consistently rejected.

3. Creation of new institutions and/or strengthening of existing organs within the OAS

As previously noted, the rigid provisions and administrative complexity of the Pact of Bogota have mitigated against either its use or even its restructuring. With regard to existing formal peaceful settlement mechanisms utilized in the past, there has also been manifest among OAS members in the last decade a tendency to shy away from these permanent institutionalized instruments. In the light of an historic wariness relative to extending political functions to OAS organs, even a proposal to revitalize the Inter-American Committee on Peaceful Settlement for use in disputes between small states seems fated for oblivion.

Suggestions for the creation of additional mechanisms have not met with success. At various points, a permanent peace observation mission has been proposed. Nevertheless, while the utilization of ad hoc peace observer groups became quite common in the 1950s and lasted into the 1970s with the El Salvador–Honduras conflict, OAS members have rebuffed efforts to institutionalize such a group. Many have, in fact, likened such a body to a de facto Inter-American Peace Force (IAPF) which is a concept in strong disrepute among most Latins because of its overtly interventionist connotations and because of a Latin fear that such an organ would become an instrument of U.S. policy. The nonmilitary character of the OAS is indicated by the fact that only once in the history of the inter-American system has such a force been established—for deployment in the 1965 civil war in the Dominican Republic. There was bitter criticism of this force, which was composed predominantly of North Americans. As a result of that experience, as well as of past almost unanimous opposition to an IAPF, the 1979 U.S. proposal to send an IAPF to restore order and democracy into the strife-torn *somosista* Nicaragua was soundly defeated at the OAS. Likewise a strengthening of Rio Treaty provisions would be unlikely to gain wide acceptance for similar reasons, since the Treaty itself is actually designed for collective security purposes and requires the determination of an aggressor.

Overall, even aside from reluctance to rely on permanent mechanisms, in the short run the strengthening of these organs or establishment of new instruments are not viable options. Given an eventual concensus on a need to revitalize the peace system, the working out of details would necessitate lengthy negotiations and compromise. Once in final form, an amended treaty or treaties would need ratifications and deposits thereof entailing at least another five years before they could be used. In the meantime, the OAS Charter continues to offer a flexibility that can be effectively employed if its members are so inclined.[8]

4. Maintenance of the present inter-American peace system

In the light of the changing character of regional disputes (e.g., now frequently centering on pressure for revolutionary change within states) and a general disinclination to use treaty mechanisms, there has developed a need to resolve these issues, not with formal procedures, but more by flexible political methods relying on just and prudent statesmanship and diplomacy. Clearly, if an issue becomes involved with, or is perceived to involve, a conflict of interest between the United States and the Soviet Union, the possibility that either formal or informal procedures will be effective is severely circumscribed. The nonparticipation of Cuba in OAS activities has raised the issue of the organization's competence to deal with questions concerning that country. It has been argued that the reincorporation of Cuba into the OAS would, in the long run, facilitate OAS settlement procedures. But the "Cold War" of the 1980s is very different from that of the 1950s. During the earlier years the United States was a superactor with an overriding psychological advantage in pressuring for a utilization of OAS mechanisms. Today the United States is not viewed as so powerful a figure.

States in an ideological minority are unlikely to turn to the OAS for the settlement of controversies. The limits of "ad hocism" must be recognized. We may have to accept as a fact of life that no regional institution may be able to settle, or even effectively manage, controversies involving a Cuban-style regime. Nevertheless, in the broadest sense of hemispheric dispute resolution, while it may appear at first glance to be a haphazard method for dealing with regional disputes, at least in the decade of the 1980s, the most viable method of conflict management within the hemisphere lies in reliance on the prior body of precedents, which created ad hoc instrumentalities and which extended into the 1970s in the form of more informal methods of settlement. To the extent that these procedures avoid the glare of the media spotlight, which tends to accentuate perceived differences in viewpoint, it is in the best interests of hemispheric peace.

With the greatly expanded nature of problem areas susceptible to serious conflict in this hemisphere, both quantitatively and qualitatively, the challenge to institutions and to the informal dynamics of governance are formidable. The pacific settlement process has already become fragmented. The danger today lies in not recognizing the institutional role of the OAS in the evolution and continuing viability of existing informal settlement procedures for the management of crisis and the encapsulation of conflicts. The strength of OAS conflict management in the past has been its flexibility, combined with a healthy reliance on the interpersonal relationships of skilled diplomats to that organization. Given the increased self-assertiveness of Latin American foreign policies today, this is the most realistic method for pursuing peaceful settlement.

NOTES

1. Dispute settlement refers to the resolution of a specific disagreement, which takes the form of claims and counterclaims between parties. Conflict resolution is concerned with the resolution of a condition of general hostility in which particular differences seem as much a result, as a cause, of tension.

2. Joseph S. Nye in *Peace in Parts* (Boston: Little Brown, 1971) p. 3, defines encapsulation of conflicts as preventing conflicts from becoming intertwined with insoluable global conflicts. See also Amitai Etzioni, "On Self-Encapsulating Conflicts," *Journal of Conflict Resolution* 8 (1964) 242–55.

3. Often described as the "American" doctrine of nonintervention, the principle of nonintervention has become not only a cornerstone of the inter-American system, but also a concept difficult to reconcile with some of the procedures of pacific settlement as they have evolved: Ann Van Wyen Thomas and A. J. Thomas, Jr., *Non-Intervention: The Law and its Import in the Americas* (Dallas: Southern Methodist University Press, 1956). In recent years the issue of the protection of human rights has led to breaks with this doctrine. E.g., a notable exception occurred at the time of the 1979 Nicaragua civil war during the OAS debates over the Somoza regime.

4. The latter projects were the source of serious dispute between Argentina and Brazil for years.

5. The Protocol of Amendment to the Inter-American Treaty of Reciprocol Assistance (Rio Treaty) has not yet come into force.

6. Tom J. Farrer, "Limiting Intraregional Violence: The Costs of Regional Peacekeeping," in Tom J. Farrer (ed.), *The Future of the Inter-American System*, (New York: Praeger Publishers, 1979).

7. Ernest B. Haas, "The United Nations and Regionalism," in Kenneth J. Twitchett (ed.), *The Evolving U.N.: A Prospect for Peace?* (London: Europa for the David Davies Memorial Institute of International Studies, 1971), pp. 120 ff.

8. The exclusion, through Article 8 (Revised Charter), of certain regional states from membership or active participation within the OAS because of pending disputes limits the ability of the organization to deal with controversies (especially those concerning boundaries).

11

The Acquisition of Arms and Western Hemisphere Relations

Caesar Sereseres

INTRODUCTION

Given the state of political and military affairs in the Western Hemisphere today, there is very little likelihood that the demand for arms or the willingness to supply arms (for whatever the purpose) will diminish significantly. This does not mean, however, that the Hemisphere is to be subjected for the next two decades to a series of "mini arms races." Conflict will become more intense throughout the area as various issues are settled: internally in terms of changes in the social order, along borders between sets of nations as territorial/population/resource disputes are managed, if not settled, and subregionally as groups of nations seek out political accommodations as a means of resolving ideological, economic, and leadership conflicts.

The acquisition of military technology—by Sandinista Nicaragua, revolutionary Mexico, authoritarian Chile, oil-rich Venezuela, financially weak Peru, budgetary strained Dominican Republic, or socialist Cuba—plays a meaningful role in the internal politics and diplomacy of each country. Even Costa Rica has demonstrated that, given the right moment in history, a critical geopolitical location, and the resources of other nations, arms acquisitions and transfers can make a difference in local political conflicts. It seems that few nations can escape contact with, or the consequences of, the seemingly never-ending flows of weapons into the Western Hemisphere.

Could such trends evolve differently during the next two decades? Probably not. This, however, does not mean that some attempts could not be made to establish mechanisms to facilitate cooperation among the nations of the hemisphere to cope better with the realities and challenges of arms acquisitions in the region. How realistic such proposals might be depends on probable adjustments to the global, regional, regime, and institutional dynamics of arms acquisitions.

THE ARMS ACQUISITION LEGACY

While concerns grow about the apparent relationships between arms acquisitions and the rise of armed conflicts, human rights violations, and authoritarian military regimes, Latin American nations continue to purchase new-generation weapons—from supersonic jet fighters, guided-missile frigates, submarines to helicopters and tanks. Yet, there appears to be a significant discrepancy between the political controversy generated by the concern for arms transfers to the region and the comparatively low level of Latin American arms acquisitions. Latin American countries have participated in the global surge of arms transfers, seeking advanced weapon systems from U.S. and European suppliers. Yet by most quantitative indicators, Latin America remains a lightly armed region where military expenditures and acquisitions have grown rather slowly, compared with other third world regions.

No single country seems to be excessively armed, and the pace of acquisition does not seem at variance with historical development, obsolescence, and local capabilities to absorb advanced technology. Arms races characterized by spiraling expenditures and swelling inventories do not exist between any two countries. Overall probabilities of regional border conflicts and arms races may be rising—but more slowly than in other areas of the world. The arms transfer "numbers" that have been updated yearly for more than three decades mean little by themselves. The "numbers" provide symbolic as well as factual bases for discussing qualitative issues. Thus, Latin America, though a minor quantitative consumer of the global transfer of arms, allows one to consider possible qualitative explanations of the central policy issue that *arms acquisitions and military development may increase the prospects for dangerous costly arms races, for local border conflicts and possibly wars, and for the strengthening of military dictatorships that violate human rights.*

However, there is another dimension to the acquisition of arms that must be considered when examining possible alternatives in the governance of the transfer of military technology to the Western Hemisphere. Since at least the mid-1960s, arms transfers have been influencing factors on the political relations between nations of the hemisphere. For the next several decades, arms transfers will continue to be an important element of Western Hemisphere relations. The prevalence of military regimes in the region only adds greater emphasis to this point. Within the region prestigious weapons are fast becoming as significant for diplomatic symbolism as for operational military capabilities in affecting relations between neighbors. Among other things, arms acquisitions must also be seen as a form of diplomacy in hemispheric relations. To understand this dimension of arms acquisitions, one must examine the changing *global* context of the Latin American region.

THE CHANGING GLOBAL CONTEXT OF THE WESTERN HEMISPHERE

Since the mid-1960s, the Western Hemisphere has been increasingly affected by fundamental changes in the international order—including the decline of global bipolarity, the lessening of U.S. economic hegemony, and the diversification of Latin America's international political and economic relations. Seeking political, economic, and security relations with extraregional powers offers more and entails less risk for Latin American nations than at any time since World War II. The changing perceptions of "friends" and "enemies" account for this diversification. For the most part, Latin American governments between 1941 and 1970 shared perceptions of a common external enemy with the United States—Germany, Russia, and, later, Cuba. These perceptions, though they differed from country to country, helped to unify Latin American foreign policies with each other and toward the United States. However, by the late 1970s, the threats faced by Latin American regimes failed to produce such unifying effects.

Today, the United States is the preponderant hemispheric power, but its influence and prestige in Latin America are diminished and its policies often countered or ignored. The decline in U.S. economic and military assistance, the increased presence of non-hemispheric nations, the growing capabilities of the Latin American governments, the emergence of regional powers (such as Mexico, Cuba, Venezuela, and Brazil) and the perceptions of new political elites contribute to this diminished influence and tarnished image.

For several decades after World War II, Latin America was commonly regarded as a valuable wartime reserve of foodstuffs and raw materials for the United States. However, military technology appeared to make Latin America irrelevant as a geopolitical consideration. In a nuclear war, these countries were considered strategically remote and unimportant as military objectives. Thus, Latin America was generally seen as a region that had a low value compared to other regions in the world. For the 1980s, however, the strategic value of Latin America is being determined somewhat less by "Cold War" considerations and more by such factors as energy. Petroleum reserves in Mexico and Venezuela, not to mention other mineral resources in the Andes and Amazon areas, raise the strategic stakes that the United States and other industrialized nations have in the Latin American region—especially if problems persist in the Middle East and in the Persian Gulf.

Together, these interrelated trends contribute to the strategically significant change in the global context of Latin American countries. The implications of this are three-fold. (1) The new external context intensifies the concerns among the Latin American nations for their relations with each other. Indeed, the weakening of the U.S. presence in particular appears to be indirectly enhancing the significance attached to intraregional relations on a number of issues, ranging from Andean Pact cooperation to the resurgence of old border disputes and historic rivalries. (2) The changes in the world context permit flexibility among the Latin American nations in their dealings not only with the outside world, but also with each other. Global trends toward political and economic multipolarity make shifting alliances on specific issues a likely outcome in intraregional affairs. (3) While improving the incentives for intraregional cooperation and integration, the United States contributes to the destabilization of the region by its diminished presence. In the past, U.S. power and influence served to dampen rivalries and potential conflicts. Given the world environment of the 1980s, however, regional actors such as Argentina, Brazil, Venezuela, Mexico, and Cuba are more likely to compete for regional leadership and local spheres of influence.

Compared to the 1950s and 1960s, today nations in the Western Hemisphere are operating within a distinctive and new international and regional setting that affects U.S.–Latin American relations. In many respects the opportunities for higher levels of cooperation are presenting themselves. Yet at the same time the potential for political, economic, and military conflict continues to increase. One very parochial point should be kept in mind as one discusses the possibilities of arms governance in the region. The Latin American policies of the United States have for more than a century alternated between extremes of inattention and closely scrutinized paternalism. Nevertheless, even changing global geopolitics have not changed the longest-lived foreign policy concern of the United States: namely, securing the Western Hemisphere from external influence. After this concern comes the desire to see Latin America, of its own choice, emulate the U.S. political and economic system.

In addition, while concrete geographic, economic, political, and military interests can be explicitly identified and debated, psychological interests are also fundamental to the national security concerns of the United States. The United States and Latin America have a unique psychological relationship that rests on the belief and experience that the United States is the dominant power in the Western Hemisphere. Successful opposition to the United States in the region implies a weakening, not only of its position in Latin America, but in the global posture of the United States as well. Despite the "imperial" connotations of this geopolitical reality, it is an historical fate from which neither the United States nor its hemispheric neighbors can escape.

THE LATIN AMERICAN ARMS MARKET: DEFENSE EXPENDITURES AND ARMS RACES

The highly publicized arms purchases by Latin American nations since the early 1970s have given the impression that the region's market is rapidly growing. The progressive increase in the absolute value of Latin American arms acquisitions seems to support such views. However, this situation is not as it appears to be. Not only are the dollar value increases more the function of rising costs of technically advanced weapons and sophisticated support equipment, but normalized indicators suggest that in *aggregate* terms arms acquisi-

tions patterns in the late 1970s resembled those of the late 1960s.*
Taken as a *region*, the relationships between Latin American arms
purchases, defense expenditures and Gross National Product could be
stated in the following manner:

1. Military expenditures as a proportion of Gross National
   Product remained constant throughout the 1960s and
   1970s.

2. Arms acquisitions as a percentage of Gross National
   Product and as a percentage of military expenditures rose
   significantly in the early 1970s (the result of deliveries
   ordered in the late 1960s) and by the late 1970s began a
   slow return to late 1960 levels.

Perceptions of conventional arms races in the Western Hemisphere are often a response to the *introduction of modern weapons*,
inflated prices for sophisticated military equipment, and *the entry
of new suppliers* into the region. This latter trend reflects the
efforts of Latin American nations to establish a network of multiple
arms suppliers for reasons of diplomacy, politics, economics, and
dependency diversification. Thus, the dramatic increase in the
number of suppliers since the late 1960s does not reflect a significant
growth in the arms market but rather further division of the existing
market.

Furthermore, perceptions of an ability/willingness to acquire
arms are also influenced by the steadily growing levels of Latin
American defense budgets. For the most part, marked increases in
defense expenditures since the late 1960s seem to reflect the increased
costs of maintaining and operating a military institution (increased
manpower, higher salaries, food, expensive fuel, newly created
pensions and social services, advanced training) rather than being
primarily attributable to purchases of new weapons.

Since the end of World War II, three phases of major arms
acquisitions can be identified. The first, in the postwar decade,
concentrated largely on jet aircraft, the second, in the late 1950s, on
a naval craft, and the third, in the late 1960s and early 1970s was a

---

* For specific data see Mike Mihalka, "Super-Client Patterns in Arms Transfers,"
in S. Neuman and R. Harkavy, (eds.), *Arms Transfers in the Modern World*,
New York: Praeger Publications, 1979, pp. 49–76.

period of intense purchasing that included air, sea, and ground combat weapons and support equipment.

This third phase of military purchases began in the mid-1960s when navies and air forces of the hemisphere decided to upgrade inventories and modernize equipment. Combat aircraft tended to dominate the early years of this purchasing period. Tanks, armored personnel carriers, and artillery were also bought, and in 1973 Peru received several hundred tanks from the Soviet Union.

By the late 1960s, the region (actually the six major South American countries) turned to Europe, a former supplier of military equipment. Throughout the late 1960s and 1970s, Argentina, Brazil, Chile, Colombia, Peru, and Venezuela accounted for roughly 90% of all military equipment orders placed by the Latin American region— two-thirds of the suppliers being Western European.

Several factors accounted for this shift. First, there was a European willingness to sell new, advanced weapons systems such as supersonic fighter aircraft and a variety of tactical missile systems. Favorable, if not concessionary, financing terms offered by European suppliers (contrasted to U.S. legislative and executive policy constraints on arms transfers to Latin America) accelerated the move to European sources. There was also the trend in Latin America toward asserting greater independence from the United States, manifesting itself by a desire to diversify the sources of arms.*

The higher costs of new military hardware and technological sophistication, together with inflation, pushed Latin American defense budgets to levels five times those of the 1950s. Even Cuba, despite its distinct relationship with its supplier, the Soviet Union, did not escape these same trends. Cuba is estimated to have imported $590 million in arms during this decade, an increase from an average of $22 million a year in 1968–72 to an average of over $100 million a year in 1974–1977.

Latin American government expenditures for the acquisition of military hardware, support equipment, and services averaged $180 million a year during the late 1960s and early 1970s. By the mid-1970s, purchases reached a high of $500 million. By 1977, arms sales to Latin America reached another record high, in excess of $1 billion dollars, twice the 1972–75 annual average. In the late 1970s the $1 billion Latin American arms market represented 5% of the

---

* See David F. Ronfeldt and Caesar D. Sereseres, "U.S. Arms Transfers, Diplomacy and Security in Latin America," in Andrew J. Pierre, *Arms Transfers and American Foreign Policy*, New York: New York University Press, 1979, pp. 121–92.

global arms market.* And, while military hardware, services, and training were supplied by some 27 nations, the United States (though having its share of the market substantially reduced since the mid-1960s) remained the *single* most significant supplier for the region. For example, in 1978–1979, the United States delivered $150 million in sales and $40 million in commercial exports. Estimated *deliveries* from other suppliers to the region ran about $600 million. These figures, of course, tell us little about the political, diplomatic, and economic dimensions of the flow of arms from supplier to client.

The pattern of purchasing from a diversity of suppliers will not change. Latin American nations continue to demonstrate a reluctance to depend upon any one nation as the sole supplier of military equipment and spare parts. Consequently, new acquisitions will continue to reflect a pattern of diversity—accepting maintenance, training, and standardization problems that come with such diversity.

The single most important reason for the acquisition of arms is force modernization and the replacement of aging equipment. Despite the transfer of equipment since the 1950s, the majority of Latin American military material dates from World War II and in some cases even earlier. Most of the armed forces in the hemisphere, especially the six major South American nations and most probably Mexico, are concerned about the inability to function with obsolete equipment. The impact of operationally deficient military symbols on professional morale and national sovereignty are quite evident.

Despite the increases in absolute terms, military expenditures for Latin America averaged less than 2% of GNP for the 1970s, a level not appreciably greater than for the 1960s. Even though regional arms spending quadrupled since 1940, Latin American military expenditures demonstrate the same basic pattern for over 30 years: expenditures remain less than 2% of Gross National Product. This is lower than any other region in the world. Furthermore, the total value of arms imports represent about 2% of total imports—again, the lowest of any region.†

Demand for new military hardware will continue throughout the 1980s. Despite two decades of purchases, the military establish-

---

* For an historical overview of arms acquisition patterns in Latin America see Luigi R. Einaudi, *Arms Transfers to Latin America*, Santa Monica, California: The RAND Corporation, 1973.

† See U.S. Arms Control and Disarmament Agency, *World Military Expenditures and Arms Transfers*, 1969–1978, Washington, D.C., December 1980.

ments of Latin America still possess large inventories of aging and obsolescent equipment. Difficult and costly to maintain, this equipment will need to be replaced, or at a minimum rehabilitated, during the 1980s. These modernization efforts to upgrade present inventories will be extremely costly. Advanced technology, increased raw material costs, and inflation have combined to accelerate the prices of new weapons. For the foreseeable future, the patterns of military expenditures demonstrated over the past decade will continue as military budgets follow the growth of the Gross National Product.

For the most part, the pattern of the past several decades suggests arms acquisitions are based on perceived service needs, motives of national sovereignty, and occasionally on the potential for conflicts with neighbors, rather than on a perceived extrahemispheric security threat. In some cases, new sources of wealth (oil, mineral, commodities) reinforced by perceived national and institutional needs will produce a new round of spending for upgrading and expanding the armed forces of the hemisphere.

Future procurement patterns seem certain. Arms demands may level off but will probably not decline. Rising political tensions between neighbors, internal warfare taking place in Central America, sovereignty over 200-mile territorial waters, expansion of the Soviet naval presence in the South Atlantic and Caribbean, the demonstration of Cuban military assistance in Angola and elsewhere,* cyclical high prices for commodities and raw materials are a few factors that will stimulate arms demands. The demand for precision-guided munitions (PGMs) is likely to grow, since these are highly effective but relatively low-cost items that are suited to defensive missions. Their utility was clearly demonstrated in Vietnam, in the Arab–Israeli wars, and in Angola. Demands will also develop for attack-type helicopters, ASW aircraft, and transports, and several countries may very well seek to purchase the F-16. *The emphasis will be more on force modernization than on force build-up.* The cycle of replacing obsolescent equipment, though slowing down, has not come to an end.

---

* For a discussion of Cuba's Angola venture and its possible ramifications for the Western Hemisphere, see Edward Gonzalez, "Castro and Cuba's New Orthodoxy," *Problems in Communism*, Vol. XXV, January–February, 1976, pp. 1–19. Also see Gonzalez and Ronfeldt, *Post-Revolutionary Cuba in a Changing World*, Santa Monica, California: The RAND Corporation, R-1844-ISA, December 1975, pp. 71–78.

PERSPECTIVES OF SOME MAJOR ARMS SUPPLIERS

The fact is that no general consensus exists among the major suppliers that the proliferation of conventional arms is a dangerous development. Moreover, Latin American nations, for the most part, view efforts by the arms-exporting nations (especially efforts by the United States) to restrain, control, or for that matter, monitor the flow of arms as being interventionist, paternalistic, discriminatory, and even imperialistic. European governments base their arms transfer policies on interests distinct from those of the U.S. government. Since each European country represents a limited domestic market, weapons are normally designed with export in mind. Thus government arms sales policies are primarily directed to garner foreign exchange, to lower procurement costs for the home military forces, to defray the research and development costs associated with modern weapons technology, and to keep domestic labor employed.

France in particular designs major weapons systems for their exportability and requires high exports in order to finance research and development costs. Almost 30% of France's arms production is exported. Thus the French might well view efforts to curtail their efforts as implicit attacks on their national sovereignty, economic well-being, and military self-sufficiency.

By way of contrast, West Germany has followed a policy of restraint, based on a determination that large arms exports lead to foreign policy complications and make the home industry vulnerable to shifting external conditions. As a rule, Germany has declined to sell into "areas of tension." However, the German government has recently relaxed this policy in order to allow sales of submarines to Latin American countries. What motivated this shift in Germany's policy was the threat of increased unemployment in Germany's shipyards. Economic realities prevailed over political ideals. Furthermore, West German firms are actively courting coproduction arrangements, especially in Brazil, that allow margins of freedom from foreign policy constraints existing inside Germany.

Because of the weight of such economic incentives, the West European governments appear unlikely to follow U.S. initiatives to control the quantitative and qualitative dimensions of arms sales into the Latin American region. France has already declined to agree to unilateral arms sales reductions as proposed by the United States. And European purchases of new fighter aircraft and tanks may release a new generation of surplus equipment that the Europeans will want to sell in Third World areas.

In general, political and security interests tend to guide U.S. arms sales policies toward Latin America. Economic incentives usually hold a secondary significance. This also seems to apply to Soviet policies. Thus, while the major European suppliers pay lip service to the concern for restraining arms sales, the United States may stand a better chance of reaching some limited understanding with the Soviet Union than with the West Europeans. But the incentives are not clear for the Soviets to enter into arms restraint agreements. The expansion of a global Soviet politicomilitary presence is closely linked to its capacities for making quick, concessionary arms transfers to Third World countries. Also, Soviet reequipment programs at home may release quantities of weaponry for transfer abroad. However, the Soviets might be more willing to agree to arms restraints in Latin America (excluding Cuba from such discussions) than in other regions, where Moscow's interests and involvements are stronger.

Even if the United States can convince other major suppliers to establish multilateral arms restraints, energetic new suppliers provide alternative sources. Israel in particular has high-quality weapons to offer, is making strenuous marketing efforts, and will not prove easy to restrain. In addition, Brazil as well as Argentina are developing military industries at home, based partly on coproduction arrangements with the advanced industrial manufacturers, for assembly or fabrication of jet aircraft, transport aircraft, helicopters, tanks, armored cars and personnel carriers, frigates, submarines, patrol boats, and surface-to-surface, surface-to-air, and air-to-surface missile systems. In fact, some Brazilians expect their arms exports to be a billion-dollar business by the mid-1980s.

While the perspectives of the various supplier nations may differ on the utility of arms control and the consequences of arms transfers, these nations do have several things in common: (1) arms sales are an integral part of part of foreign/economic policy, (2) weapon exports are linked to the viability of an independent arms industry, and (3) they see the arms market as limited and thus highly competitive, if not zero-sum for suppliers. This, of course, applies to the *major* arms suppliers selling *major* military items. The small-arms dealers (including the vast black market in light weapons and related products) is another little known aspect of the acquisition process. This further compounds prospects for serious efforts in the regulation of arms flow to the Western Hemisphere—especially to the smaller nations that rely more extensively on the private small arms dealers.

ARMS CONTROL AND CONFLICT MANAGEMENT

The potential for intraregional conflicts has increased in Latin America. For some South American military institutions, external defense missions have gained priority over internal security, although the latter remain important. Small-scale war in the Latin American region is not an unrealistic scenario. Indeed, current trends are similar to trends in the 1930s, when several border engagements and one protracted conflict took place in South America. At present, there is a decline of U.S. power and presence, the diversification and expansion of Latin American relations with nonhemispheric nations, and locally rising tensions based in part on geopolitical perceptions. Earlier decades of peace, from the end of the Peru-Ecuador conflict in 1942 through the Honduras-El Salvador clash of 1969, may be attributed in part to U.S. hegemony and to the greater priority that Latin American governments gave to relations with foreign powers over relations with their neighbors.

Governments purchase weapons for a variety of reasons, ranging from generational obsolescence of existing inventories to reactions stimulated by assessment of acquisitions by neighbors. Some country pairs, such as Peru-Chile, Ecuador-Peru, Argentina-Chile, and Venezuela-Colombia, are more sensitive than others, for historical and geographical reasons. Some balancing and emulation is occurring —but no two countries have yet engaged in a spiraling arms race that consumes large expenditures and leads to swollen arms inventories. Furthermore, there are no reliable formulas for judging whether arms transfers are likely to alleviate conflict potential or stimulate arms races. Assessment in this area becomes especially complicated when a country such as the United States provides arms to two neighbors—as in the cases of Peru-Chile, Venezuela-Colombia, and Honduras-El Salvador—for defense against an internal or external threat, when in fact the two neighbors become more interested in using the weapons for defense against each other. However, it is not necessarily true that an influx of weapons raises the risks that political disagreements will be more likely to turn to armed conflict. The limited knowledge that we now possess regarding individual cases does not suggest that arms transfers contribute more to an armed conflict than do local political conditions.

In the past, the argument could be made that an exclusive or highly dominant supply relationship represented a form of U.S. arms control. Accordingly, such a supply relationship would enable the United States to influence the type and rate of local arms orders and to curtail supplies in the event of an unwelcome local conflict.

During the 1950s and early 1960s, the United States did in fact attempt to follow a policy of regional arms balancing and limitation. In this respect, the Military Assistance Program and the allocation of Foreign Military Sales credit assistance were used to try to establish some parity among neighboring militaries and to keep the level of weapon sophistication reasonably low. Such a policy is no longer viable.

THE ANDEAN DECLARATION OF AYACUCHO

Partly as a result of major arms acquisitions in the late 1960s and early 1970s, the Latin Americans have not ignored the very real need for arms control efforts in the region. One regional effort was initiated in South America. Following a proposal from Peru to freeze arms purchases for ten years, the six Andean countries of Chile, Bolivia, Ecuador, Peru, Colombia, and Venezuela (along with Argentina and Panama) signed the Ceclaration of Ayacucho in 1974. The signatories committed themselves to "create conditions which permit effective limitations of armaments and put an end to their acquisition for offensive warlike purposes in order to dedicate all possible resources to economic and social development."*

Since 1974, several technical meetings have been held in Lima, Santiago, and La Paz in the attempt to implement the Ayacucho Declaration. As a result of these meetings, attended by technical representatives of the respective countries, agreement was reached on the following: a ban on certain types of advanced weapons not now present in Latin America, further study on limiting the acquisition of other major weapons, and consideration of a treaty to strengthen peace in the region. In addition, the possibilities were also discussed of reducing border forces, establishing demilitarized zones, and monitoring weapons inventories. Despite the fears and concerns expressed in 1974, by the late 1970s these recommendations were still being taken "under consideration" by the governments of the Ayacucho Declaration. Meanwhile, purchases of, or attempts to purchase, Soviet SU-22 attack-bombers by Peru, Israeli Shafrir air-to-air missiles by Chile, and Israeli Kfir high-performance jet fighters

---

* For the complete text of the Ayacucho Declaration see "Eight Latin American Governments Sign Declaration Aimed at Limiting Armaments," in *U.N. Monthly Chronicle*, March 1975, pp. 54-57.

by Ecuador suggest that there still remains a wide gap between Ayacucho intent and local national security concerns that require the purchase of modern weapons of both a defensive and offensive nature. While the Ayacucho declaration did not slow the acquisition of arms, U.S. support became a new decision-making factor in favor of restraining arms transfers into the Andean region.

As an adjunct to the Declaration of Ayacucho, the countries of Bolivia, Chile, and Peru engaged in their own discussions about arms limitations and conflict management. In the mid-1970s, high-level military personnel from these three countries issued a communiqué to state that they had (1) agreed in principle to find ways to consult regularly and exchange information in advance about military activities along the three borders, (2) acknowledged Bolivian concern for an outlet to the sea, and (3) supported the Ayacucho arms limitations talks. Although their Tripartite Conferences have further proposed establishing an early-warning system along the borders and possibly the signing of a nonaggression pact, the outlook for these arms control measures seems dim. Meanwhile spokesmen from all three countries have variously blamed foreign/extracontinental powers and arms salesmen for fomenting the widespread rumors of a renewed War of the Pacific.* Moreover, denials have emanated from each country that it is engaging in an arms race or harbors military ambitions; the dominant rationales for new arms demands have continued to be the modernization of obsolescent equipment and the maintenance of local power balances that discourage warfare and deter surprise attacks.

FUTURE PROSPECTS FOR ARMS CONTROL AND CONFLICT MANAGEMENT

Formal arms control agreements among suppliers, recipients, or both seem unlikely. Most, if not all, Latin American governments would

---

* The U.S. position on the Ayacucho Declaration and the Tripartite negotiations was to keep at a distance because of the sensitivities of these nations. The fear is that a strong U.S. involvement and/or encouragement would be perceived as an effort to keep these countries militarily weak and dependent on the United States. See the Hearings before the Subcommittee on Foreign Assistance, *International Security Assistance*, U.S. Senate, 94th Congress, 2nd Session, Washington, D.C., 1976, p. 26.

surely resent the imposition of a suppliers' agreement, or treatment as an arms control laboratory by the great powers. The United States and Western European countries seem unlikely to agree on arms limitations for Latin America. It is difficult to spot significant direct gains for the Europeans from entering into such an agreement for the distant Western Hemisphere.

While European interests in arms sales to Latin America appear to be primarily economic in nature, this is not the case with other important potential suppliers. In particular, the Soviet Union and Israel, and possibly Brazil in the not too distant future, seem to have political interests that militate against their potential agreement to arms control constraints. An arms control agreement does not seem to fit into Soviet interests, for the expansion of its politicomilitary presence as a great power in the developing world is closely linked to its capacity for arms transfers. USSR sales to Peru, and offers to several other Latin American countries, indicate that the Soviet Union is interested in gaining a foothold by penetrating a regional market heretofore, with the exception of Cuba, off-limits to Soviet arms. Soviet success in penetrating the Latin American market has been confined to Peru. Even favorable terms and Soviet promises of quick delivery of equipment, combined with local interests to assert independence of the United States, have not contributed to more Soviet sales in the region.

The assumption is made that a suppliers' agreement to curtail arms transfers would be likely to reduce conflict potential in Third World regions. Even if a suppliers' agreement could be fashioned, the consequences might exacerbate regional tensions and raise the potential for local military conflict. How might that be possible? In a number of cases in Latin America, Africa, and the Middle East, the acquisitions of advanced weapon systems seem more significant for their diplomatic symbolism than for their military capabilities. Depriving these governments of diplomatically useful symbols might increase the difficulties they may have in avoiding local politico-military disputes or negotiating their pacification. Moreover, intermediate and traditional weapon systems would probably remain available through indigenous production and secondary suppliers, both of which might well be boosted in case of a major suppliers' agreement. In fact, Latin American militaries would be more likely to focus on developing operational preparedness and to overreact militarily if serious diplomatic disputes arise. If such results seem possible, then peace might not be served by a suppliers' agreement to curtail arms transfers.

Latin American governments do have considerable interests in arriving at subregional arms control agreements. Arms acquisitions and rising border tensions have contributed directly to the deterioration both of the Andean Pact and of the Central American Common Market, two major efforts at integrated economic development. Yet the experiences involving the Ayacucho Declaration indicate that the outlook for institutionalized arms controls is dim. (More likely is the establishment of institutional mechanisms for conflict management, such as early-warning systems, command-and-control systems, and consultation bodies.)

Yet, despite the poor prospects for arms controls, military-diplomatic efforts made in their favor are still worthwhile to aid balancing, lessen chances of arms races, promote instances of self-restraint, and improve communications about intentions and capabilities among rivals (at the risk of confirming suspicions). Discussions and negotiations can be useful; symbolic temporization can help to pacify the current of affairs. Indeed, it is not inconsistent to arm for war and negotiate for peace at the same time. Having weapons may in fact be a precondition to having a voice in peace discussions, as has been illustrated in the past. At the inter-American conference convened in 1942 to settle the Peru–Ecuador conflict that cost Ecuador a piece of its territory, Ecuador was sternly criticized for having depended on the principles of international law and Pan Americanism for protection. The Ecuadorian representatives were admonished that these principles "exist to solve problems. You are not a problem for America. You, with your lack of military resistance, have not made your problem an American problem."* A recent episode is reminiscent of Ecuador's earlier experience. In 1978, after learning that the United States had blocked the sale of Israeli Kfir jets to Ecuador, its Minister of Foreign Affairs reportedly accused the United States of criminal action in selling arms to some countries while leaving others defenseless.

Any effort at arms control must thus deal with the basic fact that arms acquisitions are diplomacy by other means. Having arms, especially prestigious arms, appears to be essential for the successful conduct of traditional diplomacy. The acquisition and display of advanced weapons have seemed useful not so much to prepare for war as to gain effective diplomatic leverage in negotiating and resolving conflicts. For example, Guatemala's acquisition of Israeli arms

---

* The admonition of Ecuador for its inability to defend itself against Peru is described by Bryce Wood, *The United States and Latin American Wars, 1932–1942*, New York: Columbia University Press, 1966, p. 315.

lent greater credence to Guatemala's intentions and capabilities with regard to the Belize issue. The lessening of U.S. influence in Latin America and the expansion of intraregional relations probably mean that military diplomacy, based in part on the acquisition of prestigious weapons, will be increasingly significant in the conduct of intrahemispheric relations and in the resolution of potential conflicts. Particularly in South America a country deprived of arms modernization may well become diplomatically as well as militarily defenseless.

Thus in 1979 Peru's Foreign Minister said that arms purchases constitute a guarantee for the survival of his country. He noted that ". . . we are surrounded by countries which sometimes have had interests in conflict with those of Peru." In estimating the value of Peru's natural resources along its northern and southern frontiers to be in excess of $40 billion, de la Puente concluded that the approximately $1 billion spent on arms purchases in recent years represented ". . . an insurance premium cost at the rate of 1 to 40."

INTERNAL WAR, ARMS, AND HUMAN RIGHTS

Under the Carter Administration, policy guidelines sought to curtail arms transfers to governments that were found to be systematically violating human rights. The premises were that U.S. military programs should not help, even indirectly, to sustain such governments, that the denial of arms *might* provide some external leverage for inhibiting repressive practices in some countries, and that in any case U.S. ideals and interests would be better served by minimizing contact and association with security forces blamed for violations of human rights.

To some extent, the issue of human rights represents a reaction to the failure of democracy as the antidote both to dictatorship and to revolution. As authoritarian regimes undermined the hopes for democracy in the hemisphere, protest against violations of human rights became the central issue, and arms transfers were signaled out as a tool for leverage and punishment.*

---

* The fundamental premise of the human rights advocates within the Carter Administration was that "the way a regime treats its own people has to affect the quality of its relations with the United States." For a discussion of the debate over human rights and U.S. efforts to pressure foreign governments see "Human Rights and the 'National Interest': Which Takes Priority?" *Philosophy & Public Policy*, Vol. 1, No. 2, Spring 1981, pp. 6–8.

One Brazilian newspaper labeled U.S. human rights policy as representing realism for the strong and idealism for the weak. Indeed, human rights policies proved difficult to apply in an even fashion, since so many governments engaged in internal security tactics of "counterviolence." In practice, it was easiest to affect the smaller, less important governments, or those that are "inefficient" at violating human rights. It was most difficult to apply arms sanctions to the larger nations of the hemisphere.

Historical experiences suggest that, as a lever or instrument for changing the behavior of the arms recipient, the potential effectiveness of the human rights provision seems doubtful. It extends the tradition of restrictive legislation that has sought in the past to inhibit excessive resource diversion from economic development, to prevent the arming of oppressive military dictators, and to punish failures to compensate for expropriated U.S. policy. The provision is also in keeping with U.S. moves in the 1960s to influence local government successions or policies by suspending assistance and/or diplomatic recognition, for the intended purpose of levering outcomes that would be more in keeping with liberal democratic practices. These earlier paternalistic measures proved to be relatively ineffective, and their application often cost the United States political goodwill beyond the immediate case at hand.*

Such considerations indicate that U.S. curtailment of arms transfers does not lead to successful sanctions against government tendencies to violate the human rights of its citizens. Leaders of several governments in Latin America—most notably the Southern Cone countries of South America—have shown that they prefer to postpone or diminish relations with the United States over the short run rather than to succumb to U.S. influence and relinquish the use of techniques that have unfortunately proven brutally effective for destroying terrorist movements. U.S. human rights policies, these leaders insist, represent intolerable infringements of national sovereignty and intervention in domestic matters. Some changes in harsh

---

* The target of some restrictive amendments was not only Latin America but the Executive branch of the U.S. Government, which, from a variety of Congressional views, seemed lax in utilizing military and economic assistance to protect U.S. investments, tuna boats, human rights, and democratic government and discourage Latin American purchase of expensive and sophisticated military hardware. An excellent review of past efforts to dictate behavior via the supposed "leverage" obtained from U.S. assistance programs is provided in Herbert Goldhamer, *The Foreign Powers in Latin America*, Princeton, New Jersey: Princeton University Press, 1972, pp. 260–302.

government policies have been announced in several Southern Cone countries, but these changes have been largely cosmetic and carefully attuned to improving national images abroad.

Whether these unilateral efforts by the United States to improve the human rights conditions in numerous countries of the hemisphere could have been more effective with the cooperation of European arms suppliers is open to conjecture. The fact was that each regime subjected to an arms cut-off by the United States found, for the most part, other sources for its military needs. What kind and level of *cooperation* would it have taken to make the U.S. position on human rights prevail in the Western Hemisphere? What kinds of weapon acquisitions need to be targeted for denial? The least detectable, least expensive weapons, which are *operationally* used in the violation of human rights? Or, the larger, more expensive, easily detected weapons that fulfill *symbolic* military functions? The most significant portion of dollar value arms acquisition goes for sophisticated weapon systems (aircraft, seacraft, missiles, etc.) that have little, if anything to do with human rights violations.

THE GOVERNANCE OF ARMS ACQUISITIONS: A FRAMEWORK FOR DISCUSSION*

Given the particular circumstances of the symbolic functions of modern, sophisticated weapons, the festering conflicts along various borders, and the cyclical nature of the internal warfare in the Western Hemisphere, it would seem that efforts to bring about *restraints* in the acquisition of arms must start at the *subregional* level, among groups of countries. To be effective, an *arms restraint regime* would have to:

1. develop over a period of time on the basis of a common set of technical military standards;

2. satisfy the basic national defense requirements of each nation;

3. gain the cooperation of the *major* (from some 25 nations) arms suppliers for the hemisphere.

---

* For a critical review of arms control efforts and arms sales policies see Richard K. Betts, "The Tragicomedy of Arms Trade Control," *International Security*, Vol. 5, No. 1, Summer 1980, pp. 80–110.

The basis of such a regime is *not* to prevent the acquisition of arms by Latin American nations, nor to cut out the extrahemisphere arms suppliers, but to gain the acceptance of numerous sets of subregional arms arrangements by the parties involved. In terms of *arms acquisition volume* for the Latin American region as a whole, "The Big Seven" consumers (Cuba, Venezuela, Ecuador, Peru, Chile, Argentina, and Brazil) receive 75% to 85% of the dollar value of weapon imports, and "The Big Seven" suppliers (United States, Soviet Union, France, United Kingdom, Federal Republic of Germany, Italy, and Israel) provide over 90% of the transfers in hardware, support, training, and technical assistance. To propose an effective framework for the governance of arms acquisitions in the hemisphere, the focus is on a small number of supplier and consumer nations. To talk in terms of a region is thus the first conceptual error that should be corrected.

To be able to operationalize a series of arms restraint regimes in the hemisphere, three interrelated pillars would be essential. The basic premise of this approach is that *arms restraint initiatives must begin with the arms-acquiring nations*—otherwise, such efforts at governance are doomed to failure. The elements of an arms restraint regime include *institutions* for consultative dialogue between sets of nations and a *paradigm* for negotiation that maintains standards in three areas of arms acquisitions—the *quantity* of weapon transfers, the *quality* of the military hardware, and the level of *military expenditures.* Such an approach would reflect the particular circumstances of the subregion desiring the implementation of an arms restraint regime.

It would be misleading to suggest that arms restraints promote domestic peace, resolve border disputes, and establish regional stability. The minimal first step of an arms restraint regime would be to seek acceptance of such ideas as *information exchange*, *consultative meetings*, *arms acquisition paradigm*, and the *political will to negotiate* on matters of military hardware procurement.

Again, the fundamental idea would not be to prevent the acquisition of weapons but to establish a system that would encourage *consultation* prior to an anticipated purchase. A further concern would be to establish a paradigm that accounts for the military and economic disparaties between groups of nations—thus providing a flexibility for the appropriate *qualitative* modernization of individual armed forces. The purpose is to help reduce anxiety and suspicion brought about by the constant drama of the global arms business and to minimize the likelihood of surprise purchases of major weapons by neighbors.* For the most part, the collateral problems associated with the acquisition of arms have to do with the reactions of nations along common borders. The only exceptions are Cuba and, most recently, Nicaragua. Arms acquisitions by both are looked upon by many noncontiguous nations as threatening and destabilizing for ideological reasons.

While the arms restraint initiative must of necessity originate with the recipient nations of the hemisphere, supplier cooperation will eventually have to be forthcoming. The economic requirements of the European suppliers, along with the legitimate defense needs of the hemisphere, can be accommodated within a series of arms restraint regimes. Suppliers would be guaranteed access to the Latin American market and, just as importantly, the nations of the hemisphere would be guaranteed access to arms and logistical support. The obligations of the supplier nations would be involvement in subregional consultative discussions, cautious promotion of new weapon systems, and willingness to accept any arms acquisition standards set by a group of nations making up a subregion.

This approach can only offer a beginning for the just governance of arms acquisitions in the Western Hemisphere. Any notion of a global arms control policy is unrealistic and possesses numerous political shortcomings. Arms will remain a vital element of diplomacy and politics for both the suppliers and consumers of arms in the Western Hemisphere for the remainder of this decade, if not beyond. Thus, we should strive for modest progress in the *management*—not the prevention—of arms acquisitions.

---

* One popular view of the global arms market and the unrelenting merchants of modern weaponry is depicted by Anthony Sampson, *The Arms Bazaar*, New York: The Viking Press, 1978.

12

Nuclear Trends in Latin America

John Redick

INTRODUCTION

The consumption of energy by developing countries will, by most estimates, increase dramatically in the next two decades.[1] Whether nuclear energy will be providing an increasing percentage of the total for developing countries is questionable. According to a recent World Bank study, less than 2% of the electricity currently consumed by developing countries is supplied by nuclear power. Installed nuclear capacity in developing countries is centered in Argentina, Brazil, India, The Republic of Korea, and Pakistan, to be followed within several years by units in Mexico, The Philippines, Romania, and Yugoslavia.[2] By the year 2000, approximately 30 developing countries could be providing nuclear power according to the International Atomic Energy Agency (IAEA).[3]

A variety of problems are retarding the growth of nuclear energy in developing countries, including expense and difficulty of international financing, rising domestic environmental and safety challenges—enlarged by the impact of the Three Mile Island accident in the US—and problems of scale—small national grids relative to the large units, 600 megawatts (MWe) and up, which are available from foreign vendors. However, the dramatically rising costs of crude oil and the vulnerability of many countries to interruption of foreign supplies (i.e., Brazil relative to oil from Iraq) provides nuclear energy with continued appeal to energy-deficient developing countries.

In the view of some experts, the Latin American region may be one of the most favorable areas in the world for the expansion of nuclear power. One respected U.S. trade publication has recently identified Latin America as "the largest export market for reactor vendors in the next twenty years" and suggests there could be 20 to 30 operating power reactors and 30 to 40 under construction by the year 2000.[4] The former Executive Secretary of the Inter-American Nuclear Energy Commission (IANEC) of the Organization of American States (OAS) has argued that nuclear energy, already an important factor in Argentina, Brazil, and Mexico, can and should be justified for introducion in the next ten years for electric power in Venezuela, Colombia, Peru, and Chile.[5]

Despite these and other optimistic views on nuclear power's future in Latin America, at least two cautionary observations should be made. First, Latin American countries as a whole are and will continue to be dependent on oil and gas for their major source of energy throughout the decade (over 60%), whereas nuclear's projected share is not significant. Coal is significant in Colombia and hydropower in Brazil and to a lesser extent in other countries.[6] Non-conventional and new and renewable sources of energy amount to less than 1% of the region's current total and could be increased somewhat in the future. However, by the mid-1980s it is estimated that less than 5% of Latin America's total power will be supplied by nuclear facilities.[7]

Second, the development and application of nuclear power by the more advanced Latin American nations has been an unhappy and excruciating process, marked by bitterness and frustration. In Argentina, Brazil, and Mexico nuclear energy has meant expensive cost overruns, delayed completion dates, and, more seriously, highly undesirable clashes with advanced supplier countries, particularly the United States. Other countries at an earlier stage of their nuclear development, such as Peru and Chile, have also experienced similar frustrations, though on a smaller scale. To this must be added a growing sensitivity to environmental and safety concerns, producing, in some cases, unwelcome internal opposition (a growing factor in Brazil).

However the commitment of major Latin American countries to nuclear power is growing. Argentina, Brazil, and Mexico are or will be operating nuclear power reactors by 1981–1982, with the former two countries making significant strides toward independent control of the nuclear fuel cycle as well as development of heavy reactor support industries (especially Brazil). Active nuclear research programs and pilot reactors exist in these three nations and, at varying levels, in nearly every other South American nation and Cuba. There is also growing interest in small and medium-sized power reactors, raising the possibility of cooperative efforts among Latin American countries.[8] Growing Latin American nuclear programs are accompanied by varying degrees of commitment to the international nonproliferation regime as evidenced by the Tlatelolco Treaty of 1967 and the Non-Proliferation Treaty (NPT) of 1968.

This chapter describes current nuclear programs of Latin American countries, with particular attention given to the significance of the May 1980 nuclear agreement between Argentina and Brazil. The danger of nuclear weapons development and the position of Latin American countries regarding international and regional nonproliferation efforts are considered. Finally, attention is given to existing Latin American institutional arrangements associated with nuclear energy and proliferation, and possibilities are suggested for their future evolution.

LATIN AMERICAN NUCLEAR PROGRAMS

Argentina

Argentina retains a position of leadership among Latin American countries in the development and implementation of nuclear power. Insulated from domestic challenges, the Argentine nuclear program has been characterized by steady progress toward well-defined objectives. In early 1981, it remains the only Latin American country with an operating nuclear power reactor, a small fuel fabrication plant, and a pilot heavy water production facility. Moreover, Argentinian experts have gained some useful early experience with reprocessing technology.

While Argentina has been affected by the global rise in energy costs, the impact has not been extensive relative to countries having far greater dependency on imported petroleum. Argentine oil output is increasing, and some Argentine sources estimate that the nation will reach self-sufficiency in the early 1980s. In 1980, nuclear power accounted for approximately 4% of the total national electric production and is projected to contribute approximately 10% by 1995.

Current details on the Argentine nuclear program are included in the appendix.

Argentina's first power reactor, a 370-MWe German-supplied natural uranium unit, has been in operation since 1974. The nation's second power reactor, a Canadian-supplied 600-MWe natural uranium unit (Embalse), is scheduled for completion in May of 1981. A third power facility (Atucha 2), a 750-MWe unit supplied by the German company KWU, is scheduled for completion in 1987. Following its completion, current plans call for at least three additional plants of approximately 600-MWe in capacity to be operational in 1991, 1994–5, and 1997.

Argentina's decision of October 1979 to award its third reactor contract to the Federal Republic of Germany and an accompanying heavy water production contract to a Swiss company has created subsequent difficulties for Argentina in its relations with the United States. A number of factors contributed to Argentina's choice of Germany over the prime competitor, Canada. These include a very favorable operational experience of the German-supplied Atucha 1 and a variety of economic and political obstacles that have surrounded and delayed construction of the Canadian-supplied second unit now nearing completion in Cordoba province. However, the critical factor leading to the Argentine decision for the somewhat larger and more expensive German unit was Canadian insistence on fullscope safeguards, in contrast to the more flexible German approach. Argentina split its order, thus avoiding fullscope safeguards from either the Swiss or Germans.

Carter administration officials were particularly concerned over the fact that the Argentines would escape fullscope safeguards and would gain access to industrial-scale heavy water technology. Consequently, considerable pressure was exerted on both Switzerland and Germany to require very tight defacto safeguards.[9] An additional method of pressure utilized by the United States in 1980 was a hold-up in approval of a reactor vessel subcontract, which was to be supplied by the U.S. firm Combustion Engineering (CE), as well as a hold-up of U.S.-supplied low enriched uranium for an Argentine research reactor.

In an effort to appease the United States (and possibly obtain an Argentine commitment to more stringent safeguards), the German government in the spring of 1980 temporarily refused to grant an export license to the German company KWU. Argentina reacted to U.S. and German pressure by sending a high-level CNEA delegation to the Soviet Union to explore the possibility of Soviet supply of components for nuclear plants and low enriched uranium, and by reopening discussions with Canada regarding the possible supply of the next several power reactors (which Germany had been considered likely to supply). The Argentine nod toward the Soviet Union was generally considered a ploy to divert U.S. pressure. Confronted by the Soviet move into Afghanistan (and Argentine grain sales to the Soviets), the Carter administration did approve, in June 1980, with the support of the U.S. Nuclear Regulatory Commission, shipment of a small order of low enriched uranium to Argentina. This shipment was approved despite the fact that the March 10, 1980, deadline mandated by the Nuclear Non-Proliferation Act of 1978 had passed. However, reflecting the deep divisions in the Carter administration regarding Argentina, the U.S. firm Combustion Engineering was prevented from obtaining the Argentine subcontract, which was awarded to a German concern in August 1980.[10] In early 1981, Argentina contracted with the Soviet Union to receive a supply of heavy water sufficient for its purposes until a Swiss-built industrial scale unit becomes operational in 1983.

The Argentine commitment to complete an independent development of the nuclear fuel cycle seems irreversible. Argentine policy makers have adroitly managed to take advantage of commercial rivalries and variations in nonproliferation policies among major nuclear suppliers (Canada, the United States, Germany, Switzerland) to gain access to advanced nuclear technology. And, despite divisions in many other areas, the Argentine leadership appears united that nuclear energy is vital to the nation's future development and security and that it will continue to be an important tool for pursuing other regional and international foreign policy goals.

Brazil

Brazil's current leadership remains committed to a strong nuclear program, although internal criticism, both within and out of government, is increasing. There is rising sensitivity to safety issues, with the Three Mile Island accident having a definite impact. In addition there are enhanced environmental concerns, with considerable regional opposition expressed to government plans for future siting of nuclear power plants. However, the dominant factor influencing the nuclear program is the devastating impact of rising costs of imported petroleum. In the short term this is causing a discernible slowdown in the ambitious and highly publicized nuclear program.

According to Brazilian government sources, in 1979 the nation produced 15% of the oil it consumed and imported 1 million barrels per day at a yearly cost of between $6.5 and $7.5 billion. In 1980 this amount reached $11 billion and is expected to reach $13 billion in 1981. The impact of this on the nation's balance of payment and overall economic health has prompted the government to undertake ambitious programs for alternative fuels, including alcohol, and to emphasize hydroelectric development further. Currently hydropower provides around 15% of Brazil's total consumed energy, with an equal amount contributed by wood, bagasse, and charcoal. According to recent estimates, hydropower will contribute around 33% of total energy consumption by the year 1987 and be reduced to 28% by the year 2000; wood, bagasse, and charcoal will decline to 16% by 1987 and 8% by the year 2000.[11] It is planned that nuclear power will make up the difference between the demand for electricity and the capability to supply it (primarily through hydro as well as other energy sources). Nuclear's contribution to consumed electricity will be about 5% early in the decade, reaching 10% by the end and as high as 32% by the year 2000 (electricity's portion of the total energy consumed in Brazil is currently around 30% and will reach 45% by the year 2000).[12]

Testing was undertaken in 1980 on the nation's first (Angra 1) 626-MWe U.S.-supplied light water reactor, with start-up time scheduled for May 1981. Work on Angra 2, the 1245-MWe light water unit supplied by the Federal Republic of Germany, was postponed to mid-1980 due to structural and seismic problems, with a completion date set for late 1980s. A new site for the second German unit, Angra 3, was selected in mid-1980, with a completion date optimistically set for 1988. Sites on the Atlantic coast of the state of São Paulo for the third and fourth German units (units 4 and 5) were announced by President Figueiredo in the summer of 1980.[13]

Cost estimates for the German contract have risen dramatically (now above $30 billion) and this, as well as rising environmental and safety consciousness, is exacerbating opposition to nuclear energy. In 1980 alone there were several congressional investigations of the nuclear program, mounting press criticism, continuing opposition within certain scientific circles, and growing criticism of the nuclear program from other hard-pressed government agencies. Nuclear supporters reacted by blaming a variety of internal and external sources for the opposition, including the United States, the Soviet Union, Jewish influence, and so forth. It is obvious that by early 1981 costs more than any other factor will necessitate a slow-down of the timetable for implementation of the nuclear program. Current details on the Brazilian nuclear program are included in the appendix.

Other questions persist for Brazil's nuclear program, including the contract with URENCO (from which it is to receive enriched uranium for the German power units). Construction delays for the German supplied power units have caused the projected Brazilian demand for enrichment services to be much less than the original amounts covered in the contract, which will now need to be renegotiated. In addition, there is a related if somewhat cloudy issue of a plutonium storage arrangement, which, according to the original agreement required by the Dutch through URENCO, must be in place before enriched uranium is supplied.

The Brazilian nuclear program confronts many challenges, not the least of which is growing economic constraints. It is likely that the program will face further revisions in the near future, but barring some major and unanticipated economic reverse the nation seems committed to continued introduction of nuclear energy and eventual control of all aspects of the nuclear fuel cycle.

Mexico

Mexico's policy toward nuclear power development is cautious, reflecting its extensive petroleum reserves. Until 1974 a net importer of oil, Mexico is currently estimated to have reserves in excess of 200 billion barrels. Oil and gas production in the first quarter of 1980 was approximately 2 million barrels a day, with a maximum of 2.5 million set for 1980 (70% of Mexico's total oil imports are sent to the United States, although Mexico would like to reduce this percentage to 60%).[14] Petroleum currently accounts for 52%, hydro for 21% and coal for 20% of total energy consumption.[15]

Mexico's first nuclear power plant, a 654-MWe U.S.-supplied light water unit, is set for May 1982 start up with an identical U.S.-supplied unit scheduled for one year later. When completed, the two units will supply nearly 10% of the nation's total electric power needs. Similar to the more newsworthy disagreements over natural gas, the construction of the U.S.-supplied reactors has led to considerable friction between the two countries. Perennial Mexican suspicions were enhanced by a perception that the United States was seeking to interfere with their nuclear program through the requirements of the Nuclear Non-Proliferation Act of 1978. The first unit was scheduled to be completed by 1977, but problems relating both to U.S. legislation as well as to construction obstacles led to a long delay in issuing an export license (for ultimate delivery of the enriched uranium) until February of 1979. Mexican officials strongly resent such restrictions as unnecessary and unwarranted, due to the involvement of the IAEA in the arrangement, the fact that the entire Mexican program is under fullscope safeguards, and Mexico's leadership in nonproliferation (particularly with respect to the Latin American nuclear-weapon-free zone agreement).[16]

It is also notable that, while Mexico did award the contract for its first nuclear power unit to the United States, it insisted that the enriched uranium be obtained under IAEA auspices, the first such request in history to that body for fuel for a power reactor. The core for the first unit will be fueled by uranium purchased by Mexico from France and enriched by the United States (with which Mexico now has two ten-year enrichment contracts). Future uranium will be Mexican, and enrichment services may well be purchased from European producers. The important point in the view of Mexican policy makers was to emphasize the involvement of a multilateral agency, the IAEA, and to minimize any dependence on one foreign supplier, particularly the United States.

Mexico possesses 11,000 tons of proven uranium reserves, with estimated reserves as high as 600,000 tons. Yellowcake production is projected to be 385 metric tons by 1981.[17] A small fuel fabrication facility does exist, with plans for a larger facility in the indefinite future (the United States currently supplies fabrication services). A small reprocessing facility was constructed several years ago with the assistance of the IAEA. Mexico lacks domestic capabilities for heavy component manufacturing, although a recent Swedish study suggested that the nation could establish complete independence by the 1990s.[18] Recent programs for cooperation with Spain and France for uranium exploration and development have also been negotiated.

Mexico is discussing with a number of foreign suppliers (Canada, France, Sweden) the next steps in its nuclear program. U.S. companies appear to be out of the running for this contract. Differences of view and a degree of uncertainty currently exists within Mexico as to how quickly the country will implement the next phase of its nuclear program. In early 1981 there was growing speculation that Mexico would call for bids for up to 2400 MWe in 1982, as part of an eventual goal of 20,000 MWe by the year 2000.[19]

It is anticipated that nuclear energy will supply nearly 30% of the nation's total energy requirements by the turn of the century. Mexico will continue to view its nuclear energy program as one component of an energy diversification program and will avoid becoming linked to one supplier for advanced nuclear technology, as has Brazil. Current trends would also suggest that the country will put considerable emphasis on the domestic production of uranium as well as independent control of the nuclear fuel cycle, moving eventually toward manufacture of heavy components. In its arrangements with more advanced nuclear supplier countries, Mexico will use (and already is using) its oil as leverage. It would also be very much in keeping with Mexico's traditional foreign policy emphasis to develop a linkage with multinational organizations such as EURODIF and COREDIF rather than an individual supplier for its enriched uranium. Mexican investment in multinational nuclear arrangements, as well as the possible spearheading of a regional cooperative effort in the nuclear fuel cycle among the Latin American nations, is a distinct possibility in the future.

Chile

After Argentina, Brazil, and Mexico, Chile has the most advanced nuclear program in Latin America and is closest to having the technical ability to develop nuclear weapons. The Tlatelolco Treaty is not in force for Chile, and that nation rejects the NPT. A 5-MW research reactor purchased from Great Britain operates at the outskirts of Santiago, and a larger test reactor located at the foothills of the Andes, approximately 15 miles from Santiago (Aguirre), was constructed with the assistance of the Spanish nuclear energy commission. The initial load of enriched uranium at 80–90% was supplied by France. However, under U.S. pressure, highly enriched uranium is no longer available, and the facility was shut down while Chilean engineers sought to convert it to function on low enriched uranium.[20] Chile hopes ultimately to bring the unit up to 10 MW, assuming it is able to obtain enriched uranium from the United States or elsewhere.

Chile is also undertaking a careful planning program with the assistance of the U.S. consulting firm Dames and Moore, pursuant to construction of the nation's first nuclear power reactor. However, economic constraints and clear differences of view between the Chilean Nuclear Energy Commission (COCHEN) dominated by the military and the more civilian-oriented energy commission have caused delays. In early 1980, the Chilean minister of mines and energy announced that the nation would postpone until 1985 a decision to begin studies on a 600-MWe nuclear power plant, because coal and petroleum still remained cheaper than nuclear in terms of the nation's energy needs.[21]

Unlike U.S. relations with Argentina and Brazil, the nuclear issue has been fully eclipsed by human rights considerations, primarily as a result of the Letelier assassination. The result has been virtually no U.S.–Chilean cooperation in the nuclear area for several years, despite clear Chilean indications of a willingness to divorce nuclear from other political issues and conceivably to accept fullscope safeguards and Tlatelolco membership without reservations. The decision by the Reagan administration in early 1981 to improve relations with Chile may also lead to renewed cooperation on nuclear issues.

Peru

In contrast to its southern rival Chile, Peru is a party to both NPT and the Tlatelolco Treaty. However, the Peruvian representative startled participants in the August 1980 NPT Review Conference (Geneva) by announcing that his nation would seriously consider withdrawing from the global nonproliferation agreement if rapid progress toward disarmament and the sharing of nuclear technology was not achieved in the near future. (The Peruvians have argued in earlier forums that the Tlatelolco Treaty with fullscope IAEA safeguards is sufficient to ensure a nonproliferation status).

The Peruvian program administered by the Instituto Peruano De Energia Nuclear (IPEN) has been defined by Peruvian officials as focusing on basic support, including uranium prospecting and planning (through 1982), basic internal training and development of a trained group of scientists and technicians (mid to late 1980s), and installation of nuclear power units (late 1980s).[22] In late 1980, IPEN was designated to become the lead body for the Latin American uranium exploration program of the OAS. It is designed to promote cooperative efforts to identify new uranium deposits in Argentina, Chile, Ecuador, and Peru.

Considerable attention has been given to Peru's 1977 agreement with Argentina, whereby the latter provided training as well as a zero power reactor. Argentina also supplied 14 kg of U.S.-origin enriched uranium under IAEA safeguards, which was to be returned ultimately to Argentina. Also under the supplemented agreement, Argentina is receiving a 10-MW test reactor, scheduled to be in operation in 1982. As is true with Chile, the nation has uranium deposits of uncertain amounts and is enlarging its mining facilities in the Andes. In June of 1980 the United States and Peru signed an agreement whereby Peru will receive enriched uranium.

Colombia

Colombia is a party to the Tlatelolco Treaty but has not ratified the NPT. However, it has completed a program of fullscope safeguards with the IAEA under the Tlatelolco Treaty. The nation possesses adequate deposits of coal and petroleum and has recently initiated major hydroelectric and thermal projects designed to cover the nation's energy needs through the late 1980s. However, until around 1982 Colombia will need to import some petroleum to meet its energy needs. Interest is growing in nuclear energy with increasing indications of significant uranium deposits. Contracts for uranium exploration exist with France and Japan, and in 1978 a major contract was signed with Spain for a $500 million investment in a new state-controlled company for exploration and production of uranium. Uranium production was expected to begin in 1980. Long-term plans call for establishment of the nation's first nuclear power facility between 1990 and 2000.

Venezuela

Venezuela is a strong supporter of nonproliferation, being a party both to NPT and to Tlatelolco. Recently Venezuela's apparent lack of interest in nuclear energy, as a result of its vast petroleum reserves, has shifted, and there are growing indications that the nation may purchase one or more nuclear power units in the future. Venezuela has agreements with Italy and the Federal Republic of Germany for nuclear cooperation. Significant uranium and thorium deposits exist in the eastern provinces, particularly in those also claimed by Guyana. In 1979 Venezuela signed nuclear agreements with both Brazil and Argentina. Both agreements called for cooperation and transfer of information on research and power reactors to Venezuela. Brazil's motivation in part was a desire ultimately to trade nuclear technology for access to Venezuelan oil.

Cuba

The Soviet Union is training Cuban scientists and technicians and is constructing an 880-MWe facility (2 units of 440 MWe each), to be completed by 1990. It has been suggested that the center could ultimately be expanded to 4 units. Some initial work was begun on the center as early as 1976, with an estimated completion date in the early to mid-1980s. However, there have been a series of delays in actual construction because of seismological concerns and economic constraints. In 1980 Cuba also completed, with Soviet assistance, a zero-power reactor incapable of producing militarily significant quantities of plutonium. The two nuclear power units will be built in Czechoslovakia and shipped to Cuba.

Cuba is a party neither to Tlatelolco nor to the NPT. However, it is a member of the IAEA and on May 5, 1980, signed a safeguards agreement with that organization in relationship to an agreement with the Soviet Union for construction of the aforementioned nuclear plant. The agreement "corresponds in substance to those of other safeguard agreements concluded by the Agency in recent years with nonnuclear-weapon states not party to the Non-Proliferation Treaty (NPT)."[23] It is likely that Soviets will require return of spent fuel, as it routinely does for its other Eastern European clients.[24]

The Soviets have ratified Protocol II of the Tlatelolco Treaty, which no doubt has impacted on Cuba's previous rigid opposition. Cuban statements made before the First Committee of the UN General Assembly in 1978 and to the UN Disarmament Commission in May of 1980 indicate a gradual softening of attitudes and may foretell eventual Cuban adherence to the regional agreement, assuming a relaxation of tension with the United States.[25] Discussions have continued between Mexico and Cuba, including a 1980 visit by President Portillo, which resulted in a significant Cuban–Mexican oil technology agreement in December 1980. U.S.–Cuban contacts on Tlatelolco have continued, and Cuban officials have stressed the importance of resolution of other bilateral differences (including the return of Guantanamo); the United States has stressed that Tlatelolco is not a bilateral issue between the two countries.[26] The worsening of U.S.–Cuban relations with the advent of the Reagan administration has reduced chances of Cuban adherence to Tlatelolco.

Ecuador

Ecuador is a party to the NPT and Tlatelolco, having been a leader in the efforts to create a regional nuclear-weapon-free zone. The nation has considerable petroleum reserves and this, as well as a small national grid, has not, until recently, resulted in much interest in nuclear energy. However, the probable existence of rich uranium reserves led to a decision in 1979 by the Ecuadorian atomic energy commission (CEEA) to begin an accelerated program of uranium exploration and development.[27] The CEEA also signed an agreement with the Spanish nuclear energy agency in 1979 for the construction of a nuclear study center in Ecuador, including a research reactor.

Bolivia

Bolivia is also a party both to the NPT and to Tlatelolco. The nation has a wealth of mineral resources that have traditionally been the subject of both Argentine and Brazilian interest. Bolivia signed an agreement for nuclear cooperation with Argentina in 1970, which has been supplemented in 1978 and again in 1980. Bolivia had contracted earlier with a British concern to supply a 1.5-MW research reactor, but this agreement was apparently eclipsed by the 1980 agreement with Argentina. Under that agreement, Bolivia will receive a sub-critical unit, followed by a research reactor of between 3 and 10 MW and possibly a larger unit at a later point. Bolivian experts will be trained in Argentina and assist with construction. The director of the Bolivian nuclear energy commission (COBOEN) has stated that nuclear power could be feasible for the nation around 1995 or later.[28] Italy has a cooperative arrangement with Bolivia for uranium exploration, and domestic investment in uranium production was significantly increased in 1980.

Uruguay

While a national commission on nuclear energy was established only in 1979, the nation has benefited by nuclear cooperation with both Argentina and Brazil. Some nuclear training has been supplied by the United Nations Development Programme (UNDP), which has also given aid to other Latin American countries such as Peru and Chile. A 1-MW research reactor has operated since the mid-1970s. In late 1980, Uruguay signed an agreement for nuclear cooperation with Chile to include exchange of personnel, materials, and equipment. Uruguay is a party to the NPT and Tlatelolco.

Paraguay

Considerable uranium deposits are thought to exist in the nation. This has led to much foreign interest, especially on the part of private concerns from South Korea, Taiwan, and the United States. Taiwan appears to be looking to Paraguay as a major potential future source of uranium for its ambitious nuclear power program. In early 1980, a major agreement was signed, by which a U.S. company will provide 50%, with 25% each from South Korea and Taiwan, for exploration and development of hundreds of thousands of acres of Paraguayan land thought to hold high reserves of uranium.[29] Paraguay is a party to the NPT and Tlatelolco.

REGIONAL TRENDS:
TRANSFER OF TECHNOLOGY

The development of nuclear technology in the Latin American region is resulting in three discernible emerging trends: (1) a movement by Latin American countries away from cooperation with the United States; (2) more bilateral nuclear cooperation among Latin American countries; and (3) growing instances of cooperation between Latin American and non-Latin American countries. A fourth trend of even greater significance, Argentine–Brazilian nuclear convergence, is covered in a following section.

Latin American nations are clearly shifting away from a close nuclear relationship with the United States. This is particularly true of the more advanced nations—Argentina, Brazil, and Mexico—which are demonstrating a clear preference for closer relations with European suppliers. These nations argue that U.S. policy, rather than their own policy preferences, have driven them from cooperation with the United States. The important point is that this represents a fairly dramatic shift away from nearly total U.S. dominance in the region, beginning with the Atoms for Peace Program and through the late 1960s. Several Latin American countries—Argentina, Brazil, Colombia, Chile, Venezuela—were initially tied to the United States through the purchase of test reactors and subsequent enriched uranium contracts. However, the 1968 decision by Argentina to purchase a

German natural uranium power unit over lower-cost bids from the United States symbolized the beginning of a trend.

While a U.S. vendor was successful in securing Brazil's first power unit, as has been noted earlier, subsequent units will come from Germany and enriched uranium from URENCO. Argentina is committed to Germany and Canada for its future reactor needs. Mexico, after purchasing its first two power units from a U.S. company, is leaning toward France and has given clear indications of not intending to purchase again from the United States. Each of these three Latin American countries has experienced difficulties in relations with the United States over nuclear issues, with the Brazil–U.S. 1975–76 dispute becoming a major flash-point contributing to President Carter's Nuclear Power Policy Statement in 1977 and to the passage of the Nuclear Non-Proliferation Act (NNPA) of 1978. Carter's policy guidelines and the NNPA requiring renegotiation of all existing agreements for nuclear cooperation have engendered friction between the United States and Latin American countries and considerable doubt as to the reliability of the United States in its contractural arrangements. The U.S.-led Nuclear Supplier Guidelines have also produced great resentment in Argentina and Brazil. In summary, Latin American leaders have widely perceived U.S. policy to be one of technological denial, and the resulting resentment and ill feeling has probably not enhanced the goal of nonproliferation in the region.

Bilateral nuclear cooperation among Latin American countries and growing examples of transfer of nuclear technology have been referred to at various points earlier in this chapter.[30] Both Argentina and Brazil have developed cooperative nuclear arrangements with other Latin American countries, driven in part by larger geopolitical or economic goals. Of the two, Argentina has been the more active and for a longer period of time. Argentina hopes to become a regional supplier of heavy water (following completion of the Swiss unit), research reactors, and other nuclear material. Its most significant agreements are with Peru and Bolivia, for which it is supplying small research reactors. Agreements also exist with Chile, Ecuador, Venezuela, Colombia, Uruguay, and Paraguay.

Brazil's commitment to bilateral cooperation has become more sustained since 1979. The principal emphasis has been economic—a need to utilize its idle heavy nuclear manufacturing capability imported from Germany, as well as a hope of trading advanced nuclear technology for oil. Brazil's first tangible effort was a 1979 agreement with Venezuela, which raised the prospect of possible sale of Brazilian components for power reactors in the future.[31] Oil was also a major incentive for a low-level 1979 agreement with Mexico. In March of 1980, Brazil and Colombia signed a preliminary agreement for nuclear cooperation as part of a more extensive arrangement pursuant to exploitation of Colombian coal reserves.

Of greater political interest were steps initiated in early 1980, which could result in a Brazilian-Chilean agreement for transfer of some Brazilian nuclear equipment in exchange for permission for Brazilian petroleum prospecting on Chile's southern continental shelf. Chile's interest was clearly prompted in part by a desire to convey the impression of Brazilian support for its long-festering territorial dispute with Argentina, as well as a fear that its northern rival, Peru, was making rapid strides in nuclear development with the assistance of the United States and Argentina. While Brazilian officials have reacted cautiously to the Chilean interest, an agreement for nuclear cooperation was negotiated as part of a package arrangement during President Figueiredo's visit to Chile in late 1980.

Agreements for nuclear cooperation between Latin American and developing countries from other regions are also increasing. In a number of cases these non-Latin American countries are not fully covered under the nonproliferation regime, and some are correctly considered threshold countries. Spain, a country that is not party to the NPT and has at least one facility not covered by IAEA safeguards has been particularly active in Latin America.[32] Agreements for cooperation exist between Spain and Chile, Ecuador, Mexico, Argentina, Brazil, and others. An Argentine agreement with India, a "PNE" state that has taken a similar approach to the nuclear fuel cycle, has evoked interest, as has a similar arrangement with Libya. In February of 1980, Argentina signed an agreement for sharing nuclear power development information with South Korea, also considered by many to be a threshold country despite the fact it is an NPT party.

Both Argentina and Brazil previously had close involvement in the Iranian nuclear program, until the fall of the Shah. Brazil's 1980 agreement with Iraq (from which it, until recently, received nearly 50% of its imported oil) raised a concern of some that Brazil might at some future point transfer sensitive technology received from Germany. These, and other examples that could be cited, are a part of a trend toward gradual reorientation of Latin American policies toward cooperation with advanced developing countries from other regions. It also represents an enhanced international involvement and interaction on the part of Latin American countries in which nuclear power is but one small component—although with large implications for peace and security.

REGIONAL TRENDS:
ARGENTINA-BRAZILIAN NUCLEAR CONVERGENCE

Argentina and Brazil signed an important agreement for nuclear co-operation on May 18, 1980. At the time of the signing the Brazilian newspaper *O Estado De Sao Paulo* editorialized that no one had hurt the Brazilian position in Latin America more than had former U.S. President Richard Nixon when he declared some years ago that "where Brazil leans, so will Latin America." While Nixon's statement had conveyed an impression of Brazilian subimperialism in Latin America as a U.S. proxy, the true implication of the recent Argentine-Brazilian nuclear agreement, according to the editorial, was "where Brazilian-Argentine relations lean, so will Latin America." [33]

The agreement, which covers far more than nuclear power, represents a historic step toward more orderly and predictable bilateral relations, as well as a dampening of the two nations' long nuclear rivalry. When implemented, the agreement could contribute significantly to the overall stability of the Latin American region and to the goal of nonproliferation.

Geopolitical competition, particularly in the Southern Cone of South America, is an important concern to both countries. This is clearly illustrated in the nuclear area with early installation of nuclear power yielding clear advantages to Argentina, which in turn moved to consolidate them through agreements for nuclear co-operation with other Latin American countries. The Argentine-Brazilian competition, however, has stood in sharp contrast to other more troubled areas such as South Asia (India-Pakistan) and the Middle East (Arab-Israel) due to relative absence of armed conflicts in modern times, lack of official rhetoric, and considerable mutual restraint. That nuclear energy should ultimately serve as the catalyst for rapprochement has a certain logic, given the historic context of the Argentine-Brazilian relationship. That is, nuclear energy is the one significant area where Argentina retains at least a short-term superiority over its surging northern neighbor. An agreement, with nuclear energy as the capstone, allowed Argentina the opportunity to trade something of perceived value—a subtle but important component in the chemistry of Argentinian-Brazilian relations.

Disputes over the development of the immensely rich River Plate Basin had been a critical issue dividing Argentina and Brazil for nearly two decades. Solution of these protracted issues, particularly as related to the construction of hydroelectric dams, have long been considered a prerequisite to possible cooperation in the nuclear area. An October 1979 agreement between Argentina, Brazil, and Paraguay over dams on the Paraná river paved the way for cooperation in a number of areas, including the May 1980 nuclear agreement.[34]

Active cooperation in the nuclear area has earlier precedent in the nonproliferation postures of the two countries.[35] Since the mid-1960s, the two countries have often assumed parallel positions in international forums (United Nations, Geneva disarmament discussions, Latin American nuclear-weapon-free zone negotiations. IAEA Board of Governors), motivated by a desire to prevent external limitations on their nuclear development.[36] In the 1970s global nonproliferation efforts shifted toward cooperative attempts among nuclear suppliers to prescribe certain sensitive portions of the nuclear fuel cycle from threshold countries such as Argentina and Brazil. This produced significant resentment and a shared Argentine–Brazilian perception that the advanced nuclear supplier countries, particularly the United States, were practicing a form of technological colonialism through denial of access of nuclear materials necessary for their economic advance. Gradually, and over a period of years, the conviction grew among some Argentine and Brazilian leaders that their common stances on certain nonproliferation measures should be translated into positive cooperation and mutual assistance in the development of nuclear energy.

The 1976 dispute between the United States and Brazil over the German sale of the complete nuclear fuel cycle helped to stimulate a drawing-together of the two Latin American nations on nuclear issues. The strong U.S. opposition to the Brazilian action prompted statements of support for Brazil and suggestions for cooperation both in the Argentine press and by government officials. Preliminary talks, which occurred in January of 1977, produced a communiqué signed by the two Foreign Ministers, stressing the need for cooperation in nuclear matters. While Argentine officials, especially the President of the Argentine Nuclear Energy Commission (CNEA), Admiral Castro Madero, continued to push the idea of technical exchanges in early 1977, Brazil was reticent until the River Plate disputes were resolved in 1979.

While a number of factors can be identified as contributing to current Argentine–Brazilian nuclear convergence, personalities were a vital part of the process. Castro Madero, a naval officer with considerable influence in the Argentine military leadership, had long been deeply committed to the desirability of peaceful cooperation with Brazil. In part the May 1980 agreement is a result of his persistence within his own government and a sense of timing regarding Brazilian receptivity. In addition, Brazilian President Figueiredo, having lived in Argentina for many years, came into office in 1980 committed to the need for establishing a more predictable relationship and regular consultations with Argentina. On the Brazilian side, economic incentives, including problems in implementing their own nuclear program, enhanced the desirability of a nuclear linkage with Argentina. Confronted with a loss of government resources, an idle NUCLEP (the joint company established by Brazil and Germany for heavy nuclear industry), as well as pressure from private Brazilian companies designed to service the nuclear industry, Brazilian nuclear officials welcomed Argentina as a future nuclear customer. The possibility of supplying materials and equipment for three planned Argentine power reactors to be constructed over the next 20 years could help compensate for the growing likelihood of a slowdown in Brazil's ambitious nuclear program.

The bilateral nuclear relationship has evolved in several stages, beginning with a January 1980 visit to Brazil by Castro Madero in which he met with all appropriate officials, toured Brazilian facilities, and laid the foundation for subsequent agreements. A second stage was a return visit to Argentina several months later by the NUCLEBRAS president and the president of the Brazilian nuclear energy commission to arrange details of the historic visit by President Figueiredo to Argentina to sign the May 1980 agreement.

The agreement includes a master treaty, two arrangements for cooperation between the nuclear energy commissions of both countries, and a protocol on industrial cooperation. This agreement actually established the framework for specific agreements that were to follow. The most recent stage of the process occurred in late August of 1980 during a state visit by President Videla to Brazil in which agreements were signed implementing specific portions of the May agreement.

The most important aspects of the nuclear agreement are the following:[37]

1.   NUCLEP will supply the core vessel and other heavy components for Argentina's next reactor (Atucha 2). The Argentine reactor is also being constructed by the same German firm, KWU, supplying all of Brazil's equipment.

2.   The Argentine CNEA will lease up to 240 tons of uranium concentrate, to be delivered at 120 tons per year in 1981 and 1982. It will be utilized in Brazil's first reactor starting in 1981, and Brazil will reimburse Argentina in uranium concentrate when its uranium processing plants go into operation in 1982.

3. Argentina will supply zircalloy tubes (100,000 meters) "and parts for nuclear uses, particularly pertaining to manufacture of fuel elements."

Other aspects of the agreement include an exchange of technicians and personnel training, and exchange of information on component fabrication, nuclear plant security, physical protection of nuclear material, exploration and production of uranium, nuclear safety, and research reactor design. Argentina will gain access to the Brazilian Computerized Information Center containing significant technical and scientific information in the nuclear area, which will be connected to data processing centers in Argentina. Cooperation will also proceed in basic and applied nuclear physics research in advanced nuclear technology, including thorium utilization and breeder development.

The implications of the nuclear agreement are numerous. The agreement stresses the peaceful uses of nuclear energy and the goals of the Tlatelolco Treaty and should contribute to nonproliferation efforts. That is, while a variety of factors could impel either country to develop nuclear explosive devices, the most important dynamic is bilateral competition. Thus a major payoff of the agreement is increased security: a greater degree of confidence and mutual understanding of the other's actions, and a reduced danger of misconception and miscalculation.

However, on the negative side of the nonproliferation ledger there is concern that advanced nuclear technology each country will receive from Germany (and in the case of Argentina, industrial-scale heavy water technology from Switzerland) might be freely shared with the other. There are, of course, restrictions built into each country's agreement with Germany, but the fact that in both cases the same German company is involved may result in an informal closeness and sharing of information on sensitive technology. While Castro Madero has stated that Argentina will not gain access to information supplied by Germany under its contract with Brazil, nor Brazil have access to foreign information conveyed to Argentina, "Brazil and Argentina are free to share practical experience." Moreover, Brazilians have noted with interest that Argentina was far more successful than they, for a variety of reasons, in gaining significant concessions from the Germans. Currently, according to Brazilian officials, an overall triangular safeguards agreement between Argentina, Brazil, and the IAEA is not contemplated, but rather specific safeguards on supplies of individual equipment are to be worked out on a case-by-case basis. Finally, Castro Madero has on several instances during the agreements' implementation made specific mention of retaining the right to detonate PNEs, whereas Brazilian officials have been far more restrained in their comments by emphasizing the current lack of applicability of such devices.

An additional implication of the nuclear agreement is the benefit it will provide, as perceived by the two parties, in enhanced ability to resist nuclear supplier pressure and to counter restrictions on advanced technology. The agreement contains the significant phrase:

> The parties will pursue talks concerning situations of mutual interest which arise on the international scene in relation to the applications of nuclear energy for peaceful purposes, with a view to coordinating their positions when this is desirable.

This implies a far closer form of regular consultation and coordination in nuclear policies as related to the more advanced supplier nations. For the Argentine leadership this was an important motive for the agreement, a view the Brazilians appear to be slowly adopting. Argentina would also like to draw Brazil into active cooperation with the so-called nonaligned nuclear consumers group. Brazil did attend, for the first time (as an observer) a meeting of this group in Buenos Aires in June 1980. Argentina would also like to promote a Latin American coordinating group for nuclear energy similar to EURATOM, an idea Brazil has resisted in the past.

A further implication of the agreement is that it may ultimately lead to more substantive nuclear cooperation. Argentine officials have expressed the view that their nation would look favorably on purchasing enriched uranium from the German-supplied enrichment facilities in Brazil in the future, in order to curtail their dependence on the United States, the Soviet Union, or other advanced supplier countries. In addition, a longer-run possibility exists of cooperation at the back end of the nuclear fuel cycle. While the agreement offers no hint of this, cooperation between Argentina and Brazil for establishment of a plutonium storage facility (which could be situated in a neighboring country, such as Paraguay or Uruguay) is conceivable. It is of note that the creation of a plutonium storage facility is a requirement of Brazil's contract for enriched uranium with URENCO.

An additional result of the agreement is the preeminent role of the Federal Republic of Germany. As the principal nuclear supplier of both countries, Germany is well positioned to capitalize on increased cooperation for lucrative business opportunities. Despite the fact that both countries (especially Brazil) are developing an indigenous capacity to produce nuclear components, Germany, through its existing contracts and joint ownerships with Argentina and Brazilian companies, is in an enviable position. The German position on nonproliferation, which to this point has been far more flexible than that of the United States—in, for example, not requiring full-scope safeguards—will therefore assume an ever greater importance as the Argentine–Brazilian relationship matures.

Finally, the nuclear agreement must be considered in the larger context of increasingly close bilateral relations between the two nations in a variety of areas. Nuclear energy provided the cutting edge for agreements in other sectors, including armaments manufacture, joint exploitation of hydroelectric resources, increased trade, technology exchanges in such areas as food, paper, plastics, leather, alcohol for energy, and so forth. The relationship will also open new opportunities in terms of standardization and marketing approaches for transnational companies operating in both countries. While the vast structural differences in the Argentine and Brazilian economies and internal markets cannot be ignored, cooperation between these two significant countries appears to be gathering distinct momentum into the 1980s.

NONPROLIFERATION AND CONTROL

International Nonproliferation Efforts

The principal international nonproliferation efforts at the present time are the Nuclear Non-Proliferation Treaty of 1968 (NPT) and the International Atomic Energy Agency (IAEA) and its system of safeguards to insure the peaceful intent of nuclear energy programs of member countries. Related to the above are the International Nuclear Fuel Cycle Evaluation (INFCE, a two-year international study of the nuclear fuel cycle which completed its final report in February 1980) and a planned major international Conference on the Peaceful Uses of Nuclear Energy scheduled for 1983. A brief review of the current contribution of Latin American countries to these international efforts is useful in evaluating their commitment to nonproliferation.

The NPT currently has 114 parties. Under the agreement, non-nuclear-weapon states pledge not to receive or develop nuclear weapons and subject their entire nuclear program to IAEA safeguards. All Latin American countries except Argentina, Brazil, Chile, Colombia, and Cuba are parties to the agreement. Argentina and Brazil have been particularly adament in their opposition to the NPT as an unequal agreement under which non–nuclear-weapon states are asked to foreswear forever developing nuclear weapons, whereas nuclear weapon states are asked to do relatively little.

An August 1980 Review Conference for the NPT was attended by most Latin American countries, and Mexico, Venezuela, Ecuador, and Peru participated actively in the preparatory committee. Unfortunately, as nonparties Latin America's two most advanced countries (Argentina and Brazil) did not participate in the discussions (although both countries, as well as Colombia, sent observers). Mexico, and to a lesser extent Peru, were active as leaders in the non-aligned efforts in seeking to impress upon the nuclear-weapon states the importance of fully complying with Article IV (guaranteed access to the peaceful uses of nuclear energy) and Article VI (progress by the nuclear-weapon states toward early curbing of the nuclear arms race) requirements. The collapse of the conference without a final document led many current Latin American parties to question the long-term efficacy of the NPT.[38]

The IAEA currently has 108 members, including all major Latin American states. In 1980, all existing nuclear installations in Latin America are covered by IAEA safeguards.[39] These include facilities in non-NPT parties: Argentina, Brazil, Chile, and Cuba. However, these nations have not accepted "fullscope" safeguards de jure, thus in effect leaving their options open to develop unsafeguarded installations in the future.

The International Nuclear Fuel Cycle Evaluation (INFCE) was an important international effort involving all major nuclear supplier and consumer nations, including Argentina, Brazil, Mexico, and Venezuela. However, only one, Argentina, made an active contribution, and it remained skeptical as to INFCE's overall worth.[40] In addition, the Agency for the Prohibition of Nuclear Weapons in Latin America (OPANAL) submitted a position paper both to INFCE's final plenary session and to the NPT Review Conference. Perhaps the principal result of INFCE was a period of reduced tension and needed dialogue among nuclear suppliers *and* with principal consumer countries. The need for a post-INFCE mechanism for supplier–consumer consultation was widely acknowledged, and the result was creation of the Committee on Supply Assurances (CAS) under the auspices of the IAEA's Board of Governors. While there are questions as to the ultimate impact of CAS, it has appealed to Latin American countries, which comprise 6 of the 34 members of the IAEA's Board of Governors (a body in which Argentina and Brazil have exercized strong influence). The extent to which the CAS becomes a real forum for serious discussion and decision making, as opposed to remaining a low-level consultative mechanism, will impact on the amount of Latin American and nonaligned support for this mechanism.

A desire for an assured and reliable supply of nuclear technology and material provided the impetus for the decision by the 34th UN General Assembly to convene by 1983 an international conference for promotion of cooperation in the peaceful uses of nuclear energy. Latin American countries, including those with strong nonproliferation records such as Mexico and threshold countries such as Argentina and Brazil, have given firm support to the Yugoslavian-led initiative. The conference would be designed for key nuclear supplier and consumer countries as a sort of "political INFCE" and would attempt to resolve vital issues regarding supply of nuclear materials. Latin American and nonaligned countries view the CAS as an important stepping-stone toward the 1983 conference. Despite the reticence of the United States and some other major nuclear supplier countries, there are high expectations for the 1983 conference among many non–nuclear-weapon states.

Latin American countries have been active in the several international nonproliferation forums discussed above. Despite many differences among the major Latin American countries there are shared—and deeply serious—concerns that the nuclear weapon states are failing to control their own upward surge in nuclear armaments, while at the same time seeking to impose ever greater restrictions on the nuclear programs of countries that lack nuclear weapons. They argue that if this trend continues, it will lead to the inevitable unraveling of the nonproliferation regime following the 1983 conference. In the event this happens, the importance of Latin America's own regional nonproliferation regime—the Tlatelolco Treaty—can only intensify.

Tlatelolco Regime

The Tlatelolco Treaty (Treaty for the Prohibition of Nuclear Weapons in Latin America) is an important instrument that has significantly contributed to achieving a complete nonproliferation status for the entire Latin American region. Under the requirements of the treaty, which entered into force in 1969, Latin American countries pledge to keep their territories completely free of nuclear weapons; neither to develop, nor to test or import such weapons. The agreement is more comprehensive than the NPT in that no foreign nuclear bases are permitted, and binding protocols for both nuclear weapon states and states having territorial interests in the Americas are an integral portion of the treaty. Also included under the terms of the treaty are IAEA safeguards over the entire nuclear program of all parties.

Currently 22 Latin American countries are full parties to the treaty, whereas four significant countries—Argentina, Brazil, Chile, and Cuba—are not full parties. However, Argentina and Brazil have both stressed their dedication to the goals of the treaty through their recent nuclear agreement. International (non-Latin American) support for the Tlatelolco Treaty, as reflected by ratifications of accompanying protocols, is significantly widespread and diverse. Tlatelolco is the only major nuclear arms agreement supported by the three major nuclear weapons states, the United States, the Soviet Union, and China. These nations and Great Britain and France have ratified Protocol II, by which nuclear-weapon states pledge not to use or threaten to use nuclear weapons against parties to the treaty. The other protocol (I), designed for nations with territorial interests in the Americas, has been ratified by the Netherlands and Great Britain. The United States and France have announced their intent to ratify.

Brazil and Chile have technically ratified the Tlatelolco Treaty, and Argentina has signed and announced its intent to ratify, whereas Cuba has neither signed nor ratified. However, under the treaty's ratification arrangements, Brazil's and Chile's ratification is conditional in the sense that the agreement will not enter into force for them until all appropriate Latin American states have ratified and all states having territorial interests in the Americas and nuclear-weapon states have ratified the relevant protocols. The remaining obstacles to Tlatelolco's full implementation are: Argentina's ratification, Cuba's signing and ratification, and ratification by the United States and France of Protocol I (a territorial dispute preventing Guyana from ratifying is not considered a major obstacle). Assuming the final objectives are completed, Argentina, Chile, Brazil, and Cuba would become full parties and would by most interpretations be bound to accept fullscope IAEA safeguards over their entire nuclear program, as well as special inspections as required by other parties of the Treaty for Prohibition of Nuclear Weapons in Latin America. It is notable that several Latin American countries, Colombia, Barbados, and Trinidad and Tobago are not parties to the NPT but are fully covered under Tlatelolco. In a similar fashion, a number of Tlatelolco parties—Colombia, Grenada, Haiti, Jamaica, Paraguay, and Surinam

—have not adhered to the Limited Test Ban Treaty of 1963 prohibiting underground nuclear testing. The fact that these nations have given up the option for underground testing under Tlatelolco is not insignificant.

The nuclear-weapon-free zone is in effect for the territories of the 22 countries that have ratified it. The prospect for the aforementioned obstacles being overcome and the complete zone coming into creation is debatable. The likelihood for Cuban ratification has been referred to earlier in this chapter as being tied, at least in part, to the status of U.S.–Cuban relations. Soviet ratification of Protocol II, the recent signing of a safeguards agreement with the IAEA, and continued Mexican pressure on Cuba suggest that ultimate Cuban ratification is likely, although immediate prospects are poor. In a similar fashion timing for French ratification of Protocol I is not yet established, but when complete the remaining French territories in the Americas will become completely denuclearized.

Completion of U.S. ratification of Protocol I has, unfortunately become a protracted and complex affair. President Carter announced in April 1977 the intent of the United States to ratify this protocol with appropriate interpretations, and in 1978 the Senate Committee on Foreign Relations discussed but delayed final action. The delay, in part due to a dispute between the Committee and the National Security Council regarding access to certain documents, ultimately became intertwined and buried in the SALT II debate. U.S. ratification of Protocol I remains both technically necessary and symbolically vital to the success of the Tlatelolco Treaty. The failure of the United States to act has raised questions as to the sincerity of U.S. dedication to nonproliferation in Latin America and provided legitimate excuses for Cuba, Argentina, Brazil, Chile, and others for not fully adhering to the agreement.

The posture of Argentina and Brazil is critical to the ultimate success of the nuclear-weapon-free zone and therefore deserves careful study. Neither country is yet fully committed to the agreement. Argentina joined the original Tlatelolco negotiations considerably after most of the other current parties and then worked to stiffen a number of the provisions of the treaty, including the ratification procedure. It did sign the agreement in September of 1967, but at this writing is still the only holdout among Latin American nations that had taken part in the actual negotiations. Both Brazil and Chile have taken the technical step of ratifying the treaty without taking advantage of paragraph 2 or Article 28, which permits certain requirements to be waived and the agreement to come into full force (an action taken by all the other 22 parties). Brazil and Chile's ratification is important because, although the treaty is not fully in force for them, they have by both actions and words indicated they will take no measures contrary to the spirit of the treaty.

In 1977 President Videla announced that Argentina would ratify the agreement. However, Tlatelolco ratification became an issue in U.S.-Argentine disagreements over access to sensitive equipment, particularly the German/Swiss sale of a reactor and heavy water technology in 1979. The United States wanted Argentina to ratify Tlatelolco and agree to fullscope safeguards, and the Argentines came to view their ratification as valuable currency.

Argentina has raised a series of issues regarding Tlatelolco that are substantive but have also served as a delaying tactic. These include questions regarding the "interpretations" utilized by the nuclear weapon states in signing Protocol II, the completeness of the required IAEA safeguards, and PNEs. Some Argentine experts say that the "interpretations" that have accompanied U.S., Soviet, and British ratifications have had the result of modifying the rights of Latin American parties to the treaty.[41] Interrelated with this "interpretation" in the view of the Argentines is the question of legality of PNEs under the treaty. Most Tlatelolco parties share the views of the nuclear weapon states that PNEs are not permitted under the terms of the treaty. However, Argentina has continued to argue that Tlatelolco's Article 18

> recognizes the right of the contracting parties by their own means or in association with third parties to carry out explosions for peaceful purposes including explosions which may call for the use of instruments similar to those used in atomic weapons.[42]

CNEA President Castro Madero continued to endorse this view strongly in recent months, following the Argentine–Brazilian nuclear agreement.[43]

Finally, Argentina has sought to use the safeguards required under Article 13 of the Tlatelolco Treaty as somewhat of a smokescreen. That is, the negotiating history and clear intent of the Tlatelolco negotiators was that the agreement would encompass fullscope IAEA safeguards. Yet Argentina has attempted to draw a sharp distinction between NPT safeguards, which they interpret as fullscope and reject, and Tlatelolco safeguards, which they are interpreting as applicable only to their current nuclear facilities. Argentina has deliberately drawn out negotiations with the IAEA to delay final agreement and avoid any legal commitment to de jure fullscope safeguards. However, it is most likely that Argentina will ratify Tlatelolco in the near future and therefore be in a comparable position to Brazil and Chile. At that point, despite ambiguities in its positions regarding safeguards and PNEs, its commitment to a nonproliferation status and the Tlatelolco regime will be enhanced.

In contrast to Argentina, Brazil has maintained a relatively favorable posture without fully embracing the agreement. Brazil authored the first resolution for a Latin American nuclear-weapon-free zone at the UN in 1962 and was an enthusiastic supporter of Tlatelolco's Preparatory Committee (COPREDAL), which began its work in 1963. However, with the 1964 military takeover Brazil's support shifted to a somewhat more obstructionist stance, and that nation was instrumental in inclusion of provisions dealing with PNEs and for the somewhat unwieldy ratification process.

Brazil has signed and ratified the agreement, although as noted earlier the treaty is not yet in force for that nation. However, Brazilian ratification has more than symbolic significance, as was made explicit in a formal government statement on nuclear policy, the *Brazilian Nuclear Program*, issued in 1977. In the statement Brazil declared that: "having signed the treaty, Brazil has committed itself, according to the canons of international law, not to perform any act which defeats the objectives of the treaty. . . ." The statement also expressed Brazil's views that full enforcement of Tlatelolco depends on the commitment of external powers, particularly nuclear-weapon states, as expressed in support for Protocols I and II.

Brazilian officials have continued to stress in the last several years their dedication to the goals of the Tlatelolco Treaty and have emphasized this in the evolving nuclear relationship with Argentina. It is also important to note that Brazil shares with Argentina the position, opposed by most Tlatelolco parties and the nuclear-weapon states, that PNEs are legally permitted under the treaty. Yet there are shades of differences between the Argentine and Brazilian position on this and clear division within the Brazilian government as to the value of PNEs. For example, in the Spring of 1980, Brazilian Foreign Minister Saraiva Guerreiro stated: "we maintain the position of the right to use nuclear energy for peaceful purposes including explosions" and other official foreign ministry spokesmen noted that use of PNEs is envisaged and regulated by the Tlatelolco Treaty. However, at the same time Brazilian officials were clearly disturbed by strong statements by CNEA President Castro Madero emphasizing PNEs, and both the chairman of the Brazilian nuclear energy commission (CNEN), Hervasio de Carvalho, and Minister of Mines and Energy, Cesar Cals, came out in public opposition to use of PNEs.[44]

In summary, there appears to be at least an attitudinal difference between Argentina and Brazil in that the latter is predisposed to view Tlatelolco as a positive Latin American endeavor, while being less concerned over seeking practical utility for PNEs.

INSTITUTIONAL DEVELOPMENT AND NUCLEAR ENERGY[45]

As this chapter has illustrated, the issue is not *whether* Latin American countries will turn to nuclear energy, but rather what pattern will be followed as they do so. Latin American nations are making rapid advances in nuclear energy and are clearly committed to it in the future. Hemispheric institutions have had a limited but still important role in the development and control of nuclear energy in the region. Institutions can play a far more important role in the future in promoting cooperative efforts in the development and control of nuclear energy, and deserve encouragement by the United States and other countries committed to the goals of nonproliferation. The linkage to the Tlatelolco regime is essential and will contribute to regional peace and security.

Currently there are two Latin American institutions having somewhat overlapping responsibility in the nuclear energy area: the Inter-American Nuclear Energy Commission (IANEC) of the OAS and the Agency for the Prohibition of Nuclear Weapons in Latin America (OPANAL). These organizations having specific responsibility in the nuclear area (or a new coordinating organization) are most likely to provide future direction in the development of nuclear energy in Latin America.

Other Latin American institutions with broader responsibilities have shown little interest in encouraging national nuclear development projects or regional nuclear cooperation. These include the Latin American Free Trade Association (LAFTA), which has recently been subsumed into the Latin American Integration Association (ALADI), headquartered in Montevideo, and the Sistema Economico Latinoamericana (SELA), with headquarters in Caracas. The Organizacion Latinoamericana de Energia (OLADE), which seeks to serve as an instrument for cooperation, coordination, and consultation in the utilization of hemispheric energy sources, has also carefully refrained from direct involvement in nuclear issues.

Subregional efforts may have some promise for the future. These include the Plata Basin Group—Argentina, Brazil, Paraguay, Uraguay, and Bolivia—designed to promote cooperative efforts in the River Plate Basin, and the Amazon Pact countries—Bolivia, Colombia, Ecuador, Brazil, Guyana, Peru, and Venezuela—which have organized to promote development and cooperative efforts in their shared Amazonian regions. However, nuclear cooperation is not now envisaged as an element of either of the above subregional efforts.[46]

Inter-American Nuclear Energy Commission (IANEC). IANEC is a technical organ of the OAS, created in 1959 with the objective of supporting the peaceful uses of nuclear energy in Latin America. With a small staff located in Washington, D.C., it hosts conferences and supports cooperative efforts in the following areas: utilization of radioisotopes and radiation, exploration and processing of radioactive ores, training of human resources for nuclear electric programs, nuclear information, and nuclear safety. With limited resources, IANEC offers support for some nuclear training in Latin American countries and sponsors a number of technical conferences with the assistance of other organizations such as the American Nuclear Society. A recent example was the Conference on Utilization of Small and Medium-Sized Power Reactors in Latin America, held in Montevideo in May 1980. A major meeting of all members is held every two years, the most recent of which was its eleventh meeting in Santiago in July 1979.[47] At the meeting, a 1980–81 "action plan" calling for ambitious nuclear cooperative efforts was adopted, as has been the case in previous meetings. While IANEC has the strong support of OAS Secretary-General Orfila, its efforts have been limited due to lack of support by some Latin American countries and the United States and inadequate funding.

Agency for the Prohibition of Nuclear Weapons in Latin America (OPANAL). OPANAL was established in 1969 in Mexico City as an integral part of the Tlatelolco Treaty (Article 7). The three principal organs of OPANAL are the General Conference of all members, a Council of five members elected by the General Conference, and a Secretariat administered by a Secretary-General with a small support staff. The General Conference provides overall guidance for OPANAL's operations, and the Council has specially defined responsibilities with respect to inspections and other related matters.

The central purpose of OPANAL is "to ensure compliance with the obligations of this treaty" (Article 7). The Secretariat is in continuous operation in Mexico City, and the General Conference meets every two years, with its most recent sixth meeting in April of 1979 and the seventh scheduled for April of 1981. Among the responsibilities of OPANAL is to verify compliance of Tlatelolco parties, with Article 13 requiring IAEA safeguards. OPANAL also receives semiannual reports from Tlatelolco parties, stating that no activity prohibited under the treaty has occurred in their respective territories (Article 14). Of potential future interest (and OPANAL involvement) are thus far unapplied portions of the treaty, including Article 15, by which special reports can be required of Tlatelolco parties, Article 16, outlining circumstances for special inspections to be carried out by the Council in the territory of a party suspected of an illegal activity, and Article 18, outlining specific methods of control and observation by OPANAL in the event that a party decides to detonate a PNE.

While the emphasis of OPANAL's work is on compliance with the treaty, there is growing interest in emphasizing the agreement's involvement with ensuring the peaceful benefits of nuclear energy to all Latin American nations (specifically outlined in the Preamble and Article 17). There is definite interest on the part of some Latin American nations that OPANAL should evolve into an organization for the coordination, management, and planning of Latin American efforts in the peaceful uses of nuclear energy. This was a strong recommendation of the fifth session of OPANAL's General Conference, which met in 1977.[48] Moreover, OPANAL's Secretary-General continues to advocate the view that

> the course taken in giving the Tlatelolco Treaty an important part to play in connection with the peaceful uses of nuclear energy in Latin America and in making OPANAL their regional planning and coordinating centre for such matters opens up prospects of the highest interest.[49]

Support for an enhanced role for OPANAL is tempered by the fact that this would require a considerably expanded and technically trained OPANAL staff. Moreover, if this were undertaken, there would be an inevitable duplication with IANEC. If OPANAL's role is to be enlarged, it will also require far greater financial support by Latin American nations than it is currently receiving.

Coordinating Nuclear Energy Institutions. OPANAL is a political organization with a nonproliferation objective, seeking to move into the more technical area of hemispheric coordination of peaceful uses of nuclear energy. IANEC, a technical/scientific organization, also seeks a coordinating role in what is a highly politicized area. A combining of the two organizations would, at the surface level, appear highly desirable for nonproliferation objectives and in development of the peaceful uses of nuclear energy. IANEC would contribute a technical orientation and contacts with hemispheric scientific circles, whereas OPANAL would help to ensure support of important advanced nuclear countries having nonproliferation concerns. Latin American countries would not be asked to continue to support two organizations with similar objectives.

Working counter to a merging of the two organizations is the background of the Tlatelolco negotiations, in which several countries, especially Mexico, opposed any formal role for IANEC in the treaty. Some Latin American countries had suggested that IANEC could serve as the control mechanism, but most felt such a move would be contrary to the spirit of the Tlatelolco effort, which was to divorce the Latin American region from nuclear confrontation between the super powers. IANEC, as part of the U.S.-dominated OAS, would lack sufficient independence.

Limited consultation was established between the two organizations in 1978, and their representatives now attend each other's meetings. A possible avenue for further cooperation is seen as falling in Tlatelolco's Article 19, paragraph 3, which states:

> The contracting parties may, if they see fit, request the advice of the Inter-American Nuclear Energy Commission on all technical matters connected with the application of this treaty, etc.

Nonetheless the problem of duplication remains unresolved and was referred to in a resolution passed by the Eleventh Meeting of the Inter-American Nuclear Energy Commission in 1979 when it pointed out:

> In relation to Resolution 127 adopted by the Sixth Session of OPANAL that many of the aspects to be included in the survey requested are already being examined in depth by the working groups of the advisory committee of IANEC.[50]

While the need for a more unified institutional approach for nuclear energy development and control in the hemisphere is clear, merger between OPANAL and IANEC is unlikely. A better pattern for the future may be the creation of a new regional coordinating institution, in which OPANAL and IANEC would be affiliated. A regional coordinating mechanism could have responsibilities similar to those of EURATOM, which, among other things, seeks to facilitate the smooth flow of nuclear materials among its Western European members as well as the promotion of European nuclear industries. A Latin American coordinating unit could also encourage joint and multilateral efforts in the nuclear fuel cycle, such as small or medium-sized power reactors serving two or more contigious countries with limited grids, or spent fuel or plutonium storage facilities.

Under such a proposal, IANEC could serve as the scientific/technical affiliate or department of the coordinating institution by undertaking research and training in the development of nuclear science and technology, the transportation of nuclear material, and safety. OPANAL, working in cooperation with the IAEA, would provide overall safeguarding of all joint and multilateral facilities under the management and control of the coordinating unit.

A possible step toward the creation of a coordinating unit took place at the Inter-American Nuclear Law Association meeting in Buenos Aires in November 1979, with a proposal for the formation of a South American Nuclear Collaboration Agency (SUDATOM). The proposal, which was limited to South American rather than all of Latin America, envisaged the need for regional approaches to nuclear research and development, cooperation in nuclear power plants, the establishment of a more integrated nuclear industry, and cooperation in the nuclear fuel cycle. The proposal, which paralleled the beginning of significant Argentine–Brazilian nuclear cooperation, provoked considerable interest and discussion. It also echoed an earlier unsuccessful effort led by Argentina to create a Latin American coordinating group in nuclear energy within the context of the IAEA. The abortive effort, the Reunion De Autoridades Nucleares De America Latina (RANDAL), held one meeting in 1976 and attempted to promote a coordinated effort among all Latin American countries in nuclear energy.[51]

An extension of the SUDATOM concept encompassing the entire Latin American region and with formal links to OPANAL and IANEC has considerable promise. It would build on established regional institutions and reinforce current Latin American tendencies toward greater bilateral nuclear cooperation. It could help promote confidence among Latin American countries by relieving the anxieties over their respective intentions in the sensitive nuclear area. Finally, it could provide Latin American nations with positive leverage for dealing with more advanced nuclear supplier nations, which will be more predisposed to share sophisticated technology.[52]

CONCLUSIONS AND RECOMMENDATIONS

Tlatelolco Implementation

Quiet support for the Tlatelolco Regime should be the bedrock of all countries supporting nonproliferation in the Latin American region. In this effort, policy makers should bear in mind that the principal motivation for the nuclear-weapon-free zone was to prevent disruptive non-Latin American involvement in the hemisphere. This common denominator for Latin American support—a desire to avoid the effects of a superpower nuclear confrontation—gives a defensive character to Tlatelolco. The 1962 Cuban Missile Crisis provided Latin Americans with the necessary stimulus, underscoring the fact that the existence of nuclear weapons in the region *and* the close linkage of a Latin American country to a superpower will threaten to make them all targets. The Cuban Missile Crisis was in fact an exception to a prevailing trend of lack of superpower/Cold War pressure on the region relative to other more troubled areas of the world.

An enhanced level of superpower competition or pressure on the region, including the development of new or closer security arrangements, would inevitably weaken and eventually undermine Tlatelolco's foundations. It would do this by shattering the cooperative environment necessary for the nuclear-weapon-free zone and heightening tension among Latin American countries.

In order to provide support for Tlatelolco and the overall goal of nonproliferation for the region, the following activities should be encouraged:

- the development of a consensus between the two superpowers that support for the Tlatelolco Regime and nonproliferation in Latin America is in their mutual interest and that confrontations and increased competition will be counterproductive;

- early ratification of Protocol I by the United States and France;

- the encouragement by nonproliferation-supporting countries of principal Latin American holdouts, Argentina and Cuba, to ratify Tlatelolco as an important step toward full implementation of the agreement;

- support of the Tlatelolco Treaty by nuclear supplier states without directly linking it to specific nuclear negotiations with Latin American countries; too close a linkage with specific negotiations can undermine Latin American support for Tlatelolco by conveying the impression of a treaty imposed from outside the region rather than negotiated from within.

Cooperation among Supplier Nations

Nuclear supplier nations currently supplying nuclear materials to the Latin American region need to coordinate their efforts better. Of these the Federal Republic of Germany with its dominant relationship with Argentina and Brazil is of principal importance, followed by the United States, Canada, France, and Spain. This is not to argue for a Latin American specific supplier's cartel, but rather the need to develop a consensus on broad issues such as the NPT, Tlatelolco, safeguards, reprocessing and recycling of plutonium and adequate protection of supplied nuclear materials to theft and terrorism.

It may also be preferable for the United States and all other supplier countries to accept de facto fullscope safeguards (over all *existing* facilities) as the basis of a nuclear relationship with Argentina and Brazil, much as have the Federal Republic of Germany and France. Both Argentina and Brazil currently equate de jure fullscope safeguards (in perpetuity over existing and *future* facilities) with efforts to impose the NPT, which they reject. Insistence on de jure fullscope safeguards as the price of a nuclear relationship may not be a productive posture. It gives a competitive advantage to some vendors, while not necessarily achieving the apparent goal of denying sensitive nuclear equipment to certain nations.

In the longer run, the Tlatelolco Treaty may prove a more successful means of achieving safeguards in perpetuity for Latin American nations. That is, supplier countries can quietly recommend that all Tlatelolco parties live up to the obligations of *their* treaty, given the fact that most Tlatelolco parties interpret the agreement as requiring de jure fullscope safeguards (and prohibiting PNEs). It is also conceivable that a situation could evolve where Latin American supporters of Tlatelolco would pressure their reluctant regional neighbors to assume a complete nonproliferation status under the agreement. If some of the pressuring Tlatelolco supporters were oil-producing countries, such as Venezuela and Mexico, this could provide particular leverage. In any event, such an occurrence will only prove possible in the absence of overt supplier country pressure.

Fuel Cycle Cooperation

Cooperative development of the nuclear fuel cycle should be encouraged in Latin America. The United States should, in concert with other supplier countries, provide a receptive international environment for the development of Latin American institutions in the nuclear fuel cycle, with particular attention given to spent fuel storage and regional plutonium management facilities. While the creation of joint or multilateral fuel cycle ventures is not now envisaged as a part of the emerging Argentina–Brazil nuclear arrangement, such a pattern could prove possible in the future. As noted earlier, the Brazilian–URENCO agreement includes the requirement of a plutonium storage facility. The important point is that supplier countries have been neutral to mildly negative thus far as regards to development of fuel cycle cooperative efforts or centers in the Latin American region, a policy that has only served to reinforce purely national programs. Cooperative efforts should be supported wherever possible.

Argentine–Brazilian Convergence

The historic significance of this emerging relationship to Latin American politics can hardly be exaggerated. The creation of commercial and institutionalized linkages between the two countries should help reduce the likelihood that nuclear issues will exacerbate traditional geopolitical rivalries. Rather, nuclear cooperation can help create a web of relationships between the two countries, contributing to a more predictable and stable pattern of peaceful development in the Southern Cone.

It is conceivable that their cooperation could take a negative turn, such as cooperation in development of a PNE.[53] However, a negative posture by supplier countries toward the growing nuclear relationship—such as interpreting it as a "nuclear axis of military dictatorships"—could result in a self-fulfilling prophecy. Rather, supplier nations should welcome and support the evolving Argentine-

Brazilian relationship, unless clear evidence suggests a different interpretation.

Institutional Evolution

Finally, creative support should be given to the evolution of Latin American machinery devoted to development and control of nuclear energy. The two existing Latin American institutions, IANEC and OPANAL, deserve more attention and tangible economic assistance. An example of the kind of support that would be acceptable is the proposal by OPANAL's General Conference for the creation of a voluntary fund for Protocol signatories, which could be used to support operations, training, staff expansion, and planning for future evolution. Also, enhanced training programs for Latin American scientists and technicians to study at the institutions of nations with more advanced nuclear programs could be channeled through IANEC. An alternative would be a special IAEA fund earmarked for support of OPANAL and IANEC in respective areas of safeguards and technical assistance. The important point is that the support be undertaken in a manner so as to encourage, not dominate, either organization.

In the longer term, support should be given to the creation of a coordinating institution similar to EURATOM, in which IANEC and OPANAL could serve as vital components. Support will mean a willingness to share advanced nuclear technology with Latin American countries, so long as adequate safeguards exist. The scope and content of a coordinating institution will be for the Latin Americans to determine. But the ultimate posture of the more advanced supplier nations will do much to determine whether institutional development in the nuclear field can make a positive contribution to peace and stability in the region.

NOTES

1. According to the Overseas Development Council's most recent annual study, *The United States and World Development, Agenda, 1980,* effective demand for conventional energy in the developed countries is expected to increase 50% in the next twenty years, whereas developing countries will experience an increase of 200–250% (page 48).

2. The World Bank, *Energy in the Developing Countries*, August 1980, page 47.

3. As quoted in Harlan Cleveland (editor), *Energy Futures of Developing Countries*, New York: Aspen Institute, 1980, page 52.

4. "Latin America: Emerging Nuclear Market," *Nuclear News*, September 1979.

5. Marcelo Alonso, "Inter-American Cooperation in Nuclear Energy," Paper presented to the American Nuclear Society's Executive Conference, Pan American Nuclear Technology Exchange, Miami, April 1979. For equally optimistic assessments see M. B. A. Crespi: "La Energia Nuclear En America Latina: Necesidades y Possibilidades," *Interciencia*, Volume 4, Number 1, January–February 1979, and "Nuclear Energy—A Matter of Survival?" in *Development Newsletter*, Organization of American States, June 1980.

6. On Latin American Energy, see Peter R. Odell, "Energy Prospects in Latin America," *Bank of London and South America Review*, May 1980. A major study is Leonardo da Silva, *Latin American Energy and Oil: Present Situation and Prospects*, Volume 1 and 2, Inter-American Development Bank, 1978.

7. For a discussion on alternative Latin American energy sources see The Stanley Foundation, *Conference on Energy and Nuclear Security in Latin America*, April 25–30, 1978, St. John's, Antigua, Vantage Conference Report.

8. The special interest of Latin American nations in small and medium-sized nuclear power reactors was the subject of a recent Conference on the Utilization in Latin America of Small and Medium-Sized Power Reactors, May 12–15, 1980, Montevideo, Uruguay (see *Nuclear News*, September 1980, and *Nucleonics Week*, June 5, 1980).

9. The German-Swiss sale of 1979 to Argentina is discussed in greater detail in John R. Redick, "Latin America: Policy Options Following INFCE," Rodney W. Jones (editor), *Next Steps After INFCE*, U.S. International Nuclear and Non-proliferation Policy, Washington, D.C.: Georgetown Center for Strategic and International Studies, 1980.

10. Opposition from the U.S. Arms Control and Disarmament Agency and human rights supporters in U.S. State Department was attributed with responsibility for delaying any recommendations being made to the NRC, despite the fact that Argentina was known to be ready to place the order for the equipment with the U.S. company. *Nucleonics Week*, June 26, August 21, 1980.

11. Octava Du Temple, "Non-Proliferation and Safeguards Views on Brazil," Paper presented to the International Executive Conference on Non-Proliferation and Safeguards, September 7–10, 1980, Mexico City.

12. *Latin American Regional Report (Brazil)*, May 30, 1980; Octave Du Temple, *Nuclear News*, May 1980.

13. *Nucleonics Week*, June 12, 1980.

14. *New York Times*, April 24, May 5, 1980.

15. Daniel S. Lipman, International Energy Associates, Ltd, "Information Inventory—Mexico," unpublished study, September 1980.

16. For a recent statement of Mexican support for the Latin American nuclear-weapon-free zone see Alfonso García Robles, *The Latin American Nuclear-Weapon-Free Zone*, The Stanley Foundation, Occasional Paper 19, May 1979. For thoughtful statements outlining reasons for Mexican resentment of U.S. nuclear policies see: Dalmau Costa, Director General, Mexican Institute for Nuclear Research, "Transfer of Technology and the Fuel Cycle," American

Nuclear Society's Executive Conference, Pan American Technical Exchange, April 1979; and Antonio Gonzalez de Leon, "Las Relaciones Mexico–Estados Unidos: El Caso De La Energia Nuclear," *Foro Internacional*, Volume 19, Number 2, October–December 1978.

17. Lipman, op cit.

18. *Nucleonics Week*, May 8, 1980.

19. *Nucleonics Week*, January 15, 29, 1981.

20. Interview by the author with Max von Brandt, former President of the Chilean Nuclear Energy Commission, during a tour of the Aguirre facility in late 1978.

21. *Nucleonics Week*, February 21, 1980. For details on the Chilean nuclear program see papers prepared for a conference sponsored by the Chilean Nuclear Energy Commission, most of which are reproduced in Orrego V. and Armanet A. (editors), *Estudios Internacionales, Politica Nuclear*, (Institute of International Studies, University of Chile, Santiago, 1979).

22. Author's notes of address by Max de la Fuente, Head of the Department of Nuclear Affairs, Ministry of Foreign Affairs, Peru to Santiago Conference cited above in footnote 21.

23. "Safeguards Agreement with the Republic of Cuba," IAEA Press Release, PR80/10, April 30, 1980.

24. Jorge F. Perez-Lopez, "The Cuban Nuclear Power Program," *Cuban Studies*, January 1979.

25. "Note Verbale Dated 19 May 1980 from the Permanent Mission to Cuba to the United Nations Addressed to the Secretary-General," UN Disarmament Commission, A/CN.10/16, May 19, 1980.

26. *Treaty of Tlatelolco*, Hearings before the Committee on Foreign Relations, U.S. Senate, August 15, 1978.

27. "Increased Interest in Uranium Exploration Noted," Foreign Broadcast Information Service, Worldwide Report, Nuclear Development and Proliferation, Number 51, July 11, 1980.

28. "Argentina, Bolivia to Expand Nuclear Cooperation," Foreign Broadcast Information Service, Worldwide Report, Nuclear Development and Proliferation, Number 52, July 15, 1980; "Argentina to Aid in Bolivian Nuclear Plan," Number 55, August 8, 1980.

29. *Latin American Economic Report*, June 30, 1980; *Nuclear News*, February 1980.

30. The horizontal transfer of nuclear technology between Latin American countries is dealt with in greater detail in John R. Redick, "The Tlatelolco Regime and Non-Proliferation in Latin America," *International Organization*, Winter 1981.

31. Embassy of Brazil, *Brazil Today*, November 2, 1979.

32. In early 1981 IAEA sources reported that Spain had agreed to place all its facilities under safeguards while still not agreeing to the NPT.

33. "Brazil and Argentina in the American Context," Foreign Broadcast Information Service, Worldwide Report, Nuclear Development and Proliferation, No. 47, June 10, 1980.

34. The May 1980 nuclear agreement was preceeded by an exchange of visits by the Head of the Argentine and Brazilian Air Forces and a decision by the two nations to cooperate in the production of commercial and military aircraft. In a related sensitive area the two countries appeared to be moving toward cooperation in space development, including possible joint efforts in earth satellites.

35. The background of Argentine–Brazilian nuclear cooperation is discussed in greater detail in John R. Redick, "Regional Restraint: US Nuclear Policy and Latin America," *Orbis*, Spring 1978.

36. A prime example was Argentine–Brazilian cooperation after 1964 to stiffen ratification procedures and develop a common position permitting detonation of peaceful nuclear explosions (PNE's) under the Tlatelolco agreement.

37. The complete text of the Argentine–Brazilian nuclear agreement can be found in Foreign Broadcast Information Service, Worldwide Report, Nuclear Development and Proliferation, No. 49, June 25, 1980.

38. For a discussion of the major issues before the NPT Review Conference see The Stanley Foundation, *Non-Proliferation: 1980s*, Vantage Conference Report, January 29–February 3, 1980. For a perceptive description of what occurred at the NPT Review Conference see William Epstein, *Report on the Second NPT Review Conference*, to be published in *Bulletin of the Atomic Scientists* and *Survival*.

39. *IAEA Bulletin*, August 1980. However, several Latin American countries party to the NPT have not completed negotiation of the IAEA-administered safeguards.

40. See for example, A. J. Carrea, "Views from Argentina," presented to American Nuclear Society, International Executive Conference on Non-Proliferation and Safeguards, September 7–10, 1980, Mexico City.

41. Juan E. Guglialmelli, "Argentina Ratifica el Tratado de Tlatelolco, Mientras Las Superpotencias Condicionan su Adhesion al Segundo Protocolo Adicional," *Estrategia*, May–August 1978.

42. UN Document A/C.1/PV15, October 10, 1967.

43. Carlos Castro Madero, "Argentina. Situacíon Nuclear Actual," *Estrategia*, March–April, 1978, and "Castro Madero Discusses Nuclear Policy," Foreign Broadcast Information Service, Worldwide Report, Nuclear Development and Proliferation, No. 62, September 18, 1980. In early 1981 Argentina continued to insist on retaining PNE rights as part of its negotiations, with the Federal Republic of Germany and Switzerland implementing the 1980 agreement.

44. "Roundup of GOB Statements on PNEs; Accord with Argentina," Foreign Broadcast Information Service, Worldwide Report, Nuclear Development and Proliferation, No. 47, June 10, 1980.

45. This section focuses on hemispheric institutions. However, the IAEA, which has been mentioned throughout this paper, has performed a vital role in both the development and control of the peaceful uses of nuclear energy in Latin America. This role will be enhanced in the future in support of the Tlatelolco Regime, in application of international safeguards, and in support of peaceful nuclear energy development in Latin American countries.

46. Some support may be provided in the future from the World Bank and Inter-American Development Bank for nuclear energy projects in Latin America.

47. *Eleventh Meeting of the Inter-American Nuclear Energy Commission*, Final Report, July 2–7, 1979, Santiago, Chile.

48. OPANAL Document 22, September 1970.

49. H. Gros Espiell, "The Non-Proliferation of Nuclear Weapons in Latin America," *International Atomic Agency Bulletin*, August 1980.

50. Ibid., footnote 55. It is of note that the final documentation of the 6th Session of OPANAL's General Conference included far less emphasis on the

coordination of peaceful uses of nuclear energy than had been true of earlier sessions (OPANAL Document S/INF 164 April 24, 1979).

51. The RANDAL effort and the reasons for its failure are discussed in Jose Enrique Greno Velasco, "Tecnologia Nuclear y Cooperacion Regional en el Cono Sur," *Revista de Politica Internacional* (Madrid), January–February 1977, and in John R. Redick, "Regional Restraint: US Nuclear Policy and Latin America," Op cit.

52. Resentment of the perceived effort of nuclear supplier states to deny access by nonnuclear weapon states to nuclear technology has stimulated cooperative efforts among nonaligned countries, including Latin American countries. The first such tendencies in this direction took place in the meeting of Non-Nuclear Weapon States in Geneva in 1968, followed by meetings of the nonaligned countries in 1976 and 1977. In an April 1977 nuclear energy conference in Iran, an informal coordinating group among nonaligned nations was organized with strong Argentine leadership to provide a counterweight to the London supplier's club. This effort languished but was again revived by Yugoslavia, Argentina, and others in a meeting in Belgrade in 1978. The most recent effort took place in June of 1980 in Buenos Aires, in which 15 nonaligned countries (Algeria, Argentina, Cuba, Egypt, Gabon, Indonesia, Iraq, Libya, Nigeria, Pakistan, and Yugoslavia) along with observers (Brazil, Peru, and others) developed a common position for the then upcoming August NPT Review Conference. The meeting's final document condemmed efforts to restrict the transfer of nuclear technology and outlined a great many areas for multilateral nuclear cooperation among nonaligned countries. Efforts for nonaligned nuclear cooperation will continue to be pursued—although with uncertain promise—in the future. The emphasis is more likely to be on developing a common position relative to nuclear supplier countries in international negotiating fora, including the IAEA's Committee on Supply Assurances and relative to the forthcoming 1983 International Conference on the Peaceful Uses of Nuclear Energy.

53. In the event of a negative turn in the Argentine–Brazilian nuclear cooperation leading to joint development of a PNE, it should be recalled that the Tlatelolco Treaty incorporates a method for management and control of such detonations. Article 18 defines the methods whereby PNEs can be detonated in Latin America, establishing public procedures with an international presence by OPANAL and the IAEA at any such explosions. The Treaty therefore provides a means whereby the political impact of a PNE could be minimized, thereby containing its military and strategic impact. Having once contained the efforts within a set of regional procedures, it could then prevent a final step toward production of actual nuclear weapons. While a PNE is to be discouraged and, hopefully, avoided, it is fortunate that Tlatelolco provides Latin America with a containment option totally absent in other more volatile regions of the world.

APPENDIX

Argentine Nuclear Program

Argentina has ample deposits of uranium, sufficient to meet its own projected needs through 1990 as well as for export purposes. In 1979 the nation produced 159 tons of yellowcake, with 1000 tons per year planned for 1984.*

Argentina has a small fuel fabrication facility that currently supplies a portion of the needs of the nation's one 370-MWe (Atucha) power reactor. An industrial-scale facility is under construction, with plans calling for its completion in the early 1980s. Argentina has recently initiated a pilot facility to produce zircaloy, an alloy of zirconium (used as fuel rod cladding surrounding nuclear fuel material), to be followed by an industrial-scale unit. Under an agreement implemented in early 1980, the Soviet Union is supplying technology and some on-site technical experts for zircaloy production. Under the May 1980 agreement with Brazil, the Argentine Nuclear Energy Commission (CNEA) will supply "facilities for the production of zircaloy tubes and parts for nuclear uses, particularly those pertaining to the manufacture of fuel elements."†

Argentine nuclear experts have some limited operational experience in reprocessing technology, having previously constructed a laboratory-size facility that separated small amounts of plutonium but was subsequently shut down in the early 1970s. Reprocessing is a critical bargaining point with the United States, and Argentine officials are aware of the leverage and are often ambiguous in their statements about future reprocessing plans. According to a recent interview, CNEA president Castro Madero stated that an experimental reprocessing plant of 20 kg/day capacity will undertake cold tests in 1981 and begin actual operation in 1982 (amounting to an enlarged pilot facility).‡ Aside from potential military applications, Argentine interest in reprocessing is based on the possible use of mixed oxide fuel in its natural uranium reactors and more generally in relation to its ambitions to become an exporter of nuclear technology in Latin America.

---

* Letter from Octave du Temple, Executive Director of the American Nuclear Society, *Nuclear News*, May 1980.

† *Text of Brazilian–Argentine Nuclear Agreement*, Foreign Broadcast Information Service, Worldwide Report, Nuclear Development and Proliferation, Number 49, June 25, 1980.

‡ *The Energy Daily*, September 24, 1980.

Argentina is making important advances in obtaining and mastering heavy water technology, a "sensitive" portion of the nuclear fuel cycle and an essential part of the nation's chosen route of natural-uranium-based power reactors. Work is nearing completion on a small pilot heavy water facility in close proximity to Atucha, which will produce 3 tons per year. This will be augmented by a Swiss-supplied industrial-scale facility with an annual capacity of 250 tons (which will begin operations in 1983).

Brazilian Nuclear Program

Construction began in early 1979 on a pilot nozzle enrichment plant supplied by Germany, with operational tests scheduled for 1982–83. A larger demonstration plant should be operational by 1987, to be followed by a full commercial-scale plant. The objective is to be able to meet the nation's own enrichment requirements as well as developing an export market in the Latin American region. (Text of *NUCLEBRAS Annual Report for 1979*, Foreign Broadcast Information Service, Nuclear Development and Proliferation, Number 4, June 13, 1980). A small pilot facility was also slated for transfer from Germany to Brazil's Nuclear Technology Development Center in Belo Horizonte for initial operation in 1980. According to some sources, 6 months after initial testing of the pilot unit a decision will be made as to whether or not to build a larger plant.

Plans, financing, and site location for a pilot reprocessing unit were completed in 1979, but construction has been postponed and the original start-up date of 1984 seems unlikely. Brazilian engineers received training at the German reprocessing plant in Karlsruhe in 1979, and in 1980 established a laboratory in São Paulo. The laboratory is designed for analyzing "cold material" and is a necessary first stage to establishing an operating reprocessing facility.* While Brazilian officials have deemphasized the need for a commercial-scale reprocessing facility far into the future, there is little doubt that they, as well as the Argentines, are gaining rapid operational know-how in research and utilization of plutonium.

Brazilian uranium reserves, long a subject of speculation, now

---

* "Sao Paulo Trains Personnel to Reprocess Nuclear Fuel," Foreign Broadcast information Service, World-wide Report, Nuclear Development and Proliferation, Number 56, August 18, 1980.

seem to be firmly established as extensive, with amounts estimated by NUCLEBRAS as 215,300 metric tons in 1979 (Argentine claims approximately 120,000 metric tons). Brazil will produce approximately 550 metric tons of "yellowcake" by 1981, which it will send to Great Britain for enrichment in one of the European gas centrifuge facilities managed by URENCO. By the late 1980s, Brazil hopes to be supplying a considerable portion of its own enrichment needs.

Discussion in late 1979 on the possibility of a partial curtailment of the German order by the then newly installed government of President Figueiredo led to considerable consultation and an implied German threat not to transfer enrichment and reprocessing technology. Strains in the German–Brazilian relationship continued as it was revealed in the Brazilian press that secret arrangements gave the German exporting company practical control over the so-called joint company (NUCLEN) set up as part of the original 1975 contract to oversee the transfer of nuclear information to Brazil. It was also pointed out that the actual transfer of nuclear technology had been to NUCLEN, and that the Brazilian government nuclear establishment or research centers had benefited little. In early 1981, Brazilian government officials seemed determined to proceed with the full German order for 8 power units, although extending the time period for its completion until at least the year 2000. However, Brazilian officials emphasized that all aspects of the fuel cycle must be transferred to Brazil by 1990, the deadline established when the agreement was signed in 1975, regardless of the number of nuclear plants in operation by then.* Moreover, the delay in the construction of the German-supplied units have provided an unanticipated benefit to the Brazilians by giving work that had been thought would be undertaken by the German parent company, KWU, in Germany, to the Brazilian–German equipment company, NUCLEP. NUCLEP, which had been idle, began in 1980 to fashion components for the second and third units and will supply Argentina with heavy equipment and the reactor core vessel as part of that nation's arrangement with Germany.

In late 1980, NUCLON was created as a subsidiary of NUCLEBRAS, with the objective of managing the construction of nuclear power plants, previously the responsibility of the national electric utility's subsidiary FURNAS.

---

* "Controversy Erupts in Brazil—FRG Nuclear Transfer Deal," Foreign Broadcast Information Service, Worldwide Report, Nuclear Development and Proliferation, Number 53, July 21, 1980.

13

Human Rights
in Latin America

Bryce Wood

INTRODUCTION

The Organization of American States (OAS) established in 1960 the
Inter-American Commission on Human Rights (IACHR) for the
purpose of promoting respect for human rights in its member states.

In consequence of World War II, the notion became widely held
that governments most observant of human rights within their own
countries were least likely to attack their neighbors. As a result of
atrocities committed during the war, the charters of the United
Nations and of the OAS, and the Genocide Convention expressed
concern for the protection of human rights. In the Western Hemisphere, while the American states as early as the Lima Conference of
1938 had stated a desire for the protection of human rights, it
remained for the simultaneous development of democratic forces in
the late 1950s in Peru, Venezuela, and elsewhere to provide the
motivation for the founding of the IACHR. In 1959, at the fifth
meeting of consultation of ministers of foreign affairs of the American Republics, resolutions were passed that called for the drafting of
a convention on human rights and for creating a commission that
would base its authority in a statute until the convention went into

effect. In 1965, the statute was revised, and the IACHR was made a "principal organ" of the OAS.

In 1978, the revised American Convention on Human Rights went into effect with its ratification by 11 states—Colombia, Costa Rica, Dominican Republic, Ecuador, El Salvador, Grenada, Guatemala, Haiti, Honduras, Panama, and Venezuela. The IACHR is thus based on a treaty among the ratifiers of the Convention, and the court of human rights has been set up in San Jose, Costa Rica. Sixteen countries have now ratified the Convention.*

What are human rights? The term has been used to describe application of the writ of habeas corpus, and to set forth claims to cultural development and family stability. It has even been suggested that human rights is a "buzz term" for which an accurate definition, or alternative expression, should be found. For the IACHR, however, the term does not embrace the so-called "social" rights but is rather strictly limited to political and civic rights. Among these latter, some are described as "basic," and the IACHR has been directed to devote special attention to those provided in Articles 1 (life), 2 (equality before the law), 3 (religion), 4 (speech), 18 (right to a fair trial), 25 (right of freedom from arbitrary arrest), and 26 (right to due process of law) of the American Declaration of the Rights and Duties of man. Protection of these rights has been delegated by the OAS to the IACHR. The fostering of other rights is primarily the concern of the Economic and Social Council and other agencies of the OAS.

ACTIVITIES OF THE IACHR

The IACHR is a body of seven members, who are not governmental delegates. They are nominated by governments and selected by the Permanent Council of the OAS as individual citizens, who are free from orders by governmental officials. It meets for a maximum of eight weeks a year, and membership is only a part-time occupation. Members are elected for four-year terms and may be reelected. The commission staff is small, although of high quality. Its budget is of the order of $600,000 per year, and the staff is a part of the secretariat of the OAS. Through 1975, over 2000 complaints were given case numbers, and that figure has greatly increased in the past five years.

---

* Five additional countries have signed the Convention but not yet ratified.

Complaints

The IACHR is seized of situations, and may take cognizance of complaints of violations of human rights made by individuals, national and international private associations such as Amnesty International, and government members of the OAS. Acceptance of complaints from individuals is an extremely important aspect of the work of the IACHR, since it is not dependent upon political constraints that may affect the attitudes of public or private institutions.

The Commission may reject any given complaint as being insubstantial, or for other reasons. A complaint may be the basis for requests for information from a government, and it may be grounds for recommendations or suggestions by the Commission to a government. The Commission may thus be an official mediatory body between individuals and their own governments, a particularly valuable function when the individuals in question have not been given a hearing at home.

A complaint may also be the basis for a request to a government for a visit to the country by one or more members of the IACHR to investigate the situation. Usually such a request will be based on more than one complaint; and, in all cases, the government concerned may refuse the request for a visit. Even if a visit is refused, as in the case of Brazil, complaints may provide information utilized in an annual commission report on that country.

Visits

The IACHR may make two types of visits. The first is to study the situation giving rise to complaints, especially in cases of, for example, inhumane treatment in prisons, where redress would not be afforded by slow procedures of the exhaustion of local remedies. An example of this type of visit is that to Argentina in 1980.

In addition, the Commission has visited countries, again at their request, to assist in the protection of human rights in wartime, civil or international. Visits for this purpose were made to the Dominican Republic in 1965–66, and to Honduras and El Salvador in 1969.

In making visits, the members of the IACHR by no means deal only with officials—there are no possibilities of "potemkin villages." The members visit prisons, tape-record conversations with prisoners, interview wives of prisoners, visit military courts at times of trials. In Chile, in 1974, the Commission made its members available to over

400 persons who made oral reports and were encouraged to write official complaints against the Pinochet regime.

The acquiescence of states in visits by the Commission is encouraged by the Commission's informing them that it is preparing a report on the local human rights situation. Since 1974, invitations to visit have been received from Argentina, Chile, El Salvador, Haiti, Nicaragua, and Panama, among others. These governments presumably considered that they might make a better case for themselves if the Commission saw the conditions on the spot rather than depend solely on complaints from individual citizens.

Reports

Five types of reports are made by the IACHR: (1) a report of proceedings at each session; (2) annual reports to the General Assembly of the OAS—these are substantial documents of over 100 pages; (3) special reports on the human rights situation in individual countries; (4) special studies that are articles or essays by Commission members; (5) *Inter-American Yearbooks on Human Rights.*

These reports are given full publicity by the IACHR. Special regulations affect publicity for the third type of report. An example will indicate the careful procedure followed by the Commission. Charges that a labor leader in the textile industry, Olavo Hansen, had mysteriously died while in the custody of the Brazilian police were sent in 1970 to the Brazilian government, which had denied the Commission access to Brazil for a study. The Commission concluded that the Brazilian reply to the charges was inadequate, and after allowing the required period of 180 days to pass without receipt of further information from Brazil, the Commission assumed that the accuracy of its information, as charged, was confirmed. In 1973, it therefore reported as its formal judgment that the Brazilian government had been responsible for "exceedingly grave violations of the right to life." Thus Brazil was "named" by the commission, and details of the Olavo Hansen case were given.

Similarly, in the report of the IACHR to the General Assembly in 1980, it was stated that "numerous serious violations of fundamental human rights, as recognized in the American Declaration of the Rights and Duties of Man, were committed in the Republic of Argentina during the period covered by this report—1975 to 1979."*

---

* *Report on the Situation of Human Rights in Argentina* (1980), 263.

Publicity

The giving of publicity to reports such as these has created serious tension among the American states. The Brazilians ignored the 1973 report of the Commission, despite its publicity, because the issue did not arise in the General Assembly. By 1980, however, the situation had so changed that Argentina could not cover itself so quietly.

The change in the position of the IACHR was dramatically manifested during the session of the General Assembly in Santiago, Chile, in 1976. Then, for the first time, the work of the Commission was recognized and given serious attention. Ever since 1960, the reports of the IACHR had been routinely accepted, without debate. The Chairman of the Commission was not accorded the opportunity to present the report, nor to speak from the platform. In Chile, however, the Commission's report on Chile was published in full by the local newspapers; the Chairman spoke on the work of the Commission; and a debate was held on the Commission's report. Resolutions "named" Chile, asked its government to respect human rights and to provide guarantees to persons providing testimony on human rights issues, and thanked the Commission for its reports.

In the course of the debate, Secretary of State Henry Kissinger stated that the record of the IACHR showed that "it deserves the support of the Assembly in strengthening further its independence, evenhandedness, and constructive potential." He proposed that the budget and staff of the IACHR be enlarged and said that the United States would make a voluntary contribution of $102,000 to enable the IACHR to engage in new activities.*

Later, in Grenada in 1977, a resolution was passed by a bare majority of 14 to none (8 abstentions, 3 absences) expressing approval of the work of the IACHR, doubling the resources available in 1966–1977, and recommending cooperation with the work of the Commission by members of the OAS. The majority for this resolution consisted of Barbados, Costa Rica, Dominican Republic, Ecuador, Grenada, Haiti, Jamaica, Mexico, Panama, Peru, Surinam, Trinidad and Tobago, the United States, and Venezuela.

At the same meeting, a resolution proposed by Colombia passed by 18 to none. It noted that earlier states of economic development and capital formation in certain states had created "serious tensions

---

* Text of speech in Department of State Publication 8866, June 1976. Kissinger added that "the condition of human rights as assessed by the Inter-American Commission on Human Rights has impaired our relationship with Chile and will continue to do so."

and a political climate that is not conducive to the necessary respect for and protection of human rights." It asked the IACHR to explore means of analyzing human rights violations based on principles that were respectful of "the juridical equality of states." This apparently meant that the IACHR was being asked to cease issuing reports that pointed the finger of criticism at individual states. The Commission has not yet completed this study.

TENSIONS

The IACHR is concerned with individual human beings, not regimes, and it continues under its mandate to press for the primacy of the rights to life and humane treatment. The Commission maintains that exceptional conditions of war or public danger do not authorize "deprivation of life, torture," and other deprivations of human rights.*

These claims are strongly and explicitly opposed by the military regimes in Argentina, Chile, and elsewhere.

The problem was recognized in the American Convention on Human Rights, which states (Art. 27) that governments may "take measures derogating from their obligations under the present Convention to the extent and for the period of time strictly required by the exigencies of the situation." The IACHR is free to condemn, but the states are free to "derogate" and for as long as it pleases them. The Chilean government went further and justified its actions by asserting that, if it could not defend the Chilean people against the enemies of the regime, the "basic rights" of the Chilean people would be endangered.

The main issue for the OAS in this matter is to find ways for accommodation between its aim of fostering the protection of human rights and demands by member governments for freedom to violate those rights when the rights of individuals stand in the way of what governments deem essential to ensure national security, the stability of a given regime, or both.

The issue became very clear at the General Assembly's session in November 1980, when the IACHR's report on Argentina was considered. The Argentine delegate declared that if the report, highly

---

* IACHR, *Report on the Status of Human Rights in Chile* (1974), 3.

critical of Argentina, were accepted by the General Assembly, he would leave the meeting, withhold payments to the OAS, and recall the Argentine ambassador to the OAS. Indications were that he would probably be followed by other countries, including Bolivia, Chile, Paraguay, and Uruguay. The debate was lengthy and delicate, but the opposition, headed by the United States, finally accepted a resolution that, while mentioning Argentina and other countries by name, did not condemn them for violating human rights.

The Argentines and others viewed the reports of the IACHR as contravening the principle of nonintervention. Further, they viewed the final resolution as a victory over both the IACHR and the United States, since it was weaker than previous resolutions against Chile, for example, in which the General Assembly had "named" Chile for abuses of human rights.

The United States ceased pressing for a stronger resolution when it found it did not have sufficient votes and because, to use the words of the Argentine foreign minister, Carlos Pastor: "political and military sectors at the highest level in the United States were primarily concerned with avoiding any dangers to the system of Inter-American security."* Pastor added: "If our Organization is led to consider itself to have super-national jurisdiction, that it can judge governments and assume the stance of a political body superior to the governments themselves, we shall have found the best way to destroy it."†

Emboldened by this diplomatic victory, the Argentines threaten to attack the essential base of the power of the IACHR and to reduce its capability to make and publish special reports that charge individual countries with violations of human rights. Foreign Minister Pastor said at the end of the General Assembly session that at the coming meeting of the Council of the OAS he would endeavor to curtail the freedom of action of the IACHR, which, as he noted, took a political view of human rights, by asserting that their protection depended on the existence of a democratic regime in a given country. The United States may have to defend the Commission against this expected Argentine assault in 1981.

The IACHR is now on the defensive. Its position is illustrative of the principal, long-range, continuous problem in inter-American affairs: the struggle between nonintervention and control. This is the problem of governance. The Latin American states, beginning in

---

* *Informativo* (Press Notices), Nov. 28, 1980, OAS, 3.
† Address to the Tenth General Assembly of the OAS, Nov. 20, 1980, OAS, 4.

1933 at Montevideo and culminating in 1948 at Bogota, secured from the United States, first a declaration, and finally a treaty obligation to refrain from intervention, directly or indirectly, in the internal or foreign affairs of other signatory states. The obligation applied to all American countries, but the charges of intervention were chiefly made against the United States.

The United States tried to find ways around both the declarations and the treaty, but in vain. The Committee for Political Defense of the Americas was terminated in 1945; the Rodriguez Larreta Doctrine authorizing joint action in defense of democracy was rejected in 1946 by Latin America; the Inter-American Peace Committee was shorn of its informal powers to act in a conflict between two American states and, most recently, collaborative action in the Nicaraguan dispute was decisively refused by the OAS.

The work of the IACHR is the most recent of the OAS-sponsored international activities to come under attack by Latin American countries and to be defended by the United States. How strong will that defense be? Given new life and funding by the Ford administration in 1976, and strongly supported by the Carter administration, the outlook is, at the best, for "quiet diplomacy" by the Reagan Administration in defense of human rights. The recent trend of the IACHR has been toward public, noisy diplomacy, and the support previously given by the United States may therefore be subdued, if not entirely absent.

THE POLICY OF THE UNITED STATES

The policy of the United States on human rights may be divided into two sections: (1) that toward the IACHR, and (2) that taken as unilateral action.

Policy toward the IACHR

Up to 1980, the United States has been positively supportive of the role of the IACHR in giving publicity to its condemnation of violators of human rights. This does not mean that it has interfered in the work of the IACHR, but at meetings of the General Assembly it has favored approval of the agency's reports. It withdrew this strong measure of support in November 1980, in order to maintain the unity of the OAS as a regional organization within the United Nations system for keeping the peace, under Article 51 of the Charter of the UN. There might be a future occasion, comparable to the Dominican Republic affairs of 1965, when the United States would wish to bring to the OAS a case or incident that could not, because of a Soviet veto in the Security Council, be handled satisfactorily by that body. Inter-American solidarity for purposes of national security, in other words, is more important to the United States government than support of the decisions of the IACHR *à outrance*.

The Inter-American Commission on Human Rights may be expected to continue its independent, rigorous manner of upholding human rights principles and denouncing those who abuse them. The publicity given its reports on individual countries can probably not be prevented, even though the General Assembly may take action on them like that in the case of Argentina in 1980. The IACHR will remain "a boil on the body politic" of the OAS unless its capabilities are removed. Such action may well require an amendment to the Charter of the OAS, which would be extremely difficult, given the strong support for the Commission among the American states.* However, the issue is sure to come up in one form or another at succeeding General Assembly sessions.

Reports on individual countries will continue to be made. Such reports have been made on the following states, based either on complaints from persons or associations, or on visits by the Commission: Argentina (one), Chile (three), Cuba (five), Dominican Republic (four), El Salvador (one), Haiti (five), Guatemala (one), Nicaragua (one), Panama (one), Paraguay (one), Uuruguay (one).

The attitude of the United States toward the IACHR has been somewhat equivocal. Senator Edward Kennedy has said: "I can conceive of no more important organ within the Organization of American States than the Commission [on Human Rights]. ... In our relations with other [sic] Latin American nations it is invaluable to have an inter-American agency with the prestige of the Commission available to investigate, report, and make recommendations with regard to the condition of human rights within the hemisphere."† Assistant Secretary of State for Inter-American Affairs, William Rogers, asserted: "Its success—the extent to which the Commission

---

* See T. Buergenthal, "The Revised O.A.S. Charter and the Protection of Human Rights," 69 *AJIL*, 835. October, 1965.
† *Congressional Record*, S19100, Nov. 3, 1975.

can indeed nurture, protect and enhance respect for human rights in the Hemisphere—could come to be considered the most significant accomplishment of the Inter-American System in the years to come."*

To a question put by Senator Kennedy as to whether the United States was "using" the IACHR "as a mechanism now to try and protect human rights," early replies by the Department of State were unresponsive; finally, William Buffum, Assistant Secretary of State for International Affairs, said that, with respect to a resolution on Chile: "In fact it is very helpful to have this matter pending before the Human Rights Commission [of the UN] because it gives us a natural point of departure in raising and initiating discussions with some of the countries concerned." † This same argument would, of course, be applicable to resolutions adopted by the General Assembly of the OAS respecting human rights, and it highlights the advantage for the United States of having a preliminary decision made by a respected international agency, on a matter of concern to the United States government.

It is true, of course, that the United States cannot "use" the Commission in the sense of manipulating it. The Commission is independent, and is thus entirely different from the UN Commission, which consists of governmental delegates. Efforts by the United States to bring influence to bear upon the Commission, whose members are rightly jealous of their independence, could hardly be effective. The United States could, however, "use" a recommendation by the Commission after it had been made as the basis for negotiations with respect to a Latin American state's policy. The action taken by the IACHR would provide a disinterested, international platform from which the pursuit of more humane policies by a member government could be encouraged or enhanced by Washington's persuasion.

Unilateral Policy of the United States on Human Rights

Beginning in 1973, former Representative Donald M. Fraser and Senator Kennedy took the lead in inducing the Congress to adopt

---

* Address to Pan American Society, Boston, Nov. 4, 1975.
† "Hearings on Review of the U.N. Commission on Human Rights, before the Subcommittee on International Organization and Movements of the House Committee on Foreign Affairs, 93rd Cong. 2nd Session, June 18, 20, 1974.

legislation to attempt to make military and some economic aid dependent on a recipient country's observance of human rights. Development aid was prohibited after 1975 to "the government of any country engaging in a consistent pattern of gross violations of internationally recognized human rights" unless "the aid will benefit needy people." Military aid to Chile and other countries violating human rights was prevented after 1974; and severely limited economic aid could be doubled only if the President certified that Chile did not engage in "a persistent pattern" of violation of human rights and that it had allowed "unimpeded investigation" by international commissions of alleged abuses of human rights.

This latter provision opened the possibility that sanctions might be applied by the United States in order to implement some decisions of the IACHR. However, subsequent decisions in this field have not hardened into firm policies.

In 1976, the Congress expressed as "the policy of the United States . . . to promote and encourage increased respect for human rights and fundamental freedoms for all . . . by all countries."* This statement was not purely rhetorical, since it instructed the President to avoid identification of the United States, through its security programs, with regimes that disregarded the human rights of their citizens; and, in addition, directed the Department of State to provide annual reports on "the observance of and respect for internationally recognized human rights in each country proposed as a recipient of security assistance." This latter provision was drafted as a result of the Department's having ignored a similar request in 1975; it had produced only a general account of human rights situations abroad, without reference to individual countries. Subsequently, the Department complied and made extensive reports, with details on each country, that gave the Congress the means for judging the accuracy of the government's statements about security assistance and human rights.

In addition, legislation was passed establishing a Bureau of Human Rights and Humanitarian Affairs, headed by an Assistant Secretary of State, Patricia M. Derian, who served throughout the Carter administration's term. Her function was to raise the issue of human rights in all decisions of the Department that related directly to countries regarded as guilty of violations of human rights. She also gave extensive publicity, through speeches and special publications, to charges of such violations.

---

* International Security Assistance and Arms Export Control Act of 1976, H.R. 13680, 1976.

This remarkable fusion of congressional and official concern for human rights was supported by a strong constituency of religious and other private organizations that carefully watched situations abroad that affected human rights and brought pressure to bear on Congress and the administration to take action within their legal capacity. "The Latin American rights lobby 'approaches the Jewish community in its effectiveness.'"*

In addition to publishing its annual review of human rights performance in Latin American and other countries and to making speeches, the Department of State and the Congress have carried out two types of deprivations of assistance to those regarded as responsible for persistent abuses of the rights of their citizens. The first is to prevent the offering of security assistance to Argentina since 1978, to Bolivia since July 1980, to Chile since 1976, to Guatemala since 1977, and to Uruguay since 1976.

The second is that at the multilateral level the United States government has opposed 18 and supported 2 out of a total of 20 loan applications submitted by Argentina to the Inter-American Development Bank (IDB). With respect to Chile, the United States voted in the negative on all IDB loans since 1977. It should be noted, however, that these negative votes did not prevent the loans being made by the IDB or the World Bank, which, in general, follow a policy that loan applications should be judged solely on the basis of their economic promise. At the local level, however, since 1978 the United States has approved large-scale financing of exports to Argentina through the Eximbank.

With the presidential election of 1980, there were signs of a change in the policy of the United States government. President Carter maintained his policies with a firm speech at the November 1980 meeting of the General Assembly of the OAS; in the following month Clergy and Laity Concerned, a body represented by 71 prominent American religious leaders including 12 bishops from various denominations, addressed a letter to President-elect Ronald Reagan, stating that

> The greatest Christmas gift you can give the world will be a strong and unequivocal statement affirming this nation's historic commitment to peace with justice, democracy, and human rights, making it clear that however your policy on human rights may differ from

---

* Patricia M. Derian, quoted in Sandy Vogelgesang, *American Dream Global Nightmare: The Dilemma of U.S. Human Rights Policy* (New York: Norton, 1980), p. 147.

that of the previous Administration it will neither condone nor tolerate the use of torture, murder or violent suppression of dissent on the part of governments which receive our friendship and support.*

On the other hand, encouraged by some speeches made by Mr. Reagan during the presidential campaign, there were heard voices in opposition to the human rights policies of the Carter administration. David Rockefeller spoke for the business community, favoring a concern for human rights, but opposing "our Government's *application* of 'human rights' policies around the world."† Specifically, he did not believe that "repeated lecturing and public condemnation" of regimes would be effective. Further, he opposed the United States effort to impose its "own standards by threatening to curtail foreign aid and trade." Finally, he pointed to the inconsistency of giving little criticism to some totalitarian regimes "with full-blown Gulag Archipelagos," while singling out for "special opprobrium" some Latin American countries—"authoritarian nations which have posed no threat to us and were even inclined to be friendly."

On the first point, Mr. Rockefeller may have been correct. President Carter referred to "disappointments" resulting from his policies; and Ms. Derian admitted in October 1980 that in Argentina, Guatemala, and Chile the human rights situation remained serious, with little improvement. On the other hand, it does not appear that critics of the policy have been able to point to any serious number of specific instances in which the Carter policy has been of substantial disadvantage to United States national interests.

An unspoken element of Mr. Rockefeller's objection to the Carter policies was probably that they adversely affected United States business enterprises in dealing with Latin American counterparts. He might have said that North American arms firms were hampered in their dealings with Argentina and Chile because of the lack of public financing for purchases. Similarly, antipathy aroused by the policies of the United States may, in more general terms, result in business being directed toward European, Japanese, or other sources rather than to United States banks and businesses.

On the other hand, Jacobo Timerman, an Argentine publisher jailed and tortured in Argentina, has stated that: "'Quiet diplomacy

---

* *The New York Times*, Dec. 18, 1980.
† Letter, *The New York Times*, Dec. 5, 1980.

is surrender. The Carter human rights policy—an outspoken policy—saved thousands and thousands of lives in Argentina.'"* He also credited Ms. Derian with having saved many lives, because she went to Buenos Aires and made "'a great scandal' about human rights."†

The Reagan administration has made several moves indicative of a different, less public approach to issues of human rights, although some of the points mentioned above have not yet been finally answered.

In a speech to the Trilateral Commission on March 31, 1981, Secretary of State Alexander Haig stated that the United States opposed the "violation of human rights by ally or adversary, friend or foe. We are not going to pursue a policy of selective indignation." However:

> We should distinguish between the deprivation of national rights through aggression and the deprivation of personal rights through oppression. . . . It does little good to remedy the grievances of a few if that brings down worse oppression on the many. . . . We should adopt a sense of proportion in dealing with violators—the authoritarian versus the totalitarian regime.

Mr. Reagan made a statement embarrassing to his staff in saying that "the United States should not negotiate with any country unless the subject of human persecution is on that negotiating table." This is the strongest statement in favor of human rights made by the new administration, but the President's aides said this did not mean that he intended to "alter his policy of playing down the rights issue in foreign relations." A conference of the aides was called about "'what was said, what was meant and how it would be read.'"‡

The administration has proposed to Congress the elimination of the existing ban on arms exports to Argentina. However, the appropriate committees in both the House and Senate have voted to tie permission to sell arms to Argentina to that country's record on human rights and have asked the President to make a statement on the Argentine record in this regard. It remains to be seen what action will be taken on this proposal by the Congress as a whole. Over objections by Secretary Haig, human rights restrictions were also placed on aid to El Salvador. The President would be required by the committees to state in two annual reports "that the Government of El Salvador is not engaged in a consistent pattern of violations of

---

* Quoted in *The New York Times,* May 24, 1981.
† Tom Wicker, "Mr. Lefever's Colors," *The New York Times*, May 22, 1981.
‡ *The New York Times*, May 1, 1981.

human rights." The action was intended by the committees to be helpful to President Napoleon Duarte of El Salvador, who, however, later characterized it as "intervention in 'an internal political problem.'"*

Finally, the administration supported its candidate, Ernest W. Lefever, to succeed Ms. Derian as Assistant Secretary, to the end of his confirmation hearings, when he withdrew his name from further consideration after an adverse vote in the Senate Foreign Relations Committee. Mr. Lefever was known to have favored the elimination of laws setting up human rights standards for the action of the United States government, and to have been a partisan of "quiet diplomacy" in dealing with states charged with human rights abuses. There were other elements affecting the action by the Committee, so that its vote was not clearly based on the nominee's views on human rights.

It should be noted that the Inter-American Commission on Human Rights was not mentioned in the press in the voluminous reporting of the Lefever nomination hearings. The closest the hearings apparently came to the IACHR was after Mr. Lefever had said he would speak out against Soviet abuses, "But as to other countries, he would use 'quiet diplomacy' except in 'egregious circumstances.'" Senator Rudy Boschwitz, Republican of Minnesota, asked: "What egregious circumstances in the last couple of years would have led you to speak out?" Mr. Lefever responded that he preferred "'not to mention particular countries. . . . It is not in good taste for me to identify friendly and allied nations.'"† Given the strong condemnation of Argentina in the report of the IACHR, this was an opportunity for Mr. Lefever to have mentioned both of them in answer to the Senator's question. At the present time, the administration does not appear to have decided whether to nominate another person for the Assistant Secretaryship or to leave the position unfilled.

PROSPECTS FOR THE FUTURE

It has been said that the IACHR will continue to receive complaints and to make blunt, outspoken, published reports on the observance of principles of human rights to individual countries.

---

* *The New York Times*, May 13, 1981.
† Anthony Lewis, "Advice and Consent," *The New York Times*, May 21, 1981.

The IACHR will continue to be attacked by such authoritarian regimes as are now in control in Argentina, Chile, and Guatemala. If the Commission is to be maintained with no abatement in its powers, the policy of the United States will be crucial to its effectiveness in coming years.

Even under the Carter administration, the United States maintained a certain distance from the IACHR. It did not, for example, base its judgments about human rights in Latin America directly on the recommendations of the Commission, but it made its own determination of the situation, which it published, as a guide for withholding arms or economic aid. However, in the OAS itself, official representatives gave their full support to the actions of the Commission. This action apparently meant that the administration did not wish, by accepting a Commission judgment on one country, to lose the "flexibility" that it desired in dealing with certain situations in which other considerations, such as national security, were regarded as compelling.

Under the Reagan administration the portents are that authoritarian regimes in the Americas will receive more friendly treatment from Washington than in the past, and that efforts will be made to restrain the IACHR in the OAS and to change the legislation that currently inhibits the freedom of officials in their dealings with such regimes. Further, the adoption of methods of "quiet diplomacy" will probably be attempted with respect to human rights. Such methods are opposed by those who support individuals against governments as being a surrender to brutal official actions and with little effect in saving lives, as compared to the open protests by the Carter administration.

The IACHR is one of the most effective agencies of the OAS at the present time. In the governance of the Western Hemisphere, it is a vital and fundamental means of minimal international control over the efforts of governments to torture, murder, and hold without trial members of the opposition. It represents the conscience of men of good will, and their responsibility at least to speak out against inhumane methods of tyranny. The IACHR stands for the view that torture is torture, whether committed by a communist country like Cuba or a military regime such as Argentina's.

Concern for basic human rights is a global cause. There is nothing uniquely American or Western in denouncing imprisonment without trial, government-sponsored torture and political, religious or ethnic massacres. Abhorrence for these outrages is so widespread that even governments that permit them are ashamed to confess it.*

Fearful of a shift of emphasis in the national policy on human rights, Representative Don Bonker, Democrat, Washington, writes that

> To abandon our human rights policy would be a terrible blow to freedom everywhere. In a turbulent world, the forces of liberty are desperately struggling for survival. Dictatorial regimes, whether friend or foe, reject the concept of a free and open society. They uphold values that are as inimical to our country's long-term national interests as those of our avowed enemies.†

Finally, to emphasize an essential difference between the Western democratic and Soviet systems of governance, the United States should adopt firmly and openly a position that makes very clear that it is strongly opposed to the violations of human rights by any government of whatever character. As Secretary Haig has said: "We are not going to pursue a policy of selective indignation." If that is so, then let us make no efforts to distinguish among different types of regimes to justify different attitudes toward their commission of identical crimes.

It is said that we should not embarrass a regime like Argentina's by mentioning that 5000 to 6000 persons have mysteriously disappeared there without trace in the past five years. But the Argentine regime should be embarrassed at such damning statistics, and no weakening of the IACHR should be permitted that would eliminate the possibility that Argentina, among others, should be pilloried by the IACHR for its misdeeds.

The reasons adduced for being tender toward Argentina's "sensitivity" over human rights include the opinion that the Argentine navy could be of value in the South Atlantic in case of conflict. This seems a very doubtful thesis. In the past two world wars, Argentina adopted a policy of unbenign neutrality, and there is no assurance that its policy would be any different in a third World War.

It is a diplomatic technique that is counterproductive for the United States member of the IACHR to be its chairman. Further,

---

* *The New York Times*, May 24, 1981.
† *The New York Times*, Dec. 22, 1980.

he should not have given the Argentine delegate the opportunity to make some caustic remarks about United States charges, by reading the case of the IACHR against Argentina at the 1980 meeting of the General Assembly. These gaffes, however, may be remedied.

The main proposition remains, that the IACHR should be retained as a principal organ of the OAS, and that the United States government should give its strong support to the IACHR as the international spokesman for the defense and promotion of human rights in the Western Hemisphere. The separation of the IACHR from the OAS would mean a surrender to violators of human rights, much as would "quiet diplomacy." The IACHR would then again be ignored, as it was before 1976, and its protests and recommendations would go unheard and unheeded. It presently performs a noble function that cannot be ignored by member states of the OAS, and that is as it should be.

14

Export Performance and Promise in Latin America: Substance and Institutions

Sidney Weintraub

INTRODUCTION

Two measurably distinct but conceptually linked trends dominated the export sector of Latin American economies in the past several decades—the absolute growth of intraregional trade and the significant internationalization of trade (especially exports) beyond the hemisphere. The linking is inevitable, since as export competitiveness improves on a world scale, it will also on a regional scale, even absent agreements providing for intraregional trade preferences. In relative and absolute terms, the world market overwhelms the regional market. Latin America sent 78% of its exports to developed countries in 1979 and 16% to other countries of the region.[1] There was relatively greater growth in intraregional trade in manufactures than in other types of goods. What happens on the world scene thus matters a great deal in Latin America. Turning inward to the region can be an accompaniment to this international role, but not a substitute for it if the region is to grow at an acceptable rate.

These trends underscore the wariness with which hemispheric countries should view trends that gained currency during the 1970s. These parade under various guises: industrial policy, the need to organize markets or to reach orderly marketing agreements, the need for "fair" trade or bilateral "reciprocity" in each sector, or that the future of Latin American economic growth rests principally on increased regional trade. Each is a formula or an excuse for restricting imports in developed country markets, particularly of manufactured goods.

The purpose of this chapter is twofold: to examine the export prospects of Latin American (and Caribbean) countries[2] for the foreseeable future (say, over the next decade), which must involve looking at what they produce and with what efficiency, and prospects and impediments in export markets; and, in the light of the substantive projection, to examine the adequacy of existing institutions dealing with international trade. The intent is to be analytic and prescriptive rather than statistically comprehensive.

Several cautionary comments should be made at the outset. Trade affects, and in turn is affected by, other variables. Exports help a country earn the wherewithal to purchase imports, which in turn are necessary to achieve growth objectives, and, in its turn, economic growth is a necessary even if insufficient condition for adequate employment creation. Industrial and agricultural policies not only affect trade, but help to determine where people will live (in cities or rural areas) and how they will earn their livings. The growth in external debt of Latin American countries has helped to finance imports, and hence growth, but the explosive growth of such debt during the 1970s also has imposed a burden, which impedes growth, on some countries.[3] Each of these considerations must be kept in mind when examining trade, even if they are not explicitly cited at each point in the following exposition.

Trade, in other words, is interwoven with the most vital aspects of economies and political structures. Whether a country has an import bias or an export bias is a technical issue,[4] to be sure, but it also influences overall economic growth, employment, distribution of income, and even the distribution of power within societies.[5]

One final caution should be cited. Countries obviously vary in the composition of their trade, in their trade potential, and in the relative importance of trade to their income and employment. Space does not permit dealing with the trade prospects of each country. Aggregation will involve some simplification. In order to avoid gross distortion, however, some distinction will be made between large countries, whose trade weight on the world scene can be significant, middle-sized countries that have a more modest weight, and very small countries whose weight is negligible. Treatment of all countries in the same manner—which the most-favored-nation principle implies —creates its own inequities.

TABLE 14.1. GDP and Export Growth in Latin America (Average Annual Percentage Variations)

	1961–70	1971–75	1976	1977	1978	1979	1980
GDP	5.7	6.6	5.3	4.7	4.6	5.8	5.4
Exports[1]	5.0	2.4	8.4	9.0	8.7	6.3	4.6

Source: *Economic and Social Progress in Latin America, 1980-81 Report,* Inter-American Development Bank, p. 9.

[1]Exports of goods and services.

INTERNATIONALIZATION AND REGIONALIZATION OF ECONOMIES: SOME FACTS

Some important changes took place in Latin America's trade during the 1970s. During the 1960s and early 1970s, GDP for the region as a whole grew more rapidly than exports. Since 1976, the reverse generally has been the case. The comparisons are shown in Table 14.1.

As a consequence, exports as a percentage of GDP first declined and since the mid-1970s have been on the increase. This makes the region more vulnerable to economic activity in the rest of the world. Table 14.2 provides the data.

TABLE 14.2. Export/GDP Ratio in Latin America

		1960	1975	1980[2]
Exports	(millions of 1980 dollars)[1]	23,197	42,133	60,177
GDP	(millions of 1980 dollars)	169,922	403,943	519,493
Export/GDP ratio (percent)		13.7	10.4	11.6

Source: *Economic and Social Progress in Latin America, 1980–81 Report,* pp. 400 and 403.

[1]Exports of goods and services.
[2]Preliminary.

This pattern holds also for the big three countries, Argentina, Brazil, and Mexico. Their ratio of exports to GDP on the same basis as in Table 14.2 went from 8.0% in 1980 to 6.9% in 1975, and rose to 8.8% in 1980. In 1980, these three countries accounted for 52.5% of all exports of goods and services from Latin American countries and 69.5% of the region's GDP. For middle-sized countries, such as Chile, Colombia, and Peru, exports typically make up a more significant portion of GDP than for the three large countries. The pattern of Table 14.2 holds for Peru, generally for Chile in that exports as a percentage of GDP rose substantially in the latter 1970s, but does not for Colombia, although the divergence from the pattern for the latter 1970s is modest (and may be explained by nonrecorded exports). Venezuela is a special case because petroleum and its products make up more than 90% by value, of exports.

Food and raw materials still account for the overwhelming majority of the value of Latin American merchandise exports (more than 80% throughout the 1970s), but manufacturing has been the most dynamic sector (Standard Industrial Trade Classifications 5 through 8). During the 1960s, manufactured goods accounted for about 12% of the value of Latin America's merchandise exports, and in the latter 1970s they were more than 18%. This increase of manufactures in the share of total exports took place despite the large growth in the proportion of fuel exports (26.5% as an annual average between 1961 and 1966 to almost 35% between 1972 and 1977), which means that all other categories of exports (food and other raw materials) declined substantially as a proportion of the total.[6]

I will revert to this point because the protectionism that exists in world markets, and that which is threatened, is concentrated in manufactures. The threat to Latin America's manufactured exports comes also from economic slowdown (which itself fosters protectionism). Manufactured exports by Latin America as a percentage of total exports declined sharply in 1974 and 1975, the years of recession in the industrial countries, and then recovered again as worldwide economic activity picked up. It is this double vulnerability—to economic slowdown in the industrial countries and to import restrictionism, which flourishes at precisely such times—that has encouraged many in Latin America to look to increased regional trade as an antidote. Increased regional trade can be a palliative, but not a cure during the next decade, and probably well beyond that.

The development of the destination of Latin American exports is shown in Table 14.3, the destination of Latin American manufactured exports in Table 14.4. In combination, Tables 14.3 and 14.4 show the continuing overwhelming reliance by Latin America on

TABLE 14.3. Destination of Latin American Exports (Annual Average Percentages)

	1963–69	1973–79
Industrial countries	76	72
of which: United States	(34)	(36)
EEC[1]	(28)	(22)
Latin America	17	19

Source: Economic and Social Progress in Latin America, 1980–81 Report, p. 49.

[1] For all years includes the European Economic Community of nine as expanded in 1973.

world markets but also the significant potential of the regional market for manufactured goods. The push for regional and sub-regional integration in Latin America has been mainly a drive for industrial integration (and physical integration in such forms as transportation, communications, and electricity-generating facilities). As Table 14.4 shows, regional trade integration is occurring. This is significant. But Table 14.4 also shows that two-thirds of Latin America's manufactured exports still go outside the region, overwhelmingly to the industrial market economies. This, too, is significant.

It is important to keep in mind that the most diversified economies are those of the larger and middle-sized countries. These are the countries, particularly the larger ones, best able to take advantage of the drive for regional trade integration. For Latin America as a

TABLE 14.4. Destination of Latin American Manufactured Exports (Annual Average Percentages

	1973–74	1975–78
Western Europe	25	25
United States	30	26
Latin America	30	36

Source: Economic and Social Progress in Latin America, 1979 Report, p. 26.

whole, manufacturing as a percentage of GDP averaged 25.8% in 1980. Only two countries were above the average (Mexico and Brazil), but in seven other countries manufacturing as a percentage of GDP exceeded 20% (in descending order, Peru, Argentina, Nicaragua, Uruguay, Costa Rica, Chile, and Ecuador).

It is not that there has not been economic evolution and diversification in the other Latin American countries. There has been, varying from very little in the smallest and the poorest countries, to a significant amount in the middle-sized countries. However, the big three—or the big seven if the four most populous Andean countries are included (Chile, Colombia, Peru, and Venezuela)—dominate the statistics of economic regionalization and internationalization. I will revert to this point because it is a significant datum to be kept in mind in looking at what the Organization of American States (OAS) has called "horizontal" integration, that is, either regional or subregional. Bolivia's integration and internationalization interests are not the same as Brazil's, or Nicaragua's the same as Mexico's, or those of the ministates of the Eastern Caribbean the same as those of any of these.

If one focuses just on Latin America, the degree of trade internationalization looks impressive, at least for the larger countries. Between 1950 and 1977, average annual real growth in Latin America's exports was more than 7%.[8] For Brazil, following the shift in economic policy between 1964 and 1974 (that is, until the oil shock and the recession in the industrialized countries), the annual growth in exports in constant U.S. dollars was 12.5%; in industrial products it was almost 25%.[9] For Brazil, and for other Latin American countries, growth in nontraditional exports responded to the shift away from the overwhelming import bias inherent in the import substitution model of industrial development to a greater emphasis on export promotion. The crawling peg movement of exchange rates adopted in Brazil, Chile, and Colombia in the 1960s had much to do with encouraging exports, since it counterbalanced the export-impeding influence of earlier overvalued exchange rates.

The Latin American performance looks less impressive, however, when compared with that of developing Asia, where export promotion and the encouragement of competitive industry was a tenet of policy before it was adopted in Latin America. Despite its absolute growth, Latin America's share of world exports has declined steadily since the 1950s. Table 14.5 shows this.

The foregoing data are distorted by oil exports. During most of the 1970s, growth in manufacturing production has been higher in developing Asia than in Latin America, as has been the growth of

TABLE 14.5. Latin America's Share of World Exports

	World Exports (billions of dollars)	Latin American Exports (billions of dollars)	Latin American Share (%)
1958–62	127.6	10.1	7.9
1973–77	803.0	47.9	5.9
1978	1,190.3	65.7	5.5

Source: Organization of American States, *Hemispheric Cooperation and Integral Development,* 6 August 1980, p. 46.

Asian manufactured exports. Internationalization of Latin America's exports of manufactures came later than in developing Asia, but in recent years (since the mid-1970s), the growth in exports of manufactures by Latin America has been catching up with that of developing Asia.[10] The scope for further internationalization of Latin America's trade and for further penetration of world markets for manufactured goods is substantial. By the same token, mutterings about a reversion to import substitution industrialization are heard more in Latin America than in Asia. This discussion of greater reliance on import substitution is stimulated by concern that slow growth in the industrial countries, and the protectionism this might encourage, could stifle the burgeoning internationalism of Latin American economics. It is stimulated as well by an intellectual current in Latin America that argues that center–periphery relations that have accompanied this internationalization have been a major cause of the social and economic inequalities existing in Latin American countries.[11]

TRADE OPPORTUNITIES AND PROBLEMS

It already has been noted that the composition of Latin America's exports has been shifting over the past two decades. The share of food and raw materials has been declining and the shares of fuels and manufactures increasing. Table 14.6 shows this.

TABLE 14.6. Composition of Latin American Exports (In Percentages)

	1963-68	1973-78
Food	41	34
Raw materials	18	12
Fuels	27	35
Manufactures	12	15
Other	2	4
	100	100

Source: *Economic and Social Progress in Latin America, 1980–81 Report,* p. 50.

Different factors predominate in the markets for the different types of commodities. For most foods and raw materials exported by Latin America, world supply and demand conditions are the main determinants of trade and hence of export earnings. There is, however, substantial governmental interference in world markets for sugar, beef, and food and feed grains, and in the European Community for bananas.[12] For fuels, the actions of OPEC, the conservation measures of importing countries, and the state of the world economy are the most significant elements determining export earnings of oil exporters. For manufactures, the market is overlaid with extensive restrictive devices that impede imports.

The problems of primary product exporters, particularly those whose export earnings, depend heavily on a few such products, are well known. Market fluctuations were substantial for these products. Markets (prices) were exceedingly strong in 1973–74, exceedingly weak in 1975, reasonably good through mid-1977, bad again through most of 1978, then recovered in 1979, especially for oil and metals, and have since declined. There was no dynamic upward trend in the real level of primary commodity exports from the region during the 1970s. The conclusion that one must inevitably reach is that despite the continuing importance of primary products for the region's export earnings, dynamism for growth in export earnings must come from diversification into manufactures. Even for the oil exporters, for which this statement regarding growth in export earnings is not true, diversification is essential for job creation.

Just as the markets vary for different types of commodities, so do countries differ in their reliance on the various export products and, indeed, on the importance of exports in relation to GDP. As a general rule in Latin America (as elsewhere), big countries are less reliant on exports than small countries. Table 14.7 shows this. (The figures in parentheses are the actual percentages.)

The big countries predominate in an absolute sense in the most dynamic part of the export market (other than for oil), namely that for manufactures. This domination is even more pronounced for the export of sophisticated manufactures, such as the machinery and capital equipment. The data are shown in Table 14.8.

Some conclusions that emerge from these facts are the following:

1. For the small- and medium-sized countries, there is no substitute for the internationalization of their economies if overall growth rates are to be sufficiently large to absorb labor and meet the economic and social aspirations of their populations. Regional integration provides no escape from this conclusion. In both the Central American Common Market (CACM) and the Caribbean Community (CARICOM), trade with partners grew more rapidly than trade with the world until the early 1970s, but in both cases this intraregional trade growth then slackened. There were various reasons for this slowing of growth (political in Central America, skewed benefits in favor of Trinidad and Tobago in CARICOM), but one clear reason

TABLE 14.7. Exports of Goods and Nonfactor Services as a Percentage of GDP, 1978

Up to 10%	10–19%	20–29%	30–39%	40% & above
Brazil (7)	Argentina (14)	Chile (21)	El Salvador (30)	Antigua (51)
	Bolivia (17)	Costa Rica (29)	Honduras (38)	Belize (86)
	Colombia (16)	Dom. Rep. (21)	Montserrat (39)	Dominica (52)
	Mexico (11)	Ecuador (24)	Nicaragua (33)	Grenada (56)
	Paraguay (13)	Guatemala (22)		Jamaica (40)
		Peru (22)		Panama (40)
		Uruguay (20)		St. Kitts-Nevis (53)
		Venezuela (29)		St. Lucia (56)
				St. Vincent (57)
				Trinidad & Tobago (47)

Source: World Bank, *World Development Report, 1980*, pp. 118–119; various World Bank economic memoranda.

was the narrow limit to the potential size of the integrated market. In the Andean group, trade induced by integration has been marginal.[13] The early dynamism of intraregional trade in the Latin American Free Trade Association (LAFTA) benefited mainly the large countries, and that was one of the reasons for the eventual demise of the association. None of the integration movements was significant in adding to the competitiveness of Latin American countries in world markets.

It is recognized now that the original conception of regionalization, that which gave birth to all-inclusive preferential trade arrangements such as LAFTA, was not only too ambitious in the degree of intraregional trade liberalization contemplated, but also badly conceived. Trade benefits went inexorably to a few countries, usually in the form of trade diversion that Viner had analyzed was one of the potential consequences of trade integration. This meant that the less competitive countries paid higher prices for many of the manufactures they had to import, while receiving no counter-stimulus for the development of their own manufacturing industries. Various schemes to force governmental direction of industry location (going under various names, such as complementation agreements, integrated industries, and others) did not resolve the issue, indeed, probably further complicated it by requiring a degree of supranationality for which the Latin American countries was not ready. The thrust in

TABLE 14.8. Manufactured Exports from Latin America by Size of Country (In Percentages)

	All Manufactures		Metal Mechanical Machinery and Equipment	
	1970	1977	1970	1977
Large countries	66	74	82	83
Medium countries	10	13	8	9
Small countries	24	13	10	8
	100	100	100	100

Source: CEPAL, America Latina en el umbral de los anos 80, p. 61.

Note: The large countries are Argentina, Brazil, and Mexico. The medium-sized countries are Chile, Colombia, Peru, and Venezuela.

favor of inclusiveness gave way to subregionalism, of trying to integrate like-powered nations. This has been particularly important for the small countries.

Regionalism is also taking another and probably more fruitful form, that of physical integration and the practice of businessmen from different countries working together. There are many examples of both these phenomena. Physical integration has included improved transportation networks in Central America and the Caribbean, joint generation and distribution of electricity in the Southern cone and between Brazil and Paraguay, and the improvement of direct communications systems among countries of the region. Businessmen from different countries and from many industries have developed the habit of meeting together to plan future production and cooperation. Central bankers are doing the same. The report to the OAS in August 1980 by its group of experts refers to the "multidimensionality" of regional integration, by which it means using a flexible and pragmatic approach to problem solving in many fields.[14]

2. Because of limitations that presently exist for regionalization as the main engine of growth, international protectionism exacts a heavy price on Latin American development. Efforts have been made to quantify the value of exports lost because of protectionism, but this is inherently difficult.[15] There is adaptation to protection by product and market diversification, and this may offset the cost; and, on the other hand, the fear of protection may inhibit some investment, and this leads to understatement of the cost. There is no doubt, however, that the cost is high and growing.

Most current import protection in the industrial countries affects labor-intensive products such as clothing and shoes. Protection takes primarily nontariff form, such as the quantitative limits by categories of textiles and apparel in the Multi-Fiber Arrangement and "voluntary" quantitative restraints negotiated with exporters on additional labor-intensive products.[16] These products are produced, or can be produced, by most Latin American countries, including the very small ones. The impact of protection is greatest on the small and medium-sized countries because of their greater reliance on exports than the large countries and the lesser degree of diversification in their industrial structures.

3. We are witnessing a more complex phenomenon in the relationship between the large Latin American countries and the industrial centers. There is tension between the deeper integration of the large countries into the center, which would be a logical outcome of the growing sophistication of their economies, and the concern by center countries to protect many of their key industries. The large

countries now export parts of automobiles, have growing steel industries, and contemplate building substantial primary and secondary petrochemical industries. There are manifestations of protectionism in industrial countries in each of these areas. These take the form not just of orderly marketing agreements or other types of direct quantitative restraints, but also a more rigorous enforcement of subsidy and antidumping procedures. Much of the export drive of the large countries has relied on subsidized exports (as was true elsewhere in the world, for example, South Korea). In the case of Mexico, subsidies (taking many forms, such as providing oil and gas at below-market prices or tax abatements) are to be a main stimulus for growth for the large industrial complexes that are contemplated.

The effect to date of industrial country protectionism on the more sophisticated exports of the large Latin American countries has been modest, and the looming concerns may never eventuate. If they do, however, they could have a profound effect on the internationalization of the economies of these countries and, indeed, on their entire future direction. The issue is a substantial one.

Concerns about the acceptance of the increasing internationalism of the Latin American economies thus arise not only from internal intellectual resistance but also because of the external economic scene Latin America faces. To cite the staff of the International Monetary Fund: "The world economic picture is rather grim."[17] Inflation accelerated in the industrial countries in the latter 1970s and is still not under control. Their overall economic growth is currently low and is projected by the Organization for Economic Cooperation and Development to remain that way for at least another year, in the order of 2 to 3%. The World Bank expects economic growth in industrial countries between 1980 and 1985 to be lower than over the previous two decades.[18] These projections are subject to large margins of error, particularly those looking decades ahead, but they are the base from which planning takes place. This global milieu does not augur well for combating protectionism in the main markets for Latin American goods.

INTERNATIONAL GOVERNANCE

The main substantive issues regarding Latin America's international trade discussed in this essay can be summarized as follows:

1. Internationalization of the Latin American economies must continue to expand if countries are to achieve rates of economic growth large enough to incorporate productively their growing labor forces. The path of internationalization will differ, depending on the nature of the country. For the large countries, internationalization entails expansion of sales of relatively sophisticated products. Some of these, such as in the automotive industry, are in fields vital to the structure of the industrial countries and in which these countries may be losing their competitiveness. For the middle-sized countries, internationalization involves less sophisticated products (for now), but exports are more significant in relation to GDP than for the large countries. For most small countries, the economies already are thoroughly internationalized and what they have to sell are primary products, services (tourism, banking, and migrant workers), and products from labor-intensive industry.

2. Alongside this need for internationalization, there is a large potential for further regionalization of economies (for horizontal integration). This is particularly true for the small and medium sized countries, but can be important as well for the large countries (which, in fact, have benefited most from the trade, industrial, and physical integration that has occurred). Regionalization is mostly in the hands of the Latin American countries themselves, while internationalization obviously requires the cooperation of the industrial countries.

3. It is precisely this cooperation that is threatened by the protectionist pressure stimulated by anticipated slow economic growth accompanied by relatively high unemployment in the industrial countries.

These international issues have their domestic counterparts. Competitiveness in international markets for manufactures can be achieved and maintained only if real effective exchange rates (that is, on the export side, the exchange rate plus export incentives, adjusted for inflation from some base) are not overvalued, and if high costs brought about by protecting inefficient domestic industries do not destroy the competitiveness of more efficient industries. Internal issues are influenced by the international system (such as by the pressure the IMF can exert on exchange rates when countries seek credit), and national practices can run into conflict with international usage (such as the use of subsidies to alter the effective exchange rate for exports).

It is the international substantive issues, and how to deal with those internal ones that conflict with international rules, that must be addressed in the system of international governance.

The array of existing bodies in the trade field is imposing, in fact confusing. There is tension between those bodies dominated by the industrial countries (such as the General Agreement on Tariffs and Trade and the IMF) and those controlled by the developing countries (the UN bodies, such as the United Nations Conference on Trade and Development, the Committee of the Whole, and the UN General Assembly itself). There is a division between operational, decision-making institutions, such as GATT and the IMF, and those that essentially debate and pass resolutions (the General Assembly and UNCTAD). This is not a neat division, however. The idea of the developing countries is to use the Committee of the Whole (COW) to engage in global "negotiations," involving as well some second-guess oversight authority over the more functional "negotiating" institutions; and it is precisely the issue of what is meant by negotiation in each type of institution that is in dispute between industrial and developing countries. It also is too simple to label one group of institutions as debating and the other as negotiating, because there is much interplay between the two types. Debate and confrontation in UNCTAD often lead to negotiated concessions in the GATT (such as for tariff preferences for developing countries), in the IMF (such as the successive improvements of the compensatory finance facility), or in ad hoc frameworks (such as the establishment of the common fund for commodities).

The governance system involves continuous negotiation in many forums, often on the same issues, with each group of countries (the developed and the developing) seeking to concentrate the action in bodies that it dominates. There is simultaneous pressure by the developing countries to obtain more power over decisions in the functional institutions in which they are a numerical majority (counting by sovereignties) but a minority in the power wielded. Governance in the international trade field resembles a kaleidoscope in which the design varies depending on the way the instrument (the institution) is turned, but in reality the same set of facts is being viewed from different perspectives.

Trade rules tend to be global in applicability, but there is scope as well for regionalism. The regional integration movements in Latin America are examples of this. Regional negotiation is common, such as between the European Economic Community and developing countries, although this is really more than regional since the negotiation extends to all the countries in Africa, the Caribbean, and the Pacific of the Lomé II agreement. In the Western hemisphere, much regional negotiation takes place in the Organization of American States and its affiliated bodies. This takes the form both of negotiation with and confrontation against the United States (for example, to expand the list of products for which tariff preferences are given).

Trade relations between developing and developed countries in the Western hemisphere do not involve special privileges for the developing countries that are not generalized to all developing countries. (President Reagan's Caribbean Basin Initiative, if carried out, would provide special tariff preferences only for countries defined as being in the Caribbean Basin.) The EEC system, by contrast, does involve special preferences for countries associated with it in the Lomé II agreement.

A word about confrontation is useful to understand the workings of the governance system. Confrontation quite clearly works. Three substantive concessions already cited (trade preferences, establishment and steady improvement in the compensatory finance system, and the common fund) probably owe their existence to developing country confrontation of the industrial countries. In hemispheric relations, it is doubtful that the Inter-American Development Bank or the original coffee agreement would have come about without some confrontation in the 1960s. Yesterday's confrontation often resulted in today's agreement or cooperative institution. The powerful rarely make significant concessions gratuitously. It is this reality that has motivated the steady pressure of Latin American countries acting jointly against the United States for trade concessions and the Group of 77 in the United Nations acting jointly against the industrial countries to the same end.

Confrontation, however, has a price. It sours relationships. There was a conscious turning away from the OAS in the economic field by the United States since this was seen as a stacked forum, a place for pressure, of all against one, rather than for resolution of mutual problems. The United States shuns doing its trade business in the United Nations or its constituent parts like UNCTAD because this rarely involves a negotiation with an exchange of concessions and obligations. What is sought are one-sided concessions. (This is not true in negotiations on individual commodity agreements between producers and consumers, which UNCTAD sponsors.)

A simplified summary of current international governance in the trade field can be set forth as follows: The governance structure involves competing sets of institutions. The most powerful of these (GATT, the IMF) are dominated by the industrial countries, and the rules in these were formulated mainly by these countries. There have been derogations from these rules, such as from the most-favored-nation principle and reciprocity in trade negotiations, and these have come about because of pressure exerted by the developing countries, both in these institutions and in the competing institutions they dominate. The industrial countries prefer to negotiate on issues that will affect their trade—and hence their incomes and employment—in the institutions they dominate, and for the same reason the developing countries prefer to negotiate in the institutions they control. (It goes almost without saying that, over time, developing countries hope to achieve domination of the GATT and the IMF.) There is much interplay among the institutions, between debate and resolutions in one place and concrete concessions in others; and it is necessary to be aware of events in many bodies to comprehend what is occurring.

This is a complicated arrangement, and from time to time recommendations are made to tidy up the governance system. The Brandt Commission, to cite the most recent example, suggested merging UNCTAD and GATT.[19] This fetish for neatness is probably misplaced. It certainly misreads the nature of the power struggle that brought on this multiplicity of institutions and which gives meaning to this variety. Whose rules would prevail if GATT and UNCTAD were unified? Who would dominate? The current complexity of governance mirrors reality, and that is why proposals for drastic surgery are generally ignored.

The trade institutions in the Western hemisphere are not quite a replica of the global bodies, but rather of the second group in which the developing countries dominate. The United States rarely sends in its first team for regional trade negotiations. It saves these players for the global negotiations, in GATT and in the IMF.

The real pressures for change in this governance structure come not from lack of neatness but from the profound substantive changes that are taking place. These are the issues set forth earlier in this chapter.

If protectionism is not contained, this is a contradiction of the trade policy embodied in the articles of GATT. Why have GATT if its rules cannot be enforced? What sense is there to domination of GATT by the industrial countries if they make new rules outside the structure to meet what they deem to be their own requirements? The Multi-Fiber Arrangement was a derogation from the preexisting rules, and the rules were changed. Voluntary restraints forced on exporters under threat of even more severe import restrictions were not even incorporated into the rules. These nontariff restraints are imposed without suffering the penalties GATT would require if bound tariffs were increased. The nontariff codes agreed to in the Tokyo round of trade negotiations represent an effort to enlarge the scope of GATT through general propositions to be made more precise through case law, but the outcome is uncertain. In any event, the greatest danger to GATT and its rules of governance is that GATT will, in effect, be abandoned by the very countries that dominate it as these countries seek to contain pressures brought on by high unemployment, low growth, and diminishing competitiveness in some core industries.

The bargaining unity of the developing countries is losing its logic, in the Western hemisphere as elsewhere. The large countries— Brazil in particular because of its sophisticated industrial structure but the other two as well—are now in neither camp, that of the less developed or the industrial countries. They have less in common in their industrial structures with the very poor countries of Central America and the very small countries of the Caribbean than they have with the United States. They will have to opt soon (most probably during the decade of the 1980s) about their alliances; and when this occurs, it will alter the nature of North–South confrontation in the hemisphere. This transformation is taking place on the global scene as well, as middle-income countries in other areas find themselves divorced from old relationships.

This will be translated into substantive decisions in many ways. Why should the tariff preferences of the industrial countries benefit almost exclusively a few middle-income countries, as is now the case? It is one thing to tolerate substantial export subsidies given by countries with really infant industries, say in Central America, and quite another when the export drive via subsidies is mounted by the large countries. Nonreciprocity in trade negotiations is acceptable in bargaining with poor countries, but is this still appropriate for the large, middle-income countries of the hemisphere and elsewhere?

Altering the governance structure will not in itself contain growing protectionist pressure. (Protectionism could subside on its own if economic growth rates in the industrial countries recover, if vital industries such as automobiles and steel are revitalized, and if declining productivity growth in manufacturing is reversed, but it would be pollyanish to count on these developments.) The GATT articles contain a combination of rewards (tariff concessions) and punishments (compensation must be provided for not applying a bound tariff), and adjudication procedures when there are trade disputes. The new GATT codes seek to extend the adjudication process to nontariff barriers. It has been suggested that punishments should be applied to countries when they insist on voluntary export restraints by others, perhaps in the form of monetary compensation for the trade damage inflicted.[20] This hardly seems practical. Countries use protective techniques not sanctioned by GATT precisely to avoid the penalties prescribed by GATT. The trade restrictions are applied mostly against developing countries that insist on nonreciprocity in negotiations and it would be hard for legislatures in industrial countries to accept that penalties also should be non-reciprocal, that is, apply to industrial countries using protective devices but not to developing countries, particularly the more advanced among these, which use them much more extensively. Retaliation against protection, which GATT also permits, is not a device that can be used extensively since this would signify defeat of the trade liberalization objective.

Avoiding the worst scenarios of protectionism is less a question of altered governance than of exerting sustained pressure within the present system to prevent these outcomes and hoping that the good sense of national leaders will prevail. While protectionism has become more entrenched in recent years, it has not gotten out of hand as many feared it would during the recession of 1974–1975. The current proposals in the United States for bilateral and sectoral "reciprocity" are a reflection of an age-old protectionist pheno-menon in times of recession. It is not yet out of control, but the danger is there.

If the analysis is correct that the large countries in Latin America will increasingly be faced with the choice between maintain-ing present alliances for pressure purposes against the United States (and other industrial countries) or altering their tactics to reflect their growing economic strength, this will of course entail a changed pattern of governance. Should the change be rushed? Talk of co-optation into the center of the large countries implies that it should. Opposition to cooptation argues that it should not.[21] If forced, the large countries almost certainly will seek to retain the benefits accru-ing to developing countries for as long as they can. This is what Mexico did in declining to join GATT. The choice probably will come almost imperceptibly and be decided by the objective situation.

There are rules changes that could alter the benefits that now go to the more prosperous middle-income countries, or to those with the most sophisticated industrial structures. Some examples are graduation from preferential treatment for exports by those countries to industrial countries and stricter rules for middle-income than for low-income countries in the use of export subsidies and the use of local-content requirements. The purpose of these rules changes would not be to force cooptation (although it may accelerate it), but rather to provide benefits to countries that most need them. The terms of the Multi-Fiber Arrangement contemplate somewhat better treatment in quota determination for poor countries with small textile and apparel industries than for the more prosperous countries with larger industries. This, like graduation generally, may be desirable to carry out. There would be protests on the grounds that special and differential treatment *among* developing countries would be a deliberate device to smash their cohesion. It might well do that. On the other hand, the current practice of treating all developing countries alike for trade purposes means that the more prosperous obtain the overwhelming bulk of benefits. There is no doubt, however, that graduation would alter the governance system as it is practiced today. This is why it is so vehemently opposed by the Group of 77.

It is often asserted that because trade is international in scope, special regional rules have no role in the governance system. We know that this is not completely the practice, since regional integration schemes are a permitted departure from the rule of one world. So are the special preferences granted by the countries of the EEC to the developing country signatories of the Lomé II agreement. Should the United States provide special preferential treatment to developing countries in the Western hemisphere? Or, to state the question more narrowly, since what is stated in the previous sentence has often been rejected: Is there scope for special treatment for the poorest or least-developed countries of the region, say in the Caribbean Basin (that is, the islands of the Caribbean proper and countries bordering on the Caribbean)? This special treatment could be granted not just by the United States (as has been proposed by President Reagan) but by other more developed regional countries.[22]

It would be terribly divisive if this were done. Nor is it clear that preferential treatment of Caribbean Basin countries would result in benefits for them significant enough to risk disrupting trade practices developed laboriously for the last 50 years. However, there are options for stimulating the exports of these countries short of abandonment of the most-favored-nation principle. Graduation, already mentioned, is one such option, since it would provide trade benefits to all countries in the same economic situation, no matter where situated. Other such options include larger quotas in bilateral agreements under the Multi-Fiber Arrangement for the poorer Caribbean Basin countries and special encouragement for investment in these countries in promising export industries.

There are thus several options available. One is to provide explicit trade preferences only for Caribbean Basin countries. Another is to respect the fundamental rules in the system of governance for the conduct of international trade, but to bend them in a nonfundamental way to benefit the most needy countries of the region, whether in the Caribbean Basin or elsewhere in Latin America. If the second alternative were accepted, the details of the benefits could be negotiated over time.

One final comment on future governance deserves mention. What is argued in this essay is that a system of governance involving a combination of confrontation and negotiation is altogether normal in trade relations between industrial and less-developed countries. However, there are many areas in which the interests of the various countries are not antithetical. The development of energy resources, other minerals, and food production are examples. There is substantial scope for hemispheric cooperation in these essentially non-conflictive sectors. This is the central theme of the report to the OAS of the group of experts on "Hemispheric Cooperation and Integral Development."[23] These areas of cooperation deserve stress in a paper dealing with hemispheric trade because they deal with critical trade problems—the growing energy imports and the rising food imports of Latin American countries. This cooperation may not require establishment of new institutions, although the essential point is not this but rather devising new ways of governance to secure the necessary cooperation.

CONCLUSIONS

There are four themes stressed in this chapter. The first is that Latin American countries cannot turn away from the internationalization of their economies if their growth and distribution objectives are to be achieved. This in no way negates the scope for greater regionalization in trade and other economic relations, but as a complement to rather than a substitute for internationalization. The second point flows from this, that the threat to internationalization comes from the danger of protectionism in the industrial countries. It is not that protectionism is out of hand, but it is more deeply entrenched today than at any time since the end of World War II, and the entrenchment might get deeper and more extensive because of the dismal economic outlook for the years ahead. The governance consequences of these related themes are not that new institutions, or new rules in old institutions, can arrest the protectionist danger—since protectionism creates its own rules—but rather that the existing governance structure must exert constant pressure to limit the growth of protectionism.

The third theme relates to the need for the governance system to differentiate among countries more than it does now, so that benefits from special trade treatment to developing countries will accrue not only or primarily to the large countries in Latin America but also to those in a less advantageous position. This requires seeking out measures that will benefit these latter countries, even if it means diluting benefits to the more affluent. Graduation need not be unthinkable.

Finally, there is ample scope for hemisphere-wide cooperation in some crucial sectors that can deeply affect trade volumes and patterns, in particular in energy and food production.

Radical shifts in international governance are rare. They occurred immediately after World War II. The changes since then have been gradual, but steady. It is obvious from the proliferation of new agencies and alterations in power in existing ones, such as the United Nations, that these changes have been numerous. A radical change in governance can be expected to follow a radical change in power relationships, whereas gradual changes follow incremental alterations in the power structure. The assumption in this essay is that governance changes will be incremental and not revolutionary.

NOTES

1. *Economic and Social Progress in Latin America, 1980–81 Report* (Washington, D.C.: Inter-American Development Bank, 1981), p. 49.

2. When the phrase "Latin American countries" is used, it should be read to include Caribbean countries as well.

3. Brazil and Mexico are good examples of this. Each has a debt service ratio (debt service as a percentage of exports of goods and services) of 50% or more, and a majority of their debt is relatively short-term at variable interest rates.

4. The question of bias towards import substitution or export promotion is developed in Anne O. Krueger, *Foreign Trade Regimes and Economic Development: Liberalization Attempts and Consequences* (Cambridge, Mass.: Ballinger, for the National Bureau of Economic Research, 1978), p. 88 and throughout.

5. The relationship between trade protection and power is a familiar theme. Adam Smith dealt with this extensively. One strong passage is the following: "The capricious ambition of kings and ministers has not, during the present and preceding century, been more fatal to the repose of Europe than the impertinent jealousy of merchants and manufacturers." *The Wealth of Nations* (New York: Modern Library Edition, 1937), p. 460.

6. Figures come from *Economic and Social Progress in Latin America*, 1978 and 1979 reports. If fuels are excluded, manufactures as a percent of total exports rose from about 5% in 1955 to more than 25% in 1977.

7. *América Latina en el umbral de los años 80*, Cepal, Naciones Unidas (E/CEPAL/G.1106, Noviembre de 1979), pp. 15–16.

8. Ibid., p. 21. The figure given is for non–petroleum-exporting countries.

9. William G. Tyler, *Advanced Developing Countries as Export Competitors in Third World Markets: The Brazilian Experience* (Washington, D.C.: The Center for Strategic and International Studies, Georgetown University, 1980), p. 17.

10. *Economic and Social Progress in Latin America, 1980–81 Report*, pp. 24–31. This aggregation by region obviously masks differences in performance of individual countries in each region.

11. Some recent essays on problems of internationalization are Hector Assael, "The Internationalization of the Latin American Economies: Some Reservations," *CEPAL Review*, No. 7 (April 1979), pp. 41–55; and Aníbal Pinto, "The Periphery and the Internationalization of the World Economy," *CEPAL Review*, No. 9 (December 1979), pp. 45–67, and "The Opening Up of Latin America to the Exterior," *CEPAL Review*, No. 11 (August 1980), pp. 31–56. Raul Prebisch, in a series of articles in *CEPAL Review* (the final essay, "Towards a Theory of Change," is in issue No. 10, April 1980, pp. 155–208), attempts to analyze how capitalism developed in Latin America and how this was influenced by interaction with the center.

12. Latin America's main primary commodity exports are petroleum, coffee, sugar, copper, corn, bananas, bauxite, cocoa, and fish meal.

13. See Department of State, Bureau of Intelligence and Research, "Evaluating Regional Schemes for the Promotion of Inter-LDC Trade," Report No. 1362, April 14, 1980.

14. Organization of American States, "Hemispheric Cooperation and Integral Development," August 6, 1980 (OEA/Ser. T/II, GTC/15-80), p. 118.

15. Pedro I. Mendive, "The Export of Manufactures," *CEPAL Review*, No. 10 (April 1980), pp. 21–31, is an example of such an effort. Mendive estimated that in 1976, nontariff barriers in the United States, Japan, and the EEC resulted in exports of manufactures being $1.4 billion less than they could have been, and that elimination of tariffs above 5% would have led to an increase of manufactured exports by Latin America of $420 million.

16. Gary P. Sampson, "Contemporary Protectionism and the Exports of Developing Countries," *CEPAL Review*, No. 8 (August 1979), pp. 103–17, contains a discussion of current forms of protectionism.

17. International Monetary Fund, *World Economic Outlook* (Washington, D.C., May 1980), p. 3. The statement is even more valid in mid-1982, as this is written.

18. Robert S. McNamara, address to the Board of Governors, Washington, D.C., September 30, 1980, p. 3.

19. *North–South: A Programme for Survival*, Report of the Independent Commission on International Development Issues under the chairmanship of Willy Brandt (Cambridge, Mass.: MIT Press, 1980), p. 185.

20. Jagdish Bhagwati, "Market Disruption, Export Market Disruption, and GATT Reform," in Bhagwati, ed., *The New International Economic Order: The North–South Debate* (Cambridge, Mass.: MIT Press, 1977), pp. 159–91.

21. An argument in favor of cooptation policy is contained in C. Fred Bergsten, et al., *The Reform of International Institutions* (New York: The Trilateral Commission, 1976). An argument against this policy can be found in Roger Hansen, "North–South Policy—What is the Problem?" *Foreign Affairs*, Vol. 58:5 (Summer 1980), pp. 1104–28.

22. Venezuela and Mexico did just that in their agreement of August 1981 providing aid for Central American and Caribbean countries to help finance the cost of imported oil.

23. See note 14.

15

Latin America's Debt: Problem or Solution

Albert Fishlow

INTRODUCTION

Since 1973, the world has learned to live, if somewhat precariously, with high-priced oil and record international payments imbalances. One of the reasons is the increased debt of developing-country oil consumers that has been a partial offset against the huge surpluses accumulated by a handful of oil producers. Between 1973 and 1980, developing country indebtedness has grown at an average annual rate of more than 20%.

As a consequence, their medium and long-term debt (including Mexico's, only recently an oil exporter) probably exceeded $350 billion at the end of 1981. Latin American countries are responsible for about half of this total. Brazil and Mexico not only lead the region, but the world as a whole, and Argentina and Chile in recent years have also become leading debtors.[1]

The importance and vulnerability of Latin American borrowers are highlighted by measures like the ratio of interest and amortization payments to export earnings and the ratio of debt to gross domestic product. Their current debt service ratio of about 40% is four times larger than the level for non-Latin American oil-importing, developing countries. Their debt–GDP ratio of .3 is half again larger than the .2 characterizing others. The relatively greater burden of Latin American debt service is explained by the importance of private credit, with its higher charges, and by import substitution policies that have reduced exports as a proportion of total product compared to other developing countries.

This indebtedness has not escaped notice. Comment has ranged from warnings of an impending financial Armageddon to soothing assurances that market forces are in full command. Concerns have varied from preoccupation with debtor capacity to meet outstanding obligations to fears that shortages of financial capital will limit economic growth, of borrowers and industrial countries alike.

This paper addresses itself to clarification of some of these issues raised by the level of Latin American indebtedness. Although written before the unfolding of the August 1982 Mexican crisis, and its subsequent ramifications, the discussion remains timely. Successive sections deal with the evolution of the debt, the burden the debt confers, the diverse national experiences with indebtedness, and the implications for United States policy. In the last analysis, the question posed is whether the debt that helped reduce international economic dislocation in the 1970s will become a problem in its own right in the 1980s.

FACTS ABOUT THE LATIN AMERICAN DEBT

Two trends dominate the Latin American experience. One is the explosion of debt in the 1970s. The other is the progressively larger role of private financial flows, especially from commercial banks. Both are clearly evident in Table 15.1.

During the last decade, debt increased more than seven-fold, compared to a doubling in the 1960s. Deflated for price change and subtracting the growth of product, the differences in the two periods amount respectively to 117% versus a mere 8%. Reliance on external finance has demonstrably increased, while foreign direct investment expanded more slowly: between 1956 and 1965, direct investment exceeded loans; between 1976 and 1980, investment amounted to 20% of borrowing. Debt has become the predominant form of capital transfer.

The access to capital markets evolved in two phases. In the first, before the oil crisis, surpluses in the Eurodollar market became newly available to selected larger countries whose growth experience and export performance conferred creditworthiness. Current account deficits could be used as a planned basis for mobilizing external

TABLE 15.1. Latin American Medium and Long-term Debt

	1960	1967	1970	1973	1976	1978	1980
Public or publicly guaranteed	5.5	10.7	15.8	24.8	53.1	82.7	104
Official	n.a.	5.9	8.0	11.0	17.4	22.7	n.a.
Private	n.a.	4.8	7.2	13.8	35.7	60.1	n.a.
Financial markets	n.a.	2.2	3.7	10.0	30.3	51.5	n.a.
Banks	n.a.	n.a.	2.6	8.4	27.9	44.8	n.a.
Non-guaranteed	2.9	3.9	6.5	12.3	21.7	30.7	51
Banks	n.a.	n.a.	n.a.	n.a.	16.3	23.0	38.3
Total disbursed	8.4	14.6	20.8	37.1	74.8	113.4	155

Excludes Venezuela and Trinidad and Tobago.

Sources:

Public and Publicly Guaranteed External Debt:

1960: Inter-American Development Bank, *Economic and Social Progress in Latin America.*

1967–1978: World Bank, *World Debt Tables.*

1980: International Monetary Fund, *World Economic Outlook*, p. 102, change for Western Hemisphere, 1978–1980.

Total Disbursed Debt:

1960–1970: Balance of payments based estimates of cumulative capital inflows, reported in an earlier working paper ("Debt, Growth and Hemispheric Relations") adjusted upward by 1.02. This factor is the relationship between the earlier 1973 estimate and the new direct 1973 estimate.

1973–1978: National Foreign Assessment Center, Central Intelligence Agency, "Non-OPEC LDC's: External Debt Position" to which public debt of Ecuador has been added.

1980: 1978 estimate incremented by estimated capital flows less foreign investment, as reported in *World Economic Outlook.*

Non-Guaranteed Debt: Total minus Public and Publicly Guaranteed.

Non-Guaranteed Bank Debt: Proportion of bank loans to non-guaranteed debt for Brazil, 1977/78, in *World Debt Tables,* Supplement 3, 1979.

savings. In the second, after 1973, borrowing was of another kind, a response to the rising costs of oil and other imports and less vigorous expansion of world trade that penalized exports.

Borrowing was not the only option in the face of the sudden increase in oil prices. One alternative was to use less oil. Individual countries could also compensate by importing less of other products, helped along by the reduced real incomes resulting from adverse terms of trade, or by exporting more. They could thus self-finance their higher oil bill by adjusting other trade accounts. To some extent, and especially as time went on, the Latin American countries took such measures. But early on, in the midst of industrial-country recession that made exports less certain, and since the other measures reduced growth rates and invited political opposition, a debt strategy was a more attractive one to follow. Gradual adjustment made good economic sense at the national level. At the international level, there was no choice: the oil country surpluses had to be matched by deficits elsewhere, or global income would fall. Some countries were required to borrow.

The Latin American choice to do so affected not only the volume of debt but also its composition. During the early 1960s, the principal sources of Latin America's new infusion of capital were United States loans and grants under the Alliance for Progress. In the 1970s they were private bank loans, after 1973 partially intermediating petrodollar surpluses. Two-thirds of Latin America's debt now is owed to banks, more than twice the level in 1970.

This substitution of private for official finance did not prejudice the growth of the public sector in Latin America. Quite the contrary. Governments, state enterprises or firms with public participation, and official banks remained the principal recipients of private loans. Public guarantee was an important attraction to banks, providing an unprecedented access to capital for the state sector and underwriting its expansion. This was a far cry from the 1950s, when Latin American governments pleaded, largely in vain, for official capital to finance public projects.

Private capital is also available quickly and at lower spreads as competitive forces have reduced the charges for intermediation. It comes with fewer political strings than bilateral aid—at least until doubts about creditworthiness emerge. Then banks have been concerned, and press unabashedly for orthodox and conservative policies, political as well as economic. This asymmetry, and even bias, is still a long way from a full dependency view of the adverse implications of bank finance: "Bank loans, open-door regimes and repressive policies have frequently coincided. ... The technocratic posturing and apolitical rhetoric of bank officials is merely a mask for far-reaching political actions."[2] That view presumes that an export orientation is necessarily bad, fails to see balance of payments problems as even partially the consequence of disregard of market forces, and interprets authoritarian solutions as wholly of international capitalist imposition rather than related to populist failures.

This is not to argue that private finance does not impose additional burdens. One is a market interest rate that is higher than charged for official loans. Another is a shortened debt maturity structure, as few as the average of 4.3 years Brazil experienced in 1977. A third is the flexibility of interest rates, subject to readjustment at six-month intervals. That uncertainty has large quantitative implications. A one-percentage-point change in nominal interest rates can change Latin American service costs by almost one billion dollars.

THE NATURE OF THE PROBLEM

On balance, because money was cheap during the peak borrowing of the 1970s and because new inflows far exceeded return payments, reliance on debt clearly seemed a sound policy. Now, with interest rates persistently positive instead of negative and debt service mounting, does the same judgment hold?

To answer that question requires a differentiation between two types of debt problems. One is where the real rate of return on the foreign resources falls short of their cost. The other is a foreign exchange cash flow or liquidity constraint.

For money borrowed in the 1970s, even allowing for higher interest rates to be paid in the 1980s, the average costs are low enough, and even negative in the mid-1970s, so that real return on their investment does not seem to be the central issue. But a fundamental limitation of a debt strategy is that one never knows the real cost until the loan has been repaid. This is true not merely because future interest rates may change, but also because the real resources required by the future exports needed to liquidate the debt depend on unknown price trends. If export prices move adversely, then debt repayment will turn out to be more onerous than anticipated, and the margin of gain smaller.

Even with these uncertainties, it is likely that the real rate of return on Latin American debt will continue to exceed the cost. There is no similar assurance about the ability to meet short-term service requirements. A positive differential between returns and costs does not imply that foreign exchange will be available when payments fall due—even though the debt more than repays itself considered over the full lifetime of its investment. In the short term, there may not be the increase in exports needed fully to satisfy debt service. Only if it is possible to borrow to meet interim obligations can the long-run advantages be realized.

Continuing access to capital markets is therefore essential if debt finance is to produce its potential benefits. In the medium term, access to export markets is equally essential. Export growth must not only meet import requirements but also be sufficient to slow down the high rates of recent debt expansion. Financial and real markets are linked: Debt exposure cannot be reduced without expanded exports.

The looming Latin American debt problem is therefore not that costs, even though rising, will outstrip returns, but that capital may be unavailable in adequate quantities, even at higher prices. Respected bankers warn that they are overcommitted and more reluctant to lend as their developing-country loans mount to significant multiples of their net worth. Since 1975, American banks have increased their lending to non–oil-developing countries at a rate of 17% a year, more rapidly than the expansion of their capital base. Even this has not been enough. United States banks have not maintained their market share, especially in the last two years. Only the willingness of late-comer European and Japanese banks to expand their loans at 40% a year has met demand. Such a rate is not sustainable, leading one industry authority to predict a future limit to nominal growth—at current rates of inflation—of no more than 15% a year.[3]

World Financial Markets estimates at the same time that 12 major non–oil-developing country borrowers have needs that will be likely to expand at annual rates ranging downward from 22 to 16.5% between 1981 and 1985. There is thus an inconsistency between demand and supply that can be averted only by higher industrial country growth and developing country exports, or by new financial intermediation.

For Latin America as a region, my own projections suggest that a regular 15% increase in finance could meet requirements, despite slower export growth in the next few years. There would be a reduced rate of economic expansion, but not as severe for Latin America as elsewhere.

Two special reasons for this result are important. One is the demonstrated capacity of the industrially advanced Latin American countries to restrict imports and substitute domestic supply when export earnings and capital flows together fall short of requirements.

This flexibility reduces the otherwise fully adverse effects on income. A ceiling of 15% on capital flows would, however, mean a significant reversal in the larger place of imports in many countries.

The second factor is the progressively reduced weight of petroleum imports for the non-oil countries of the region because of the new prominence of Mexico and Peru as oil exporters. Indeed, net imports have now been converted to a small net export surplus for these non-oil countries. This transformation insulates the region, taken as an aggregate, against the effects of oil price increases. It facilitates intraregional arrangements that only a few years ago seemed impossible. Mexico and Venezuela have recently offered new direct assistance to nine countries of Central America and the Caribbean adversely affected by oil price increases, in addition to earlier Venezuelan assistance through the Venezuelan Trust Fund of the Inter-American Bank and the Puerto Ordaz Agreement providing long-term finance for oil imports to many of the same countries. During his visit to Brazil in August, 1980, President Lopez Portillo suggested expanded Mexican exports of oil in exchange for Brazilian iron ore, bauxite, and food.

This better situation of the region on average does not eliminate its vulnerability to even small declines in export earnings. Debt service payments are now a regular and large obligation that will continue to come over the next several years to more than 40% of export receipts. They are the inevitable and predictable consequence of earlier borrowing. Uncertainty about short-term export prospects calls for potentially greater compensating capital flows, while the forecast is for smaller. Indeed, the supply of private finance is likely to be least for those countries facing a liquidity problem.

In emphasizing the importance of continuing and growing indebtedness in the next several years as a solution, I do so mindful that it is not a panacea. In the first place, inflation is not the cushion in easing future repayment that it once was. Now that interest rates have adjusted for inflationary expectations and the preponderance of the debt is subject to variable interest rates, inflation becomes a disadvantage. That is because higher interest rates anticipate amortization and effectively reduce the maturity of the loan. Current debt service ratios are higher than they would be under stable prices.

Secondly, reliance on debt can complicate and distort the domestic economic policy of borrowers. Real exchange rates seem to follow a systematic cycle of undervaluation and overvaluation. In the first phase, lending is attractive because of improving export performance; with increased capital flows the exchange rate tends toward overvaluation, sustained by the preference of domestic borrowers for contracting loans abroad when the exchange rate fails to accompany domestic inflation. Sooner or later overvaluation adversely affects exports and prejudices their diversification. Then the prospect of devaluation discourages borrowers and lenders both, hastening its very need. Large credit flows mean the exchange rate is embedded in a more complicated economic structure involving financial assets and liabilities as well as merchandise flows, and that it is easier for disequilibria to occur and to persist.

Thirdly, the debt model requires a present commitment to future export without certainty of the conditions they will confront. Slower industrial country growth can be compensated by greater capital inflows in the short term, but if that slower growth unleashes a new surge of protectionism, it will be to no avail. The positive accomplishments of the Tokyo Round have not fully allayed fears of diminished market access. New and more effective restrictions remain a threat. They can frustrate an otherwise sound debt strategy.

Lastly, reliance on debt postpones but does not prevent imposing hard domestic requirements: raising oil prices, accepting lower real incomes, shifting resources from consumption to investment and exports, cutting back on national expenditures. Postponing these adjustments may not make them easier. Obvious issues of distribution present themselves: Whose consumption will be constrained, how will export incentives be distributed, what compensation will energy consumers receive, what role will be taken by state and private enterprises in the new structure of production, and so forth. In a period of transition to greater popular and civilian participation in politics in some countries, these questions admit to no easy answers.

These additional considerations make even clearer that a model of development with large infusions of debt, as many Latin American countries have embarked upon, involves a delicate and difficult balance. Solution and problem are intertwined.

We return to policies that can appropriately supplement market forces in a concluding section. Beforehand, it is necessary to add to these general, but consequently artificial, regional impressions by referring to actual national experiences.

A NATIONAL FOCUS

There are obviously large differences in indebtedness and in political difficulties among countries in the region. In the first place, debt is highly concentrated. Five countries—Brazil, Mexico, Argentina, Chile, and Peru—account for almost 90% of the total Latin American (excluding Venezuela) debt. Their debt service ratios range upwards from 30 to 70%.

In the second place, there are countries whose current debt levels, given their export and income levels, are far below regional norms. With the prominent exception of Colombia, this list is denominated by smaller and poorer countries whose open economies and relative lack of attraction to private lenders have enforced conservative economic policies.

Thirdly, the two principal debtors, Brazil and Mexico, both seem to be straining their debt limits with debt service ratios that far exceed those of the other large borrowers. Yet such static ratios can mislead. Mexico continues to be a favorite in world capital markets, while Brazil-watchers speculate about when it will be forced to go to the International Monetary Fund for help.

The different situations of these countries epitomize the advantages and limitations of debt finance. Mexico's political stability, economic performance, and proximity to the United States had long enabled it to borrow from private sources. By the mid-1970s, and quite independently of the oil price increase, it was obvious that debt levels had reached troublesome proportions in the minds of creditors. Mexico was faced with a liquidity crisis, exacerbated by a long over-valued exchange rate and capital flight induced by heightened investor concern with seeming populist policies. It was forced to borrow from the Fund, devalue, and accept restraint in further borrowing and in domestic expenditure. Prospects were for a prolonged and possibly quite difficult domestic adjustment.

The verification of large petroleum reserves and the advent of a new Mexican administration rapidly restored creditworthiness. Agreed restraints were breached and growth accelerated, financed by new injections of external finance. More certain prospects for repayment justified large capital flows and made possible continuing balance of payments deficits. The crisis of 1975–76 was forgotten.

Debt adds an essential degree of freedom to economic policy by underwriting imports without counterpart exports. Mexico can afford to follow a conservative oil production and export strategy because it is now easy to borrow against oil in the ground that is appreciating in value. That strategy is the more attractive if the terms of borrowing are cheap and their prospective returns in real productive capacity are high. Mexican policymakers now face an elastic supply of foreign capital, and hence they have an ability to borrow short-term while investing in long-term projects.

Mexico still cannot ignore management of its debt. Under a continuing policy of limited oil exports, the economy's high import elasticity can only be satisfied by a substantial rise in external liabilities. They will in turn create return interest and amortization obligations. If Mexico were again to fall into disfavor, a new crisis would be much more severe. What averts it is confidence in export capability and continuing capital inflow.

The liberating role of debt increase in the Mexican case stands in contrast to the constraint debt service now represents in the Brazilian. Interest and amortization payments have risen sharply in the past two years and come to about two-thirds of export earnings, with prospects for a further rise. This increase has occurred despite a spectacular gain in exports over this period. Brazil confronts a burden like Mexico's, but with the fundamental difference that oil appears in the import—not the export—side of the accounts. Lenders recognize Brazil's vulnerability to external circumstances and seek to limit their exposure, despite an impressive export performance and favorable long-term prospects. To be sure, diminished confidence in economic management has contributed. A rate of inflation over 100% hurts, but perhaps less than the deliberate creation of overly optimistic expectations and their subsequent frustration.

Even apart from such a reaction, Brazil's difficulties were predictable. Its access to capital was certain to become more circumscribed as soon as debt service increased to such high levels. Once capital supply becomes inelastic, long-term returns become irrelevant. All that matters is short-term risk. That is obviously present in the Brazilian situation. A $5 increase in the price of a barrel of oil translates into $1.5 billion in additional foreign exchange requirements; a hike in interest rates of 5 points adds some $2 billion. Balance of payments difficulties cause creditors to shy away and to precipitate the very liquidity crisis they fear.

Brazil's problem, like Mexico's and Peru's before it, is a familiar one. It will be resolved, whether it goes to the Fund or not, by new assurances that external obligations can be met so that capital can flow again in larger amounts. Such assurances in the Brazilian situation will probably take the form of slowed economic growth and hence imports. Promises of a diversified export potential will not satisfy. That is why the Mexican oil finds were so significant: They made capital flow again without a long and costly adjustment.

If Brazil goes to the Fund, it will be because that route promises to guarantee the needed supply of private capital more effectively than direct negotiation. Debt will continue to grow and will be likely to double by 1986. Large and mandated interest and amortization charges on outstanding debt mean that even rising exports cannot reverse the debt service ratio in the next few years. Rescheduling will do little good if significant new capital is not also forthcoming.

On its side, the liquidity crisis causes Brazil to shorten its adjustment to high-priced oil and credit. Its efforts to substitute other sources of energy for oil, and to conserve, must be accelerated. Resources must be shifted more rapidly in favor of the diversified exports that are the only means of slowing down further external indebtedness. Domestic savings must be mobilized in significant amounts to replace the resources now transferred by an excess of imports over exports.

These requirements are as essential as a certain supply of capital. They make clear that going to the Fund to reassure creditors will only work if at the same time a national consensus can be reached on the austerity program to be followed. That consensus now must include newly active labor unions and political parties, not only narrow elites. Inadequate attention to the politics of adjustment can cause the best technocratic schemes to fail.

Mexico's oil bonanza cannot work for everyone. Others, like Brazil, must rely on more complex strategies. Many more Latin American countries fall into this second category. What both circumstances share in common is a continuing short-term reliance on external finance, even as debtors reduce their dependence in the long term.

There can be no guarantee of unlimited supplies of capital to every country all along the way. But it is essential that there be sufficient finance in the aggregate and that the horizon of lenders be long enough. Those are responsibilities that the free market alone will not necessarily fulfill.

POLICY IMPLICATIONS

The problem posed by the current levels of indebtedness of some Latin American countries is not a new one. Two decades ago the Economic Commission for Latin America prepared a report on external financing that concluded rather pessimistically that the capital needed because of high debt service would not be forthcoming "inasmuch as a higher proportion of [Latin America's] foreign exchange receipts on current account is now absorbed by the servicing of capital previously invested in the region."[4] Need destroys its own supply.

What helped to prove the prediction wrong was a significant increase of official United States capital under the auspices of the Alliance for Progress. No sooner did the positive impulse of bilateral economic assistance on generous terms begin to wane in the late 1960s when new and larger opportunities were presented by the Eurodollar market. On the merchandise side of the accounts, growing exports after a decade of stagnation were an important source of relief.

Those solutions are no longer available today, at a time when the burden of Latin American debt service is twice as great. The United States is in no position to play the role it did in the early 1960s. For one thing, its own economic relations with other developing countries have broadened. Special attention to Latin America contends with the need for a general policy that also responds to United States interests in other continents. For another, United States bilateral assistance now amounts to an insignificant proportion of Latin American net capital inflow, less than 2% in recent years compared to more than 35% in 1961-65. Except for Israel and Egypt, such assistance is relevant only for the smallest and poorest countries. They on the whole do not confront a debt problem, because they never were creditworthy enough to borrow much in private capital markets.

Private sector financial innovation that underlay the great expansion of the Eurocurrency market in the late 1960s and 1970s does not seem likely to recur. Indeed, it is the possibility of less rapid growth of such lending in the future that is a principal source of concern. Caution is now the hallmark of private banks; it makes itself felt in shorter maturities, larger risk premiums, and smaller commitments. Banks now have a far greater exposure in developing countries than they ever intended, and few are eager to be as aggressive as they once were.

Another surge in exports to compare with the results of the new outward orientation that began in the 1960s seems equally unlikely. At that time the markets of the industrialized countries were expanding at much higher rates than are projected for the 1980s. International trade continues to grow relatively more rapidly than world output, but continuing slow increases in production take their toll on exports. Latin American countries confront new and less favorable prospects: a potential reduction in world export growth from 8% in the 1965-1975 period to 5% in the 1980s.[5] Despite a commitment to greater exports, and despite a still small share of world trade, these countries in aggregate will find it difficult to have foreign exchange earnings outstrip debt service requirements in the next decade.

Former sources of relief cannot therefore be relied upon. At the same time, the dimensions of the problem are demonstrably greater. Debt and debt service are larger. Price fluctuations of export products are wider. Oil price increases are a constant threat to the best-laid plans of oil importers. Interest rates have varied substantially in response to United States credit conditions and introduce another relement of instability.

New policies to cope have therefore been advocated. They are self-interested. Debt illustrates the reality of interdependence. Lending countries are also vulnerable to a generalized inadequacy of finance. They are not only directly affected, with much of the burden falling on private banks, but also indirectly, through the broader impact of reduced import demand of debtor countries contracting their economies.

Such policies seek to ensure an adequate supply of credit to developing country borrowers under more certain conditions and for longer terms. Various proposals differ in their attention to each of these objectives and in the form official intervention takes. Three broad approaches can be identified. One is to make private lending more attractive. The second is to augment the participation of official institutions, principally the World Bank and the International Monetary Fund. The third is to facilitate direct recycling of the oil exporter surplus without the intermediation of financial markets.

Common to efforts to encourage continuing private lending is a search for ways to reduce individual bank risk. One recent suggestion by A. W. Clausen of the Bank of America (before his designation as Robert McNamara's successor at the World Bank) calls for an insurance pool funded by the IMF to protect banks with large developing country exposure. Another proposal is for a separate institution that could directly guarantee the debt of developing countries. I have suggested elsewhere transferring part—but not exclusively the most vulnerable part—of the commercial bank portfolio of developing country loans to the World Bank, in exchange for longer-term World Bank bonds. That would create capacity for additional private lending, while at the same time the repayment of the loans would increase resources at the disposition of the Bank. Still a fourth alternative emphasizes the potential significant expansion of co-financing, that is, formal joint participation of private and official banks in lending for a specific project. Developing countries have greater reason to avoid a loss of creditworthiness with official institutions than with any single bank.[6]

These possibilities share the attractive feature of bolstering the efficient private intermediation of recent years. Cofinancing already has been practiced and may become more appealing to some banks now hesitant to commit larger sums. But it will do little to change country lending limits or the fear of generalized financial over-exposure. Sharing of risk already occurs among banks in Euromarket participations. Insurance or guarantees, to be effective, must be selective. If all loans are guaranteed, bank regulators will hardly be satisfied; if all banks are insured, without regard to the risks they individually decide to undertake, then there is no reward for prudence. There is also the important issue of who shall pay the premiums or provide the guarantee.

These proposals have not evoked an enthusiastic response from many officials who see them as ways of bailing out the commercial banks at public expense. They do not have to be. Schemes that pool risk, even if the banks directly pay the cost, may still be an efficient way of inducing greater lending.

Yet even were some of these steps taken, they would not address the problem in its entirety. Short-term, private bank credit, even in large volume, forces the borrowing countries to live with high debt service ratios and the continuing threat of sudden crisis. Longer-term and more certain finance are also necessary components of an adequate financial strategy.

An enhanced role for the official institutions has therefore been proposed. So far, it seems to have been more productive. The World Bank has already voted to double its capital stock, from $40 billion to $80 billion, and authorization to borrow against assets rather than capital exclusively has been discussed. A ratio of loans to assets of 2:1 would lead to a further doubling of the Bank's lending capacity. The IMF has also increased its quotas for developing countries by about $10 billion apart from the creation of the Witteveen Facility. In addition, it has been proposed that the IMF be allowed to borrow from the financial market directly.

These changes to some extent restore the relative position of these institutions to what they had been before the great increase in private lending. More than a restored market share is involved. Beyond the change in the composition of debt, a larger role for the official institutions gives scope for their surveillance function. Individual countries, in appealing to the private capital market, can get themselves and their lenders in trouble. Unlimited finance is not necessarily desirable. Less monitoring has been done in recent years than has been appropriate. There is considerable evidence that bank assessments of risk, and risk premiums, do not serve that purpose.

These steps to reconstruct the financial system have had broad support from developed and developing countries alike. They may suffer only partial implementation, however, under a Reagan administration much less sympathetic to multilateral lending. They may also fall victim to developed and developing country conflict about the relative roles of the International Monetary Fund versus the World Bank.

Commercial bankers have tended to feel more comfortable with the former than the latter, while the contrary is true for the developing countries. Thus, confronted with the prospect of inadequate private bank lending, Morgan Guaranty's *World Financial Markets* calls for an expanded IMF presence: ". . . the Fund must be prepared to accept programs of current account adjustment that lead to a more than short-term use of its financial resources." Morgan Guaranty also suggests that the IMF "must show greater willingness to modify the targets it sets for particular countries when changing external circumstances invalidate the assumptions on which adjustment programs are built."[7] The Brandt Commission goes so far as to recommend a new World Development Fund, although Edward Heath, one of the members of the Commission, in recent testimony has made clear his preference "that the existing institutions adapt themselves, the World Bank in particular, to program lending. . . ."[8]

The distinction between the Fund and the Bank begins to blur as the latter enters into program lending for structural adjustment while the former extends the maturity of its credits and the flexibility of its conditions. Nevertheless, there will still be, and there should be, differences. There is a place for shorter-term management and a place for medium-term strategy. Permitting the IMF to borrow in capital markets will give it the resources to enable it to deal more effectively to anticipate liquidity crises. With an enlarged Bank as well, the international capital markets of the 1980s can take on a different and more adequate aspect, in which public and global objectives can supplement private profit maximization.

The third set of proposals to modify the present financial system focuses on tapping OPEC surpluses more directly. This approach has gained wider support in recent years as those surpluses have again increased and seem likely to remain large. Bypassing the Eurocurrency market would preclude the need for banks to assume the risk of intermediation; the surplus countries would instead bear it. This would involve these countries in financing the deficits corresponding to their surpluses without leaving the burden of adjustment to others.

Some proposals call for new international funds, or new facilities at existing institutions. Other variants favored by many developing countries are preferential prices and concessional loans tied to oil imports. Mexico, Venezuela, and Trinidad and Tobago are now doing so with Central American and Caribbean countries. Other oil exporters have also increased their direct financial involvement. Kuwait has taken an equity position in Volkswagen do Brasil; Saudi Arabia contributed more than any other country to the Witteveen Facility; OPEC-based banks have increased their lending to developing countries; and so on. These commitments are in addition to concessional bilateral assistance, which, though largely limited to the Muslim world, represents a higher percentage of GNP than is true of the OECD countries.

Less helpful to the developing countries is the increasing tendency of the surplus countries to find new channels of investment in the industrialized countries. The low real cost of borrowing that has made Eurocurrency loans attractive and advantageous to developing countries has also meant low returns to deposits. Surpluses that are recycled by way of the industrialized countries may not wind up so readily in the developing: Part of the thrust of these proposals is to ensure that they do.

Yet there is also a political cost attached to a larger OPEC role that the financial advantages should not obscure. Equity participation in developing countries, loans from OPEC-based banks, and contributions to new multilateral facilities all grant the surplus countries greater power. It may be explicit through pressure for larger OPEC voting participation in international institutions. It may be implicit through a larger say on a range of issues that may extend from the legitimacy of a Palestine state to views on broader development strategy. That is another side of OPEC oil power, the exercise of which has until now been limited. Private bank intermediation has neutralized the financial threat, even while the cartel has determined prices. The industrialized countries should consider how deeply they want OPEC involved, and what the full range of tradeoffs is between alternative financial arrangements and greater OPEC assumption of responsibility.

It is for this very reason that some have sought to link recycling proposals to a broader global agreement that would at least include the price of oil. The Brandt Commission speaks of a package that "could include price indexation related to world inflation, denomination of the price in a basket of currencies or SDRs, and guarantees of the value and accessibility of financial assets which oil producers receive."[9] Others have been skeptical of enforcing such a deal when oil prices are subject to independent demand and supply conditions and not subject to direct determination. They are afraid that an oil price policy will be seen as a substitute for the measures that oil consumers must take to reduce demand and make it more elastic, and to develop alternative sources of supply.

Yet the relationship between financial recycling and the price of oil cannot be ignored. The abruptness of oil price increases both in nominal and real terms, and the attendant uncertainty, has contributed to generally lower rates of economic growth throughout the world. Conversely, low rates of return on financial assets tend to encourage oil producers to leave the oil in the ground. This means higher prices and unnecessary social cost.

It is possible to establish such a linkage short of a global bargain.[10] A modest alternative would be a special lending facility administered by the World Bank, which would pay OPEC depositors a return tied to the real price of petroleum. The higher the price climbed above an agreed-upon level, the lower would be the percentage of indexation on OPEC deposits to compensate for inflation.

Such deposits would be long term to permit lending for the long term to developing countries. Such loans would necessarily also require correction for inflation. The real borrowing rate could be fixed at modest levels, say 2%. Depositors might be paid a higher rate, in order to stimulate continuing increases in oil production. The difference could be made up by a levy on World Bank members in proportion to their share of capital.

The surplus–oil-exporting countries, only a handful dominated by Saudi Arabia, have an interest in such an arrangement, because it offers them a prospect of a better return on their assets than they have experienced. Their position within OPEC has always been on the side of moderation because of their large stake in financial stability. Such an arrangement formalizes, and provides monetary incentive for, behavior toward which they already lean. The developing countries have an unsatisfied demand for longer-term and more certain borrowing, and the inflation adjustment they must accept is a modest cost. The industrial countries pay the bulk of the interest rate subsidy, of a modest magnitude compared to current direct assistance, and receive in return assurances of greater oil price and financial market stability.

These three approaches to ensuring an adequate supply of capital to developing countries in the 1980s are not mutually exclusive. On the contrary, they are reinforcing. Finance for development must have elements of private and public interests and expertise if it is to perform its task. Banks, official institutions, and direct intermediation of the surplus all have a place. There is every reason to believe that these measures would avert an aggregate shortage of funds in the next decade.

Individual countries would not be fully guaranteed against short-term problems, but there would be no generalized inability to continue the borrowing that is necessary. Under reasonable assumptions, the debt for the Latin American non-oil countries (including Mexico) may rise by almost as much as 50% in real terms over the next decade. That will still be much slower than the 1970s, indicative that the burden is of manageable proportions.

The principal danger is not the instability of developing-country debt and the possibility that it may bring the financial system crashing down. Rather it is that because of its very stability, there will be a tendency not to take even modest steps to supplement what private financial markets left to themselves will provide. If that proves inadequate, then it will be the largest debtors—many of them Latin American countries—who will be most exposed. They will have to bear the brunt of the adjustment burden themselves. Because they can do so, at the cost of unnecessarily slower growth to be sure, and because interdependence is still asymmetric, the pressures on the developed countries to reform the system will not necessarily command a response.

The role of the United States in averting such an outcome is no longer a direct financial one. It is now the more difficult one of leadership in advancing cooperative reform. Even for the Caribbean Basin, where United States public assistance can make an important difference, such a multilateral emphasis is indicated. Beyond the potential political gain, a multilateral approach involving donor countries and international institutions is better able to cope with the debt problem of countries in the region. The needed programming of total resource inflow over a period of years, and debt renegotiation, are more likely to emerge from such an arrangement than from largely bilateral economic aid.

In many ways the debt issue is one of the easier problems on the North–South agenda to confront. The mutual stakes are transparent, and the potential remedies are at hand. If we cannot deal with the Latin American debt to ensure that it remains solution rather than problem, prospects for other international economic problems and for coping with other regions are more remote.

NOTES

1. This estimate of disbursed debt and service payments excludes the Mediterranean countries commonly calculated in the World Bank estimates. It includes private nonguaranteed loans. The 1980 total debt takes as its base a

1978 level of $216 billion (National Foreign Assessment Center, Central Intelligence Agency, *Non-OPEC LDC's: External Debt Positions*, January, 1980, p. 3) to which net external borrowing of $87 billion in 1979–80 has been added. (The latter estimate is derived from International Monetary Fund, *World Economic Outlook*, May 1980, p. 101, after adjustment for the capital flows to the Mediterranean countries.)

The most inclusive estimate of developing country debt, including the oil exporters as well as the countries excluded above, would come to more than $400 billion.

Differences in country coverage and concept (disbursed vs. outstanding; publicly guaranteed vs. total; medium and long term vs. total foreign liabilities) bedevil discussions of the debt situation. The resulting numbers can alarm or placate according to preference.

2. Jonathan D. Aronson, ed., *Debt and the Less Developed Countries* (Boulder, Colo.: 1979), pp. 203, 205.

3. *World Financial Markets*, September 1980, p. 8.

4. Economic Commission for Latin America, *External Financing in Latin America*, (1965), p. 202.

5. These estimates for the 1980's derive from the World Bank, *World Development Report*, 1980, p. 7. The rate of growth for the world exports is put at 5.4% annually for the high-case projection of industrialized country growth at 3.6% per annum. The low case of 3.0% would bring world trade growth below 5%.

6. For a description of some of these proposals see Roger Leeds, "External Financing of Development—Challenges and Concerns," *Journal of International Affairs* (Spring/Summer, 1980) pp. 34 ff. For my portfolio swap suggestion see Albert Fishlow, et al., *Rich and Poor Nations in the World Economy* (New York, 1978) pp. 67–68.

7. *World Financial Markets*, September 1980, p. 11.

8. *North–South Dialog: Progress and Prospects*, Hearings before the Subcommittees on International Economic Policy and Trade and on International Organizations, Committees on Foreign Affairs, House of Representatives (96th Congress, 2nd Session), p. 183.

9. *North South: A Programme for Survival* (Cambridge, Mass: 1980), p. 279.

10. For an initial exposition of this proposal, see North–South Dialog, pp. 27, 34, and the ensuing discussion.

16

Agricultural Development Issues in Latin America

Montague Yudelman

INTRODUCTION

Latin America and the Caribbean have a population of around 350 million people, living in a far from homogeneous region that ranges from the humid tropics of the Amazon to the temperate grasslands of the Pampa and from the high altiplano of the Andes to the low-lands of the Llanos of Colombia and Venezuela. The economies of the region encompass highly sophisticated agricultural production systems such as those used by coffee growers of San Paulo as well as near-subsistence systems followed by the potato producers of the Peruvian Andes. In addition, the countries of the region range from those that have a highly devloped industrial capacity and market of a size to manufacture sophisticated inputs for agriculture, such as chemical fertilizers, to those that have little industrial capacity and have to rely almost wholly on inputs.

The sections that follow start with some discussion of agricultural development in the region; this is followed by a consideration of problems of migration and rural poverty. Thereafter, the paper briefly stipulates the necessary conditions for agricultural development and concludes with a look at the role of regional institutions and the very limited role they can play in resolving the major agricultural problems of the region.

The main conclusion is that increasing food production and raising rural incomes depend, in good measure, on government actions. Regional institutions can only provide support to national governments, whether this support be intellectual, financial, or technical. Given the magnitude of the rural problems, such support might be important, but at best its impact is marginal. The likelihood is that there will be increased imports of grain by the more affluent countries of the region; the probability is high that these imports will come from outside the region. Regional trading "arrangements" can have little impact on supply of basic staples so long as the major suppliers of grain are outside the region, as they are at present and probably will continue to be in the foreseeable future.

AGRICULTURAL DEVELOPMENT

Food Production and Trade

The region as a whole had a very high rate of population growth during the 1960s and early 1970s. During that period, food production increased at a rate well in excess of population growth in Central America and South America but fell substantially below the rate of population increase in the Caribbean (see Table 16.1). On the face of it, the region as a whole should be in a strong position to meet the food needs of the 600 million plus inhabitants who are expected to inhabit South and Central America and the Caribbean by the year 2000. Overall the population/natural resource relationship is considerably more favorable than in Africa or Asia. It is estimated that the acreage currently under cultivation could be doubled, the area under irrigation can be substantially expanded, and the 13 million hectares of land currently irrigated can produce close to double its current output. Present yields are below world averages and can be raised substantially, and the large livestock population of the region can yield much more than at present. In brief, with the exception of parts of the Caribbean and Central America, there is no physical resource constraint, as such, to increasing production, and there appears to be a resource base in the region capable of yielding a substantially larger food and agricultural product than at present.

The region as a whole has a substantial trade balance in favor of agricultural products; over the 1973/78 period, the ratio of exports to imports was about 3:1, with a favorable balance in 1978 amounting to US $16 billion (see Table 16.2). Most of these exports consist of tropical beverages and fibers, coffee being the largest. The largest imports are cereals and foodstuffs. Excluding Argentina, the region's ratio of cereal sufficiency has dropped and is now 80%; Latin America now relies on the outside world (largely the United States) for one-fifth of the grain consumed in the region. Even when Argentina is included, the region is still a modest net importer of at least one million tons—a far cry from 25 years ago, when the region was a substantial net exporter of grains. There is good reason to assume that grain imports into the region will increase over the coming decades unless governments make special efforts to raise their agricultural output.

The changes in the region's grain trade reflect changes in the world at large. Prior to World War II, there was relatively little international trade in grain; most of the world was self-sufficient, and the trading that did take place was largely between the United Kingdom, Canada, Australia, and Argentina. Since then—and more especially in the last 20 years—there has been a substantial growth in the international grain trade. Whereas, in 1956 only 5% of global production of grain was traded, by 1975 close to 11% of a much larger output was traded. This expansion in trade was from 33 million tons in 1956 to 193 million tons in 1979—an 8% average growth rate per year.

A main source of world grain exports was once Argentina; it is now North America. While the United States and Canada produced about one out of five tons of grain grown in the world, exports have risen because of high productivity and the ability to provide export surpluses in response to growing market opportunities throughout the world, including countries such as Venezuela and Mexico. As a result, US grain exports rose by more than 10% a year between 1955 and 1975; the other traditional exporters, especially Argentina, Mexico, and Brazil, failed to participate fully in the growing market. Argentina's exports grew at a much lower rate, around 3% a year, so that its share of the world market declined substantially. Mexico has become a net importer and as petroleum-based incomes rise is likely to follow the path of other oil producers and become a very substantial importer of grain. Brazil has yet to exploit its potential as a corn exporter. The growing importers Venezuela and Mexico are closer to the United States than to the major regional exporter Argentina; transport costs give U.S. grain a marked CIF edge.

TABLE 16.1. *Agricultural and Food Production Indices. Total and Per Capita. Latin America and the Caribbean, Selected Countries – 1970, 1975, and 1978 (1961-65 = 100)*

	Agricultural Production			Food Production			Agricultural Production per Capita			Food Production per Capita		
	1970	1975	1978[1]	1970	1975	1978[1]	1970	1975	1978[1]	1970	1975	1978[1]
Mexico	126	151	159	137	169	175	99	100	94	107	112	104
Dominican Republic	115	131	150	122	133	148	97	94	100	99	95	98
Haiti	99	90	97	102	92	99	87	72	72	90	73	74
Jamaica	84	83	84	84	84	83	76	69	67	76	69	67
Trinidad and Tobago	97	78	90	96	78	89	82	63	72	82	63	71
Caribbean	107	111	123	109	112	122	92	86	90	94	87	90
Costa Rica	148	176	192	160	197	208	118	124	127	128	139	138
El Salvador	117	141	165	136	172	197	92	94	101	107	115	120
Guatemala	121	167	191	141	187	204	99	119	125	116	133	133
Honduras	127	121	162	127	110	148	100	80	97	100	73	89
Nicaragua	118	149	172	132	160	178	97	107	113	108	114	118
Panama	147	151	164	149	153	166	119	107	107	121	108	109

326

Central America and Panama	127	152	176	141	162	183	103	106	113	114	113	117
Argentina	115	123	148	117	127	152	105	105	121	106	108	125
Bolivia	120	150	156	118	142	150	98	108	103	97	102	99
Brazil	121	155	168	136	170	189	99	111	111	112	122	125
Chile	127	129	125	129	132	127	108	100	92	105	103	94
Colombia	121	149	165	125	160	176	98	108	111	102	116	119
Ecuador	118	129	138	115	127	134	97	91	90	94	90	87
Guyana	97	112	116	97	112	116	83	85	83	83	85	83
Paraguay	124	140	175	125	129	153	103	101	117	104	93	101
Peru	105	101	98	116	113	108	86	70	63	94	79	69
Uruguay	107	101	96	112	111	103	104	96	90	108	106	97
Venezuela	142	172	200	145	175	202	113	117	124	115	119	125
South America	119	141	156	127	149	167	100	104	107	106	110	115

[1]Preliminary.

Note: The index formula is explained in the source, cited below.

Source: U.S. Department of Agriculture, *Indices of Agricultural Production for the Western Hemisphere, 1969–78*, Statistical Bulletin No. 622.

327

TABLE 16.2. Trade in Agricultural Food Products, Selected Countries, Latin America and the Caribbean, 1975–1978

	Latin America		Argentina		Brazil	
	Value[1]	%	Value[1]	%	Value[1]	%
Exports						
1973	12505.3	100	2457.1	19.7	4180.6	33.4
1974	15837.3	100	2859.2	18.1	4869.3	30.7
1975	16750.6	100	2175.5	13.0	4875.1	29.1
1976	19032.4	100	2845.2	14.9	6112.1	32.1
1977	23591.1	100	4173.7	17.7	7566.7	32.1
1978	24412.5	100	4690.9	19.2	6557.9	26.9
Imports						
1973	4170.4	100	251.4	6.0	770.0	18.5
1974	6463.0	100	242.9	3.8	1133.5	17.5
1975	6091.5	100	238.6	3.9	887.9	14.6
1976	6230.3	100	191.0	3.1	1155.0	18.5
1977	6665.5	100	263.5	4.0	942.3	14.1
1978	8201.4	100	242.0	2.9	1563.7	14.1
Balance						
1973	8334.9		2205.7		3410.6	
1974	9374.3		2616.3		3735.8	
1975	10659.1		1916.9		3987.2	
1976	17802.1		2654.2		4957.1	
1977	16925.6		3910.2		6624.4	
1978	16211.1		4448.9		4994.2	
Growth Rate of Exports						
1973–1974		26.6		16.4		16.5
1974–1975		5.8		−24.0		.1
1975–1976		13.6		30.8		25.4
1976–1977		23.9		46.7		23.8
1977–1978		3.5		12.4		−13.3
Growth Rate of Imports						
1973–1974		55.0		−3.4		47.2
1974–1975		−5.7		−1.8		−21.7
1975–1976		2.3		−20.0		30.0
1976–1977		7.0		38.0		−18.4
1977–1978		23.0		−8.2		65.9

[1] U.S. $ million (current).

Colombia		Mexico		Venezuela		Others	
Value[1]	%	Value[1]	%	Value[1]	%	Value[1]	%
816.6	6.5	991.5	7.9	41.1	.3	4018.4	32.1
951.2	6.0	1060.7	6.7	75.0	.5	6021.9	38.0
1096.7	6.6	976.6	5.8	64.5	.4	7562.2	45.1
1323.3	6.9	1334.3	7.0	58.1	.3	7359.4	39.6
1914.8	8.1	1418.0	6.0	108.5	.5	8409.4	35.6
2536.2	10.4	1503.8	6.2	122.1	.5	9001.6	36.9
154.4	3.7	543.7	13.0	387.8	9.3	2063.1	49.5
222.7	3.4	1091.2	16.9	536.6	8.3	3236.2	50.1
151.9	2.5	925.6	15.2	718.8	11.8	3168.7	52.0
217.7	3.5	563.3	9.0	892.0	14.3	3211.3	51.5
241.0	3.9	827.9	12.4	1234.9	18.5	3135.9	47.1
294.0	3.6	1121.9	13.7	1336.5	16.3	3643.3	44.4
662.2		447.8		-346.7		1955.1	
728.5		-10.5		-461.5		2785.7	
944.8		51.0		-654.3		4393.5	
1105.6		771.0		-833.9		4148.1	
1653.8		590.1		-1126.4		5273.5	
2242.2		381.9		-1214.4		5358.3	
	16.5		7.0		82.5		50.0
	15.3		7.9		-14.0		25.6
	20.7		36.6		-9.9		-2.7
	44.7		6.3		86.7		14.3
	32.4		6.1		12.5		7.0
	44.2		100.7		38.3		57.0
	-31.8		-15.2		34.0		-2.1
	43.3		-39.1		24.1		1.3
	19.9		47.0		38.4		-2.3
	12.7		35.5		8.2		16.2

Source: Food and Agriculture Organization (FLO). *1978 Trade Yearbook,* Vol. 32, 1979

It is important to note that the major increases in grain imports in the world are coming from the higher-income developing countries such as many in Latin America (Venezuela, Mexico, Brazil, Colombia), *not*, as many seem to think, the poorest countries such as Haiti, Bolivia, or Central American countries). One important reason for the increased demand and for imports for grain is the shift in diets—a shift toward wheat products and grain-fed meat, a shift fueled by rising incomes and accelerated by growing urbanization. The use of grain intended for feeding animals has been increasing since the mid-1950s. At present around one-third of all the grain produced in the world is used to feed animals, with half of that being so used in the United States and the Soviet Union. But at the same time there is a growing trend toward grain-fed livestock in the developing world, the bulk of it in Latin America. The "better-off" consumer in rich and poor communities inside (and outside) Latin America is consuming increasing amounts of meat as incomes rise. And much of the grain to feed the animals is imported from outside the region.

An important reason for the growing gap between demand and domestic supply of meat and grain in Latin America is the comparatively low productivity of grain production. For example, grain yields in the United States are around 4 tons per hectare—twice the average level in Latin America (see Table 16.3). Output per man in the United States is much larger than anywhere else in the world—roughly 90 tons per worker, compared with 10 in the Soviet Union and less than 3 in Mexico (which is still higher than the 1 ton per Indian or Chinese agricultural worker). The differences in yields can be explained, in part, by the differences in fertilizer usage—a U.S. farmer puts four times as much fertilizer on his fields as does his Mexican neighbor and eight times as much as South American farmers in general. Higher output per man can be explained in part by the higher investment in agriculture in the United States. Broadly speaking, the level of investment in U.S. agriculture—with its 6 million rural people—is greater than that in the whole of Latin America with its 120 million people in the rural areas. The point to emphasize is that productivity is low and agriculture is grossly undercapitalized, especially the food producing sector (as opposed to parts of the export-oriented sector, especially beverages and fibers). If incomes continue to rise, then—unless more is done in the food sector—food imports will increase, and the region as a whole will become a still larger net importer of grains. And if present patterns continue, these imports will come from North America.

TABLE 16.3. Consumption of Fertilizer (Nitrogen, Phosphorus, and Potassium–Nutrient Basis), Latin America and the Caribbean, 1974 and 1976

	1974[1]	1976[1]	1976[2]
Mexico	922	1,165	42
Cuba	303	361	116
Dominican Republic	98	75	76
Jamaica	25	14	54
Trinidad and Tobago	8	8	55
Other Caribbean	44	38	
Subtotal	478	496	
Belize	3	1	
Costa Rica	73	55	114
El Salvador	98	102	153
Guatemala	65	86	50
Honduras	19	25	29
Nicaragua	35	46	30
Panama	28	23	40
Subtotal	321	338	
Argentina	71	72	2
Bolivia	6	3	1
Brazil	1,716	2,371	63
Chile	158	116	20
Colombia	249	247	48
Ecuador	41	77	15
Guyana	15	11	
Paraguay	2	129	39
Peru	142	129	39
Surinam	6	6	
Uraguay	35	63	33
Venezuela	128	161	
Subtotal	2,569	3,257	
Latin America	4,290	5,256	

Source: U.S. Department of Agriculture, Food and Agriculture Organization, *Annual Fertilizer Review*, 1977; and International Agricultural Development Service, *Agricultural Indicators*, 1980.

[1] In thousand mt.
[2] Per ha of total cropped area (in kg).

Urbanization and the Rural Sector

Any strategy for dealing with agricultural and food related-problems in the region has to take account of the great shifts that are taking place in the distribution of population and the reasons why these shifts are occurring.

There are two coincidental shifts of population under way. The first is the high rate of urbanization, and the second is the declining proportion of population in the rural sector. Urbanization has proceeded at an explosive rate in Latin America; between 1950 and 1980, the proportion of population living in urban areas rose from 40% to 65%. Both Mexico and Brazil set the pace, with the urban population in the two countries rising from about 40% of total population to close to 66%. By the year 2000, it is expected that more than 70% of the population will be urbanized, and there will be at least 16 cities in the region with a population in excess of five million (compared with one in the 1950s: Buenos Aires).

Most of the increase in urban population is coming from natural increase within the urban areas; however, all the evidence indicates that a substantial part is due to rural–urban migration. Research suggests that most people move because they want to improve their economic situation; rural inhabitants seek better opportunities in the industrial and service sectors of the economy. The patterns of investment throughout the region have been such that these opportunities tend to be in the urban areas.

The movement of people out of agriculture is a feature that is common to all economies where people have freedom to move, as is the case in most of the region. Economic growth is generally accompanied by a reduction in the relative size of the rural labor force. Agriculture tends to be a supplier of labor, with the numbers remaining in agriculture diminishing as average per capita incomes rise. Figure 16.1 shows this quite clearly; the "richer" the country, the smaller the proportion of the labor force in agriculture; it also shows that the levels of development vary considerably and with them the problems related to rural development. A uniform regional policy prescription is difficult where population distributions vary so greatly. This is not a problem for the United States and the European Economic Community as a whole, where the labor force in agriculture represents less than 5 to 10% of the total labor force.

One of the major differences between the impact of the migration of people out of agriculture in the region and in the developed countries is that the absolute number of people in the rural areas has *not* declined in the region. During the 1970s, the proportion of the labor force in agriculture fell by 5% in South America (to 33%) and

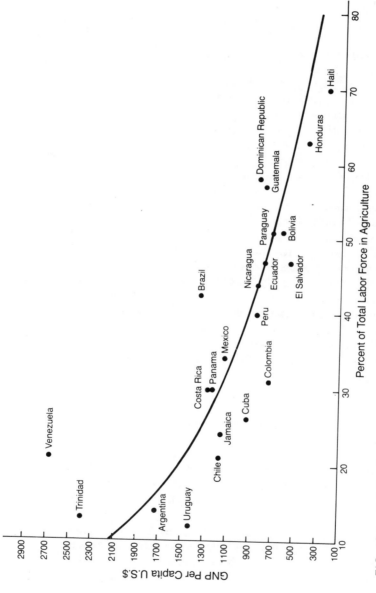

FIG. 16.1: Relation between per Capita GNP and Percent of Total Labor Force in Agriculture—Latin America and the Caribbean, 1977

by 6% in Central America (to 40%). At the same time, the agricultural population increased by ten million. In other words the natural increase of population has been such that despite a rapid outmigration the numbers in the rural areas increased, so that *more* rather than fewer employment opportunities had to be created in the rural areas. This is not the experience of the industrialized countries. Another and related important difference between the experience of developed countries and developing countries relates to urban employment. The greater migrations out of the rural areas in the West were accompanied by a rapid expansion of industrial employment and growth in the service sector. Migrant laborers helped to provide the workers in factories and other industries. By all accounts, while there has been rapid industrial growth, it has not been able to absorb the rapidly expanding labor force (with the one exception of Venezuela). The consequence is, of course, that there is a large amount of open unemployment in the urban areas.

The pattern of population distribution and employment problems make it clear that job creation has to be part of any strategy of development in the region. Job creation in the rural areas, of course, has to include measures that reduce labor displacement and encourage labor-intensive techniques of production. The techniques of the West, which are primarily labor saving, are thus not necessarily those best suited to much of the region. At the same time, though, as is pointed out below, the urban explosion is leading to a tremendous increase in demand for a marketable surplus. But there is little in current experience to indicate what regional arrangements can contribute to reducing unemployment when it is pervasive throughout the region.

Rural Poverty

Recent analysis indicates that approximately 100 million people in Latin America are living below an absolute poverty line. The characteristics of this group are well known: malnutrition, illiteracy, absence of health or sanitary facilities, lack of adequate housing. Perhaps less widely known is the fact that well over half of these people consist of families with large numbers of children, and that the great majority live in rural areas that contain around one-third of the total population. Put differently, over half of all rural people in the region live in absolute poverty, compared with one quarter of the inhabitants in urban areas.

Scattered evidence tends to show that the mixture of sources of earnings for the rural poor varies considerably among the countries in the region. In Peru, 80% of the rural poor are subsistence farmers of distinct ethnic backgrounds. Subsistence farmers are mostly Indian, Quechua or Aymara speaking, and in 1961 about 70% were illiterate. Their principal source of livelihood was on the average about 0.9 hectares of Sierra cropland, three head of cattle, and some other livestock. Most earned some cash income by seasonal labor on larger farms or occasional sales of livestock products. In Colombia, approximately half of rural households in poverty are small producers, the rest landless labor. Nevertheless, even small producers gained at least two-thirds of their earnings as wage labor on larger farms.

In contrast to Peru, where most rural poor are subsistence farmers, the evidence in Northeastern Brazil shows that most of the poor are landless. According to the survey undertaken jointly by the Brazilian government and the World Bank, only 1.7 million of the 6 million rural labor force (heads of households plus working family members of landowners) own land. Of this 6 million, about three million have no access to land and subsist on temporary employment or eke out a living on lands so poor or remote that they were not captured by any of the censuses or cadastral surveys. These three million families constitute the hard core of poverty in the Northeast. Most landowners (even if they own only two or three hectares of land), sharecroppers, renters, and permanent workers realize real incomes at or about the absolute poverty line, but the remaining persons presumably do not, and this situation is traceable, in good measure, to their lack of access to land.

The above evidence shows that rural poverty cannot be characterized by a single simple occupational classification. Small farmers are not necessarily at the core of rural poverty in all countries, as is frequently believed. For many countries, landless or near landless labor is at least equally represented in the poverty group, and wage earnings represent an important component of income, even in the case of subsistence farmers. Indeed, a recent study indicates that the share of rural households that are landless or near landless in many countries in the region is higher than that in India and, in some countries, as high as in Bangladesh—around 75% of the total; these data reinforce the significance of creating off-farm employment.

Finally, it is important to know whether rural poverty is increasing or decreasing. No one knows for sure, but fragmentary evidence is not very encouraging. Information on income distribution in certain South American countries shows that the poorest 20% of the population have received a declining share of the national income over the past decade or so; at the same time, the richest 10% have been receiving an increasing share of the national income. An exception appears to be Colombia, where the poorest 20% have been receiving an increasing share while the richest 10% have been receiving a decreasing share.

Mexico's experience during the last 25 years is a relatively well-documented illustration of what appears to be a worsening situation for the rural poor. A variety of factors have acted as a drag on potential growth in rainfed areas—regions that contained the majority of Mexico's poor and small farmers, but which also provided most of the food consumed by the urban poor. By 1960, the largest 0.5% of all farms produced 33% of total agricultural output and accounted for almost 50% of all incremental production since 1950; this concentration has increased since then. Today, the modern large farms (7.1% of the total) generate 3 to 5 times more income per hectare and 8 to 20 times more per capita than traditional and subsistence farms. As a result, in 1975, 76% of all agriculture families (2.4 million) lived below the poverty level. Most of these families have to rely on off-farm earnings to make ends meet: 850,000 rural families own no land whatsoever, a number that reflects a substantial increase over past years.

Evidence indicates that, at best, income inequality may not have worsened over recent periods of sustained economic growth. Although the fraction of people in poverty has declined, there has been a constant *absolute* number of people in poverty and some increase in the number of people malnourished. It is estimated that, in Latin America, some 100 million people will remain in absolute poverty by the year 2000 unless special efforts are undertaken to correct this situation.

Rural poverty is, of course, linked to the absence of employment and to low levels of investment in the rural areas. It is also linked to the distribution of wealth especially land. Alleviation of rural poverty requires a combination of increasing agricultural output with a focus on ensuring that low income producers participate in any such program, as well as the creation of off-farm employment through the decentralization of industry and other employment creating activities.

THE NECESSARY CONDITIONS FOR RURAL DEVELOPMENT

The preceding somewhat sketchy analysis touches on some of the characteristics of the region that come to mind when thinking about any policy on rural development. In brief, we see the region as a rapidly urbanizing area that is becoming less and less self-sufficient in food-stuffs with large numbers of rural unemployed and one that has made few significant inroads on the problem of rural poverty and malnutrition. Clearly, increasing both rural incomes and the supply of food must be given priority; such a result would help reduce urban poverty through the generation of more abundant and cheaper food supplies and by mitigating the forces that push labor out of the rural areas into the overcrowded urban centers. Ideally, a strategy for rural development would center around fulfilling the twin objectives of increasing food production available for domestic subsistence consumption, thereby driving down relative food prices, and raising incomes of the rural poor, including those with and without access to land.

The incomes of many low-income producers are highly dependent on their access to land and their security of tenure. It is well known, too, that land distribution in much of Latin America is skewed, and that the redistribution of land can well reduce poverty. All the evidence indicates that there is considerable scope for redistributing income and eventually increasing output where idle or under-utilized land is redistributed to smallholders who are provided with the means for productive use of the land. However, as we look ahead to the future, it is important to appreciate that there are limits to the extent to which land redistribution can solve the problem of poverty. For example, a careful study of Northeastern Brazil, where half of that country's lowest-income group live, shows that even an extremely radical land reform can only have a limited impact on alleviating overall rural poverty. If productive assets were reallocated so that all land-owning families would have an average per capita income of around $150, there would be a 20% decrease in the number of households living below the poverty line. Thus, despite a program of redistribution that would create close to 800,000 new farms, four million members of the rural labor force of six million would remain in absolute poverty.

The point to be emphasized is that land redistribution *can* improve the lot of millions, but that the scale of problems faced by the millions of landless or near landless precludes making agrarian reform alone the solution. Employment and poverty problems in the rural sector cannot be resolved on the land alone—other productive opportunities are needed to absorb migrants arriving in central and regional urban areas as well as in the rural areas themselves. Much of the additional effort required will involve creating full and part-time off-farm rural employment. To this end, creating industrial growth poles, fostering agrovilles and market towns and systems such as the vertically integrated kombinats of Yugoslavia must be accelerated. Regional planning must become part of every *program for rural development*. There is a great need for measures that look beyond agriculture alone and deal with both on- and off-farm investment and employment. This is a general area where experience is limited and many governments are groping for ways and means of implementing this facet of development.

At the same time, much more needs to be done to assist low-income groups who do have access to land, to help meet the food needs of the region. Much more is known about how to deal with this part of rural development. In the past five years there has been a growing awareness throughout the region about what is required to meet these objectives. In the first instance, it is recognized that there is a hierarchy of requirements to increase agricultural output that must begin with the farmer himself. The producer, large or small, is a rational decisionmaker. Some of the necessary conditions for the farmer to increase output are dependent upon:

- more effective technical packages that are applicable to prevailing physical conditions at the micro-level;

- an extension service to spread the knowledge to farmers:

- a credit and distribution system that enables the farmer to acquire the inputs he needs;

- a transport and marketing network for the farmer to move his output.

Most important of all, there has to be a pricing system that gives the farmer an incentive to undertake the additional effort, risk, and investment involved in increasing his production.

These general considerations apply equally to large and small producers. In many instances, however, the available services have been tailored to meet the needs of larger farmers. This must change if rural poverty is to be reduced or if small farmers are to produce a much-needed market surplus. Research must be focused on technology appropriate to the small nonmechanized farm; extension must be designed to reach small producers; credit programs and institutions have to be directed to reach small farmers and low-income groups; and such credit projects must not only increase earnings but should also provide low-income producers with mechanisms for savings. Experience indicates that it is possible to have an effective strategy that meets the objectives of rural development, such. as increasing food production and raising the incomes of small producers; usually, such a strategy is based on the development of support services, ensuring that small farmers have access to these services and that there is the incentive to use them to increase production.

Some of the short-term expansion of agricultural and food production will come from opening new areas; increasingly, though, higher output will have to come from a more efficient use of land now under cultivation. Whatever the means of raising output, all experience indicates that there are limited opportunities for low-cost agricultural expansion. In many parts of the region the rate of public investment in support of agriculture is basically not enough to offset the physical depreciation that is occuring in erosion, poor maintenance of irrigation systems, deterioration of roads, depreciation of machinery, and the like. Government services—the heart of the support system for farmers—are woefully inadequate. It is true that in some countries the private sector has invested heavily, especially in the export-oriented tree crop industries, *but* by and large agriculture throughout the region is grossly under-capitalized; there is a great need for additional investment in agriculture. One estimate is that it would require $26 billion to double irrigation capacity in the next decade. Investment in the past decade was around $10 billion.

In the main, the path to development calls for a much greater and more effective support system. Governments have to provide the services—technical, educational, advisory, marketing, and credit that help the producer to increase his output. The producer, in turn, must have the incentive to increase output. Most of these services have to be national—there is very little opportunity for interregional activities other than through provision of scarce manpower for research. Even so, experience has indicated that international research efforts have to be complemented by national efforts because of the location-specificity of agriculture. There can be little substitute for a strong national effort in agricultural development to establish the necessary conditions for rural progress.

THE ROLE OF REGIONAL INSTITUTIONS

I have set out what I believe to be the primary challenges that must be met in Latin America if agriculture is to play its full role in the development of the region through provision of increased food and raw materials for domestic consumption and export and generation of the basis for expanded employment in rural areas. In addition, and perhaps more importantly, there is the challenge of achieving a more equitable distribution of the fruits of economic growth. I turn now to the question of whether international arrangements or institutions are relevant or necessary in addressing these challenges. In considering this, four types of public institutional arrangements might be identified:

1. those related primarily to trade, which are set up solely at the initiative of governments within the region, such as LAFTA, SELA, OLADE, CARICOM, SIECA, and the Groupo Andino;

2. those related to financing and, to a lesser extent, technical assistance and training, which, with one or two exceptions, are designed to mobilize extraregional capital for investment in the region. The World Bank would be included in this class, along with the IDB, CABEI, and the Caribbean Development Bank. The nature of these institutions dictates that their management reflect the views of both the member nonborrowing countries (from outside the region) and borrowing members within the region;

3. those related mainly to research, technical assistance, and training. Again, these are generally international rather than regional institutions, such as UNDP, FAO, UNESCO, or the Consultative Group for International Agricultural Research; the activities of those considered regional, such as OAS, IITA, CATIE, are for the most part indistinguishable from those that are international in scope.

The role of these institutions is difficult to assess. The regional trade organizations have had little impact on intraregional agricultural trade or on prices; intraregional trade is relatively limited. It is considerably less than the $20 billion of exports and $8 billion of imports that make up the region's "external trade," which is dominated by exports of beverages, fibers, vegetables, oil seeds, and sown wheat, with the EEC importing over $6 billion a year and the United States even more than this amount. The largest intraregional trade in agriculture, about 25% to 50%, is the export of Argentinian wheat to Brazil; but the grain importers whose imports are growing most rapidly—Venezuela and Mexico—import from North America (to which they export their oil). There is no explicity "rural development" theme in proposals for expanding trade other than the notion that expanded trade benefits all. However, one of the major reasons for limited intraregional trade is that most countries in Latin America produce a wide range of similar commodities, so, when faced with rural underemployment and poverty, they strive to increase their self-sufficiency as a means of dealing with these problems. (This is clearly illustrated in Mexico's most recent food plan, which envisages a doubling of corn prices to promote self-sufficiency, despite much less costly suppliers being available in the United States). One of the great differences between the region in comparison with the EEC is that the EEC cannot produce tropical products; another is that the EEC, with only 6% of its population in agriculture, can be concerned with maintaining high farm incomes rather than increasing production and reducing rural unemployment. The problems of increasing intraregional trade in the region extend well beyond the tariff structure—they relate to a host of activities starting with uniform pricing and increasing agricultural productivity, as well as lowering of costs of distribution. Raising productivity depends largely on improving national development efforts.

If one were to look specifically at food products among the members of these trade groupings, and the steps I have suggested for addressing these issues, it *is* possible that trade policies in agricultural products and inputs could be designed to make some contribution to their resolution. There could be regional investment programs in large-scale fertilizer plants (where economies of scale are important) and special efforts to develop regional distributional facilities. There is little in the record to suggest this has been done to date. Insofar as trade and rural poverty is concerned, the role of these institutions in resolving rural poverty will be constrained by the fact that most of the trade covered by agreements that do exist is not in commodities that affect a majority of the rural poor (e.g., citrus fruits). In addition, the bulk of the agricultural export and imports has been, and will continue to be, with countries such as the United States and the European Economic Community, whose policies are unaffected by intraregional trade groups.

On the international financing side, major efforts have been made by institutions such as the World Bank and IDB to channel external capital resources and to engage Latin American governments in dialogue on the rural development issues I have described. For example, in the past ten years the World Bank has made 102 loans for agricultural development in the region for more than U.S. $3 billion, with about half going to Mexico and Brazil. It has taken active steps to pioneer, in conjunction with governments, innovative approaches to development designed to raise food production and reach the rural poor; examples include ongoing programs in Mexico, Colombia, Brazil, and Honduras aimed at raising incomes of about three million rural people living under conditions of absolute poverty. Total Bank lending for this purpose is expected to reach approximately 10–15 million people in Latin America between 1980 and 1985.

The remaining groups of international agencies are those whose influence is exerted on national policy makers and technicians through the written or spoken word. The research, training, and technical assistance provided by this array of agencies may well have had an impact on current policies for agricultural and rural development. For example, FAO, CEPAL, ILO, and OAS have made philosophical and technical contributions to resolving current issues. Likewise, institutions such as the CCIAR centers, IICA, and CATIE have made important breakthroughs in developing technical packages suitable for subsistence farmers. But these disparate efforts are frequently marginal. An important but unexplored area where regional efforts might be effective is to pool experience on what is a regional phenomenon—the problems of linking rural production to the requirements of a rapidly urbanizing society. This will be a central issue in the 1980s, and effective distribution systems will be important in holding down urban food prices. The social and political consequences of ignoring this dimension of the problem can be very high indeed.

Regional or international agencies could undoubtedly be more relevant in dealing with rural poverty, food supply, and accelerated agricultural growth in Latin America. I would like to repeat the conviction that, in the final analysis, solutions to rural poverty or sluggish agricultural development come from national administrative and technical capacity to tackle difficult political and social questions.

International intergovernmental organizations can help in conceptualising the issues, facilitating information exchange, channeling capital and technical resources, formulating internationally acceptable norms to gauge development performance (at project, sectoral, or national levels) in such terms as enhanced economic growth, equity, social participation, or human dignity, or exploiting economies of scale in certain activities such as fertilizer manufacture or agricultural research and training. Regional governance, interpreted as collective decision making by governments of the region, is somewhat tangential to the central issues I have sketched in relation to rural development and increased food production. The situation may well be different for other sectors. If one is concerned with international "trade" in ideas, knowledge, or even moral values to strengthen national government capacity or political resolve, and associated mobilization of capital and human resources to cope with rural poverty and efficiency in agriculture, then there appears to be little to choose between those institutions that may be termed international, such as UN bodies, and those considered regional, such as the OAS. However, one thing is clear: Greater efforts are required to make the research training and technical assistance more immediately relevant to the development needs of the countries of the region.

A more coherent and practical framework should be evolved to enable such initiatives to provide more constructive support to the formulation and execution of national policies. One avenue suggests itself—a closer relationship between these regional or international institutions and governments and the international or bilateral financing institutions in the design and execution of research, training in support of planning and execution of programs, and investments for agricultural and rural development. But these activities are all supporting activities—supporting the efforts of national governments. In the final analysis it is the national governments that have to take the necessary actions to promote rural development.

17

Natural Resource Development in the Americas

William Glade

INTRODUCTION

As the Americas move into the third Development Decade, it would seem to be an especially opportune time to look at the adequacy of the institutional structure of contemporary development efforts for ensuring the availability of and access to requisite national resources. This kind of concern, of course, is not new. The whole school of economic thought known as physiocracy placed land at the very center of the economic process. Even Ricardo, who wrote when capital and labor factors had also been more clearly recognized as creative agents in growth, worried over the implications of diminishing returns to land factors, which were expected to become even scarcer with the passage of time. Later still, the so-called stagnationist thesis of the 1930s saw the possibilities for continued increases in aggregate output being throttled back by, among other things, a disappearance of the land-related investment opportunities that had long been associated with a moving frontier.

Leaving these more historic concerns to one side, we may date our contemporary era's monitoring of resource availabilities to the period immediately following World War II, an event that had prompted a greatly heightened awareness of the importance of supply continuity in the natural resource field.[1] Reflective of this new appreciation was the monumental tome called, somewhat ethnocentrically (since it dealt only with the United States), *America's Needs and Resources*. The volume was prepared by Frederic Dewhurst and associates. This landmark work, sponsored by the Twentieth Century Fund, was comprehensive in its focus and touched upon both replenishable (renewable or flow) resources and exhaustible (nonrenewable or fund) resources in ways that were both prescient and awry. Recognition of the probably enduring importance of large-scale coal resources, for example, was one of the better judgments, as was the study's stress on the dwindling domestic supplies of economically usable liquid hydrocarbons. Farther from the mark, however, was its view of the feasibility of tapping oil shales for petroleum, thought to be economic if the then-low costs of producing crude petroleum in the midcontinent and Gulf Coast areas should rise 50 to 100%. Farther still off-target were the sanguine expectations of that day regarding nuclear energy. The general tone of the study, in its treatment of natural resources, was summed up thusly:

> It is inevitable, of course, as time goes on, that our supplies of mineral resources will come nearer to exhaustion and that our needs will be satisfied with less ease and at higher cost than before. Given a system that permits free access to the world's resources, however, there can be no question of a raw material supply adequate to support an expanding American economy for many decades to come. And even if we should be forced to rely on our domestic mineral deposits to a much greater extent than in the past, no reason exists for believing that depletion is so extensive that it would necessarily become a serious barrier to the maintenance of high levels of production and employment in the future.[2]

It is interesting that an up-dated edition of *America's Needs and Resources*, published in 1955, backed off little if at all from the largely optimistic tenor of the first edition. Indeed, in some ways, the revised second edition was even more optimistic—perhaps because it introduced a new chapter on "Technology: Primary Resource." This chapter was nothing if not exuberant in its foretelling of all the fruits that could be expected to be harvested from the accelerating advance of science and technology. Taking a retrospective look at the first half of the twentieth century, the chapter's authors, Dewhurst and J. A. Waring, Jr., correctly perceived the pivotal role of these factors, which might appropriately be called cultural resources, in product development, and the movement to higher levels of productivity in the methods of production. No less significant, they felt, was the dynamic effect of technological progress on the process of resource creation as well as more efficient extraction and use. "Technology is also constantly adding to our supply of basic resources by discovering new materials and ways to put them to use and new uses for existing materials. . . . The increase in variety and substitutability of raw materials, is, in fact, a good index of technological progress."[3] The point is one to which we shall have occasion to return later on.

If the present era opened on a relatively bright note in its general apprehension of resource prospects, it is understandable, if nevertheless somewhat curious, that this major resource survey, *America's Needs and Resources*, made practically no allowance for a possible growth of competing national demands in the international markets for natural resources. Doubtless the predominating influence of the United States in global trade accounted for this foreshortened perspective, the transitory nature of the dominance not having been fully appreciated at the time. Reference was made to the economic development of underdeveloped areas in much of the literature of the late 1940s and early 1950s, but it is interesting to note that what is today called the Third World was relegated to scarcely more than a passing mention in the Twentieth Century Fund's assessment of the situation.

As for Latin America, thinking about resource policy during the 1940s and 1950s was dominated by the run-up of prices on its raw materials exports during the Second World War and the Korean War and a widespread belief that, apart from such exceptional circumstances, the long-run terms of trade for primary commodity exporters were fated to deteriorate. This view, which became an article of faith among most development planners in the region, obviously assumed a situation of relative resource abundance for the foreseeable future. No little energy was therefore devoted to propounding the advantages of various commodity stabilization schemes as a means of enhancing the regional capacity to import the investment goods needed for implementing national development programs. Beyond this, the 1940s and 1950s witnessed a progressive spread of nationalistic policy preferences in Latin American public opinion and policy communities as country after country sought to subordinate natural resource utilization to the priorities of national development policy. The general view of resources that emerges from the early development literature, as in the World Bank's country mission reports, is that of latent wealth waiting to be tapped, or exploited more efficiently, to provide much-needed foreign exchanges to finance agricultural modernization and industrialization efforts.

AN EVOLVING RESOURCE PROBLEM

A number of developments have conspired to bring the question of natural resource supplies to the forefront of hemispheric attention in recent years, bringing to an end the easy optimism of the late 1940s and early 1950s. A review of these should be a particularly helpful way of exposing different facets of this complex matter and, at the same time, to locate the *problématique* in its appropriate social, political, and economic setting.

As the first Development Decade got underway, in the 1960s, heightened public awareness of the demographic explosion building up in less industrialized regions, particularly in Latin America where the Alliance for Progress drew regional problems into a sharper focus, led to concern over the adequacy of production of food, fiber, and other crops in the low-income economies. Thus, doubts about the adequacy of land resources were the first to surface. Shortfalls in agricultural production seemed to threaten national efforts to raise rural (and urban) incomes and fueled the forces of inflation, while placing additional strains on balance of payments positions already overtaxed by import requirements for capital and intermediate products. Primitive agricultural production methods not only thwarted the drive toward a higher standard of living but also placed at risk much of Latin America's soil and forest resources. What, with care, could function more or less indefinitely as a flow resource appeared destined, instead, for depletion in the manner of a fund resource.

Land settlement and expansion along the extensive margin, through techniques of slash-and-burn agriculture and low-technology grazing, combined with a growing demand for fuel-wood to denude an ever widening area of its sylvan cover.[4] Erosion often accompanied the process, and in not a small portion of the former tropical woodlands climactic conditions interacted with soil structure to produce a form of land degradation that has left vast stretches of territory bereft of even its limited former productive potential. Only in comparatively recent times has the meager regenerative capacity of tropical forests come to be fully appreciated, but public policy has yet to reflect this fuller apprehension of how both soil and forest resources have been brought to the point of exhaustion. The introduction, in more recent times, of agribusiness operations has not so much changed the basic disparate relation between social costs and private gains as simply accelerated the momentum with which this disparity moves to a larger scale. Elsewhere, in regions populated for a longer time, population crowding, poor cultivation techniques, and the progressive fragmentation of minifundia plots led to a similar form of soil mining, with erosion of increasing severity as rural settlement crept up the steeper gradients. To some extent commercial farming has suffered from ecological misuse, but the effects have been especially pernicious for the subsistence sector.[5]

In places, profitable export-oriented ranching and livestock production for the limited but growing domestic urban markets intensified the displacement of cropping to lands ill-suited for tillage (and hence especially vulnerable to erosion). Meanwhile, in more than a few regions the rising man/land ratio pushed farming further into semiarid and arid zones, where complementary water resources are either scarce or expensive to develop and, in some instances, where water resource development must be geared to multiple uses if serious problems, of the sort exemplified in the drought quadrangle of the Brazilian Northeast, are to be avoided. In no small degree the problem of persisting low agricultural productivity is bound up with institutional factors of an exceptionally complex nature, but from at least the 1950s on the realization has grown that resource limitations, both quantitative and qualitative, have also posed obstacles of considerable magnitude as population growth has proceeded apace in Latin America. For years, rightist groups had maintained that the key to regional agricultural progress lay in opening up new lands to settlement, a filling-up of the empty spaces that would emulate, in form and economic effect, the westward movement of the United States and Canada. Brazil, in fact, even enshrined this belief in public policy and launched its own *marcha para oeste* with construction of a new national capital. Leftists, for their part, generally ascribed the poverty of agriculture to a land tenure system that was unarguably inequitable and almost certainly counterproductive. Yet both were, at least partly, trading in illusions by exaggerating the resource value of Latin America's land resources (that is, the combined effects of soils and climates as conditioned further by location and topography). On the whole, Latin America is not particularly well endowed with agricultural land, notwithstanding the fertility of much of the River Plate region and scattered zones of favorable soil-and-climate combinations elsewhere.

Overcrowding in the Latin American rural sector, and the deleterious resource effects associated therewith, are by no means the end of the story. Concern also began to mount during the 1960s over the adverse environmental consequences of pell-mell urbanization and industrialization, a process that has produced a truly stunning degree of congestion and pollution in such urban centers as Mexico City, Monterrey, Bogotá, Rio de Janeiro, São Paulo, and Santiago.[6] For the larger metropolitan complexes, both household and industrial consumption of water rose rapidly, as it had in the United States and Canada, forcing municipal suppliers to draw water from sources more distantly located, and to begin to pay more attention to the quality of water resources located nearer at hand. Provisioning the ever more numerous urban households with staples placed additional pressure on archaic foodcropping systems.

Stimulated in part by the rise of environmentalism in the United States, critical observers began to remark that the negative by-products of rapid growth in Latin America appeared no less damaging to air and water resources in the central and southern parts of the hemisphere than they had in the northern portion. The difference, of course, was that the smaller economic surplus in the former region made the social opportunity costs of environmental protection higher than they were in the United States and Canada.

One other adverse effect of industrial development was in evidence by the end of the 1960s, even though its magnitude was not clearly understood until the following decade, and it was, in any event, concentrated in one country. This was the conversion of still another flow resource into a fund resource, at least for the time being, when the rapid escalation of the Peruvian fishing boom—trumpeted far and wide as a success story in market-induced export diversification—resulted in overfishing and a drastic decline in the size of the annual catch. At first the significance of what had happened was masked by a natural phenomenon: Namely, a sporadic diminution of the fishing catch occasioned, over the years, by shifts in ocean currents. As time went by, however, it became painfully clear that a failure to practice conservation measures had in fact brought about a substantial depletion of the once-rich offshore fisheries. While nothing on quite this scale was to occur over the next decade anywhere else in the Americas, there was evidence during the 1970s that some of the fishing banks in North America had dropped off considerably from their former abundance, while technological advances in exploiting offshore fisheries in Mexico unexpectedly undermined the shoreline fishing on which not a few poor communities regularly depended for their livelihood.

In view of the potential of fish products as a major protein source for low-income people in Latin America, where the net animal protein deficit is now estimated at some two million tons a year, a number of experiments—as yet inconclusive—were undertaken to develop new ways of processing fishmeal and other fish products for popular consumption. Moreover, with one eye cocked toward eventual imposition of conservation measures and the other on more immediate fiscal benefits, several of the Latin American republics began to press for a major extension of national jurisdiction into the sea. Even so, much remained to be done of a more immediately practical nature to make better use of Latin America's fishing resources—for example reduction of the large amount of spoilage incurred in fish processing, more effective use of the fish varieties caught but often discarded as a by-product of shrimping operations, improvement of inland distribution systems, popular dietary education, and so on. Peruvian experience, in other words, sounded an alert for other countries, serving as a caution not to neglect maritime resources, but only slowly has the lesson been digested and translated into effective public policies.

Two further developments, both in the 1970s, served to bring the resource question into sharper focus still. The first of these was the prolonged petroleum shock associated with the oil embargo of 1973 and OPEC's aggressive pricing policies, which hit Latin America with a double-barreled impact and even caused the United States to shake off some of its traditionally Promethean cultural assumptions. The recessionary impacts of OPEC policies on the major industrial nations of the world had a detrimental influence on all Latin American countries by depressing demand in their principal export markets; in only a few of the Latin American republics—Venezuela, Ecuador, and Mexico, mainly—were there offsetting advantages through the increased earnings on petroleum exports. In addition to this export-market effect, the majority of the countries in the Americas were hard hit by the steep rises in the prices of imported petroleum, especially in the instances in which industrial policy and consumption policy had held down the prices of petroleum and petroleum derivatives and in so doing had artificially boosted demands.[7] (An unfortunate side effect of these policies was to retard development of Latin America's fairly abundant hydroelectric potential and thereby to substitute reliance on nonrenewable energy sources for reliance on renewable energy sources.) Considerable strain was consequently put on the balance of payments positions of most of the Latin American countries. Financing the flow of imported oil—and gas, in some cases—was a factor in pushing external indebtedness to such high levels in countries such as Brazil. In Latin America as in the United States the sharp and repetitive increases in the price of petroleum products were also a factor, albeit probably a minor one, in inflation. In addition to provoking, at least in some countries, a turn to more realistic pricing policies, the oil problem helped set the stage for more explicit attention to other resource aspects of development.

The second circumstance that, during the 1970s enhanced consciousness of the resource base of development was the whole "Limits of Growth" controversy. To a degree that, earlier on, many external—and some internal—observers would not have thought likely, Latin American industrialization took firm root and moved strongly ahead, racking up historically high rates of growth in the late 1960s and the 1970s, just as it had in an earlier phase during the 1940s and 1950s. The total 1979 gross regional product of Latin America of $421 billion (in 1978 dollars) was, for example, almost three times the equivalent figure for 1960. In the process, however, substantial industrial growth and population increase together produced quite a rapid rise in the volume of resources being used, particularly to support a rising standard of living among the ever more numerous urban middle- and upper-income households. Moreover, since for a whole variety of reasons, development policy throughout Latin America tended to bias the factor mix in production methods in the direction of greater capital intensity, the industrialization that took place tended to be relatively energy intensive as well.

Much has been heard of late about the voracious appetite of the United States for natural resources and the disproportionate share of the world's resources that is used by the consumerist society of this country. On two counts serious questions have been raised: (1) the sustainability of the present and expected future rates of resource consumption in the United States and (2) the generalizability of the U.S. pattern of resource consumption (that is, the degree to which other countries can step up their rate of resource use in emulation of the U.S. structure of production and consumption). Great as has been the absolute rise in resource use by the U.S. economy over the postwar period, in many instances the *rate* of increase in resource consumption in Latin America has been much higher. There, too, a certain profligacy has crept into resource allocation patterns. In consequence, the assult upon the hemisphere's resources triggered by economic growth throughout the Americas, owing to the success of Latin America's industrialization efforts, and continued—if slower—expansion in the huge U.S. economy, has finally begun to promote a reexamination of many dimensions of hemispheric development. To the millions of trees felled for reasons mentioned earlier, for example, one must add the further sizable incursions into woodlands occasioned by accelerated logging and pulping operations. To the existing pressure on land for the production of staples of grains and legumes, one must now add the diversion of additional cropland to pasturage to provide the meat and dairy products desired by more affluent consumers in the home market as well as by consumers overseas, or to specialty crops such as flowers and strawberries, which are also in increasing demand at home and abroad.[8] To the rising demand for fuel oil to run thermal-electric generating facilities, one must add the demand for gasoline and lubricants to service a veritable population explosion in motor vehicles. So strong has been the growth in this industry, for instance, that Brazil has already emerged as the ninth-largest vehicle producer in the world.

Finally, to add to the growing picture of resource uncertainty, the end-of-decade disintegration of an uneasy equilibrium in the Middle East and festering social and political conflicts in sub-Sahara Africa have made extrahemispheric supply sources of several natural resources (including energy resources) increasingly unreliable for the foreseeable future.

THE COMPLEXITY OF THE RESOURCE PROBLÉMATIQUE

This is not the place to add yet another doomsday prediction to the many we have already heard in recent years. Neither does one want to suggest that we must rush to fabricate and install some fancy new system of crisis management. Yet, it does seem reasonably certain that critical conditions lie ahead in the field of natural resource development in the Americas, and it is no less clear that the devising of effective measures to ameliorate these conditions will be fraught with difficulty—as, for example, the sluggish pace of agrarian modernization has illustrated. The reason, as the preceding section of this paper has endeavored to make plain, is that the contemporary patterns of resource use that set the course of future developments, *ceteris paribus*, and hence the problems now abuilding, are deeply embedded in the whole matrix of institutional relations and policies. Further, as was suggested above, the problems now appearing over the horizon (or already visible in some instances) are partly the result of past policy successes, not just an outgrowth of failures.

To be sure, the situation is not equally troublesome in all countries. It is not even the same among all the smaller and poorer countries, or among the set of more developed countries, although, in general, these latter turn out to enjoy certain advantages owing to their more ample resource endowments.

Among the latter, for example, Mexico and Venezuela are both relatively well endowed with petroleum resources, have some remaining undeveloped potential in hydroelectric power resources, and possess an assortment of other resources to support their national development. While agricultural resources are the most vexing matter in Mexico, in Venezuela the greater resource challenge for the next two decades will probably be that of finding ways to turn its heavy oil deposits to account. Brazil, which appears to be blessed with the widest variety of resources (among Latin American countries) to support its future industrial plant, will have to act far more concertedly than it has in the past to safeguard its remaining forest resources and to develop innovative forest management techniques to make the most effective use of the tropical moist forest. However, its Achilles heel, as is well known, lies in the limited petroleum resources discovered to date. There the central task of resource policy for the next two decades will, accordingly, be that of pioneering the use of alcohol as fuel for motor vehicles, switching to peanut oil instead of diesel, electrification of its rail lines, and various other energy operations to tap even more fully its substantial hydroelectric potential and to press ahead on development of the technology of oil shale extraction. For Colombia, the distinctive centerpiece of its resource policy over the next decade or so will probably be stepping up exploratory drilling for petroleum and capitalizing on its emerging strength in coal production. Assuming that Argentina is able to up its output of petroleum (an increase that should not be difficult to bring about) and to cash in on its hydroelectric power potential, its generally balanced resource picture is such that the main problems facing the country are more likely to inhere in the institutional order than in the natural order—as has been the case for several decades. To some extent the same may be said of Chile, although there the energy picture seems rather less ensured so far as the hydrocarbons are concerned.

A country-by-country audit of the smaller and, in most cases, poorer economies would be too tedious to include at this point. Suffice it to call to mind the fact that they are all, for a number of structural reasons, much more tied in with international trade and more constricted in their range of development options than are the larger economies, and to take note of their diversity in other respects. Among the least fortunate cases would seem to be Haiti and various ministates of the Caribbean, in most of which the resource base is exiguous and therefore extremely confining. On the other hand, Paraguay, which has slumbered in economic obscurity for most of its national existence, is soon to become a major energy exporter (of hydroelectric power) and should be able thereby to finance a considerable expansion of economic activity on an otherwise rather restricted resource base. Ecuador, too, would seem to enjoy comparatively favorable resource prospects as a stepped-up rate of exploratory drilling enlarges proven reserves, as projected large new hydroelectric power installations are constructed and put into operation, and as the fishing and wood products industries continue the notable growth they have experienced in recent years.

In short, it is impossible, on account of the diversity of resource positions and the multiplicity of interests in Latin America, to define a single set of priorities for the region as a whole, let alone for the still more varied country situations of the entire Western Hemisphere. Nevertheless, there may be some common interests on the basis of which a dialogue in search of new policies may be launched.

THE INSTITUTIONAL FRAMEWORK FOR IMPROVED RESOURCE POLICIES

Taking into account the intercountry variations just mentioned, the question of how adequate will be the available supplies of natural resources for the hemisphere's economic growth from now until the end of the century leads over two distinct types of institutional territory. On the one hand, there is the market, the chief allocative mechanism even in this age of intervention. On the other hand, there are the congeries of organizations, both national and international, that *tout ensemble* function as agencies for the conscious social management of economic processes.

As for the market, it does not seem amiss to conclude that it has gained some ground over the past decade or so as a source of signals for resource allocation, even if, in some instances, the human costs of this policy shift have been appalling. Certainly, in the three Southern Cone countries a number of domestic interventionary structures have been dismantled and the national economies have been opened up to somewhat broader and less-filtered interaction with the outside world. At this time, it seems quite likely that Peru and, possibly, Bolivia will also veer in this direction, reducing further the number of economies engaged in a managed interaction with others in the hemisphere. Mexico, too, seems slated to interact more and more with other parts of the industrialized world over the years ahead, thanks to its huge petroleum and natural gas resources and to the emerging export capability of its industrial structure, in which case it will tend to gravitate away from the Latin American economic constellations with which it has been linked in the past.[9]

Moreover, most of the regional integration schemes that once looked toward consolidating trading blocs around particular development strategies are now on the wane. The Central American Common Market, first weakened by the Honduran–Salvadoran conflict, has been further shattered by the radical shift of economic policy in Nicaragua and the contemporary paralysis of development programming in El Salvador and, in lesser measure, Guatemala. The Caribbean Free Trade Association has fared no better. Chile and Bolivia have parted company with the Andean Group, and, although the Pact still contains Gran Colombia and Peru, it does not seem any longer headed toward the closely planned integration that once characterized the scheme. Meanwhile, what remains of the old Latin American Free Trade Association are mainly some useful industrial complementation agreements but little else. The Institute for Latin American Integration recently reported, in fact, that of the more than 11,000 concessions negotiated on a product-by-product basis among the member nations under the LAFTA system, only 30% are currently in use, while only 5% of the 7,000 special concessions made in favor of the less developed countries are in use. For all practical purposes, efforts to draw up a common list of free trade products ceased in 1964.

Whether the newer Latin American Economic Systems will ever amount to much remains to be seen. The inspiration behind it might be credited with the agreement signed last August, whereby Mexico and Venezuela undertook to supply nine energy-short countries (the six Central American republics and three Caribbean nations) with petroleum on concessionary terms. Most probably, however, special purpose agreements of this sort will hold more promise for the future of multinational collaboration in Latin America than the failed broad integration schemes of the past.

Underlying all the foregoing tendencies has been a gradual reintegration, during the past dozen years, of most of the Latin American economies into the world economy, an "opening up to the exterior," as it has been called. With these more outward-directed development strategies has come an increased emphasis on promotion of nontraditional exports and a more moderate and nuanced approach to import-substituting industrialization.[10] While this reorientation of policy does not represent an about-face and, in fact, is a logical evolution from the previous policy style, it does imply that market signals will henceforth necessarily play a comparatively larger role in allocating the region's resources than they did from, say, the 1930s through the mid-1960s.[11]

Doubtless, there is much in this partial turn toward the market that will help alleviate some aspects of the resource development problems discussed previously. The reduction of various price subsidies will, for instance, aid in curtailing overconsumption and encourage shifts to substitute resources that are relatively more abundant. By the same token, the general rise in primary commodity prices, including energy, will surely impel both industrial and household users to be more sparing, or efficient, in their use of these resources and firms to become more aggressive in their search for additional supplies thereof—as well as more innovative, where this be applicable, in developing improved secondary recovery techniques. If, as seems likely, energy intensity and capital intensity go together, there may even be certain employment-enhancing benefits over the longer run in the form of a gradual shift to more labor-intensive methods of production, particularly if countries come to recognize the unintended adverse effects on employment of several of the favored development-promotion techniques of the past. All this is, of course, standard fare in a neoclassical reading of the situation.

There is reason to doubt, however, that markets will fully reflect all future interests in present allocation decisions involving both nonrenewable and renewable resources. Efficient intertemporal resource allocation is, in other words, by no means automatic, even when markets are more comprehensive and function with somewhat fewer imperfections than they have had hitherto. For a variety of reasons, the market institution can be remarkably inattentive to high-priority social needs.

In the first place, the historical record makes it clear that in the unregulated exploitation of renewable and nonrenewable resources alike there has often been a considerable divergence between private money costs and returns on the one hand and social real costs and returns on the other (thanks both to the operation of externalities and to the existence of unemployment and underemployment). Given the additional complications that the knowledge or information dimension of resource markets in Latin America shares the general characteristic of underdevelopment and that product and factor markets are not uncommonly fragmented, there is little reason to expect short-run money costs and prices to express long-run social opportunity costs with any degree of accuracy. What is more, the degree to which all claims, future as well as present, on natural resources are adequately mediated through existing markets depends in part on the acceptability of the prevailing distribution of income, and nothing could be clearer than the fact that it is precisely the existing distribution of wealth, income, and access to the social opportunity structure that constitutes the major focus of political contention and even overt conflict throughout most of the hemisphere. So obvious is this point that it could only be overlooked by economic policy makers who are so enamored of free-market doctrines that they have come to mistake revealed preferences for revealed truth.

For that matter, the distributional battle is joined at both national and international levels. Thus, if national price structures are institutionally suspect because of a fundamental lack of consensus on the division of the national income, so, too, is the international price structure, biased as it necessarily is by the superior purchasing power and preferences of the economies of the industrial center. Within countries, in other words, substantial segments of the population are, *de facto*, disenfranchised wholly or in part when it comes to registering market preferences concerning resource use, and within the operation of the global economy the structure of relative prices and the consequent patterns of resource allocation likewise reflect a broad disenfranchisement and a relative ignoring of the needs of vast populations and regions. In economies like those of Latin America, wherein the external sector figures large, market-induced conservation and resource development measures will almost unavoidably be skewed in the direction of the needs of the major foreign trading partners and of that segment of the local population whose consumption patterns approximate those of the advanced industrial countries. The much-discussed "basic needs" strategy of development, for instance, would almost certainly imply a substantially different configuration of resource use and research-and-development priorities from those that guide the course of economic activity in the hemisphere at present.

It is, finally, difficult to escape the conclusion that at least in the area of resource policy a very strong case can still be made for modifying the operation of the price system through conscious and discriminating measures of social guidance, particularly those aimed at fostering resource conservation and promoting a much larger local and regional investment in resource prospecting, in improved methods of resource extraction and utilization, and in the development of new mineral, marine, forest, and agricultural resources, including, of course, unconventional energy resources. The range of projects is considerable: from the large watershed management program now underway in Panama to Brazil's promotion of alcohol-burning motor vehicles and the Brazilian–Paraguayan Itaipu project, from the promotion of solar heating devices on the fuel-scarce *altiplano* of Peru and Bolivia to the manufacture of fishmeal *pasta* products and to massive programs of rural education and agricultural extension (of the sort long talked about but seldom implemented).

The precise policy instrumentation most suitable for carrying out these aspects of development planning remains to be determined, but already certain probable if general outlines are visible: national indicative planning along something resembling the French model, a substantial strengthening of research organizations in the scientific/technical fields, the formation of networks to promote cross-national linkages among such institutions, and a continued and possibly increased reliance on more effectively managed public enterprises, mixed enterprises (of public and private capital), joint ventures (involving capital of different national origins and comanagement), and even multinational Latin American undertakings such as OLADE, the CDB, the CAF, and the BID. To speak of activities that all imply a continuing active role for the public sector, *un estado rectora* at the national level and multilateral public institutions at the international level, may seem oddly out of place under the present circumstances when, for the moment, privatization processes seem to be in the ascendant. Yet, more than ever before, the informational, technical, organizational, and human resources necessary for improved macroeconomic management and indigenous technological and scientific production are available, thanks to the institution-building and other development accomplishments of the past three decades, including the learning-by-doing that has grown out of the many planning episodes that have occurred during this period.

Since it is highly unlikely that the Latin American private sectors will be able to absorb all these new cultural resources fully, the safest bet is that a kind of Say's Law of bureaucracy will come into play, as it has so often in Latin American history: supply (in terms of organizational and personnel capabilities) will generate its own demand.

Fortunately, however, the prospect now is that this process will play a rather more constructive social role than it has in times past, when the public payroll grew mainly to build constituencies and coopt those whose discontent would be politically destabilizing.

Unlike the previous era of export-led growth, in which the development of natural resources was captained by foreign enterprises and ran far ahead of the development of indigenous cultural resources, this time around the advances realized during recent decades in the region's accumulation of cultural resources, a phenomenon not yet fully appreciated outside the region, will almost certainly be harnessed to steer natural resource development along lines of greater eventual benefit to society. As we in the United States veer, at least for the time being, in a more market-oriented, private-sector direction, we should not make the mistake of interpreting temporary institutional aberrations in Latin America—which contain, however, a measure of healthy policy correction—as a permanent change of course in that region. To do so would simply ensure that the failures of communication that have so plagued hemispheric relations in the past will be transferred intact to the future.

NOTES

1. We may plausibly date the present era from the mid-1940s for a variety of reasons. In the United States the Employment Act of 1946 explicitly committed the government to more active economic management than it had hitherto accepted as a normal function, while in Europe and Latin America economic planning and interventionist policies were gaining far more widespread acceptance, especially in the latter region, after the establishment of the UN Economic Commission for Latin America. The Marshall Plan, product that it was of special circumstances, gave additional impetus to the concept of a development process (or, more accurately, a redevelopment process) led by public authority rather than unfettered market forces. Together with the Point Four program and the I.B.R.D., the Marshall Plan introduced international development collaboration as a new dimension of global interaction, although some of this had been prefigured by wartime technical assistance missions from the United States to Latin America and the development-related loans of the Export-Import Bank. All of this was, of course, predicated on a wartime experience that had precipitated an increased recognition of the importance of short-term supply elasticities while, by drawing down minerals reserves in the United States, it raised the general consciousness that longer-term supply availabilities would be in question.

2. J. Frederic Dewhurst et al., *America's Needs and Resources*, New York: The Twentieth Century Fund, 1947, p. 598. This remarkable study was followed, a few years later, by a second major resource audit, this time in the guise of the official Paley Commission report of 1952 (The President's Materials Policy Commission).

3. J. Frederic Dewhurst et al., *America's Needs and Resources, a New Survey*, New York: The Twentieth Century Fund, 1955, p. 877.

4. The Brazilian Trans-Amazon Highway, the Peruvian Trans-Andean settlement schemes, and Bolivian occupation of the eastern marches of that country are among the best-known examples of the penetration of the forests by colonization both planned and spontaneous. The process is, however, actually much more widespread and has been going on for years, albeit on a smaller scale than in the last three decades. Among the areas so affected are the Mexican coastal plains and Chiapas highlands, the Guatemalan region between the highlands and the Petén, the Guanacaste region of Costa Rica, the Caribbean coast of Colombia, the Pacific coast of Ecuador, and so on. In El Salvador, population expansion even outran the capacity of the national territory to provide peasants with small plots, leading to Salvadoran encroachment on unused Honduran lands and, eventually, the so-called Soccer War of the late 1960s, the first overt demographic war in Latin America.

5. The subsistence sector has often been pushed onto marginal lands where substantial capital investments in the form of leveling, terracing, contouring, irrigation, and drainage expenses would be needed, together with outlays for highways and storage facilities, to confer much resource value on the land. At the same time, however, altitudinally controlled variations in climate do provide in a number of resource-short areas possibilities for tree cropping, assorted horticultural products, spice growing, raising ornamental plants, and other forms of diversification that could be commercially remunerative over the long haul were improvements of these types installed.

6. As an awesome indication of the historically unprecedented pace of urbanization, it might be observed that never before the growth of Mexico City in the 1970s had there been a net addition of six million people to the population of one metropolitan area during a single decade.

7. A number of countries held petroleum products prices relatively low as an economic subsidy to industrial development and a political subsidy to the urban electorate, with the additional argument, in some cases, that such a policy would reduce consumption of fuelwood and, hence, deforestation.

8. The growing import requirements of Latin America as it moves to higher per capita income levels have set up a cruel choice in respect of land use patterns. The millions of malnourished and undernourished poor are being crowded out of the market for foodstuffs by competing demands from upper- and middle-income families in the same countries and by foreign consumers of speciality exports whose preferences must be attended to maintain the flow of export earnings needed to procure industrially related imports. Evidence of this systematic contradiction, for example, is discernible in the current Mexican situation.

9. This recasting of Mexico's external economic policy would have been formally consolidated had the López Portillo administration decided to join the General Agreement on Trade and Tariffs, a step that once seemed likely and would have represented a movement toward a more market-constrained development strategy. Even so, the decision to stay out of the GATT does not imply a significantly closer interaction with other Latin American economies. Structural factors will almost certainly intensify its connections with the advanced industrial nations, even though there also is scant interest in Mexico in association with some type of North American common market. Indeed, the very concept arouses considerably antipathy.

10. While intervention may abate somewhat, it will hardly decline substantially. Parastatal enterprises will surely continue their singularly prominent

role, and public policy sanctions will continue to be utilized to hasten the reintegration process. For example, multinational enterprises will probably find that they will be under increasing government pressure, as a condition of doing business in Latin American markets, to organize an expansion of Latin American exports, and public institutions much as the Latin American Export Bank and the Banco do Brasil will also play a prominent role in this new phase of development.

11. Ironically, now that Latin America is moving in the direction of a relative liberalization of its foreign economic policy, the United States may well be entering a neoprotectionist phase that will pose a special threat to Latin America as the most advanced Third World region. This, together with the role of certain Latin American borrowing countries in the impending shake-out in the world financial system, seems to guarantee a continuation of policy conflicts within the hemisphere.

18

Latin American Environment and Development

Kirk Rodgers

Latin America in the last two decades of the twentieth century will be a region facing the realities of rapid growth. Among the consequences of the growth that is likely to command increased attention is its effect on the environment of the region. The push for development to supply the needs of rapidly expanding populations while attempting to raise millions above the level of poverty will continue to be the central concern of most governments, but more and more the so-called environmental consequences of development will require examination and action by countries individually and collectively. Few other issues have the potential to promote more cooperation between governments than the issue of sustained development of shared natural resources and the need to manage the region's environment to the benefit of future generations. Development efforts that are shortsighted, overly sectoral, or poorly planned can pre-empt later development, and these are matters of common concern. In the next decade countries are likely to draw closer together in their attempts to find a more balanced approach to environment and development. The role for regional governance will continue to expand to support these efforts.

LATIN AMERICA'S MAJOR ENVIRONMENTAL PROBLEMS

The environmental problems of Latin America are becoming well documented. They cover an enormous range of issues from deforestation and soil erosion to surface and groundwater pollution to salinization of irrigated land to overfishing, overgrazing, and desertification to air pollution and improper disposal of hazardous wastes.

For the purpose of this chapter, four broad problem areas that incorporate some of the most serious issues of environment and development with which governments will have to deal in the next five to ten years have been selected. The effects of these problems and government responses to them will be discussed in terms of both large and small countries. Particular attention will be focused on environmental problems with consequences that transcend international boundaries and which therefore may require additional response of international governance.

DEFORESTATION

Consensus is growing that deforestation is taking place on such a massive scale that by 1990 it will constitute one of the major problems for Latin America. Indeed, many government officials and scientists believe that it already is "the most important environmental concern in the region."

Natural forests represent more than just a stand of trees. Forest ecosystems provide "free" goods and services, such as soil stabilization, flood control, habitat for valuable animal species, ecosystem and climatic regulation, which are necessary if true development is to be maintained. Deforestation, and therefore the disruption of these goods and services, occurs in clearing land for agriculture and pasture as well as for lumber and firewood. It takes place both on a large-scale basis for agricultural projects and cattle ranching and on a small-scale basis as "slash-and-burn" subsistence agriculture whenever access is provided to new areas.

Particular attention has been focussed on the Amazon Basin, since it contains the world's largest remaining forest reserve of any size. The margins of the tropical rain forest have been pushed back significantly in the past decade, and the Brazilian Congress of Botanists has warned that the Amazon forest will be devastated unless immediate actions are taken. Their 1975 report calculated that

200,000 square kilometers were being cut over every year and that eventually the climate of the whole region would be altered, potentially cutting the annual rainfall in half.*

Controversy has surrounded this issue as well as the claim that the Amazon forest constitutes the "lungs of the world." There is general agreement, however, that much of the soil of tropical forests is of very poor quality for growing anything other than tropical forests. These soils are easily degraded upon removal of vegetation, and the return of deforested areas to present nutrient balances could take thousands of years. Because of this and other problems, Brazil has begun to take active measures to control deforestation by large commercial agricultural and forest interests. Other countries may be successful in doing the same. The difficult problem, however, is control of spontaneous colonization by poor farmers and land spectators.

Perhaps the classic case of the effects of deforestation, an example that also illustrates the dilemma of a small country with high population and limited agricultural land base, is seen in Haiti. As a colony, Haiti once exported more food, wood, spices, and minerals to France than the 13 original colonies in North America did to Great Britain. In the 1980s this small country had a relatively large population, which has continued to grow, but the nation's history has been turbulent and its economic and social development has been limited. Today its population of over five million has reduced much of its forests to bare, nonproductive land. Rural Haitians cook with charcoal obtained by a practice of burning and then cutting the hillside forests. The then denuded slopes are subject to soil erosion and leaching, which results in degraded soil conditions unfit to support vegetative growth. Without forest cover to control runoff, the frequent rains produce flash floods, which carry even more soil to the sea. Recent efforts to reforest and reclaim the hillsides have been made, but the deforestation process goes on. Many are beginning to feel that Haiti has passed the environmental point of no

---

* Deforestation in the tropics would allow the escape of water from the normally tight regional and local hydrologic cycle through the increased runoff of rainfall. According to A. H. Gentry in a recent article in *Science* magazine, the long-predicted changes in climate and river flow in the Amazon may already be beginning. The height of the annual flood crest of the Amazon at Iquitos has increased markedly in the past decade. The accelerating rate of deforestation, especially in the Upper Amazon in Bolivia, Peru, Ecuador, and Colombia, where populations have doubled in 10 years, is expected eventually to reduce the transpired water available for rainfall and may eventually convert parts of the Amazon to near-desert.

return—a grim prospect for the country's five million people, the poorest in the hemisphere.

Deforestation is the conspicuous "environmental" problem, but the root cause lies in the fact that the population of this small country outgrew the carrying capacity of the land. This basic set of environmental and socioeconomic problems faces many of the island nations of the region as well as other small but densely populated countries such as El Salvador. By the end of the decade, all of these small countries will be forced to confront these realities. The problems of population growth and poverty, leading to serious and perhaps irreversible declines in the productivity of renewable natural resource systems, are among the most serious issues to be facing Latin America in the next 20 years.

An important result of severe degradation of the land base in countries with high population density, as seen in this example, is migration across national borders. The flight of Haitian "boat people" to Florida and illegal immigration of Salvadoraneons to the western United States have been triggered in part by this phenomenon. It can be expected to increase significantly in the next ten years and to constitute an exacting challenge for governance in the western hemisphere. In extreme circumstances, movements of people across borders may even strain the peace-keeping machinery in the Latin American Region.

Water Resources

A further set of major problems that Latin American governments will face in the next five to ten years pertains to the region's water resources. These interconnected problems range from water supply shortages for industry, agriculture and domestic uses, to pollution of surface and groundwater, to floods.

The Global 2000 Report has the following to say:

> Regional water shortages will become more severe. In the 1970–2000 period population growth alone will cause requirements for water to double in nearly half the world. Still greater increases would be needed to improve standards of living. In many LDC's water supplies will become increasingly erratic by 2000 as a result of deforestation. Development of new water supplies will become more costly virtually everywhere.

In 1979, USAID estimated that 25% of the city dwellers in Latin America have no direct water supply, despite great expansion of city water systems over the past two decades. Goals set at the UN World Water Conference held in Mar del Plata, Argentina, in 1977 calling for safe drinking water for the entire world population by 1990 are not likely to be met. Part of the problem is that population is flocking to Latin American cities at such a rate that even the best-financed water supply systems are unable to keep up. The poor urban dweller living on the outskirts of Latin American cities, who has migrated there from depressed rural areas, soon contributes to his own water supply problem as his untreated sewage pollutes ground water supplies and nearby lakes, rivers, and streams. Serious health problems result.

His rural counterpart is no better off, since many rural areas are suffering serious water supply problems due in part to industrial pollution of rivers as well as industrial competition for water supply. Deforestation, of course, will continue to reduce the capacity of land to absorb, store, and regulate the flow of water in rivers. Because rivers and ground water acquifers do not respect national boundaries, many of these problems are of regional significance. In 1980 it can be expected that disputes between countries will have intensified over the issue of water use and water pollution. It took more than a decade of negotiations to conclude agreements between the United States and Mexico to treat the issue of high saline content in the Colorado River crossing into Mexico caused by irrigation in California. As irrigated agriculture expands, and industrialization continues, many future conflicts may be expected in international river basins. After nearly two decades of negotiation, punctuated by near-confrontations between some of the major countries, Brazil and Argentina, Bolivia, Paraguay, and Uruguay are now beginning to cooperate in development of the Plata River Basin. The key issues are the allotment of irrigation water between countries, the development of the vast hydroelectric potential, the displacement of populations as reservoirs fill, the determination of boundaries given ever-changing water courses on flat terrain, and problems of sedimentation and changes in water flow caused by upstream activities. To date, problems of contamination crossing national boundaries have not been significant because of the high dilution potential of the rivers and the sparse population and lack of development over much of the basin. These, however, will shortly change as development efforts increase.

Water resource problems will affect all countries in the next five to ten years but will be particularly grave in the small countries with limited resources. The islands of the Caribbean face a special problem. Their small land areas and limited water resources demand special care in development, since through poor control of land development, deforestation, and pollution they can shortly arrive to a very precarious situation of water supply inadequate to meet needs. Equally important from a regional standpoint is that the Caribbean Sea is being adversely affected by pollutants and siltation contributed by both its island and coastal states. This issue has already catalyzed the undertaking of the Joint UNEP/CEPAL study, which resulted in an Environmental Action Plan for the Wider Caribbean Area. Coordination of the Plan, funding of its many activities, and the cooperation of numerous national and international institutions will challenge the existing system of regional response.

Urbanization

The rapid pace of urbanization in Latin America is bringing with it problems of such magnitude that the subject of "Human Settlements and the Environment" was singled out as one of the seven areas of priority concern for the Americas in the 1980's.* The report says: "It is beyond question that while Latin America has experienced significant economic growth in recent decades, its human habitat has deteriorated considerably. . . ." Human settlements, and the large metropolitan areas in particular, have suffered a severe loss in environmental quality." The social and political consequences of these difficulties are a matter of escalating concern in the Americas, particularly given the dramatic predictions of growth for the major cities in the Region over the next ten years.

One has only to visit the cities of Mexico, Sao Paulo, Caracas, Buenos Aires, Lima, Guayaquil, and others to see the problem in all its dimensions: serious air pollution from auto and factory emissions, which obscures the view of the cities' skylines or surroundings and endangers health, the change of urban rivers to urban sewers, the contamination of adjacent estuaries, bays, and even the sea, inferior housing, refuse and congestion. All of these problems are consequences of urban growth. The costs of correcting these mistakes are now evident throughout the region. Cleaning up the pollution of

---

* Hemispheric Cooperation and Integral Development Report of the Group of Experts to the General Secretariat of the OAS, July 1980.

Guanabara Bay, the natural harbor of Rio de Janeiro, is costing $300 million, just to start. SANEGRAN, the plan for cleaning up São Paulo that deals mainly with sewerage treatment in the Tiete River, is projected to cost $4.5 billion before the year 2000.* Although few countries can bear such costs without adversely affecting their overall development, not to do so also restricts development as well as the quality of life of very large populations.

Air pollution in major Latin American cities is another result of industrial growth and the increased use of automobiles. It came as a surprise to very few when in 1979 an international group of air quality experts found that air pollution in the Valley of Mexico City is potentially one of the most serious in the world. Efforts to control air pollution in Mexico are complex and expensive. A positive result of experience, however, is that the lessons being learned are promoting better spatial planning of development throughout the country. Improved development planning that considers the environment from the outset is receiving increased attention.

Air pollution, like water pollution, shows no respect for political boundaries. Air contaminated by industrial effluents that crosses frontiers is likely to command attention in the near future along the borders of Colombia and Venezuela, Mexico and the United States, and elsewhere.

Unplanned and uncontrolled urban expansion is also having multiple environmental consequences, even in relatively small cities like Port of Spain, the capital of Trinidad. Careless eastward expansion of the city appears to be overwhelming the whole central part of the island, bringing about loss of productive agricultural land, deforestation, and serious erosion of the southern flank of the Northern Slopes Range of the island. The sediment from this erosion is carried by streams that flow through the city. Dredges are permanently located on certain streams to keep them open so that they will not flood surrounding urban areas. The costs of dredging and engineering works to control erosion, plus reforesting and rehabilitating the Northern Slopes Range, will be a heavy price even for an oil-wealthy nation like Trinidad. Few other small countries can easily absorb the negative economic effects of such unwise urban development.

Urban development associated with the tourist industry is creating problems in many other Caribbean countries, in some cases

---

* World Environment Center report on "Environment—Latin America," to be published in 1981.

affecting the very resources that attracted the tourists to begin with. Dredging of mangrove areas to build tourist facilities has destroyed wetlands that nourish fish populations and simultaneously brought about siltation of the coral reefs the tourists came to see. Conflicts in coastal zone use between urban development, industry, tourism, and agriculture are seen as one of the major problems of the Caribbean islands in the near future. Better spatial planning of development is of critical concern.

Fisheries Resources

Fish protein forms a significant part of the protein intake of large populations in Latin America and in some countries constitutes a major element of the national economies. The combination of over-fishing and destruction of marine habitats is building toward a major problem in some parts of Latin America. In the countries making up the greater Caribbean Area, coastal mangroves, estuaries, and coral reef communities play a very large role in providing nutrients and breeding grounds for many species of fish, mollusks, and crustaceans. The destruction of these habitats through the construction of marinas, harbors, and coastal resorts, coupled with inland activities such as construction of dams, has substantial environmental implications. Offshore drilling, the transport of large amounts of oil, and the installation of refineries and petrochemical complexes in the Caribbean form another escallating risk for fisheries and other marine resources. There is good probability that one or more major crises will occur in this decade, although perhaps not of the magnitude of the oil-well blowout at IXTOC-1 in the Bay of Campeche in the Gulf of Mexico in 1979, which had a major impact on the coastal shrimp industries of the United States and Mexico.

Development of coastal and inland areas in Central America is also having major effects on the marine resources of both the Caribbean and the Pacific coastal areas. Construction of dams and other hydraulic works that alter both the flow and nutrient content of rivers is having an effect on populations of valuable marine species such as shrimp. There is great potential for the development of shrimp fisheries in the Gulf of Fonseca, if Nicaragua, Honduras, and El Salvador could control negative environmental effects and agree on controlled joint exploitation of the resource.

At the other end of the continent, Argentinian ecologists have warned of another danger—the overfishing of krill, a tiny crustacean that is an important part of the food chain in Antarctic waters. There is concern that continued overfishing could damage the entire southern ocean ecosystem, which supports a large fish, bird, whale, and seal population. The Argentine Antarctic Institute put it very well: "The goal is not to obtain the maximum possible yield of the species considered (krill), but of the entire ecological system in such a way that stability and future exploitations are not affected."

The sea is often referred to as "the global commons." Cooperation in the management and conservation of marine resources is one of the most obvious items on an agenda of international and regional governance.

HOW WILL NATIONS DEAL WITH THESE NEEDS AND DEMANDS?

The selected problems of environment and development cited previously, in combination with many others that have not been discussed in this chapter, have already impelled most governments in the western hemisphere to initiate corrective action. An agenda for national governmental action was first outlined at the UN Conference on the Human environment in Stockholm in 1972. It has received much attention in subsequent international and regional meetings and has been the subject of a very large number of publications and documents. One of the most recent and most comprehensive outlines for action is contained in the World Conservation strategy, an undertaking of the International Union for the Conservation of Nature, the United Nations Environment Program, and the World Wildlife Fund, published in 1980.

The World Conservation Strategy lists the "Priority National Actions" as follows:

1. preparation and implementation of national and/or subnational conservation strategies;

2. adoption of anticipatory environmental policies;

3. adoption of cross-sectoral conservation policy;

4. inclusion of nonmonetary indicators of conservation performance in national accounting systems;

5. preparation of ecosystem evaluations;

6. advance assessment of the likely environmental effects of all major (development) actions;

7. adoption of a procedure for allocating land and water uses based on ecosystem evaluation and environmental assessment;

8. review and strengthening of legislation concerning living resources to ensure that it provides sufficiently for conservation, paying particular attention to enforcement;

9. review and improvement of the status, organization, funding, and staffing of agencies with responsibilities for living resources;

10. establishment of a soil and water conservation body at the policy-making level;

11. establishment of new organizations, or of special measures to coordinate existing ones, for comprehensive management of marine living resources;

12. review and strengthening of training facilities at the professional, technical, and user levels;

13. increased research to improve the management of living resources;

14. greater public participation in decisions concerning living resources;

15. environmental education campaigns and programs;

16. rural development, combining short-term measures to ensure human survival with long-term measures to safeguard the resource base and improve the quality of life.

Looking across this ambitious list, one must acknowledge that while much has already been accomplished, or will be, in the next 5 to 10 years, the agenda will be inadequately treated in most Latin American countries by the end of the decade. While progress will be made on the establishment of environmental policies, institutions, and legislation, and many studies will be completed, difficulties will be encountered in fully staffing these institutions with qualified personnel, enforcement of laws and regulations, and adequate financing of governmental agencies charged with environmental responsibilities.

But even if successful, all of this will only partially satisfy the problems surrounding environment and development. A great deal needs to be done in revising the philosophies, organization, mandates, and operations of the development and planning institutions themselves. For example, one of the most challenging tasks will be the incorporation of the environmental dimension in the implementation process: from goal setting through survey and identification of development possibilities to implementation of prefeasibility studies of individual projects and programs and then to implementation of development itself. Governments will continue to face the predisposition of many people to treat environment as an externality to development rather than as a necessary dimension of development. The tendency to treat development as a series of sectoral considerations, that is, agriculture, forestry, water supply, fisheries, industry, urban development, and so on, constitutes one of the major obstacles to effective treatment of environmental issues that are essentially multisectoral and interrelated. Professional education is basically sectoral in its focus, and administrative institutions tend to be organized similarly. It is no wonder that the integrated approach required to manage the environment and develop it rationally is so difficult to implement.

There are sharp financial constraints on taking these actions as well. Some of the smaller or less advantaged countries will be faced with such serious economic difficulties by the end of the decade that government institutions will have little capacity to deal with mounting environmental problems. As the experience of many highly industrialized countries demonstrates, the cost of corrective action to repair environmental damage is many times greater than the initial cost of prevention. Beyond this, the damage is sometimes irreversible, and the resulting social costs have been found to be unacceptable. In a few cases countries will be quite helpless to take any effective action whatsoever without outside help.

Environmental problems, while national in origin, are frequently regional or even international in their impact. National boundaries make no difference to the movement of water, air, migratory species, fish, or the sea, and this applies to people as well, when they become hungry or desperate enough. The possibilities for conflicts between nations over these issues are growing daily. Some of these conflicts can and will be resolved bilateraly, but many lend themselves to multilateral treatment. Some examples to emerge from the preceding discussion include management of the resources of the wider Caribbean area, development of major international river basins such as the Plata, the Amazon, and the Orinoco, trans-frontier air and water pollution, the major migration of people across national borders in response to exhaustation of resources and degradation of environments and migrating species. The illegal traficking of valuable species of fauna and flora, the so called "dumping" of dangerous goods and industrial residuals, and even the broader questions of CO_2 build-up and ozone depletion in the atmosphere should also be added. In all of these the need for international and/or regional action is clear.

Other areas of cooperative action are also indicated. There is a large potential for useful interchange of the results of experience of the successful management of the environment, methodologies for studies, research results, and even legislation. For the Latin American region, with its cultural and linguistic similarities, this is particularly significant. Likewise, on the subject of training there is ample opportunity for cooperative action to establish networks of training centers and to take advantage of economies of scale for training in certain fields.

THE RELEVANCE AND IMPACT OF EXISTING INTERNATIONAL ORGANIZATIONS AND INSTITUTIONS: THEIR STRENGTHS AND WEAKNESSES

The Latin American Region is served by a large number of international, regional, and bilateral institutions providing assistance on developmental and environmental matters. An excellent review of the relative capacities of these institutions was made by the International Institute for Environment and Development (IIED) in 1978 in its study entitled "Banking on the Biosphere—A Study of the Environmental Procedures and Practices of Nine Development Financing Agencies," and in its recent (1981) study of several bilateral aid agencies "Aiding of the Environment." The agencies included in the first study that serves Latin America include: the World Bank (IBRD), the Inter American Development Bank (IDB), the Caribbean Development Bank (CDB), the Organization of American States (OAS), and the United Nations Development Program (UNDP). Those that were included in the second study were the Development Assistance Agencies of Canada, the Federal Republic of Germany, the Netherlands, Sweden, the United Kingdom, and the United States. The remarks that follow quote liberally from these studies but include updated information in some cases.

World Bank

The IBRD received high marks in the IIED study, which stated: "The Bank has the most advanced environmental policy and practices of any aid organization included in the study and undoubtedly exerts intellectual leadership on environmental matters in the whole international development community." Based on policies established by President Robert McNamara in the early 1970s, the IBRD routinely examines the environmental and health implications of every project that it funds, although the degree to which this procedure is successful is hampered by the large number of projects funded by the Bank and small "environmental" staff available to review each project fully. By forcing high environmental standards for development projects, the Bank encourages all countries seeking loans to incorporate environmental considerations into their development actions. The Bank has also financed some of the major environmental rehabilitation projects in the Americas, including the massive São Paulo environmental clean-up. It also offers limited technical advice and training on incorporation of environmental considerations into project formulation. If there can be any criticism leveled at the IBRD, it is one that must be applied to all development banking institutions, namely, that they take a traditional sectoral approach to development for the most part and provide very limited multisectoral lending. The latter could result in a more comprehensive set of integrated development actions in relation to environmental parameters.

Inter American Development Bank

While the IDB has recently established a policy and project guidelines for including environmental considerations in its lending decisions (based largely on IBRD experience), it has not shown the degree of commitment or sense of urgency on the matter demonstrated by other institutions. Environmental considerations are to be given attention by traditional project review staff in the Bank, but there is no central review office dealing with the environment, as is the case in IBRD. The IDB has a wider mandate than IBRD for providing technical assistance and training services to member states. It has not as yet made significant use of this capacity to assist governments on environmental matters. Overall, IDB has much more potential for support to countries in the region than it has utilized.

The Caribbean Development Bank

While the CDB is a relatively new institution, it has taken many positive steps to incorporate environmental considerations into its development lending and does not seem to have adopted the defensive posture of others. The countries of the Caribbean in general seem to have greater environmental awareness than some of their neighbors to the south, which may account for this. The fragility of the ecosystems of the small island countries served by the CDB will demand special caution in development lending and a better-integrated approach than bankers are usually noted for.

The Organization of American States

The OAS, despite its small size and presently too fragmented technical assistance program, is generally given good marks by the IIED study. As it says, "environmental quality objectives are now almost routinely included in technical assistance missions at the reconnaissance and prefeasibility planning level, and all regional planning courses and seminars given by the training centers connected with the Program of Regional Development include a unit on environmental protection." It goes on to say, however: "OAS dependence on national requests (for technical assistance) continues severely to limit its initiating role." The quality of the work of the OAS in natural resources survey, river basin development, and regional planning has begun to attract attention, and the fact that the Group of Experts Report to the OAS on "Hemisphere Cooperation and Integral Development" recommended that environment and natural resource development be major focal points for the Secretariat in the 1980s may result in a greater concentration of OAS talents in these fields in the future.

United Nations Development Program (UNDP)

The IIED report states: "Because of UNDP's decentralized nature and the autonomy enjoyed by the Specialized Agencies that execute the great bulk of UNDP projects in project preparation, responsibility for environmental planning is difficult to locate. The UNDP rarely acts alone or has undisputed control over a project." Nevertheless, by the magnitude of its financing and the broad character of its mandate, UNDP has significant potential to expand its services to Latin America on environmental matters and is beginning to do so. Country requests for assistance and the policies of the specialized agencies are the determining factors of its future role.

United Nations Environment Program (UNEP)

While charged with a broad mandate for international action and empowered to undertake a wide range of initiatives and actions of regional coordination, UNEP has been somewhat of a disappointment. Where the agency was once seen as a significant catalytic force for regional action in combination with other agencies, it is coming to be known as a weak and unstable partner, plagued by financial difficulties and poor management. ECLA, which was to perform important regional functions for UNEP, has in turn been constrained in its actions by the weakness of UNEP. There are bright spots, however. Despite great initial political and management difficulties, the Joint UNEP/ECLA Project for Environmental Management in the Wider Caribbean Area has produced an impressive blueprint for future action involving a wide array of international and regional agencies and bilateral programs. In this subregional project of great significance, UNEP has fulfilled its intended role as catalyst for action. The present economic plight of UNEP, however, does not bode well for the future, and stronger leadership is still needed in the Americas to coordinate and reinforce the actions of agencies that are supporting governments on matters pertaining to environment and development.

U.S. Agency for International Development

As the "Aiding the Environment" report says: "Concern about environment and natural resources problems arose within AID in the early 1970s and the National Environmental Policy Act made protection of the environment part of the mandate of AID." The agency has provided leadership on these matters and substantial financing on a country-by-country basis through individual development projects. The current "environmental profiles" being prepared for many Latin American countries are an important contribution to understanding of the region's problems. USAID is limited by the fact that it is providing (in accordance with Congressional mandates) assistance to less than half of the countries in the region. It is further restrained by the difficulties of supporting regional or subregional projects where non AID supported countries are involved. Its financing relating to the environment can probably be more effective if ways can be found to link it to the action of other multilateral agencies.

POSSIBLE NEW POLICIES, MECHANISMS, AND COOPERATIVE EFFORTS TO ASSIST GOVERNMENTS

Some of the problems outlined in the first part of this paper are already provoking important reactions of international agencies and the interamerican system. One of the broadest-based and most significant policy responses has been the recent signature by the world's major development finance institutions of the "Declaration of Environmental Policies and Procedures Relating to Economic Development." This document, signed on February 1, 1980, calls on these agencies to "institute procedures for systematic examination of all development activities, including policies, programmes and projects under consideration for financing, to ensure that appropriate measures are proposed for "ensuring the sustainability of economic development." It directs that the development finance institutions "enter into cooperative negotiations with governments and relevant international organizations and agencies to ensure integration of appropriate environmental measures in the design and implementation of economic development activities" and mandates that the agencies will "provide technical assistance, including training on environmental matters to developing countries at their request, thus developing their indigenous capacity, and facilitating technical cooperation between developing countries." The development lending institutions whose financing is measured in billions of dollars per year can exert considerable leverage over economic development decisions. Their determination to incorporate environmental considerations systematically into lending decisions is strongly reinforcing government policies to promote sustained economic development. The follow-up action to this agreement has been particularly vigorous by the agencies serving the Latin American region. IBRD, IDB, the Caribbean Development Bank, OAS, UNDP, and UNEP, who were among the original signatories, now meet periodically to coordinate their environmentally related actions and undertake joint efforts of benefit to Latin America. Particular attention is being given to exchange of information, studies, and research results to improve criteria for project evaluation, plus environmental guidelines and check-lists. Inter agency committees will be organized to evaluate environmental performance of selected development projects from prefeasibility through execution stages, with the objective of improving criteria and procedures of technical assistance as well as development lending.

Methodologies for preinvestment studies need great improvement so that environmental problems are not confronted for the first time when decisions on implementation of development projects are about to be made. Head-on conflicts between development and environmental goals can usually be avoided by early consideration of environmental factors when identifying development possibilities. Agencies such as the OAS have provided leadership in the design of methodologies for reconnaissance and prefeasibility studies that incorporate environmental considerations from the outset.* Regional agencies that have had a long continuity of experience in assisting Latin American countries in planning natural resources development are in an advantageous position to catalyze the interchange of experience from one country to another.

Much needs to be done also to promote exchange of development experience in Latin America. Post audits of completed development projects when exchanged between countries are of enormous value in avoiding the repetition of mistakes. Models of how common problems have been tackled successfully are greatly needed.

Additional regional mechanisms of cooperation and exchange of information are needed on the whole range of issues of environment and development treated in the "Declaration of Environmental Policies and Procedures." The spectrum of development assistance institutions, from banks through multilateral and bilateral technical assistance agencies to nongovernmental institutions, must all be involved, as they have much to learn from each other and they have a large responsibility for increasing the flow of information and experience between the countries of the region. It is important that

---

* See, for example, *Environmental Quality and River Basin Development: A Model for Integrated Analysis and Planning* Organization of American States, 1978.

many other agencies, especially the bilateral ones, sign the declaration and become involved in the efforts of regional coordination that are underway.

Throughout the first section of this paper attention was drawn to the importance of integrated planning of development and to some of the adverse environmental consequences of sectorially oriented development thinking. The spatial effects of development were also stressed, not only within countries but between countries as well.

A particularly valuable example of cooperation between a group of countries focusing on a set of environmental problems in a large physical region is the Wider Caribbean Action Plan. One of the reasons for the relatively positive response of governments and agencies to this effort is the fact that the wider Caribbean is a physically interrelated piece of space where cooperation between governments is obviously essential. Regional institutions like OAS, PAHO, and IICA are playing a key role in this effort, a role that must be expanded in this decade. Other geographic subregions in Latin America, such as the great Chaco region of Paraguay, Bolivia, Argentina, and Brazil, where desertification is a common problem, should likewise become the focus of attention of Latin American regional institutions.

The large river basins in the Americas, such as the Amazon, Plata, and Orinoco, offer a golden opportunity and large challenge to the mechanisms of regional governance. They constitute another situation in which integrated development planning and resource management is required if development is to occur without negative environmental effects and explosive political consequences. The OAS has played an important role in the Plata River Basin, assisting countries individually or collectively in execution of preinvestments studies and facilitating exchange of information between countries about natural resources, environmental conditions, and socioeconomic data needed for rational planning of development. To a certain degree the OAS has functioned as an institutional umbrella under which member governments were able to collaborate on specific development and avoid conflict. It is interesting to note the expansion of the organization's traditional peace-keeping function evident here. The OAS has a rather good track record of helping countries to resolve disputes in border areas. Here we see the organization in a role of helping to prevent such disputes while encouraging rational development. The need to expand this function is evident. New opportunities are likely to be provided in the Amazon and Orinoco river basins before the end of the decade. Additional opportunities will also be provided in border areas between two or more countries where coordinated development efforts are planned, as for example the borders of Haiti and The Dominican Republic, Panama/Colombia, Panama/Costa Rica, and so forth.

Disputes arising from transfrontier pollution of air and water are likely to intensify by the end of the decade. The law of the sea negotiations and the recent extension of country jurisdictions to a 200-mile economic zone along coasts have added a further area for conflict and controversy. Mechanisms for resolving these conflicts will have to be developed, and there is a large role here for the institutions of regional governance. Reliance on regional rather than international mechanisms for mediation of such conflicts has clear advantages in many cases.

The issues raised in environment and development will also require legal solutions. There must be a review of the coverage and effectiveness of international law relevant to shared natural resources, and development of new laws where deficiencies are identified. Simultaneously there must be increased efforts at implementation of existing laws such as the Convention on the Prevention of Marine Pollution by Dumping of Wastes and Other Matter, the Convention on the Regulation of Long-range Trans-boundary Air Pollution and of analagous regional conventions for Latin America.

Another critical area of concern for the 1980s is the whole subject of environmental training. While in the past decade many countries have established new facilities or strengthened existing ones, for training related to the environment, the supply is still quite inadequate to meet the demand. Of equal importance there is very limited interconnection between these institutions. A network of training facilities must be developed to strengthen and make more efficient the institutions working in this broad field. Specific help and coordinating is needed from agencies such as UNEP, OAS, and USAID. A cooperative effort of many multilateral, bilateral, and nongovernmental and governmental agencies is required to accomplish the task, for it is already evident that such an approach will be more cost-effective than the isolated effort of a large number of national institutions.

One could go on almost indefinitely to enumerate the possibilities for responses of international and regional governance to the issues raised by environment and development. This is true, because the issue itself is all-encompassing and because cooperation between nations is essentially unavoidable. There will either be cooperation or there will, in time, be conflict. There is no escaping the confines of our spaceship earth and its life-support systems. Nations will either cooperate or suffer the collective consequences of a degraded environment. Many actions must be taken on a global basis, but the opportunities for use of the mechanisms of regional governance are extensive. If the past decade is any indicator, the international institutions will continue to fall short of accomplishing the task. The institutions in the Interamerican system have a great opportunity—if they accept the challenge.

19

Population, Urbanization, and Migration in the Americas: An Overview of Recent Trends

Alejandro Portes

POPULATION GROWTH

In 1980, the population of Latin America and the Caribbean was estimated to be about 370 million and to have grown during the last decade at an average annual rate of 2.8%. While economic growth during the decade reached 6% per year, the fast population increase reduced the rise in *per capita* growth to 3.2%, below the original targets set by the Second United Nations Development Decade. By the end of the 1970s, there were indications that the rate of population growth was beginning to drop and that the decrease was relatively rapid, not only for the traditional low-growth countries of the Southern Cone, but also for others that had experienced vigorous demographic expansion in the past.[1]

The decline in population growth may be attributed, in part, to the fact that officially sponsored population planning programs are beginning to take hold. More important, however, are changes in the economic and social structure of these countries, including urbanization and the increasing incorporation of rural areas into the money

The paper was written while the author was a Fellow at the Center for Advanced Studies in the Behavioral Sciences. The cooperation of the Center's staff is gratefully acknowledged.

economy. For low-income groups, increasingly dependent on wage labor, it may become less rational to continue to bear large families. These trends can be expected to continue in the future and to lead to further declines in the rate of population growth, down to about 2% by the end of the century. According to present estimates, the population of Latin America and the Caribbean will reach about 600 million by then.

Because of rapid population growth in the past, the rate of increase in the labor force during the next two decades will be faster, averaging an estimated 3% annually. However, this figure conceals wide disparities among countries. According to a recent estimate by the Projections Centre of CEPAL (UN Economic Commission for Latin America), a group of countries including Argentina, Chile, Uruguay, and Cuba will experience average population growth rates of less than 1.5% with somewhat higher rates of labor force increase, though these will also decline by the end of the century. A second group, including Brazil and Colombia, will experience rapid declines in rates of population growth, but their labor force will continue to increase by about 3% until year 2000. A third group, comprising Mexico, Central America, and some South American countries, will maintain vigorous population growth, with annual rates of about 3% and still higher increases in the labor force; both rates can be expected to decline by the end of the century.[2]

In general, the trends toward rapid urbanization, incorporation into the money economy, and diffusion of birth control methods can be expected to lead to a significant decline in rates of population growth for the region as a whole. More urgent, however, is the problem of absorbing hundreds of thousands of new entrants into the labor market. The problem is acute since the rates of unemployment and underemployment in most countries are already very high, and since about 49% of the families in the region already live under conditions of extreme poverty.[3]

It is clear that the present model of economic development, pursued with individual variations by most Latin American and Caribbean countries, will not produce the necessary rapid increases in labor demand. The required policies demand a significant reorientation of national states toward the goals of development and a changed role for these countries in the international economy. The present model of economic development affects not only the labor growth problem but also related ones such as internal migration, urban growth, and international migration. For this reason, the nature of present policies and alternatives to deal with the current situation will be discussed in connection with these other problems in the next sections.

INTERNAL MIGRATION AND URBAN GROWTH

Patterns of recent urbanization in Latin America and the Caribbean are well known. Accelerated migration from the countryside has produced rates of urban growth exceeding in every country those of the total population. As a result, the continent has increasingly become one of urban dwellers. Between 1960 and 1970, the proportion of the Latin American and Caribbean population defined as "urban" increased from 32.5% to 40%; in turn, 76% of the urban population lived in cities of 100,000 or more. These aggregate figures obviously conceal wide disparities: The urban population in Uruguay and Argentina is close to 70% of the total, while in Guatemala it is 18% and in Haiti, 7%.[4]

By the year 2000, however, it is estimated that about 80% of the population of the region will be urban and that the figure will not be less than 50% for any country. About two-thirds of the total population will live in cities of over 20,000.[5]

Despite recent evidence on the rapid growth of intermediate cities, the process of urbanization has generally led to the concentration of the population in a few centers, accentuating the phenomena of urban primacy and regional imbalance. Disparities among countries in the proportion of the urban population are sharply reduced when one considers the proportion of the urban population living in large (100,000+) cities: In no country is this figure less than 50%, and in most it exceeds 70%. Representative cases include those of Paraguay, where 92% of the urban population is concentrated in one or two large cities, Haiti, where the figure is 78%, and, at the other extreme, Argentina and Uruguay, where the proportions are 82% and 75%, respectively.[6]

The phenomenon of urban primacy registered parallel increases in both large and small countries. In 1974, the population of metropolitan Buenos Aires was estimated at almost 9 million, or four times the combined population of the three next-largest Argentine cities. In the same year, Mexico City had close to 11 million inhabitants, three times the combined populations of Guadalajara, Monterrey, and Leon. In Brazil, São Paulo and Rio combined had about 10 million people in 1970, or double the population of the six next-largest cities. The same pattern was true for the small countries: The population of Santo Domingo triples that of the next three Dominican cities; that of Panama City quadruples the same figure; and that of Guatemala City is about seven times the population of Quezaltenango, Escuintla, and Puerto Barrios, combined. In Latin America, only Colombia approximated a log-normal distribution of the urban population, but even this exception is being challenged by the rapid growth of Bogotà.[7]

Internal migration and urban growth are, intrinsically, neither good nor bad. Such assessments depend on the specific social context and, in particular, on the point of view that one adopts with respect to the interest of different classes and institutional actors. A case can be made that, in the short run at least, the present trends of rural-urban migration and urban concentration are functional for a wide assortment of groups.

First of all, these processes are functional for the migrants themselves. Within the constraints of peripheral economies, where opportunities for paid employment in the countryside and small towns are limited, migration to the city emerges as a viable and frequent sole alternative. The very size of these cities creates a wide variety of economic opportunities, if not in the formal economy, at least in the growing informal sector. For private firms in manufacturing and services, migration and urban growth are functional for three reasons: First, they expand, albeit in a limited manner, the urban market for a variety of products; second, sustained migration ensures an abundant supply of labor, which contributes to maintain low wages; third, and perhaps more important, the informal sector, although apparently unrelated to the established firms, represents a central mechanism to further reduce their labor costs.

Informal enterprise provides workers with access to goods and services that would otherwise be unavailable to many. Access to consumption through easier credit or lower prices in the informal sector permits the maintenance of wages bearing little relation to the costs of goods and services in the formal market. In addition, established industries frequently subcontract part of their production process to informal entrepreneurs, thus saving the costs of social security protection and taking advantage of the subremunerated labor of informal workers.[8]

Rural–urban migration also benefits entrenched landowning classes by providing a safety valve for pressure on the land and peasant mobilization. Finally, political parties and even the government itself have taken advantage of the urban masses created by migration to generate social movements and political constituencies with which to further their own aims.[9]

Neither can the view that rural–urban migration is negative be based on the argument that it necessarily empties places of origin and weakens their economies. There is considerable evidence at present that places of outmigration need not lose population nor suffer permanent economic stagnation as a result of the flow. The occupational skills and savings accumulated by migrants in the city have been frequently invested in places of origin, helping to activate their economies and attracting population from other areas.

Contrary to generalized views, return migration to rural places need not be a reflection of the "defeat" of migrants in their struggle for survival in the city but may represent exactly the opposite: the means by which successful migrants can put their urban-acquired resources to use for further economic advancement. Hence, while rural stagnation provides the original push for migration, the crisis need not be accentuated by this outflow.[10]

The negative characteristics of mass internal migration and urban concentration emerge only when we assess their long-term effects against two criteria: (1) returns on an alternative model of development and (2) the quality of life for the mass of the urban population. The concentration of peasants and workers from all over the country in one or two cities, employed in activaties of minimal productivity for which the only "edge" is the minimal cost of labor, amounts to an obvious waste. It is a double waste: of the country's physical resources, underutilized or abandoned, and of the energies of its population.

The accelerating contradictions in urban space have to do primarily with the inability of the state to accommodate the rapid increase in population within the legal framework of land ownership and to prevent the increasing deterioration of services and the environment.

The pattern of urbanization in Latin America in the early twentieth century resembled that predominant in North American cities. The poor, city-born, or migrants rented quarters in the deteriorating fringe surrounding the urban core. This type of housing, variously called "vecindades," "cites," "conventillos," and "solares," soon proved insufficient to accommodate the new migrant waves. The inability of the existing housing supply to provide shelter for this new population led to the breakdown of the existing legal structure of land ownership and the emergence of unregulated settlements, such as private urbanizations, organized land invasions, and spontaneous occupations.

It is a misconception to define the causal relationship between migration and unregulated urban settlements as a direct one—that is, one where migrants created the settlements as their own "reception centers" in the city. In fact, new migrants often go to live in established low-rent quarters in the city, and the settlements emerge only through the actions of the older migrants and the city-born. The basic impact of rural–urban migrations has been to drive up rents of working-class housing, putting pressure on *both* migrants and the city-born.

Simultaneously, even the most modest housing that is for sale has increased in price beyond the reach of these groups. This prevents the more established workers from moving out of rental housing into home ownership by legal means. Different types of uncontrolled settlements thus respond to different needs: they are the creation of the poorest groups, migrant and city-born, in search of minimal shelter in the city *and* of more established members of the working class in search of some form of home ownership.[11]

It is equally wrong to regard uncontrolled settlements as an "inevitable" consequence of mass migration. The private construction industry in Latin America and the Caribbean has responded alertly to the demand generated by the urban upper classes. Wages received by the mass of the population, usually below one or two minimum salaries, do not create a profitable demand for this industry. They are so low that most workers are priced out even from subsidized public housing. In this situation, illegal occupation of land and the spontaneous self-construction of shelter by the poor emerge as the only viable alternatives. They are, therefore, tolerated and even sponsored by the state through various informal means. Recently, governments and international organizations have collaborated in the creation of what are, in fact, officially sponsored squatter settlements through the so-called "site-and-services" programs.[12]

The point is that, contrary to conventional views, the emergence of squatter settlements, land invasions, and sites-and-services programs is not the consequence of "excess" numbers but of a given wage structure. These settlements reflect the fact that wages paid to a sizable segment of the urban labor force bear no relation to the market cost of a basic consumption item: shelter for the individual and his family. Seen from this perspective, the self-construction of housing in peripheral urban settlements can be appropriately defined as a "subsidy" to employers in the formal sector. The unpaid efforts of weekend construction gangs in the settlements are, ultimately, means to perpetuate returns to labor that exclude the real market costs of a place to live in the city.

This statement can be challenged by arguing that the bulk of the population in the urban peripheral settlements is unemployed or precariously employed, and that they would not qualify for regular housing even on the most generous terms. While this argument represents conventional wisdom, it does not square with the facts. The proportion of the unemployed in peripheral settlements has been found to be consistently low and generally not higher than for the total urban labor force. The reason is that open unemployment is a luxury that few can afford: Men and women of the working class must do "something" in order to earn a living. Similarly, peripheral settlements are not inhabited exclusively by individuals in the lowest echelons of the labor market. Most studies to date indicate that they possess a considerable internal occupational diversity.

A probability survey of Caracas' "marginal" settlements found declared unemployment to be 9.1%, lower than for the city as a whole. Self-employed activities, typical of the informal sector, accounted for 13.6% of total employment. The bulk of the employed population, 56.3%, were workers in manufacturing, services, and transportation. White-collar workers accounted for a sizable 27%— 16.2% in private firms, and 10.8% in government.[13]

A representative survey of four peripheral *poblaciones* in Santiago de Chile found that 13% of family heads had white-collar jobs in government or private enterprises. An additional 45% were employed as skilled and semiskilled workers in formal sector firms. Declared unemployment was only 6%, not significantly different from the figure for the Santiago labor force at the time.

These and similar figures show that the problem of peripheral settlements is not primarily one of unemployment and poverty, but one of poverty-in-employment: the fact that returns to labor are frequently below those required to meet basic consumption needs, including minimal shelter. Furthermore, these figures show that the wage structure affects not only informal sector workers, but also those in regular industrial employment and even white-collar and government employees.

The deterioration of services and the environment in cities accompanies the growth of peripheral settlements as the second major contradiction produced by migration and urban concentration. The contradiction here lies in the fact that urban industrial expansion and economic development do not lead to better life conditions for the mass of city dwellers but actually worsen them.

Skyrocketing rents and land costs price an ever-growing segment of the urban population out of the conventional housing market. Lower-income groups are expelled to the urban periphery and forced to live in areas ever more remote from the urban center and from places of work. Three- and four-hour rides each way to work are not uncommon. The transportation system, antiquated and unreliable to begin with, is strained to the limit under the pressure of increasing distances. In cities like Rio de Janeiro and São Paulo, popular frustration at accidents and delays in the suburban train system has exploded in a series of spontaneous riots where a number of stations and trains have been destroyed.[15]

Other basic urban services, such as electricity, water, sewage, police and fire protection, hospitals, and recreational parks also fail to keep pace with the rate of urban growth. These services are distributed along a social gradient, with high-income areas receiving the best and most reliable ones and peripheral settlements receiving the worst. With urban growth, the existing urban infrastructure and social services are forced to cover larger areas and handle greater numbers. The fraction of the population covered by these services frequently diminishes.

In São Paulo, the most industrialized of Brazilian cities, only 55% of dwellings in 1975 had running water, and only 35% were connected to the sewerage system; corresponding proportions in the Northeast city of Recife were 61% and 13.7%. In Santiago de Chile, running water was available in 85% of the dwellings, but the sewerage system covered only 47%. Similar proportions were reported for Buenos Aires and Mexico City. The number of hospital beds per thousand inhabitants in major cities was estimated circa 1970 at 4.0 in Chile, 3.2 in Colombia, 2.4 in Mexico, and 1.8 in Peru. A comparable figure for large U.S. cities in the same year was 16.5.[16]

Industrial concentration in major cities and the absence of government regulation have led to levels of environmental pollution that make some of the most polluted cities in the advanced world look healthy by comparison. Two of the largest industrial cities in Latin America, Mexico City and São Paulo, represent the best examples of the accelerating contradictions in urban development: peripheralization of the working class, urban congestion, insufficient and unreliable public transportation, insufficient infrastructure and deteriorating social services, environmental pollution, and a chaotic, unplanned pace of urban expansion.

The processes of accelerated migration and urban concentration, whether evaluated as positive or negative, did not just "happen." As suggested above, these processes are integral parts of a model of development that, though adopted by most countries in the region, is neither necessary nor inevitable. The model stresses rapid industrialization, with a strong export orientation. It also emphasizes agricultural modernization, including the breakup of traditional productive arrangements and their substitution by capital-intensive enterprises. Modernized agricultural production is supposed to lower domestic food costs and simultaneously to make exports more competitive in world markets.

With significant local variations, this model of development has been adopted by all major and most middle-sized countries in Latin America. Its application has had two profoundly negative consequences for the condition and aspirations of the working classes. First, industrialization and agricultural modernization have been based on a capital-intensive model that reproduces in these peripheral economies processes of production originally developed for the advanced countries. The overall consequence of these externally-led processes has not been to absorb labor, but to displace it. Artisan and labor-intensive industries producing for the domestic market have been rapidly displaced by larger firms, national and foreign-owned, employing more efficient production methods.

Peasants have similarly seen their livelihood threatened by absorption of their lands and by the absence of supplementary employment, given the lower labor needs of mechanized agriculture.[17] No serious provision was made in any country to absorb the labor displaced by the new industries and commercial farms. Instead, the argument was advanced that rapid economic growth would generate multiple effects, "trickling down" in the form of expanded employment opportunities. This thesis has proven incorrect, even after years of application of the model, unless one is willing to consider the swelling informal economy as evidence of the "trickling down" effect.

Second, industrialization and agricultural modernization have not been accompanied by a systematic effort to expand the internal market. Instead, they have been oriented to satisfy a restricted domestic demand and to increase the volume of exports. This model of development is based, ultimately, on the existence of an abundant supply of low-wage labor. This gives manufacturing exports from peripheral countries their main real edge in world markets. It is also the central argument employed to attract industrial investment from abroad: the availability of a labor force able to perform tasks similar to those of industries in the advanced countries at a fraction of the cost.

Several estimates in the 1970s compared returns to different categories of industrial labor in the United States with those for comparably trained labor in Third World countries. U.S. manufacturing wages exceeded the average in Latin America by a factor of 5 to 1; they tripled average wages in the relatively advanced countries such as Argentina, Mexico, and Venezuela. For relatively less advanced countries, such as Peru, Ecuador, and Colombia, the ratio was close to 10 to 1. The data also show that Brazilian wages for unskilled labor ca. 1975 were one-tenth and for skilled industrial labor one fifth of those paid in the United States.

A model of development based on labor displacement and the containment of wages at a fraction of those predominant in the advanced economies will lead inevitably to the patterns of urbanization and rural-urban migration observed in Latin America. Industrial investments tend to locate in those few cities where the necessary infrastructure is available. These are also the cities where the limited domestic market concentrates and where the available industrial labor force is accessible. A peasantry displaced by agricultural modernization has little choice but to move to the same cities. Since employment in capital-intensive industries and other segments of the formal economy is limited, many migrants end up as a source of labor for the informal economy. The latter thus assumes the dual function of keeping these workers alive and of supplying a demand based on low wages in the formal sector.

While returns to labor in peripheral countries are a fraction of those in the advanced economies, prices of formal sector goods and services are not. Hence, industrial workers constitute a weak source of expansion of domestic demand. As seen above, low industrial wages also bar workers from access to the housing market and force them to search for shelter through informal means.

The point is that accelerated migration and the "hyper-urbanization" of Latin American and Caribbean countries are not symptoms of the breakdown of the economic system. Instead, they are integral components of that system and routine aspects of its operation. This pattern of urbanization fits the requirements of the existing model of development and the short-term needs of a variety of economic classes and institutional actors. For this reason, it can be expected to continue, at least in the immediate future. A reversal of these trends will require significant changes in the groups in control of the state and the adoption of a very different set of policies.

The contradictions brought about by the present model of development have already created pressures in that direction. In Mexico, a pioneer in the application of the model, up to 50% of the population is estimated to be underemployed. For Latin America as a whole, the total underutilization of labor has been estimated at 30% of the economically active population.[19] Agricultural modernization has not produced the anticipated increases in food supplies and reduction of food costs. Between 1970 and 1978, agricultural production for the region grew at 3.5% per year, below total economic growth and the original targets for the decade. While there are significant differences among countries, the general trend has been toward displacement of the peasantry and toward concentration on exports, a process that has led to food shortages and to a need to increase imports.

An alternative model of development must have, as its basic premise, the urgent need to increase employment and the level of real earnings of labor, preventing the perpetuation of an economy based on very low wages. Policies necessary for dealing with rapid population growth thus converge with those required by accelerating migration and urban concentration.

The reversal of present urbanization trends in the region would require the application of four interrelated policies: (1) reactivation of the small-scale agricultural sector through provision of land, credits, and technology to the peasantry—attention to this sector would help discourage further migration, encourage return migration, and increase domestic food production; (2) promotion of new industrial centers and "development zones" as a means to rechannel migration away from primate cities and put to use underutilized resources; (3) effective control of urban land and housing speculation to discourage further unproductive investment and the continued expulsion of low- and middle-income groups from the city; (4) increases in real wages to a level compatible with a minimum standard of living, including shelter. Combined with other policies aimed at labor absorption, this expansion of the domestic market should lead to rapid increases in employment, both in the industrial and agricultural sectors.

The application of these interrelated policies confronts many obstacles. Several countries attempted to implement one or more during the 1960s and early 1970s, but abandoned them for the model of development outlined above. Additional discussion of these alternative policies and their obverse, as being applied today, will be postponed, for they also bear on our final topic of discussion.

MIGRATION ABROAD

The concept of international migration comprises, in reality, a number of separate flows. Broad reports of migration, say from Chile to Argentina or from Mexico to the United States, generally fail to clarify the specific character of the movement and, hence, do not provide a reliable basis for analysis. In recent years, for example, sizable emigrations originating in Latin America have involved such different groups as refugees escaping political upheavals in their home country, highly skilled professionals in search of better opportunities abroad, and manual workers, legal and illegal, coming to fill labor shortages in the host country.

Even within these categories, the specific characteristics of migrant flows defy generalization. A rough "map" of recent international migrations from Latin America and Caribbean countries may give an idea of the complexity of these movements. Without being exhaustive, such a map would include the following:

Labor migrations from Chile, Bolivia, Paraguay, and Uruguay to Argentina, each having different origins, destinations, and functions; professional and technical emigration from Argentina, Colombia, the Dominican Republic, and the British-speaking Caribbean to the United States, Europe, and the rest of Latin America; political refugee flows from Cuba to the United States and to Puerto Rico, and from Argentina, Chile, and Uruguay to the rest of Latin America, the United States, and Europe; rural contract labor from Haiti to the Dominican Republic, from Mexico to the United States and Canada, and from the British West Indies to Florida; undocumented labor flows, both rural- and urban-bound, from Colombia to Venezuela and Ecuador, from El Salvador to Honduras, and from Mexico, the Dominican Republic, Haiti, Colombia, the British Caribbean, and Central America to the United States.[20]

The following discussion will have to do only with international labor migrations, primarily manual labor flows but also professional and technical emigration. Political refugee movements, though important, have a different and more fortuitous character, which would require separate analysis. At present and for the foreseeable future, labor migrations represent both the more numerous and more predictable movements. They are also the ones more directly traceable to the changing articulation of countries in the international economy.

There are several notions about the character of labor migrations that should be considered first. These include the assertion that migrations occur from the "periphery" to the "core" of the international system, the description of undocumented flows as a response to poverty in the most backward regions, and the metaphor of migration as an irreversible escape from misery. The first notion runs against significant labor flows between peripheral countries.

Unless one is willing to consider rural areas of Venezuela, the Dominican Republic, or Honduras as part of the "core," existing migrations toward them will provide convincing evidence against the first generalization.

The usual description of undocumented migration as involving impoverished peasant labor from the most backward regions runs against a body of evidence that shows that a substantial proportion of these flows comes from urban and metropolitan areas. Further, neither rural- nor urban-origin undocumented migrants tend to come from the most impoverished strata of their respective populations. Recent studies of undocumented Colombian migration to Venezuela, Mexican migration to the United States, and Dominican migration to New York provide evidence of these trends.[21]

The idea of international migration as an irreversible escape from poverty is also contradicted by the fact that many migrants, legal and undocumented, return to the source country after a period of time. The available data indicate that substantial proportions of undocumented migrants from Mexico, Colombia, and the Dominican Republic return to their country. There is also evidence of a pattern of recurrent cyclical migrations in which workers move back and forth across an international border according to labor demand in the receiving areas and the requirements of crops and other investments back home.[22]

Also questionable are sweeping statements defining labor migrations as a reflection of inequalities in the world system and the "dependency" of particular countries. These statements lack the required specificity to account for concrete flows. They fail, for example, the basic test of explaining why only a minority of the population in a dependent or exploited country actually migrates. Their rhetoric would lead us to expect much larger out-migrations from these nations than those that actually take place.

An exhaustive analysis of labor migrations must proceed at two interrelated levels: the level of broad structural determinants setting the preconditions and directionality of the flow and the level of microstructural circumstances affecting the context in which individual decisions are made. At the first level, one of the few permissible generalizations is that labor migrations tend to occur toward areas of higher relative wages. Despite its almost tautological character, this statement can serve as a useful point of departure for analysis.

At the second level, migration may be broadly characterized as a dynamic process that both recreates and depends on the existence of social networks across space. Participation in such networks is frequently the decisive factor in individual decisions to migrate. The consolidation of social networks, frequently spanning vast geographical distances, is also a primary determinant of the resilience of migrant flows, even after the original economic incentives have changed or disappeared.

At the structural level, the analysis of migration requires joint consideration of the demand and supply of this labor. The existence of higher relative wages in places of destination implies the existence of labor demand. The nature of this demand varies in terms of a series of factors such as sector of the economy, seasonality, and contractual arrangements. It is possible, however, to distinguish between two basic types of demand: The first is a situation of absolute scarcity of labor, which requires importation of workers to fill a domestic shortage. It is the case, for example, of the demand for physicians, nurses, engineers, and other professionals in the advanced countries. Labor migrations under these conditions generally occur through legal channels, and migrants are accorded rights and privileges similar to those of domestic workers.[23]

The second type is a situation of relative scarcity where a domestic labor supply exists, but where it cannot be tapped at the wages offered. Migration represents in this case a device to preserve low wage levels in particular sectors of the receiving economy. This is accomplished both by the direct employment of migrants and, indirectly, by weakening the organizational efforts of the domestic working class. It is the case of most current undocumented flows, such as that of Mexicans to the agroindustries of the U.S. Southwest; Mexicans, Dominicans, and others to industrial and service firms in U.S. cities; and of Colombians to the sugar industry in Venezuela.

Though historical circumstances vary, migrations responding to this second type of demand tend to occur either surreptitiously or under temporary labor contracts. In both cases, migrant workers are denied the rights, legal protection, and perquisites to which domestic labor is entitled. Illegality and temporary contracts are, ultimately, means to preserve the legal vulnerability of these workers. The threat of summary expulsion from the host country has proven an effective weapon in weakening the organizational efforts of migrants and preventing them from joining forces with domestic labor organizations.[24]

In recent years, the slow expansion of the international economy and a growing supply of trained domestic manpower in the advanced countries have led to a decline in absolute demand. In the United States, for example, this trend has led to the end of active recruitment abroad for most types of professional workers. The same condition of slow growth has led, however, to increasing pressure on employers in competitive sectors of the economy to reduce labor costs.

These efforts take the dual form of attempting to control direct wages and to reduce the indirect or "fringe" wages and protection to which workers are legally entitled. This process helps to explain the apparent paradox of high levels of unemployment in the United States, especially among those minorities traditionally hired by the competitive sector, along with the massive presence and hiring of undocumented workers from a number of countries.[25]

The analysis of labor supply from sending countries can also take as its point of departure the fact that migrations take place toward areas of higher relative wages. As seen above, migrants do not necessarily come from the most backward regions, nor do they generally belong to the most impoverished strata. Additional data from the United States indicate that undocumented migrants were seldom unemployed in the country of origin prior to emigration.

There is also evidence suggesting that many undocumented and contract labor migrants perform tasks in places of destination that are below their qualifications and occupational experience in the country of origin. As a report on the program supplying Jamaican labor to Florida agriculture stated: "many of these laborers would never cut sugar cane in Jamaica since they are themselves small farmers or urban workers."[26]

This evidence suggests that the "push" toward migration from Latin America and the Caribbean does not originate exclusively or even primarily in unemployment, but in the earnings level of employed workers. Returns to labor are frequently so low that they make the paltry wages and harsh working conditions in places of destination appear attractive by comparison. At this pont, however, a cautionary note should be added.

It is a common practice to attribute the push to emigration to absolute wage differentials between receiving and sending countries. This kind of analysis runs counter to many instances, historical and contemporary, where migration has failed to occur despite vast disparities in returns to labor. Little professional emigration to the United States was registered from Mexico, Brazil, and Chile at the time when there were sizable professional outflows from Argentina and Colombia, despite the fact that absolute disparities in salaries were, in every case, quite significant.[27] In contrast to the other Central American and Caribbean countries, little labor migration, legal or undocumented, has taken place so far from Costa Rica, despite a significant absolute gap in wage levels with the United States.

The significance of earnings in the "push" for emigration is not the invidious comparison with outside levels but the internal assessment of their relationship to costs. This relationship has, in turn, two major aspects: (1) the availability of other sources of income, monetary and nonmonetary, and (2) normative standards of consumption for the country or region.

A given wage level if it is the sole means for acquisition of necessary goods and services for the household means something ensirely different from a wage level that represents only part of a "package" of such means. Additional ones may be monetary, such as independent production and sale of goods, or nonmonetary, such as direct subsistence production. In general and with specific exceptions, the trend in peripheral economies has been toward proletarianization of the labor force, including increasing reliance on wages as the sole or primary means of livelihood. This does not imply the elimination of other activities, which continue to proliferate in the informal sector, but a restriction of their relative earnings potential. As a rule, workers in the formal sector have come to depend primarily on wages, with other activities having an ancillary character in the overall economic strategy of the household.[28]

Another feature of the model of development dominant in the region is a corollary of its outward orientation: the importation of consumption standards predominant in the advanced countries. Specific items are added, with a greater or lesser lag, to the normative consumption package. In the extreme, a situation can be anticipated of consumption expectations (and prices) at a par with those in the advanced countries together with peripheral wage levels.[29] In the less extreme cases that exist today, there is still a contradiction between the penetration of consumption expectations that become defined as part of the normal life style for different categories of workers and the fact that "normal" earnings bear little relation to their cost.

Paradoxically, these contradictions are often more acute in relative advanced urban areas than in backward rural regions, and among regularly employed workers with some skills than among the unskilled and marginally employed. Exactly the same contradiction underlies the push toward emigration among professionals who are frequently even more exposed to the contradiction between normative consumption standards and real earnings.[30]

The point suggested by this analysis is that the existence of a migrant labor supply in peripheral countries cannot be automatically imputed to a "traditional" rural sector, left behind by the process of modernization. Instead, many of the pressures giving rise to a ready supply of migrant labor are continuously recreated by this process itself and frequently affect the most "modernized" workers. This helps explain why sources of undocumented and contract labor migrations appear to be located increasingly in cities and among segments of the urban working class.

During the next decade, it is likely that the pace of labor migration will be maintained and even accelerated. The direction of these flows will continue to be toward the traditional higher-wage countries: the United States, Venezuela, and Argentina. To these may be added significant flows from Central America to Mexico and from Colombia to Ecuador. Professional emigration is likely to decrease in importance, unless propelled by political instability. The reason is not the disappearance of conditions giving rise to a ready supply of would-be migrants, but the slackening of demand for this type of labor in the advanced countries, particularly the United States.

The bulk of labor migration in the immediate future will be through undocumented or "informal" channels and through temporary contract programs. The reason for their continuation is three-fold: (1) the persistence of demand for low-wage labor in the competitive sector of receiving urban economies and in agriculture, in particular labor-intensive harvest work; (2) the likely intensification of the contradictions giving rise to a ready labor supply in the sending countries; (3) the consolidation of social networks and established migration patterns between communities of origin and destination. As noted above, the existence of such networks give to migrant flows a measure of autonomy from changes in economic incentives and in the broader structural context.

The magnitude that international labor migrations have acquired in this continent and the fact that many of the larger flows are illegal should have led long ago to greater attention by the political and economic institutions of the Inter-American system. Tales of exploitation and abuse against migrants are innumerable and rival in gruesomeness those that have given rise to international concern about political repression. It is bad enough that individuals and families are forced out of their country by economic necessity to withstand, in addition, abuses, persecution, and arbitrariness by those profiting from their work.

It is a task of the greatest urgency for the Inter-American system to set up the necessary institutional machinery to deal with this issue. Among the functions that have not been performed by international organizations and that demand their immediate attention are: (1) monitoring the size, character, and direction of international labor flows; (2) drawing up legal instruments establishing the rights of migrant workers, legal or undocumented, in the countries of destination; (3) sponsoring bilateral or multilateral agreements between governments aimed at legalizing undocumented migrant flows and protecting the rights of migrants; (4) investigating violations of existing agreements, abuses committed against migrant workers in the receiving *or* sending countries, and actions by employers aimed at bypassing protective labor legislation.

These actions are necessary to respond to the most pressing short-term problems of labor movement across national borders. In the long-term, however, the contradictions underlying the presence of a mass of workers ready to abandon their country in search for higher wages would require major shifts in state policy. Such shifts coincide with those required by the rapid growth of the labor force, mass internal migration, urban primacy, and uncontrolled urban growth. They all point to the need of abandoning a model of development based exclusively on export promotion and returning to one based on the expansion of the internal market through employment creation and increases in returns to labor.

As noted above, the impact of earnings on the supply of migrant labor is not based primarily on invidious comparisons between their domestic and external levels, but in the internal comparison with their actual acquisition power. A redistributive policy aimed at bringing returns to labor into balance with a minimal normative standard of living for different classes of workers represents the only effective means of reducing outmigration in the long run.

Ultimately, the question is one of alternative conceptions of development: aggregate output growth based on the continuous impoverishment of the labor force and the expulsion of part of it abroad, or growth governed by the need for protecting living standards for the mass of the population.

CONCLUSION

The analysis above indicates that specific issues of population growth, urbanization, and international migration cannot be tackled in isolation from a global approach to the problem of development. Since the latter is not the specific topic of this paper, it has not been possible to explore its many significant aspects in detail. However, a few concluding remarks are in order.

In the past, lip service has been paid to the need for a redistribution of the fruits of economic growth, but few concrete steps have been taken in that direction. In fact, the extraordinary influence exercised by international economic organizations, both public and private, on Latin American and Caribbean countries has generally been directed toward encouraging policies with the opposite effect. To preserve or regain their international credibility vis-à-vis financial institutions, countries have been directed to implement policies that go directly against the interests of their most vulnerable sectors.

In some countries of the Southern Cone, the application of the ideology of "opening up to the exterior" threatens to subvert many of the painfully gained achievements of industrialization, returning their economies to a role not too different from the one they occupied at the beginning of the century. Under apparently reasonable banners such as "efficiency," "comparative advantage," and the control of inflation, this ideology is leading to a situation close to that outlined above: international prices and expectations and peripheral wages.

A model of development based exclusively on the promotion of exports cannot but accelerate the internal contradictions giving rise to underemployment, mass rural–urban migration, urban primacy, slum growth, and out-migration. Proponents of this model argue that a strategy based on income redistribution and the internal market is unfeasible at present. However, they fail to note other important facts, which include: (1) that the strategy of the "opening" has conspicuously failed in several of its central goals, including the control of domestic inflation and income redistribution through an increase in labor demand; (2) that there is no evidence that the self-imposed elimination of protective tariffs by peripheral countries necessarily leads to a more advantageous position in the international economy; (3) that those countries that have been more successful in the promotion of nontraditional manufactured exports are precisely those with the largest internal markets and the longest experience in domestic industrial production.

As several economists have recently noted, the choice between development based on export promotion or on the internal market may be ultimately a false one. Unless countries are willing to settle for industries of the "export platform" type, the industrial firms in the best position to seek external markets are those that have first developed by supplying internal demand. The case of the Brazilian auto industry is a well-known example.[32] While the dilemma between export promotion and the internal market might well prove illusory, the consequences of orthodox application of the "opening" strategy are not. They fall most heavily on the urban and rural working classes and perpetuate the cycle of low wages, weak internal demand, and growth governed by the ups and downs of the international market.

It is impossible here to go into what an alternative development strategy would entail and the obstacles that it would confront. In general, the point of such a strategy would not be the vain pursuit of economic autarchy, but the implementation of policies that integrate the promotion of exports with internal development. Such policies would not relegate fundamental social goals to the category of secondary considerations to be handled through trickle-down effects.

The implementation of this alternative model in Latin America and the Caribbean is not unfeasible, at present, though its specific form will depend on the degree of economic autonomy available to each country. Larger and more industrialized countries and those with unique resources, such as oil, will be in a better position; smaller and less developed countries will require the prop of regional markets created through intergovernmental cooperation.

The role of economic institutions of the Inter-American system must be to support the effort of governments embarked in redistributive policies and to help countermand short-term financial pressures aimed at reversing them. The continuation of a strategy of growth-and-inequality will necessarily lead to the aggravation of existing problems of underemployment and poverty and to long-term social and political instability. An effective policy must depart from the assumption that a peaceful domestic and international order can only be preserved through real improvements in the living standards of the mass of the population.

NOTES

1. Projections Centre, CEPAL, "Economic and Social Development in the 1970s: Experience and Lessons," *Cepal Review* 11 (August 1980); 7–30.

2. Ibid., p. 14.

3. Enrique V. Iglesias, "Latin America on the Threshold of the 1980s," *Cepal Review* 9 (December 1979): 7–43.

4. *Statistical Abstract of Latin America, 1977*, Los Angeles: UCLA Latin American Center Publications, 1978, Table 104, 629.

5. Projections Centre, CEPAL, op. cit., p. 14.

6. *Statistical Abstract of Latin America*, op. cit., Table 104.

7. Ibid., Table 626.

8. For a more detailed presentation of this argument and supporting evidence see "Unequal Exchange and the Urban Informal Sector," Chapter 3 in Alejandro Portes and John Walton, *Labor, Class, and the International System*, New York: Academic Press, 1981.

9. On this point see Manuel Castells, "Multinational Capital, National States, and Local Communities," Working Paper No. 334, Institute of Urban and Regional Development of the University of California at Berkeley, November 1980. See also David Collier, *Squatters and Oligarchs, Authoritarian Rule and Policy Change in Peru*, Baltimore: The Johns Hopkins University Press, 1976.

10. For supporting evidence see Bryan R. Roberts, "The Provincial Urban System and the Process of Dependency," pp. 99–131 in Alejandro Portes and Harley L. Browning (eds.), *Current Perspectives in Latin American Urban Research*, Austin: Institute of Latin American Studies of the University of Texas, 1976. See also Lourdes Arizpe, *Migración, etnicismo y Cambio Economico*, Mexico D.F.: El Colegio de Mexico, 1978.

11. See "The Economy and Ecology of Urban Poverty," Chapter 2 in Alejandro Portes and John Walton, *Urban Latin America*, Austin: University of Texas Press, 1976. Wayne A. Cornelius, *Politics and the Migrant Poor in Mexico City*, Stanford, CA.: Stanford University Press, 1975.

12. Collier, op cit. John F. C. Turner, *Housing by People*, London: Marion Boyars, 1976.

13. Magaly Sanchez, *La Ségrégation Urbaine à Caracas*, These de Doctorat, Université de Paris, 1980, as cited in Manuel Castells, op. cit.

14. Alejandro Portes, "Occupation and Lower-Class Political Orientations in Chile," pp. 201–37, in A. Valenzuela and S. Valenzuela, *Chile: Politics and Society*, New Brunswick, N.J.: Trans-Action, 1976.

15. Jose A. Moises and Verena Martinez-Alier, "A Revolta dos Suburbanos," pp. 13–63 in CEDEC, *Contradições urbanas e Movimentos Sociais*, São Paulo: Paz e Terra, 1977.

16. Ibid. *Statistical Abstract of Latin America*, op. cit., Tables 810, 906.

17. Arizpe, op. cit. M. R. Redclift, *Agrarian Reform and Peasant Organization on the Ecuadorean Coast*, London: Athlone Press, 1978. Bernardo Sorj, "Agrarian Structure and Politics in Present Day Brazil," *Latin American Perspectives* 24 (1980): 23–34. S. Gudeman, *The Demise of a Rural Economy*, London: Routledge and Kegan Paul, 1978.

18. *Statistical Abstract of Latin America, 1970*, Los Angeles: UCLA Latin American Center Publications, 1971, pp. 97, 356. *Statistical Abstract of Latin America, 1977*, op. cit., Table 1400. A. Brown and J. P. Ford, *Brazil: Today's Business Opportunity*, London: 1975, p. 124.

19. Francisco Alba, "Mexico's International Migration as a Manifestation of its Development Pattern," *International Migration Review* 12 (Winter 1978): 502–513. Projections Centre, CEPAL, op. cit.

20. For a partial review of the evidence on international migration see Adriana Marshall, "International Labour Migration in Latin America: the Southern Cone," paper presented at the Conference on International Migration, Bellaggio, Italy, June 1979. Alejandro Portes (ed.), *Illegal Mexican Immigrants to the United States*, Special Issue of the *International Migration Review*, Vol. 12, 1978. Josh DeWind, Tom Seidl, and Janet Shenk, "Caribbean Migration, Contract Labor in U.S. Agriculture," *NACLA, Report on the Americas* 9 (Nov.–Dec. 1978): 4–36. Ramiro Cardona and Carmen Ines Cruz, *El Exodo de Colombianos*, Bogota: Ediciones Tercer Mundo, 1980. Gabriel Murillo, *La Migración de Trabajadores Colombianos a Venezuela*, Bogota: Ministerio de Trabajo y Seguridad Social, 1979. Terry L. McCoy, "The Political Economy of Caribbean

Workers in the Florida Sugar Industry," paper presented at the Fifth Annual Meeting of the Caribbean Studies Association, Curaçao, May 1980. Antonio Ugalde, Frank D. Bean, and Gilbert Cardenas, "International Migration from the Dominican Republic: Findings from a National Survey," *International Migration Review* 13 (Summer 1979): 235-254. Saskia Sassen-Koob, "Formal and Informal Associations: Dominicans and Colombians in New York," *International Migration Review* 13 (Summer 1979): 314-332.

21. Antonio Ugalde et al., op. cit. Gabriel Murillo, op. cit. Saskia Sassen-Koob, op. cit. Francisco Alba, op. cit. Alejandro Portes, "Illegal Immigration and the International System, Lessons from Recent Legal Immigration from Mexico," *Social Problems* 26 (April 1979): 425-38.

22. Wayne A. Cornelius, "Mexican Migration to the United States: The View from Rural Sending Communities," Center for International Affairs, M.I.T., 1976. Ina R. Dinerman, "Patterns of Adaptation among Households of U.S.-Bound Migrants from Michoacan, Mexico," *International Migration Review* 12 (Winter 1978): 485-501. Luz Marina Diaz, "Reproducción de la Fuerza de Trabajo Migrante Colombiana en Venezuela," paper presented to the Second Latin American Seminar on Labor Migrations, Cali, Colombia, December 1980. Ugalde et al., op. cit.

23. Alejandro Portes, "Modes of Structural Incorporation and Present Theories of Labor Immigration," paper presented at the Conference in International Migration, Bellaggio, Italy, June 1979. Alejandro Portes, "Determinants of the Brain Drain," *International Migration Review* 10 (Winter 1976): 489-508.

24. Robert L. Bach, "Mexican Immigration and the American State," *International Migration Review* 12 (Winter 1978): 536-558. Manuel Castells, "Immigrant Workers and Class Struggles in Advanced Capitalism: the Western European Experience," *Politics and Society* 5 (1975) 33-66. McCoy, op. cit.

25. For a more detailed presentation of this argument see Alejandro Portes, "Migration and Underdevelopment," *Politics and Society* 8 (1978): 1-48.

26. Florida Sugar Cane League, "Off-Shore Workers in the Sugar Cane Industry," *Fact Sheet* 2, 1979 cited in McCoy, op. cit.

27. For evidence on this point see Alejandro Portes, "Determinants of the Brain Drain . . . ," op. cit.

28. Immanuel Wallerstein, William M. Martin, and Terry Dickinson, "Household Structures and Productions Processes," working paper, Fernand Braudel Center, State University of New York at Binghamton, 1979. Paulo Renato de Souza, *A Determinação dos Salarios e do Emprego nas Economias Atrasadas*, Tese de Doutoramento, Universidade Estadual de Campinas, São Paulo, 1980.

29. Anibal Pinto, "The Opening up of Latin America to the Exterior," *Cepal Review* 11 (August 1980): 313-56. Francisco Alba, op. cit.

30. Alejandro Portes, "Illegal Immigration . . . ," op. cit. Alejandro Portes and Adreain A. Ross, "Modernization For Emigration: the Argentine Medical Brain Drain," *Journal of Inter-American Studies and World Affairs* (November 1976): 395-421.

31. Constantine Vaitsos, *Intercountry Income Distribution and Transnational Enterprises*, London: Oxford University Press, 1974. Edmar Bacha, *Os Mitos de Uma Decada*, Rio de Janeiro: Paz e Terra, 1976. Enrique V. Iglesias, op. cit. Anibal Pinto, op. cit.

32. Ibid. See Hollis B. Chenery and Helen Hughes, "La Division Internacional del Trabajo: El ejemplo de la Industria," *Trimestre Economico* 39 (July-September 1972): 415-60.

20

Unemployment in Latin America: Priority Areas for International Action in the 1980s

Juan Buttari

At the risk of excessive simplification, unemployment in Latin America involves four distinct—yet intertwined—dimensions of policy action.* They are:

- the creation of sufficient jobs for a rapidly growing labor force; the jobs should entail adequate income levels—this area relates to long-run growth and development strategies;

- the stabilization of cyclical and seasonal fluctuation in employment—this area implies integrating fiscal, monetary and trade policies with measures addressed to sectorial and regional development;

- the linking of prospective employers and employees—this area encompasses establishing public employment services,

---

The views expressed in this paper are those of the author and do not necessarily in any way reflect those of the International Labour Office.
* In this paper the term Latin America is meant to also include English-speaking Caribbean countries.

acting on the obstacles that affect the role of the labor market as an allocator of productive resources, and manpower planning;

• providing employment services for the special needs of members of population groups with very low incomes.

This paper will touch on these four dimensions without focusing on any one of them.

Employment is a means to expand a country's economic output by making a fuller use of its productive resources; as a means it also serves for the attainment of standards of living judged as desirable. Yet, in a way, employment can also be seen as an end in itself. For the individual, the status of being "employed" can be a precondition for self-respect. In this last sense, it has been written that long-term unemployment can be equated to a form of social rejection.

While the relevance of conceiving employment as a means needs no elaboration, the notion of employment as an end is more elusive. The distinction between both perceptions is not trivial. In cases where a trade-off may exist between high growth and employment objectives, a government should determine the weight it is going to assign to each of the objectives. Moreover, emphasis on seeing employment exclusively as a means leads to the need of evaluating an employment strategy against alternative means that might serve the same ends more efficiently. For instance, under certain conditions, alleviating the plight of the unemployed via income transfers might be preferable, in view of opportunity costs, to relying on employment creation for the same purpose.

Furthermore, the conceptual distinction between employment creation as a means and as an end has a bearing on whether development should treat employment generation as a by-product of output growth, or whether explicit development strategies are to be set around specific employment goals. In this connection, while considerable lip service is paid to the high priority employment generation deserves in development planning, quite frequently projects purportedly designed to deal with the issue of unemployment are evaluated on the basis of conventional cost-benefit analyses in which little value is assigned to the generation of employment. In these instances, the employment impact of such projects (or plans) is assessed after the fact, if at all. Obviously, when attacking unemployment is the main goal, this is an awkward procedure.

In this light, it would seem that a fundamental realm for action by international agencies relates to the assistance they could offer national governments in the assessment of potential trade-offs between employment creation and other major objectives.*

GENERAL ASPECTS OF THE
UNEMPLOYMENT SITUATION IN THE REGION

There is wide across-country variation in unemployment levels; nevertheless, the rate of open unemployment for the average country may be placed at approximately 8%. More meaningful concepts of unemployment make it possible to establish that the degree of overall underutilization of the labor force is around 27%.† This situation is not likely to change significantly during the 1980s.

The causes of unemployment are diverse, and their interrelation is complex. In regard to Latin America one could mention, as salient factors, high rates of population and labor force growth, a neglected agricultural sector, the limited capacity to absorb labor by high-growth modern manufacturing sectors, and an inadequate development of its human resources. In turn, these factors are causally twined together with technological processes, noncompetitive production structures, distortions in the relative prices of production factors, and the overall performance of labor markets.

In reference to the incidence of unemployment, the following points are worth noting. Although one does find evidence of significant unemployment among relatively well educated persons, in general the correlation between education and unemployment is negative. This may be due to higher skill requirements by evolving technologies or to the fact that, in markets where there is a substantial excess supply of labor resources, industries will tend to upgrade their skill demands for specific occupations. Undoubtedly both causes are at work. Overall, family heads are not the persons most affected by open unemployment, which falls, primarily, on the young, the inexperienced and women.

---

* In no way this should be interpreted as implying that a trade-off between growth and employment objectives is likely to exist. Fortunately this is often not the case.

† See Programa Regional del Empleo para América Latina y El Caribe (PREALC), *El Problema del Empleo en América Latina: Situación, Perspectivas y Políticas*, (Santiago de Chile: PREALC, 1976).

Probably the most dramatic change taking place in the Latin American labor market is the increase in the labor force participation rates of women. While the strength of this rise differs across countries, the trend is quite clear for the majority of them. Even though the nature of the causal relations is not well understood, the change is surely related to modifications in fertility patterns, to a widening of educational opportunities, and to alterations relating to the role of women in society. The social implications of the changing pattern in the labor supply of women, along with the apparent existence of wage and occupational discrimination by sex has attracted the interest of the academic community and the international agencies. The issue should continue to deserve priority attention.

Another important happening worth noting also refers to the internal functioning of the labor market. The last twenty years have evidenced that an increasing proportion of the labor force finds employment in small-scale industry and services, which, together with construction, might serve as the entry port into the urban sector for rural–urban migrants. It is estimated that these small-scale units, sometimes generically identified as the informal or casual sector, absorb around 35% of the urban labor force in Latin America. The limited information that exists supports the contention that rural–urban migrants experience a rise in their relative income and productivity levels.* This event has also aroused the attention of researchers and policymakers; this interest is warranted and should be encouraged. Helping governments to assess the interactions between labor market conditions, migration flows, and the ports-of-entry into the labor market should lead to consequential policy guidelines.

THE SPECIFIC AREAS

Two broad types of areas for policy action, each consisting of a set of three areas, are outlined in the chapter. The first type relates to setting or strengthening the infrastructure for employment planning; the second refers to priority sectors. In dealing with the issues that are mentioned below, the countries would be also addressing themselves to the four basic policy dimensions mentioned at the beginning of the chapter.

---

* Relative to the levels experienced prior to migration as well as to the levels of comparable nonmigrants at the place of origin.

Naturally, priorities will change across countries. In general, the countries that are behind in the development process should probably place a greater emphasis on aspects relating to the infrastructure; these countries will collectively be referred to as relatively less developed countries (RLDCs). In comparison, for the remaining countries a greater effort might be directed to the policy sectors. It probably goes without saying that differences in the priorities established for each group of countries is just a matter of degree, and that both sets of policy areas are relevant for all countries in the region.

It is felt that through attention to the areas mentioned, and to the policy issues involved, progress will be made toward the attainment of long-run employment objectives, as well as in the achievement of goals pertaining to short-time horizons.

The Groundwork for Policy Design and Implementation

The areas sketched in this subsection refer to the institutional structure, the preparation of training programs for employment planning, and the data base. The rationale for the selection of these areas is that they are an essential part of the foundation for effective policy actions. Much of what is mentioned is relevant for policy making related to social issues in general.

Strengthening the Institutional Structure

There is considerable need to integrate the work of the agencies that have a major responsibility for providing inputs for employment planning. A frequent experience international "experts" encounter when called to provide technical assistance to governments is the lack of adequate institutional arrangements through which employment strategies may be designed and implemented. The emphasis here is not on technical competence but, rather, on authority and efficient organization. As it unfortunately happens in many other instances of development planning, when they exist, employment policies are frequently made on a piecemeal basis that results in a motley of inconsistent objectives and guidelines.

Although in principle labor ministries are responsible for identifying the employment issues that call for priority attention (shortages and surpluses of specific skills, for example), for carrying useful records of employment conditions, and for suggesting or setting basic guidelines for the employment strategy, more often than not these ministries are ill suited for these tasks and, in a significant number of cases, no serious attempt is made to carry them through. Likewise, planning ministries are supposed to integrate employment objectives and related project and policy guidelines in national development plans; moreover, it is presumed that they have, at the minimum, some say in the implementation of such guidelines. Yet, the region development plans are frequently decorative documents, planning agencies have scarce real power, and there is often little functional communication and integration in the work of both ministries.

The situation relating to the interaction with other fundamental agencies, such as the ministries of education and finance, is similar. As the wide scope for employment projects and policies requires the collaboration of practically all major agencies, the lack of interagency cooperation is of transcendental significance.

A simplified version of an effective scheme for employment planning could be seen as follows. Together with the labor ministry, and with the collaboration of the authorities responsible for the fiscal and monetary policies, the ministry of planning would set the macroeconomic employment goals and related objectives pertaining to the welfare of specific population groups. In these endeavors both ministries would work jointly with the National Statistical Agency, which would bear the main responsibility for the collection, processing, and initial analysis of the relevant data. In turn, once preliminary objectives are set, individual ministries—and, to some extent, other public and private institutions—would submit projects geared to the attainment of the objectives established. These projects would be evaluated by the planning ministry and by interagency committees.

In practice one sees little coordination, with individual agencies going along separate ways. Labor Ministries, for instance, frequently play no significant part in the adoption of policies designed to stimulate employment; their role is commonly limited to advising on social legislation, intervening in collective bargaining processes or labor disputes, and operating labor exchanges.

In view of the above, it would seem that basic assistance to many national governments by international agencies should be geared to strengthening interagency links and communication channels, to helping allocate the responsibility for employment planning among agencies, and to helping specify the planning process.

Training for Public Officials

The importance of forming cadres of competent technical officials in RLDC's can hardly be exaggerated. Although it is unfair and inaccurate to make across-the-board statements, it can be stated that, in general, in RLDC's government officials in technical positions are deficiently trained. This weakness should not be surprising, given the traditional shortcomings of educational systems in these countries.

The lack of appropriate training limits the benefits that national technicians could derive from working alongside international counselors and, moreover, prevents them from following agreed guidelines on their own. A complicating factor is that government is often not able to compete with the private sector for well-trained personnel because of adverse wage structures and the absence of a well-established civil service system offering reasonable prospects for career development. A net result of this combination of elements is that innovative capacity is too limited, and tasks are done on a routine basis.

As a consequence of the points that have been made, technical assistance relating to policy-making in social issues often falls short of its goals. International technical advisors can stay in aid-recipient countries frequently for only short periods. It is assumed that, working in conjunction with national counterparts, they will make a positive contribution to the determination of priority issues and to the determination of methodological approaches or technical procedures needed to arrive at relevant answers. Ideally, after a period of collaboration, national technicians would be able to proceed independently. Unfortunately, it often does not work out that way. Instead, after the departure of the international advisors, who frequently bear the brunt of the work involved in identifying issues and in providing answers, little else is accomplished.

Granted that the modus operandi according to which technical assistance is offered is also frequently deficient; there are unfortunate instances in which, for example, international advisors are ill suited for the tasks to which they have been assigned. But this is a different issue. It would seem, nevertheless, that most of the problem lies in the inadequate training of officials in technical positions as well as in the failure to see international technical assistance as a means for technological diffusion instead of simply as a way of obtaining free man-hours resources. The high priority that correcting this misconception deserves is clear to many seasoned field officers.

The solution would seem to lie in a two-pronged approach, according to which greater weight would be placed by technical assistance and donor agencies in promoting the training of middle- to high-level personnel in technical positions, and in contributing to the organization of an efficient civil service system. The neglect of the latter aspect would probably lead to high turnover, as these persons leave the government sector for more attractive work opportunities, thus resulting in the loss of many of the benefits that could result from the provision of increased training to public service officials.

Presenting the outline of training programs in manpower issues lies beyond the scope of this paper. Nonetheless, it is appropriate to indicate basic characteristics that such programs might have.*

One aspect of these programs is the institutions to which they should be addressed. As has been indicated, almost all government agencies have a role to play in the design and implementation of employment policies, and, accordingly, all could benefit from training schemes. However, given the fact that resource constraints will surely limit the number of agencies that may be reached during a comparatively brief span of time, it is proposed that training for employment planning be directed mainly to the ministries of planning, labor, and education. It is assumed that the essential responsibilities for determining what employment issues have priority and for setting basic policy strategies rests with these agencies.

A second aspect relates to the type of training. In this connection it would seem that training programs should be designed to make up or compensate for the emphasis on memorization and the dogmatism so typical of education systems in many RLDC's. Accordingly, training programs should accentuate problem-solving aspects and the application of technical procedures. Probably a first stage, at which basic aspects of statistics, survey and sampling techniques, and principles of project administration were taught would serve as an adequate preparatory phase for subject areas directly related to employment issues. Courses dealing with such issues as techniques for the evaluation of the employment effects of projects and the range of technological alternatives in specific industries (and the cost of such alternatives), as well as in manpower planning and the application of labor-market economic models would fit well in a second phase.

A third aspect that ought to be mentioned relates to the convenience of launching national or regional training programs. The former programs would be directed exclusively to officials of a given

---

* Obviously much of the need for these programs would cease to exist if the formal educational systems were efficient and in tune with country necessities. While helping reform educational systems is certainly an area for international assistance, the undertaking involves a long-term horizon; these are approaches that could be developed in relatively short periods of time.

country; the latter would include as participants officials from a set of selected countries. Each type of program has relative advantages and disadvantages. However, attempting to structure both types of programs so that one would complement the other seems a meritorious idea. One way of accomplishing this objective would be to include in regional programs only the more complex techniques and to invite to them participants who have excelled in the national programs.

Strengthening the Statistical Base

The third major priority area for international action relates to the need of improving statistics relevant to policy making for employment creation. Information that permits the timely identification of changing labor market conditions and the tracing of the impact of policy measures is needed. This means detailed, periodic, and dependable data.

Approximately 20 years ago, President Kennedy referred to the tasks of the Presidents' Committee to Appraise Employment and Unemployment Statistics in the following terms:*

> These statistics are of vital importance as measures of the economic health and well-being of the Nation. They serve as guides to public policy in the development of measures designed to strengthen the economy, to improve programs to re-employ the unemployed, and to provide assistance to those who remain unemployed.

The case for these statistics is even more compelling in connections with RLDC's; their data systems can be described as incomplete, too limited in coverage, obsolete, and of doubtful reliability. The following deficiencies have recently been underlined by the International Labor Office: †

● Employment, unemployment, and underemployment concepts and definitions as used in industrialized countries are

---

* President's Committee to Appraise Employment and Unemployment Statistics, *Measuring Employment and Unemployment* (Washington: Government Printing Office, 1962) p. 9. Taken from Sar A. Levitan and Robert Taggart III, *Employment and Earnings Inadequacy a New Social Indicator* (Baltimore: The John Hopkins University Press, 1974), p. 2.

† See International Labour Office, Bureau of Statistics, "Recent Experience in Labour Force Sample Surveys in Developing Countries", in James Brown, et al. (editors) *Multi-Purpose Household Surveys in Developing Countries* (Paris: Organization for Economic Cooperation and Development, 1978), p. 159.

grossly insufficient for adequate analysis of employment in developing countries.

• The quality of the information is poor. Data on labor and nonlabor income is a good example: Information about it is frequently obtained indirectly by interviewing only available household members. These persons may not be well informed about income (and other labor market aspects) relating to other household members.

• Processing and tabulation of data often takes so long that it frequently loses much of its relevance for policy action.

• As sampling errors are not estimated (or reported), the precision of the data collected is indeterminate.

A more complete data base would call for the collection of information on such aspects as: people's perception of labor market opportunities, employment and income histories; personal mobility; labor force or employment status according to various specifications; rural-urban origin of younger and older generations; precise marital status; family income; opportunity cost of out-of-household female labor; parent's occupation and family status; characteristics of place of work including establishment size; level and type of education; sources of funds during first months of rural urban migration; source of information about labor market conditions and job opportunities; reservation wage or income; number of children per family; hours and earnings per industry; and credit sources for specific establishment types and industries. Much of this type of information should be collected on a periodic basis; it should also be amenable to relevant breakdowns such as by regional and urban-rural classes. Data relevant for the identification of population groups whose incomes are inadequate to satisfy basic needs deserve special attention.

In connection with the data needs that have been mentioned, the importance of surveys is enormous. Surveys supplement census data in a more expedient and less expensive fashion; moreover, as they make use of better trained and experienced personnel, the margin for human error is reduced.

Until recently, in Latin America only Costa Rica, Chile, Panamá, Venezuela, and Brazil carried out periodic national surveys covering both urban and rural areas.* In other countries, national household

---

* This and the following comments in the section are based on Programa Regional del Empleo para América Latina y El Caribe (PREALC), *Técnicas para la Planificación del Empleo en América Latina y El Caribe*, Working Papers Series (Chile: PREALC, 1980).

surveys with a national coverage have taken place only occasionally, if at all, and generally their coverage has been limited to selected cities or regions.

Establishment surveys are also an important source of information for employment planning. In most countries in the region, periodic establishment surveys have taken place, especially in connection with the manufacturing sector. One important gap in these surveys is the lack of information pertaining to small-scale establishments (usually establishments with less than five workers) by industry. While the difficulty of identifying these establishments is considerable, information on their characteristics and mode of operating is important in view of the significant potential that this type of establishment might have for the creation of productive employment in certain industries.

The construction of indicators or indexes appropriate for the assessment and changes in employment situations within short-term time horizons—a year, for example—is most important. On the basis of such assessment, corrective or compensatory measures directed to specific sectors or populations groups could be adopted. Naturally, in addition to the use of data on labor market aspects, the type of short-term policies referred to should be based on the analysis of other types of economic information (such as estimates of GNP, prices, and inventory changes). Moreover, much of the necessary information should be regularly gathered, at intervals of a few months.

Labor market indicators of the type mentioned have been classified as follows:*

1. Indexes relating to employment conditions:

   • open unemployment rate;

   • underemployment rates;

   • equivalent unemployment rates;

   • indicators of the distribution of the labor force by occupational category, establishment size, sector, region, age, sex, education, and number of hours worked.

2. Indexes relating to the income situation of population groups:

   • proportion of workers earning incomes equivalent to minimum wages;

---

* Each index, in turn, can be defined in various ways. See PREALC, op cit.

- median income of workers by education, sex, and age class;

- income or wage concentration indexes;

- indexes of disposable income.

3. Indicators of labor force supply conditions:

- proportion of school-age population registered in educational institutions;

- composition of the working-age population by age, sex, and education;

- estimates of migration inflows and outflows, by region;

- labor force participation rates by sex, age, education, and region;

- composition of the working-age population according to labor force status (inactive, employed, unemployed);

- proportional changes in the number of international immigrants by age, sex, and education.

The Sector Areas

The areas discussed in this subsection have been signaled for priority action on the grounds that they relate to current issues of strategic importance and that they are felt to be relevant for all countries in the region. These areas consist in rural development small-scale industries and technology and the close issues of human resources development and labor market information systems.

Rural Development for Employment

In contrast to the prevailing position of approximately ten years ago, the view that what seemed to be a deterioration in employment conditions in developing countries actually has basically been a transfer of disguised unemployment from rural to urban areas is now respectable. Regardless of whether rural–urban migrants improve their lot by migrating, as indeed seems to be the case, the limits to the provision of "adequate" employment and income in urban areas has placed the need for rural development back into the limelight. This is fortunate. Not only do rural activities seem to offer a wide range of alternatives for the generation of productive employment, but rural stagnation is a major stumbling block to economic growth and development.

As pointed out by FAO and ECLA, at the end of the 1970s the agricultural sector in Latin America was very different to what it used to be in 1950. The volume of agricultural production is currently more than 2.6 times what it was then, and the technological change has been significant. Yet, this advance notwithstanding, it is estimated that probably over 47 million persons suffer from malnutrition; moreover, because of institutional factors, the benefits of technological change have been fundamentally restricted to medium to large rural enterprises. As a result, poverty, income distribution, and unemployment in rural areas have not been as positively affected as they otherwise could have been.* Furthermore, stimuli to inappropriate technology might have had a perverse impact on rural employment.†

As discussed in other chapters, the general approach to rural development is inextricably linked to the wider issues of efficient exploitation of natural resources and comparative advantages in a dynamic setting. Yet the point that ought to be emphasized is that, as has been repeatedly indicated before, the attainment of a significant increase in productive rural employment requires the provision of various needed ancillary services as well as changes in land tenure systems. In recent years commendable attention to these issues has been given by international agencies; nevertheless, there is still much to be done. What is involved are additional efforts toward the creation of agro-based industries, the improvement of training and educational services, the construction of main secondary and feeder roads, and the development of facilities for the provision of credit and technical counseling services especially directed to the small farmer. Also, rural work programs could play an important role in generating productive employment opportunities for the most needy. They may also be used as a powerful instrument for compensating seasonal fluctuations in agricultural employment. To these ends rural work programs would be a useful complement to a careful selection and combination of crops, to crop rotation, to an increase in irrigation facilities, and to the use of adequate fertilizers.

---

* See Naciones Unidas, CEPAL, *América Latina en el Umbral de los Años 80* (1979) pp. 43-54.

† For an elaboration of this point in the context of a Latin American country please refer to Felipe Pazos, "Development and the Underutilization of Labour; Lessons of the Dominican Republic Employment Mission," *International Labour Review* (March 1975), pp. 235-249.

In addition to the issue of marked seasonal fluctuations in overall agricultural employment, a point that should be borne in mind is that, especially in countries in which agriculture still absorbs more than 50% of the labor force and which rely on one or two major crops, the simultaneous occurrence of rural labor shortages and surpluses in different areas is a field claiming for policy attention. In this context, projects aimed at identifying suitable crops with different harvest periods, as well as at setting irrigation systems that would make an increase in the number of crops per year possible, are most valuable. Attention should be also given to the potential contribution of cattle raising which, although not a labor-intensive activity, is at least a source of permanent employment.*

Much has been written about the importance of land reform/ redistribution plans, and it is not necessary to belabor the point here. It may be added, however, that in many countries the prospects for carrying out these schemes are not good unless accompanied by fair compensation.† Naturally, what is to be understood by "fair compensation" may be a moot point. A related aspect is that in countries where cultivable land is available, or where it could be made available if well integrated with other development efforts, projects for land rehabilitation may be a valuable source of employment and income creation.

Lastly, it should be mentioned that rural development for employment creation has few possibilities unless care is taken by governments to do away with policies that tend to discriminate against the rural sector. Examples of such policies are long-term measures adopted to stimulate manufacturing activities and certain patterns of public expenditures: While the former tend to raise the relative cost of agricultural production, the latter are frequently biased in favor of urban areas. At the country level, international agencies should intensify their efforts to raise government awareness of the negative implications of such types of policies.

Employment in Small Manufacturing Firms, Technology, and Related Aspects

The recent literature on unemployment has paid considerable attention to the closely related issues of identifying industrial activities in

---

* The author is grateful to Alberto Hintermeister of the ILO/PREALC staff for enlightening discussions on these points.
† Needless to say, this is not a sufficient condition.

which labor-using production techniques are efficient, the assessment of the factors that determine the selection of production techniques, and the potential that small-scale firms may have for the generation of productive employment opportunities. Concern with these issues has also led to still very limited research on the relative importance of product growth, the sector composition of industrial production, industrial concentration, and the size distribution of industrial establishments, on the generation of employment opportunities.* It must be emphasized that, for Latin America, evidence on these issues is still too fragmentary for categorical statements.

The scarcity of solidly based information notwithstanding, whatever evidence is available does suggest the following points:

1. There is a substantial range of activities in manufacturing in which labor-using methods are efficient. This relates both to the substitution of labor for capital in the central activities of specific industries, and to the application of labor-intensive procedures in such peripheral activities as handling of materials, packaging, storage, and the like. However, one feels that the adoption of precise and effective policy measures still calls for further investigation at the industry, subindustry, and activity/department levels. Also, additional investigation efforts are needed in connection with the relative importance of factor price distortions, deficient market information, and fear of social-institutional disruptions for decisions on production techniques.

2. Production growth seems to be more strongly correlated with employment creation than changes in the productivity of labor. Obviously, among other factors, these changes are related to technological processes and modifications in the sectorial structure of production. This, of course, does not imply that in Latin America, the impact of these latter factors on employment creation has been weak; certainly it has been substantial. What it does mean is that a long-term employment creation strategy should be designed in

---

* On these matters see, for example, David Morawetz, "Employment Implicatins of Industrialization in Developing Countries: A Survey," *The Economic Journal*, (September 1974), pp. 491–542; A. S. Bhalla, *Technology and Employment in Industry* (International Labour Office, 1975); and Juan J. Buttari (Technical Coordinator), *El Problema Ocupacional en América Latina; Concentración Industrial, Tecnologia v Empleo, Estudio ECIEL* (Buenos Aires: Ediciones STAP, 1979).

a context of high production growth. This aspect once again points out the importance of shedding light on potential trade-offs between employment-creation and production-growth mixes that might result from different policy combinations and emphases.

3. Concentration within industries (i.e., oligopolistic conditions in specific industries) seem to be positively associated with the use of capital-intensive technologies. Furthermore, it also appears that a positive correlation exists between industrial concentration and industry wage levels; in this connection, it makes sense to assume that industrial concentration probably affects the performance of labor markets by inducing distortions in the wage structure. It thus would seem that, other things being equal, industrial concentration might hinder the attainment of employment goals. Accordingly, policy stimuli for more competitive product markets may be important ingredients in employment planning.

4. In reference to small manufacturing firms, it has been pointed out that they:*

• tend to be more labor intensive than larger firms;

• have significant effects in terms of indirect employment creation;

• are the most efficient form of organization in many activities;

• have advantages in meeting the demands of low-income population groups—in part these advantages result from the fact that they may be better suited to differentiating products according to individual tastes and needs and are able to establish themselves near to where consumers are;

• are vehicles for entrepreneurial action.

Given these characteristics, it is obvious that tending to small-scale industries may be important for the generation of employment. This action course requires efforts directed at offsetting the major

---

* A summary of the case for small firms can be found in World Bank, *Employment and Development of Small Enterprises*, Sector Policy Paper (Washington DC: World Bank, 1978) and in A. S. Bhalla, "Technology and Employment: Some Conclusions", *International Labour Review* (March-April 1976), pp. 189–203.

problems faced by small firms; among these problems, a deficient access to conventional credit facilities and to marketing and training public programs may be mentioned. In addition to stimulating relevant research, international assistance agencies should encourage the exploration of areas for efficient subcontracting by large to small firms, foment the creation of financial intermediaries that would make credit accessible to small firms at reasonable rates, and work on the development needed to evaluate the economic potential of small firms.

Two factors that ought to be considered for these lines of action are that: (1) while in general there does seem to be a positive association between size and labor intensity, the relation is not necessarily monotonic and, in some industries, the positiveness of the association is not at all clear; (2) the economic potential of small firms has to be examined in a dynamic context as current prices might not be adequate indicators of the real costs. Both considerations underline the significant specificity by industry that measures directed at small firms might require.

Human Resources and Employment Systems

This area relates to the issues of skills development and their optimum allocation in the labor market. While the author considers that unemployment in Latin America is essentially a problem of too few jobs and as such not a consequence of labor market inefficiencies, surely policies addressed to high-need segments of the population and to the improvement of labor market performance will have an impact on the lot of the poor. Rather than commenting on a wide range of relevant subjects, the present subsection focuses on aspects referring to the provision of training, to the articulation of training programs directed toward the special problems of the poor and long-term unemployed (including the hidden unemployed), and to mechanisms that link people with jobs.

An approach that integrates general education and training programs with measures to encourage employment creation and industrial growth targets is needed. Present practices are quite deficient.* The determination of manpower requirements, of the supply of skills, and of efficient training programs, as well as the

---

* In part because of data constraints.

improvement of the flow of information in the labor market require a dynamic, interconnected, and coherent frame.

The interaction between training and production skills is complex. Technological change and modifications in the sectorial structure of production usually tend to alter the mix of skills required. Accordingly, insofar as the educational and training systems fail to deliver the skills demanded, growth and development are blocked. Yet, in contrast to how it has traditionally been perceived, the direction of causality between production and skills is not unidirectional.

The development of certain skills is likely to induce changes in the production structure. Education is a case in point. In addition to being a vehicle for imparting knowledge in specific disciplines, education affects values, attitudes and the capacity to reason. Thus it surely influences motivations and patterns of action and has an impact on variables directly related to economic production.

As is well known, the weight that should be given to education and training as tools for development has been an issue of recent controversy.* Yet, even if some of the effects attributed to education are questionable, the point being raised here is that the system for delivering skills should not be portrayed solely as a dependent variable of the production structure; such a system can also play the role of an independent variable.† The implication of this perspective is that while conventional manpower planning tends to estimate skill requirements as a function of projected changes in the economy, it fails to take into consideration the probable "forward-linkage" effects on the economy of education and training systems. In the context of manpower planning for long-run development, this omission would be corrected by a dynamic and systemic approach. Research-wise, this area, of immense potential implications for development and employment policies, is virtually virgin in Latin America. The fact that it seems that many governments are not able or willing to raise much more the proportion of resources assigned to education, and the shortcomings of educational systems in the

---

* One suspects that much of the controversy has resulted from misplaced emphasis; in the argument, the way a given educational system operates, and hence its output, have often been confused with the role of education at large.

† Of course, if as mentioned in the text, failure to deliver the skills required by a changing technology blocks growth and development, in an indirect way education would also be playing the role of an independent variable vis-à-vis production. The argument emphasized in this paper is that there is a *direct* way in which this role is performed.

region, add to the urgency of rethinking these aspects and achieving a more efficient approach.*

In a systems approach to manpower and employment policies, the role of placement centers becomes more complex. In addition to matching skills with jobs, these centers must play a central role in the design of training programs, as well as in linking the programs with the poor long-term unemployed. In fact, it is better to refer to an "employment system" rather than to placement centers.†

Traditionally the role of the placement centers has consisted in registering, testing, and counseling applicants for employment, as well as referring them to potential employers. As part of their new responsibilities, they must also be active in identifying activities in which the supply of jobs is likely to expand and the skills they would require; moreover, they must be able to assess the needs and relevant characteristics of the poor and long-term unemployed.‡ Moreover, for the sake of effectiveness, close ties have to be developed between the "employment system" and the business community. It is to be noted that because they lack the "right connections" to the extent that the channels of employment more frequently used are referrals from present employees, business associates, relatives, and friends of employers, the poor are at a disadvantage.§ This, of course, accentuates income distribution disparities.

The high priority of directing employment services to the poorest segments of the population has been emphasized throughout this chapter, and the importance of identifying the characteristics of the poor and long-term unemployed has also been mentioned. The rationale for this latter point is not hard to see. It might happen

---

* Overall, as implied in an earlier section, educational systems in Latin America do not seem to be geared to the development of the capacity to reason and of initiative. This must have an impact on entrepreneurial drives. Moreover—or because of it—as ECLA has pointed out, as recently as in 1975, in Latin America, less than 50% of the children who six years previously had become enrolled in primary education cycles actually finished such cycles; furthermore, more than 50% of those who failed never went beyond third grade. The source of these statistics is CEPAL, *América Latina en el Umbral de los Años 80*, p. 102.

† Actually, the term "employment system" is already being used in several Latin American countries.

‡ With regard to these issues, the changes needed are analogous to the efforts made in the United States in connection with the "disadvantaged minorities." See Sar A. Levitan, Garth L. Mangum and Ray Marshall, *Human Resources and Labor Markets*, 2nd ed. (New York: Harper and Row, 1976).

§ The author owes this point to Mr. Allen E. Broehl of the United States Agency for International Development.

that individuals belonging to different population groups would react differently to given employment and training opportunities. For example, faced with a program of job creation, the labor supply reaction of individuals belonging to a family unit would determine whether the corresponding family income would be raised or not. The outcome would hinge on factors such as how efficiently information flows in the labor market, as well as on the perceptions of the relative costs and benefits of working versus alternative activities. These perceptions might vary across population groups. The variation could be due to differences in preference maps, as well as to differences in the way persons of given demographic and socio-economic characteristics perceive labor market conditions and associated work opportunities. To the extent that social, cultural, and demographic factors have a bearing on the decision to engage in "socially productive" work, the objective of raising family income through employment opportunities might have to be complemented by policy approaches tuned to specific population groups. In addition to human development policies, the range of such approaches would include measures designed to affect family-specific costs of joining the labor market.*

---

* A more elaborate treatment of these points is contained in Juan J. Buttari, "The ECIEL Research Project on Economic and Demographic Determinants of Labor Supply in Latin America" (mimeo, 1978).

21

Education, Training, and Human Resources

Raul Allard

In this chapter, we shall deal first with some ideas about education and development and, in the second and third parts, with the most important problems of education at various levels both now and in the future as well as approaches to training, employment, and related topics. In the fourth part, we shall mention four multilateral international cooperation mechanisms in the field of education, both with regard to activities already accomplished and future policies. In the last part we will propose some conclusions. In view of the scope and variety of topics, the coverage in this chapter will necessarily be condensed and schematic.

EDUCATION AND DEVELOPMENT

In recent decades, especially since the end of the Second World War, Latin America has undergone a period of economic growth and expansion in its educational systems. Despite the efforts that have been made, the impoverished conditions in which the large majority live have not yet been overcome. The regional development strategy that originated in the 1950s and was elaborated on in the 1960s was structured with a view to establishing advanced economic sectors and geographic areas, particularly with regard to industrial productive capacity, but also including scientific, administrative, and communication areas, in the conviction that these advanced areas would stimulate the more traditional sectors. In the beginning, no importance was attached to either educational or social investment under this strategy. Later, education was conceived of as an economic growth factor, as an investment that would increase the growth rate. The sector was no longer considered as an expense limiting society's investment capacity, but came to be seen as an investment in the human resources that are needed as basic elements in creating and accelerating development. A number of government declarations, such as those that gave rise to the Alliance for Progress and the Declaration of the Presidents of America in 1967, stressed giving priority to education.

Toward the end of the 1960s, limits had been encountered both with regard to the possibility of modernization by import substitution and the view that investment in education resulted almost automatically in economic growth. The education policy of that decade tended toward improving the general internal efficiency of the system and improving external efficiency with respect to production of the capabilities and aptitudes required for accelerated economic development, expansion of enrollment at various levels, and a modernized curriculum reform. Based on that strategy, an unprecedented quantitative expansion of the formal system was achieved, along with renewal in various aspects, but without attaining universal basic education or reducing the low educational level of the adult population remaining outside the system. Moreover, curriculum, structural, and administrative factors continued to have a negative impact on educational performance, for example, failure to achieve closer adaptation of the educational system to the work world and employment possibilities. These aspects were especially serious in rural areas and marginal urban areas in the large cities, which underwent a disorganized process of urbanization.

The experience of recent years has given rise to a revision and expansion of the development concept, stressing its integral nature and the fact that it is primarily people who develop. Hence, development cannot be measured only by the goods or resources available to the community, but must basically be assessed in terms of the quality of the people who produce and use it. This approach was taken by the Latin American and Caribbean Ministers of Education, who defined a developed country in 1979 as one whose population is "informed, educated, efficient, productive, responsible and solidary."[1]

In 1980, the Ministers of Education stressed that "the process of educational development should be defined with a broad concept of integrated, harmonious and independent development whose central theme is the enhancement of the various dimensions of the individual and the satisfaction of his basic needs, with special emphasis on the promotion of the disadvantaged social sectors."[2]

In 1980, the World Bank stressed a comprehensive approach to development, underscoring the importance of education in three interrelated ways: as a basic human need, as a way of attaining other basic needs, and as an activity sustaining the speeding up of overall development.[3]

Education involves formal, nonformal, and informal processes designed to improve the current and potential capacity of human beings so that they may be able to achieve their own destiny and functions within the society. *Formal education* is institutionalized and systematized by the State and public or semipublic agencies. *Nonformal education* is systematized but not State-institutionalized. *Informal education* is not systematized and is provided through a number of channels and media, such as radio, the press, TV, experts training their apprentices, parents training their children, and so forth. Education involves the individual responsibility of each person to achieve his full human potential and to educate himself systematically in his youth and throughout his life, the responsibility of the family to initiate education and provide a formative environment propitious for development of the body and the mind, the responsibility of educational systems to train citizens imbued with a spirit of service to the community and the values of respect for human dignity, the responsibility of educators to formulate objectives and prescribe tasks that will harmoniously train the student to utilize his creative and productive capacity, combining theory and practice, research and action, knowledge and work, assimilation of traditions, creativity and social change, and the responsibility of the cultural and the mass communications media to transmit ethical and aesthetic values and inform and entertain in a responsible manner. Education appears to be a complex phenomenon, with a social function that has an impact and provides feedback on all other functions, shaping the human resources that will take part in various human activities. There is a tendency to go beyond viewing the educational system as a closed pyramid system, with the university at the peak and primary education at the base. Education appears to be both a set of formal and nonformal mechanisms, as well as a common responsibility that must be assumed by the entire society. There is also stress on education that concentrates on the subject who is learning, and emphasizes learning rather than teaching. Knowledge is viewed as a way of personal and collective creation rather than merely a cumulative acquisition of information. Such concepts involve changes in the practice of teaching, which should train the student to investigate, integrate, and select available information instead of confining itself to transmitting knowledge. The teacher's function is restated and becomes active and inductive, with a recognition that the student is an active agent in his own education.

PROBLEMS AND TRENDS IN
LATIN AMERICAN EDUCATION

Two Factors Having an Impact on Schooling: Demographic Growth and Urbanization

According to recent statistics, Latin America and the Caribbean had an annual population growth rate in the 1960s and 1970s of 2.8%, the highest in the world. It is important to stress that the share of Latin America and the Caribbean in the total work population rose from 7.1% to 8.4% in 1980.[4]

This annual growth rate is largely concentrated in five countries, representing 69.9% of the region's total population: Brazil, Colombia, Mexico, Peru, and Venezuela, which grew at a 3.1% rate.

In absolute figures, these growth rates meant increasing from a population of 211 million in 1960 to 366 million in 1980, a 73.5% rise in 20 years. If the estimated 2.6% annual demographic growth rate for the next 20 years is accepted, Latin America will have 612 million people by the year 2000, or 9.8% of the world's population. This demographic growth is reflected in the age structure and geographic distribution of the population, as shown in Table 21.1.

The table shows the population structure and growth rate in the 5- to 24-year age group, which is the group requiring primary, secondary, and tertiary education (basic, intermediate, and higher). The population of this age group has risen 3% a year in recent decades. Its share of total population has risen during this period as

TABLE 21.1. Structure of Latin American and Caribbean Population for 1960–1980 and Projections to the Year 2000 (in Millions)

	1960	1970	1980	1990	2000
Population in Millions	211	278	366	473	612
Urban %	48.6	56.8	63.7	69.4	75.0
Rural %	51.4	43.2	36.3	30.6	25.0
0–4 Years					
m	36	45	56	73	95
%	17.1	16.2	15.8	15.5	15.5
5–24 Years					
m	92	126	166	215	278
%	43.6	45.3	45.4	45.5	45.5
25 Years and over					
m	83	107	142	185	239
%	39.3	38.5	38.8	39.0	39.0

Source: Quantitative education and enrollment projects for the educational systems of Latin America and the Caribbean. 0/79 MINELAC/Ref. 2, 1979.

follows: In 1960, this age group (5–24) accounted for 43.6% of the population; in 1980, it reached 45.5%. For the world as a whole, these percentages reached 40 and 45%, respectively. This shows that the pressures to expand the educational systems were strong in the region in recent decades for purely demographic reasons, without taking into consideration the already existing shortfalls due to the time-lag problem.

Another factor bearing on the level and demand for schooling in Latin America is the relatively high rate of urbanization. As shown in Table 21.1, the region's urbanization rate, which in 1960 was 48.6%, rose to 56.8% in 1970, and was projected at 63.7% for 1980. Hence, urban population rose 4% and rural population about 1%. The average world-wide urbanization rate was projected at 41% for 1980, with a 30% average for the developing countries. Latin America's rates (particularly in Argentina, Chile, Uruguay, and Venezuela) did not differ markedly from those of the developed countries, which reached an average urban population of 72% in 1980.

TABLE 21.2. Relationship between Total Number of Students Enrolled in Latin America and the Caribbean, and the World, for 1950-1975 (Millions)

Region	1950	1960	1970	1980
Latin America and the Caribbean	17.0	31.1	56.7	74.2
World-wide	221.5	329.1	492.7	569.2
Ratio of Latin America and the Caribbean/World (5)	7.7	9.5	11.5	13.0

Source: *Yearbook Statistique,* UNESCO, 1978.

Educational Systems and Enrollment Trends

The educational systems of Latin American countries differ considerably with respect to the age of entry into the system, the number of years at each level, and the total length of schooling. The age of entry into the basic system ranges from 5 to 7 years. The length of basic education ranges from 5 to 9 years. In most countries, it is 6 years, although there is a trend to extend and modify basic education, the most recent case being that of Venezuela. At the second level (intermediate or secondary education), there are also differences, owing to the splitting-up of this level into a first and second cycle. Entry into secondary education occurs between 11 and 15 years of age, as a result of the differences noted in basic education.

The increase in school enrollment is a world-wide phenomenon, as shown in Tables 21.2 and 21.3.

Latin America and the Caribbean have increased their percentage share of world-wide school enrollment from 7.7% in 1950 to 13% in 1975.

It can be seen that the relative decrease in the number of students in basic education as compared with total number of students is a world-wide trend. This trend, which would be natural for countries that have already achieved efficient universal basic education, is adverse for those developing countries that continue to have deficits at the primary level. (See Table 21.4.) Primary enrollment rose from 27 million in 1960 to 60 million in 1977; secondary enrollment, from 2.8 million in 1960 to 14.7 million in 1977; and higher education, from 546,000 in 1960 to 4.3 million in 1977.

TABLE 21.3. Structural Changes in the Educational System Compared to
Total Enrollment at Each Level, 1970–1974

Level of Education	World		Latin America	
	1950	1975	1950	1975
Primary	80.0	66.9	88.5	78.5
Secondary	17.2	26.5	9.8	16.6
Higher	2.8	6.6	1.7	4.9

Source: Education in Latin America and the Caribbean, Enrollment and Rates of School
Attendance 1960–76. UNESCO–CSR–E–33; June 1979.

Adult Illiteracy

Illiteracy in the population over 15 years of age is a particularly
acute problem for the region. Although there is a continuous reduction in relative or percentage figures, the absolute number of adult
illiterates is very high, which has a human, social, and economic
impact. (See Table 21.5.)

In analyzing illiteracy, a number of factors must be taken into
consideration: (1) Its incidence differs in the various countries of the
region, as shown in Appendix 1; (2) The relative reduction in illiteracy
is the result of two parallel trends: first, new generations reaching
15 years of age have had better opportunities for schooling than
previous generations and they are more numerous; moreover, some
massive adult literacy campaigns (for example, in Brazil) have been

TABLE 21.4. Growth by Educational Levels in Latin America

	1960–65	1965–70	1970–75	1960–75
Basic Education	5.6	5.4	3.9	5.0
Secondary Education	10.4	8.3	9.3	9.3
High Education	9.8	12.4	16.1	12.7

Source: Education in Latin America and the Caribbean, Enrollment and Rates of School
Attendance 1960–76, UNESCO–CSR–E–33; June 1979.

TABLE 21.5. Illiteracy in Latin America and the Caribbean for 1960–1980 and Projections up to the Year 2000

Years	Total Population (Millions)	Population (-15 years)	Population (15 years +)	Illiteracy (Millions)	% Illiteracy (15 years +)
1950	156	62.9	92.7	38	41.0%
1960	211	90	121	40	33.1
1970	278	119	159	44	27.7
1980	366	151	215	43	20.0
1990[1]	473	195	278	38	13.7
2000[1]	612	249	363	36	10.0

[1]Projections

Source: "Evaluacion cuantitativa y proyecciones de matricula de los sistemas educativos de America Latina y el Caribe. EO–79/MINEOLAC/REF.2 1979" Análisis Demográfico de la situación educativa CELADE ST/ECCA/CONF.10 L.8. 1962.

successful; (3) Estimates for the coming years are based on both natural trends and the assumption that, according to the policies and programs announced by the governments, the countries will make intensive organizational and economic efforts in this field (even so, by the year 2000 there will be 36 million illiterates—in other words, 10% of the population over 15 years of age—projected for that year); (4) Other structural aspects of illiteracy in the region show its relationship to urban-rural, age, and sex distributions. In general, the analyses made by the OAS and UNESCO conclude that in Latin America, the greatest disparity in illiteracy is observed, on the average, in rural areas as compared with urban areas and in populations over 20 (slightly higher for women).

In recent years there has been a firm political resolve by the countries to initiate massive literacy programs, within a more comprehensive approach that includes not only reading and writing, but also postliteracy training, specific training, and basic job training through a number of modalities. This resolve is reflected in the Declaration of Mexico and the CIECC resolution on the Development of Education in the Eighties. Both of these declarations at the ministerial level headed their priority courses of action with the one "to eradicate illiteracy before the end of this century and to devise strategies for covering the marginal sectors of the population whose level of schooling is unsatisfactory."

Basic or Primary Education

Development centering on man necessarily requires a real effort to enable the entire population to attain the minimum levels of schooling that they are entitled to and that will enable them to participate as agents in the development process.

The population between 6 and 11 years of age constitutes the theoretical demand for basic education. Between 1960 and 1976, as a result of substantial effort by the countries, school enrollment for this age group increased from 57% to 78%. During that same period, primary education expanded at a 4.1% rate, which, while significant, is less than the growth rate for previous periods. Eleven million children between 6 and 11 years of age remained outside the school system in 1970/77.

The future demand for basic education will be expanded by two factors: the increase in this age group, which will grow from 51 million in 1975 to 90 million in the year 2000, and the fact that large population groups over 11 years of age (adolescents and young adults) must also be educated at this level. The latter fact explains why school enrollment in some countries exceeds 100% of the total number of children in this age group.

A number of studies show a general uptrend in the countries with respect to enrollment of school-age children. Thus, for example, in 1960, ten countries had enrollment rates under 50%: Bolivia, Brazil, Colombia, El Salvador, Honduras, Mexico, Nicaragua, Peru, Guatemala, and Haiti. In 1970, one country (Haiti) had a school enrollment rate under 40%, and three countries (El Salvador, Guatemala, and Nicaragua) had a rate ranging from 50 to 40%, while in the other countries, rates had risen considerably.

There are still no exact figures for 1980, but projections show that the improvement in some countries, like Mexico, Panama, Costa Rica, Ecuador, Peru, Dominican Republic, Bolivia, Brazil, Colombia, and Nicaragua, has continued. At the upper end, five countries had rates higher than 90% in 1970: Argentina, Barbados, Cuba, Chile, and Jamaica. This accelerated evolution, which constitutes the global demand for primary education, will mean a strong pressure for greater financial, material, and even more, human resources. Up to the end of the 1970s, this quantitative expansion was partly absorbed by increases in the sector's yield—in other words, by obtaining enrollment growth rates that were higher than resources growth rates for this level. This was possibly largely because of the use of physical infrastructure in more than one shift, the change in teaching methods, the improved assignment and upgrading of teachers, better techniques for planning, and management of educational resources. In addition it was also necessary to expand the physical infrastructure, the number of classrooms and staff.

Dropouts and Repeaters in Primary Education

At the regional level, only about 500 out of every 1,000 children enrolled during the last decade in the first year of primary school completed the fourth grade. The problem was even more serious 20 years ago. In 1960, of every 100 children who entered the first grade of primary school, 37 reached the fourth grade, and 26 the fifth grade. Of 100 students entering school in 1970, 47 reached the fourth grade in 1973, and 41 the fifth grade in 1974.

The retention rate in primary school over the last decade ranged from over 80% (Guyana and Uruguay) to over 40% (Brazil, Colombia, Guatemala, and Nicaragua). Aside from the socioeconomic and internal reasons for dropouts, this situation is attributable to the fact that the schools, particularly in the rural area, do not offer all grades (incomplete schools).

A recent study[5] stresses the internal cause of dropouts, implying that the problem can be reduced in a number of ways: provide an educational content more relevant to the students and their parents, train teachers to provide a more individualized education adapted to the living conditions of the child, furnish texts, equipment, and school libraries, and improve the student's self-esteem.

Repeaters also offset the improvement in primary educational coverage. In 1970 and 1975, the repeater rate in the first five years of primary education was 15.7% and 13.6%, respectively, which, in absolute figures, means over 6 million repeaters in that last year. The key problem in this case is not so much the dilemma of whether to promote or not to promote but rather improving the level of children with low performance and predicting and preventing scholastic failure.

Intermediate, Secondary, or Second-Level Education

The population that is theoretically included in the secondary level of education is the 12 to 17 age group. According to estimated growth rates, that group will rather rapidly grow up to the year 2000. In fact, the population of 43.7 million in 1975 is expected to reach 80.6 million in the year 2000, an 84.4% increase, or a 2.48% annual rate over the last quarter of the century. The effective demand for secondary education also includes those who are over that age, either because of late enrollment or repeaters.

Secondary education enrollment expanded at a high rate in the 1970s, rising from 8 million students in 1971 to approximately 16 million in 1978. If that trend continues, enrollment will rise from 12.1 million in 1975 to 37.1 million in the year 2000, increasing 207.8% over that period. The progressively larger number of students who complete primary school will increase the pressure on secondary school enrollment. The expected demand at this level will represent a strong pressure for greater financial, material, and human resources, especially teachers, teacher's aides, and administrative personnel. Until the end of the 1970s, these services had been able to expand in general education largely because of improved performance of the sector. However, the number of teachers also increased significantly. Vocational-technical education at the secondary level has as a general rule suffered from a shortage of equipment and contents that are inadequate to the possibilities of the productive sector. Other countries have modernized this sector, in many cases with the assistance of international aid and financing agencies.

Some countries have extended primary education, in response to numerous recommendations by international conferences, by absorbing the first two grades of traditional secondary education. Other educational reforms have divided the secondary level into two cycles, from 2 to 3 years each, with a basic cycle that is more or less standard and a second cycle that provides more diversified vocational training.

As Table 21.6 shows, the majority of students continue to choose "general" and humanistic education. Twenty-seven percent of the students at the secondary level attended technical schools in 1975, half of them taking business courses. In most countries, farm or agriculture courses accounted for less than 10% of secondary enrollment. These trends do not appear to have changed over the last 20 years.

TABLE 21.6. Enrollment by Type of Secondary Education (Percentages)

Type	1960	1970	1971
General	64.8	71.2	65.7
Technical	25.7	23.4	27.5
Teacher Training	9.5	5.4	4.8

Source: UNESCO estimate

Diversified Cycle of Secondary Education

This cycle prepares the student for going-on studies and for entering the labor market. There are three choices in secondary vocational education and in nonuniversity higher education in the countries:[6] (1) full vocational training for the entire student body at these levels to prepare them to enter the labor market directly—this involves problems of high cost and the difficulty of overcoming rigidity in the national technical school structure, which hampers the adaptation of those schools to the productive sector's requirements; (2) basic technical training for the entire secondary school population, with later specific training replacing out-of-school vocational training or training in the work place, which involves the risk of reducing the technical content of the training and preparing insufficient manpower for the labor market; and (3) diversification of options—full vocational training or basic technical training.

Higher Education

The 18- to 23-year-old population constitutes the potential demand for higher education. Between 1970 and 1977, school enrollment at the various levels rose from 55 million to 78.7 million. The largest percentage growth rate was in higher education (171%), while secondary education increased 91%, and primary education 30%. University growth rates exceeded those of secondary education in the last decade, and there was a trend to expand the supply at higher levels. Higher education enrollment rose from 600,000 students in 1960 to about 4 million in 1978.

According to demographic estimates, the 18- to 23-year-old population will rise from 36.5 million in 1975 to 69.9 million in the year 2000. Since 2.5% of that age group attended universities in 1961 and that percentage increased to 9.6% in 1975, it is estimated that by the end of the century, if these trends continue unchanged, 19.9% of that age group (or 13,851,000) will be in a position to enroll in the universities.

An OAS meeting of nongovernmental experts[7] identified a number of problems in higher education: pressures for increased enrollment as a result of a number of socioeconomic and educational factors; the explosive increase of knowledge and information, especially in scientific and technological fields; structural and operational problems of present higher education institutions; the fact that more vigorous economies have not resulted in an equivalent increase in the demand for professional workers; and the complexity of economic and social development, which causes a trend toward diversification of specialties.

These and many other situations require viewing higher education as a complex system of institutions and mechanisms within which the university plays an important but not exclusive role. Rational decentralization of university activities has also been tried out through regional or provincial universities or centers to avoid overcrowding. Diversification in the course of studies offered in higher education can be achieved in a way that does not create rigid academic structures tending to perpetuate themselves. Lastly, progress in scientific knowledge requires updating the teaching methods used in the universities and a more active role of the student in his own learning.

Vocational Training System

Depending on the country, this system is under the ministry of education or labor, or is connected with autonomous agencies or public or private companies. The vocational training system primarily provides in-service training for those already in the labor force and to a lesser extent for those who are laid off or are seeking work for the first time. Short courses designed for specific jobs are usually offered. It is essential for the choices provided to tie in with immediate requirements and with the changing labor market situation.

From the standpoint of curriculum organization, vocational training is an open system that serves all occupational levels: unskilled, semi-skilled, skilled, and highly skilled workers. In addition, the 14 to 18 age group is regularly trained through "apprentice systems." Courses are given at vocational training centers, in businesses, through mobile units, and so forth.

In some Latin American countries, vocational training institutions give courses for middle-level technicians. Analysis of this sector shows the diversity of these institutions, now numbering 27, established during the last 25 years in the region. The first courses were offered by CONET in Argentina and by SENAI and SENAC in Brazil in 1955. Between 1955 and 1975, participants in these programs increased from 175,000 to 1,800,265, expanding coverage in 1978 to 3,168,657. This spectacular growth, especially in 1975/78, occurred in Bolivia, Brazil, Colombia, Chile, Ecuador, Honduras, and Venezuela, which more than doubled their coverage. Despite the considerable effort made by vocational training institutions in the region, their impact on the total number of the labor force is still insignificant in most countries. Regionally, participants in these programs represented only 2.3% of the labor force in 1973, increasing to 3.26% in 1978. This ratio ranged from 0.24% for Bolivia to 8.87% for Colombia.

Preschool or Initial Education

In 1970/75, preschool education rose at an annual rate of 96% in Latin America. However, in absolute figures, it only totaled 2.3 million children, an insignificant proportion of the total number of children between 1 and 6 years of age. It is at this stage that the bases for the child's cognitive processes are established and the basic characteristics and structure of his personality take shape. Other studies show that negative environmental factors and nutritional deficiencies have pathological impacts on the intellectual development and physical growth of the child. It is being recognized in Latin America that massive development of preschool education makes it possible to reduce the differences in the set of skills with which children enter elementary school.

The countries of the region are trying out various kinds of preschool education. Some are more institutionalized and tied in with formal education, other are nonformal or not given in school, with the latter prevailing. In specific cases these efforts are also promoted and supervised by the ministries of education. In the case of the OAS, there is a growing demand for technical assistance in preschool education as well as in special education for handicapped children.

Planning, Administration, and Decentralization

As a general rule, educational policies are set by the central government. Ministries of education are responsible for the development of these policies and are usually organized at three levels: (1) the highest policy level, composed of the minister, his immediate advisers, and usually a national educational council and a planning office; (2) an administrative level, composed of bureaus in charge of the various levels of education and specific programs; and (3) an implementation level coordinated at the provincial, regional, or local level.

This outline of course refers more to unitary countries than to countries with a federal system.

In the 1960s, great importance was attached to educational planning as a tool, and almost all of the countries have sectoral planning offices that formulate medium and short-range sectoral plans or, as required, assist the Central Planning Office, although this coordination has serious limitations in practice. A significant lack of coordination has been detected between the planning and administration stages.

In recent years, as a reaction to administrative centralization, a number of countries have set up regionalization or decentralization systems with various objectives, including better adaptation to socio-geographic characteristics of the environment in which the educational institutions operate and providing equal service to all regions. Under this trend, actions with varied specific objectives can be envisaged for the 1980s, according to the situation and policies in the individual country: administrative decentralization and deconcentration; nuclear school systems; greater emphasis on the educational role of regional and local agencies; mechanisms for community participation in support of the local school; adaptation of educational planning and curriculum development to adjust educational activities to the requirements of the environment; specific plans in pilot areas, and so forth.

Qualitative Change

A number of countries in the region have undertaken change or reform programs. Some are comprehensive and affect even goals of the system, while others are more specific and relate to a particular level, such as increasing the number of years of basic education, diversifying secondary education, introducing educational technology, establishing vocational guideline policies, changing the teacher training system, modernizing the universities, establishing middle-level technical training systems, employing open education, etc. International cooperation mechanisms have helped with the introduction of changes and innovations, especially in training the specialists required for implementing them.

Despite the progress made, the great challenge for the next decade is to review the contents or programs that still maintain their encyclopedic character, lack of adaptation to educational objectives, rigidity, and inadequate psychological bases. Some programs have an excessively detailed normative character that does not leave sufficient room for the teacher's initiative. General secondary education appears to be designed almost entirely as a stepping stone to higher education and lacks real terminal character. A recent CIECC resolution stresses the need for qualitative curriculum changes that include the flexibility required to adapt them to the various situations in each country, greater pertinence of contents and improvement in evaluation systems, incorporation of scientific-technological, ecological, and cultural variables in the curricula at each level, enhancing the value of work, and using participatory methodologies that favor reflection, a critical spirit, and creativity.

Any qualitative change must have a counterpart in improvements in the teaching staff. The total number of teachers at various levels rose from 1,183,000 in 1960 to some 3,200,000 in 1975. In 1960, twelve countries in the region had 30% or more primary teachers without degrees, while only six countries were in that position in the following decade. Starting in the 1960s, there was a trend to training teachers, even elementary school teachers, in the universities. Currently, a number of countries are revising this approach, and the trend is to stress the use of a variety of institutions to train teachers (universities, teacher colleges, and institutes). A recent study recommends establishing national teacher training systems, aimed at coordinating three approaches: (1) actual educational training, which is given in the above-mentioned institutions; (2) basic and advanced training of in-service teachers, both by training institutions and by specialized centers under the ministries of education; and training centers and self-training of teachers at the local level; (3) a third approach is that of follow-up, detecting training gaps and requirements, and strengthening the programs being offered. This proposal is based on the fact that teacher training is one of the areas where the concept of continuing education can be best applied. Both planning and administration needs and qualitative change needs require information, statistics, and a research system for decision making. After two decades of experience, a network of public and private research and educational information training centers is beginning to develop in Latin America.

EDUCATION, TRAINING, AND EMPLOYMENT

Other Forms of Adult Education and Training

Along with professional training systems that are very structured and aimed primarily at the modern sector of the economy, Latin America and the Caribbean have a number of forms of job training and adult education. The latter are embodied in the concept of continuing education, which is predominantly nonformal and stresses the aspects of equity and social justice inherent in this type of education. Through its Education and Work Action Plan, the OAS has just compiled a number of job-training modalities that have been analyzed in basic studies and subregional seminars. In summary, these efforts show a variety of types: literacy campaigns, with a broader conception than traditional approaches; postliteracy programs; basic education and job training; national adult education systems, such as those in Bolivia, which involve both public and private efforts; systems for providing assistance by national agencies to local organizations to improve adult education, such as MOBRAL, in Brazil; programs combining the educational variable with marketing, social, health, and nutrition-productive elements in comprehensive rural development activities; various kinds of on-the-job training and training through work; specific training in various trades through short courses designed to meet specific regional or local requirements; vocational training; family education; university extension; training by radio and television combined with direct action with adults through monitors and group leaders; programs presented through art centers; night schools for those wishing to take self-improvement courses beyond formal education.

In higher education, there is an interesting trend toward open universities.

Education and Work

Educational systems in the region have been criticized for not adequately training students for the workplace. We have already seen three dimensions in the relationship between education and work: work as a value to be considered in education at all levels (page 438), education for work as preparation for a specific job, in vocational-technical training and in the diversified cycle (pages 433 and 434) and in vocational training systems (page 435); and the association of education and work as part of adult continuing education (page 439). The Consensus on Education and Work approved by CIECC at its ninth meeting in 1978 stressed a number of experiments that have been conducted and that might be put into widespread use: utilization of human and physical resources of production sector for educational purposes; certification of experience gained in the workplace; training and refresher courses for in-service staff; polyvalent centers integrating education and production; and technical centers where the practical part of the training is given in the industries themselves, and so forth.

Education and Employment

With regard to employment problems, the expectation that the industrial sector would absorb a large proportion of manpower has not materialized, partly because of the type of technology employed. In fact, this sector has employed a constant 14% of a labor force over the last three decades. While unemployment ranges from 5.5% to 6%, the underemployed labor force is estimated at 27%. Most of the population remains in the traditional or informal sector (subsistence agriculture, handicrafts, workshops, small businesses, independent labor, etc.), which represents a challenge for the educational system because those working in these activities are mostly unskilled.

Unemployment is beginning to be found at various levels of skills. There is also the phenomenon of deflation of certificates, that is, more years of schooling are required to obtain the same job as compared with a generation ago. Added to these problems is the fact that a dynamic economic reconversion changes employment structures, which requires a constant learning readaptation during the employee's work life.

Productivity Studies

The need to promote education for disadvantaged persons as part of a comprehensive development strategy has to some extent been supported by studies conducted mainly by the World Bank on social rates of return. A study of 20 countries in various regions of the world shows that investment in education has a high social rate of return and that it is higher in basic education (26.2%) than in secondary education (13.5%) or higher education (11.3%).

A 1980 World Bank document on sectoral policy[8] states that arguments of both economic efficiency and equity support continuing investment in primary education. "At least some form of formal schooling appears to be necessary for later training."

Moreover, as indicated by PREALC, expansion of educational opportunities at the secondary level is not sufficient to generate employment or change income distribution. The lack of qualified personnel conspires against employment, but the primary factors in the situation continue to be economic.

Higher-Level Human Resources
and Migration of Professional and Technical People

Some studies on the percentage distribution of the unemployed in Latin America show relatively low unemployment rates at the two extremes of education: illiterates and university graduates, while there are high rates in the middle sectors: persons with completed or incomplete primary or secondary education.

Table 21.7 shows estimates for all of the developing countries, giving the urban unemployment rates compared to schooling (assigning 100 to those having more than 12 years of education).

The relatively high rate of employment for university professionals often involves other factors, such as working at lower levels or in jobs other than those for which the person is trained. There is also a higher percentage of professionals in the service sectors and in government. In 1970, 25.90% of university graduates had degrees in

TABLE 21.7. Urban Unemployment Rates Compared with Schooling

Over 12 years schooling	100
6 to 11 years of schooling	280
1 to 5 years of schooling	170
Illiterate	130

Source: *International Labour Review,* Vol. 92, No. 6, 1975.

the humanities, teaching, and the fine arts, while 32.3% had degrees in law and the social sciences, including economics. This shows clearly the adaptation of students to the importance of the services sector.

Existing maladjustments are due both to the fact that the distribution of graduates is not in line with development requirements and to the inadequate translation of potential job market demand into educational requirements.

The emigration of Latin American professionals and experts is a very complex phenomenon, and available data are fragmentary. Although in the analysis of the ratio between educational system supply and development requirements, the migratory flow is small, its impact can be significant when considering particular specialties or sectors rather than the total labor force.[9]

Existing studies do not usually consider reverse migration or the return flow to the country of origin. Most Latin American professionals emigrate to the United States. In 1961/75, some 80,000 Latin Americans classified in the occupational group of "professionals, technicians, and related workers," were admitted into the United States, according to the official figures of the Immigration and Naturalization Service. Not counting emigration from Cuba, the total was 60,500.

Breaking down the data by sectors, emigration of professionals to the United States in 1965/70 is shown in Table 21.8. The table shows an increase in occupational selectivity, favoring engineers and paramedics.

The figures for some countries such as the Dominican Republic, with 1,474 professionals officially admitted by the United States in 1971/75, and Haiti with 1,430, show a very serious situation, especially when compared with countries with much larger populations, such as Argentina and Brazil, with official figures of 939 and 600 for the same period.[10]

Setting policy in this area is highly complex. Attempts to establish in the country of origin working conditions similar to those of the country of destination are usually not feasible. Attempts to reformulate human resources training plans to bring them more in line with local requirements should be done very cautiously to avoid producing negative effects. Obviously, only a combination of many factors can be effective in reducing the outward migration and encouraging the return of emigrants.

FINANCING OF EDUCATION

Financial Aspects and Educational Costs

Public spending on education in Latin America increased between 1965 and 1976 from U.S. S3,386,000 to U.S. $14,759,000, reflecting the significant increase in coverage during the period. This 335% increase in growth compares with the 426% increase in educational spending throughout the developing world and shows the importance of education in those countries' development strategy.

Educational expenditures amounted to 3.1% of the gross national product in 1965 and increased to 3.6% in 1976. Recent

TABLE 21.8. Emigration of Professionals to the United States, by Sectors

Categories	1965	1975
Total	100	100
Engineers	8.4	11.4
Specialists in natural and social sciences	4.4	4.8
Doctors, surgeons, and dentists	11.0	10.0
Nurses and paramedics	10.0	20.2
Professors and teachers	24.7	14.6
Lawyers and members of religious orders	3.7	6.9
Others	37.8	32.1

Source: United States Immigration and Naturalization Service.

resolutions at the ministerial level in UNESCO and the OAS propose a progressive increase of this share to 7 or 8% in order to meet the growing needs of education.

The proportion of public spending allocated to education varies widely: In 1976, six countries allocated between 10 and 15%, six, between 15 and 20%; three, between 20 and 25%, and five, over 25%.

Sources of Financing

The sources of financing for education are the public sector, which is the largest contributor, the private sector, the family sector, the community sector, and the bilateral and multilateral external sector.

Public investment is mainly contributed by the central governments. Municipal, provincial, or state participation is significant in Brazil, Colombia, and Argentina and, to a lesser extent, in Venezuela. Chile has started a policy of transferring primary schools to the municipalities.

Private education (both lay and religious) is of some importance, more in secondary and higher education than in primary education. In Argentina, Uruguay, Chile, Bolivia, and Ecuador, private enrollment in primary schools was over 15% in 1975; in eight other countries, the proportion ranged between 10 and 15%. At the secondary level, private education accounted in 1975 for over 26% of enrollment in Ecuador, Colombia, Brazil, Paraguay, Nicaragua, El Salvador, and Argentina. There are government subsidies, whose amounts are difficult to specify. Private universities contribute their own resources, although 25% also receive government support.

Educational Spending by Levels of Education

Public spending in the region shows a higher growth rate for secondary and higher education than for primary schools from 1965 to 1975, but the trend is not uniform for all countries. In countries with a great increase in primary school enrollment, such as Mexico and Colombia, spending at that level was 42.2% and 39.6%, respectively, of the total educational budget in 1965 and increased to 45.2% and 44.2% in 1975. The proportion of education expenditures for secondary education rose sharply in Argentina, Colombia, and

Panama. The proportion of expenditures for higher education increased markedly in Venezuela and Costa Rica.[11] Although available data are very fragmentary, the cost of secondary technical education is estimated at almost half the overall average.[12]

As to the breakdown of expenditures, a study shows that on the average, 70% of current public expenditures on education are budgeted for salaries of professors and teachers.[13] Another study shows that faculty salaries represent over 85% of public spending in 18 countries of the region at the primary level and in 12 countries of the region at the secondary level.[14]

TECHNICAL ASSISTANCE FOR EDUCATION IN LATIN AMERICA AND THE CARIBBEAN

OAS Assistance to Education

Since 1969, the OAS Regional Educational Development Program (PREDE) has represented a multilateral and systematic attempt by the countries of the region to cooperate and help each other. PREDE has provided reciprocal and horizontal technical assistance among the developing countries of the region. The program is financed by the voluntary fund of the Multilateral Special Fund for Education, Science and Culture (FEMCIECC).

Nature and Content of Projects

PREDE conducts its multinational and national projects through existing institutions in the region, and its contributions are not reimbursable.

Some multinational projects have selected in developing countries of the region "Multinational Centers" to be strengthened in order to provide specialized and basic training to fellowship students from the various member states and furnish technical assistance to third countries. Others have been integrated through joint national actions tackling a particular problem area, with common objectives and philosophies. The special projects financed by the Mar del Plata Account are interdisciplinary and employ existing infrastructure to solve socioeconomic educational problems. National projects are called on to resolve specific problems and needs. Projects comprise support from international and local experts, technical courses and seminars, research, teaching materials, equipment, fellowship, and internships.

Action in the 1970s

PREDE allocated U.S. $59,786.50 to education in 1971/80, as indicated by the breakdown in Table 21.9. These data do not include contributions from the OAS Regular Budget, national counterpart funds, or OAS participation in the administration of projects by other agencies, an item that amounted to $3,100,000 up to 1980.[15]

The OAS Department of Educational Affairs has a staff of specialists at headquarters and in the field assisting projects and various missions and has recently acted as the executing agency for three educational projects financed by the World Bank and one by the IDB. In addition, it has been initiating a technical assistance project with IDB funds in the Dominican Republic and will assume partial execution of a World Bank project in Guatemala.

Because of the nature of the program, its activities have tended to finance qualitative improvements and not investment expenditures,

TABLE 21.9. *Regional Educational Development Program (in Thousands of U.S. Dollars)*

	1969/ 1970	1970/ 1971	1971/ 1972	1972/ 1973	1973/ 1974
FEMCIECC Projects: national and multinational	4,682.1	5,276.2	3,491.3	3,235.4	4,424.5
MAR DEL PLATA ACCOUNT Special projects					
Special Funds 33 and 37					
TOTAL	4,682.1	5,276.2	3,491.3	3,235.4	4,424.5

These figures represent 18 months due to change in fiscal year.

and it has been especially active with regard to specialized training for the staff of various educational areas, the incorporation of educational innovations, and the dissemination of experience among the various countries.

Projects having the greatest impact in the first decade of PREDE were aimed at improving primary and secondary education curricula, training personnel in educational technology, and introducing innovations, improved planning, administration and educational research, and improved science teaching, as well as the improvement of vocational-technical and adult education in their various ramifications. As to special projects, the program's greatest impact is in the integrated development of border areas, better coordination between education and work, and emphasis on disadvantaged adults. Noteworthy also are the projects on curriculum development and science and mathematics education in the Caribbean.

Recent Trends

In 1978, the Program undertook a review of its activities. The Ninth Meeting of CIECC, held in Santiago, approved the program guidelines

1974/ 1975	1975/ 1976	1976/ 1977	1978	1979	1980	TOTAL
3,521.3	3,819.4	6,647.4	4,879.1	4,591.9	4,686.0	49,254,6
2,237.0	2,237.0	2,940.8	1,428.1	1,436.1	1,558.2	11,837.2
	3.9	62.7	94.0	400.7	702.8	1,264.1
5,578.3	6,060.3	9,650.9	6,401.2	6,428.7	6,947.0	62,355.9

for 1980/81, establishing three courses of action that were later repeated and expanded for 1982/83: (1) promote the opening of educational opportunities for all sectors of society, giving priority to projects favoring rural populations and urban marginal populations, programs aimed at returning dropouts to school, and so forth; (2) strengthen agents and instruments taking part in the educational process and identify both conventional and nonconventional agents with the greatest potential for innovation; and (3) promote educational change in the triple dimension of using appropriate educational technologies, incorporating scientific and cultural elements into the curricula and tying in education, work, and productivity at the levels of technical education, adult education, vocational training, and higher education.

Important among the guidelines given by CIECC annually to educational processes is the resolution on Prospects for the Development of Education in the 1980s, adopted in Bogota in 1980.

New program fields have emerged, such as educational regionalization, qualitative improvement of basic education, preschool and special education, rural education, and improvement of university teaching, which supplement previous programs while giving strong stimulus to projects for both formal and nonformal job training. New special projects include Adult Education for Integrated Rural Development, in which 17 countries participate in a joint action including direct work with grass-roots communities. Demand for technical assistance in 26 countries results in some tendency toward dispersion of efforts, which the program endeavors to offset through greater precision in program guidelines and in the types of priority projects.

Educational Activities of the Inter-American Development Bank

In the Act of Bogota of 1960, members of the Inter-American Development Bank (IDB) recommended that measures for social improvement and economic development should be supported. In 1965, the Fund for Special Operations was set up, which took over the functions of the previous Trust Fund. The purpose of the FSO is to promote "economic infrastructure" and "social infrastructure" projects, particularly in public health, housing, and education.

Development of IDB Educational Activities

The IDB began to make small loans to universities based on the concept that only by transforming higher education would it be possible to develop the expert personnel and the awareness required for expanding the systems. Early in the 1960s, there was a significant demand for qualified professionals and a favorable environment for reform of the university structure and teaching methods. In a few years, loans and technical cooperation actions multiplied (20 projects from 1962 to 1965) for higher education, and the IDB program financed projects in all countries of the region. Unquestionably, the Bank was involved in the modernization of many universities. The programs were aimed at construction of facilities and laboratories, staff training, support for university development designed to achieve more integrated education, and the inclusion of science and technology. It was necessary for the universities to support full-time work of their faculty members. The projects could be devoted to advanced training in agriculture, engineering, natural resources, and economic and administrative urban and rural development.

In the second stage, the Bank endeavored to expand vocational-technical training to meet the needs of modern industrial complexes that had been established under development policies and the requirements of upwardly mobile social groups. In the first years of the 1970s, loans for universities began to decrease significantly and those for vocational and technical training, particularly at the secondary level, began to increase. Starting in 1967, 19 technical education projects were financed in 13 countries of the region. These projects have stressed adapting programs to the demand for jobs, modernization of teaching media, and institutional flexibility. Later, many of these projects were expanded to rural areas, where agricultural transformation needed to be supported by trained human resources. The loans combined capital investment (equipment, facilities, and construction) with technical assistance (about 10% of the total number of projects).

Work Performed

In its first decade, the Bank is estimated to have persuaded the governments, based on the favorable results from social projects, to implement a balanced development effort. The Bank also helped to introduce discipline in formulating projects in sectors accustomed to grow through budget allocations. The second decade was dominated by the relative scarcity of concessional funds and the need to give preference to the less developed countries. Funds for assistance to those countries accounted for two-thirds of the total.

TABLE 21.10. IDB Action in the Science and Technology Education Sector

	No. of Projects	Amount IDB Contribution
Higher education	61	308,231.6
Educational credits	8	25,000.0
Vocational and occupational training	17	135,050.0
Special education	8	84,552.6
	94	552,809.2

Source: Data from "IDB Action in the Science and Technology Education Sector" prepared by the Project Analysis Department. The figures indicated would be double
if local contributions to the project were considered.

In this second decade, stress continued to be placed on social programs, while many countries gave priority to directly reproductive investments.

In summary, up to June 30, 1980, the IDB had conducted 94 projects in the educational area (we have excluded science and technology projects, which were also undertaken, because there is a specific OAS regional program in that field), totaling $552,809,200. The breakdown by type of projects is shown in Table 21.10.

Recent and Future Trends

Starting in 1976, the IDB adopted a new financing policy for the education sector: Instead of confining its efforts to educational fields, general basic objects were set: (1) human resources training for the managerial occupations and functions required by the countries' socioeconomic development in each particular case; (2) equality of opportunity for the entire population; (3) rationalization of educational systems to achieve maximum effectiveness of investments in the sector.

Recently, integrated rural development programs have included seven basic education projects, together with investments coordinated with other social and productive sectors. Haiti and Argentina are implementing projects to reform their rural educational systems.

A recent address by the President of the IDB pointed out the need for Latin America to meet three challenges: to provide basic education for the great majority of the population, to increase secondary school attendance, and to provide the technical and managerial staff required for the development process.[16]

UNESCO and the UNDP

A number of United Nations agencies take part in education in Latin America, the main one being the United Nations Education, Science and Culture Organization (UNESCO), which provides world-wide guidance by furnishing technical assistance through its programs and by implementing projects financed by other agencies, especially the United Nations Development Programme (UNDP). This UN program also acts throughout the developing world. In 1979, the UNDP allocated a total of U.S. $546,600,000 for programs in all areas, of which U.S. $36,009,000, or 6.9%, were earmarked for education.

The UNESCO regional office in Santiago, Chile, is directly under the Deputy Director General for Education. That office has performed work in basic and advanced training of teachers, assistance in formulating and implementing educational plans, technical support to experts and UNESCO projects in the region, studies and research on educational problems and trends, and operation of information services.

In 1971/79, UNESCO helped to prepare and start a number of projects, with external financing as indicated in Table 21.11. Activities

TABLE 21.11. *UNESCO Activities in the Field of Education*

	32 projects financed by the UNDP in 19 countries and 3 regions
	6 projects financed by the World Bank in 6 countries
	5 projects financed by the UN Population Fund
	3 projects financed by the FIT in 2 countries
	1 project financed by the BIT in 1 country
Total	50 projects

Source: *UNESCO Activities in the Field of Education in Latin America and the Caribbean since the Conference held in Caraballeda in 1971.* 1979

carried out by UNESCO itself include what are known as the ordinary program and the participation program, which conduct regional activities of various kinds.

The UNDP acts through national projects based on an indicative figure set by country and regional activities of various kinds.

UNESCO Direct Activities

These activities are concerned with: (1) personnel training, through assistance to courses, seminars, study visits, and so on; (2) aid to member countries at the request of their governments, which accounts for most of the resources provided in terms of time and available technical staff; (3) publications such as the biannual Educational Bulletin, the monthly Bibliographic Bulletin, and the Statistics Bulletin. UNESCO exerts a considerable impact through the publications issued at its headquarters in Paris, resolutions of its World Conferences, and reference publications such as the World Statistical Yearbook.

Projects Implemented by UNESCO with Funds from Other Agencies

The report cited on UNESCO activities in Latin America since 1971 gives a summary of extra-budgetary activities in 1971/79 as shown in Table 21.12. As can be seen, UNESCO's work as executor of projects has followed the fluctuations and the crises of UNDP financial resources. Currently, the decline in UNDP resources is primarily affecting regional projects.

Analysis of national projects distribution by field of activity shows that most of them have dealt with the following areas, in the order given: planning, administration and supervision of education (11 projects in 10 countries); integrated programs on general education; technical education and vocational training; education in the field of population and teacher training.

The following are examples of regional activities and projects: the Regional Project on the Training of Education Planners and Administrators (project RLA/700/507), which started in 1970 and lasted for five years; and the Project on Development and Education in Latin America and the Caribbean (Project RLA/74/024), to which UNESCO contributes, which is connected with the planning process —in its first phase, it received UNDP financing of U.S. $858,999 and

TABLE 21.12   UNESCO Funding in the Field of Education

	PNUD			WB, IDB,	Total
	National	Regional	Subtotal	UNDPF, FIT	(Rounded off)
1972	2,312	560	2,872	104	3,000
1973	1,824	580	2,404	1,033	3,400
1974	2,027	48	2,075	1,849	3,900
1975	3,594	137	3,731	2,058	5,800
1976	3,473	317	3,790	1,461	5,300
1977	1,398	443	1,841	1,451	3,300
1978	1,294	551	1,845	1,219	3,100
Total	15,922	2,636	18,558	9,165	27,700

Source: UNESCO activities in the field of education, op. cit.

is jointly executed with ECLA and the Project on Educational Systems Network for Development in Central America (RLA/72/100), which endeavored to help improve education, especially by establishing subregional coordination and support mechanisms.

Future Trends

The Caraballeda Meeting at the ministerial level in 1971 urged the countries to carry out joint efforts to improve education and make it more democratic. The Declaration of Mexico issued by the Ministers of Education and Planning meeting called by UNESCO in 1979 was a strong appeal to overcome by the end of the century the educational backwardness of the masses.

World Bank Educational Policy and Action in the Region

Because of the nature of World Bank operations (officially the International Bank for Reconstruction and Development), it has no education program specifically for Latin America. It has, instead, a world-wide program that conducts projects in our region as well.

History of the World Bank's Action in Education

The Bank began to make loans to education both directly and through the International Development Association in 1963. From 1963 to 1970, its activities concentrated on vocational and technical training at various levels and, in general, on secondary education to meet the human resources needs for the development plans of that period. The emphasis was on equipment and construction.

From 1971 to 1974, policy was set by the 1971 Working Document, which recommended systematic studies of the education sector as a requirement for loans and began to provide technical assistance to include new areas of education, such as nonformal education, training by radio and television, and so on.

Between 1975 and 1978, the policies set forth in the 1974 working document criticized the excessive stress that economic modernization policies were placing on secondary and higher education to the detriment of basic education and the education and training requirements in rural areas. Stress was placed on the need to provide basic education and later training in line with the human resource needs in crucial areas.

In 1963/78, the Bank contributed U.S. $2.6 billion in aid to education world-wide. The priority for secondary education projects continues to be high (43% in 1975/78), but much less than in the 1960s, when it reached 84%. Increased aid was given to primary education (14%) and nonformal education (17%). The picture for project content by inputs in the 1960s showed that 59% went to construction and 28% to equipment. In 1978, the percentage for construction and equipment was 48% and 39%, respectively, while the technical assistance component had risen from 3% to 13%.[17]

Action in Latin America

In 1971/80, the World Bank and AID lent Latin America a total of U.S. $14,884,500,000 for all programs, with particular stress on electric power, agriculture and rural development, water supplies, and transportation. During that period, educational projects received U.S. $374,200,000.

The breakdown of activities in the region shows that between 1963 and 1978, the Bank made 40 education loans to 18 countries, 14 to Latin America, 3 to the English-speaking Caribbean, and 1 to Guyana, totaling U.S. $412,800,000.[18]

Many projects are aimed at various levels or specialties of education, particularly general secondary education, vocational and technical training, teachers training, and agricultural education. Seven projects were devoted to basic education, mostly concentrating on secondary education and technical fields. The most important work was as follows: Brazil III projects on vocational training, with U.S. $32 million in support; the Peruvian project on general secondary education, with U.S. $24 million; the El Salvador IV program on basic rural education, training of in-service teachers, teaching materials, curriculum development, administration, and the postsecondary technological level, with U.S. $235 million; Trinidad and Tobago III project on Secondary Basic Education, curriculum development, and the Center for Faculty Development, with U.S. $20 million; and Colombia III project on agricultural basic education, general secondary education, postsecondary technical training, teacher training, and rural development, with U.S. $21.2 million.[19]

Future Trends

In recent years, the World Bank has stressed the concept of basic needs, including education and a direct attack on poverty.

The Bank proposes a balanced growth in education, aimed at providing basic education for all children and adults as soon as feasible; increasing productivity and promoting social equity; strengthening internal efficiency of educational systems; tying in education with work and the environment; and creating capacity in the countries for the design, management, and evaluation of education and training programs.[20]

Also proposed is an increase in the technical assistance component of loans up to about 20% in 1979/83. Within this component, educational research is being stressed as a basis for planning and decision making.

Incidence of Loans and Contributions of Financing Agencies

A study sponsored by the IDB[21] shows that for Latin America external loans approved by international agencies (including IDB, the World Bank, and the USAID) reached 13% of investment in the education sector in 1962/77. That percentage is significant in that it shows the importance of policy guidelines agreed upon by international agencies.

It should also be stressed that this chapter has only considered multilateral cooperation mechanisms. Analysis of the Rockefeller Foundation's work throughout the world shows that 60% of external aid for education in 1970 went to bilateral mechanisms, 16% to multilateral institutions, and 24% to private nonprofit institutions. The analysis shows that in 1975 those percentages reached 65%, 21%, and 14%, respectively.[22]

FINAL OBSERVATIONS AND CONCLUSIONS*

This brief analysis enables us to say that the countries of the region have made a great effort over the last two decades to expand and renovate their educational systems, having had significant supplementary contributions in the form of external assistance, which has varied in nature according to the type of institution that has provided it.

Despite this, grave problems, the nature and seriousness of which vary from country to country, still persist and drag on without resolution, and others appear as a result of the demand generated by the growth of the population, the dynamics of economic and social development, and the very expansion of the educational system itself.

The challenges this presents are varied; some are general in nature and some more specific. The former include:

1. Integral development centered on man requires action by a number of sectors, of which education is only one variable, in a constant interaction with other variables and sectors of society. At the same time, it means giving preferential attention to the disadvantaged who have greater educational deficiencies, in order to promote their complete development as participant, aware, and productive citizens and individuals.

---

* These and the other observations throughout the document are the personal views of the author and do not necessarily represent the opinions of the Organization of the American States.

2. Educational change and manpower training—in other words, the maximum development of human potential—require an overall strategy for educational development covering all levels and both the formal and nonformal modes, so that any partial changes can be framed within a preconceived strategy.

3. The qualitative challenge requires that there be a closer relation between the objectives of the system and social needs, and that models adopted in the past that no longer respond to the region's current realities or potential be discarded.

4. The difficulties in predicting the precise demand in the labor sector and production in no way invalidate—indeed, they strengthen—the need for curricula and educational programs to consider the variety of opportunities—and limitations—in the production sectors of a particular country, be they traditional or modern.

The specific challenges that appear both from what we have discussed above and from the goals the countries themselves have set in recent international declarations in the OAS and UNESCO include:

1. Providing universal basic education by the end of the century. This type of education is the cornerstone for democratizing the whole system and lays the foundations for any subsequent training or education. In the present decade, it is the public formal education system that will continue to bear the greatest burden: private education, although important at the secondary and higher levels, is insignificant at the level of basic free education for the poorest urban and rural sectors. Unless internal and external resources are increased, there will still be numbers of children who have no access to or never complete their basic education. However, coverage might still be expanded by making more adequate use of the physical infrastructure and existing teachers and by improving the retention rate by increasing efficiency. In countries that have serious underenrollments in basic education and whose allocations to education in terms of the GNP are below the regional average, the situation will become worse, unless special programs and resources are provided: These countries will find themselves faced with redistributing their allocations

to education toward basic education. Even this mechanism has its limitations, however, because of the progressive extension of the entire system, and particularly of secondary education, to more and more people.

2. Ending illiteracy by the end of the century. Unless special resources and programs are provided, illiteracy will drop in percentage terms, but will remain the same in absolute figures during the present decade. The challenge means linking the literacy education process to job training and basic education systems that are tailored to adults.

3. Ending the gap between urban and rural education. The deficiencies in basic education in rural areas and in agricultural secondary education are such that it is not enough to redistribute the resources for these levels internally. Agricultural workers' education is a good candidate to be supplemented by nonformal methods using an intersectoral and community participation approach.

4. Improving the quality and effectiveness of the educational system and making the structure more flexible. This challenge is related, among other things, to the relevance of the subject matter taught at all levels; the introduction of educational technologies appropriate to the region; the introduction of new values and attitudes; a reduction in the drop-out and repetition rates; new teacher training systems; and the structuring of systems that will make for vertical and horizontal linkages between the various modes and levels, intermediate exit levels, and reentry into the system by those who wish to continue their education.

5. Improving the relationship between education, work, and employment. There are various facets here, including set-up machinery for coordination between the formal system, particularly technical education (which will continue to have an important role to play during the present decade, despite the difficulties it has had in coordinating itself with the requirements of the production sectors) and the vocational training systems (which should expand their area of action to include the traditional sector of the economy) and other modes of nonformal education, which will have a major role to play in the integrated rural development

programs and in modular courses designed to combat unemployment among the young and give another opportunity to drop-outs from the formal system. There must also be links between the various public and private agencies that promote and finance these efforts, and certification mechanisms must be established for them. Higher education systems must be diversified. Universities will be called on to provide basic scientific and technological education that will fit their graduates to adapt to various specialties and jobs, and will also have to link their research, teaching, and direct community action to needs of the country and region in which they are located. Examples of cooperation between the university and the state and the university and the production sector must be found.

If the indicated challenges in the areas of education and manpower training are to meet with success, it will not be enough to maintain the resources allocated to external cooperation at current levels. Greater internal and external resources will be required, and at the same time there must be substantive changes, using conventional and nonconventional strategies, and the system must optimize its efficiency. The inflexibility of the countries' regular education budgets, which are allocated almost entirely to wages and administration, place limits on their ability to test major qualitative changes or to give special training to the personnel who must make the changes, particularly in the relatively less developed countries. This underscores the need for international cooperation and technical assistance such as that provided by the OAS and UNESCO-UNDP, and which also appears in IDB and World Bank loans (not counting bilateral aid or aid from other regional or subregional agencies.) International financial cooperation for investment and equipment is also needed, both to keep up the new lines of cooperation and loans that have been given over the last five years and to help in the new tasks and challenges of the 1980s.

Let us conclude with some words about the question of what future action international agencies should take in the field of education in the region:

1. The fragmentation action among the various agencies noted in the 1960s and the beginning of the 1970s has generally given way to a single idea that favors projects that open up educational opportunities to the mass of the

population. At the same time, the agencies are tending to be more flexible in their action and not to concentrate on any particular level of education.

2. Instruments of cooperation must be flexible and versatile; there must be many of them, and they should combine technical assistance and research with educational equipment or materials, training with the direct solution of problems or preinvestment studies, foreign with national experts, support for the formal system with aid to non-formal mechanisms, and so forth.

3. The multilateral regional agencies such as the OAS are in an advantageous position both to serve as a forum in which to find solutions to common problems and to carry out horizontal multinational actions that encourage joint efforts and make use of the experience of countries that are relatively more advanced in any one area.

4. Starting from the principle that only the countries themselves can coordinate the international aid they request and receive, we might suggest some ideas that are consonant with that principle and at the same time expand on it, to the benefit of the countries of the region:

    a. There is a potentially high degree of compatibility between the financial agencies and the agencies that basically give technical assistance and that have permanent teams of experts;

    b. Mechanisms can be set up to facilitate use by the agencies of studies on educational realities in the region. These could serve as the basis on which to design cooperation projects (including projects prepared by bilateral agencies such as AID or CIDA or subregional or Latin American agencies);

    c. The possibility could be explored of holding joint intergovernmental and interagency working sessions every five years, to ensure that the policies set by the governing bodies of each agency are compatible; to determine possible coordination action or to review existing coordination procedures; and to exchange information. These meetings would be in the form of working encounters, and would not be international conferences.

NOTES

1. Declaration of Mexico adopted at the Regional Conference of Ministers of Education and Ministers responsible for Economic Planning of the Member States of Latin America and the Caribbean, organized by UNESCO in Mexico City, December 1979.

2. Resolution entitled "Prospects for the development of education in the eighties." Resolution 486/80 adopted by the Inter-American Council for Education, Science and Culture, CIECC/OAS, Bogota, July–August, 1980, operative paragraph 2.a.

3. World Bank, *Education Policy Paper*, Washington, April 1980, p. 13.

4. "Selected World Demographic Indicators by countries, 1950–2000." UN–New York, May 1975, *Statistical Yearbook, UNESCO*, 1980.

5. Ernesto Shiefelbein, "Elements for a systematic discussion of strategies examining the external and internal causes for school drop-out, 1980." Prepared for the OAS, Meeting on educational needs and prospects for Latin America and the Caribbean in the eighties. Panama, 1980.

6. OAS, Meeting on educational requirements and prospects for Latin America and the Caribbean in the eighties. Panama, May 1980. Final Report.

7. Ibid, footnote 6.

8. World Bank, *Education Sector Policy Paper*, op. cit., p. 44.

9. United Nations, "Reverse transfer of technology: dimensions, effects and policy questions," *Study of the UNCTAD Secretariat*, October 1975, and UN Publication, ECLA, *Education, human resources and development in Latin America*, New York, 1968.

10. The actual figures for the countries listed, and particularly for Argentina and Brazil, may be larger than the figures shown, because of the fact that some professionals are in the United States as nonimmigrants, e.g., as guests of universities and government agencies, staff of international agencies, and so forth.

11. Information based on the *UNESCO Statistical Summary, 1977*, pp. 559–661.

12. Oscar Corvalán, "Nuevas prioridades de la educación técnica y la formación para el trabajo en América Latina," prepared for the IDB. San José, Costa Rica, 1980, p. 10.

13. José Dagnino Pastore, "Nivel y estructura de los costos y del financiamiento educativo en America Latina," in IDB Publication, *Financing of Education in Latin America*, Economic Cultural Fund, Mexico, 1978, pp. 155–156.

14. L. Ratinoff and M. Jeria, "Estado actual de la educación en América Latina y el Caribe y sus repercusiones para la educación," IDB Working Document, 1979.

15. Between 1981 and 1980, the sum of U.S. $12,400,000 was allocated in the Regular Fund for education activities. Subtracting 25% for secretarial and administrative support, the remaining $9,000,000 financed the staff experts in the Department of Educational Affairs who participate directly in project execution, supervision, and technical assistance, without their basic remuneration being charged against the projects. Hence, if we take the contributions shown in Table 21.9, the allocations from the Regular Budget, and the projects administered with funding from other agencies, the round total for OAS action in education during the last ten years was U.S. $74,500,000.

464 / GOVERNANCE IN THE WESTERN HEMISPHERE

16. Antonio Ortiz Mena, President of the IDB, "El financiamiento de la educación superior en América Latina. Problema y estrategias," Paper presented to a CAMESA meeting, Petrópolis, Brazil, February 1980, p. 11.

17. Data taken from: World Bank, *Education Sector Policy Paper*, op. cit., table, p. 80.

18. Data taken from the list of loans given by the World Bank and the IDA, *Education Sector Policy Paper*, op. cit., pp. 125-140.

19. Ibid.

20. World Bank, op. cit., p. 86.

21. Rolando Castañeda and Maritza Izaguirre, "Características del sector educativo en los países de América Latina," in *El problema del financiamiento de la educación en América Latina*, IDB, 1978, pp. 48-49 and 69.

22. H. M. Phillips, *Educational Cooperation between Developed and Developing Countries*, The Rockefeller Foundation, New York, 1977.

APPENDIX 1. *Latin America and the Caribbean. Illiteracy Rates in the Countries among the Population Aged 15 and Over (Censuses Conducted in the 1970s)*

	Both Sexes (20 Countries)		Men (19 Countries)		Women (19 Countries)	
Less than 10%	Uruguay	6.1	Trinidad and		Argentina	8.3
	Argentina	7.4	Tobago	5.3	Uruguay	5.7
	Trinidad and		Argentina	6.5		
	Tobago	8.3	Uruguay	6.6		
10–19%	Costa Rica	11.6	Chile	11.1	Trinidad	
	Chile	11.7	Costa Rica	11.4	and Tobago	10.3
	Colombia	19.8	Paraguay	14.9	Costa Rica	11.8
	Paraguay	19.8	Peru	16.8	Chile	12.8
			Colombia	18.0		
20–29.9%	Panama	2.7	Venezuela	20.3	Colombia	20.2
	Venezuela	23.5	Panama	21.0	Panama	22.2
	Mexico	25.8	Mexico	21.8	Paraguay	24.5
	Ecuador	25.8	Ecuador	22.7	Venezuela	26.6
	Peru	27.2	Bolivia	24.8	Mexico	29.6
30–39.9%	Dominican		Brazil	30.6	Ecuador	30.4
	Rep.	21.7	Dominican		Dominican	
	Brazil	33.6	Rep.	31.2	Rep.	34.3
	Bolivia	37.3	El Salvador	39.2	Brazil	36.9
					Peru	38.2
40–59.9%	Nicaragua	42.1	Nicaragus	42.0	Nicaragus	42.9
	El Salvador	42.9	Guatemala	46.1	El Salvador	46.4
	Guatemala	53.8			Bolivia	49.0
	Honduras	40.5				
60% or more	Haiti	75.0	Haiti	71.3	Guatemala	61.5
					Haiti	81.6

22

Science, Technology, and Western Hemisphere Governance

Aaron Segal

INTRODUCTION

The movement of scientific and technological goods, services, and talents is as rapid, smooth, and large within the Western Hemisphere as it is anywhere in the world, except for the European Community. The movement over the last 25 years has grown more rapidly than the national economics involved and total hemispheric trade. However, it is a movement that continues to be dominated by one participant, the United States, as seen in Tables 22.1 and 22.2. Although globally the U.S. predominance in science and technology is slipping, it remains predominant in the Western Hemisphere, absolutely and relatively. Moreover, U.S. predominance characterizes both the formal and informal flows, whether government to government, private sector to private sector, nonprofit to nonprofit, or the various combinations. Although major advances are occurring in science and technology capabilities in Argentina, Brazil, Canada, Mexico, Venezuela, and other states, these have yet to alter U.S. predominance. Nor have the major global competitors in science and technology to the United States—Japan, West Germany, and France—yet come to displace its influence in the Western Hemisphere.

TABLE 22.1. Global Distribution of R&D Capacity, 1973

Region	Funds (billion dollars)	Share of World Total (percent)	Scientists, Engineers in R&D (thousand)	Share of World Total (percent)
Developing countries	2.77	2.9	288	12.6
Africa (with South Africa)	0.30	0.3	28	1.2
Asia (without Japan)	1.57	1.6	214	9.4
Latin America	0.90	0.9	46	2.0
Developed countries	93.65	97.1	1,990	87.4
Eastern Europe (with USSR)	29.51	30.6	730	32.0
Western Europe (with Israel and Turkey)	21.42	22.2	387	17.0
U.S.A. and Canada	33.72	35.0	548	24.1
Other (with Japan and Australia)	9.01	9.3	325	14.3
World Total	96.42	100.0	2,279	100.0

Source: Jan Annerstedt, 1979

CURRENT PROBLEMS

Four major problems confront the governance of science and technology in the Western Hemisphere at present and for the forseeable future. These are (1) conflicts over the transfer of proprietary technology; (2) support problems related to the emergence and consolidation of indigenous research and development (R & D) capabilities; (3) persistent imbalances in the demand for and supply of science and technology; (4) new science- and technology-driven problems resulting from innovations and new products. The governance of these problems will require changes in attitudes in regional and international organizations as well as national policies. Science and technology will provide some of the key tests to the viability of hemispheric practices.

Present smooth flows depend upon limited international and regional organization. United States, Canada, and several other states are members of GATT; elsewhere the Andean Pact, Caribbean Community, Central America Common Market, and the Latin American Free Trade Association facilitate visible and some invisible trade. The World Bank, Inter-American Development Bank, and Caribbean Development Bank provide credits for technology transfers, as does the private sector. The Organization of American States (OAS) operates a modest science and technology program that supports research, professional exchanges, and fellowships. An impressive if somewhat fragile network of nongovernmental professional associations, journals, science societies, and other organizations concentrates on promoting person-to-person contact as well as research dissemination. One might conclude that at present science

TABLE 22.2.   Research and Development in the Western Hemisphere, 1980

Country	Researchers (full-time equivalent)	R&D Expenditures (U.S. $)	R&D % of GDP	Technology Exports % Total Exports
United States	600,000	65 billion	2.5	60
Canada	35,000	1.2 billion	1.1	30
Brazil	12,000	800 million	0.8	25
Mexico	8,000	600 million	0.7	15
Argentina	7,000	400 million	0.6	20
Venezuela	3,000	250 million	0.4	5
Colombia	2,000	90 million	0.3	15
Chile	2,000	75 million	0.2	15
Cuba	1,500	50 million	0.25	5

The other 20 independent states of the Western Hemisphere each have 500 or fewer researchers, spend $10 million a year or less on R&D with these expenditures accounting for less than 0.1% of gross domestic product, while technology exports are 0–20% of total exports. The science and technology problems of the smaller states are thus of a fundamentally different nature. This table represents very crude estimates based on data from national science and technology plans, OECD, UNESCO, and National Science Foundation sources. There is little data on "shop-floor" industrial R&D in Latin America, and it is probable that private sector R&D has been underestimated.

and technology in the Western Hemisphere is not much governed as it is prodded and pushed along.

Present controversy centers on proprietary transfers of technology and the alleged disadvantages for developing country purchasers. Mexico, Venezuela, and the Andean Pact as a group have adopted legislation that provides for government screening of imported technology, particularly to "unbundle" technological packages of goods and services, and limit or eliminate other restrictions. Meanwhile the trend toward joint ventures, especially with parastatal entities or governments, has become more pronounced, sometimes overriding national technology transfer concerns. While demands continue for Multinational Codes of Conduct for Technology Transfer, the evidence suggests that the principal importers are putting into place at the national level the technology screening devices considered appropriate, for example, in Brazil.

There has been little or no resort to international arbitration, even by the multilateral banks, in cases of conflict. Nor have the serious problems of the smaller states who lack the capability at national levels to screen technologies been addressed. UNCTAD has floated the idea of regional centers with little response, the UNECLA (Economic Commission for Latin America) has provided some technical training, and SELA (Latin American Economic System) has discussed a regional information and documentation network, but prospective importers short of information in Bolivia, Panama, or elsewhere still have no reliable source to which to turn. The low-cost provision of information on alternative technologies to the smaller states remains an important job without an institutional home.

An emerging and eventually more serious conflict is that over the failure of multinational corporations to invest in R & D in their regional subsidiaries. Table 22.3 indicates the paucity of such funding. Pressure is mounting in Canada, Brazil, Mexico, and elsewhere to compel MNC's to do research abroad, especially where low-cost national scientific and engineering talent is available. Few MNC's, from the United States or elsewhere, have been responsive to date, and one can predict the continued use of carrots and sticks to change attitudes and practices. The private sector Council of the Americas and various Latin American and Canadian business groups have looked at this problem with little forward movement. Canada and Brazil can be expected to take the lead, with national fiscal incentives and other legislation to promote overseas R & D. It could become the leading source of conflict during the 1980s, replacing the transfer of technology issue with that of its implementation abroad.

TABLE 22.3. R&D Expenditure by U.S. Affiliates of Foreign Companies: 1974 (U.S. Dollars in Millions)

Country and Industry	Expenditures
By country of foreign parent	
Total	13
Developed countries	694
Canada	53
Europe	611
European Economic Community	456
France	14
Germany	46
Netherlands	285
United Kingdom	107
Other EEC countries	4
Other Europe	155
Switzerland	140
Other	15
Japan	29
Australia, New Zealand, and South Africa	*
Developing countries	119
Latin America	117
Middle East	1
Other Africa, Asia, and Pacific	2
By industry of U.S. affiliate	
Total	813
Petroleum	111
Manufacturing	574
Wholesale trade	78
Finance, insurance, and real estate	10
Other industries	40

*Less than $0.5 million.

Note: Detail may not add to totals because of rounding.

Source: Department of Commerce, *Foreign Direct Investment in the United States,* vol. 1, "Report of the Secretary of Commerce to the Congress," 1976, p.54.

A related emerging issue is that of the legal framework in which R & D functions: copyrights, trademarks, and patents. Bolstered by UNECLA and UNCTAD studies there is a growing conviction among hemisphere users that present legal regimes favor providers of technology. Hence Mexico and other governments have adopted new laws that patent rights, limit copyrights and trademarks, and reduce the amounts of royalties. This is another issue that does not lend itself to international or regional arbitration. Instead, one forsees the specialist lawyers and law firms involved arriving at the modus vivendi, following the codification and implementation of new laws and decrees. Technology exporters may charge higher initial prices to offset lower rates of long-term payback.

The final issue concerning proprietary technology transfer is the most difficult of all. Essentially, a wide range of mostly labor-intensive industries are being displaced from the United States to elsewhere in the region, whether on the Mexican–U.S. border, in the Caribbean, or in Brazil. This is a logical and desirable movement over time, but it is an extremely painful movement for the industries, workers, and employers involved. Various protectionist and pseudo-protectionist devices have been advocated and some used in the United States to delay or stall this movement. Meanwhile the U.S. legislation to indemnify or compensate U.S. employers and workers from displacement due to imports has been proven limited and unsatisfactory. No suitable regional or international forum has emerged in which this problem can be intelligently discussed, and bilateral negotiations are often bitter and protracted. Here is an opportunity for serious study to consider which industries the United States might be willing to relinquish to the rest of the Hemisphere over a 25 year period, and how such a displacement might best occur. The Latin American Studies organizations in North America and Latin America might separately undertake such a study. It is imperative that trade unions, employers' organizations, and other directly interested parties be involved. The Caribbean and Mexico–U.S. Border Industries programs offer ample evidence of what has and has not been done.

OPTIONS AND STRATEGIES

The establishment and consolidation of R & D in the rest of the Hemisphere is at very diverse stages, as illustrated in Tables 22.4,

22.5, and 22.6. While Argentina, Brazil, and Mexico have sophisticated and effective R & D complexes, albeit with many problems, and Venezuela, Chile, and Colombia are rapidly building infrastructures, the other, smaller, and mostly poorer states are struggling years to light-years behind. The efforts of UNESCO, UNECLA, the IBRD, IDB, OAS, and other organizations have succeeded in promoting a striking national consciousness and awareness of the importance of R & D. Yet the human resource and the institutions are still in very short supply. Rather than enumerate the many shortcomings and needed steps, let us examine only three that are of particular hemispheric interest.

One of the most painful questions is whether to use English, Spanish, or Portuguese as the language of science and technology. At present the literature is overwhelmingly in English, many researchers prefer to publish in that language, and a reading knowledge is indispensable to do advanced work in many fields. However English is adequately taught mostly to private, city students from affluent backgrounds. Thousands of future researchers are halted in their tracks by the lack of access to the learning of English. The U.S. Fulbright Program, the binational cultural councils, Canadian agencies, and other organizations provide English-language instruction, but the need and demand overwhelms the supply. The teaching of English as a scientific language, that is, the mastery of sufficient English to read journals and papers, is in its infancy in the region and desperately needs to be encouraged. The alternative is that researchers will continue to come from a much too limited social stratum, often divorced from national problems, and more inclined to emigrate.

Another alternative would be to promote a scientific and technical literature in Spanish and Portuguese, especially as markets for journals and texts grow. Linguistically, both languages can adequately be used for advanced literature. However the lead of English, regionally and globally, is so great that a major investment in other languages appears to be very risky. This is an issue that should attract the attention of OAS, the Inter-Ciencia Association of the National Association for the Advancement of Science, the Fulbright Program, and others. Although probably it may be culturally healthier to launch a science-in-Spanish drive, realistically the teaching of scientific English may take precedence. One way or another, advanced students and professional staff must have the linguistic skills needed to keep up-to-date in their own fields. The problem of keeping up-to-date is one of access to effective hemispheric information systems and networks as well as language skills. Present networks are primarily focused on the United States and

TABLE 22.4. Scientists and Engineers Engaged in R & D by Field of Science

Country	Year		Natural Sciences	Engineering and Technology	Medical Sciences	Agriculture	Social Sciences and Law	Humanities Education Arts	Total
Cuba	1969	FT	–	226	–	274	–	20	520
		PT	188	1054	300	–	46	198	1766
		FTE	166	1033	190	274	34	153	1850
Guatemala[1]	1972	FT	1	3	–	1	11	–	16
		PT	–	8	–	–	32	4	44
		FTE	1	8	–	1	23	2	35
Mexico	1971	FT	859	451	396	585	307	123	2721
		PT	301	229	189	40	584	–	1343
Argentina[2]	1969	FT	2290	711	1027	867	402	121	5454[3]
		PT	963	464	24111	290	826	311	5373[3]
		FTE	1688	532	991	627	448	134	4452[3]
Chile	1969	FT	1538	705[4]	530	489	579[4]	403[4]	4244[4]
		PT	417	265[4]	633	129	214[4]	322[4]	1980[4]
		FTE	1577	793[4]	742	532	650[4]	510[4]	4904[4]

474

Country	Year								
Colombia	1971	FT	188	154	127	348	323[5]	—	1140[5]
		PT							
Peru	1970	FT	445	76	267	494	151	—	1522[3][6]
		PT	100	13	125	24	54	—	318[3][6]
		FTE	496	83	330	507	180	—	1686[3][6]
Uruguay	1971/1972	FT	184	356	359	253	132	28	1537[3]
		PT	1150	142	285	239	253	93	16[3]
		FTE							
Venezuela	1970	FT	365	297	489	246	173	107	1677
		PT	14	25	119	34	28	28	248
		FTE	370	306	542	255	186	120	1779

FT: Full-time PT: Part-time FTE: Full-time equivalent

[1] Data are for the University of San Carlos and refer to permanent personnel only.
[2] Not including data for private enterprises; data refer to net man-years; architecture is included with engineering.
[3] The total does not correspond to the sum of the component items owing to the inclusion of other fields of science.
[4] Not including data for education; law is included with humanities and arts.
[5] Not including data for law, humanities, education and arts.
[6] Not including data for humanities, education and arts.
Source: Unesco Office of Statistics and Unesco Statistical Yearbook 1973.

do not permit researchers within the region to know each other's work. SELA, through its proposed regional technical information systems (RITLA), is attempting to network Bolivia, Brazil, Peru, Mexico, and Venezuela. Other embryonic networks include the Association of Caribbean Universities, the Association of Latin American Universities, and many professional groups. The U.S. National Bureau of Standards, the U.S. National Library of Medicine, and the National Agricultural Library also network various regional users.

The use of satellites, computers, data-processing equipment, and other technologies can revolutionize the hemispheric dissemination of information at relatively little cost. Universities, industries, and research centers struggling with a handful of journals and several hundred books can quickly have access to storehouses of information. Networks are already being established, usually from the capital cities to North America and through the liason of national science councils. Again the risk is that the poorer countries and the provincial cities and towns will be left behind. One would like to see the OAS and the IDB combine on a comprehensive study of regional information system needs and possibilities. The Canadian experience with the use of satellites for television and other purposes in the Arctic could be helpful.

Networking ultimately is most effective on a person-to-person, scientist-to-scientist basis. Although many valuable voluntary organizations such as Inter-Ciencia are working to fill this need, much, much more is needed. Funds to attend meetings and conferences and to present papers, workshops on regional and subregional research topics, exchanges of staff, subsidies for journals, textbooks, cassettes, training of science-oriented journalists, are all important activities carried out at present on a miniscule scale. Indeed, only seven Caribbean and Latin American states have national associations for the advancement of science in order to network at home.

The priority for voluntary organizations should be science education at all levels. This means training and recycling of teachers (a UNESCO project), provision of texts, learning aids, audiovisual materials, organization of science clubs and science fairs, and many other activities. Women in Latin America are particularly deprived of opportunities to study science and technology and should receive special attention. A considerable experience with science education has been acquired in Brazil, Chile, and the United States, and it should be shared hemispherically. As sluggish as are most national ministries of education, the momentum behind science and education will have to come from voluntary groups, concerned parents, and

TABLE 22.5. Sectors of Performance According to Some National Surveys

Chile 1969	Venezuela 1970	Argentina 1969	Uruguay 1971
1. Higher education 2. Government	Public 1. Production of goods and services 2. Higher education 3. NP (nonprofit) establishments Private 1. Production of goods and services 2. Higher education 3. NP establishments	Sector 1. University 2. Public (decentralized) 3. Public (centralized) 4. Private working for public good 5. State and semi-public enterprises 6. Mixed	1. Ministries and central government 2. Other government departments 3. University 4. Private sector

Colombia 1971	Mexico 1970	Mexico 1973	Peru 1971
1. Government 2. Higher education 3. Productive sector 4. NP establishments	1. Higher education 2. Public and semi-public 3. Private 4. International organizations	1. General government 2. Enterprises 3. Higher education 4. NP establishments 5. Foreign establishments	1. Government 2. Higher education 3. Productive sector 4. NP establishments

Source: UNESCO, *Statistics on Science and Technology in Latin America, 1974*

477

TABLE 22.6. *Branches of Science in Different National Surveys*

Mexico 1970	Mexico 1973	Argentina 1969	Peru 1971
1. Mathematical sciences	1. Natural sciences	1. Natural sciences	1. Agriculture
2. Physical sciences	2. Agricultural sciences and technology	2. Engineering sciences and architecture	2. Natural sciences
3. Chemical sciences	3. Engineering sciences and technology	3. Medical sciences	3. Medical sciences
4. Biological sciences	4. Medical sciences and technology	4. Agricultural and veterinary sciences	4. Engineering sciences
5. Social sciences	5. Social sciences and humanities	5. Social sciences	5. Social sciences
6. Bio-medical sciences		6. Humanities	6. Legal and administrative sciences
7. Agriculture			7. Humanities and arts
8. Earth sciences			
9. Marine sciences			
10. Engineering sciences			
11. Communication sciences			
12. Technological applications and industrial development			

478

Chile 1969	Colombia 1971	Venezuela 1970	Uruguay 1971
1. Natural sciences	1. Natural sciences	1. Natural sciences, medical sciences	1. Exact sciences
2. Engineering sciences and technology	2. Engineering and technology	2. Physical and mathematical sciences, including:	2. Natural sciences
3. Medical sciences and technology	3. Medical sciences	Agriculture	3. Social, human and behavioral sciences
4. Agricultural sciences and technology	4. Agriculture	Engineering sciences	4. Engineering technology
	5. Social sciences and law	3. Social sciences and humanities	5. Medical technology
	6. Law, humanities		6. Agricultural technology
	7. Fine arts		7. Social engineering
			8. Humanities and Fine arts
			9. Other branches

Source: UNESCO, *Statistics on Science and Technology in Latin America, 1974*

sympathetic regional and international organizations. While the brunt of the effort must be national and local, international and regional groups can be of value through facilitating contacts, partly funding experimental programs, providing research and documentation services, and organizing conferences.

The demand for and supply of science and technology in the Western Hemisphere is substantially out of line. The United States, for instance, has substantial excess capacity, especially in the higher education system, while the Caribbean and many Latin American states with acute demands have no means of tapping this supply. Ironically, the major Latin American states, especially Brazil and Argentina, are demanding the transfer of technology to establish a civilian nuclear capability—technologies that the United States has become most reluctant to export. Another demand-and-supply disparity is the felt need in the region for technologies that will foster both economic growth and income distribution: decentralized, labor-intensive technologies that have long since gone out of style among technology exporters. The smaller countries are also seeking science and technology policies and infrastructures relevant to their size and needs, and these, too, are in short supply. There are few if any regional or international organizations that take up these demand-and-supply questions, and most actual transactions occur through bilateral channels. The result is often to perpetuate present disparities.

Through its own policies, the United States has tied itself up in knots that prevent mobilizing its science and technology for hemispheric use. This produces an enormous unused supply, especially in higher education where enrollment is static, young doctorate holders cannot find academic positions, and schools of engineering depend on foreign graduate students for research assistants. The 1972 doctrine of "Basic Needs" for U.S. aid, concentrating programs on the poorest of the poor, eliminated from assistance all Latin American middle-income countries including Brazil, Mexico, Argentina, and Venezuela. Yet these are the countries most capable of utilizing U.S. proprietary and public sector technology. Elsewhere the emphasis on basic needs has resulted in the exclusion of universities and even technical schools from AID programs and in an emphasis on rural development, rural health, and other low-technology efforts where the United States has no particular expertise nor experience.

The excess U.S. capacity can only be mobilized through joint multilateral or bilateral funding efforts to provide science and technology. For instance, young U.S. scientists and engineers could be made available to teach in the region where they are urgently needed, provided that some provision were made for the eventual reentry to the U.S. labor market, as is done for French volunteers. U.S. senior faculty could be made available to supervise research and advanced student exams through more flexible Fulbright and Binational funding. The Latin American Scholarship Program at American Universities (LAPAI), an effective effort to train Latin American graduate students in the United States to return to university teaching at home, could be greatly expanded. U.S. and regional research centers could be linked to work on a number of vital topics of mutual interest.

The reliance of the U.S. proprietary technology in its hemispheric relations means that the countries possessing foreign exchange (Mexico, Venezuela) or able to borrow it (Brazil) will be the principal beneficiaries. Technologies such as remote sensing developed with U.S. public sector funds will be available strictly for cash rather than need. Most importantly, the largest, finest higher education system in the world will operate at much less than capacity, while unfulfilled regional demand grows. The problem remains to convince the American public and politicians that the provision of U.S. science and technology on a noncommercial basis is in the national interest. Such provisions could provide amply for shared and joint funding, use through voluntary and multilateral channels, and other devices.

Ironically, certain technologies that some Latin American states are willing to purchase on a proprietary basis, the United States refuses to sell. The most important consists of nuclear reactors, where Brazil has obtained West German assistance and Argentina has obtained technology from Canada and recently Switzerland. The U.S. fear over the proliferation of nuclear energy is understood but not appreciated in the region, except in Canada. There is a desire to master nuclear technology, both as an important source of energy and as a concomitant of keeping up in a high-technology world. The prospect of continued dependence on the United States for high-grade uranium is as poorly viewed in the hemisphere as it is elsewhere in the world. Mexico may shortly also become a reactor customer, and the United States will either have to forego a major sale or change its own rules.

Related to the nuclear debate is the discussion over the export of U.S. products banned for use at home or subject to severe restrictions. It is the self-assertion of what technologies will or will not be allowed on the market, without consultation with interested buyers, that is so annoying. The decision may very well be sound not to export these products, especially to countries lacking a technology screening capability. However, a regional consultative process is needed before such decisions are unilaterally announced. The Pan American Health Organization (PAHO) might serve as a vehicle for regular consultation on undesirable drugs and other exports.

As the U.S. economy drifts, the desire to retain monopolies over important technologies may grow, especially if they have military value. Yet the sharing of science and technology, including nuclear energy, has been one of the most important strengths of the open U.S. society. The discussion over U.S. patent laws and university–industry connections needs to include the desirability of continuing to share U.S. innovations widely.

The problem of reconciling economic growth with income redistribution is one of the most intractable in the Western Hemisphere. It is in part a technological problem, and the search continues for reconciling technologies. For instance, 4-HP minitractors may be much more suitable for smallholders and tenant farmers than 16-HP tractors. Used industrial equipment, which employs more labor, may be cost-effective in many parts of the region compared to new, capital-intensive items. The recognition of the growth-redistribution technological problem has produced some limited research supported by the IDB on agricultural mechanization, a handful of "appropriate technology" groups in several countries, and some agricultural research at the International Maize and Wheat (CIMMYT), Tropical Agriculture, and Potato centers located respectively in Mexico, Columbia, and Peru.

Most imported as well as indigenous technologies, though, are capital-intensive, function best in urban environments, and require skilled labor and professionals. Underemployment and unemployment, the desire of women to enter the labor force, overurbanization, and other problems are simply not being addressed technologically. One place to start would be the construction industry, where low-cost, labor-intensive technologies should have a place. As private-sector R & D grows, one hopes that in the textile, leather, and other industries it will be concerned with redistributive technologies. In addition, IDB, together with the international agricultural research centers and the national governments, needs to mount a crisis technological effort to assist rainfed smallholders with food crops. Here are veritably the "poorest of the poor," next to their landless neighbors, and their problems do have a vital technological dimension that has not been resolved.

Just as technologies are needed for the rural poor, so are science and technology policies and practices needed for the poorest and smallest countries (20 of 30 independent states in the region). These countries need to select 2 to 3 research problems of national priority, put together a critical mass of researchers and technicians, network them to the best facilities in the world, and provide consistent 3-5-year funding. These efforts could then benefit from regional and international aid, especially where centers of excellence developed that could serve a wider region, such as marine biology in the Dominican Republic, oceanography in Costa Rica. The elaborate national councils of science and technology and bureaucracies erected in Brazil and Mexico are not needed. Instead, competent surveys of natural resources, using remote sensing where available, manpower inventories and plans, and firm funding decisions could get the show under way. At present in scores of countries there is little or no research, the few trained researchers emigrate, and demands are met by imported and sometimes unsuitable technologies. The handful of regional Central American research centers for nutrition, industrial research, and public administration provide examples of what small states can do by pooling their resources and maximizing external aid. The smaller states have enormous demands, which simply cannot be met through existing changes. They must be helped to create their own R & D capacity, which takes account of the international situation but accords with national realities.

AREAS OF SPECIAL CONCERN

Forecasting the evolution of science and technology is a hazardous enterprise. Still, several present or near-term developments can be seen to have the capability to alter hemispheric governance. We are anticipating situations in which science and technology are the driving forces bringing about changes in human organization, as in the case of television or the automobile. The potential for S & T-driven change seems greatest in telecommunications (computers and satellites), earth sciences (climatology and oceanography), and biology and agriculture.

The computer revolution is here, and Latin America is anxious to take part. Brazil has launched its own minicomputer industry after failing to induce IBM to enter a joint venture. The trend toward less and less expensive, smaller and smaller computers has enormous implications for the region. It may be possible to bypass high capital costs and to buy in on advanced technologies without paying the full research price. It is imperative that the region avoid getting stuck with obsolete hardware that will only accentuate its technological gap.

Communications satellites will soon have the capability to transmit TV signals into homes around the world. Linked to computers, satellites can provide fingertip information to the entire region. Argentina and Brazil have modest space research capabilities, and Canada has its own satellite, but U.S. technology through COMSAT continues to predominate. Studies are urgently needed of possible satellite–computer links and how they might be used to the benefit of research. Again the prospect exists of major cost savings, provided that technologies are shared. The IDB has done some research in this area and could move faster with Canadian help.

The earth sciences are on the verge of improving our understanding of our planet and our ability to predict its foibles. Perhaps the most challenging science for the hemisphere is seismography, which offers the still-awaited prospect of earthquake prediction. Regional seismographic research and training centers are needed for Central America and the Andean Pact countries, with greatly improved instrumentation. Cooperative research can be vastly expanded through the U.S. National Science Foundation and its national counterparts. The dilemma of what to do with predictions, and how to provide for human responses, needs to be urgently examined. The United States should continue its open science policy toward seismography and earthquake prediction, while assisting the region to participate fully in the field.

Oceanographic studies are widely dispersed throughout the hemisphere, but national capabilities vary enormously. The commercialization of the oceans, with or without a Law of the Seas, is harnessing the scientists to national needs. As our knowledge of ocean resources grows and technologies improve for their exploitation, old conflicts may reemerge. Already fishing disputes are a frequently recurring problem while knowledge of fish stocks and cycles remains inadequate. The problem is to build an oceanographic hemispheric data bank open to all to provide information for policies. This may not prevent a fight over deep-sea minerals or fishing rights, but it may facilitate a compromise. Thus cooperative research, shared facilities, regional centers of excellence, journals, conferences, and such should be the order of the day for oceanography.

Probably the most frightening science-driven problems are in climatology. Present uncertain studies point to the possibility of CO^2 resulting from industry accumulating in the atmosphere, destroying the ozone layer, and changing the earth's climate. Other studies suggest that rapid destruction of tropical rain forests may also bring about major climatic changes. While still in the realm of scientific conjecture, these possibilities indicate the need for new hemispheric forums for their discussion. Perhaps Inter-Cienca and its national science associations will take the lead? Again we need much more systematic data-gathering and shared hemispheric effort to solicit new information. And we need to begin to think about the possibility of alternative technology and spatial distributions of industry. The Amazon Basin Treaty of bordering states is a good start, which needs also to be followed up by cooperative research on those climatological problems.

The Green Revolution, which originated at the CIMMYT research center in Mexico, has brought about dramatic increases in agricultural yields. These are achieved through plan breeding of hybrid seeds and use of fertilizer and pesticides. Unfortunately this technological package favors those farmers who have existing resources. It is also a package with a high cost energy content and where returns to yield may be approaching biological ceilings. Together with agricultural mechanization, the Green Revolution package constitutes a massive source of social change throughout the region. It probably also contributes to the urbanization of the landless and tenant farmers.

Some observers speculate that the next agricultural revolution will result from current scientific work in biogenetics. This work is directed at helping plants to do better what they already do well: that is, improving plant photosynthesis and nitrogen fixation properties, and breeding plants that will thrive in saline soils. Similarly, the biological control of pests seeks their genetic sterility rather than relying on chemical pesticides. Much of this research is still at the basic stage, and no timetable exists for its maturation. The research is concentrated in a few universities and other centers in the United States and other postindustrial countries.

The biogenetics revolution in agriculture may never occur, but some new technologies will soon be needed to replace the Green Revolution. The region needs to invest in biogenetics research rather than waiting for the appearance of mature technologies. Brazil has already begun, through its work on nitrogen fixation. The designation of several regional centers, exchange of researchers, workshops, journals, and other techniques could enable the region to get aboard at this early stage, where it can still fully participate. International aid to facilitate such participation from the IDB and other sources is justified.

A host of challenges are altering the ways in which we manage science and technology in the Western Hemisphere. We are not doing badly, but we will have to do much better in the future.

23

Industrialization and Industrial Policy

Werner Baer

INTRODUCTION

Since the early 1950s, the policy makers of Latin America's major countries have relied upon industrialization as the principal strategy for achieving economic growth and development. The purpose of this essay is to examine the past impact of the industrialization process in Latin America, including its positive and negative aspects, current problems facing the industrial sector, and the future role of industry in the region's domestic and international growth.

Historical Antecedents

Until the twentieth century, Latin America fitted into the world division of labor as a supplier of primary products and few attempts were made to promote industry. There was little political desire to change the structure of the economies because favorable external markets for the region's primary exports benefited the elites of those days. In the nineteenth and early twentieth century, moreover, Latin American countries did not have the entrepreneurial classes, the skilled labor force, economic and social infrastructure, market size and administrative capacity to cope with industrialization. Finally, in a number of countries European powers had enough leverage to force governments to maintain free trade policies, which effectively blocked any possibility for the development of industries, as domestically produced manufactures could not compete against lower cost and better quality imports.

Latin America did not, however, remain completely devoid of manufacturing activities prior to the 1930s. In the latter part of the nineteenth century, workshops and small factories appeared in the textile, clothing, and food products sectors in Argentina, Brazil, Mexico, and a few other larger countries; machine tools and spare parts workshops were started to service railroads, sugar refining mills, and other economic activities. The early industrialists were often importers who turned to producing goods they had formerly bought abroad. They were able to do this by investing their accumulated profits, and their main motivation was the growing size of the market. On the eve of World War I these light industries had grown to such an extent that most local textile and food products consumption in the larger countries was already furnished locally. Interruption of supplies during World War I spurred domestic manufacturing, and installed capacity was used intensively. In the 1920s, however, industrial production stagnated as a result of U.S. and European competition and the refusal of Latin American policy makers to protect domestic industries. It was believed that World War I had been an aberration from the natural order of things, and governments were thus reluctant to impede the movement back to the apparent "normalcy" of the nineteenth-century world division of labor.

Until the great depression of the 1930s, no Latin American country had undergone a process of industrialization. Although some industries made their appearance in certain regions, export agriculture remained the leading and dominant sector of the economy. One can hardly speak of this process as industrialization, since industry did not become the economy's leading sector, causing pronounced structural changes.

For some countries, such as Argentina and Brazil, the great depression marked the beginning of an industrialization process. Industry became the leading sector of the economy and substantially increased its share of the GNP. Industrialization at the time was, however, more the result of a defensive policy—that is, of attempts to deal with the impact of the world depression on the balance of payments—rather than of deliberately choosing industrialization as a method for promoting economic development.

THE RISE OF INDUSTRIALIZATION

It was only after World War II that industrialization was adopted as the strategy for economic development. The type of industrialization pursued became known as Import Substituting Industrialization (ISI). It consisted of establishing domestic production facilities to manufacture goods that had formerly been imported. Most of the large Latin American countries explicitly or implicitly accepted the CEPAL (Economic Commission for Latin America) analysis of the futility of gearing their economies to the traditional world division of labor. Continued reliance on the export of food and primary products was thought to be inimical to economic development because of the market instability of such exports and the slow growth of world demand for them, which, it was agreed, would turn the terms of trade against them. ISI was viewed as introducing a dynamic element into the Latin American economies, which would increase their rates of growth. The latter was deemed essential to deal with the population explosion of the region and to meet the demands of the increasingly urban population for the ways of life of the masses in more advanced industrial countries. It was also thought that ISI would bring greater economic independence, with self-sufficiency in manufactured goods placing Latin American economies less at the mercy of the world economy and the economic fluctuations originating in the industrial centers of the world.

The principal policy instruments used to promote and intensify ISI consisted of: protective tariffs and/or exchange controls to restrict the imports of consumer goods; special incentives for domestic and foreign firms importing capital goods for new industries; preferential import exchange rates for industrial raw materials, fuels, and intermediate goods; government construction of infrastructure especially designed to complement industries; and the direct participation of government in certain industries (especially heavy industries such as steel) where it was assumed that neither domestic nor foreign private capital was willing to invest.

The promotion of ISI industries was indiscriminate. No attempts were made to concentrate on industrial sectors that might have had a potential comparative advantage. Some countries followed a sequence that began with the promotion of consumer goods and building materials products, which used a relatively simple technology; this was followed by consumer goods using a more sophisticated and capital intensive technology, and, finally, by heavy and capital goods industries. This road was followed by such countries as Argentina, Chile, and Colombia. Other countries, like Brazil, followed policies that stressed a maximum amount of vertical integration— that is, they simultaneously promoted final consumer goods, intermediate goods and capital goods industries.

An important feature of Latin American ISI has been the participation of foreign capital. Although its proportion of investment was often below 10%, it was instrumental in setting up key manufacturing industries by transferring know-how and organizatinal capabilities. This was also the case with infrastructure and heavy industry investments by government-owned enterprises, which depended on foreign financing and technical aid.

The ISI policies were responsible for high real rates of economic growth in the 1950s in many of the region's major countries, among them Brazil, Mexico, and Colombia. Even where overall growth rates were not very high (e.g., Argentina), industry was usually the leading sector. By the early 1960s it had surpassed agriculture's share of GNP in all the major countries.

Shortcomings of ISI by the Early 1960s

Some economists have viewed ISI as an inefficient way of using resources to achieve growth. The more conservative among them believe that since world production can best be maximized by having each country (or area of the world) specialize in sectors where it has its greatest comparative advantage, Latin America should have continued to concentrate on the production of primary products. This would have maximized world output and made possible a higher level of income in all parts of the world.

Because of the declining share of food and primary products in world trade, more moderate criticas recognized the need for some ISI. Their main objection is to the indiscriminate way in which it was carried out, with the across-the-board promotion of industries without regard even to potential comparative advantage. The Latin American ISI strategies are seen as drives toward national self-sufficiency, with total disregard of the advantages of a possible international division of labor along newer lines. This emphasis on autarky was considered as prejudicial to rapid economic growth for a number of reasons.

Given the small markets, limited capital, and a dearth of skilled manpower, autarkic industrial growth leads to the development of inefficient and high-cost industries. This is especially the case in sectors having high fixed costs. They require large-scale output to bring costs down to levels prevailing in advanced industrial countries. Outstanding examples are the steel and automobile industries, which have been established in many Latin American countries. In the case of automobiles, the situation was worsened because many countries permitted the establishment of a large number of firms, thus completely eliminating the possibility of economies of large-scale production. Even in the largest market, Brazil, only in recent years have a few of the major manufacturers achieved the economies of scale regarded as normal in the older industrial countries. The reason for such large numbers of firms was the impression of policy makers that this would bring on the benefits of competition. If the latter existed at all, it was overcome by the lack of scale economies. In the latter 1960s and the 1970s a number of smaller countries substantially reduced the quantity of automobile firms operating within their borders.

Inefficiencies in the industrial sectors have also been the result of overprotection. In many countries the rate of "effective protection" has been much greater than "nominal" protection. The latter measures only the percentage by which prices of protected goods exceed their world prices. "Effective" tariffs indicate the percentage by which value added ". . . at a stage of fabrication in domestic industry can exceed what this would be in the absence of protection, in other words, it shows by what percentage the sum of wages, profits, and depreciation allowances, payable by domestic firms can, thanks to protection, exceed what this sum would be if the same firms were fully exposed to foreign competition."[1] Thus, if a product uses a considerable amount of imported inputs on which there is no tariff or on which the tariff rate is lower than the tariff on the finished product, protection is higher than is indicated by the nominal tariff, since the margin available for domestic value added is larger than the difference indicated by the tariff. In a number of Latin American countries the effective tariff on consumer goods was much higher than for intermediate or capital goods. (At one time in the 1960s effective protection for manufactured products in Brazil was about 250%, as compared with nominal protection of about 100%). Such high levels of effective protection eliminate incentives to increase production efficiency and make it difficult to bring the cost of production to international levels.

It has been argued that the stress on autarky in the region's industrialization (that is, the maximizing of internal vertical integration of industry, promoting not only final goods production, but also intermediate and capital goods) impedes growth because resources are not used in sectors where they will produce the highest possible output.

The promotion of industry has been prejudicial to the agricultural sector in a number of countries. The allocation of investment resources to new industries has often meant that fewer resources were available to increase agricultural productivity. Overvalued exchange rates, which favored industries by providing cheap imported inputs, hurt agriculture by making its goods less competitive in the international market and/or by making it less profitable to produce for the agricultural export sector. The combination of higher industrial prices caused by protection and the price control of agricultural goods, moreover, turned the internal terms of trade against agriculture. All these factors hurt agricultural production and exports. (Argentina is probably the outstanding example of ISI taking place at the expense of agriculture.)

Neglect of Exports

Until the 1960s, Latin America's policy makers concentrated exclusively on ISI. They neglected the export of traditional goods and made no effort to diversify the commodity structure of exports in accordance with the changing internal economic structure that ISI had brought about. It gradually became obvious, however, that ISI had not made Latin American countries self-sufficient. It had only changed the nature of their trade linkages with the outside world. Whereas previously imports were principally made up of final consumption goods, they now increasingly consisted of raw materials and capital goods. The latter represented imported inputs into the newly established industrial sector which could not be obtained domestically.

It was thus ironic that the net result of ISI placed Latin American countries in a new dependency relationship with the advanced industrial centers and a more dangerous one than before. In former times a decline in export receipts acted as a stimulus to ISI. Under the new circumstances, a decline in export receipts not counterbalanced by capital inflows can result in forced import curtailments, which, in turn, can cause an industrial recession. This has been experienced by a number of Latin American countries. Most of the major Latin American countries gradually perceived that to adjust to this situation, they would have to make efforts to diversify exports.

Post-ISI Adjustments

During the 1960s and 1970s, attempts were made to adjust to some of the shortcomings of ISI. The export of nontraditional, especially manufactured exports was promoted by the use of both fiscal incentives and subsidized credits. By the late 1970s, these efforts proved to have been fairly successful. The share of manufactured goods in the value of Latin America's total exports increased from 13% in 1970 to about 25% by the late 1970s. Especially notable was the share of manufactures in Brazil and Mexico's exports, which in the late 1970s amounted to about 33%.

The smaller countries of Latin America that had industrialized faced many problems because of their small internal market size, which prevented them from benefiting from economies of scale and thus eventually producing at competitive prices. These countries were the most fervent advocates of regional economic integration, which was seen as a way out of their narrow market. When progress of LAFTA became stalled, the smaller countries of South America formed the Andean Group. One of its basic goals was to rationalize the existing industrial base of member countries to provide for future integrated growth. These countries, for instance, substantially reduced the number of automobile firms in their respective countries, and those firms permitted to stay on had to fit into an agreed-upon division of labor for the production of various types of vehicles and their parts. Central American economic integration, which began even prior to the Andean Group, was promoted in order to get the industrialization process started, since the very small size of Central American countries precluded even the beginnings of many manufacturing industries.

THE CURRENT ROLE OF INDUSTRY

In the contemporary major Latin American economies industry plays a key role. Manufacturing accounts for over 35% of the domestic product in Argentina, about 30% in Brazil and Mexico, 25% in Peru, and about 20% in Colombia. Including construction and public utilities would substantially increase this share: For all of Latin America it would rise from 27 to 39% in the late 1970s. Much of the region's manufacturing was concentrated in three countries— Argentina, Brazil, and Mexico—which accounted for 78% of its value added (while they contained only 65% of Latin America's population).

The industrial achievements of Latin America are impressive in absolute terms—that is, amount of transport equipment produced, tons of steel, output of consumer durables, of capital goods, or petrochemical products. Over the last decade there has also been a noticeable diversification of the industrial structure away from the traditional sectors (especially textiles and food products). In the late 1970s machinery and equipment accounted for 30% of industrial value added in Brazil, 24% in Argentina, and 20% in Mexico; while chemicals amounted to 13% of industrial value added in Argentina, 12% in Brazil, and 14% in Mexico. As already mentioned, there has been an impressive growth of manufactured exports in the 1970s, which includes even some exports of capital goods and industrial projects, especially from Argentina and Brazil. In absolute terms, there also exists a large and by now well-trained skilled industrial labor force and a substantial amount of engineering and managerial capabilities.

The nature of Latin America's industrialization has, however, brought problems and/or aggravated already existing ones, which defy short-run solutions. Let us examine some of them.

Employment

The employment impact of industrial growth in most countries of Latin America has been disappointing. The rate of growth of industrial output (especially in the manufacturing sector) has been substantially higher than the rate of growth of industrial employment. By 1978, while industry's share of the GDP in Argentina was 45%, it only employed 29% of the labor force; for Brazil the difference in the ratio was 37 and 33%; for Mexico 37 and 26%; in the United States the ratios in the late 1970s were 34 and 33%, while in West Germany they were 48 and 48%. This low labor absorption capacity of the industrial sector has to be viewed in the context of a high rural–urban migration in most countries of the region. Thus, a large proportion of the urban labor force has been forced to find employment in the low-productivity urban sectors, especially in services. (Industrial-urban growth, of course, calls for the expansion of many complementary service jobs. But even the latter have not expanded at a satisfactory rate relative to the labor supply).

The principal reason for the low job-creating capacity of industry is its capital-intensive technology. There was little adaptation of imported technology to local factory supply conditions. The reason for this rigidity has never been satisfactorily established. Some economists have claimed that developing countries have artificially distorted factor prices in their desire to stimulate ISI. In other words, they have made the price of capital artificially low relative to that of labor, thus stimulating the introduction of capital-intensive technology. This argument, however, has never been satisfactorily proven. In fact, in the early ISI spurt, much of the imported equipment was second-hand, and one could thus argue that at the time a choice was made favoring relatively more labor-intensive technology. Yet even with the latter, industry's labor absorption was low.

With the advent of nontraditional export promotion in the 1960s and 1970s, both domestic and multinational firms in Latin America switched to new equipment in their investment programs in order to compete more effectively in the international market. The cost of diversifying exports was thus to make the industrial sector even less labor absorptive than before.

Income Distribution

In Latin America the distribution of income has traditionally been very concentrated, and industrialization has tended to accentuate this characteristic. In fact, in the major industrial countries, periods of high industrial growth rates have brought about substantial increases in the relative inequality of the income distribution. This may have been caused, in part, by the capital-intensive nature of newly-built industries. A high capital/labor ratio means that a large proportion of the increment in the national income contributed by the industrial sector goes to non–wage-earning groups. Within the wage earning groups, moreover, a high capital intensity may favor certain types of skilled labor at the expense of poorer workers. Since the industrial sector is the most dynamic in the economy and since its capital/labor ratio is higher than the national average, growth (ceteris paribus) will inevitably favor the nonwage sector (even if average wages in the dynamic industrial sector are higher than the national average).

The traditional justification for industrialization policies that resulted in these trends in the distribution of income is that concentration increases the capacity of a society to save (i.e., the upper income groups have a higher propensity to save than the lower ones), making it possible to invest in new productive capacity. With time, the total productive capacity will be large enough to support both a continuing high rate of growth and a more equitable distribution of income. There is, thus, at first, a negative relation between growth and equity, but beyond a certain point this conflict may disappear as growth makes all groups better off.

The experiences of the large countries of Latin America have thrown some doubts on this argument, even if we ignore the political power to resist change that may be generated by increasing inequality. The type of industrialization that takes place under conditions of increasingly concentrated income will not necessarily be adequate for a possible future situation of greater equality. Latin America's actual production profile reflects the demand profile, which, in turn, is influenced by the distribution of income. How flexible is the productive apparatus built up to accommodate a specific structure of demand? Could it be used under new socioeconomic conditions that would result in a changed demand profile? Obviously the basic economic infrastructure and industries in the capital goods and steel sectors would have more flexibility than other industries that are further downstream (i.e., closer to the consumer). Finally, one should also take into account the firms with a vested interest in the existing productive structure: How effectively would they resist reforms that would threaten their markets?

Regional Concentration

Regional disparities in the growth of economic activities and the distribution of the national product have been a common feature in large Latin American countries. The process of industrialization has accentuated this concentration and made redistribution more difficult.

There is a logic to this trend. Since industrialization in a poor country begins with a small market with few opportunities for economies of scale, especially if export opportunities are regarded as limited, any attempt at regional deconcentration in the early stages will tend to increase the difficulties in making the new sector efficient. One should also consider the various external economies associated with geographical concentration, which also contribute to decreasing the cost of industrial production. There are thus obvious conflicts between regional balance and rapid and efficient industrial growth. To date the latter has usually been given priority.

Multinationals

Since rapid ISI was possible only with a substantial influx of foreign capital, it is not surprising that in many dynamic sectors multinational corporations became vehicles for such investments. Some countries allow only subsidiaries of multinationals to function with local participation (e.g., Mexico), while others allow them to be totally owned by the parent company. Regardless of the formal rules of operation, however, there can be little doubt of the important role multinationals continue to play in the dynamic industrial sectors of Latin America.

Although multinationals were a fundamental factor in enabling Latin American countries to industrialize rapidly—in providing capital, technology, organizational skills, and, at a later stage, in providing marketing outlets for the export of manufactured goods—their presence has raised a number of issues that affect not only relations between multinationals and the host governments, but also relations between the government of the host country and the government of the parent-firm country. The major problems are the following:

Profit Remittances

In addition to the issue of what would be a reasonable maximum profit remittance per year that the host government could impose, there is also the question of control. The phenomenon of "transfer pricing" makes possible hidden transfers of profits. The technique is used to understate profits in the host country not only to circumvent profit remittance controls, but also to decrease tax payments. Disputes about such practices are bound to rise in the future, since it is difficult for any control agency to make unambiguous rules for pricing imports from the parent companies or for pricing technical assistance from parent to subsidiary.

Technology

Multinationals have been accused of not adapting the technology they implant to Latin American conditions—that is, making it more labor intensive. Yet, as discussed above, it is not clear whether such adaptation is either feasible or desirable.

Emphasis on old or artisan-type technology, however, may not satisfy the desire of policy makers to strengthen their country's economic and political position vis-à-vis the industrial centers of the world. Many feel that only modern technology and the capacity for generating new technology within their countries will improve their relative position.

Although multinationals have responded by introducing fairly up-to-date technology, they have been reluctant to engage in genuine research and development activities in the host countries. Most "R & D" of multinationals takes place on the parent company's home ground. A major reason for this is that technology is the strongest card a multinational has in its international bargaining position, and this advantage is thus to be guarded carefully.

Meanwhile, for the host country, it is important to acquire the capacity to produce technology to increase its relative bargaining position and to reduce the cost of importing technology.

Thus the development of local "R & D" capacity will be an increasing bone of contention between major Latin American countries and multinationals in the next decades, as the ambition of these countries grows from merely building new industries to acquiring a share in the world's technology-producing capacity.

The Role of State Enterprises

A notable feature of Latin America's industrialization has been the role of state enterprises and state financial institutions.[2] In most countries a large proportion of the steel industry is owned by state enterprises; most public utilities are run by state companies; the state owns mining operations and derivative firms; in a number of countries it has a monopoly of oil exploration, and state petroleum companies have a large stake in refining and petrochemical industries. Development banks are state-owned, as is a significant proportion of commercial banks.

Direct state participation in economic activity is largely due to national industrialization ambitions, which required development of a number of basic industrial sectors with large capital requirements and long gestation periods. Few local private groups had the financial and technical capabilities to launch such ambitions, and multinationals were reluctant to commit huge sums to projects that would only begin to pay off in the distant future, if at all. Consequently, governments were forced to organize state enterprises to do the job. In certain cases, of course, governments entered for other nationalistic reasons; For example, it was deemed to be against the national interest to have such sectors as petroleum and mining under foreign control.

In a similar fashion, the large presence of the state in investment and commercial banking is linked to the industrialization process. Rapid ISI required an adequate financial system to provide funding for both the private and the state sectors. As capital markets were still underdeveloped, the founding of state financial institutions became a necessity.

In most cases in the hemisphere, the domestic, private sector, the multinational corporations, and the state enterprise sectors have worked harmoniously together. They have largely complemented rather than competing against each other. It is doubtful that the state will—or can—reduce its share of economic activities in the short or even medium-run, since there are still few sources of funds to permit the private sector to buy out large state undertakings, and since it would be politically unfeasible to sell these to multinationals.

The present state of knowledge on how state enterprises operate is still rudimentary. For example, it is unclear where decision-making powers lie concerning pricing, investments, imports or equipment, or domestic vs. foreign procurement. The few existing studies of large state enterprises make it clear that they are not necessarily under the control of the central government. Often their own economic power makes itself felt on the decisions of government ministries, rather than vice versa.

A recent trend, which merits further examination, is the appearance of joint ventures between Latin American state enterprises and multinationals. These have been especially prevalent in mining, steel mills, aluminum plants, petrochemicals, and some other areas. Usually the state firm has 51% control of such ventures. There are obvious advantages to both sides. The state firm has access to requisite natural resources, basic technology, and equity finance; the multinational sells equipment and supplementary technology, may provide management skills, has shares in the earnings, hence has a politically safe investment.

COMPLEMENTARITY VS. COMPETITIVENESS IN ECONOMIC RELATIONS

The recent emphasis on trade diversification, in which exports of manufactures have played a prominent role, has raised questions about the share of world markets for manufactured goods that Latin American countries will be allowed to have. The success of Mexico, Brazil, Argentina, and other countries in selling manufactured goods in the United States and Europe brought about a reaction in the late 1970s in the form of demands to eliminate various types of export incentives. Some countries (e.g., Brazil) have complied with these demands and, in compensation, have drastically devalued their currencies.

Although it is generally recognized that export diversification is important to increase the foreign exchange earnings capability of Latin American countries (which has become even more important for petroleum importing countries), most advanced industrial nations have not been very receptive to the idea of providing a permanent market for Latin American manufactured goods. One of the major issues in the next decade will be the degree of accommodation the industrial centers of the world will offer: To what extent will they agree to a new world division of labor in the production of manufactured goods?

A further issue in industrial trade relations concerns the growing vertical division of labor between Latin America and advanced industrial countries. A growing proportion of trade consists of semifinished products, many of which are goods sent from subsidiaries of multinationals to parent firms, or to other subsidiaries. For example, U.S. auto manufacturers make engines in some of their Latin American subsidiaries, which are then shipped to the United States for final assemblage. Although such a new interrelationship may have benefits from an efficiency point of view, it can also produce situations in conflict.

This trend results in some sacrifice in decision-making autonomy within Latin America, as it becomes more integrated into an international system of production.[3] The level of production of the subsidiaries of multinational corporations, especially those vertically integrated on an international level, thus depends on decisions of multinationals concerning their world production objectives, hence the international division of their activities.

International bargaining for shares in the international production scheme of multinationals is still in its infancy. On the Latin American side, the multinationals increasingly are feeling the pressure of governments anxious to push their export diversification programs. Simultaneously, multinationals remain attracted by tax incentive schemes to increase exports. Meanwhile, in the United States, there has been a mounting pressure by labor unions and other interest groups to limit the expansion of overseas production facilities of U.S.-based multinationals, on the grounds that such operations in effect "export" American jobs.

It is possible that the huge foreign debt of the major countries of Latin America may periodically have given their governments some bargaining strength. The large stake that U.S.-based and other multinational corporations and commercial banks have in the economic growth and balance of payments strength of the borrowers is an obvious consequence of their past financial commitments. It is probably no exaggeration to state that the continuing ability of the larger countries (notably Brazil and Mexico) to service their external debt is essential to the solvency of many of the principal members of the international financial community. For this reason, the past borrowing and receptivity to foreign direct investment of the major Latin American nations has given them a group of allies in their efforts to obtain favorable trade policies from the developed world and especially to facilitate the further growth of their manufactured exports.

IMPLICATIONS FOR INTERNATIONAL GOVERNANCE

Existing international organizations—such as the UN and its regional affiliate (CEPAL), the OAS, the IDB—are not structurally suited to resolve many of the issues outlined in this paper. The needs of Latin American countries to guarantee the further growth and stability of their industrial sector are: (1) continued expansion of industrial exports; (2) new policies by multinationals to minimize retrenchments in their Latin American subsidiaries during the downturns of the business cycle; (3) greater technological development within Latin America; (4) expansion of joint ventures between multinationals and local private or state enterprises. Though not emphasized in this paper, there are many implicit advantages to the United States and its industrial, agricultural, and banking sectors in seeing balanced economic growth in Latin America continue in steady fashion.

Since concrete results in these areas can only be achieved by parties with economic and political power, the creation of a new hemispheric organization is called for. It might be a hybrid of a GATT-type organization and an international equivalent of the corporatist entities found in many Latin American countries, such as the confederation of industries. The organization could, however, deal with a broader set of issues. It might be called the Inter-American Trade and Development Organization (ITDO). Delegations from each country representing the following groups might join in its periodic meetings: associations of industries, of private financial institutions, of public development banks, of unions, of state enterprises, and of governments. The objective of such meetings (which could last several months) would be to achieve international policy goals through bargaining. The meetings would include plenary sessions in which representatives would articulate general and particular problems and needs, but most of the work would be done through direct negotiations.

For example, the following illustrative bilateral deals might be negotiated:

1. Representatives of Brazilian exporters would confer with U.S. banking representatives, which have great exposure in Brazil, about ways to open U.S. markets for Brazilian goods.

2. Representatives of U.S. multinationals could bargain with Colombian government officials about abolition of import and price controls in exchange for commitments of the firms to increase local research and development expenditures.

3. Peruvian government representatives could bargain with multinationals, resulting in more lenient profit remittance policies in exchange for more equity investments by multinationals and less international borrowing by the Peruvian government.

In other words, the ITDO could provide a clearing-house for sectoral interests from all countries in the hemisphere. The representatives of interest groups might discover allies to achieve common goals or bargain for mutual favors. Bargains struck between the two nongovernmental groups could then lead to a commitment of each to obtain the necessary concessions from the respective governments.

The development of such an organization would be a logical follow-up to the era of "Import Substituting Industry" and of "foreign aid" of the 1950s and 1960s, when development often depended on aid from the U.S. government or on persuading multinational corporations to establish themselves in a protected market. The new era of international governance would involve international cooperation based on bargaining for mutual advantages. This, in the long-run, might be a sounder basis for inter-American relations. Instead of being based on a donor–receiver basis, which has always resulted in mutual resentments, the new emphasis would be on practical and concrete mutual objectives and mutual concessions, leading to a greater equality in international relations.

NOTES

1. Ian Little, T. Scitovsky, and M. Scott, *Industry and Trade in Some Developing Countries* (Oxford University Press, 1970), p. 39.

2. See: Werner Baer, *The Brazilian Economy: Its Growth and Development* (Columbus, Ohio: Grid Publishing, Inc., 1979), chapter 7, "Brazil's Extended Public Sector."

3. The following paragraphs are taken from: Werner Baer and Donald V. Coes, "Changes in the Inter-American Economic System," in *The Future of the Inter-American System*, edited by Tom J. Farrer (New York: Praeger Publishers, 1979).

24

Regionalism Reconsidered

L. Ronald Scheman

THE CHALLENGE

The Brandt Commission's recommendation to strengthen the role of regional financial institutions could well signal a major turning point in our approach to global development programs. It is the first major report commissioned by a global agency that acknowledges advantages that may accrue from delegation of responsibility to a regional level. Coming upon another recent recommendation to strengthen the International Court of Justice by creating a network of decentralized regional courts with right of appeal to the International Court, the potential of regionalism as a meaningful component of a new international development system is coming more to the fore.

Since the current international structure was designed in the post-World-War-II era, regional arrangements have been relegated in our thinking and planning to issues of peace-keeping and security under Articles 52–54 of the United Nations Charter. Indeed, the framework for world order structured in recent decades is probably

---

Dr. Scheman is Assistant Secretary for Management of the Organization of American States. The opinions in the paper reflect only the views of the author and not those of the Organization.

one of mankind's most daring experiments: the voluntary association of sovereign nations on an all-inclusive, pluralistic basis. These two elements, voluntary and pluralistic, are unprecedented in history. Combined with the growing understanding that development is the vital element in achieving world order, they mark a complex challenge to our ingenuity and will. Aside from the United Nations' Regional Economic Commissions, a small, polite bow toward regional development capability, however, little serious attention has been given to regional potential.

Rather than a diversion from the goal of universal world order, regional arrangements for development cooperation may have important potential as an essential component in a viable system of global development assistance. In this context, regional cooperation has an important, serious, and largely underestimated role in a systematic effort to spur more effective and rapid global development and as a logical stepping stone to the goal of a universal peace and development.

Its potential lies essentially:

1. as an intermediary administrative level in a global development system that is simply too vast to manage from a centralized base;

2. as a practical mechanism to enable the peoples of a region to express themselves and resolve many issues pertinent to their daily concerns that become submerged in the broad general discussions of the global fora;

3. as an essential instrument to cope with the interdisciplinary issues that require lateral communication among different professions to implement relevant and pragmatic programs on a manageable scale.

Despite our pretensions, we are well aware that our current knowledge of man's predicament is rudimentary and our efforts for international development cooperation are highly experimental. These experiments are taking place amidst radical changes in the international environment. Overwhelmed by a torrent of technological innovations and the revolution in communications, human survival has come to dominate the international agenda. Demands on finite energy and natural resources increase, the gap between the wealthy and the poor nations continues to widen, financial systems are strained, environment pollution accelerates, terrorist groups and organized crime ignore national borders with impunity, weapons of mass destruction become cheaper to produce, and, most serious, the expectations of our peoples are rising dramatically. Overlaid with new issues and new players on the scene, solutions that formerly appeared viable are becoming bogged down in competition and controversy in a world of widely divergent national interests and values.

The issues and contradictions that have come to influence our international organizations never were and could not have been taken into account in the design of our system of international cooperation decades ago:

1.   one of the principal functions of international organization has become development;

2.   a raft of smaller states established in the dismantling of colonial empires have adopted international organization as their major platform while vigorously asserting their independence and sovereignty;

3.   the realities of interdependence for planetary survival are inescapable;

4.   the divergent specific needs of different regions are becoming more pronounced;

5.   the international institutions are beginning to handle enormous sums of money, more than some of their members, in widely diverse and far-flung operations.

The sum is that a viable basis for international cooperation cannot hope to prosper without a credible mechanism to assist the developing countries achieve their own institutional basis for growth, and that this has become the specific business of the international community.

The shortcomings of UN machinery for managing development programs from a centralized base need not be commented upon here. The UN system has been termed as "more the product of history than an overall plan."[2] Sir Robert Jackson, in his "Study of the Capacity of the United Nations Development System," called the United Nations a "non-system."[3] The question is whether there are viable alternatives to strengthen and supplement our global efforts. In this regard, the concept of regionalism has been generally dismissed either as a diversion from the objective of a universal world order[4] or as a military security device that has little to do with development. The landmark study of regionalism by Joseph Nye emphasized the "conflict containing" advantage of the regional arrangements.[5] Some advocates of regionalism have distorted the immediate argument by trying to oversell it as device to surmount national sovereignty and to move beyond the nation-state.[6] Nonetheless the practical importance of this type of regional cooperation is evidenced by the increasing numbers of those organizations being formed by the governments themselves. It has been reported that 73% of the international organizations established in the period between 1956 and 1965 were regional.[7] The potential complementary and not conflictive relationship between the global and regional institutions in a multidimensional world is the subject of this discussion.

THE PREMISES

One vital aspect of our current effort to construct a world development system on a voluntary and pluralistic basis is the potential beginning of a new era of democracy *among* nations. In the past, international organization was regarded as a device to surmount national sovereignty. The enshrinement of the concept of national sovereignty within the UN Charter, however, sets the rules of the present game. Even the words—United *Nations*—define our precepts. The reality is that the nation-state is firmly part of our international structure and is probably indispensable as an administrative component of any global development system.

But we know that the nation is not sufficient. The attempt to manage global development efforts from a centralized base, without recognizing any administrative subdivision except the nation-state, is ineffective and wasteful from almost any criteria. One formula cannot be applied arbitrarily to every problem. Neither the United States, nor any other government of the world, could operate effectively without city, county, and state jurisdictions for different functions. Conversely, our efforts for international order may increase their potential enormously if we encourage interacting structures on multiple levels: national, regional, subregional, and global. Existing forces operating at various levels must be mobilized in more practical and creative ways.

This is especially relevant considering the large number of small developing nations, their diverse cultural patterns and state of readiness, and their unique needs for a practical source for technical assistance and training. Over half of the current members of the United Nations have populations under 5,000,000. Of these, 32, or one fifth of the nations, have less than 1,000,000. It has been pointed out that 148 of the next 150 nations that potentially could become members of the United Nations will have populations under 5,000,000, and 120 of these will have populations under 300,000.[8]

The role of the small states in international organization has brought fundamental changes to the nature of doing business in the international community. As one observer has noted, ". . . gradually the new nations have taken over the U.N., imbuing it with their values and cutting it to their cloth. It has become their major platform, the place where they express their aspirations and frustrations and where they mobilize world opinion."[9] In the development activities of our international institutions, this new voice, combined with the separation of voting power from the financial capacity to implement specific programs, is placing new strains on the mechanisms of governance.

While they have learned how to make more effective use of international fora, the smaller nations, fresh from a colonial past, remain wary of the degree of the confidence they can place in public multinational institutions and the dominance of the larger nations. Even where they perceive that public multilateral mechanisms may reinforce their development efforts and help constrain the power of the larger states, generating confidence is slow and difficult. What Robert Cox has called the issue of "stratification of power" will be a major concern in the design of our global systems of governance.[10] Domestic leaders will insist on maintaining manageable barriers between themselves and outside pressures, but will find themselves increasingly buffeted by forces totally out of their control operating on the national level alone.

The devolution of authority is one of the most important phenomena of our age. Having decided to let all nations speak out, their integration into a comprehensive and credible world development system is a major task. Such a system based on the voluntary association of nations must take greater account of these realities, which cannot be done by trying to apply global medicine to all of our complex maladies. Supplementing these efforts must be some means to encourage and blend activity and expression on multiple levels.

Another new and vital element in the equation lies in the international organizations themselves. Any movement toward a reconsideration of the structure of our international institutions encounters in them a new factor that did not exist when world organization was conceived. These institutions often mount highly effective defenses toward the established ways of handling their fields of specialization. A strong international civil service within the international organizations has its own interests and protective mechanisms.[11] It has become, as planned, a tremendous force for stability and continuity within the existing agencies. On one hand, it has endowed them with a spirit of professionalism and impartiality, which enables them to manage international development efforts as well as emergency situations with equanimity and confidence. On the other hand, it is a strong force that must be taken into account in any effort to change the current structure. Because the international career service is largely and deliberately composed of expatriates who have given up traditional family ties and careers in their national hierarchies, they are extremely chary of changes that might threaten their status. Before even presenting his study on the capacity of the United Nations development system, Sir Robert Jackson despaired that it would be strongly resisted by governments and international bureaucracies alike.[12]

Indeed, one of the great ironies of our world is that the international agencies, which were established to end anarchy among nations, today have greater anarchy among themselves than ever existed among nations. Nations have reasons to communicate: commerce, investment, tourism, and so on. The present structure of our international agencies, however, gives them little reason even to talk to each other. They have independent budgets, independent governing bodies, and independent financing. From the initial decision making to program execution, they are self-sufficient and autonomous.

Equally significant, the governments themselves can hardly keep track of the agencies and what they are doing. The large countries are unable to follow the many issues with coordinated policy.[13] The smaller countries are notoriously under-staffed and find it impossible to cope with the mountains of paperwork that are produced. In large measure, this situation is a serious threat to the effectiveness of all international undertakings. The reality is that governmental control of the global international machinery is an illusion. Even the top management of the institutions is unable to keep track of the far-flung activities. The staffs and technicians of the various international agencies have very little restraints other than their own high motivation and goodwill, which is, on the whole, considerable. But a more manageable scale for different types of activities is a desperate need if we are to grow to meet tomorrow's demands.

THE SCENARIO

Instantaneous communications between Peking and Paris, Kansas and Kenya, have created today a capacity to interact on multiple levels that is only beginning to impress itself upon our consciousness, no less upon the institutional structure by which we conduct our international affairs. While it is argued that this facilitates a global approach, the reality is that it magnifies our differences and makes global decision making more difficult. With the expectations of people in remote villages coming to match those of people in the most sophisticated cities, the demand for dramatic solutions to intractable problems far outstrips the capacity of our institutional structure. The persistent gap between expectations and the capacity to deliver, always a pernicious one for humankind, is especially acute in international affairs. It is wishful thinking to presume that the world's poor are going to wait 100 years to see if it can be bridged. They seek effective machinery to help deal with their more immediate day-to-day needs now.

On the other hand, great latent resources are suddenly at our fingertips. The rich strains of thought and perceptions that exist among humankind, the diversity of our peoples, the different cultures, values, and ways of doing things in different areas of the world, are one of our most valuable assets if we can motivate them toward cooperation. An international system that will facilitate expression of and reconcile our differences in culture and geography, our differing endowments of natural resources, our different systems of government, can tap unsuspected energies. It will require a coherent and sensitive mechanism that allows all these factors full expression to work together while maintaining the uniqueness of each.

The strong nationalistic motivation that persists as part of the identity of the new nations and the protective mechanisms of the old will not easily or quickly yield to international symbols. The jump from "national budgets to world development budgets"[14] is simply too great. Evolution to a broader world community on a working level will be achieved only by small, careful steps among nations with similar interests and common development problems where tangible and productive cooperation will begin to broaden ties between peoples and create interests beyond national borders. One important mechanism for this is to encourage regional and subregional efforts at developmental cooperation, moving from small, dependent economic units to larger productive areas among neighboring peoples.

A major argument against regional international organizations is that shifting the attention of nations from global cooperation to small units will be a step backward, creating other loyalties and diverting humankind from building a universal global organization. This is especially pertinent considering the decisive factors in the world environment and the current North–South issues. A strong argument can be made that regional organizations may require and foster a certain degree of discrimination against the industrialized countries and thereby be directly contrary to the interests of those countries. Another argument is that except for the superpowers, the vital interests of the smaller nations are often more in conflict among neighbors within a region than those at larger distances.

These arguments, however, ignore the reality of our condition. First, regional blocks are already an integral part of our global negotiations. But while they have become major factors in the decision-making process within global entities, we are not seeking ways of making use of regional and cultural dynamics as a functional component of global development. Second, the nation-state will only evolve slowly no matter what principles are professed. If there is conflict within a region, a rudimentary regional mechanism at this state of history is no worse than no mechanism at all. Growth requires a system in which primary responsibility falls on those most directly affected. While we are awaiting global accords, many things can be done on a smaller scale to create the environment to bring nations together. To put our thinking on a more tangible level, New York City would hardly refuse to enter into an agreement with New Jersey to share an energy network until all the cities in the United States agreed to take similar measures. Nor would the world benefit if the industrialized nations refused to take measures on the disposal of pollution until all nations agree. Then why not devise a global system that will encourage small groups of nations to move forward on many of the small practical things that must go on for the common interest, whether in forestry management or food production? Would not the world benefit if our international systems encouraged cooperation on the wide range of small practical issues that make the world run? The corollary is equally important: If we cannot get neighbors to agree, will the global accords be any more effective?

The reality is that history has proven that effective regional arrangements, far from being incompatible with building a larger global consciousness, often reinforce it, particularly in the field of development. Latin America's and Europe's experience demonstrate that clearly. In Europe, the Common Market's growth has in no way detracted from those nations' awareness of broader global needs.

Many Latin American countries that now play a major role in global fora are also leading the way for closer regional ties, as witnessed by Venezuela's role in OPEC and the Law of the Sea negotiations, and their strong leadership within the OAS, SELA, and the Andean Group, both regional and subregional groupings. We need sacrifice none of our commitment to the ultimate predominance of global institutions if we move, at the same time, to promote regional and subregional cooperation in the areas where it is appropriate. But it is essential to ensure the systematic linkage of the regional and subregional efforts to the over-all global system.

In other words, there are different needs, different capacities to act, different perceptions of the problems, and different states of readiness among the nations and regions of the world. Rather than allow these to be a hindrance to our progress, there are ways of making them an asset. This can only be done by constructing a system by which our global institutions will encourage actively all kinds of cooperation among nations as an integral part of their development strategy.

THE TASK AND THE STRUCTURE

In considering viable systems for achieving world order, it is important to define the major tasks that must be accomplished. The principal goal, clearly, is the establishment of a world community and consciousness: an awareness among humankind of our common humanity, fragility, and destiny. Out of this general goal emerge two principal areas for international cooperation: the prevention of conflict and the improvement of the quality of planetary existence. I would identify five major functions of international governance that relate to these goals:

1. policy making, both political and functional, for collective action;

2. finance and banking;

3. direct development services, such as technical assistance and training;

4. documentation and information;

5.   direct operations.

Within each of these functions, two fundamental criteria distinguish the role of an international agency: first, to bring the nations together in joint efforts and, second, to marshall the collective resources of the nations to assist each other to do what each might be unable to do for itself, or to do only at much greater cost. The scope of international arrangements to meet these needs is enormous. It ranges all the way from border commissions, arrangements between small groups of nations with a common interest, to full-scale agencies, such as the United Nations, the European Community, the OAS, the OAU, the World Bank, and the International Monetary Fund.

The roles and motivations of the different institutions required to meet these needs reveal distinct characteristics and pressures. Policy making requires free thinking, brainstorming, and uninhibited open debate. Banking and finance have specific disciplines and fiduciary relationships, which are confused with other motivations only at great risk. Technical assistance requires cost-conscious and sensitive management that knows what it wants and can ensure that it is getting value for money without losing sight of its ultimate social and developmental goals. Documentation and informational exchanges are quasi-operational programs that require substantial familiarity with the needs of both the sender and the receiver of information. Direct operations are unique international programs to deal both with inseparable global management issues such as the Universal Postal Union, the International Communications Union, the World Meteorological Organization, and the proposed World Seabed Authority, as well as special situations where the international entity maintains its independent operations, such as the Human Rights Commissions on both global and regional levels.

In general terms, a well-structured system will have institutions to deal with all levels. Some institutions must take care of large financial resource needs; others must take care of people, the human needs. It is important to examine each of these tasks in the context of the entire range of our available social and political institutions, beginning with the nation and proceeding through border commissions, subregional arrangements, regional and global organizations. The goal must be to define their complementarity, and integrate them into a comprehensive international structure through meaningful working relationships.

To begin an effective analysis, we must look at some of the principal issues involved in making these institutions work. I would set forth four criteria as relevant to evaluate the efficacy of global or regional arrangements. These are:

1. the scope of the problems with which each must deal;

2. motivating and involving the people of our nations;

3. the relevancy and practicality of the programs;

4. efficiency of administration.

In each of these it is important to compare the relative merits of different kinds of agencies in meeting the desired goals.

Regional Organizations can deal effectively with localized development problems

For stimulating a consciousness among humankind of global responsibilities, no one questions that global institutions are indispensable. They raise and spotlight issues touching the heart of every nation and making their consideration unavoidable. The question is: What is a global issue, and what is meant by a "global solution?" Some issues, especially economic ones such as monetary policy and trade, must be resolved among all the nations. Partial solutions of these issues are illusions.

Similar criteria apply to many of the political questions involving conflicting interests of the major powers and different regions. With nuclear weapons becoming cheaper and more accessible, the issue of preventing humankind from ultimately blowing itself off the face of the earth can only be handled as a global concern. The utilization of our limited natural resources, the production and distribution of energy, the control of our global environment, the control of organized crime, which has also benefited from the technological revolution in mass communications and transportation, these are all problems of global import.

But we should not blind ourselves that a series of regional solutions may help us set the stage and reinforce or indeed be prerequisite to global cooperation. World policy may be necessary for monetary matters as a result of the large number of variable and potentially disruptive sources, but is the same true for the training of public administrators to understand monetary issues? Familiarizing nations with the scope of the issues, probing ever deeper into the parameters of solutions, and, most important, placing constraints upon certain types of behavior even in small areas are major contributions to the atmosphere that will promote global solutions.

The most fundamental element for any kind of cooperation is to get along with your neighbor. Without that, is there really any hope for abstract global arrangements? A poet once mused that the only way to know the world is to know your own backyard. It is intoxicating to sit in international fora and try to influence the great powers of the world. But unless nations learn to live with their neighbors, is it meaningful? The only way to learn to work with your neighbors is to work with them. There are no magic formulas. Our international machinery must encourage this at every turn and incorporate it as basic policy for the gradual opening up of the nation-state system to a community of nations. Continue the search for solutions to the grand issues in the global fora, yes. But we must not delay seeking better ways of working on improving the quality of life with what we have at hand, in our neighborhood, city, state, and on the local, subregional, and regional level.

The application of this concept is apparent in many issues that confront the world today. For example, one of the most demanding of these issues is the control of conflicts. Nye has presented a strong case on the role of regional organization in "encapsulating conflict" and isolating it from unsolvable global issues.[15] The success of these efforts has been uneven. In the OAS it has become stronger with the recent handling of the Nicaraguan problem and the responsibility being assumed by the community of American nations, especially the subregional action of the Andean Group. In the OAU, however, the results have been less hopeful.[16] But these matters evolve slowly and the degree of encouragement from the world community could be a decisive factor in the ultimate success or failure.

Another important example is armaments. Meaningful arms control among the major powers demands global pronouncements and global pressures. But the principal motive for arms purchases of the smaller nations is the fear of their neighbors, a uniquely regional or even subregional question. Successful arrangements to eliminate violence as a means of solution of disputes among neighboring states would be one of the major building blocks in achieving global agreements on the subject. Latin America is an important example. Arms purchases today are in smaller proportion to GNP in Latin America than in any other area of the world.[17] The nations have created the institutions and have given substance to their regional commitments to one another. The recent Tlatelolco agreement on a nuclear-free zone strengthens that even further.

While political issues gather the headlines, specific development assistance comprises the bulk of the activities of our international organizations today. The amount of money devoted to technical assistance efforts is enormous and growing. The activities range from helping the nations to improve the administration of their governmental ministries, joint efforts to improve curricula in the schools, increasing capacity in technology, improving statistics capabilities, and similar programs in hundreds of specialized fields where the human and technical resources of the smaller nations are weak.

The issue for development relates to the question of *how* our public multinational development agencies get the job done. How do we begin to implement specific activities to build the educational institutions to train the teachers, the scientists, the factory workers? How do we get assistance to plan and implement fair tax systems; how do we bring neighboring nations together in joint river basin development projects; how do we help ministries of agriculture, transportation, or labor achieve better administration of their own activities; how do we begin to train technicians on the imperatives of forestry management and reforestation? These are not matters of international agreement or treaties. They require diagnosing specific problems, finding experts to work on them, defining the expert's job, determining how much it costs, and managing complex multicultural missions of experts.

Paralleling the specific assistance needs are the matters of international infrastructure such as devising treaties on the legal niceties of taking testimony in the courts of other nations, or bonding goods financed in one country and warehoused in another. These could be, but are not necessarily, global matters.[18] A wide range of the "nitty gritty" of our international business, a series of specific technical activities that affect our daily life, seem to be implemented most effectively among small groups of cooperating nations of similar cultural and institutional backgrounds. This has been demonstrated in Europe and new models are being experimented with among the nations of Latin America.[19]

Pondering the structure of our international community, we must ask ourselves whether it is worthwhile waiting for global accords on letters rogatory or whether it is better to encourage a few nations willing to move ahead to do so within an organized global/regional framework. It is similar to asking whether the Mexican–U.S. Border Commission should proceed when ready with agreements on water resources or whether they should wait for some world-wide convention on each matter.

The patterns that were developed by Jean Monnet and Robert Schuman with the European Coal and Steel Community cannot be ignored as the type of stepping stones that may serve in other areas of the world. Our global agencies must become sensitive to and actively searching for ways of identifying areas in which this type of regional cooperation can be encouraged. The Report of the Trilateral Task Force on International Institutions emphasized "that regional institutions can often help foster the evolution of constructive global arrangements. In many instances, regional—or other limited—groups among both industrialized and other developing countries can move more quickly than would be possible for the same countries on a broader scale. The creation of the European Payments Union, for example, was an important step towards the widespread restoration of currency convertibility."[20] The pattern seems to be that while talking about global solutions, pragmatic statesmen frequently look to the region for more practical solutions.

Arguments for regional approaches cutting across traditional political subdivisions are not unique to the international community. They are debated as much within nations as among nations.[21] The problem is the same whether organizing a private multinational enterprise or a public multinational development agency. The relative advantages and disadvantages of centralized or decentralized approaches are traditional in all discussions of administration. In considering our public international institutions, however, the arguments are more cogent because of the magnitude of the task. Our thinking regarding the institutions we construct and the way they relate to each other must take all levels of activity into account if we are to avoid the disillusionment of expecting certain institutions to deliver a product that they are incapable of providing either structurally or because their agenda is so full they cannot give it adequate attention.

Regional agencies have more opportunities to motivate and involve the people of the nations.

Reaching and motivating the people of the world to a greater respect and confidence in an international system is essential if an environment is to be created in which these institutions are to have credibility and national leaders will be comfortable relying on cooperation with them.[22] This is not to imply that regional or any other type of international organization will replace national loyalties, as some theorists maintain.[23] The gradual awakening of people to the potential beyond their current national centricity, however, will come only through institutions that have reasonable, meaningful, and understandable objectives and the capacity to articulate issues relevant to the concerns of the people.

In the long run the confidence of the people in the international agencies demands a wide range of tangible projects that bring their operations closer to the people and the people closer to them. The key is involvement and participation. There are two ways in which this participation can be achieved. One is by having the international agencies hire more and give greater international responsibilities to the technicians of the member state. This involves them in the activity and provides greater understanding of the benefits of international cooperation. The second is to deal with issues more closely related to national interests. Both are more manageably and meaningfully done on a regional level. That is what happened in Europe. The framework is now beginning to work in Latin America. Our global institutions could have a decisive role in helping it to occur in other regions.

The base structures of our international development framework must contain a viable mechanism to allow more technicians from the developing nations to come to work for the international organizations, participating actively in the joint efforts to seek solutions to common problems in the international context. Moreover, they must do so in a way that will add to the nations' available manpower and not become a sophisticated form of "brain drain." Some of the recent arguments for horizontal cooperation are strong endorsements of this reality.[24]

Regional organizations have a far better opportunity to do this because the technicians of the region are the ones who staff the organizations. Moreover, it keeps them close to the place of the action. The OAS, for example, is staffed 77% by Latin American technicians. The OAU is virtually 100% African. On the other hand, foreign technicians, no matter how expert, are not always more efficient. In every program there is a sender and a receiver of information, a speaker and a listener. Words spoken but not heard or applied are of little use. Because ways of communicating and getting things done are so varied in different societies, it is of little avail if high-level experts from the developed countries prepare programs that are not sensitive to these realities.

Marshall McLuhan wrote that the *way* we do things is often more important than *what* we do. This is especially applicable in our international life. Involving the technicians from the countries directly affected by the projects can do far more for the motivation of international cooperation than any study or lecture by persons from the outside.

While some question the "efficiency" of regional agencies, this is more than compensated for by the direct involvement and responsibility assumed by the nationals for their own needs. The cultural patterns and ways of "getting things done" are taken into greater account, potentially leading to more meaningful activity among responsible technicians from the nations of the region. If officials from the countries directly involved do the hiring for common programs in regional organizations, they may hire persons from outside the region when the catalytic force is desired, but they will have ample opportunity on their own to evaluate their usefulness and cultural sensitivities before assigning them to the job.

On a practical level, the idea of any efficiency of global entities dealing with thousands of small projects from a centralized base is an illusion.[25] Communications with the national governments are a source of constant problems that are difficult to deal with from a remote headquarters that has different criteria for successful project execution. Regional organisms in more direct touch with the realities of their member states are far more able to adapt to these practical conditions.

There are no easy solutions to these problems. But one important avenue is to achieve the maximum participation of the technicians and people who understand their societies, giving them greater opportunities to work in an international structure, to seek their own way in dealing with the problems that are relevant to the progress of their own societies. In that way they can most effectively build up their capability to relate their own cultural heritage to what is available in the rest of the world.

Regional organizations can adopt more relevant and practical approaches to apparently unsolvable global problems.

A serious problem in development assistance is the relevance of some of the solutions proposed by the global agencies when considering how to implement specific programs to assist in science or industrial development.[26] This was noted in the recent Report of the Brandt Commission in discussing the need for greater regionalization of the operations of the international financial agencies. Can the same staff effectively manage programs for Nigeria, Burma, and Brazil? The range of the wealth of nations, their natural endowment, and their state of readiness can hardly be compared. The very poor nations with small populations and limited resources will need very rudimentary applications sensitive to an unskilled labor force. On the other hand, the middle-class nations have entirely different needs, as do the more developed industrialized nations.

More important, the very nature of development and progress is still undefined. The question of what kind of "progress" we are currently pursuing and whether it is or should be a universal value is one of our most unsettling issues. The applications of new systems to different cultures must be sensitively applied. The attitude of different cultures and the state of readiness of different nations must be taken into account. The recent call of the Finance Minister of Peru for an inter-American regional monetary fund was a severe comment on the standard solutions of the International Monetary Fund, one of our most respected institutions, to problems of different regions. Tremendous domestic political forces are unleashed by the interventions of international agencies, which, because of the enormous resources at their disposal or the subjects with which they are dealing, ranging from finance to human rights, have now become actors on the world scene in their own right. The relevancy of the solutions by broad, centralized agencies must be carefully examined if we are to seek seriously an acceptable international structure among our nations.

The Atlantic Council, in a recent report, put the question in a slightly different light. It said:

> The U.N. system as central organization with almost universal membership can and should take the initiative on global issues, as it has done usefully in the past on food, population, drugs, peacekeeping, disaster relief, status of women, arms control, human rights, the law of the sea. But international organizations with partial membership, whether based on regional location or on functional necessity, should, where possible, take on more of the items on the new international agenda. . . . We recommend the reconsideration of the division of labor between global and regional organizations. It is timely to decide whether certain functions that have been taken up at the global level should not rather be "regionalized," and thus dealt with only by those directly affected. . . . Some regional action groupings might themselves have U.N. sponsorship as is already the case in the environmental field.[27]

A serious obstacle, some analysts argue, is the absence in other regions of the world of the tradition of political cooperation or international infrastructure as found in Europe or the Western Hemisphere. But alternatives have been suggested to resolve these structural and financial questions.[28] One possibility is for the U.N. to redirect its philosophy and actually foment and finance regional development activities, broadening the scope of the regional economic commissions and chanelling funds to the regional and sub-regional agencies. This would imply restructuring the United Nations so that the developed industrialized nations would pay their quotas to the global agency, which would then reallocate the funds among the various regional agencies responsible for executing regional development plans. The practical effect would be to give the regional entities the economic clout to undertake meaningful development programs, while, at the same time, diluting the political "power of the purse" of any individual nation. This, of course, is the essence of a federal structure, in which the agents of global federalism become the regional and subregional entities.

Regional organization is potentially more efficient and easier to administer.

An important argument for greater experimentation with regional arrangements is that they are inherently more manageable, both in size and scale, and are potentially more efficient vehicles for the delivery of development services. This argument is difficult because of the lack of any conceptual agreement on contemporary international administration. Moreover, measuring real costs is complicated amidst the many intangibles involved in administering international services. The data available for informed judgments are relatively poor since the international organizations have not been diligent in undertaking cost analyses or in publishing their data. Nor are traditional cost-benefit comparisons applicable to situations that are eminently political. The international bureaucracies have used this argument well in resisting cost-analysis efforts.

While the lack of reliable data may preclude absolutist judgments or attempts to compare international development systems with private sector efforts, it is not a valid argument to vitiate *comparative* studies among the international agencies. Criteria can and are being devised by which the efficiency of alternative means of delivery of development services can be measured, as well as the relative effectiveness of different systems and even different managers within the international system.[29]

The basic issue for all of our international development efforts is how to administer developmental assistance to ensure that we are delivering the highest quality of services with minimum waste and maximum impact upon a specific problem. Funds that national governments appropriate for international institutions must compete with priorities on the national development agenda. If our international development institutions are to succeed, they must have integrity and credibility. That means they must be effectively run. They must be fully accountable for the use of their funds; they must clearly demonstrate they produce services at least as economically as other means available to deliver similar services.

Except for the development banks that have attained high-caliber staff and operational policies, global development institutions have been weak in administrative capacity. The inefficiency of the UN system has been widely documented.[30] The issue is not only one of politics: The practical logistics are overwhelming. The techniques of international management of public multinational programs by a multinational staff are unlike anything the world has known. The staffs of the agencies are multicultural, the decision-making mechanisms are multicultural, and the field of action and implementation is multicultural.

To make matters worse, the international institutions are dealing with thousands of small projects in hundreds of countries, all with different needs and ways of doing things. There is no way top management in New York or Geneva really knows the true nature or quality of the product being delivered by technicians or professors in Korea or Bolivia. Accountability to a centralized base for a largely intangible work product cannot and does not work, regardless of how many internal or external inspection forces are organized. The result is that the staff of the global international agencies is top-heavy and largely uncontrolled.

Standard theory holds that the international organizations are not actors on the world scene but only agents to implement the desires of the member states. Theory must bow to reality. Technical assistance experts hired and deployed throughout the world largely call their own tune. Their prestige and reception in the developing countries are often far out of proportion to their real experience. Their recommendations of approval or disapproval of projects often have profound implications on the internal politics of the smaller nations. Top management of institutions allocating billions of dollars a year have no practical way of keeping track of the criteria of these judgements or the quality of the results of technical assistance missions on everything from taxation to tourism, from mathematics to musical education, from public administration to public health, in over 150 different countries.

If the issue is to husband precious resources, a centralized global base cannot work, no more than the U.S. federal government in Washington could hire the teachers for each public school in the United States. Whether diagnosing local development needs or devising programs to respond to them, institutions closer to the specific problems and more sensitive to acceptable local solutions must be given more serious attention.

The baseline of the analysis rests upon the efficiency of the various types of international vehicles for the delivery of services. However rough, statistical indicators seem to point to the greater economies of delivering services from a regional organizational base, with efficiencies both in the quality and the quantity of the benefits to be derived.[31]

Even in the functional institutions, we cannot accept without question the concept that centralized, global institutions do things best. Given the special place that functional institutions have in the strategy for international organization, their role and method of operation must be given very close attention. But concepts of centralized administration have little relationship to the realities of a pluralistic world. Nor do they have any basis in practical administrative terms. The fact is that even our functional efforts have to be rooted in regional bases, regional understanding, regional cooperation, and regional management if they are effectively to reach the goal of functional pluralism.

A good argument can be made for linking functional agencies to regional development delivery systems from the point of view of effective interaction of programs within a region. The relationship between the Pan American Health Organization and the World Health Organization, whereby the Pan American Health Organization manages all of WHO's programs in the Western Hemisphere, can serve as a useful model.[32] The bringing together of regional Ministers of Health to determine regional policy for the global programs in the field of health applies equally in the fields of food, agriculture, transportation, education, and so on.

Interdependence applies not only among nations but also among the issues. Neither economic, social, scientific, nor educational issues can be divorced from each other or dealt with in isolation. While there are certain discrete activities, such as the International Postal Union, that can be managed in a homogeneous fashion, other issues are not so easily separable. The real task of generating employment cannot be divorced from skills of the labor force, from the education system, from investment, from the transportation system. Similarly, programs of industrialization cannot be separated from training in the schools or policies to foment savings and investment. Agriculture is vitally linked to transportation, credit, and functional education. Examples are innumerable. While clearly functional divisions are practical necessities, their operation from a global base makes sectoral interrelationship almost impossible. The reordering of the operations of our functional agencies to require coordination by a regional development authority could be an important step to ensure coherent and effective regional development policies. This would not eliminate coordinating regional functional activity and productivity by experts working out of a global mechanism. In this manner, the immediate operations could be brought closer to local services and relate more directly to the state of readiness and nature of the local institutions, while remaining linked to global discussions of overriding policy issues and global monitoring of results.

CONCLUSIONS

Evaluating regional organization in the development field is not easy. It has never been seriously explored in the context of a role as an active component of global development efforts. The regional defense and security treaties after World War II seriously prejudiced our thinking. The extent to which that period gave us preconceived notions of regionalism is evident in the literature on regionalism, which relates almost exclusively to security matters. However, in discussing regional arrangements for development, we are not talking about NATO or SEATO. We are talking about public transnational development agencies that work with limited groups of countries, employing officials from those countries to deal with their common problems.

The only areas in which this has been seriously tried are in Europe, among the developed, industrialized nations, and in Latin America, where an elaborate network of international cooperation organizations joins the American nations in common efforts. The Asian Development Bank has become a major force in the financial field in Asia, but broad needs for specific development cooperation, technical assistance, and training remain unattended. Similarly, in Africa, the Organization of African Unity simply has not had the financial resources to enter into serious development programing.

The reality is that humankind's entire effort at voluntary international cooperation today must be viewed as one great experiment. Our present international institutions are nothing but an opportunity. We are all involved in probing the depths of problems with which we have little prior experience. The need for experimentation with different modes and methods of international cooperation, from bilateral commissions to a World Sea-Bed Authority, is real. On all fronts, at all levels, our search for a workable system of voluntary associations of nations must be probed and tested.

The utilization of international organizations at different levels is essential if we are to move off the plateau on which we are currently stalled in our search for more effective international cooperation. It is conceivable that if we can devise a true federalist system of interrelated institutions that are meaningful to the nations, institutions that they feel part of and responsible for, we may be able to take another step on a long path toward an international community based upon the voluntary association of all members of the world community.

In sum, the fundamental propositions are:

1. the nature of the problems of ordering a global community are of such magnitude that the transition from our current form of nationalist behavior cannot be made successfully through rigid, centralized approaches;

2. regional arrangements within a global framework hold considerable potential of making the world development system work on many issues with sufficient flexibility and adaptability to satisfy widely divergent values and patterns of living;

3. major steps to advance from a nation-state system to an international consciousness will occur most readily through establishing systems of democratic interaction among neighboring states in subregional and regional developmental cooperation.

The reality, as stated above, is that we can no more hope to devise effective global management systems without intermediary administrative mechanisms than the U.S. Government could manage without city, county, and state machinery for different purposes. The issues that the international community will confront in the next generation are of such importance that we have a real, practical need for viable intermediate mechanisms to mobilize real participation and understanding of the nations and the people. The attitudes within the global system to find new and more innovative ways to take this into account and encourage and organize it can be decisive.

NOTES

1. Independent Commission on International Development Issues, *North-South: A Programme for Survival*, Cambridge, Massachusetts, The MIT Press, 1980. See especially pp. 135, 140, 249–255. C. Maxwell Stanley. *Managing Global Problems.* Muscatine, Iowa, the Stanley Foundation, 1979. p. 27.
2. U.S. Senate, Committee on Government. Operations, *U.S. Participation in International Organization*, February 1977, p. 14.
3. Sir Robert Jackson, *A Study of the Capacity of the United Nations Development System.* U.N. Document DP-5, Geneva, 1969.
4. David Mitrany, *A Working Peace System*, London, Royal Institute of International Affairs, 1943, pp. 10 and 19.
5. Joseph S. Nye, *Peace in Parts*, Boston, Little Brown & Co., 1971.
6. Ibid., p. 15.
7. Ibid., p. 4.
8. Elmer Plischke, *Microstates in World Affairs*, Washington, D.C., AEI, 1977. See also: Yehuda Z. Blum, *The U.N.'s Ongoing Decline* in *The New York Times*, Sept. 13, 1979.
9. Jane Rosen, *New York Times Magazine*, December 16, 1979, p. 37.
10. Robert W. Cox, *The Politics of International Organization*, New York, Praeger, 1970, pp. 29 ff.
11. George Langrod, *The International Civil Servant*, New York, Oceana, 1963.
12. Sir Robert Jackson, op. cit., foreword.
13. U.S. Senate Committee on Government Operations, op. cit., p. 36.
14. C. Fred Bergston, Georges Berthoin, Kinhide Mushakoji, *The Reform of International Institutions*, New York, The Trilateral Commission, Triangle Papers: Number 11, 1976.
15. Nye, op. cit. See also: Ernest B. Haas, the United Nations and Regionalism, in K. J. Twitchett, Ed., *The Evolving U.N.: A Prospect for Peace?*, 1971, pp. 120 ff, and Ronald J. Yalem, *Regionalism and World Order*, Washington, D.C., Public Affairs Press, 1965.
16. See: "OAU Delegates Hear Recitation of Failure," *Washington Post*, July 2, 1980.
17. U.S. Arms Control and Disarmament Agency, *World Military Expenditures and Arms Transfers, 1967–1976.* Washington, D.C., 1978. See also: Latin America Weekly Report, WR 80-24, June 20, 1980, p. 4.
18. See, for example, eight new inter-American Conventions signed at the recent Conference on Private International Law, Montevideo, Uruguay, April

23–May 8, 1979, ranging from Conflicts of Laws Concerning Checks, Extraterritorial Validity of Foreign Judgments and Arbitral Awards, to Proof of and Information on Foreign Law.

19. Of particular interest is the program being developed by SELA, the Latin American Economic System, to form new multinational corporations owned by the member countries.

20. Bergston, Berthoin, and Mushakoji, op. cit., pp. 6–7.

21. See: "The Developing Commissions, Regional Network Spreads Despite Carter Criticism," in *Washington Post*, May 30, 1979, and "Regional Bickering over TVA," in *Washington Post*, July 19, 1979.

22. An important discussion of this problem is set forth in Cox, op. cit., p. 34.

23. Nye, op. cit., pp. 15, 21, 176, and 186.

24. The recent U.N. Conferences on Technical Cooperation Among Developing Countries (TCDC) are focusing wide attention on the techniques and application of this process.

25. The United Nations Development Program has reported that it has over 7,000 individual projects operating annually. The FAO has over 2,200. See: U.S. Senate Committee on Government Operations, op. cit. The Organization of American States has reported that it has over 600 individual projects operating in its $82,000,000 budget.

26. Comptroller General of the United States, *Report to the Congress: Training and Related Efforts to Improve Financial Management in the Third World*, Washington, D.C., September 20, 1979, pp. 22, 26. See also: Lincoln P. Bloomfield, Rapporteur, *What Future for the U.N.?*, The Atlantic Council of the U.S., Policy Paper, U.N. Series, Boulder, Colorado, 1977, p. 19.

27. Bloomfield, op. cit.

28. For a review of ways in which global and regional organizations could interact more effectively, see: *Regional Organization Without Big Power Participation* by "A" in International Journal of the Canadian Institute of International Affairs, Vol. XXX, No. 4, Autumn, 1975, p. 768.

29. Intensive work has been going on in the OAS to analyze the cost of delivery of services, taking into account all of the indirect and intangible costs that generally attach to any service operation. Using formulas that were carefully devised to allocate various indirect costs according to specific criteria, the Organization came up with combined overhead and indirect costs of 29%. By any criteria, these costs are fair or on the low side. Private consulting firms often run at least 50% overhead on the work that they do for the international agencies. By contrast, the overhead costs for the UN agencies, which are not directly revealed, are estimated to run over 40%.

30. See: Jackson, op. cit.; U.S. Senate Report of Committee on Government Operations, op. cit.; Robert W. Cox and Harold K. Jacobson, *The Anatomy of Influence: Decision-Making in International Organization*, New Haven, Yale, 1974. See also Comptroller General of the United States, *Report to the Congress on Improving Financial Management in the United Nations.* Sept. 24, 1979.

31. See note 29.

32. See: Agreement between the World Health Organizaiton and the Pan American Health Organization of April 22, 1949, in *Basic Documents of the Pan American Health Organization*, 13th Edition, 1979, p. 42.

About the Editor
and Contributors

VIRON P. VAKY is Research Professor of Diplomacy, School of Foreign Service, Georgetown University.

Mr. Vaky served for thirty years in the U.S. Foreign Service. His principal posts in that period were as U.S. Ambassador to Costa Rica, to Colombia, and to Venezuela as Assistant Secretary of State for Inter-American Affairs.

RAUL ALLARD is Director of the Department of Educational Affairs of the Organization of American States. From 1968 to 1973 he was President of Catholic University of Valparaiso, from which he graduated in 1961.

Mr. Allard holds a Master's of Comparative Law from Southern Methodist University. His books include: *Two Phases of Reform in Catholic Universities of Chile,* CPU Editions, Santiago, Chile, 1970.

WERNER BAER is Professor of Economics at the University of Illinois Urbana-Champaign. His most recent book is *The Brazillian Economy: Growth and Development,* (2nd edition) Praeger 1983. He is the author of numerous other articles on economics and development.

Dr. Baer holds an M.A. and a Ph.D. from Harvard University and a B.A. from Queenstown College.

JUAN BUTTARI is an Economist at the Agency for International Development. He has recently edited two books: *Employment and Labor Force in Latin America: A Review at National and Regional Levels,* Organization of American States, 1979; and *Concentracion Industrial, Technologia y Empleo,* Ediciones Siap, Argentina, 1979.

Dr. Buttari holds a Ph.D. and M.A. in Economics from Georgetown University and a B.A. from the University of Puerto Rico.

JORGE I. DOMÍNGUEZ is Professor of Government and member of the Center for International Affairs at Harvard University. Among his most recent works are: *Economic Issues and Political Conflict: U.S. Latin American Relations,* Butterworth 1982; and *U.S. Interests and Policies in Central America and the Caribbean,* American Enterprise Institute.

ALBERT FISHLOW is Professor of Economics, University of California at Berkeley. His monographs include: *Rich and Poor Nations and the World Economy,* McGraw-Hill; *Trade in Manufactured Products with Developing*

Countries: Reinforcing North–South Partnerships, Tri-lateral Commission; and *Latin America's Emergence: Toward a U.S. Response,* The Foreign Policy Association.

Dr. Fishlow holds a B.A. from the University of Pennsylvania and a Ph.D. from Harvard University.

WILLIAM GLADE is Director, Institute of Latin American Studies, and Professor of Economics at the University of Texas at Austin. His most recent publications include: "The Levantines in Latin America", *American Economic Review,* May 1983. "The International Economy and Latin America 1870–1914", a chapter in the *Cambridge History of Latin America,* Cambridge University Press, (forthcoming).

Dr. Glade holds a B.A.A., and an M.A. and a Ph.D. in Economics from the University of Texas.

ALLAN GOODMAN is Associate Dean of the School of Foreign Service at Georgetown University. Dr. Goodman is a guest columnist of the *Baltimore Sun.* His recent book, *The Lost Peace,* about the search for negotiated settlement in the Vietnam War, was published by the Hoover Institution Press.

Dr. Goodman holds a B.S. from, Northwestern University, an M.A. in Public Administration, and a Ph.D. in Government from Harvard University.

MARGARET DALY HAYES is a Professional Staff Member of the Committee on Foreign Relations, U.S. Senate.

Her books and articles include, "Security to the South: U.S. Interests in Latin America", *International Security* (Summer 1980) and "Latin America and the U.S. National Interests: A Basis for U.S. Foreign Policy", Westview Press (forthcoming).

Dr. Hayes holds a B.S. from Northwestern University, an M.A. from New York University at the University of Madrid, and an M.A. and Ph.D. from Indiana University.

ROBERT JACKSON is Professor at Carleton University in Ottawa. Among his books and articles are: *The Canadian Legislative System: Politicians and Policy Making,* with M. Atkinson (2nd edition) Toronto, Gage 1980; "Comparative Crisis Management: Theory and Cases", *Dynamics of Public Policy,* Sage, London 1976; and "Quebec Foreign Policy?: Canada and Ethno-Regionalism", *New Nationalisms,* Praeger, 1979.

Dr. Jackson holds B.A. and M.A. degrees from the University of Western Ontario, and a Ph.D. from Oxford University.

MARY JEANNE REID MARTZ is a Foreign Service Officer. She has written a number of works on conflict resolution, including "The Central American Soccer War: Historical Patterns and International Dynamics of

OAS Settlement Procedures", Ohio University for International Studies, 1978.

ALEJANDRO PORTES is Professor of Sociology at Johns Hopkins University. His books and articles include: *Urban Latin America,* University of Texas Press, 1976. "Labor Class and the International System", New York Academic Press, 1981. "Latin Journey: A Longitudinal Study of Cuba and Mexico Immigration in the U.S.," University of California Press, 1984.

Dr. Portes holds a B.A. from Creighton University, an M.A. in Sociology from the University of Wisconsin at Madison, and a Ph.D. in Sociology from the University of Wisconsin.

JOHN REDICK is Staff Consultant of the W. Alton Jones Foundation, Charlottesville, Virginia, and earlier served on the staff of the Stanley Foundation. Among his recent articles is "The Tlatelolco Regime and Non-Proliferation in Latin America", *International Organization* (special issue on non-proliferation), Winter, 1981. He has contributed chapters to two recent books dealing with nuclear arms, those edited by, George Quester, *Nuclear Proliferation, Breaking the Chains,* 1981, University of Wisconsin Press; and by Hans Gunter Brauch and Duncan Clarke, *Decisionmaking for Arms Limitation in the 1980s: Assessments and Prospects,* Ballenger, 1983.

Dr. Redick holds a B.A., M.A., and a Ph.D. in Foreign Affairs from the University of Virginia.

KIRK ROGERS is Director of the Program of Regional Development of the Organization of American States. His B.A. and M.A. degrees are from Yale University.

A specialist in natural and physical resources, Mr. Rogers has worked or traveled in every country in Latin America.

AARON SEGAL is Professor of Communications and Political Science at the University of Texas at El Paso. His most recent book, *Haiti: Cultural Splendor, Political Poverty,* will soon be published by Praeger. Others include: *Population Policies in the Caribbean,* Lexington Books, and *The Travelers Africa,* Scribner's.

Dr. Segal holds a B.A. from Occidential College, B. Phil. from Oxford University, and a Ph.D. from the University of California at Berkeley.

L. RONALD SCHEMAN is Assistant Secretary for Management of the Organization of American States. He is co-author of *The Foundation of Freedom: The Relationship between Democracy and Human Rights,* published by Praeger in 1966. He has written numerous articles on Inter-American cooperation and U.S. and Latin American relations.

Mr. Scheman holds a B.A. from Dartmouth College and a J.D. from Yale Law School.

CAESAR SERESERES is a Staff Member of the Rand Corporation's Political Science Department and Associate Professor of Political Science at the University of California at Irvine. Dr. Sereseres' latest publications are: "Military Politics, Internal Warfare, and U.S. Policy in Guatemala", (R-2996-AF), Santa Monica: The Rand Corporation; and "The Management of U.S.-Mexico Relations: Drift Toward Failure?" (co-authored, in Manuel Garcia y Griego and Carlos Vasquez, eds.), *U.S.-Mexico Relations: Selected Issues for 1980s* Latin American Studies Center, Los Angeles: University of California Press, 1980.

Dr. Sereseres holds a B.A. from the University of Santa Barbara and an M.A. and Ph.D. from the University of California at Riverside.

SIDNEY WEINTRAUB is Dean Rusk Professor at the Lyndon B. Johnson School of Public Affairs, University of Texas. Earlier he served in top policy positions at the U.S. Department of State and the Agency for International Development.

He is the author of 6 books and more than 50 monographs, articles and book chapters dealing with various economic issues. His most recent books include: *Free Trade Between Mexico and the United States,* The Brookings Institution; *Economic Stabilization in Developing Countries,* The Brookings Institution; and *Temporary Alien Workers in the United States,* Westview Press.

Dr. Weintraub holds a Ph.D. in Economics from The American University, an M.A. in Economics from Yale University, a B.J. and M.A. in Journalism from the University of Missouri, and also a B.B.A. in Accountancy from the City College of New York.

BRYCE WOOD was for 23 years Executive Associate of the Social Science Research Council where he directed Latin American and Caribbean programs. Earlier he taught at Swathmore College. Recently he has been a guest scholar at the Brookings Institution.

Dr. Wood was graduated from Reed College and holds a Ph.D. in Political Science from Columbia University.

MONTAGUE YUDELMAN has for many years been Director for Agriculture and Rural Development of The World Bank. Among his books are: *Africans on the Land,* Harvard University Press, Oxford. *Agricultural and Economic Integration in Latin America,* Fonda Cultura; and *Agricultural Development and Technological Change and Employment,* OECD.

Dr. Yudelman holds a B.S., an M.A., and a Ph.D. from the University of California at Berkeley.